The Complete Works of

HORACE

The Complete Works of
HORACE
(Quintus Horatius Flaccus)

Translated in the meters of the originals,
with notes by

Charles E. Passage

FREDERICK UNGAR PUBLISHING CO.
NEW YORK

Library of Congress Cataloging in Publication Data

Horace.
    The complete works of Horace.

    I. Title.
PA6394.P34   1983   874′.01   82-24774
ISBN 0-8044-2404-7

Contents

Preface

This volume offers, for the first time, the works of the poet Horace translated by a single hand, unrhymed, and in the meters of the originals, unbowdlerized, and with sufficient notes for a reasonably deep appreciation of the texts.

Rhyme, which was unknown to Greek and Latin poets, has been avoided as alien to the spirit of Horace. Metrical patterns for the reader's guidance appear at the head of each lyric, and on pages 14–15, there is an explanation of the uniform dactylic hexameters used throughout the Satires and Epistles. All poems have their traditional numbering, followed by the complete first line of the Latin; the originals have no titles and none have been invented. To facilitate metrical reading all but the most familiar proper names have been accented. Brief notices introduce each subgroup of Horace's works.

The Satires and Epistles were translated from the 1909 edition by Edward P. Morris of Yale, the lyric poems from the 1902 edition by Clifford Herschel Moore of Harvard. Occasionally we quote from the interpretive notes of these editors, but our notes are drawn from multiple sources and regard readers of goodwill with no more than passing aquaintance with classical civilization. In order to bring clarifying information into close conjunction with each poem we have not hesitated to repeat certain data, cross-referencing only when the material became too bulky. On the other hand, our thematic cross-referencing is considerably more extensive than that of either of the above-mentioned editors. The many place names have been geo-graphically located and, wherever possible, modern place names supplied. The peripheral matter of Horace's ethnography is succinctly dealt with in an appendix entitled "Foreign Nations." Two other appendices collect information about Maecenas and the emperor Augustus, but all other personages are identified in the notes, a few of them at fair length, e.g., Agrippa, Pollio, and the poet Propertius.

In rare instances we permitted ourselves to go somewhat afield to bring in ancient literary information of interest, but no comments of a merely appreciative nature have been included. Appreciation is sufficiently attested by the six years of almost daily application that went into this volume.

Charles E. Passage
Dansville, New York
1981

PUBLISHER'S NOTE

This volume was set by computerized composition. Special characters, such as those indicating meter, are limited in the system. We chose those that most closely resemble the traditional symbols. The rendering of the metric patterns for Horace's stanzas in this volume may still strike the reader as unusual. Thus, ∪ represents the unstressed and _ the stressed syllable.

The translator and the publisher hope that the reader still will accept with understanding this compromise with the technological age.

The Complete Works of
HORACE

Introduction

In the southward expansion of their power the Romans were repeatedly challenged by the Samnites, an Italic people closely allied with the previously conquered Sabines, until in 291 B.C., after three wars fought, a colony of Romans was established some eighty miles due east of Naples to keep the Samnites under observation. The new town, apparently somewhat larger than most such Roman colonies, was named Venúsia (modern Venósa), and there, more than two centuries later, the poet Horace was born on December 8, 65 B.C., by which time, of course, all of Italy had come to be considered the Roman heartland, as opposed to foreign provinces on three continents.

Of his racial stock Horace says not a word, but there are passages where he seems to have thought of himself, proudly, as an Italian provincial, an Apúlian, rather than as a Roman; note especially *Odes* 3.30.10–12.* He makes no mention of his mother, and apparently he was an only child, but he speaks with loving gratitude of his father, who was a former slave.

How many generations of his forebears had been in slavery is quite unkown, nor do we know how his father came to be freed.† He may, in his thrift, have saved up wages to purchase his liberty, as was sometimes done; or he may have been manumitted by his owner, perhaps by terms of the latter's will, or even in his lifetime, for faithful service done or from personal esteem. As a slave, the father would have had only a given name or a nickname, but upon liberation he would have adopted a family name. Our poet mentions no name at all for his father.

Thus it is a mystery how our poet came by the full tripartite name of Quintus

---

* The Roman colonists who settled Venúsia in 291 B.C. had descendants who found themselves in what came to be the extreme south of Samnium province and within walking distance of the borders of Lucania province and of Apulia province (where descendants of Dorian Greek colonists still spoke a variety of Greek in 65 B.C.). The intervening 225 years could so have blended these elements that Horace's ancestors may have combined any or all of these strains, but from remarks scattered through his poems we can be sure that Horace was Italian, with no admixture of overseas nationalities.
† On the basis of mere speculation, we suggest the possibility that the father or grandfather could, through misfortune or mismanagement, have gone bankrupt and, by long-standing terms of Roman law, could have sold himself into slavery to pay his debts. The father's thrift takes on new significance in the light of such a hypothesis.

Horatius Flaccus. The given name (*praenomen*) "Quintus" was common enough. The family (or clan) name (*nomen*) "Horatius" was Roman, aristocratic, and centuries old, as witness the triplet brothers Horatii who, allegedly in 670 B.C., fought the triplet brothers Curiatii in the war against Alba—the story is dramatized in Corneille's play *Horace* (1640); or again, the Horatius Cocles ("One-eyed"), who singlehanded, defended the city bridge in 506 B.C. As for "Flaccus," meaning "Flap-ear," it was a *cognomen*, one of those unflattering "extra" names that a nobleman might assign to his son, in some cases to be passed on from generation to generation. "Flaccus," in fact, was a cognomen used in at least a dozen distinguished families. Possibly the poet's father, upon liberation, adopted the family name of his former master. We do not know. Horace himself, however, was "born in freedom."

Some biographical details about him are supplied by the ancient *Vita Horatii*, translated in pages 384–87 below, but in his poems Horace tells a good share of his own life story, piecemeal and in random order. The main events to age twenty-seven or so (38B.C.) are sketched in the sixth "Satire," lines 45–88; his daily life in Rome at that stage is described in lines 111–129 of the same poem; and in the fourth "Satire," lines 105–126, there is an account of his father's method of moral instruction. These passages are best appreciated in Horace's own words, but here we shall briefly relate the biography in chronological sequence.

Scattered through the poems there are sufficient allusions to the geography and customs of the Venúsia area to indicate that he was probably in early adolescence by the time he left his native region. The boyhood adventure of surviving unharmed while lost in the mountains overnight, as told in *Odes* 3.4.9–20, implies an age of no less than ten, probably more. Let us guess, then, that Horace was fourteen or fifteen years old (51–50 B.C.) when his father brought him to Rome and put him in a school that offered the best education available. Let us guess further that his father sent him at age twenty (45 B.C.) to Athens for advanced study.

Late in 44, or in 43, the "college student" was enlisted as an officer in the army which Brutus, the chief assassin of Julius Caesar, was mustering in the name of the Roman Republic against Caesar's heir, young Octavius Caesar, and Mark Antony. After months of maneuvers in the extreme north of Greece (Macedonia and Thrace) the youthful officer, just short of his twenty-third birthday, took part in the decisive battle at Philippi, which was fought in two installments, October 23rd and November 16th of 42, to the utter defeat of the Republican army and party. Wisely the victors granted amnesty to the soldiers of the opposition, and Horace is likely to have returned to Italy early in 41. He returned, however, to find his father deceased and the paternal farm confiscated, along with many another farm, so the troops of the victors could be paid off in land grants. From that year dates Epode 16, his earliest preserved poem (unless the seventh "Satire" was composed in 42, the year of the event narrated in that "Satire").

Through all or part of the three-year period, 41 to 38, Horace worked as a clerk in the treasury department in Rome. To that experience he alludes only obliquely in S.2.6. 36–37 and even more obliquely in the autobiographical lines 41–52 of the late poem, E.2.2. There, after recalling his education in Rome and Athens and his military service, he says:

After Philíppi my service was over, but I was in want; my
Wings had been clipped, I was destitute, left without home and deprived of
Land that my father had owned, until poverty gave me sufficient
Boldness to start writing poems.

The precise meaning of the last clause is left for the reader to interpret. Presumably, the second and fourth "Satires" were among the poems he wrote at that time.

The poems caught the attention of Vergil and Varius, two poets with literary careers already launched and with connections in very high places, and they recommended him to the wealthy statesman Maecenas, patron of poets and trusted advisor to Octavius Caesar. In either 39 or 38 Horace was interviewed by Maecenas, who, after an interval, summoned him back and bade him be a member of his entourage—with stipend. Between poet and patron there developed a friendship which was to last thirty years, until their deaths in the same year, 8 B.C.

In 33 Maecenas bestowed upon the thirty-two-year-old Horace the gift of a tract of land in a mountain valley some thirty miles northeast of Rome, in Sabine country. Prudently Horace sublet most of the tract to five citizen farmers, reserving the remainder for his own use. There he built his "farmhouse," a rural retreat he mentions frequently, always with delight. Though this "Sabine farm" was ever afterward his primary residence, he maintained a house in Rome—we fancy on the slope of the Esquiline Hill, somewhere below Maecenas's new mansion at the summit—and also a house in fashionable Tibur (modern Tívoli), within ten or twelve miles of the farm. With health less than rugged, he occasionally journeyed to spas such as Baiae, on the coast west of Naples, or to Tareñtum (now Táranto) in the extreme south to escape the winter's cold. He never again left Italy, and, so far as we know, never ventured farther north than his own farm. At home or on travels, he seems always to have had his work-notebooks at hand.

Whatever poems he composed in Greek (see "Satire" 10, lines 31–33) he must have destroyed. We first meet him as a sharply witty observer of public manners in the two Books of the so-called "Satires" and as a lyric poet in search of a congenial form, in the Epodes. This early phase of his career closed in 30 B.C. Through the seven years from 30 to 23 he produced his masterwork, the eighty-eight odes or "songs", which he published together in three books in 23. Through the remaining three years of the decade he composed the twenty letters in verse, subsequently known as *Epistles. Book I*, which he issued as a collection in 20. This master decade of his career also witnessed Vergil's creation of the *Aeneid* and the transformation of the Roman Republic into the Roman Empire.

At forty-five he expressed a weariness and a wish to have done with poetry, and for two or three years he wrote little. At the wish of the emperor he emerged from semiretirement to compose the hymn for the centennial rites of 17, and again at the wish of the emperor in 15 he undertook to celebrate the momentous Roman conquests of that year in and beyond the Alps. The victory poems were fleshed out with other lyric pieces, of varying merit and apparently of widely varying dates, to make *Odes. Book 4*. In the same period a verse letter addressed to and solicited by the emperor formed the nucleus of *Epistles. Book II*; the two long, accompanying epistles—one of them the famous "Art of Poetry"—were probably republications of works from the years 19 to 17. These two final collections of odes and of epistles, seem to have been published in 13, presumably by Horace himself. After that double valedictory no further poems were composed and nothing whatsoever is known about the last five years of his life. He died November 27, 8 B.C., a few months after Maecenas, and the two were buried side by side in the gardens of the mansion on the Esquiline Hill.

In summary, Horace's published works are:

Satires. Book I	S.1	35–34 B.C.	at age 30
Satires. Book II	S.2	30 B.C.	at age 35
The Book of Epodes	Epode(s)	30 B.C.	at age 35
Odes. Books 1,2, and 3	*Odes* 1,2, 3	23 B.C.	at age 42
Epistles. Book I	E.1	20 B.C.	at age 45
The Centennial Hymn		17 B.C.	at age 48
Odes. Book 4	*Odes* 4	?13 B.C.	at age 52
Epistles. Book II	E.2	?13 B.C.	at age 52

These works enjoyed fame in their own time and place, and ample financial reward as well. Obvious merit silenced the early fault-finders, whose objection to Horace was more social than literary anyway, so by the time of the *Centennial Hymn*, 17 B.C., Horace was a national figure and acknowledged as Rome's greatest living poet, Vergil having died two years before. The first critical edition of the poems was made by Marcus Valerius Probus around 60 A.D., and by that date, if not earlier, selected poems had come to be regularly studied in schools, where busts of Vergil and Horace adorned the classrooms. Around 100 A.D. Suetonius wrote his biography of Horace, which survives only in brief digest. Soon thereafter Quintus Terentius Scaurus brought out his elaborate edition in ten Books, the tenth Book being given over exclusively to the *Ars Poetica*, under that title. (Not until the sixteenth century was that poem restored to its original place as "E.2.3.") Scholarly annotation of the works had begun before 100, but the most extensive commentary was compiled by Pompónius Porphýrio, who seems to have lived in the 200s A.D. Further commentary was added by the still later writer known as Acro. Verbal echoes of Horace's lines continued to be heard in Roman poets beyond the fall of the Western empire, as long as classical Latin was understood.

Christian monks long admired the "Satires" and Epistles and used them in their monastery schools, but the monastic scriptoria copied out the lyric poems also. Some 250 manuscripts, complete or partial, survive from the period before the invention of the printing press, the earliest being in the 700s. If the first printed text appeared in an unknown year before 1471, there were more than seventy printed editions, whole or partial, before 1500. Establishment of a correct Horatian text and refinement of interpretive commentary were achieved by numerous writers in western European countries, but three landmarks of Horace scholarship may be cited: the 1578 edition by Jacques de Crusque, professor at Bruges, who signed himself Cruquius; the edition of 1711 by the Englishman Richard Bentley; and Kiessling's German edition in three volumes of the 1890s.

Horatian influence on western European poets since 1500 has been strong, though not always continuously so. Ronsard in sixteenth-century France is a conspicuous example. In England verbal adaptations of Horace's phrases and lines may be discerned woven into the very fabric of poems from the Elizabethan lyricists to at least 1900, notably in the works of Milton, Herrick, Pope, and Tennyson; we cite a number of instances in the notes to the present translation. Until recently, however, Horace's stanza patterns have been rejected as alien to English prosody, so that translations were often loose paraphrases in what individual writers deemed "equivalent forms." A case in point is *Odes* 1.3 with its 40 lines paragraphed 8 + 12 + 20; Dryden's 1685 version used 55 tetrameter lines, mostly rhymed in couplets, whereas the 40 lines by John Conington (1825–1869) alternate 4-foot lines with 5-foot lines through ten quatrains, rhymed a–a–b–b. In such renditions one looks in vain for the "lapidary" quality which Nietzsche admired as uniquely Horatian. In this fashion the Odes were four times translated complete between 1861 and 1894, with or without the other lyric poems, and a fifth complete rendering appeared in 1880 "Englished and Imitated by Various Hands." Some of the poems, including favorite "Satires" and Epistles, have been so "Englished" over and over again. No classical author has so often been *partially* translated as Horace.

In the twentieth century there have been further anthologies of imitations by various hands, notably George F. Whicher's *Selected Poems of Horace* (1947), with nine pieces done by Professor Whicher himself. In 1959 the "Satires" and Epistles were presented complete in the racy and wittily inventive idiom of Smith Palmer Bovie. In 1960 Joseph P. Clancy offered the Odes and Epodes, and in 1965 James Michie published the Odes and Centennial Hymn, using the classical meters in thirteen cases.

Besides the value of the poems as poems, there is also the endearing personality of Horace himself to account for this perennial interest. He is Everyman's friend. Advance only a short distance into his works, and you begin to perceive him as a living personage at your side: immensely likeable, trustworthy, level-headed, compatible with almost any society, and congenial with almost any mood. Apart from the rigors of his Latin, he offers few difficulties of comprehension. No inaccessible ecstasies, no dark profundities. He was accounted erudite by his contemporaries, but the erudition appears in the details, not in the central thoughts. Averse to travel, he gathered his extensive geography largely at home and used it chiefly for ornamentation. His weather-and-star lore is commonplace information picturesquely expressed. Only his "mythology" demands effort from the modern reader. On the subjects of history and philosophy he makes statements important to him but less important to us because he was not clearly informed about either one.

In his overview of history he sometimes saw the earth and mankind as degenerated from the perfections of the Golden Age long ago and sometimes as brought slowly forward by "heroes" from an originally brutish condition into civilization. He even seems unaware of the contradiction. As for the "long ago," it sometimes appears as remote as the Ice Age, and then again it seems close to the (Greek) heroic age and the Trojan War. His factual history goes no further back than Herodotus was able to go, to about 600 B.C., and after the Persian wars (490–479) it turns into literary history. The Greek poets and dramatists were perfectly clear to him, and he was aware of the rise of Alexandria as a center of learning after 300. He knew that all Greece had been reduced to the status of a Roman province, but apart from inferring a moral parable about Greek weakness and Roman superiority he seems indifferent as to how it all came about. His Roman history is a congeries of patriotic myths rather than ordered facts, and there are moments when his chronology seems to blend the Second Punic War of 218–201 with the Third Punic War of 149–146.

By "philosophy" he usually means no more than the study of "how to live," but in at least one case (E.1.12.16–20) he understands it as natural science: "What keeps the sea at one level? What orders the cycle of seasons?/ Should we see planets as self-moved or governed by laws in their motions?" And last, "Whether Stertínius or whether Empédocles preaches sheer madness?" These two names betoken respectively the Stoic and Epicurean philosophies as Horace knew them in his own time and between which he cannot make up his mind. More than once he argues against the Stoics, yet his recurrence to them shows that he is partly drawn to their stern doctrine of moral self-control in accordance with "Nature." By temperament he inclined rather toward Epicureanism, but he shrank from full commitment there either, possibly because he misinterpreted the doctrine in the popularly shallow way as mere avoidance of the unpleasant. At forty-five he declares (in E.1.1.13–15) his independence of any "school," or, as we would say, of any sect, any denomination. Abstract thinking was not his way, he clung to day-to-day realities, and when he proposes, at age forty-six or so, to abandon poetry for philosophy we feel he is barking up the wrong tree.

He brings the day-to-day realities of his city so close before the reader that they seem only a step or two away, and those realities absolve us from "the grandeur that was Rome," about which we have heard unto weariness. At the mention of traffic jams in the Forum we grin, knowingly. We hear also of noisy theater crowds, of hazards from construction works in the streets, of rascally teenagers soldering a penny to the pavement and lurking to watch some sober citizen try to pick it up, of election candidates handshaking right and left, of barbershops and greasy quick-food kitchens, of fortune-tellers and performing mountebanks, and of trysts at nightfall on the Campus Martius and "whisperings under arcades,"

> When laughter rippling low from a shadowed nook
> Delightfully betrays that a girl is there,
> With bracelet yielded from an arm or
> Ring from a finger not quite reluctant.

Oddly enough, his urban vignettes are more vividly evocative than his rural ones: beloved scenes are more difficult to portray than scenes familiar but disdained.

If his laughter is often infectious, his dry wit is often more memorable. We quite understand about the writer "Of (whom) they say that his books and their cases supplied all the fuel/Needed to cremate him after his death." And our sympathy goes out to that 'indecent old woman of Thebes" who so

> Ordered her will that her corpse should be liberally coated with oil and
> Carried to burial over her heir's naked shoulders, to see if
> She could just once, even dead, slip away from him.

Both quotations illustrate Horace's characteristic brevity and understatement. On occasion he will tell a longish story, and tell it very well, but his hallmark is the distilled anecdote from which we reconstruct the larger story for ourselves. The same compression is to be found in his lines of pathos, glee, or loveliness, and very rarely does he overcompress to the point of obscurity. The terseness does, however, oblige slow reading. He knew all about *le mot juste*. He was aware that words had overtones in addition to denotations, and he was capable of using the subtle overtones to complete his meaning (see our note on the word *volubilis* in *Odes* 4.1.40). He could also use the sound of words themselves to enhance his meaning: his Bandusian waters *sound* in *loquaces/ lymphae desiliunt tuae* (which we try to imitate in "Lightly babbling in liquid speech").

Not infrequently a poem intricately wrought will conclude with lines still more intricately wrought in order to create the sense of a full stop. A striking case is that of the lines quoted above:

> When laughter rippling low from a shadowed nook
> Delightfully betrays that a girl is there, . . .

Our note to *Odes* 1.9.21–22 demonstrates the tour de force of the Latin counterpart. The same poem also exemplifies his unique manner of making his lines "evolve" toward a wholly unexpected ending. That ninth ode begins in wintry cold, with Mount Sorácte's snows contrasted to the blaze of a cheerful hearthfire, while with lines 18 to 24 we enter into the mood of a warm and sensuous summer night out of doors. Such astonishing transitions occur more than once, and there is no explaining them by logic. If at first encounter we are disconcerted, we soon accept this baffling kind of enchantment. The secret of the process, we suspect, lies in systematic deletions of all prosaic elements. Long before the French symbolists Horace had discovered *une alchimie du verbe*.

How all these things came out in oral delivery we can only guess. The *lyric* poems imply *lyre*-accompaniment. In *Odes* 4.6.35–36 Horace himself bids his chorus

> Keep the Lesbic rhythm and mark my thumbstroke
> Setting the cadence.

But surely the lyre did more than plunk out the rhythm, though we know next to nothing about what kind of musical continuum was used or of what flourishes and embellishments were permissible. Discreet experiments ought to be made with recitations to the accompaniment of a guitar, or possibly of a lute, bearing in mind that "ode" was the Greek word for "a song." The art of the "Satires" was, by contrast, nonlyric and elocutionary, and there is an elocutionary quality in much of the Epistles, for all that the title suggests private reading.

In the "Satires" Horace strikes the pose of a public speaker, his objective being to be the Lucilius of his own time. The mordant invective of the Epodes was intended to revive the bellicose spirit of Archílochus, but the mood of harsh invectiveness could not be sustained. We even suspect Horace of purveying "secondhand anger," not only in Epode 10 but elsewhere as well. Then, with the discovery of the true touchstone in the poetry of Alcáeus, as Epode 13 indicates, he found his way to exalted song. In the Odes he sought to create for his countrymen the Latin equivalent of the splendid repertory of Greek lyric (now almost wholly lost to us). Through an astonishingly broad range of themes and moods he sings, lyre in hand, of love and wine and friendship, of his beloved country and of the gods. About the

god of wine he has much to say, to be sure, but his personal reverence for
Mercury/Hermes is deeply felt. Laying aside his lyre at last, he entrusted earnest
thoughts and opinions to his "letters in verse," a literary device apparently of his
own invention. From semiretirement in ill health patriotic duty summoned him
forth to last efforts both lyric and elocutionary. Amid the impressive totality of his
productions we may have our individual preferences, but even the lesser pages are to
be treasured.

A Suggestion. For any poem in this book we recommend: first, a cursory reading of the text,
then a cursory reading of the accompanying notes, and then a careful reading of the poem.
Horace never composed works to be taken in at a glance.

For first-time readers of this large body of work, S.1.6 and S.2.6 establish the personality
of Horace. Old favorites among the earlier works are S.1.9 and Epode 2; for good measure
add the poignant Epode 16 and the sardonic S.2.5.

A fair sampling of the famous odes might consist of:

Book 1, Nos. 4, 9, 10, 17, 37, and 38;
Book 2, Nos. 14 and 19;
Book 3, Nos. 5, 7, 9, 11, 13, 14, 18, 23, and 26.

Beyond this, readers will easily find their own way, either at random or by glancing at the
introductions to the separate subsections.

To Horace

Toga, cowl, and periwig, in their eras,
Found your hand more true than a living brother's;
Words of yours are keys in our present locks of
        Friendship and laughter.

Human truths at odds with each other, Horace,
Were your Truth; you welcomed each man and mood, each
Song and thought, and each of the sovereign gods, as
        Jupiter's kinsfolk,

To your lyric feasts, not disbarring Folly.
And you had a "thing" about human hair, both
Lads' and minxes', seeing in each a masking
        Godling or goddess.

Mellow was your wine, without mad excesses.
Under noonday's heat you discerned the summer's
Silent music breathed by the flute of Faunus
        Over your farmstead.

Sternness too you spoke in the face of wrongs, and
Greed drew your contempt; self-respect was stoutly
Yours, and you could laugh at your own shortcomings
        Frankly conceded.

When your threads of thought on a listless morning
Frayed, or knotted up in the Dog Days' torpor,
Then in eerie stillness the son of Maia
        Suddenly stood there

Skeining out the strands of connective discourse
For you, tipping words with his wand of power
Bright from skies or dark from the land of death, as
        Journeyings brought him.

                                    —CEP

9

Satires. Book I
Sermones. Liber Primus
35 B.C.

Satires. Book I

Around his thirtieth birthday, December 8, 35 B.C., Horace issued a first collection of his poems, ten in number, in a "volume" (i.e., in a single papyrus or parchment roll), for public sale. Since No. 10 replies to criticisms of No. 4, and since No. 4 in turn alludes to criticism of No. 2, some or all of the pieces must have circulated previously, at least within limited circles. He entitled the collection *Sermones* (pronounced "sair-MON-ace"), "Talks," (singular *sermo*), yet his avowed model was the "Satires" (*Saturae*) composed by the Roman poet Lucilius between 133 and 103 B.C.

In English, "satire" implies mockery and sarcasm, which were only incidental features of the ancient form. Latin *satíra/satúra*, as in *satura lanx*, "a mixed platter," meant "a medley," or "a little bit of everything." It had nothing to do with satyrs and should not be spelled "satyra." Indeed, the critic Quintilian, writing a century after Horace, claimed that *satura* was an exclusively Roman invention, with nothing Greek about it. Its origins were remote and its evolution complex, but it is to be inferred that Lucilius was the first poet to impress literary shape and distinction upon the old form. From the thirty "Books" of his *Satires* 1,272 disconnected fragments still survive, confirming the report that those poems dealt with the greatest variety of subjects possible under the circumstances: politics, manners, individuals in the public eye, events, bits of autobiography, and the author's feelings and opinions. In short, they resembled somewhat a modern "syndicated column" in a newspaper, except that they were in verse.

Horace set out to compose a Lucilius-style miscellany for his own time. Again the verse form would be the "dactylic hexameter" (see below), which was the standard line for nonlyric poetry in Latin and ultimately derived from Homer, but without the diffuseness and technical carelessness of his model. There would be maximum variety of subject matter, except that political remarks absolutely had to be avoided in the explosively dangerous 30s B.C. Topics of public morality, moreover, needed to be generalized and treated impersonally. Thus Horace's sinners bear fanciful names, or else he cites real persons safely dead for a generation. Whether the end product is or is not "poetry" is a point discussed in S.1.4.39–64, which concludes

12

that "satire" is decidedly *not* exalted poetry but that it has a justifiable place in the literary scheme of things.

These ten first-published works are unequal in poetic merit, but Horace's technical control in all of them implies that he had discarded more than one forestudy. No. 9, sometimes called "The Bore," is the most immediately enjoyable to readers of any era. No. 6, autobiographical from line 45 on, is very moving. The swift-paced No. 5, "The Journey to Brundisium," brings us face to face with a lively personality who must have been a delight to know. If the sex-talk of No. 2 startles by its brutal frankness, the viewpoint expressed is solidly conventional. The anti-Stoic No. 3 verges on anger and seems rather removed from our own times, until we perceive that the cantankerous Stoic is a cantankerous fundamentalist of any era. No. 8 is a bizarre piece, bawdy insofar as it deals with Priápus, gruesome insofar as it deals with Canídia.

The opening poem was doubtless composed last or second to last, in order to bring the name of Maecenas into the very first line and thereby to dedicate the whole collection to him. No. 7 reports an anecdote from the early months of 42 B.C.; if it was written soon after the incident narrated, it would be Horace's earliest preserved work; but the anecdote could have been recalled and written up later. Presumably, however, it was, together with Nos. 2 and 4, among the works that caught the attention of Vergil and Varius in the years 41 to 38 and led them to bring the obscure civil servant Horace to Maecenas's attention. That introduction may have been made in 39, surely no later than 38; hence all the other pieces, by alluding to Maecenas—and, in our opinion, No. 7, which shows familiarity with the layout of Maecenas's residential property—are to be dated to the years 38 to 35. The sequence of composition is otherwise a speculative matter. Only No. 5, "The Journey to Brundisium," can be specifically dated to the winter of 38–37, because political history dates the journey itself to the autumn of 38 B.C.

Essentially, then, these ten *Sermones* are the work of an author aged twenty-six to thirty. Uneven in value they may be, but they are not negligible. Despite the author's title for them, they have been known since ancient times as "Satires. Book I," and we shall henceforth so refer to them here, abbreviating the term as "S.1."

The Dactylic Hexameter Line

Latin poetry of the classical period, like the Greek poetry it imitated, was based on the distinction of long syllables from short syllables. By definition, a "long" required twice the pronunciation time of a "short," and conversely, a "short" required half the pronunciation time of a "long."

Any hexameter line consisted of six time-units ("feet") of equal duration, each occupying the time required for the pronunciation of two long syllables. In the particular type of hexameter here under discussion the poet was at liberty to use two "longs" (a spondee) *or* one "long" and "two shorts" (a dactyl) in any or all of the first four "feet." The fifth "foot," however, had to be a dactyl (LONG-short-short), hence the term "dactylic hexameter". The sixth "foot" may be imagined as consisting of: one "long" and one "short" and a breath catch, like a rest in music, equivalent to the missing "short."

Rhyme was totally unknown in classical Greek and Latin poetry. It is of Oriental origin and, in the western world, first appeared in early Christian hymns.

English poetry is based, *not* on the principle of "long" and "short" syllables, but on the principle of stressed (or accented) and unstressed (or unaccented) syllables. The present translation imitates the meters of the Latin originals by substituting "stresses" for "longs" and "non-stresses" for "shorts."

Not, however, without problems. In the frequent cases where a Latin spondee (two "longs") is followed by a Latin dactyl ("long-short-short") there is an automatic succession of three "longs." Regular English speech does produce a succession of three stressed syllables, but neither frequently nor regularly, and more than three is impossible to contrive. Not infrequently Latin has two spondees followed by a dactyl, requiring *five* accented syllables in succession. This is impossible in English, to say nothing of cases where three or four spondees occur before the fifth-"foot" dactyl, producing *nine* accented syllables in a row. Our translation, therefore, settles for uniform lines of five dactyls, and the semi-dactyl of the sixth foot. It was either this or abandoning the principle of imitating the meter of the original Latin altogether. Our lines are, then, all:

_ ∪ ∪   _ ∪ ∪   _ ∪ ∪   _ ∪ ∪   _ ∪ ∪   _ ∪

14

In first draft the present translation did, in fact, experiment with English spondees, always with appeal to usual speech rhythms, but unless there was recourse to awkward diacritical marks (such as Robert Bridges used in his "Poems in Classical Prosody"*), the scansion of lines would have perplexed the best of readers. In revising, the translator retreated to an all-dactyl pattern, leaving the first foot of S.1.3.18 as a sample spondee; there regular English emphasis exactly suited the meaning of the text in "All day long he would snore": _ _ _ ∪ ∪ _. . . .

A few remarks relevant only to the Latin language may be added for the curious. Native Latin speakers learned from infancy which vowels in their language were "long" and which were "short;" a modern must consult a dictionary. In theory, *hīc* ("here") required twice the pronunciation time of *hĭc* ("this"); both vowels had the *quality* of English *ee*, the difference was in the *quantity*. Thus the classroom distinction between English "heat" and English "hit" makes an inexact parallel: in these English words the vowel *quality* is different. Precisely how the Latin distinction *sounded* nobody knows.

In poetry, a syllable is "long" because it contains: (1) a "long" vowel, or (2) a double vowel (*ae*, *oe*, etc.), or (3) a "short" vowel followed by two (or more) consonants, even if the second consonant comes in the following word. A "short" syllable" is one containing a "short" vowel followed by no more than one consonant. In the dactylic hexameter, however, the final syllable is deemed "short" regardless of its vowel's quantity.

Most baffling to moderns is the fact that poetic scansion often runs counter to Latin speech accent—and Latin did have a strong speech accent. In the dactylic hexameter the first four "feet" usually work *against* the speech accent, the last two "feet" usually show the two elements "harmonized." (A clear exposition of these matters may be read in W. Sidney Allen's *Vox Latina*, Cambridge University Press, 1965, pp. 89–94.)

As a testing sample, the opening of S.2.3 is offered as a problem in oral reading. Speaking angrily and, one would imagine, rapidly, Damasíppus breaks in upon the drowsing Horace with the following lines, in which *all* syllables are "long" except those italicized.

> Sic raro scribis, ut toto non *quater* anno
> membranam poscas, scriptorum quae*que re*texens,
> iratus *tibi*, quod, vini somn*ique be*nignus,
> nil dignum sermon*e ca*nas.

1.1.   *Qui fit, Maecenas, ut nemo, quam sibi sortem*

How does it happen, Maecénas, that no one, no matter what lot is
His in this life by deliberate choice or as chance has determined,
Ever is happy with that, but is always admiring the courses
Followed by others? — "Oh, merchants are lucky," a soldier of lengthy

The Poetical Works of Robert Bridges, Oxford University Press, 1936, pp. 407–472.

5   Service remarks, now a wreck of a man after years of much hardship.
     Contrariwise speaks the merchant with cargo ship tossing in southwinds:
     "Soldiers do better. And why? There's a battle, you see; in a single
     Hour swift death overtakes them or else they are victors rejoicing."
     Someone immersed in the law and the statutes is all for a farmer's
10   Life when a client comes thumping his door as the roosters are crowing;
     Dragged in from country to city, the other, in court on a bail bond,
     Swears that the only existence worth living is there in the City.
     Citing all parallel cases, and many and many they are, might
     Bore even Fabius. Not to go on over-long, let me come right
15   Down to my point. If a god should proclaim: "Here I am. Each one's wishes
     I shall perform. You who now are a soldier, I make you a merchant;
     You there, the lawyer: be changed to a farmer. Be off and away now,
     Off and away with you, changed in your several characters. — Heia!
     Why are you standing there?" See how they balk at the chance to be happy
20   Who, then, can rightly blame Jupiter if in his anger he puffs his
     Cheeks full of air and announces that he will henceforth not be quite so
     Easily summoned to listen when people come making petitions.
          Furthermore, not to go rattling off lists the way comics tell one joke
     After another, — yet what's to forbid our amusement at telling
25   Truths, the way teachers cajole little boys by awarding them cookies,
     Coaxing them on to the point where they *want* to learn more of their letters?
     Joking, however, aside, let us talk about serious matters.
          That fellow there, the one breaking up clods by the toil of the plowshare,
     Or, say, this cheat of an innkeeper here, or soldiers, or daring
30   Sailors that travel the seas: every one of them claims that he labors
     Only to serve his old age and have safety and peace in retirement,
     When they expect to have scraped up provisions enough to get by on.
     Theirs is the way of the ant, of the mightily toiling but tiny
     Ant that comes lugging as much as she can in her mouth to the stockpile
35   Already gathered in cautious awareness of times that are coming.
     Then, when Aquarius saddens the under-turned year in its round, not
     Once will she poke her head out, but will live on the stores she collected
     Wisely. But nothing keeps *you* from your moneybags, neither the raging
     Heat of the summer, nor winter, nor fire, nor the ocean or weapons:
40   Nothing can stop you while one man alive still outranks you in riches.
          What is the good of acquiring such masses of silver and gold if
     All you can do is go furtively digging a hole to conceal it?
     — "Take out a little, and all of it goes, to the last wretched penny."
     — But, if you don't, what's the use of the whole blessèd pile you've assembled?
45   Say that your threshing-floor furnishes one hundred thousand of grist-grain:
     That does not mean that your belly can hold any *more* grain than mine; if
     You were to walk in a slave-porter train with your shoulders bent double
     Under great netfuls of bread, you would not get more bread at the lunchtime
     Break than the man who has not carried any. And tell me: if someone
50   Lives within nature's own bounds, does it matter if acres are sown by

Hundreds or thousands? — "It's nice, though, to draw on a sizeable stockpile."
— But, since you leave me to draw just as much for myself from my *small* pile,
Why do you glory in granary barns as opposed to my wheat-bins?
That's as if, needing a drinking supply of no more than a pitcher
Holds, or a cup, you replied: "I prefer getting drink from a river   55
Rather than drawing an equal amount from this trickle-flow spring here."
That's how the people delighting in more than sufficient get carried
Off by the Aúfidus River, which drowns them along with its banksides;
Those taking only the needed amount find the water unmuddied,
Nor do they run any risk to their lives in the turbulent floodstreams.   60

    Still, there is many a man so misguided by greed as to claim: "There
Is no such thing as 'enough.' What you *own* is your measure of *being*."
What can you do with a person like that, but reply: "Go ahead! Be
Wretched as much as you like!" An Athenian once, so they say, both
Greedy and wealthy, would counter reproaches like this with the answer: 65
"People may hiss me, but *I* am quite proud of myself on arriving
Home and inspecting the masses of coin I have stored in my coffers."
Tántalus, thirsting forever, keeps straining to taste the retreating
Waters forever eluding his lips . . . Do you sneer? With a simple
Name-switch the story fits *you*. On your moneybags gathered from every   70
Quarter you dotingly sleep and inhale, but forbid any touching,
As with a consecrate object, or paintings meant only for viewing.
Are you aware of what money is good for? what uses it offers?
Bread can be bought with it, cabbage, a measure of wine, not to mention
Various things that the nature of man is unhappy for lacking.   75
Think of your staying awake, worried sick with anxiety; think of
Guarding by night and by day against burglars and fires and the slaves you
Fear may make off with your goods and escape: can you really enjoy this?
Those are the worldly possessions that *I* would prefer to be poor in.

    But, you say, if it so happens you're stricken with chills or the ague,   80
Or, if some other disease makes you keep to your bed, you have someone
There at your bedside to give you your medicines, call for the doctor,
Get you back up on your feet and restore you to kinsmen and loved ones.
— Neither your wife nor your son wants to see you get well again; all your
Neighbors and all your acquaintances hate you, yes, even the children.   85
Are you surprised, after ranking all else below money, to find that
No one will show you affection — which *you* have done nothing to merit?
If you imagine you can, without effort, retain the good wishes
Bred into kinsmen by nature herself and retain all your friendships,
Miserable man, you are wasting your time; you might just as well try, say,   90
Breaking a donkey to harness to run on Mars Field in the races.

    So: put a stop to acquiring and, having amassed the more riches,
Worry the less about poverty. Make a beginning at ending
All these exertions and, having achieved what you wanted, stop acting
Like that Ummídius: wealthy — this story is not very long! — so   95
Wealthy he measured his money by footage, yet cheap to the point of

Dressing no better than one of his slaves, and forever in terror
Down to his very last day that his funds might run out and he yet might
Perish from want, — but his freedwoman split him in two with an ax, for
100   She was as ruggedly brave as the bravest of Týndarus' daughters.
— "What is your recommendation to me, then? To live like a Naevius
Or Nomentánus?" — Why *must* you see only extremes in contention:
One being wrong, the reverse must be right? When I say "Don't be greedy,"
I am not saying you ought to turn wastrel and spendthrift instead. There
105   *Is* middle ground between Tánaïs' standpoint and that of Viséllius.
Things have a mean; whence it follows they also have boundary limits
Past which or short of which there is no proper or lasting position.
        Back where we started, then: how does it happen that, much like the miser,
Nobody likes what he is and begrudges the next fellow's fortunes?,
110   Pining away because somebody's nannygoat's udders are swollen
Fuller of milk than his own, not comparing himself with the vaster
Hordes of the poor, and bent only on beating out this man and that man.
This kind of climber invariably finds his path blocked by the richer
Still, as, when chariots lunge from their stalls in the wake of the racers,
115   Drivers intent on their separate teams watch the lead-horses only,
Scornful of those left behind and pursuing the ones further forward.
Thus does it happen that we can but rarely discover a mortal
Who will admit that he lived his life happily, or at departure
Willingly goes from this life like a diner replete from a banquet.
120   So, then, enough. Lest you think I have pillaged the files of the blear-eyed
Poet Crispínus, I shan't add a syllable more on this topic.

---

14   Fabius was a writer on Stoic philosophy, says an ancient commentator.
36   The year is conceived as a turning wheel; the zodiac sign Aquarius (January 21 to
      February 19) was the last sign in the old Roman year that began on March 1.
50   To live within nature's proper limits was a basic doctrine of the Stoic philosophers.
53   "Wheat-bins" = *cumeris*, which an ancient commentator explains as either wickerwork
      bins or large earthenware jars.
56   "From this trickle-flow spring here" = *ex hoc fonticulo*.
58   The Aúfidus, now the Ofánto, River flows easterly through Horace's native Apulia.
68   According to *Odyssey* 11. 582–592, Tántalus stands forever chin-deep in water which
      drains away the minute he attempts to quench his desperate thirst. The nature of his
      offense to the gods varies with different authors and Horace nowhere specifies which
      version he accepts.
69–70 *Mutato nomine, de te/ fabula narratur* became proverbial.
91   "Mars Field" (*Campus Martius*), the multipurpose park of ancient Rome, included a
      race course. See the note to *Odes* 1.8.4.
95   Ummídius is unknown; he is likely to have been a personage in Lucilius.
100   Clytemnéstra, daughter of Týndarus/-eus, slew her husband Agamemnon with an ax.
101–102 Naevius is unkown, but his name will recur in S.2.2.68. Ancient commentator
      Porphyrio identified Nomentánus with Lucius Cassius Nomentánus, a notorious
      spendthrift of the generation before Horace, but the name occurs in two fragments of
      Lucilius. "Nomentánus" means "a person from Nométum, a town just NE of Rome.
      The Nomentánus" of S.2.8 seems to be a different character altogether.

105   This unclear line may allude to some Greek saying. The text says ". . . and that of
      Viséllius's father-in-law." "Viséllius" is a real Roman name, but "Tanaïs" is the name
      of the S-Russian river now called the Don, as in *Odes* 3.4.36 and 4.15.24.
118–119   Lucretius: *On the Nature of Things* 3.938–9, asks the man afraid of death:

>   Why not, O foolish man, retire, as a dinner guest
>   who has had his fill, and take your rest in peace and quiet?
>   (*Mantinband translation*)

120–121   Ancient commentator Porphýrio says Crispínus was Plotius Crispínus, a
      voluminous poet and a teacher of Stoic philosophy. He is mentioned again in S.1.3.139
      and 2.7.45.
           "Files" = *scrinia*, cylindrical boxes in which the papyrus rolls were kept. (Morris)
           "Blear-eyed" = *lippi*, "having eye-infection", a condition elsewhere mentioned by
      Horace.

1.2.   *Ambubaiarum conlegia, pharmacopolae*

Guilds of our flute-playing ladies, retailers of nostrums, performing
Mime-artists, street entertainers, and mendicant priests,—all that class of
People are mightily mourning the death of Tigéllius the singer
"Always so free with his money!" Contrastingly, here is a fellow
So much afraid of appearing unthrifty he even refuses   5
Helping a friend with enough to prevent him from freezing or starving.
Here is a third: if you ask why he squanders his grandfather's and his
Father's enormous estate to feed gluttonous habits and even
Borrows at interest to purchase all sorts of unusual dainties,
He will reply: "So as not to be seen as a spiritless cheap-Jack."   10
Some people praise him for doing so, others unsparingly blame him.
Then there's Fufídius, dreading the label of wastrel and spendthrift,
[Land-dowered, loaded with cash, every cent of it interest-bearing];
Five percent monthly he charges on loans, plus a principal-discount,
Pressing his debtors more harshly the closer they come to their ruin,   15
Scouting out names of young men with their togas of manhood assumed but
Still under age and with hard-handed fathers in charge of them. "Mighty
Jupiter!" someone exclaims—(as who wouldn't?)—at hearing the like, "then
Outlay and intake must balance?" Oh, no! You would never believe what
Scrimping he practices—much like the father whom Terence's drama   20
Shows us half-starved from remorse after hounding his son from the house: no
Torment more cruel does this man inflict on himself, this Fufídius.
      Now, if you ask me: "What is it you're driving at?", here is my answer:
Fools who avoid any one vice go rushing to opposite vices.
Slack-girdled Málthinus walks with a dangle-down tunic, another   25
Girdles so daintily high at the waist he exposes his privates.
Breath-pills come wafting from Rúfillus, but from Gargónius, goat-stink.
Nothing half-way. There are fellows that won't touch a woman unless her
Dress has a hem with a ruffle-extension to cover her ankles;

30   Others again, only one that's lined up in a rank-smelling whorehouse.
      One of our studs, upon leaving the whorehouse, repeated the cry of
      "That's how to do it!"—(the sentiments voiced by oracular Cato)—
      "Once there's a distention of veins from compulsion of lust, it is well that
      Fellows resort to those places; it's better than grinding away at
35   Other men's wives."—"Not to *my* way of thinking!" retorts Cupiénnius,
      Known connoisseur that he is of the kind that wear white dresses only.
           "Welcome to ears of you all who desire that adulterers *not* thrive"
      Come the good tidings that everywhere they are in line to fare badly;
      Any enjoyment they get is offset by a host of vexations,
40   Chances occur only seldom, and often the risks are excessive.
      One fellow dived from a rooftop; another expired under flogging;
      One that escaped ended up as an outlaw with highwaymen cut-throats;
      One that was captured was able to buy himself off with a ransom;
      Kitchen hands drenched one in piss; there have even been cases where one has
45   Suffered the loss of his testicles and of his lecherous cock by
      Severing sword. "Served him right!" is the verdict—with Galba dissenting.
      Safer by far are the dealings with those who belong to the second
      Class—I mean freedwomen—those that Sallústius goes just as crazy
      Over as any adulterer. If a man wants liaisons with
50   That sort and craves to be told he is "kindly" and "generous,"—taking
      Into account both his means and good sense, and a due moderation,—
      Then he should pay them an adequate sum, stopping short of self-ruin
      Or a bad name. If there's one point a man of that kidney will often
      Boastfully make, it's: "I simply won't touch any woman that's married."
55   So did Marsáeus of old, who was Órigo's lover and gave that
      Mime-actress all his ancestral estates and possessions, saying,
      "Never will *I* have relations with other men's wives." It's a fact that
      Traffic with actresses no less than traffic with prostitutes injures
      Good reputation far more than it injures estates. Are you really
60   Helping yourself by avoidance of one of the pitfalls while plunging
      Into the other, which all men despise? To besmirch a good name and
      Waste an inheritance is a disgrace either way. Does it matter
      Whether you go with a prostitute or with a woman that's married?
           Víllius (back in the Fausta case), solely beguiled by the "Sulla's
65   Son-in-law" epithet, suffered inordinate penalties for it,
      Taking a beating with fists and attacked with a sword while he waited,
      Locked out of doors, for the time Longarénus was indoors with Fausta.
      If, after witnessing that many miseries, Víllius's prick had
      Asked him the question: "What *are* you about?! Have I ever demanded
70   Cunt that was born and descended from blue-blooded consuls and which was
      Wrapped in a matronly stole, when my dander was up?", what excuse could
      Víllius offer except that "The girl has a high-ranking father?"
           Vastly more wise are the promptings of Nature in all of her bounty
      When she advises the opposite course of procedure, if only
75   *You* manage matters aright and do *not* confuse things to be shunned with

Things to be sought. Do you fancy it makes little difference if troubles
Come of themselves or from wrong done by you? Then before you regret it,
Cease your pursuit of the already married, because it results in
More disadvantage than ever the business has yielded in profit.
No married woman in snowy-white pearls and in emerald beads (though   80
You may not think so, Cerínthus) is softer of thigh or of leg more
Shapely, and girls in the dark-colored togas are frequently better.
Furthermore, *their* wares are free of disguises and dyes, what they have to
Sell may be freely inspected, what physical charms they possess they
Do not go touting and flouting while keeping their blemishes hidden.   85
Kings have the habit, when purchasing horses, of covering portions
During inspection, lest excellent features, supported—as often
Happens—on unsteady feet, should befuddle the buyer with splendid
Haunches, a shortness of head, or a sinewy neck. And they're right in
Doing so! Therefore you ought not to scrutinize physical merits   90
Keen-eyed as Lýnceus while being more blind than Hypsáea in seeing
None of the shortcomings: "Oh, what a leg! And what arms!", when in fact she's
Flat in the buttocks, low-waisted, long-nosed, and her feet are enormous.
Now, with the married ones nothing is open to view but the face, all
Else—(save with Catia)—being concealed by the length of their dresses.   95
If you go after objectives enclosed as with ramparts, since those so
Wildly excite you, obstructions aplenty will stand in your way, like
Litters, attendants, and hair-dresser maids, and a bevy of gossips,
Dresses let down to the heels and a muffle of cloaks over dresses,
All of them jealously blocking your view of the principal object.   100
But, with those others, no problem. In gauzes from Cos you can see them
Practically naked: the leg is not bad and the foot is not ugly,
And you can measure a waist at a glance. Would you rather they played you
False and deceived you, collecting your money before there was any
Showing of merchandise? "Just as a hunter goes trudging through snowdrifts 105
After a hare, yet declines the same meat when it's served him at supper,"
Someone will quote, and then add: "That's the way with my love, which
Skips the already dished-up to go after a quarry still running."
         Are you still counting on verses like those to relieve you of grief and
Sorrow and feverish worries that now on your heart weigh so heavy?   110
Wouldn't you do a lot better to ascertain first what are Nature's
Limits on appetite, which are the things she will tolerate, which are
Those she would grieve at the loss of, and see what is substance and what is
Void? If you're dying of thirst, do you ask if the goblets are golden?
Or if you're famished and starving, refuse every food in the world save   115
Peacock and turbot? Then why, if your groin is distended, and right at
Hand is a slave girl or slave lad of yours that you crave in the moment's
Urgency, why would you choose to endure the discomfort of passion?
I wouldn't. *I'm* for a love that's accessible, easy to come by.
Girls (Philodémus remarked) who say 'After a while,' 'For more money,'   120
Or 'If my husband goes out,' are for old eunuch priests;" for himself, he

Wanted one not over-coy about price, who would come when you called her.
Let her be comely and straight, and with just enough elegance so as
Not to seem taller or whiter-complected than Nature designed her.
125 Once such a girl puts her left side up close to my right side, she then is
Ília to me, or Egéria—names I assign do not matter—
Nor am I scared of her husband's return from the country while I'm there
Fucking, with doors battered down, with the dog in a frenzy, with uproar
All through the house, with the woman as pale as her linen and jumping
130 Up, while in various terrors the confidante wails that she may have
Both her legs broken, the wife dreading loss of her dowry, and I my
Death. Then it's "off in a hurry!" with tunic ungirdled and barefoot,
Else it's my money, my ass, or, in future, my good reputation.
Even with Fabius judging, I'll prove getting caught is disastrous.

1–2   "Guilds" (*conlegia*) is ironic. "Fute-playing ladies" *ambubaiarum*, a Syrian word. The "mime-artists" (*mimae*) are actresses in the vaudeville *mimi*; in tragedy and comedy male actors in masks performed all roles. Mendicant priests served only in Asiatic (imported) religions, or possibly in the Orphic cult from Greece.

3   For Tigéllius see the following Satire, line 3 and note.

12   Moneylender Fufídius bears an actual Roman name, but the individual is unidentified.

13   This identical line occurs as E.2.3.421, where it is necessary to the sense. Here it is superfluous and probably represents some reader's marginal cross-reference later copied into the present text.

14   *One* percent monthly was the usual interest rate—without a principal-discount.

20   Terence's drama is the comedy of the 160s B.C. called *The Self-Tormentor* (*Heautontimoroumenos*).

32   Cato the Elder, 234–149 B.C., was the very "oracle" of puritanical virtues.

35   "Cupiénnius" was doubtless selected for its suggestion of *cupio*, "to lust after," but one ancient commentator believed it represented Gaius Cupiénnius Libo, a friend of Ocatvius Caesar.

36   Respectable matrons wore only white in public; prostitutes wore dark togas; see line 82. In the text, Cupiennius is a *mirator cunni albi*, "a fancier of white cunt."

37   A line of Ennius (239–169 B.C., whom schoolboys studied; see the note to *Odes* 4.8.20): "Welcome to ears of you all who desire that the Roman state thrive. . . ," with the word *not* intruded by Horace.

47–53   Adultery, then, can occur only between "persons of quality"! From Horace, the son of a freedman, comes the advice that freedwomen are socially acceptable mistresses! Sallústius is unidentified. The famous historian, Gaius Sallústius Crispus, died the year when this satire was published (35 B.C.), and his heir, of the same name, seems an implausible party, given the friendly tone of *Odes* 2.2, addressed to him.

55   An ancient commentator says that Órigo was a mime-actress (see the note to lines 1–2 above); Marsáeus is known only from this context.

64–67   A scandal of Cicero's time involved Fausta, daughter of Sulla. As the wife of Milo, she had concurrent affairs with Longarénus and Víllius, the latter being derisively known as "Sulla's son-in-law."

86–89   This "custom of kings," if it ever existed, is nowhere else mentioned.

91   Lýnceus ("lynx-eyed") figured in various Greek myths, e.g., he was the lookout man on the voyage of the Argonauts. Hypsáea is unknown.

101   "See-through" silks from the Greek island of Cos were famous. The text says "in Coans."

105–108 The quotation paraphrases an epigram of Callímachus, who flourished around 260 B.C. as a poet, critic, bibliographer, and probably as director of the great library in Alexandria, Egypt.

113–114 "Substance" here = the "atoms" of Epicurean physics; "void" (*inane*) = the empty space between such "atoms." Horace knew Lucretius's Latin poem *On the Nature of Things* and quite possibly the Greek source works for that poem. The sense is "shadow versus substance," or "appearance versus reality."

120 Philodémus was an Epicurean philosopher of the previous generation. His lost epigram must be inferred from the present text.

121 "Old eunuch priests" = *Galli*, the priests of Cybelē, whose orgiastic rites culminated in self-castration. See the note on Dindymenē, *Odes* 1.16.7.

126 Ília was the mother of Romulus by the god Mars; see the note to *Odes* 1.2.18. Egéria was the "goddess" whom the early Roman king Numa used to consult privately for her wise guidance.

134 Fabius is doubtless the Stoic philosopher of S.1.1.14 and note. A basic doctrine of the Stoics had it that no evil could befall a true philosopher, who stood outside of good and evil, but Horace is sure that "getting caught" *would* be recognized as an evil.

1.3.   *Omnibus hoc vitium est cantoribus, inter amicos*

Singers have one sorry habit in common: when asked among friends to
Sing for the company, nothing on earth will induce them to do so;
*Un*asked, there's no way to stop them. Sardinian Tigéllius was like that.
Ceasar, who could have invoked his authority if he had wished to,
Either by citing the friendship of Julius or citing his own, could   5
Never get anywhere with him at all. When the mood was upon him
He would intone the "Hail, Bacchus!" from egg-course to apples, now playing
High in the treble, now deep in the bass, on all four of the lyrestrings.
Nothing consistent about the man: sometimes he went at a run as
If he were fleeing from foes, then again at a pace such as Juno's   10
Cult-object bearers observe in processionals. Two hundred slaves might
Serve him at times, then again only ten. He might sometimes talk kings and
Tetrarchs and grandeurs; or else it was: "Give me a three-legged table,
Unscented salt in a sea shell container, and any old coarse-weave
Toga to keep out the cold." Yet this man so contented with little   15
Would, if you gave him a million, discover his money chest empty
Five days thereafter. At night you would find him awake till the dawn, then
All day long he would snore. There was never a man that was quite so
Fickle. —Now, maybe some person will challenge me: "What about you? Do
You have no foibles?" —Yes, only they're different ones. Lesser ones, maybe.   20
— One time when Máenius was picking on Novius' flaws in his absence
Somebody asked him: "Do *you* know yourself? If you don't, you're still no
Stranger to *us*." — "Any faults I may have, I forgive," answered Máenius.
Smugness like that is outrageous, absurd, and deserving of censure.

    Faults of your own you inspect with an eyesight all bleary from eye-salve: 25
Why peer at faults of your friends with the eye of an eagle and fix on

Them like the wise Epidáurian serpent? For, sooner or later,
Your vices too will come under inspection from others. —"But what if
One is a trifle quick-tempered, impatient of finicky critics?

30 Maybe a toga that drapes like a rag, or a countrified haircut
Makes him ridiculous, maybe he shuffles along on account of
Ill-fitting shoes." — But he *is* a good man, you won't find any better,
And he is also your friend, with a first-rate intelligence too, for
All of his outward uncouthness. Just shake out your own toga-folds and

35 See whether Nature may not have implanted some faults in yourself when
You were created, or whether bad habits have not introduced some:
Untended fields go to weeds and at times need a good burning over.

　　　Turning the subject somewhat, let us note how a lover is blind to
Blemishes found in a mistress, and even may find them attractive,

40 Just as the nose-wart on Hágna delighted Balbínus. I wish we
Made that mistake in our friendships! I wish terminology used in
Ethics had furnished a kindlier name for that error! We really
Oughtn't to shrink with aversion before the defects of our friends, but
Treat them as fathers treat sons: if a boy is born squint-eyed his father

45 Gives him the nickname of "Blinky": a son that is wretchedly small is
"Chicky," — Mark Antony kept such a runt in his household and called him
Sísyphus; one that has misshapen legs will be "Bandy"; and one with
Ankles so twisted he hardly stands upright, his father calls "Stumpy."
Now, let us say there's a man a bit close with his money: then call him

50 "Thrifty." One given to playing the clown and the show-off, let *him* be
Hailed as "Amusing" by friends. For a man who is tactlessly rude and
Brusque in his judgments, a better description is "Fearless" or "Forthright."
One is hot-tempered: enroll him among the "high-spirited." *I* feel
This is how friendships are made in the first place — and kept after making.

55 　　　Yet we go on switching excellent qualities bottom-sides-up and
Even take pleasure in getting a clean jar encrusted with wine-lees.
If in our midst lives a man that is honest and utterly gentle,
Him we deride with such catchwords as "slow" and "dull-witted," but take one
Smart at eluding a snare and whose flank is not open to side-thrusts, —

60 Such is the world that we live in, with envy so keen, and with quick-tongued
Vilification so rife, that instead of our saying he "shows good
Sense and is not without prudence," we say he is "crafty" and "two-faced."
Some are well-meaning but thoughtless, — like me on occasion, Maecénas,
Blurting out some insignificant comment or other while you are

65 Reading or silently lost in the train of your thoughts: of a pest of
This sort we say "He's a nuisance and lacking in tact altogether."
We are too hasty, alas!, making rules to our own disadvantage.
No one is born without faults, and the best man among us is he with
Fewest upon him. A friend who is fond of me properly weighs my

70 Good points agatimst my defects; let the heavier weight of my good points
　— If they indeed are the heavier — lower that scale of his balance
If he desires my affection: then *his* shall be weighed in like manner.

Anyone asking his friends not to take notice of *his* warts
Must forgive *them* for their pimples; when craving indulgence for faults of
Ours, it is no more than fair to show similar patience with others.   75

(The poem now gradually passes to a critique of the Stoic doctrine that all crimes are
equally heinous, e.g., that killing a rooster is as evil as murdering one's father.)

Since, then, the fault of bad temper is quite inextractable from us,
Just as the vices inherent in fools are beyond all excision,
Why not let Reason apply its own standards of measures and weights and
Mete out the penalties as individual cases may warrant?
Say that a host bade a slave take a platter away, and the slave stood   80
Eating the left-over fish on the platter and licking the gravy:
Anyone having him crucified for it might well be considered
Madder than Labeo. How much more crazy and how much more heinous
Would be, however, a crime such as this: say a friend has committed
Some slight offense that you churlishly will not forgive; you avoid his   85
Company out of distaste, — like the man that owes money to Ruso,
Who, when the miserable first of the month rolls around and he cannot
Scrape up the interest or pay on the principal, stoops like a captive
Under the yoke and submits to historical readings by Ruso.
Someone, while drunk, may have peed on my couch, or have broken a certain   90
Priceless antique with a handle worn smooth by the thumb of Evánder,
Or in his hunger have reached to the side of the dish nearest me and
Taken my serving of chicken: shall that man be any the less my
Jolly good friend? What on earth do I do if he steals? or goes blabbing
Secrets confided to him? or declines to abide by a promise?   95
People who rate all offences as equally wicked are brought up
Short when they face actualities: private and public opinions
Find that abhorrent and scarcely of use to the general welfare, —
Which is the matrix of justice.

(Without transition, the Stoic doctrine under attack is now countered with the
Epicurean concept of social evolution.)

When creatures first crawled from the primal
Earth, without speech and unsightly, to squabble for acorns and lairs, they   100
Fought with their nails and their fists, then with cudgels, and then with the
                                                                weapons
They had devised in the course of experience, until they discovered
How their ideas and feelings could be represented by verbs and
Nouns they invented; and then they desisted from warfare and started
Settling in fortified towns and establishing law-codes forbidding   105
People to rob or to steal, or to practice adultery either,
For, in the times before Helen, the female was foulest excuse and
Pretext for war. But those rapists of earlier days died obscurely;
Seizing a woman for random coitus in animal fashion,
They were killed off by more powerful rivals, as bulls kill each other.   110

Fear of injustice brought law into being, as anyone grants who
Troubles to read and investigate records of previous ages.
    Nature, however, can not differentiate just things from unjust
As she distinguishes things to be shunned from the things to be sought for.
115   Neither will Reason claim guilt of identical kind and degree for
Breaking off tender young cabbage stalks growing in somebody's lot and
Coming by night to rob temples of things that belong to the gods. Fair
Punishments need to be meted by scale in proportion to crimes, lest
Someone deserving a whip gets chastised with your dread cat-o'-nine tails.
120   I have no fear of your using a cane on a man whose offenses
Merit a flogging, when mere petty larceny ranks among you as
Equal with piracy, and when you threaten to prune with the same sized
Sickle both vine-stalk and tendril, — once people put *you*, as you say, in
Charge of the state. But if only the wise man is wealthy, and only
125   He is a cobbler of skill, and in beauty unique, and a king, then
Why do you crave what you already have? — "You lack knowledge (says he) of
Master Chrysíppus's words: 'A philosopher maketh him neither
Sandals nor slippers, yet wisdom the shoemaker hath, nonetheless.'" — Eh?
"Just as Hermógenes silent is nonetheless master of song and
130   No less supreme as a harpist, and just as the clever Alfénus,
After discarding his tools and withdrawing from shoe-repair business,
Still was a cobbler. In *this* sense the wise man is master of every
Trade, without equal, and truly a king." — And yet mischievous street boys
Grab at your long flowing beard; if your cane can't disperse them, you stand there
135   Trapped in a circle of jostlers and hecklers, my poor, sorry fellow,
Barking your head off and bursting with rage, O my greatest of monarchs!
    Not to prolong this unduly: while you are off wending your kingly
Way to the one-penny bath house with no one but silly Crispínus
For a companion, my lenient friends will perhaps bear my presence
140   While in my unphilosophical way I persist in misconduct.
Follies of theirs I will cheerfully live with in turn, and so doing,
I shall live happier as mere private person than you in your kingship.

3   Tigéllius is the recently deceased singer and lyre player of the previous Satire, line 3. Cicero's letters call him "Sardinian" (*Sardus*) Tigéllius, perhaps a derogatory epithet. His real name was Hermógenes Tigéllius, suggesting a Greek with a Roman patron. See the note to Line 129 below.

4–5   "Caesar" = Octavius Caesar, who assumed that name in 44 B.C. as specified in the will of his recently assassinated great-uncle Julius Caesar, posthumously his legal "father." Not until 27 B.C. will he become "Augustus" and Emperor.

7   "Hail, Bacchus" (*Io Bacche*) is a drinking song. "From egg-course to apples" = the modern "from soup to nuts."

10–11   For the cult objects, see the note to *Odes* 1.18.12–13. The bearers walked while balancing the *containers* of the objects on their heads.

11–12   In S.1.6.16 Horace's very modest supper, when "eating in," is served by *three* slaves.

13   "Tetrarchs" here means "Oriental rulers," as does "kings" in line 12. The word is Greek: *tétra*, "four," + *arkh*-, "rule," and meant the ruler of the fourth part of a territory

under Roman control. New Testament Herod the Great was "in the news" when the present poem was published (35 B.C.), having been recognized in 40 B.C. as Tetrarch of Galilee; in 30 B.C. he was confirmed by Rome as King of the Jews, ruling all four parts of the Jewish territory: Galilee, Samaria, Judea, and Perea (Trans-Jordan).

13–14   Only round tables supported on a single central pedestal were elegant. Compare *Odes* 2.16.13–14 and note:

> Living well on little is he whose whose father's
> Silver salt-dish gleams on a frugal table.

A mere sea shell for a salt container would indicate extreme poverty. The more affluent added perfume or other flavorings to salt.

22–23   A triple pun is involved: *ignoras te?* (Do you *not* know yourself?), *ignotum*, "stranger," and *ignosco*, "I forgive."

27   The Serpent at the temple-and-sanatorium complex at Epidáuros in Greece might (somehow) convey oracles of Aesculápius, god of healing, or might be the god himself in serpent form. For the wisdom, compare Genesis 3:1: "Now the serpent was more subtil than any beast of the field."

Perhaps there is confusion here with the Erichthónian serpent, which Athéné removed from her shield and bade it cleanse the ears of Teirésias with its tongue so Teirésias might understand the language of prophetic birds.

A generation after Horace, Ovid (in *Metamorphoses* 15.626–744) tells how "long ago" the Epidáurian serpent was brought to Rome and installed there in his own shrine.

37   "Weeds" = *filix*, "wild fern," the pest of Italian agriculture.

40   Like many names in the *Satires*, Balbínus and Hágna are unidentified, but "Hágna" (Greek '*Agné*, "chaste") is known to have been a common name among freedwomen.

45–48   "Nickname" equals *cognomen*. Upper-class Roman males had a given name (*praenomen*), a family—actually a clan—name (*nomen*), and frequently a distinguishing *cognomen*, which was usually anything but flattering. History remembers famous Romans with *cognomina*: *Paetus* (blinky), *Varus* (bandy-legged, knock-kneed), and *Scaurus* (club-footed, "Stumpy"), but *Pullus*, "Chick(y)," may have been a nickname in the modern sense. Horace himself was Quintus Horatius *Flaccus*, "Flap-ear(ed)," a very common *cognomen*. The complimentary *cognomina* proposed by Horace in lines 49–53 were *not* in use.

91   Evánder (Euándrus, Greek for "good man") was the legendary king who welcomed Aeneas to the site of (future) Rome. The American parallel might be one of the turkey platters used by the Pilgrim fathers at the first Thanksgiving.

96–99   "People who rate all offences as equally wicked" are the Stoics. Their doctrines were first preached around 300 B.C. in the Stoa *poikíle* (the "Painted Porch") in the market-place of Athens by Zeno (who may have been a Phoenician Semite). Cicero's "Speech on behalf of Murena" (63 B.C.) recounts some of their chief concepts, including the claim that they considered killing a rooster as morally equal to murdering one's father.

99–112   The social evolution here described reflects, in a very general way, the whole last half of Lucretius's fifth Book (lines 782–1457) of *On the Nature of Things*, published probably in the early 50s B.C.

Horace prefers to see morality as the rational collective adjustment to man's collective experiences "since the beginning of time," rather than as a matter of individual conscience-searching.

114   The same phrase (*fugienda petendis* as in line 75 of the preceding Satire. "Things to be shunned" (*fugienda*) are harmful, "things to be sought for" (*petendis*) give pleasure.

118–123   All crimes being equally wicked to the Stoics, all punishments, to their notion, should be equally harsh. Horace finds this idea outrageous.

124–125   Cicero's "Speech for Murena" (note to 96–99 above) went on to say that the Stoics claimed to be the only truly wise men (philosophers): in extreme ugliness they were handsome, in extreme poverty they were rich, in extreme subjection they were "kings," all by virtue of their wisdom. Their basic concept was total self-control in harmony with Nature, as achieved by examination of conscience. To them, Nature and Conscience were the sole realities; pleasure and pain were alike superficial—mere "accidentals."

127   Master (*pater*) Chrysíppus (ca. 280–204 b.c.) was a major Stoic writer.

129–130   Hermógenes Tigéllius, the younger, was a still living musician and either a freedman or the adopted son of "Sardinian" Tigéllius in line 3 above.

130–132   Alfénus Varus, consul in 39 b.c., was said to have abandoned his cobbler's trade at Cremona to become a lawyer and a successful politician.

133–139   With abrupt contempt Horace dismisses his unnamed Stoic, whose sole friend is "the blear-eyed/Poet Crispínus" of S.1.1.120–121; see also S.2.7.45.

Readers may wish to transpose lines 96–142 into terms of a confrontation between a genial man of the world and a dour reformer, religious or political.

1.4.   *Eupolis atque Cratinus Aristophanesque poetae*

All the great names that comprise the Old Comedy roster of poets,
Such as Cratínus and Eúpolis and Aristóphanes, when they
Knew of a man that deserved designation as rascal and thief, or
Cut-throat or whoremaster — any notorious character, did not
5   Hesitate using those terms with a great deal of freedom and candor.
All of Lucílius depends on them; they were the models he followed,
Altering only their meters and rhythms, but brilliantly witty,
Keen in his thinking and language, and often rough-hewing his verses.
Now, on this last-mentioned score he was much in the wrong; he would sometimes
10   Dictate as many as two hundred lines without moving a muscle;
Flowing so silted and muddy, that river had need of some straining;
Wordy, diffuse, and too lazy to work his lines over with care as
Good verse requires; that he wrote great amounts is indifferent. — Ah, but
Here is Crispínus to offer me odds: "If you're willing, go fetch your
15   Tablets, and I will fetch mine; let a place and a time be agreed on,
Get us some proctors, and then see which one of us does the more writing."
Thanks to the gods, I was blessed with an unteeming mind, unexcessive
In its pretentions, and given to speaking but few words and rarely.
You go ahead, in the way you prefer, and perform like a goatskin
20   Bellows or wind-bag, and blow up a fire that will fairly melt iron.
Fannius gets all the readers, however, I warn you, with books and
Even his bust on display free of charge, whereas no one reads *my* books.
I am reluctant, in fact, to give readings in public because so
Few people take any pleasure in my sort of writing — though most could
25   Profit from censure. Pick anyone out of the crowd here at random:
Either he suffers from greed or he suffers from wretched ambition;
This one is crazy for other men's wives, and the next one is boy-crazed;
One dotes on silverware's gleaming, while bronzes leave Albius awe-struck;
One will trade goods from the upspringing sun to the regions where evening
30   Sunlight is warm, carried headlong through perils and swept ever on, like

Dust that is caught in the spinning of whirlwinds, forever in dread lest
Capital slip from his grasp and forever intent on more profits.
All of these people find poetry scares them; they hate any poet:
"Careful! (they say) He's got hay on his horns! All he's after is raising
Laughs, and there isn't a friend in this world he would not make his victim.   35
Once he has scribbled a thing on those papers of his, he is gleeful
Having it known to all persons returning from wells and from bake-shops,
Slaves and old women alike." — A few words, if you please, in rebuttal!
     First, I exclude my own name from the roster of genuine poets.
Merely composing a metrical unit is not, you would say, what   40
Qualifies someone; you would not consider a "poet" a man who
Wrote about matters belonging in mere conversation, as I do.
Only on genius commanding the mind and the lips to deliver
Utterance fit for a god would you ever bestow that distinction.
Thus it is questioned by some whether comedy may or may not be   45
Poetry, given the fact that its manner and matter lack any
Vivid intensity; save for the metrical pattern not found in
Commonplace discourse, it *is* only commonplace discourse. — "A father
Rages with fervor, however, when scolding a profligate son for
Madly rejecting a bride with a sizeable dowry for some mere   50
Prostitute's sake and parading the streets in the daytime with torchlight,
Drunk and disgracing himself." — Would Pompónius hear any softer
Screed of rebuke if that father of his were alive? For that very
Reason it does not suffice to write poems in everyday language
Which, when you look at it closely, has actual fathers all raging   55
Just like the fathers in masks on the stage. If from lines such as *I* write,
Or from the lines that Lucílius composed long ago, you extracted
Rhythms and metrical quantities, varied the order of words, put
Early words late in the line and the latter ones toward the beginning,
You would not find that a poet had ever been rent and dismembered,   60
As you would find if you did that to: "After foul Discord in fury
Burst from the portals of War, wrenching door-posts of iron asunder."
     So much for that. As to whether it's poetry, that shall be left for
Later discussion. Right now I shall merely inquire as to whether
My sort of writing deserves the disdain that you feel for it. Sleuthing   65
Súlcius and Cáprius, police snoopers both, prowl around with indictments,
Hoarse-voiced from questioning, one and the other a terror to highway
Robbers, but honest and clean-handed people abhor and despise them.
Even supposing you *were* like the highwaymen Cáelius and Bírrus,
I'm no informer like Cáprius and Súlcius, so why should you fear me?   70
Writings of mine are displayed on no pillars and sold in no shops for
Sweaty-palmed rummagers such as Hermógenes son of Tigéllius;
Nor do I read them to any but friends, and then only when forced to,
Not just to anyone, any old time. There are those who give readings
Right in the midst of the Forum, and some at the baths, where enclosing   75
Walls lend their voices a flattering resonance. Fatuous people

Find that so pleasing they never consider good taste in the matter
Or if the time is appropriate. — "But you enjoy giving pain!", you
Say,"and what's more, you're malicious on purpose."— Now,why do you make that
80   Charge against me? Is it someone I know that has given you grounds for
Such accusations? — "A man who will slander a party not present
Or who avoids standing up for a friend under censure, a man who
Tries to raise laughs out in company so as to show himself clever,
One who invents things he knows never happened, who can't keep a secret, —
85   *I* mean to tell you the fellow's a rotter: beware of him, Roman!"
Often three couches at dinner accommodate four to a couch, with
One party present who loves to bespatter the others with insults;
No one is spared but the host — who gets splashed later on when the drunken
Guest, at the impulse of truth-telling Liber, hides feelings no longer.
90   This fellow *you* say is "genial," "urbane," "uninhibited," yet to
Me you apply the word "poisonous." Just for my frivolous quip that
"Breath-pills come wafting from Rúfillus, but from Gargónius, goat-stink,"
I am, by *your* lights, a spite-goaded backbiter? But, let one word be
Said in your presence concerning Petíllius Capitolínus
95   And his embezzlements, and you defend him at once, as your way is:
"Capitolínus and I have been friends since our boyhoods, his house has
Often received me, and many a favor he's done as requested
Too, and I'm happy to know that he lives in this City unharmed, — though
I am astonished he ever escaped a conviction and jail term."
100 This is as black as the ink that the cuttlefish squirts, this is downright
Rust and corrosion. That I shall keep malice like that from my pages —
And from my heart in the first place — I promise as surely as I can
Make any promise of anything. Then, if I do speak too bluntly
Or too facetiously, you will allow it and even forgive me.
105 It is a habit I learned from my wonderful father, who used to
Point out particular cases of vice so that I would avoid them.
When he would urge me, for instance, to thrift and frugality so that
I would be able to live and be happy with what he could leave me,
"Look," he would say, "at how wretchedly Álbius' son has to live, how
110 Shabbily Báius exists. Those are perfect examples of why no
Person should squander a father's estate." To deter me from whores as
Mistresses, he would say only, "Don't *you* be another Scetánus."
Steering me clear of adulterous wives when permissible love was
There to be had, he would say, "Good repute did not stay with Trebónius
115 Once he was caught. Maybe wise men can give you the reasons why one thing
Should be avoided, another pursued; as for me, I am wholly
Satisfied carrying on in the ways of our ancestors and, as
Long as you still are in need of a guardian, keeping your life and
Good reputation from harm; later on, when your mind and your body
120 Come to maturity, you will not need to use cork-bark when swimming."
Thus by his precepts he molded my boyhood. And when he would say, "Do
This or do that," he would also say, "Here's your authority for it,"
Pointing to one of the judges assigned to a difficult law case.

When he said *not* to do something, he asked me, "Well, do you or don't you
Think it was shameful, what so-and-so did, now you see him ablaze with   125
Scandal?" A neighborhood funeral strikes terror in persons diseased with
Gluttony, till, out of fear of their own deaths, they look to their health: so
Too the disgraces of others will often deter youthful minds from
Mischief. The upshot of that kind of training has been to preserve me
Safe from the ruinous vices and leave me with only the middling   130
Sort, which I trust you will pardon. Perhaps even those can be largely
Banished with time, and a friend who is candid, and sober reflection.
I am not one to neglect myself, either while reading in private
Or during strolls in the portico. "That way, I think, is more fitting." —
"Doing it this way, I'm far better off." — "Here's a thing to delight my   135
Friends with." — "That wasn't a very nice action: I wonder if *I* might
Ever, from thoughlessness, do such a thing?" Then I ponder the matter,
Lips pressed together, and mull it all over; when leisure time offers,
Then I start marking up paper with poems. It's one of those lesser
Vices of mine that I mentioned before. If you cannot condone this   140
Practice, an army of poets stands ready to lend me support, — we
Are, after all, the majority these days, outnumbering critics,
And, like the Jews, we will simply compel you to be of our circle.

1–5   From obscure beginnings in the 6th century B.C., Greek "Old Comedy" flourished in
        the 5th century, down to 404, characterized by exuberant fantasy, rollicking choral
        songs, irreverent burlesque of myth, and biting political satire. Tradition cited three
        primary masters: Cratínus (ca. 490 to ca. 420), Eúpolis (445 to some date before 404),
        and Aristóphanes (ca. 445 to some date after 388), parallel to the tragic masters:
        Aeschylus, Sophocles, and Euripides.
             Of the works of Cratínus and Eúpolis (and other writers) only fragments now
        remain; from the extensive production of Aristóphanes eleven complete comedies are
        preserved, nine of them in the Old Comedy manner (*The Birds*, *Lysistrata*, *The Frogs*,
        etc.), as well as almost a thousand fragments from the others.
             "Middle Comedy," a much tamer art, flourished from the political downfall of
        Athens in 404 until 338. Five centuries later, more than 800 'Middle comedies' were
        reported as still available in libraries, but only fragments of these now survive, plus the
        last two plays of Aristóphanes, *Ecclesiazusae* and *Plutus*.
             "New Comedy," essentially a Comedy of Manners, flourished after 338, primarily
        in the name of Menánder (342–1 to 291–0). Again a large repertory, by numerous
        authors, is known only from fragments and from Latin adaptations by Plautus (ca.
        254–184; 20 complete plays preserved) and by Terence (ca. 195–159; 6 complete plays
        preserved).
6–8   Gaius Lucílius (?180 to 103, 102, or 101 B.C.) composed 30 "Books" of *Saturae*, chiefly
        in dactylic hexameters, not in meters used in comedy.
             As a wealthy bachelor Lucílius lived most of his adult life in Rome, where his
        connections were with the most prominent men of the time, though he himself seems
        not to have been a Roman citizen; he was Latium-born, from Sinuessa, just short of the
        border of Campania; see the note to S.1.5.40. Yet his brother was a Roman senator, his
        niece married the historian Strabo, and his sister was the grandmother of Pompey the
        Great. He was also a close friend of Scipio "Africanus," the Younger, who destroyed
        Carthage in 146 B.C.
             The Loeb Library *Lucilius* prints 1272 disconnected fragments of Lucílius's work
        as quoted by later authors.

14   Crispínus is the blear-eyed poet of S.1.1.120 and the "silly Crispínus" of S.1.3.139.

19–22   Neither the overlong works of Crispínus nor Horace's own (succinct) works can match the popularity of Fánnius. This last is known only from these lines and from "ridiculous Fannius" in S.1.10.79.

   In the text, "books" (line 21) is *capsis*, "buckets" (with handle and lid), containing several papyrus rolls, i.e., multivolume works. The bust of Fannius is a "promotion" device of the book dealer's, if not of Fannius himself.

37   Public bakeshops and public wells were frequented by Rome's poorer apartment dwellers.

61–62   The quotation is from the *Annals* of "Father" Ennius (239–169 B.C.), a work studied in school. In peacetime the temple of Janus was closed, in wartime it was open; the poet visualized "Discord" as a Fury wrenching open the doors in sign of war.

70   Horace is no "FBI agent" quoting secret information in poems.

71–72   This line was written while the *Satires* were still circulating in multiple copies among a limited circle and before Horace decided on publication of his first collection and sale in bookshops.

72   Hermógenes Tigéllius the younger, as in S. 1.3.129–130 and note.

78–104   Where lines 39–64 addressed the question: is satire "poety?", and where lines 64–78 denied that satire divulged secret information, the unnamed interlocutor now raises a third issue: satire, he claims, is malicious.

> 86   Nine dining couches usually accommodated nine men at a formal dinner: see the diagram in the endnote to S.2.8; or perhaps three couches accommodated three men each. The unusual "four to a couch" is unexplained.
>
> 88   In the text "the host" = *eum qui praebet aquam, "him who provides the water"* (for washing hands, since people ate with their fingers), thus carrying "the water figure" one step further.
>
> 89   Liber is Bacchus/Dionysus, as often in the *Odes*. Originally "Father Liber" was distinct from the Greek Bacchus, as an old Italian divinity of fruitfulness.
>
> 91–93   Line 92 quotes S.1.2.27 and the rest of the statement shows that *Satire* 2 (and other poems of Horace) had limited readership before the publication of Book I in 35 B.C.; see the note to lines 71–72 above.

94–99   Petíllius is presumably the Quaestor (elected assistant to a Consul) of 43 B.C. who was acquitted of an embezzlement charge, apparently against the evidence. S.1.10.26 below alludes to his "diffult case" (*dura causa*).

109–114   Álbius, Báius, Scetánus, and Trebónius must be persons alive in Horace's youth, under their real names or substitute names. The Álbius of *that* time is probably not the Álbius cited in line 28 above as a collector of antique bronzes in "present" time.

115–116   "Wise men" means "philosophers." The phrasing of ". . . why one thing/ Should be avoided, another pursued" varies the wording of S.1.3.114 (and note) and of S.1.2.75.

143   The line implies a Judaism that was still actively seeking converts. Cicero's "Speech for Flaccus" of 59 B.C. mentioned the large numbers of Jews in Rome. See the note to S.1.9.69 below.

1.5.   *Egressum magna me accepit Aricia Roma*

Seemingly random recollections from Horace's journey from Rome to Brundisium comprise this *Satire* 5; actually the episodes were selected to provide readers' amusement and a maximum of contrast and variety. Surprising to modern minds, the poem is not a spontaneous recording of personal impressions but a deliberate imitation of a *satura* from Lucilius's Book 3, as ancient commentator Porphyrio states. In the older work Lucilius described a journey from Rome to Capua and thence on to the Sicilian Strait, and from that poem some forty disconnected fragments survive.

Horace's journey occupied about two weeks of the autumn of 38 B.C.; the poem must have been composed late in 38 or early in 37. For somewhat more than half the distance the travelers followed the Appian Way, "queen of roads," but after Benevéntum they took a secondary route to Barium and along the Adriatic coast. The Appian Way itself was 495 km/310 m long, requiring 3 1/2 days for relay couriers, 9 for unencumbered travelers, and 16 or 17 for merchant transports.

Except for lines 28–29 there is no hint that three of the named personages are making the journey as a political mission of the utmost importance to the Roman state. Maecenas, Cocceius, and Fonteius Capito, as representatives of Octavius Caesar, are on their way to negotiate with Mark Antony. Why Horace and Vergil and other literary men are accompanying the statesmen is not clear; we assume that theirs is a private junket organized at the whim of Maecenas. Understandably Horace does not discuss the delicate political mission in this poem, but we regret that he has so little to say about two weeks spent in Vergil's company.

First of the towns after Rome to receive me, Arícia put me
Up at a plain little inn; my companion was Heliodórus,
One of the very most learnèd of Greek rhetoricians. The next was
Appius' Forum, a place full of bargemen and inn-keeping rascals.
Thus far we sluggards had taken two days for what livelier steppers   5
Cover in one, but the Appian Way is less hard on the slow-paced.
There, on account of the water, the vilest I ever have tasted,
War was declared between me and my stomach and I was left fretting
While my companions ate supper. Now night began shrouding the lands in
Shadows and setting out star-constellations all over the heavens.   10

(19 miles by canal barge: Appius' Forum to [modern] Terracina)

Arguments started to rage between slaves on the docks and the bargemen:
"Here! Pick us up over here!" — "But three hundred on board is too many!"
— "Hey! That's enough!" A whole hour is lost in collecting the fares and
Getting the tow-mule in harness. The pesky mosquitos and swamp frogs
Ruin all sleep, while our pilot, exalted with dregs of the vintage,   15
Sings of his far-away girl-friend; the mule driver out on the tow-path
Sings competition. The driver got tired and dropped off to his slumbers,
Whereat our lazybones pilot unbridled the mule to its grazing,
Fastened the ropes to a rock, and lay down on his back for some snoring.
Daylight already had come when we saw that the barge wasn't moving.   20
One of the passengers angrily jumped to the shore, took a willow
Cudgel, and with it proceeded to whack both the mule and the pilot
Head-side and rump-side alike. Even so, we made port close to noontime.
Faces and hands we then laved in thy fonts, O Ferónia goddess.
After some lunch we did three miles of crawling along, till at last we   25
Climbed up the precipice crowned with the far-gleaming city of Anxur.
There both Maecenas and worthy Coccéius had promised to join us,

They being deputies charged with significant matters and skilled at
Bringing estrangements of friends in contention to order again. There
30   I, with my eye-inflammation, applied some collyrium ointment.

(*The diplomats arrive; Fundi; Formiae; the literary men arrive and join the party at Sinuessa; on to Capua.*)

Meanwhile Maecenas arrived with Coccéius, and so did Fontéius
Cápito, who was a gentleman right to his fingertips, someone
Antony trusted more fully than anyone else for his friendship.
Fundi, the town where Aufídius Lúscus was mayor, we left quite
35   Willingly, laughing at how his preposterous clerk did the honors:
Purple-edged toga and pan of hot coals for the kindling of incense.
Wearily then we found rest in the city of all the Mamúrras,
Cápito furnishing meals and Muréna providing us lodgings.
Welcome indeed was the following dawn, because that was the day which,
40   At Sinuéssa, brought Plótius, Várius, and Vergil to join our
Party, all three of them spirits more noble and rare than the world has
Ever produced, and to each of the three I bear equal devotion.
Oh, what embracings then followed, and oh, what tremendous rejoicings!
While I have sense, I say nothing compares with a cheerful companion.
45   Close by the bridge as you enter Campania there was a tiny
Lodge for our shelter, with government stewards to furnish the common
Fuel and salt. On to Capua next, where the mules were unloaded.
There it was sports for Maecenas, while Vergil and I preferred napping;
Workouts are not for dyspeptics, and ballgames are bad for the sore-eyed.

(*Entertainment by clowns at a villa*)

50   Next came a stop at Coccéius's farm, with its bounty of foodstocks
Beating all Cáudium's hostelries. Now, O my Muse, I would have thee
Briefly recall how the jester Sarméntus met combat with jester
Méssius Roostercomb, stating the names of these champions' fathers.
"Méssius comes of illustrious lineage — Oscan; Sarméntus'
55   Previous owner — a lady — still lives." Now with forebears like that, both
Champions entered the fray. First to speak was Sarméntus: "It's *my* guess
You are the beast we call Unicorn." (Laughter.) — "And what if I am?" asked
Méssius, wagging his head. His opponent came back with "I wonder
What you would do if you still had your horn? Even *de*horned, you're pretty
60   Threatening." (I should explain that a mean-looking scar had disfigured
Méssius's forehead just under the shag and a bit to the leftwards.)
Volleys of quips about scars, such as: "Was it 'Campania sickness?' ",
"You could perform in a mime, you're a ringer for 'Cyclops as Shepherd'
Just as you are, without mask and without a tragedian's buskins."
65   Roostercomb got in his licks: would Sarméntus be hanging his slave-chain
Up in the shrine of his house-gods?; promoted to scribe he might be, but
How were his mistress's ownership rights any less over *him*?; and
Why had he ever attempted escape in the first place, when one-pound

Rations of flour sufficed for so mincingly dainty a body?
Downright delightful that suppertime was.   70

    *(On to Benevéntum in Samnite country; eastwards across a section of Horace's native
province of Apulia, then down the Adriatic coast road to Brundisium.)*

                         By the highroad we traveled
On till we reached Benevéntum. Our host there almost set his house on
Fire with his diligent turning of thin little thrushes on hearth-spits.
Embers stacked up in volcano-formation collapsed, and the ancient
Kitchen was showered with flames that went licking their way to the rafters.
There was a scene: famished visitors, slaves in a panic, all grabbing,   75
Trying to salvage a meal and extinguish a fire that was spreading.
    Onward again, and Apulia gradually opened before me
Prospects of mountains familiar of old and scorched brown by sirocco;
Crawling out through them might well have undone us, except that a farm not
Far from Trivícum afforded us rest for the night, — though the hearth-smoke   80
Made us shed tears, as the fuel was all of green wood with the leaves on.
There, like a fool, I stayed up a good half of the night for a wench that
Promised and lied when she promised, till sleep took away the erection
Venus delights in; and then to my dreams came an off-color wraith of
Fancy, who left me with stains on my nightshirt and down-pressing belly.   85
    Twenty-four miles of the following stage we went whisking by carriage,
Passing the night in a hamlet that cannot be named in this meter,
Though it is easy to guess from the following: water, the cheapest
Thing in the world, is dispensed for a price, but bread is so good that
Foresighted travelers buy it by armloads; the bread at Canúsium   90
Tends to be gritty, and water no jugful less easy to come by,
Even if brave Diomédes of old did establish that city.
That was where Várius sadly took leave of his friends amid weeping.
    We were exhausted arriving at Rúbi, that being a longish
Stretch of the way, not to mention the rains on that lap of our journey.   95
Weather improved after that, but the road was much rougher as far as
Fish-teeming Bárium. Then to Gnátia, built when the nymphs of
Water were angry, and where we found matter for banter and laughter:
People there tried to persuade us that incense dissolves without fire as
Soon as it passes a consecrate threshold. Apélla the Jew may   100
Credit that miracle, *I* don't. I've learned that the gods exist care-free,
And, if a marvel does happen in Nature, that petulant gods have
Nothing to do with dispatching it down from the heavenly rooftop.
    Long journey's end was Brundisium, — also the end of this poem.

Itinerary
(The regular notes follow below.)

1 ARICIA (now Ariccia), ca. 30 km/20 m S of Rome on the Appian Way and near the
    Álgidus Ridge of the Alban Hills and the shrine of Diana; see the note to *Odes* 1.21.6.

4   APPIUS' FORUM, another 30 km/20 m of the Appian Way. (In Acts 28:15 Saint Paul was met at Appius' Forum by a deputation of Roman Christians.)

11-25   The roadside canal, called *Decenovium* ("Nineteener") for its 19 miles, traversed the Pomptine/Pontine marshes, 750 sq. kilometers of malarial swamp, drained and settled by Mussolini's government, 1932–39.

26   The southern terminus of the canal was at Tarracina (now T*e*r-), but on the overlooking hill was the ancient Volscian town of ANXUR, with its imposing temple to Jupiter Anxur, built in 80 B.C. The temple ruins were revealed by archeologists in the 1960s.

34   FUNDI (now Fondi), some 16 km/10 m inland, to avoid a large coastal swamp.

37   FORMIAE (now Formia), some 20 km/13 m back out to the coast; here called "the city of all the Mamúrras"; see the note to this line below.

40   SINUESSA, some 30 km/19 m farther down the coast; its ruins lie just N of modern Mondragone and at the foot of Monte Massico; see the note to *Odes* 1.1.19. This was the last town in Latium before the border of Campania province.

47   CAPUA (now Capua Vetere), some 34 km/15 m east and inland, the chief city of Campania and the original terminus of the Appian Way in 312 B.C.

50-51   CAUDIUM, a small town three quarters of the way to Benevéntum, in Samnium province. The villa of Coccéius was presumably not far from there.

71   BENEVÉNTUM (now Benevénto), due E of Capua in the Apennine mountains and chief city of Samnium province.This is approximately the half-way mark of Horace's journey.

77-90   From Benevéntum to Canusium (line 90) the itinerary is vague. At some point, apparently short of Horace's native Venusia, the party took a secondary road. To judge by E.1.18.20: "Roads to Brundisium: Minutian or Appian: which route is better?", this secondary road was "the Minutian Way." Presumably it went N to (unmentioned) Herdónia and then abruptly turned SE for Canúsium. For the unmetrical town-name, see the notes.

90-104   The poem now hurriedly summarizes the last third of the journey: CANUSIUM (now Canosa di Puglia) was in Apulia province and on the Aufidus River; see S.1.1.58 and note. RUBI (now Ruvo) and the seaport BARIUM (now Bari) were also in Apulia, and GNÁTIA/EGNÁTIA was the last Apulian town before the border of *ancient* Calabria.

104   BRUNDISIUM (now Bríndisi), in *ancient* Calabria, was the regular sailing port for Greece.

2-3   Heliodórus is unknown; his erudition is whimsically exaggerated.

5-6   Forty miles in two days, with slave attendants and presumably some baggage, implies a vehicle or two. Alone, Horace might travel on muleback, as in S.1.6.105, or on horseback, as in E.1.15.10–13. Slave-porters on foot, as in S.1.1.47–49, would accompany a larger party.

7-9   Stomach upset here, eye-inflammation in lines 30 and 49, and so on; Horace pokes fun at his own lack of ruggedness.
      The companions must be Heliodórus and the slave attendants.

9-10   Grandiose epic description introduces the scene (11–23) of the rough-and-ready canal town, as the grandiose line 24 concludes the episode. Stylistic jolts, perhaps in Lucilius's manner, particularly mark this poem.

24   Ferónia was an ancient Italian goddess of groves and waters, also a patroness of freedmen.

27   Lucius Coccéius Nerva became consul two years later, in 36 B.C.; he was the great-grandfather of the future emperor Nerva (ruled 96–98 A.D.).
      Morris infers that Maecenas and Coccéius had been in conference with Octavius Caesar at some estate near Ánxur-Tarracína.

28-29   The estranged friends are Octavius Caesar and Mark Antony. Two years before, in 40 B.C., their 13-year rivalry had been accommodated by a partition of the Roman world between them: Caesar was to rule the Dalmatian (Yugoslavian) coast and everything west of it, Antony was to rule Greece and the Near East. The weak third

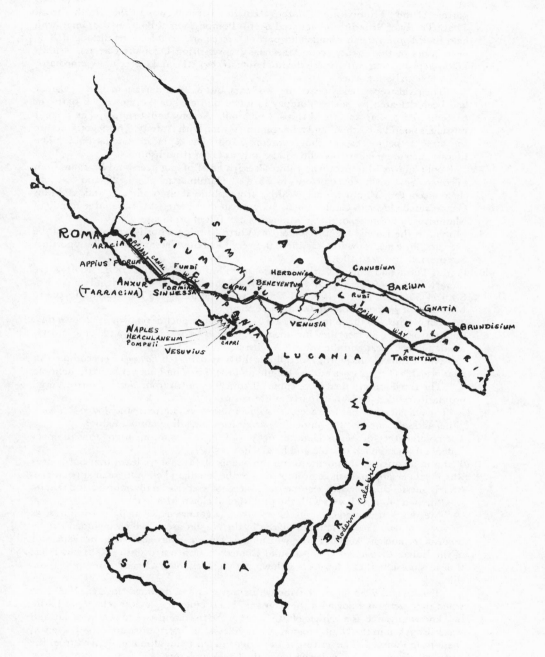

partner of the "Triumvirate," Marcus Aemélius Lépidus, was to rule North Africa. That "Treaty of Brundísium" ignored Sextus Pompey, son of Pompey the Great, who held the Mediterranean islands and part of Greece and could not be dislodged. The negotiators of that treaty were Maecenas (representing Octavius Caesar), Asínius Póllio (representing Antony; see the final note to *Odes* 2.1), and Coccéius as a mediator acceptable to both parties.

The rivals kept uneasy peace for two years, but in 39 and again in 38 B.C., Caesar had been defeated by Sextus Pompey in naval battles. For the showdown battle to come in 37 B.C. Caesar needed ships, which only Antony could supply. The present mission is bound for Athens and a bargaining session with Antony. The negotiators are the same as before, except that Fontéius Cápito has replaced Asínius Póllio. The literary men are mere extras who will go only as far as Brundísium.

37   The only known Mamúrra was Julius Caesar's chief of engineers and he came from Formiae. Seventeen years before, in 55 B.C., Catullus (in poems 29 and 57) had denounced *that* Mamúrra as wealthy from plunder, as profligate, and as Julius Caesar's male lover in Gaul. Line 37 may mean that there was still a large family of Mamúrras in Formiae, or that Formiae is a city full of profligates.

38   Muréna is the Lucius Licínius Teréntius Varro Muréna who, 15 years later, will be executed for conspiracy to assassinate the very Octavius Caesar he is now supporting. See the note to *Odes* 2.10.1.

40   Plotius Tucca and Lucius Varius Rufus—the "Plotius and Varius" of S.1.10.81—were literary friends of Vergil's and publishers of the *Aeneid* after his death in 19 B.C. S.1.6.54–55 states that Vergil and Varius were the men who introduced Horace to Maecenas (a year or so before the present poem).

For Varius, see the note to *Odes* 1.6.1–4. He was a poet of renown in his own day, but his works are all lost; they included a tragedy, *Thyestes* (29 B.C.), and "epic" poems about Julius Caesar and the wars of Augustus.

At the time of this journey Vergil was thirty-two; his ten *Eclogues* were complete or nearly so, his *Georgics* were not yet begun, and the *Aeneid* had not yet been thought of.

The three literary men have come 50 km/30 m north from Naples, where Vergil ordinarily resided, to join the party at Sinuessa.

45–47   The official party has free access to a government waystation: "tiny lodge" (*villula*). "Fuel and salt" means "the immediate necessities, including animal fodder.

49   The commentary of Aelius Donatus on Vergil, ca. 350 A.D., mentions that the poet suffered from stomach trouble and headaches.

51–70   From an ancient commentator on the poems of Juvenal we learn that Sarméntus was a real person, an ex-slave promoted to scribe, small and effeminate in appearance. Morris guesses that he was a secretary in Maecenas's service on this journey and that he was "invited" to match wits with the professional clown Messius.

Messius is surnamed Cicírrus: Greek *kíkirros*, "gamecock," which we paraphrase as "Roostercomb." The scene takes place "in the Naples area," which included Atella, home of the ancient Atellan Farce, which many believe to have been the lineal ancestor of the Italian *Commedia dell' arte* (Guild Comedy) not attested until 1500 years later; thus it is possible that Messius is a clown with a stock role. "Oscan" here is an ethnic slur.

The Oscans were an Italic tribe whose fortunes had declined since ca. 1000 B.C., when they were on a par with the Romans. Their language, a close relative of Latin, had known prestige as a vehicle of literature in the third and second centuries B.C. and was still spoken in the Naples region. Some 200 Oscan inscriptions are extant, a few of them from Pompeii. The writing is from right to left in an alphabet derived from the Etruscan alphabet, itself a derivative of the Greek alphabet.

62   "Campania sickness" puzzled even ancient editors of Horace.

65–66   The slave-chain would be dedicated as a relic of the past, parallel to the arms of the retired gladiator Veianius in E.1.1.4–5, or "the dripping-wet clothes" of the man who escaped drowning in *Odes* 1.5.13–16.

82–85   Morris's Latin edition of 1909 omits these lines altogether, without comment.
87   Ancient commentator Porphyrio says the town was Aequum Tuticum, but this has been disputed. Porphyrio adds that the little joke imitates Lucilius's "inability" to name a certain holiday; see Fragment 252–3 in the Loeb Classical Library *Lucilius*.
97–100   Gnátia/Egnátia, on the Adriatic coast as it was, lacked fresh water—"the nymphs were angry." Pliny's *Natural History*, 2.107, 240, reports a variant form of the miracle: the altar wood caught fire of itself.
100–101   When Moses and Aaron offer sacrifice in Leviticus 9:24, "there came a fire out from before the Lord, and consumed upon the altar the burnt offering and the fat," and in 1 Kings 18:38 a similar fire consumed Elijah's offering when his pagan opponents could produce no fire from Baal. Conceivably, garbled versions of these events could have reached Horace. See the note to S.1.9.69 below.
101–103   Horace has in mind Lucretius's *On the Nature of Things* 5.76–90, especially line 82: ". . . who have learned that the gods live care-free." The three-line statement here is a forthright profession of Epicurean beliefs.

1.6.   *Non quia, Maecenas, Lydorum quicquid Etruscos*

Never, Maecenas, was Lydian comer of old to Etruscan
Settlement regions more nobly descended and born than yourself, whose
Forebears on both sides, your mother's and father's alike, in the days of
Yore held command over powerful legions; and yet, unlike most, you
Never have turned up your aquiline nose at a person obscure of   5
Origin such as myself, who was born of a freedman. By showing
Such unconcern about any man's parentage, only so long as
He was himself of free birth, you display your awareness that slave-born
Tullius reigned as a king, while before him a great many men, not
Issued from eminent ancestors, nevertheless in their time lived   10
Lives of esteem and were honored with offices. Contrariwise you
See how Laevínus, for all he derived from Valérian stock which
Once expelled Tarquin the Proud from the kingship, was still, in his own right,
Never considered a pennyworth higher in value for that, not
Even by lower-class voters, who often, as you are aware, heap   15
Honors upon the unworthy and grovel to fame in their folly,
Awed by the death-masks of ancestors, each with its listing of titles.
How, then, should *we* act, who live on a plane far removed from the rabble?
Granting that people would rather elect a Laevínus to office
Than to see Décius the newcomer there, and that Áppius the Censor   20
Would have barred *me* from the senate on grounds of a father not free-born:
I must agree with them — *if* I play lion while being a donkey.
        But to her glittering chariot Ambition has shackled both mean and
Mighty and drags them along in her wake. So what good did it do you,
Tillius, starting from tribune again up to senator's purple?   25
Envy of you has built up, but retire, and it will diminish.
Anyone crazy enough to go lacing the black leather thongs to
Mid-calf and draping his chest with the broad senatorial purple

Stripe must hear queries like "Who is this man?" and "What rank was his father?"
30   Then it's as if he had Barrus's trouble, the Barrus who always
Wants to be thought of as handsome, so when he puts in an appearance
Girls are agog with inquiries about his particular features
Such as his face, and the calves of his legs, and his teeth, and his hair-style.
That's what a candidate has to put up with when vowing to safeguard
35   Citizens, City, Italian dominion, and shrines of the gods, and
By so declaring he forces all mortals to ask with concern what
Rank he acquired from his father and whether his mother was base-born.
"*You* there, the son of a Syrus, a Dama, or some Dionýsus,
Dare to have *Romans* thrown over a cliff or subjected to torture?!"
40   — "How about Novius, my colleague? He sits only one row behind me
Though he is now what my father once was." — "Does that make you a Paulus
Or a Messálla? Why, Novius shouting at two hundred wagons
Stalled by three funerals crossing the Forum could drown out their horns and
Sirens completely, and that's what we like in a man that holds office."
45   Let me come back to myself as the son of my father, a freedman,
Carped at and picked at enough as the son of my father, a freedman,
Now for frequenting your household, Maecenas, but also before that
For my command of a legion and holding the rank of a tribune.
These are two disparate charges. My holding an officer's rank may
50   Well have been open to question, but not so my friendship with you, who
Always take special precaution to choose only worthy companions
Lacking all self-serving motives. Nor would I agree it was luck or
Merely a random coincidence that has produced such a friendship;
Nothing like random coincidence brought us together, for Vergil,
55   Noblest of men, and then Varius, had told you long since all about me.
When I at last came before you I stammered some short little statements —
Infantile bashfulness would not allow me to speak any further —
But I did *not* say I had an illustrious father, nor did I
Talk about riding my Tárentine pony around my estates: I
60   Merely declared what I was. Whereupon you replied, as your way is,
Briefly, and I took my leave. After nine months of time you recalled me,
Bidding me be of your circle of friends. That I met with your standards
Gratifies me, since you judge between honor and shabbiness not by
Status of fathers but rather by conduct and how a man's heart is.
65   Yet, if my character — sound enough generally — does show some little
Medium-serious vices, deserving no harsher reproaches than
Birthmarks or moles here and there or an otherwise excellent body,
And if I cannot be fairly accused as a miser or someone
Having bad habits and haunting the dens of iniquity, and if
70   (In my opinion) I live a clean life and have friends who esteem me,
I have my father to thank for it. Poor, with his few meager acres,
He would not send me to Flavius, whose school was attended by lordly
Scions of veteran sergeants established on government land-grants,
Each with a bookbag and tablet slung leftwards and over his shoulder

And on the Ides of the month coming in with his eight-coin tuition;   75
Rather, he dared bring his boy up to Rome for instruction in higher
Subjects that senators wanted their sons to acquire, or the high-placed
Men of equestrian rank. If amid all those numerous people
Any took note of my clothes and my slaves in attendance, they must have
Fancied those things had been furnished and paid for with riches ancestral.   80
Acting himself as my most incorruptible watchdog, he met all
Teachers of mine. But what use would it serve to enlarge on these matters?
Prime among factors of manhood he held me to decent behavior,
Keeping me not from wrongdoing alone but from rumor of scandal.
Nor did he fear its reflecting on him if I later took up some   85
Minor profession, — presiding at auctions or, as in his own case,
Gathering taxes. I would not myself have complained if I had, but
As it turned out, I owe all the more thanks and respect to him for it.
While I have sense, I shall never regret such a father; nor will I
Plead my defense like so many, who mourn that it was not through any   90
Fault of their own that they missed having parents both famous and free-born.
My line of thought and my manner of speaking are wholly at odds with
Those people's. If, indeed, after attaining one age or another,
Nature's command were to live to that stage of existence a second
Time, giving each of us freedom to choose other parents to suit our   95
Vanities, I would be perfectly happy with mine; I would not want
New ones entitled to escorts and chairs of authority. Vulgar
Judgements may say I am "crazy," but "sane" will perhaps be what *you* would
Call my refusal to shoulder — unpracticed — a burden so dreary.
I would at once feel the need for acquiring a much larger fortune;   100
Mornings would go into interviews; this one and that one would then have
Claims on my company such that I never could be by myself when
Going abroad or on country excursions; then ponies to feed, and
Grooms to attend them, and four-wheeler transports to shepherd in convoy.
Now, if I like, I can ride a plain mule all the way to Taréntum,   105
Saddlebags over his sides and the weight of his rider to gall him.
No one will twit me with cheapness, moreover, the way they do you there,
Tillius, when all in your magistrate's pomp on the road out to Tibur
Five slaves attend you to carry the cook-pot and hamper of wine jars.
There is where I, mighty Senator, live in more comfort than you, and   110
Thousands of other ways too. When I feel so inclined, I go out for
Walks by myself; I inquire about prices of cabbage and flour;
Late afternoons I may stroll by the Race Course and look at the jugglers,
Or in the Forum; I stop to watch tellers of fortunes, and then go
Home to a bowlful of scallions and chickpeas and flour-and-oil pancakes.   115
Three slaves suffice me at supper; my table, a slab of white marble,
Holds my two goblets and ladle; at hand are a sea shell for rinse-dish,
Cruet and saucer for oil, and Campanian earthenware dishes.
Off then to bed, with no worry of getting up early tomorrow
Morning to meet someone down by the statue of Mársyas — posed to   120

Signify how he abhors the appearance of Novius Junior.
Mornings I sleep until ten; then I stroll for a bit, or I read or
Write in enjoyable quiet, and then have a rubdown with olive
Oil, — not the kind that old Natta saves up from the lamps that he filches.
125 After I'm tired from my workout, the heat of the sun shows it's time to
Go for a bath, but I pass up Mars Field and the three-handed ballgames.
Lunch is a modest affair, just enough so the stomach will not be
Empty the whole of the day; after that, I may putter at house chores.
Such is the life of a man disencumbered of sorry ambition;
130 By the same token I feel I shall live a more pleasant existence
Than if my grandfather, father, and uncle had all served as quaestors.

1–4   Herodotus 1.94 (before 400 B.C.) says that half the population of Lydia (west-central Turkey), chosen by lot after prolonged famine, sailed off to colonize Italy N of Rome, where they called themselves Tyrrhenians. For "Tyrrhenian" = "Etruscan" see *Odes* 3.10.11 and 3.29.1 and notes. Archaeology tends to support Herodotus and to date the immigration after 900 B.C.; see Paul MacKendrick: *The Mute Stones Speak*, St. Martin's Press, 1960, pp. 27–29.

In *Odes* 1.1.1 and note Maecenas is said to be descended from Etruscan kings, but history reports nothing about distinguished service *to Rome* by Maecenas's ancestors.

Servius Tullius ruled 578–534 B.C. as sixth of the seven early kings of Rome. "Servius," a name not unique with this king, was understood as "slave-born" (from *servus*, "slave"), but Livy's History 1.39 (composed 29 B.C. ff.) tried to discredit this old notion.

12–13   No Valérius Laevínus is known, though many illustrious members of the Valerian family are mentioned over the centuries, including one who was active in the expulsion of Tarquin the Proud, seventh and last of Rome's early kings, in 509 B.C.

17   Wax death-masks of distinguished ancestors, each with its list of offices held, were displayed in the main room of a noble Roman houshold.

20   Publius Decius Mus, military hero of 340 B.C., was a *novus homo* ("new man"), i.e., the first of his family to win high office.

Appius Claudius Pulcher, Censor in 50 B.C., purged the senate of all sons of freedmen and even of many aristocrats with deficient family credentials.

27–28   Senators' shoes were cross-laced to the calf of the leg by four black leather thongs; their broad purple toga-borders were draped diagonally across their chests.

38   Typical slave-names: Syrus ("Syrian"), Dama (as in S.2.5.18), and Greek Dionysus. Most slaves were foreigners, often captives of war.

39   Formerly, condemned criminals might be thrown from the Tarpéian Rock, a cliff at one end of the Capitoline Hill, but by Horace's time the practice had been discontinued. "Subjected to torture" paraphrases "turned over to Cadmus," whom an ancient commentator identies as the public executioner.

40–44   "Novius" is probably a coined name, reflecting *novus homo*, as in the note to line 20 above. The Paulus and Messalla families were of the highest social rank.

Theater seats were, to some degree, allotted by social rank; see the note to Epode 4.16; also E.1.1.62–64.

The funeral processions would halt in the Forum for delivery of eulogies. The number of wagons and funerals is comically exaggerated.

48   In 42 B.C. Horace, not yet twenty-three, was a "tribune of soldiers" (*tribunus militum*) in the army of Brutus. At that time a legion might number 4200 to 6000 Roman citizens and about 300 cavalrymen; command rotated among six "tribunes of soldiers." See *Odes* 2.7.1–16 and the notes to lines 1–2 and 9–12. The specific rank is named in the *Vita* of Horace by Suetonius.

55   For Lucius Varius Rufus see S.1.5.40–42 and note.

59   "Tárentine pony" = *Satureiano caballo*. Even ancient readers had to be told that *Satureia* was the region around Taréntum. Note the "Romance" word *caballus*, "an inferior horse."

61   "After nine months of time" = "after quite some time." Compare the "nine years" of E.2.3.388.

72–73   The Latin says only "lordly boys born of lordly centurions." Centurions were commoners promoted for merit to command a hundred troops (a *centuria*); a legion of 6000 men had 60 centurions, or "sergeants." Grants of farmland comprised their retirement pay. See the story of "farmer Oféllus" in S.2.2.112–136.

76–77   The "higher subjects" included early Latin poetry (E.2.1.69) and the *Iliad* in Greek (E.2.2.41).

81   I.e., his father acted as his *paedagogus*, escort and guardian of a respectable schoolboy; usually a trusted slave performed this function.

86–87   Horace's two terms are *praeco*, "auctioneer," and *coactor*, "tax collector." In Suetonius's *Vita* of Horace, variant manuscripts make the poet's father either *exactionum coactor*, "a subordinate official in the collection of taxes," or *auctionum coactor*, "a collector of money at auctions." (Morris's footnote)

101   Interviews, i.e., with *clientes*, as in S.1.1.10 and elsewhere. Persons in a rich man's pay reported to him daily at dawn for political or business assignments or to bring in the results of previous assignments.

108   The fashionable resort town of Tibur (now Tívoli), 24 km/15 m E of Rome.

113   The Race Course (*circum*) is the Circus Maximus, bgun in 329 B.C. and ultimately accommodating 250,000 spectators; it lay over the Palatine Hill from the Forum; excavated ruins are still to be seen.

115   "Home" is clearly in Rome, we suspect on the slopes of the Esquiline Hill, due E of the Forum, and since there is no mention of the Sabine farm, the poem may be dated between 38 and 33 B.C.

116–118   Three slaves (perhaps cook, waiter, and wine server) contrast with "Sardinian Tigéllius's" minimum of ten in S.1.3.12.

    The "slab of white marble" (*lapis albus*) probably was supported on *three* legs; compare S.1.3.13 and note.

    The two goblets and the ladle indicate a mixture of wine and water in varying proportions. Doubtless a larger wine container was also near by.

    "A sea shell for rinse-dish" = *echinus*, "a sea urchin," a word which puzzled ancient commentators. Compare S.1.3.14; also *Odes* 1.7.22–23, where conch shells hold oil.

    The "saucer" (*patera*) may have held the oil cruet (*guttus*).

    Campanian earthenware was the cheapest crockery.

120–121   The statue of Mársyas stood in the banking area of the forum; its typical pose was the uplifted and averting hand.

126   Mars Field was the public athletic grounds. Horace also avoided the ballgames at Capua in S.1.5.48–49. Three-handed "catch," without use of bats, was the typical Roman game.

131   Twenty annually elected *quaestors* served as treasurers and document keepers, and, in the army, as quartermasters and paymasters. The office was the lowest on the political ladder, hence its contemptuous mention here.

1.7. *Proscripti Regis Rupili pus atque venenum*

Amid the turmoil and uncertainties that followed upon the assassination of Julius Caesar on March 15, 44 B.C. the senate chose to appoint the chief conspirator, Marcus Junius Brutus, Governor of Crete, a humiliatingly minor position. Brutus sailed in July, went nowhere near

Crete, but made for Athens, where, either then or later, he recruited Horace for the army he intended to raise. For soldiers and money, however, he turned to Macedonia (northern Greece) and the rich province of Asia (the western half of modern Turkey), with such success that by February of 43 the senate recognized his *de facto* control of those areas. Meanwhile the other chief conspirator, Gaius Cassius Longinus, after leaving Rome in October of 44, had made himself master of Syria in 43. Late in 43 the two Generals held a strategy conference at Smyrna (Izmir). The present poem relates an anecdote from the winter of 43–42 when Brutus was apparently sitting as itinerant Judge at Clazoménae, a now uninhabited site near Smyrna, and hearing a lawsuit between a Roman and a Greek.

The Roman was Publius Rupílius Rex, from Praenéste (now Palestrina) just SE of Rome, who had learned that he had been "outlawed" and marked for death by Octavius Caesar and Mark Antony. As an anti-Caesarian he fled to Brutus, who made him a member of his staff.

The Greek was Persius, "a half-breed"; ancient commentators explain that he had a Greek father and a Roman mother.

Outlawed Rupílius, with surname of "King," with his poisonous malice,
And his subjection in turn to the malice of Persius the half-breed
Must be old gossip in barbershops and to all eye-trouble patients.
     Persius was wealthy from multiple businesses at Clazoménae,
5   Where he was also embroiled with this King in some bothersome lawsuits;
He was a hard man to deal with, addicted to quarrels as King was,
Loudmouthed and sure of himself, with as nasty a tongue in his head as
Any Sisénna or Barrus — outstripped them, in fact, like a race horse.
And, as for King, he would hear of no compromise short of a court case.
10 (Bullheads in nose-to-nose challenge are quite as entitled to rights as
Champion heroes of old in those duels where one of them perished.
Rage was so fierce between mighty Achilles and lofty-souled Hector,
Scion of Priam, that only the death of the one or the other
Could have concluded it, simply because, on the score of their prowess,
15 Each was ranked foremost. If two who are cowards get into a jangle,
Or if a poorly matched pair get involved — Diomédes when faced with
Glaucus the Lycian, for instance, — the weaker backs down and may even
Placate the other with gifts.) Now it seems that when Brutus was hearing
Cases as Judge in the province of Asia, Rupílius and Persius
20 Fought out their lawsuit, more evenly matched than our Bácchius and Bithus.
     Fiercely each entered the courtroom with mighty display of dramatics.
Persius presented his case amid laughter from everyone present.
Tributes of praise went to Brutus and tributes of praise to his cadre;
Brutus, he said, was "the sunlight of Asia," the men on his staff were
25 "Stars of prosperity" — all except King, who had come like the Dog Star
Hated by farmers for bringing the midsummer drouth. On and on he
Raged, like a river in winter where axes are rare in the forest.
     Drenched in the spate of his insults, the man from Praenéste shot back in
Language derived from the vineyard, a hard-fisted vinedresser's screed that
30 Often is more than enough to scare off any passer-by who had
Started the name-calling fracas by shouting the cry of "Hey, cuckoo!"

Persius the Greek, thus bespewed with Italian-type vinegar, shouted:
"Now, by the almighty gods, I appeal to you, Brutus, and ask you:
Since you are so in the habit of murdering kings, why not simply
Murder this King? It's your chance to do something that's right up your alley."   35

3   I.e., in barbershops and drugstores.
10–18 The mock-heroic parenthesis quips at the *Iliad*, first by likening "King" and Persius
to Achilles and Hector, and then by deliberate "misunderstanding" of *Iliad* 6.119–236,
where Diomédes and Glaucus discover that their fathers were old friends and therefore
refuse battle and exchange gifts in friendship with each other.
20–21 Bácchius and Bithus were popular gladiators of Horace's own time. "King" and
Persius enter the courtroom with all the fanfare of gladiators making their bows to the
audience in the arena.
25–26 For the Dog Star see *Odes* 1.17.19 and note.
31   "By shouting the cry of 'Hey, cuckoo!' " = *magna compellans voce cuculum*. Though the
expression occurs in three different comedies of Plautus, its sense is unclear. We suspect
an obscene pun on *culus*, "the fundament."
35   Brutus had assassinated Julius Caesar because Caesar, as some people said, wanted to
make himself king.

1.8.   *Olim truncus eram ficulnus, inutile lignum*

In the early 30s B.C. Maecenas built his famous mansion on the Esquiline Hill within the
northeast angle of the old Servian Rampart, laying out its extensive gardens as a bit of
countryside within the City limits. Adjacent was a parcel of land, 1000′ × 300′, formerly a
pauper cemetery, which in turn adjoined, or had been partially reclaimed as, a vegetable
garden dominated by the garden god Priápus in his common aspect as a scarecrow. The
topography is frankly unclear and the reader will need to adjust the details to his own
satisfaction. The 50-line poem is presented as a monologue by Priápus.

Once I was only the trunk of a fig tree, and *that* wood is useless.
Up came a whittler, debating: "A privy-seat? or a Priápus? —
Better the garden god." Therefore a god I now stand, striking holy
Terror in birds and in trespassers. Thieves I expel with my upraised
Hand and this red-painted cudgel that juts from my middle so lewdly;   5
Bothersome birds I scare off with this wand of a reed on my head: it
Waves in the wind so they dare not alight in the fresh-planted seedbeds.
This is where slaves out of cramped little chambers were formerly buried,
Slave-mates contracting with funeral directors for crudely hewn coffins;
Here was the general burying place for society's poor, — for   10
Parasite-jester Pantólabus and Nomentánus the wastrel,
Posted by marker: "A thousand feet frontage by depth of three hundred,
Transfer forbidden with sale of the property hereto adjacent."
Healthful existence is possible now on the Esquiline Hill, and
People can stoll on the Servian Rampart enjoying the view, where   15

Bones used to bleach in the sun and the prospect was downright depressing.
I am myself less perturbed about grave-robbing prowlers and all those
Scavenging animals given to haunting the place than I am by
Witches that torture the souls of the living with drugs and enchantments.
20 Once let the wandering moon show her face at the full of its beauty,
I can do nothing to keep them away from here, or to prevent their
Gathering bones and collecting the poisonous herbs for their potions.
    I have myself seen Canídia, clad all in black and short-girdled,
Barefoot, with hair all disheveled, come walking about with her elder
25 Sister Sagána to utter their howlings. The pallor of both was
Ghastly to look on. They first dug a trench with their fingernails; using
Only their teeth they proceeded to rip a young she-lamb to pieces,
Draining its blood in the trench so the ghosts of the dead would be conjured
Forth at the taste of the blood and give answers to questions. A little
30 Image stood by, made of wool, and a second, of wax, was beside it,
Woolen doll larger, to torture the waxen one into submission,
Waxen doll standing in slavishly suppliant posture, like one whose
Death is upon him. To Hécatē one of the hags made entreaty,
While to avenging Tisíphonē cried out the other. You then saw
35 Hell-hounds and snakes on the prowl as the moon hid the blush of her shame in
Shadow behind many towering tombs so as not to be witness.
If I have not told the truth about this, may my head be streaked white with
Droppings of crows; may I also be pissed on and shit up against by
Julius and faggoty young Pediátia and thieving Voránus.
40 Need I go into a lot of details? how the ghosts gave Sagána
Answers at intervals, piteously squeaking in thin little voices?
Or how they buried the beard of a wolf and the fang of a spotted
Snake in the ground? how the bonfire blazed up as it fed on the waxen
Image? or how in my horror at what those two Furies were doing
45 I did not merely stand by without making some gesture of vengeance?
For, with a crack like a bladder exploding, I spread out my fig-wood
Buttocks and farted. Then back to the City they fled in a hurry.
Then how Canídia dropped her false teeth, how Sagána's enormous
Wig came undone, how their herbs and their ritual bracelets went flying:
50 That was a wonderful sight to behold, — you'd have laughed till your sides ached.

1   Doubtless the fig is the wild fig, or "goat-fig" (*caprificus*). In Epode 5, 17 Canídia's fire is made with "barren wild-fig wood that sprouts from gravestone cracks."

2–7   Priápus (Greek *Príapos*), god of gardens and vineyards, whether well carved in wood or stone or a mere tatterdemalion scarecrow, displayed an enormous erect phallus (for fertility) and often held a pruning knife aloft.

11   "Parasite-jester" = *scurra* (whence English "scurrilous"), a man who lived on free dinners to which he was invited for his repartee. The word will recur.

        Pantólabus is Greek for "Grab-all." The name of Nomentánus—"a man from Noméntum," just NE of Rome—occurs seven times in the *Satires*; see S.1.1.102 and note.

14   One of "the Seven Hills of Rome" was the Esquiline, in the E and NE section of the ancient city. It sloped down to the Forum and to the (future) Colosseum.

15   The Servian Rampart was Rome's earthworks constructed by (Etruscan) King Servius
      Tullius (578–534 B.C.), upon which a great wall of stone was built at intervals after 378
      B.C. A 300-foot stretch of it still impresses tourists near the Rome railway station (which
      occupies part of the site of Maecenas's mansion and gardens).

22–26   For Canídia see the "Note on Canídia," p. 122. Her elder sister Sagána,—Latin *saga*
      means "witch"—will appear again in Epode 5, 25. "Short-girdled" means that her dress
      (*palla*) has been pulled up and bloused over her belt to leave her legs free for movement.
      One wonders how Priápus could see the witches' pallor by moonlight.

      26   Witches left their fingernails uncut (as in Epode 5, 47) in order to dig with
      them, since witchcraft fails in the presence of iron tools.

33   Hécate was the goddess of witches. Tisíphonē ("Avenging Destruction") was one of the
      three Furies.

36   "Towering tombs" = *magna sepulchra*. Such were indeed built by the wealthy, usually
      along roadsides, and ruins of several may still be seen along the Appian Way. But in a
      pauper cemetery. . .?

39   For *fragilis Pediatia* the C. T. Lewis dictionary suggests "the delicate Miss Pediatus."
      "Voránus" is likely to mean "devouring anus." "Julius," the family name of the Caesars,
      is flabbergasting in such company.

As mentioned in the headnote, it is difficult to visualize the respective positions of vegetable
garden, Priápus figure, pauper graves, "towering tombs," and Servian Rampart, not to
mention the access of scavenging animals—Epode 5,99–100 speaks of wolves and birds of
prey. Nor can we be sure that Maecenas's mansion had yet been built.

Epode 9,4 shows that the "high house" was standing by September of 31 B.C.; lines 7–8
seem to imply that already stood in 36. Avoidance of Maecenas's name in such a context may
have been a matter of taste, but the poet's awareness of the cemetery purchase must postdate
his introduction to Maecenas in 38. We suggest dating the poem to the garden-planting
season of 35 B.C.

Fourth-century-A.D. critics Donatus and Servius knew of some 80 *Priápea*, poems to or
about Priápus, from the Augustan period; three of these, attributed to Vergil, are still
perserved. In Hérédia's *Les Trophées*, 1893, the admirable five-sonnet sequence subtitled
Hortorum Deus imitates these and uses as its epigraph: *Olim truncus eram ficulnus* from the
opening line of S.1.8.

1.9.   *Ibam forte Via Sacra, sicut meus est mos*

Down Via Sacra one time I was walking along, as my way is,
Thinking out verses and lost in my thoughts about this thing and that, when
Up comes a person I knew — knew him merely by name and no more, and
Grabs for a handshake and says, "Well, how *are* you, how *are* you, dear fellow?"
— "Tolerably well at the moment," say I, "as I trust you are also."   5
Seeing him trail right along, I inquire, "Was there something you wanted?"
— "Yes. I want *you* to know *me*. I'm a person of culture." And I say,
"All the more reason to prize your acquaintance," and try to escape, now
Putting on speed, now delaying a minute and whispering something —
Any old thing — to my slave, while the sweat, like a river, is pouring   10
Down to my heels. ("Oh, Bolánus," I think to myself, "for your lucky

Wits of invention!") My man goes right on with his chatter, however,
Praising the streets and admiring the City. Observing I do not
Answer, he says, "You're just dying, I know, to escape. I could tell that
15   Some distance back. But no use of your trying, I won't let you go. I'll
Follow wherever. Might this be the way you were headed?" — "No need to
Go to such bother. I'm visiting someone completely unknown to
You — over Tiber — he's sick and in bed — near the Gardens of Caesar."
— "Oh, I'm not busy right now, and the walk wouldn't tax me; I'll keep you
20   Company." Down go my ears like an ill-treated donkey that feels too
Heavy a load being piled on his back. So this fellow of mine starts
Off with: "As surely as I know myself, neither Viscus nor Varius
Ever could win your affections so fully. Who beats me at writing
So many poems so fast? Who can equal my daintiest dance-steps?
25   As for my singing, why, even Hermógenes listens with envy."
          Then came a chance to break in: "Do you have, say, a mother or kinsmen
Who could look after you?" — "Hardly a one. I have buried the lot." — ("How
Lucky for them! Oh, I plainly perceive that I'm all you have left, so
Finish me off! I perceive the approach of the doom that the Sabine
30   Woman predicted when I was a boy with her jarful of swirling
Lots: 'Not from poison or enemy sword shall this lad come to perish,
Nor from a cough or the pleurisy, nor from the crippling podagra:
Some day, however, a person excessively talking will cause his
Death; in adulthood he should, in all wisdom, avoid the long-winded.' ")
35   Vesta's was now just ahead and the morning was nearly half over.
Time had now come when his bail bond required his appearance in court, and
Failure to do so would certainly mean a decision against him.
"If you're my friend, stick around, you can be my attorney." — "I couldn't
Stay on my feet for so long, I know nothing at all about law, and
40   I have an errand, remember." — "I'm wondering which to abandon,
You or my law case." — "Oh, me, by all means!" — "No, I'll never do that!", and
Off he goes leading the way. Since a winner is not to be challenged,
I trail along. Then he starts a new tack: "How are you and Maecenas
Getting along? He's a man of few friends but of excellent judgment.
45   No one has ever more neatly turned luck to advantage than you have, —
But you could have an assistant, a second-role actor to you, by
Just introducing this person now speaking. You'd beat them all hollow
Then, I'll be hanged if you wouldn't! — "Our manner of living is simply
Not as you seem to imply. There is no other house so above-board,
50   None that is freer of devious doings. I tell you I never
Worry about, who is richer or who is more learnèd; there each man
Occupies *his* special place." — "That's amazing and hard to believe!" — "Well,
That's how it is." — "What you say only heightens my wish for becoming
Friends with him." — "Wishing is all that it takes, and with talent like yours, no
55   Doubt you will capture his fortress. And he is a man who can *be* won;
That's why he makes first approaches so difficult." — "Leave it to me! I'll
Bribe his attendants; and if I am barred from admission today, I

Still won't give up; I'll be watching for chances to meet him when he is
Out in the streets and escort him back home. After all, there is nothing
Granted to mortals without a great effort." Now meanwhile along comes   60
Fuscus Arístius, someone I cherish and someone who knew this
Character perfectly well. So we stop. The "Where from?"s and "Where to?"s are
Asked and replied to. I give him a twitch of his toga fold, clutch his
Unfeeling arm, and by winking my eyes and by nodding my head, I
Signal my desperate need to be rescued. The joke-loving cad keeps   65
Smiling away and pretends not to notice the fact that I'm seething.
"Surely you said there was something or other you wanted to tell me
Privately." — "Oh, I remember quite well, but let's wait till a better
Time to discuss it. Today is the thirtieth Sabbath: you wouldn't
Want to go flouting the fore-shortened Jews." — "I am free of religious   70
Scruples of that sort!" — "But *I*'m not! I'm somewhat less hardy than you — just
One of the multitude. So, till another occasion, excuse me."
Oh, that so dismal a day ever dawned! There that rascal deserts me,
Leaving me under the knife. But along comes the plaintiff by chance and
Shouts at his enemy: "Where are you off to, you scoundrel? And *you* there   75
(Turning to me), will you witness this fellow's arrest?" There I gladly
Lend him my ear. So he drags him to court, with the two of them shouting,
Crowds thronging up for the spectacle. I had been saved by Apollo.

  1   Via Sacra, "the Sacred Way," sloped gently NW by W down the side of the Forum to the
      foot of the Capitoline Hill.
 10   A gentleman rarely left his house without an attendant slave (*pedisequus*) at his side.
 18   Julius Caesar's will bequeathed an estate SW of the city proper, across the Tiber and on
      the Janiculum Hill, to serve as public gardens. In Shakespeare's *Julius Caesar*, III,2
      Antony closes his "oration" with:

               Moreover, he hath left you all his Walkes,
               His private Arbors, and new-planted Orchards,
               On this side Tyber, he hath left them you,
               And to your heyres for ever: common pleasures
               To walke abroad, and recreate your selves.

 22   Two brothers named Viscus were friends of Horace and Maecenas; see S.1.10.83. For
      Lucius Varius Rufus see S.1.5.40 and note and S.1.6.55.
 23–25 Three things abominated by Horace: poetry dashed off in a hurry, dancing by men,
      and singer-entertainers.
          Horace blamed Lucílius for writing poems too fast (S.1.4.10–13). Dancing, as in the
      modern Orient, was often a solo performance by either a male or a female; in S.2.1.
          24–25   Horace is disgusted by a man who dances when drunk.
          Hermógenes Tigéllius, the singer, is the son of "Sardinian" Tigéllius, as in S.1.3.129
      and S.1.4.72.
 29   The Sabines in the mountains E of Rome were noted for witchcraft and fortune-telling.
 35   I.e., Vesta's temple, near the lower end of the Via Sacra. Compare Ben Johson's *The
      Alchemist*, I,1, line 93: "in Paul's," that is, in Saint Paul's Church, in London.
 61   Fuscus Arístius = Arístius Fuscus; Horace occasionally inverts the order of family name
      and *cognomen*. See *Odes* 1.22 (*Integer vitae*), which is addressed to him, and the note to line
      3 of that ode. In E.1.10, likewise addressed to him, Horace says the two of them "are
      almost like twins" (line 3).

69–70   "Fore-shortened" (*curtis*) = circumcised, but "the thirtieth Sabbath" (*tricesima sab-bata*) is either whimsical invention or error. Suetonius (in *Augustus* 75) quotes a parallel error from a letter of Augustus to Tiberius: "Not even a Jew fasts so scrupulously on his sabbaths as I have done today."
　　　　　Jewish proselytism was alluded to in S.1.4.143 and note; Jewish belief in miraculous fire in S.1.5.100–101; see also S.2.3.288–295 and notes, where the ritual fasting and bathing may be Jewish. Cicero's "Speech for Flaccus," 59 B.C. (mentioned in the note to S.1.4.143) spoke not only of the great numbers of Jews in Rome at that date, but also their "barbarous superstition" and their aversion to Roman ideals.

76–77   "I lend him my ear" (*oppono auriculam*) means, *not* "I listen to him," but that Horace allows the plaintiff to touch his ear in an ancient, symbolic gesture of agreement to the arrest and to formal acceptance of legal responsiblity as a witness to the action.

78   Horace the poet is saved by Apollo, patron god of poets.

1.10.   *Nempe incomposito dixi pede currere versus*

Oh, no denying! I did say Lucílius's lines ran on clumsy
Feet. But would any Lucílius enthusiast be so absurd as
Not to admit it? And yet in that very same paper of mine I
Praised him for scouring the City with liberal doses of salt. That
5　　Homage, however, stops short of conceding him every perfection,
Else I would reckon Labérius's farces as beautiful poems.
Making an audience snicker is hardly sufficient for greatness,
Though I admit there is merit in having the power to do that.
Brevity too is an excellent thing, so the thought moves along and
10　　Listeners' ears are not burdened with verbiage till they are weary.
And there is virtue in varying style, being sad and then funny,
Playing the alternate roles of the orator and of the poet,
Or the sophisticate holding his fire and deliberately keeping
Things understated. A joke often settles an issue of substance
15　　Better and with a more telling effect than a bitter rejoinder.
That is the way the Old Comedy writers composed, and we ought to
Follow the models they set,—though our handsome Hermógenes never
Reads them at all, or that monkey whose training equips him for nothing
Other than learnèd renditions of works by Catúllus and Calvus.
20　　— "But he was brilliant, the way he mixed *Greek* phrases in with his Latin
Text." — Oh, you late-learning scholars! A difficult feat and a marvel?!
Something already achieved by that dreary old Pítholeón of
Rhodes?! — "But a blend of both languages makes the new work more attractive,
As when you flavor Falérnian wine with a tinge of the Chían."
25　　— Only in poems, you mean? Would you ever do that, I inquire, when
Trying a difficult case at the bar, like Petíllius', for instance?
Would you, I wonder, forget about homeland and old Father Latin
Even while Pédius Poplícola pleads to the court, or Corvínus,
So interlarding your language with terms and expressions from foreign

Parts that you sound like a bilingual man from down south in Canúsium?   30
I once considered composing Greek verses, for all I was born this
Side of the sea, but Quirínus appeared in a dream after midnight,
When we behold only dreams that are true, and forbade me to do so:
"Carrying logs to a forest would not be more foolish of you than
Trying to swell the already vast numbers of Greeks who write poems."   35
    So, while bombastic "Alpínus" goes murdering Memnon in verse and
Turning the Rhine-mouth to mud, I myself go on writing my lighter
Works, which will never resound in the temple of arbiter Tarpa,
Nor will they ever be seen on the stage in repeated revival.
You are, Fundánius, the one man alive who can charm us with prattling   40
Play-books where Davus the slave and the artful young girl circumvent old
Chrémes; in tragical trimeter Póllio sings of the feats of
Kings; with the power and grandeur of epic our Varius succeeds as
No other poet can do; and the Muses delighting in rural
Scenes have accorded to Vergil their elegant deftness and sweetness.   45
This kind of writing, however, — which Varro of Gaul and some others
Vainly attempted — was something that *I* could do better, though not so
Well as the man who invented it; nor would I dare to remove that
Crown which so rightly belongs on Lucílius's head in all honor.
    But, yes, I did say he flowed like a silt-laden stream that too often   50
Carried more things you would rather reject than retain. Let me ask you,
Scholarly friend, is there nothing to censure in mightiest Homer?
Does not the kindly Lucílius himself call for changes in Áccius'
Tragedies? Does he not laugh at undignified verses in Énnius,
All without saying his own works are better than those he finds fault with?   55
What then forbids me, when reading Lucílius, to raise certain questions?
Was it by fault of his own or by fault of his difficult time and
Place, that he failed to write lines of more polish and easier flow than
Someone who chose to enclose an idea in six feet of verse and,
Pleased with that much, then delighted in writing his two hundred lines or   60
So before breakfast and matching that count after dinner? Etruscan
Cassius's genius was likewise more foamy than rivers in flood time;
Of him they say that his books and their cases supplied all the fuel
Needed to cremate him after his death. If we say of Lucílius:
His was an art of refinement and grace, with a polish beyond some   65
Author rough-hewing his form unaware of the Greeks, and achieving
Higher distinction than all of our earlier poets, — I still would
Say that if fate had prolonged his existence on down to the present,
He would be filing off many a rough spot and pruning away all
Elements short of perfection, and he would be scratching his head and   70
Chewing his fingernails down to the quick to achieve that perfection.
    Do not neglect your eraser if works are to merit a second
Reading, and never mind trying to work for the crowd's admiration;
Rather, rejoice to be read by the few. Are you crazy enough to
Hope that your poems will serve as dictations in everyday schoolrooms?   75

I'm not! Applause from a knight is enough satisfaction for me, as
Fearless Arbúscula said when the audience booed her. Why let that
Cockroach Pantílius upset me, or fret that Demétrius twits me
After I leave him, or worry about what ridiculous Fannius
80   Says to defame me, that chum of Hermógenes, son of Tigéllius?
          Plotius and Varius, Maecenas and Vergil are the men whose approval
I am content with; Octavius, Valgius, excellent Fuscus
Too; and I trust that these pieces win favor with both brothers Viscus.
All adulation aside, let me also make mention of *your* name,
85   Pollio; and yours too, Messála, along with your brother's; and also
Servius and Bibulus; not to omit, honest Furnius, your own; and
Many another besides, all the men of discernment and taste whom
I have not space to include. May these poems, whatever their worth, give
Such persons pleasure, and I shall be sorry indeed if I please them
90   Less than I hope to. Be off, then, Demétrius, be off, then, Tigéllius,
Off to your wailings before the divans of your lady disciples!
Now with all haste, boy, go add these remarks at the end of my volume.

1   In S.1.4.8.
4   "Salt" as salt-water cleansing solution and as the common synonym for "wit."
6   Décimus Labérius, about a decade deceased in 35 B.C., was a knight of Cicero's genera-
     tion who was a successful writer of farces or "mimes," as in S.1.2.2 and note. About 150
     lines from his works survive as disconnected fragments.
13   "Sophisticate" = *urbanus*, a word coined by Cicero.
16   For Greek Old Comedy see S.1.4.1–5 and note.
17   Again Hermógenes Tigéllius the younger, as in lines 80 and 90 below and as in S.1.3.129;
     S.1.4.72; and S.1.9.25.
18   An ancient commentator identifies "that monkey" (*simius iste*) with the Demetrius of
     lines 78 and 90 below.
19   Caius Valerius Catúllus, ca. 84 to ca. 54 B.C. As Morris aptly says, he was "one of the four
     great Roman poets (i.e., along with Vergil, Horace, and Lucretius), inferior to Horace in
     sanity and judgment, but superior in spontaneity and brilliancy. This is the only
     allusion to him in Horace, and, while the contempt is directed against *simius iste*, it
     cannot be denied that the allusion is slighting in tone." See the note to *Odes* 3.30.13–14.
          Caius Licinius Macer Calvus, 82–ca. 47 B.C., was a lawyer, orator, and admired
     writer of epic, lyric, and epigrammatic poetry. Though less than a dozen disconnected
     lines survive from his works, a vivid impression of him is to be gained from four poems of
     Catullus to or about him (Nos. 14, 50, 53, and 96).
22–23   "Pitholeón of Rhodes" is the bad epigrammatic poet Pitholaus, whose works are lost.
24   Compare *Odes* 1.20.1–3 and note.
26   For Petíl/ius see S.1.4.94–99 and note.
28   Pédius Poplícola (or Publícola), adopted son of Julius Caesar's nephew, Quintus Pedius,
     is known primarily from this line. Some think he was the brother of Messala.
          Marcus Valerius Messal(l)a Corvínus (or Corvus, "Crow"), consul in 58 B.C., was a
     lawyer of legendary courtroom eloquence and renowned for the purity of his Latin. He is
     the Messála of line 85. S.1.6.42 mentioned the distinction of the family; E.2.3.370 will
     mention his brilliance as a lawyer; and the note to *Odes* 3.21.7 supplies further infor-
     mation about him.
30   Canúsium (now Canósa di Puglia) was mentioned in S.1.5.90–92 for its gritty bread and
     its lack of water. The area had spoken Greek—perhaps in corrupted form—for centuries,
     and to some extent Oscan; see the note to S.1.5.51–70. The town is about 40 km/25m NE
     of Horace's birthplace.

31 Perhaps in his student days in Athens, before age twenty-three.

32 Quirínus is the deified Rómulus, "founder" of the Roman people.

34 A proverb, like "carrying coals to Newcastle." (Greeks said "owls to Athens.")

36 "Alpínus" doubtless = Marcus Furius Bibáculus, who wrote an epic poem on the slaying of Memnon by Achilles and another about Gaul; S.2.5.40–41 calls him Furius and quotes one of the bombastic lines from the poem about Gaul.

38 Spurius Máecius Tarpa (the Máecius of E.2.3.387), as head of the Board of Poets (*collegium poetarum*), passed judgment on new poems in a certain "temple" (*aedis*), which ancient commentators explain as "the temple of the Muses."

40–42 Of comedy writer Fundánius we know only what these lines say, plus what may be inferred from S.2.8. The comedy situation was a frequently used one. Compare the miser Chrémes in Epode 1,33.

40–49 Reviewing the literary genres then being practiced:

> · Fundánius excels in comedy writing;
> · Caius Asínius Póllio excels in tragedy writing. His name recurs in line 85 below; for more information about this important personage see the final note to *Odes* 2.1;
> · Lucius Varius Rufus is the foremost epic poet. His name recurs in line 81 below; he was previously mentioned in S.1.5.40 and note, in S.1.6.55, and in S.1.9.22;
> · Vergil is the foremost writer of bucolic poetry, i.e., the ten *Eclogues*, which were published as a collection in 37 B.C.; see the note to S.1.5.40. If the present poem is dated to 35 B.C., as is highly probable, Vergil's *Georgics* have been begun;
> · Horace himself is the foremost living writer of "satire," though second to the deceased Lucílius.

"Satire" has been unsuccessfully attempted by others, including Marcus Teréntius Varro, distinguished from the famous scholar of the same name by addition of the epithet *Atacínus*, "of the (River) Atax," (now the Aude, near Narbonne in the extreme south of Gaul/France); we translate "Varro of Gaul."

50 That is, in S.1.4.11.

52 Since ca. 300 B.C. Homeric criticism had much occupied scholars in Alexandria, Egypt.

53 Lucius Áccius, 170 to ca. 85 B.C., a slightly younger contemporary of Lucílius, wrote the best tragedies in Latin; only fragments survive.

54 "Father" Énnius, ca. 239–169 B.C., the venerable author of tragedies and of the *Annals*, Horace quotes from him in S.1.2.37 and note and in S.1.4.61–62 and note.

61–64 These lines contain all we know about "Etruscan Cassius." "Cases" = *capsis*, as in S.1.4.21–22, meaning lidded buckets holding rolls of multiple-volume works, or possibly "slip-covers" encasing the individual papyrus rolls.

72 "Do not neglect your eraser" = *Saepe stilum vertas*, "reverse your stylus often." Writing was often done in wax contained in shallow trays, which were hinged together and shut with a clasp, the implement being a sharp-pointed "stylus." One "erased" by rubbing the blunt end of the stylus over the error. By melting the wax and letting it harden again a "clean slate" was prepared.

74–76 The early Latin poets were taught by having the pupils write them at dictation; Horace so learned them in school from "cane-wielding Master Orbílius" (E.2.1.70–71).

77 Arbúscula was an actress in farces ("mimes"), such as those of Labérius (line 6 above and note). In a letter of 54 B.C. Cicero reports to his friend Atticus that Arbúscula was a great popular success.

78–80 Horace's "enemies" include: Pantílius (unidentified); Demétrius ("that monkey" of line 18 above, and note); Hermógenes Tigéllius the younger (as of S.1.3.129 and S.1.4.72, and notes); and Fannius (as of S.1.4.21–22).

81–86 The "pro-Horace" literary faction included, besides Maecenas and Vergil:

> · Plotius Tucca (S.1.5.40 and note) and the epic poet, Lucius Varius Rufus (lines 48–49 above, and note);
> · Octavius Musa, poet and historian. (To Horace, Octavius Caesar is always either "Caesar" or, after 27 B.C., "Augustus.")

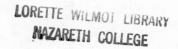

· Caius Valgius Rufus, elegiac poet; *Odes* 2.9 is addressed to him.
· Arístius Fuscus, playwright and critic; see S.1.9.61 and note.
· The two brothers Viscus were members of the Maecenas circle; one was mentioned in S.1.9.22, and one called Viscus of Thurii will be mentioned in S.2.8.20.
· For Caius Asínius Pollio, statesman, General, historian, sponsor of the young Vergil, see the final note to *Odes* 2.1.
· For Marcus Valerius Messal(l)a Corvinus, famous jurist, statesman, General, companion of Horace at "college" in Athens and in the army of Brutus, and patron of poets (including Tibullus), see line 28 above, and note, and the note to *Odes* 3.21.7;

and three more names only approximately identified:

· Servius may be the son of Servius Sulpicius Rufus, mentioned by Cicero;
· Bibulus may be Lucius Calpurnius Bibulus, son of Julius Caesar's fellow-consul and a companion of Horace while at "college" in Athens;
· Caius Furnius is mentioned by Plutarch, more than a century later, as an orator.

Morris, who furnishes these data, adds: "It is worthy of note that, with scarcely an exception, all the men here named as friends are of sufficient importance to be referred to by other writers than Horace."

91 "Divans" = *cáthedras*, high-backed armchairs with cushioned seats.
92 "Boy" means a slave, of any age; here a slave-secretary.

Satires. Book II
Sermones. Liber Secundus
30 B.C.

Satires. Book II

"Satires. Book I" (10 poems; 1,030 lines) was successful enough to warrant publication five years later, in 30 B.C., of "Satires. Book II" (8 poems; 1,083 lines). Again dactylic hexameter is the medium, but now often in dialogue form, with named characters exchanging speeches as in a play. Allusions, however slight, to political events enable us to see that Nos. 1, 5, and 6 of the new series were composed after the battle of Actium of September 2, 31 B.C., and before the publication date (not specifically known) in 30, and it is clear that the exceptionally long No. 3 was written after mid-December of 33. Otherwise the compositional sequence is obscure.

Three of the poems, Nos. 2, 4, and 8, dwell on the subject of gourmets and gourmands, while Nos. 3 and 7 present Horace as under attack from overzealous Stoic "fundamentalists," as in S.1.3. No. 5 is a sardonically witty piece in which Homer's Ulysses (Odýsseus) consults the ghost of the prophet Tirésias, as in the eleventh Book of the *Odyssey*, but with all the prophet's advice ironically updated to around 30 B.C. in Rome.

The gem of the collection, however, is No. 6, probably second to last composed of the series. Whereas the sixth poem of Book I offered Horace's *état présent de ma vie*, bringing him from childhood, youth, and military experience up to his contented status as Maecenas's pensioner-poet, yet pleased to live unostentatiously in Rome, the sixth poem of Book II offers a new *état présent de ma vie*, with Horace established as the delighted owner of his "Sabine farm." Maecenas had made him the gift of the land in 33; the "farmhouse" was, if not fully built, sufficiently habitable for Horace to come there with a provision of books and rusticate for the Saturnalia ("Christmas") season of that year, as the opening lines of poem No. 3 indicate. We may imagine him as happily living there through long parts of the years 32–31–30, alternately busy with the latter pieces of "Satires. Book II" and with his lyric poems in the manner of Archílochus, which will become part of his "Book of Epodes."

In this same period, Mark Antony was sharing the resplendent rulership of the East with Cleopatra, the thirteen-year rivalry between Mark Antony and Octavius Caesar was approaching its climax, and, in September of 31, the fate of the Roman world was decided at Actium. But of these matters we hear hardly the faintest echo in "Satires. Book II."

2.1. *Sunt quibus in satira videor nimis acer et ultra*

Alleging concern about his role as a writer of "satire," Horace presents his dilemmas to the
elderly lawyer, Caius Trebátius Testa, and asks for advice.

Some people think I am overly sharp in my satire and carry
Matters too far, and some others say every last thing that I write is
Lacking in sinew: such verses as mine, they insist, can be reeled off
Any old time at the rate of a thousand a day. What advice do
You have to give me, Trebátius?   5
              Trebátius: Lie low.
                     Horace: And completely abandon
Writing of poetry?!
      Trebátius: Yes.
            Horace: I'll be damned if that mightn't be wisest!
Only I can't get to sleep that way.
            Trebátius: Oil on the skin and a three-lap
Swim of the Tiber work wonders for any insomnia victim;
Also, the body needs thorough infusion with wine before bedtime.
Or, if the writing-bug bites you past any endurance, go pluck up   10
Courage and write about unconquered Caesar's achievements, and then you'll
Have some reward for your efforts.
          Horace: But, excellent father, my talents
Do not suffice. Not just anyone *can* describe battle formations
Bristling with lances, and perishing Gauls with their broken-off spears, and
Wounds of a Parthian horseman collapsing in death from his saddle.   15
Trebátius:
Still, you might try to portray his acumen and fairness, as wisdom
Prompted Lucílius's treatment of Scipio.
           Horace: Oh, I will surely
Do so when things come around. But the time must be properly suited,
Otherwise words from a Flaccus shall never seek Caesar's attention:
Rubbed the wrong way, he will kick like a horse for his own self-protection.   20
Trebátius:
How much more seemly, however, than giving offense with a line like
"Parasite-jester Pantólabus and Nomentánus the wastrel."
Everyone, even unscathed, is afraid of that line and resents it.
Horace:
What shall I do? For Milónius there's dancing the minute the wine has
Gone to his head and he sees every lamp flame around him as double.   25
Castor's diversion is horses, his twin since the eggshell contained them
Glories in boxers: a thousand pursuits for a thousand pursuers.
I take delight in enclosing my words in a metrical unit,
Much like Lucílius, who did it much better than I — or than you — do.
He would entrust his most personal thoughts to his writings, as though to   30
Faithful companions, and never looked elsewhere for refuge if things went

Badly or well; thus that poet of old set his total existence
Forth as in multiple scenes on a vows-tablet. He is my model,
Born though I was a Lucánian or, if you will, an Apúlian.
35 (Down at Venúsia the plowmen are never quite sure where the line is,
Colonists having been sent there, according to ancient tradition,
After the Samnite defeat to forestall the exploiting of vacant
Lands for advancing on Rome, if Apúlians or if Lucánians
Started a war.) But this pen that I wield will not harm any living
40 Being; it rather will serve to protect me the way that an undrawn
Sword gives protection; and why should I try to unsheath it, as long as
I am not being attacked by nefarious brigands? Oh, hear me,
Jupiter, father and king: may my weapon rust out in its scabbard!
Grant that no person harms *me*, because I am a creature of peace. But
45 Anyone giving me trouble will rue it: "Hands off!" is my cry, and
People all over this City will quote from my poem about him.
Cérvius, angered, may threaten reprisal by law and by ballot,
Persons Canídia hates may be in for Albútius's poison,
Túrius, thwarted, may deal with you harshly as judge in your law case;
50 All creatures terrify those whom they fear with the weapon they're best at,
Driven by Nature to do so; observe how the wolf will attack with
Teeth, how the bull uses horns to attack: is this not at the urge of
Instinct? If profligate Scaeva, in charge of his long-living mother,
Never commits any violent action against her, there's no more
55 Miracle than in a non-kicking wolf or a non-biting bull, for
Still the old lady may go by a mixture of honey and hemlock.
     So, to be brief: whether tranquil old age may await me, or whether
Sable-winged Death may already be wheeling in circles above me,
Wealthy or poverty-stricken, at Rome or in exile (if Fate so
60 Wills), be my life of what color it may: I shall write.
                                   Trebátius: Well, my boy, your
Life, I'm afraid, may not last very long, since a friend higher up may
Send you a chill to undo you.
                    Horace: How so? — when Lucílius invented
This sort of poetry *long* ago?! When he ripped lion-skins off of
Sleek-looking donkeys that strutted about and exposed the disgusting
65 Animals under those coverings, Láelius was hardly offended,
Was he? or he who from "Carthage destroyed" won his merited name? Was
Either one shocked by his genius? Or were they distressed when Metéllus
Was? or when Lupus was riddled by verses that made him notorious?
Bigwigs and commons he haled into court, by the ward and the district, —
70 Though he dealt fairly with Excellence and her supporters. In fact, when
Scipio's courage and Láelius' wisdom withdrew to retirement,
Leaving the crowds and the stage of affairs for a private existence,
They had a way of relaxing with him and of joking together
Over the vegetables cooking for supper. Whatever I am, though
75 Less than Lucílius in rank and in talents, the envious cannot

Help but concede I have lived with the great and the mighty. Moreover,
Anyone sinking a fang in me, hoping to hit on a weak spot,
Bites on a stone, — or do you disagree with me, learnèd Trebátius?
Trebátius:
No. As a matter of fact, I see nothing that I would delete here.
Nevertheless, let me warn you, the law is a sacred affair, and   80
Ignorance of it could land you in trouble; bad poems against some
Party entitle the person offended to legal recourse and
Legal reprisal.

       Horace: Agreed — if the poems are bad. But the good ones,
Poems that Caesar found praiseworthy: what about those? Say the poems
Only abused where abuse was deserved, and the poet was blameless?   85
Trebátius:
Then the indictment gets laughed out of court, and you're clear of the charges.

  1   Horace himself refers to his *Sermónes* as "satire" — and will do so again in S.2.6.17.

  7-9 Seventeen preserved leters of Cicero to Trebátius show the latter to have been witty, fond of swimming, and fond of the bottle.

  11 The phrase "unconquered Caesar" would be appropriate only after his defeat of Mark Antony at Actium, September 2, 31 B.C., thus confirming the guess that S.2.1 was composed last of its series, doubtless in 30 B.C., just before publication.

  12 "Excellent father" was a common respectful address. See E.1.6.55 and E.1.7.37–38 and note.

  22 Quoted from S.1.8.11.

  24 Compare S.1.9.24 and note.

  26-27 The twin gods, Castor and Pollux, were patrons of horses and of boxers respectively. They were born of a single egg, as were their sisters, Helen of Troy and Clytemnestra, as a result of Zeus's coupling in swan-form with their mother Leda.

  30-31 Books as an author's faithful companions, so an ancient commentator remarks, was a stock phrase: one Aristóxenus had said the same of Alcáeus and Sappho.

  32-33 The story of one's deliverance from peril might be depicted in multiple scenes on a *votiva tabella*, which would be hung in some shrine; compare the note to S.1.5.65–66.

  34-39 The parenthesis contains accurate history: Horace's native town of Venúsia was founded by colonists from Rome in 291 B.C., at the end of the third Samnite war.

  40-41 Latin *stilus*, "pen," (as in the note to S.1.10.72), yielded Italian *stilo*, (dagger), and then *stiletto*.

  48 For Canídia see S.1.8.23–50 and the "Note on Canídia" on p. 122.

  63-65 The allusion is to Aesop's fable about the donkey that wore a lion's skin, as in S.1.6.22 and note, and in E.1.16.45.

  65-68 Lucílius was a friend of Caius Láelius Sapiens ("the Wise"), consul in 140 B.C., and of Publius Cornelius Scipio Aemilianus, surnamed "Africanus" for his destruction of Carthage at the end of the Third Punic War, 149–146 B.C.

      Lucílius wrote satires against Scipio's political enemies: Quintus Caecílius Metéllus (Macedónicus), consul in 143 B.C., and Lucius Cornelius Léntulus (Lupus), consul in 156 B.C.

      Horace, tongue-in-cheek, says Lucílius never got into trouble for satirizing important persons, so why should *he*?—well aware that the two cases were utterly dissimilar.

  69 Literally: "Yet he summoned leaders of the people to court, and the people too, one tribe at a time." Rome's 35 voting districts still bore the names of the ancient "tribes" (clans), and Lucílius, in one of his satires, castigated all 35 of them.

  81-84 Trebátius has in mind an ancient law "of the XII Tables" against anyone who "sang a bad poem," that is, a spell of witchcraft. Horace blandly takes the words to mean an esthetically bad poem, and, for his lawyer's benefit, implies that even the laws "of the XII Tables" are superseded by the legal authority of Caesar.

2.2.   *Quae virtus et quanta, boni, sit vivere parvo*

Values of simple and frugal existence, good friends, is my subject, —
Not any notions of mine, but the doctrine of farmer Oféllus,
Unsystematic philosopher, schooled in no wisdom but Nature's.
This is no theme to be broached over tables of glittering platters
5   When the perceptions are dazed from the sheen of the silver and every
Mind is receptive to falsities, quite undisposed to better
Things: our discussion shall be before dinner. — "But why before dinner?!"
— I shall explain, if I can.
                    When a judge has been bribed he examines
Evidence carelessly. When you are tired from a rabbit hunt, or from
10   Training an unbroken horse, or — if soldierly sports of the Romans
Bore you, accustomed so long to the Greek type of exercise, — you were
Playing at three-handed catch without sensing how hard you were playing,
Or if your preference had you out throwing the discus, — whatever:
Come with the nonsense worked out of your system, bring hunger and thirst, and
15   Spurn simple food and insist on a wine from Falérnum with honey
Brought from Hyméttus. Your steward is out, and the fish have fought shy of
Nets in the dark winter sea. You will soon feel the growls of your stomach
Finding appeasement in bread with a sprinkle of salt. Do you wonder
How it can be so? Your gratification does *not* lie with high-priced
20   Sauces, but *in*side of *you*. For a taste-whetting relish, just once try
Sweating. The fat and the sallow from overindulgence will not find
Pleasure in oysters and parrot-fish, or in the migrating heath-grouse.
Oh, to be sure, if a peacock is served, I would hardly have strength to
Keep you from tickling your palate with peacock instead of mere chicken,
25   Awed as you are by an empty display; and that rarity sells for
Gold, not to mention the spectacle made when its tail is unfolded, —
As if those colors pertained to the matter. You surely don't eat those
Plumes you admire? And when it is cooked, what becomes of that splendor?
Bird–meat is bird–meat, with hardly a difference, and when you insist on
30   This kind or that kind, I fancy you must be deceived by the sizes.
How can you tell if this open-jaw pike swam the sea or the Tiber,
If it was caught in the buffeting currents between the two bridges
Or at the mouth of our own Tuscan river? You madman! To rave so
Over a three-pounder mullet — which must be divided in portions
35   Anyway. Outward appearance misguides you, I see. What's your point, in
That case, for scorning an overgrown *pike*? Why, the answer is simple:
Nature made pike in the heavier sizes and mullet in light weights.

Stomachs infrequently hungry disdain any commonplace victuals.
— "*I* like to look at a giant-size platter with something gigantic
On it," says he of the gullet that gapes like a ravening Harpy.   40
    And these gourmets! May siroccos blow rot on their appetite-teasers!
Even the freshest of boar-meat and turbot will stink when excess has
Jaded the stomach and over-stuffed eaters prefer to fill up on
Slivers of turnip and horseradish pickle. Not even today have
Simple foods vanished from banquets of kings; even now there is room for   45
Commonplace eggs and black olives. It's not in the *far*-distant past that
People were awed when Gallónius the auctions-man first served a sturgeon.
What! Did the sea fail to breed many turbot in those days? No, turbot
Then were quite safe, and so too was the stork in her nest, till a would-be
Magistrate started the fad of consuming them. If an official   50
Issued a bulletin now, recommending the charms of roast seagull,
Young men of Rome, ever prompt to adopt a bad custom, would serve them.
    Stingy and simple existence, Oféllus opined, were by no means
One and the same, and avoiding the former would profit you nothing
If in so doing you went to the other extreme. Take the case of   55
Avidiénus, whose nickname is Scavenger, not without reason:
Olives five years in the jar and wild cherries comprise his whole diet;
Never a wine pot of his may be opened before it goes sour, and
As for the smell of his oil, you would never be able to stand it;
Even when dressed all in white, at a wedding, a birthday, or other   60
Festive occasion, he doles out that oil on the salad himself, one,
Drop at a time from a jug that weighs all of two pounds, though he never
Skimps on his hoarded old vinegar. Here are two modes of existence:
Which shall a wise man adopt? "Face the wolf or the dog," says the proverb.
He will be elegant only enough so as not to offend by   65
Shabbiness, yet without over-concern about either extreme; nor
Will he, like old man Albútius, show temper when issuing servants
Even their first-time instructions; nor will he, like slovenly Naevius,
Pass around rinse-water scummy from previous use, — which is shocking.
    Now let me name the advantages gained by a plain sort of diet.   70
First, you feel healthier; all those assortments of dishes are harmful,
As you will realize if you recall less elaborate meals that
Used to sit well on your stomach. But once you combine many items,
Boiled foods together with roasted ones, shellfish together with thrushes,
Pleasant things turn into bile so your stomach goes sour and you bring up   75
Slow little clottings of phlegm. Have you noticed how people look pale when
Leaving a multi-course banquet? Not only the body is sluggish
Then from the overindulgence of yesterday, but there is also
Dullness of mind, and our spark of divine upper air is dragged earthward.
Quick as a wink the philosopher finishes eating and goes to   80
Sleep for a time, then arises refreshed to the rounds of his duties.
Once in a while he may step out of bounds for a bit of indulging,
As when a holiday comes in the annual cycle of seasons,

Or when he seeks to recover his strength after weakening illness,
85 Or when those years have arrived where a feeble old age makes a milder
Regimen needful. But what is to happen to *you*, who in youthful
Vigor and prime have indulged in those milder procedures beforehand?
What if bad health overtakes you, or what if old age makes you feeble?
Boar-meat gone bad was still prized by our forefathers, not that old-timers
90 Did not have noses, but rather, I fancy, because it was thought more
Proper for callers to finish it up, even spoiled as it was, than
Having the host overeat on it while it was fresh. Oh, if only
I had been born among heroes like those when the earth was in springtime!
      Do you account reputation of value? which falls on the ear more
95 Sweetly than music? Those oversize turbots and oversize platters
Also mean oversize losses of money and standing. Your uncle's
Wrath must be added to these, and your neighbors' ill will, and self-loathing
Such that you hanker for suicide — right when you don't have a penny
Left for the price of a noose. — "But by rights," someone says, "it is Tráusius
100 You should be lecturing. *I* have extensive resources and income
Such as three kings would find ample for all of their needs." — In that case,
Isn't there any more suitable way to dispose of the surplus?
Why must unfortunates suffer privation when you are so wealthy?
Why must the ancient and venerable shrines of the gods be left shabby? And
105 Why, impious creature, why *not* devote some of your hoard to your country?
You are unique, you suppose, in possessing good fortune forever —
Only to serve some fine day as the butt of your enemies' laughter!
Which of two men may the better rely on himself in misfortune:
One who from overabundance is proud both in body and mind, or
110 One well contented with little, yet wary of future mischances,
Ever preparing for war, like the wise man he is, amid peacetime?
      Now, in support of my statements, I add that I knew this Oféllus
Back in my boyhood; he lived no more lavishly then with his total
Holdings than now when his wealth is reduced; as a hireling he works his
115 Confiscate farm with his sons and his oxen, and here is his story
Told by himself:
            "On a workday my dinner has seldom been more than
Potherbs boiled up with a hambone; but if it so chanced that a distant
Visitor happened along that I had not set eyes on for ages,
Or if a neighbor dropped by because rain interrupted the farmwork,
120 We were contented with chicken or goatmeat and did not send out for
Fish that would have to be gotten from town; for dessert we had clustered
Raisins, and almonds, and figs split in halves, and the table was festive;
Last came the fun of the wine, with discretion to dictate proportions,
And, with libation to Ceres to flourish in spears of our grainstalks,
125 Wine found a way of unpuckering brows of their wrinkles of worry.
Fortune may rage as she will, and set further disorders afoot, but
How are we any worse off? In what way, O my sons, have I prospered
Less than before, or you either, for all this new landlord's arrival?

Final possession of land has been given by Nature to no man
Neither to him, nor to me, nor to anyone. Though he drove *us* out   130
Yet from mismanagement, or from not knowing how tricky the law is,
He in his turn will be surely forced out by an abler successor.
Now in the name of Umbrénus, and lately in that of Oféllus,
This is not any man's farm, but a parcel of land that will lend its
Uses to me or another. For this very reason, live bravely   135
And, when adversity comes, may you front it with hearts full of courage."

3   I.e., Oféllus followed no one "system" of philosophy, Stoic, Epicurean, or other.
10–12   Horace avoided games of three-handed catch in S.1.5.48–49 and S.1.6.126 and
note. See also *Odes* 3.24.54–58 and E.1.18.44–51.
15–16   The best wine came from Falérnum, NW of Capua (as in S.1.10.24), the best honey
from Mount Hyméttus just SE of Athens.
22   "Parrot-fish" (*scarus*); Greek *skáros*), and "heath-grouse" (*lagóis*; also Greek), are not
zoologically certain.
23–28   Cooked peacock was first served by the gourmet and orator, Quintus Hortensius,
whose fame was challenged by Cicero in 81 B.C. and surpassed in 70 B.C. The plumes
were cooked with the bird.
31–33   Gourmets prized river pike over deep-water pike, the best ones being caught
between the Aemilian Bridge and the Sublician Bridge just downstream from the
Tiber Island at a point where the city sewer drained into the river—the pike being a
scavenger fish. The passage imitates line 603 of a fragment of Lucílius given on pp.
188–9 of the Loeb Library *Lucilius*, and we follow Warmington's note there, which
contradicts Morris's.
44   "Horseradish pickle" = *acidas inulas*, "sour elecampane (root)."
47   Lucílius (Loeb Library, pp. 64–65) spoke of a sturgeon-eating glutton named
Gallónius.
49–50   Horace's readers knew who it was that first served cooked stork, but the secret is lost.
"Would-be/ Magistrate" = *praetorius*, a sly adjective suggesting a candidate who was
defeated when running for *praetor*, or "judge, magistrate."
51   "Seagull" = *mergos*, an unidentified kind of sea bird—probably unfit to eat.
56   "Avidiénus" is probably a coining from *avidus*, "greedy." "Scavenger" paraphrases
"Dog," (*Canis*), which may be a bilingual pun on "Cynic," that is an extremist Stoic.
64   Literally: " 'On one side threatens a wolf, on the other, a dog,' as they say." (*Hac urget
lupus, hac canis, aiunt.*)
67   This Albútius can hardly be the one poisoned by Canídia in S.2.1.48.
77   "A multi-course banquet" = *cena dubia*, a dinner with so many good foods that you
don't know where to begin. The phrase is from Terence's comedy *Phormio*, line 342,
from the 160s B.C.
79   Only a Stoic would use the expression "our spark of divine upper air," that is, the
"soul" imprisoned within the clay of the human body.
96   In Roman tradition uncles and stepmothers were hostile persons.
112–113   Scholars have debated whether "farmer Oféllus" (*Ofellus rusticus*) represents a
single individual or a composite of several, but since 48 B.C. many farms had been
confiscated in order to reward army veterans like the "Umbrénus" of line 133, with
results as described in lines 130–132.
123   The Romans drank wine and water mixed in varying proportions; see the note to
S.1.6.117.

Much of S.2.2 is a parody of a Stoic sermon, as indicated by the choppy sentences, by line 79,
and by the strong overstatements, but the melancholy of Oféllus's story in lines 117–136
rather undoes the comic impression.

2.3.   *Sic raro scribis, ut toto non quater anno*

For the December holidays (see the note to line 5) of 33 B.C. Horace has sought the seclusion of hs new Sabine farmhouse, bringing with him "as companions" a number of Greek comedies and the poems of Archílochus. There his privacy is invaded by a zealous convert to the Stoic philosophy, one Damasíppus, who was an actual person three times mentioned in the letters of Cicero. Long-haired, bearded, and fiercely righteous, the unwelcome visitor has hardly arrived before he demands to know why Horace is idling over frivolous lyric poems instead of getting on with the business of reforming society by writing satire.

Damasíppus:
Why, it's so rarely you do any writing at all that not even
Four times a year will you call for a parchment, — and then for unweaving
Work you had finished, annoyed because, over your wine cups and drowsing,
Nothing gets written that's worthy of mention. Where *will* this all end? And
5   Skulking out here at the holiday time! If you really are all that
Earnest, compose me a poem befitting your promises. Now! — What,
Nothing to show? No use blaming your pens, and the wall doesn't merit
Thumping: it doubtless was built under frowns of the gods and the poets.
Think of the many and mighty achievements you threatened us with when
10   Once you had leisure out here in the warmth of your snug little farmhouse.
What was the point of your cramming your luggage with works by Menánder,
Eúpolis, Plato, Archílochus, bringing them here as companions?
Can you be meaning to mollify foes by abandoning satire's
Manliness? Shame on you, wretch! Keep away from the dissolute Sloth-witch,
15   Else you will see the undoing of all you have gained by your better
Life — while you sham unconcern.
                    Horace: For your thoughtful advice, Damasíppus,
May all the gods and the goddesses send you — a barber! But tell me,
How do you know me so well?
                    Damasíppus: Since my fortune was wrecked in the market
I have been rather devoting my time to the business of others,
20   Being forced out of my own. In the past I enjoyed pricing bronzes,
Things such as crafty King Sísyphus once might have used as a foot bath,
Statues botched up by the sculptor or crudely misshaped in the casting:
I, as an expert, would then set the price at, say, one hundred thousand.
I was a broker for gardens and eminent mansions as well, and
25   Turned a nice profit when others did not, so the street-auction people
Gave me the nickname of "Mercury's boy."
                    Horace: Yes, I know. But I marvel
How you have managed the cure for your malady.
                    Damasíppus: What is still odder
Is that a new one has driven the old one away, like the common
Case where a headache or muscle-cramp turns into stomach disorder,
30   Or where a patient comes out of a stupor and beats up his doctor.
Horace:
Barring such actions as that, say whatever you like.

Damasíppus: My good man, you
Must face the fact you are mad, as are nearly all other men, *quite* mad,
If there is anything *to* all that stuff that Stertínius prattles.
It was from him I adopted those wonderful doctrines of comfort
When he advised me to grow a philosopher's beard and to pluck up   35
Courage to leave the Fabrícian Bridge and no longer be downcast.
After my failure in business I went there, intending to shroud my
Head for a suicide jump in the river: there *he* was beside me,
Saying:
(*Stertínius*) "Do nothing unworthy of you. Your chagrin is not really
Shameful: you fear being looked on as mad in a world full of madmen.   40
First, I inquire what it means: 'to be mad,' and if you are alone in
Being so, then commit suicide bravely, I won't try to stop you.
        Anyone blindly compelled by his follies, not knowing the truth of
Things, is defined as insane by the Stoa, the sect of Chrysíppus.
That definition holds true for entire populations and monarchs: 45
Only the wise are exceptions. Now listen and let me explain how
All of those people who called you insane are distraught by their follies
And in no lesser degree than in your case. When blunder leads men to
Wander astray in a forest and keeps them from finding their way, then
One man turns right and another turns left, but it still was that single   50
Blunder that takes them in various directions. Consider yourself as
Crazy in *this* sense: that any man mocking at you is himself no
Saner: he too has a donkey-tail pinned to his back. But there *is* one
Type of a fool who is frightened without any reason for terror,
Dreading a torrent, a cliff, or a fire in the midst of a meadow.   55
Equally foolish, his opposite number will rush into fire or
Torrents of rivers; his mother may lovingly call, his devoted
Sister may call, or his kinsmen, his wife, or his father: 'Be careful!
Here is a chasm!" or 'Here is a terrible cliff! Have a care!', but
He is as deaf to their cries as that drunken old Fúfius was, who   60
Slept his way through Ilióna's whole scene while the audience cued him
Twelve-hundred strong, shouting 'Mother, I summon thee!' Now let me show you
How the entire population is crazed with that kind of delusion.
        Say Damasíppus was crazy for buying up all those old statues:
Was Damasíppus's creditor right in the head? Let's assume so.   65
But, if I say to you, 'Here is some cash which you need not repay me,'
Would you be crazy for taking the money? Or would you be even
Crazier still to reject it when generous Mercury offered?
Sign up for ten with old Nérius — That's not enough: lend a hundred
More to Cicúta, the knot-tying genius; add thousands of liens: your   70
Debtor will slip every noose like a rascally shape-shifting Próteus.
Then, when you drag him to court, he will laugh at your threatened reprisals,
Changing himself to a boar, or a bird, or a rock, or a tree stump.
Granting bad management indicates madness, and managing well, sound
Mind, then Peréllius's brain must be far more befuddled, believe me,   75
Drafting the terms of a loan with no possible hope of repayment."

(Report of a lecture by Stertínius at a meeting)

    Now be so kind as to settle your togas for comfort, and listen;
Anyone pale from unworthy ambition or passion for money,
Anyone flushed with the fever of luxury, gross superstition,
80   Or with some other disorder of mind, gather closer around me
While I explain how you all, to the last man among you, are crazy.

1.   *Greed*

    Those needing maximum doses of hellebore are the diseased with
Greed. (I don't know but what Reason needs all Anticýra to cure them.)
    Heirs of Stabérius had to inscribe the amount of his wealth, in
85   Full, on his tombstone, or, failing to do so, to pay for a hundred
Gladiatorial combats, match Árrius's funeral banquet,
And make donations of grain that would equal the Africa harvest, —
'Whether I rightly or wrongly so stipulate, do not refuse me.'
(I have a notion Stabérius foresaw that they might.) But why ever
90   Should he have wanted his heirs to engrave the amount of his wealth on
Stone? In his lifetime he always thought poverty something disgraceful;
Nothing distressed him more painfully than the idea that, if he
Ever should die with his fortune reduced by so much as a farthing,
He would feel that much more sinful, while everything else among gods or
95   Men — reputation or valor or dignity — merely enhanced what
Riches conferred; and the riches amassed were a sign that a man was
Famous and upright and brave. And wise *too*? Yes, indeed! And a king! or
Anything else you can name! As if *he* had performed a great feat, he
Trusted that this would redound to his glory. Now set him beside that
100   Greek, Aristíppus, who ordered his slaves to abandon his treasure
Out in the midst of the Libyan desert because, thus encumbered
By it, they travelled too slowly. Which one of the two was more crazy?

(Other examples of greed)

    But, illustrations are futile that settle disputes by proposing
Other disputes. If a man bought up lyres and did nothing but store them,
105   Having himself not the slightest concern with the lyre or with music,
Or if a non-cobbler stocked up on shoemakers' leather and knives, or
Someone averse to the sea-faring life purchased sail cloth, they all would
Rightly be thought of as out of their heads. What distinguishes them from
Someone forever amassing more silver and gold and yet never
110   Using the hoard? in fact, fearing to touch it, as if it were sacred?
Say that a man who has gathered a giant-size stockpile of wheat stands
Guard on it uninterruptedly, armed with a monstrous great cudgel,
Yet, though he owns it and though he is starving, withdraws not a kernel,
Frugally choosing to live on a diet of bitter old herbs; or
115   Say he has Chían and mellowed Falérnian wines in a thousand —
No, that's a trifle! — in three hundred thousand containers, and yet he
Drinks only vinegar; or, say at close onto eighty years old he

Sleeps on a mattress of straw because all of his bedding is locked in
Storage to mold or to furnish the moths and the worms with a feast: no
Doubt he would seem quite insane, — but to only the few, since the largest   120
Numbers of men are consumed with a sickness no different from this man's.
Oldster abhorred by the gods, are you guarding your wines from your son, or
From an inheriting freedman who might drink it up? or from fear that
You may run short? Why, how little each day would subtract from the total
If you would merely begin to use better-grade oil on your salad   125
Greens — and to clean up your tousle of hair that is filthy with dandruff!
If the "wee bit" that you use is "enough," then why perjure yourself by
Stealing and pilfering everywhere? This you call sane?! If you started
Stoning some people to death, say, your slaves who had cost you good money,
Everyone, even the boys and the girls, would agree you were crazy.   130

(*A digression*)

What if you poisoned your mother or strangled your wife: would you still be
Right in the head? You say yes, since you neither committed the deed in
Argos nor murdered your mother by swordblade like raging Oréstes.
Or do you claim he went mad only *after* he slaughtered his mother
And that the Furies, from wickedness, drove him to madness *before* he   135
Ever thrust steel of a swordblade into the neck of his mother?
No, you feel once it was clear that Oréstes's mind was unbalanced,
He could do nothing at all that you ever would bring him to book for.
Notice he never tried turning his sword against Pýladēs or his
Sister Eléctra, but merely heaped curses on both of them, saying   140
She was a Fury and he was whatever his frenzy could think of.

(*A further example of greed: Opímius the miser*)

Then take Opímius: poor despite treasures of silver and gold, who
Used to drink second-rate Véientine wine from Campanian crocks on
Holidays — out of the dip-ladle, yet! — and sheer dregs on the workdays:
One time he drank himself into a stupor so deep that his heir, all   145
Glee and rejoicing, was running around trying keys on the strongbox.
But it so happened his quick-thinking doctor was loyal as well and
Brought him around by the following method: he moved up a table,
Emptied the moneybags out, and had various persons come up and
Start counting coin. When his patient had somewhat revived, he advised him: 150
"Look to your money! Your heir in his greed is attempting to steal it."
— "Am I alive?" — "That you are! But wake up, pay attention to business!"
— "What must I do?" — "You will perish of weakness unless you take food in
Quantity so as to bolster your stomach which is now on the brink of
Ruin. You hesitate? Come now, try eating this dish of rice-gruel."   155
— "What did it cost?" — "Very little." — "But *how* much?" — "Eight farthings."
                                                          — "That's awful!
Whether I die of disease or of robbery, what does it matter?"

(*Transition*)

Who, then, is sane? — Any man not a fool. — What if someone is greedy?

— He is both mad and a fool. — What if someone is *not* greed-afflicted:
160   Is he immediately sane? — Not at all! — But why isn't he, Stoic?
— I will explain. Suppose Cráterus said that a sick man did not have
Ulcers: does that make the patient all right? Should the patient get up? By
No means! He may have acute inflammation of lungs or of kidneys.
Any man neither a miser or perjuror owes his domestic
165   Lars the reward of a pig; but in case he's ambitious and ruthless,
Ship him to hellebore country. What difference if all that you own gets
Thrown in the rubbish pit or if you never make use of possessions?

2. *Ambition*

Servius Oppídius, possessing two farms at Canúsium, was reckoned
Wealthy by old-fashioned standards, and of him they tell that he summoned
170   Both of his boys to his deathbed to give them his final instructions.
"Aulus, (he said) I observed you one time with your toga fold full of
Walnuts for gifts and of dice for your gambling; Tibérius, I saw you
Once as you worriedly counted yours over, then hid them below ground.
I have been dreading the madnesses threatening your separate futures,
175   *You* growing like Nomentánus, and *you* taking after Cicúta.
Therefore I beg of my sons, by our family's hearth-gods, that *you* shall
Never make less, and that *you* never make any more, than your father
Deemed was enough, or than Nature imposes as adequate limits.
So, to prevent your distraction by lures of ambition, I hereby
180   Swear you by oath, that whichever of you becomes aedile or praetor
Shall be accursed and shall forfeit his legacy. You with your handouts,
Aulus, of chickpeas and lupines and beans: would you squander a fortune
So you could strut at the Racecourse in ample-fold toga or stand in
Bronze, and be — lunatic!—loser of lands and your father's possessions?
185   Would you, Tibérius, seek the applause that Agríppa receives in
Order to play the sly fox that parades in high style as a lion?"

(*Stertínius "acts out" a scene between Agamémnon and a Greek soldier at Troy;
ambition is dehumanizing.*)

"Why, son of Átreus, forbid us to bury the body of Ajax?"
— "I am the King." — "As a commoner, then, I must ask no more questions."
— "And my command is a proper one. Yet, lest I seem to be *un*just:
190   Anyone present here now may with safety declare his opinion."
— "Greatest of kings, may the gods let you pilot the fleet to the ports of
Home after Troy has been won! May we question and hope for an answer?"
— "Ask." — "Why should Ajax, the hero who, after Achílles alone, stood
Second, who rescued the Argives so often, lie rotting unburied?
195   Is it so Priam and Priam's whole nation may gloat over *him* now
Graveless, whose battle left so many Trojans unburied in Troy-land?"
— "Madly he raged against sheep, slaying more than a thousand and yelling
It was Ulysses, or else Meneláus and I, he was killing."
— "When before altars at Aulis you caused your own daughter to die in
200   Place of a cow, and yourself strewed the salt and the meal that consigned her

Head unto death: were you sane at that moment?" — "The point of your question
Is — ?" — "How was Ajax insane when he raged against sheep? For he murdered
Neither his wife nor his child; if the scions of Átreus were cursed at,
Teucer, and even Ulysses, were never molested." — "When lee-shore
Winds were detaining the fleet, I admit that I did, after thoughtful   205
Weighing of matters, shed blood — but to placate divinities." — "Madman!
That was your own flesh and blood!" — "I concede that. But *I* was no madman."

    (*Stertínius offers reflections on this interchange.*)

    Anyone holding conceptions derived from the senses, at odds with
Actual things and distorted by passion, may rightly be called "off
Balance," and whether he errs out of folly or rage is no matter.   210
Ajax, in killing those innocent sheep, lacked control of his senses;
But, when from "knowing the world" you pursue empty titles by outright
Crimes, are you really quite sane? Is your heart without vice in its turmoil?
Say that a man has a pretty pet lamb, sends it riding by litter,
Dresses it up like a daughter, assigns it allowance and maids, and   215
Calls it Pusílla or Rufa, and even engages a sturdy
Husband to marry it: judges will rule him incompetent, taking
Measures to place him in care of some kinsmen who *are* sane. Then how can
Someone be right in the head if he sends his own daughter to die in
Place of a dumb little lamb? Never claim that he is! The supremest   220
Madness is folly turned evil, and anyone who is a scoundrel
Rages in frenzy no less; and whoever is dazzled by fame and
Glory has raved in the thunder of blood-crazed Bellóna's mad orgies.

<h3 style="text-align:center">3.   Extravagance</h3>

    Now an attack on extravagance and Nomentánus, since Reason
Demonstrates wastrels to be simultaneously foolish and crazy.   225
    Here is a man who no sooner inherited one thousand talents
Than he gave fish-mongers, fruiterers, poultrymen, perfume purveyors —
All of the rabble frequenting the Tuscan Street quarter, the gullet-
Crammers, the parasites, hucksters of cheese and of oil in Velábrum —
Word to appear at his door in the morning. What happened? They came, and   230
Up spoke a pimp: "All I have in my house, all that these fellows have in
Theirs, can be yours for the asking, right now if you wish, or tomorrow."
Taking them up on the offer, the fair-dealing youth gave his orders:
"You there, don leggings and sleep in Lucánian snows over night so
I can have boar-meat for supper; and *you* haul me fish from the winter's   235
Sea. I'm a sluggard myself, undeserving this money, so take it!
Here, take a million! For you there, another! And triple that sum for
You with the wife that will come at a run if I call her past midnight."

    (*Other examples of senseless extravagance*)

    Actor Aesópus's son took a very fine pearl from Metélla's
Ear-drop and, so he could boast he had drunk the round sum of a million,   240
Downed it, dissolved in some vinegar. Which of the two is the saner,

He, or the person who throws it in swift-flowing streams or the sewer?
Or, take that pair of notorious brothers, the offspring of Quintus
Árrius, twins in their fondness for wastefulness, knick-knacks, amours, and
245   Making their breakfast on nightingales purchased at sums beyond reason:
How are their names to be listed, in white-colored chalk or in charcoal?

4.   *Love-folly (a topic not announced in lines 78-80 above.)*

Building of play-houses, harnessing mice to a miniature wagon,
Playing at Even-or-Odd, and cavorting on broomsticks called "Horsey,"
These are pursuits that are tagged as "insane" for a man in adulthood;
250   Reason persuades us that being in love may be even more childish.
Mucking around in the dirt as you did at age three: is that one bit
Different from fretting and moping, I ask, for the love of a harlot?
Or, will you follow Polémon's example, upon your conversion
Throwing away all the tokens of former disease, — all the ankle-
255   Ribbons, the elbow-rest cushions, the mufflers? They say, on returning
Drunk from a party, he ruefully tore off his necklace of flowers
After the voice of a fasting philosopher caught his attention.
Offer a petulant youngster an apple and he will refuse you:
"Have one of these, little scamp," and he won't; take them back, and he wants one.
260   How is he different from someone in love, who debates about going:
"Shall I or shan't I?", and then, going back uninvited, will linger
There by the door he detests? Like the youth in the play, he says, "Shall I
Go, now she summons me? Or, should my heart call it quits with this pain? She
Did turn me out — but she *has* called me back. Shall I go to her? Never!
265   Not if she begs me!" His slave, with more wisdom, advises him, "Sir, when
Matters are hopeless and endless they cannot be managed or kept in
Limits by logic. In love, the twin evils are warring and making
Peace, having spats and agreeing; if anyone tries to control these
Unstable elements, fickle as chance and as changeful as weather,
270   So as to give them stability, he can no more set them straight than
He can go crazy within the strict limits and measures of reason."
When you lie snapping Picénian appleseeds up at the ceiling,
Crowing for joy upon scoring a hit, is your mind on its hinges?
Tell me, are cute little names and the babytalk babbled by oldsters
275   Saner than building a play-house? Then to this nonsense add murder, —
"Raking the fire with your sword": when just recently Marius, after
Murdering Hellas, proceeded to jump to his death, was he not, I
Ask you, deranged? Would you rather, on grounds of a mental disorder,
Find him not guilty on *that* score, yet put him on trial for the murder,
280   Making distinction of crimes where, in fact, there can be no distinction?

5.   *Mind-paralyzing superstition*

There was a certain old freedman who used to go out in the morning
Breakfastless, after performing his ritual cleansing of hands, to
Pray at the street-corner shrines: "Just this once, O ye gods, I entreat you,

Make an exception: exempt me from death. It's so easy for you." His
Eyesight and hearing were good, and yet short of a lawsuit his master   285
Could not have said quite the same of his mind when he sold him. This sort of
Person Chrysíppus includes in the lunatic crowd of Menénius.

    "Jupiter, thou who dost send and who takest away these afflictions,"
So wails a mother in dread of her son after five months of illness,
"If these malaria chills leave my boy, I will stand him in Tiber   290
Naked at dawn of the day thou hast set and appointed for fasting:
Such is my vow." So if luck, or the doctor, has rescued the patient
Just when his illness was worst, the ridiculous mother will kill him
Standing him there by the icy-cold stream, reinducing his fever.
What is the matter with *her* mind? The terror that grovels at godhead!   295
*
    These are the weapons Stertínius, the eighth of the Sages, supplied me
With, as his friend, so I never again need to stand for reproaches.
Anyone calling me crazy will now find the insult returned, so
Let him examine the sack of his own faults slung over his shoulder.
Horace:
Bankrupt before, may you sell at a profit the next time, my Stoic!   300
But, since insanity comes in assorted varieties, which is
My special kind, do you think? I feel perfectly sane, I must tell you.
Damasíppus:
Well, does Agávē feel *she* is insane as she carries her own son's
Ill-fated head, which she lopped off herself in her frenzy of madness?
Horace:
I am a fool, I confess — let me yield to demonstrable fact — and   305
Even insane. But explain to me just what particular mental
Illness you think me afflicted with.
             Damasíppus: I shall be happy to do so.
First, you go in for construction, which means you are aping some "bigger
Men," though your height, from your head to your toes, does not measure two feet in
All; yet you laugh at the stride and the spirit of Turbo in arms as   310
Being too big for his body, — and look who is doing the talking!
Is it quite seemly of you to compete with whatever Maecenas
Does, when you really are not in his class and so vastly beneath him?
    Once, in a mother-frog's absence, a calf set his hoof on her tadpoles;
One, who was lucky enough to escape, told his mother a monstrous   315
Beast had come by and had trampled his brothers to death. "How big *was* this
Monster?" she asked, and beginning to puff herself up, "Was he *this* big?"
— "Oh, half again as big." — "How about this? — As she puffed herself ever
Bigger and bigger, the little frog said, "If you puff till you burst, you
Never will equal him." This is not far from your own situation.   320
    Then, take these lyrical poems of yours, to add oil to the fire: if
Any sane man could write those, I'll agree you are sane, — not to mention
All of these horrible tantrums of temper —
             Horace: Enough!

Damasíppus: — and your living

Way past your means —

Horace: Damasíppus! You mind your own business!

Damasíppus:—and all these

325 Crushes on thousands of girls, and these crushes on thousands of boys, and —

Horace:

Oh, my superior lunatic, spare this inferior person!

 2   That is, ask a slave to bring him some parchment, perhaps for final copy.

 5   The Roman "Christmas" was the Saturnalia, December 17–18–19 (later extended to the 23rd) in honor of the god Saturn ("the Sower") who presided over the Golden Age at the beginning of time.

11–12   Eúpolis was a master of Greek "Old Comedy"; "Plato Comicus" (not the philosopher Plato) was a master of "Middle Comedy," and Menánder of "New comedy"; these terms are explained in the note to S.1.4.1–5.

       These three writers might offer inspiration for the "Satires," but mention of Archílochus indicates (as does line 321 below) that Horace was engaged at this time (33 B.C.) in writing his *Epodes*. For Archílochus, see the Introduction to the *Epodes*, p. 96 below, and also E.1.19.23–25 and E.2.3.79.

18   "In the market" = *Ianum ad medium*, "by the middle Janus," i.e., an arch near the middle of the Forum in the area where the bankers' booths were located. (Morris notes the same expression—apparently a colloquialism—in Cicero's *On Duties*, 44 B.C.)

21   Not the mythological Sísyphus, but an ancient King Sísyphus of Corinth, a city renowned for its bronzes. Damasíppus specialized in "the primitives."

26   *Merc*ury was the patron god of *merc*hants and *merc*handizing.

32   Much of the poem will depend on this fundamental paradox of the Stoics: that all men are mad except the Stoic philosopher.

33   Stertínius was an actual person still alive from the previous generation, but he is known only from the present poem and a casual allusion to him in E.1.12.20.

36   The two sections of the Fabrician Bridge, now the Ponte Fabricio, still connect the Tiber Island to either shore.

37–38   One veiled one's head before committing suicide.

44   The Stoic doctrine was formulated by Zeno, ca. 315 B.C., who lectured in the Painted Porch, or *Stoa*, of the Athenian marketplace, but the doctrine was systematized by Chrysíppus (ca. 280 to 204 B.C.), who then became "the authority." S.1.3.127–8 quotes him.

53   An ancient commentator explains that prankish boys sometimes tied an animal's tail to the backs of unsuspecting persons. The text does not specify "donkey."

60–62   In a tragedy by Pacúvius (220 to ca. 130 B.C.) a mother named Ilióna is wakened by the ghost of her murdered son crying, "Mother, I summon thee!" Actor Fúfius, playing the mother, fell into a real sleep—from alcohol—so that the ghost got no reply; the audience of 1,200 then began shouting the cue line. (The text names actor Catiénus, who played the ghost on that occasion.)

69–76   Roman banking terms and procedures are too obscure to follow this much-argued passage in detail, but Peréllius is the creditor and the borrowers are Nerius (*not* Nereus, the sea-god!) and Cicúta, whose name means "hemlock" (the poison).

       The sea-god Próteus evaded all questions by changing himself into different shapes; but he would finally answer if his questioner grabbed him and held on tight despite all his transformations.

77   All the interlinear headings are supplied by the translator, who follows Morris in assuming a scene change at this point.

78–79   "Madness" is the theme of the sermon, which here announces four subheadings, in the order: 2, 1, 3, 4. Actually, the poem will deal with *five* subheadings:

1. Greed ("passion for money"), lines 82–157
2. Ambition, lines 158–223
3. Extravagance ("the fever of luxury"), lines 224–246
4. Love-folly, lines 247–280
5. Mind-paralyzing superstition, lines 281–295

The conclusion, lines 296–299, balances the "introduction," lines 77–81, while lines 300–326 bring the reader back to the "frame-tale" of lines 1–31.

82–83   The plant called hellebore was the accepted remedy for insanity. It grew near the town of Anticýra, no great distance S of Delphi, on the coast.

84–91   Stabérius is unknown, but one stone inscription of this kind is known. Quintus Árrius and his extravagant sons who breakfasted on nightingales (line 245 below) were real persons.

          "Africa" is the Roman wheat-producing area of Tunisia and eastern Algeria.

100–102   Aristíppus of Cyréné (on the coast of Libya), ca. 435 to 356 B.C., was a pupil of Socrates and a philosopher in his own right. His basic doctrine is stated in E.1.1.19 as "Seeking to subjugate things to myself, not myself unto things."

125–128   Compare S.1.6.124: "Oil — not the kind that old Natta saves up from the lamps that he filches."

131–141   The complex story of Oréstes, prince of Argos, is told, with variants, in different Greek tragedies, particularly in Aeschylus's trilogy, the *Orestéia*. In line 264 of Euripides's *Orestes* the hero calls his sister a Fury, but no preserved Greek work shows him as cursing his devoted friend Pýlades.

142–144   The name "Opímius" is probably Horace's own coining from *opimus*; "fat; abundant." Campanian dish ware, as in S.1.6.118 and note, was the cheapest and poorest. "Véientine" means "from Véii" (modern Veio) just N of Rome. By using the dip-ladle, Opímius saved the cost of a cup.

158–160   Stertínius both asks and answers the rapid-fire questions, preacher-style. It is erroneous to have Horace interrupt with questions at this point.

161   Cráterus was an actual physician of Cicero's generation, twice praised in Cicero's letters.

168   "Oppídius" ("Townsman," from *óppidum*, "town") is probably a coined name. For Canúsium see S.1.5.90–92 and Itinerary note, and S.1.10.30 and note.

175   Nomentánus (also in line 224 below) is the wastrel several times mentioned before; see S.1.1.102 and note; S.1.8.11 and note; and elsewhere.

180   Four annually elected aediles had charge of street repairs, police, firemen, and public games. Eight annually elected praetors staffed the law courts as judges.

          Votes might be "influenced" by free distribution of foodstuffs.

185   In 33 B.C. Agrippa, Octavius Caesar's principal General, in his capacity of aedile, gave such lavish public games that he was applauded by the spectators. Hence the present poem, which is set in December, must have been composed in the winter of 33–32 B.C.

186   Horace is probably varying the fable about the *donkey* that wore a lion's skin, as in S.2.1.63–65 and note.

187–207   This striking episode is not in the *Iliad* or even in Sophocles's drama *Ajax*; it would appear to be derived from mythographic tradition. See Robert Graves: *The Greek Myths*, 165 (entire).

          When both Ulysses and Ajax claimed the arms of the slain Achilles, Agamemnon awarded them to Ulysses. When the offended Ajax sought to murder Ulysses, Athena struck him with madness so that he hideously tortured and slew animals, under the impression he was killing his offenders. Upon regaining his sanity he was so horrified that he committed suicide. Thus far Sophocles, but the argument over the unburied corpse is not included in that drama.

208–213   In these lines Horace ironically uses Roman legal terminology which eludes translation.

223   The Roman goddess Bellóna was a sister of Mars, the war god. Her orgiastic rites must originally have been calculated to induce battle-frenzy, but they were assimilated to the rites of Cébelē, Dindýmenē, et al. See the notes to *Odes* 1.16.7–9.

228–229   The short *Vicus Tuscus* ran from the Forum west to the Tiber. Velábrum was a cheese-and-oil-dealers' street on the Aventine Hill, SW of the Forum.

234   Lucania was the mountainous south-Italian province adjoining Horace's native Apulia.

239–241   Aesópus was a famous actor of Cicero's time, famous, like his sons, for extravagance. Metélla was the wife of Cornelius Léntulus Spinther, a political ally and correspondent of Cicero's.

The pearl-swallowing story, Morris remarks, "is also connected with Antony and Cleopatra. But pearls do not dissolve in wine or vinegar."

253–257   After Plato's death in 347 B.C., his "Academy" was presided over by Xenócrates, and then by Polémon. The sudden conversion of Polémon upon hearing a speech of Xenócrates was a famous episode in the history of Greek philosophy.

262–271   Horace closely paraphrases (in hexameters) the text, beginning at line 46, of Terence's comedy *Eunuchus*, of 161 B.C., where the youthful hero Phaedria speaks with his slave Parmeno.

272   Apple-growing Picénum was the Adriatic coastal province south of Ancona.

281–295   The fasting and the ritual washing of hands indicate an Oriental origin for the daft old freedman, and though he prays at various shrines, some critics have thought that Horace had in mind some confused impressions of Judaism.

Menénius (287) is unknown.

"The day" may be Thursday, a fast day for strictly observant Jews; the ritual bathing is "Oriental" and possibly Jewish; see the note to S.1.9.69-70. Though the Romans had no "week," they were aware of the Near Eastern concept.

"The terror that grovels at godhead" = *Timore deorum*, literally "the fear of the gods," a phrase that renders Greek *deisidaimonía*. Horace rather arbitrarily uses the words in a pejorative sense.

296   "The *Seven* Sages" were proverbial.

299   According to a fable of Aesop, a man wears two sacks, one in front, where he puts the faults of others within easy reach, and the other slung over his shoulder, where he keeps his own faults out of his sight.

303   In *The Bacchae* of Euripides (405 B.C.) queen-mother Agávē kills her son and king during a frenzy of religious delusion, fancying he was a wild animal. She enters at the beginning of the final scene of the play, carrying the severed head ecstatically. (Horace several times alludes to *The Bacchae*.)

308   "Construction" surely refers to the newly built Sabine farmhouse. "Bigger men" alludes to Maecenas and the construction of his mansion on the Esquiline Hill.

309   In E.1.20.24 Horace mentions his short stature; the *Vita* of Suetonius calls him "short and stout," and quotes the emperor's remarks to the same effect in a letter to Horace. But Damasíppus makes Horace a two-foot midget.

310   Turbo, whose name means "Tornado," was a contemporary gladiator.

321–323   "These lyrical poems" (*poemata*) can only be the *Epodes*. "These horrible tantrums of temper" (*horrendam rabiem*) may refer to Epodes 4, 6, 8, and the like.

2.4.   (H) *Unde et quo Catius?* (C) *Non est mihi tempus aventi*

Horace:
Catius! Where from? and where to?
                                    Catius: I'm too rushed for a visit! I need to
Jot down some precepts I've heard that beat all that Pythágoras taught, or
He who stood trial, accused by Anýtus, or even wise Plato.

Horace:
Oh, my apologies, then, for untimely intrusion, but be so
Kind as to grant me forgiveness, I beg you! If any ideas   5
Do slip your mind, I am confident you will retrieve them by either
Natural gifts or rhetorical training: your skill is amazing.
Catius:
That was my problem, to memorize all of these numerous precepts,
Since they were delicate points that emerged from a subtle discussion.
Horace:
Who was the lecturer? Someone perhaps from abroad, or a Roman?   10
Catius:
I shall restate what he taught; the authority's name shall be secret:

    Always remember to serve only eggs of elongated oval
Shape for superior flavor; they also are whiter than round ones;
Hardness of shell is a sign that the male of the species is in them.
    Tastier cabbage is grown in a dry soil not close to the City;   15
Nothing so washes the flavor away as a much-watered garden.
    If you are suddenly faced with a guest in the late afternoon and
Rush to serve chicken, the meat will be tough and unwelcome to palates;
Skilled preparation immerses it first in Falérnian wine-broth:
That makes it tender. — The best kind of mushroom is found in the meadows; 20
Others are not to be trusted. — Black mulberries eaten to top off
Midday repasts will insure the most healthful of summers, provided
They have been picked from the tree before over-hot sunlight has hit them.
    Apéritifs mixed of honey and potent Falérnian wine were
Wrongly advised by Aufídius, for, when the stomach is empty,   25
Only a light wine will do: it is better the organs be moistened
First with a lighter concoction. — If sluggishness troubles the bowels,
Mussels and shellfish, both cheap on the market, relieve the congestion,
As does the smaller-leaf sorrel, but white wine of Cos should go with them.
    Slippery-type shellfish grow fat when the moon is at wax, but not every 30
Body of water produces the quality sorts; from the Lúcrine
Lake come the jumbo-size mussels surpassing the cockles of Baiae;
Oysters are best from Circéi; for sea-urchins go to Misénum;
Milder Taréntum can boast of the biggest and tastiest scallops.
    No one may lightly assert he has gained connoisseurship of dining   35
Till he has mastered the delicate science of flavors. More skill is
Needed than grabbing the highest-priced fish in the market, not knowing
Which ones to stew for their broth and which others to broil, so a guest who
Leans back replete will be freshened with zest for resuming the banquet.
    One who abominates meat that is tasteless selects only boars that   40
Pastured on Umbrian acorns to load his round platters to bending;
Boars from Lauréntum are bad, having fattened on rushes and sedge grass.
    Edible she-goats do *not* necessarily come from a vineyard.
    True connoisseurs hunt the females of much-breeding hares for their forelegs.

45   Optimum age and condition of fish and of fowl was a matter
    Never much studied till *my* palate rendered definitive judgments.
            Some persons turn their considerable minds to inventing new pastries.
            One subject only, however, should not claim exclusive attention,
    Taking great pains, for example, to see that the wines are not bad, yet
50 Being indifferent to what grade of olive oil seasons the fish dish.
            Massic wines may, if the weather is good, be exposed to the open
    Air; any bite they may have will be mellowed by overnight breezes
    And in the process the unpleasant odor will dissipate; but any
    Wine that is strained through a cloth tends to lose its bouquet altogether.
55 Clever men drop some Falérnian lees into lighter Surréntine,
    Adding the egg of a pigeon to gather the sediment up: all
    Alien matter adheres to the egg-yolk and sinks to the bottom.
            Shrimps that are fried give relief after overindulgence in drinking;
    African snails do the same. — With excesses of wine in the stomach
60 Lettuce just floats, whereas sausage and ham whip the appetite on and
    On to eat more, or in fact almost any hot dishes you send for,
    Smoking and sizzling, from one of those filthy old street-corner cookshops.
            It is rewarding to study the nature of double-mix dressings.
    Basic, of course, is the kind that consists of a quality olive
65 Oil and a wine of the heavier sort and some brine from the pickling,
    Preferably brine from a vat in which Byzantine fish have been pickled.
    This should be brought to a boil, with some finely chopped herbs in the mixture;
    Dust with Corýcian saffron, and when it has cooled, add some extra
    Olive oil pressed from the far-renowned orchards of Samnite Venáfrum.
70   Apples from Tibur are less full of juice than the kind from Picénum
    But they are prettier looking. Venúculan grapes may be jar-packed,
    Albans had better be smoke-dried for raisins. Now, I was the first of
    Hosts to serve raisins with apples, the first to serve fish-sauce with wine-lees,
    And I am credited first for the black-salt-and-white-pepper mixture
75 Sifted together on clean little plates at each separate setting.
            It is a crime to pay three thousand cash for a fish at the dealer's
    Only to crowd it on some little platter too narrow to hold it.
            Stomachs are turned if a goblet is served by a waiter with hands all
    Greasy from tidbits of food he has pilfered and then licked his fingers,
80 Or if the wine-mixing bowl has the stains of old lees at the bottom.
            Sawdust and brooms for the floor cost so little, and what does it cost for
    Cleaning-rags? Not to provide such equipment is simply disgraceful.
    Would you let precious mosaics be swept with a dirty old palm-frond
    Broom? or put Tyrian covers on badly stained dining-room couches?
85 When you consider how little in trouble and outlay of cash these
    Items require, any failure to have them is all the more heinous,
    Fancying only the homes of the wealthy could ever afford them.

Horace:
    Scholarly Catius, I beg in the name of the gods and our friendship,
    Take me, no matter how distant the journey, to where I can hear this

Man for myself! Your account of all this may be faithful to fact but 90
Hardly conveys all the subtle nuances of meaning. Besides, just
Think of his looks and demeanor! While you, lucky fellow, have seen all
That, you may well have ignored it in too close acquaintance. But *I* have
No small concern to repair to those far-away wellsprings of lore and
There to drink deep at the source of these doctrines of blessèd existence. 95

1   "Catius" may stand for a real-life Matius, a friend of Julius Caesar, Cicero, and the
    young Octavius Caesar, but the identification is uncertain.
3   Anýtus was the accuser of Socrates at the latter's trial in 399 B.C.
6   Rhetorical training included mnemonic devices for extensive recall of memorized
    material.
11 In Horace's circle this "authority" (*auctor*) was surely evident to all.
24 The Roman apéritif (*mulsum*) was honeyed wine. Aufídius is unknown.
29 Cos is a Greek island off the SW coast of modern Turkey.
31–34   The Lucrine Lake (*Lacus Lucrinus*), the resort town of Baiae (now Baia), and the
    naval port of Misénum (now Miseno) were all just W of Naples. Epode 2,49 praises the
    oysters of the Lucrine Lake; see also *Odes* 2.15.3–4 and note.
        Circéi (now S. Felice Circeo) was further N on the coast, near Tarracina.
        Taréntum (now Táranto) was on the inside of the "heel" of Italy.
41–42   Umbria is central Italy, N of Rome and E of the Tiber. Lauréntum (now an
    uninhabited marsh some 25 km SW of Rome) was the capital of Latium at the time
    when Aeneas landed.
51 Massic was a superior wine; see *Odes* 1.1.19 and note; 2.7.21; and 3.21.5.
55 "Surrentine" is from the region of modern Sorrento, S of Naples.
63–69   The "basic" (*simplex*) dressing was uncooked, the "double-mix" (*duplex*) was cooked.
    "Corýcian" = "from Corycus," a town on the S coast of Turkey. Venáfrum (now Venáfro) is
    some 75 km N of Naples, in the ancient province of Samnium.
70–71   Tibur (now Tívoli), the town 24 km/15m E of Rome, as in the not to S.1.6.108.
        Picénum, the Adriatic coastal province, as in the note to S.2.3.272. "Ven(n)ucula"
    is unidentified in my dictionary.
73 "Fish-sauce" (*allec*) may be something like caviar.
94–95   Horace slyly echoes: "I love to find fresh springs and drink from them," a statement
    twice made by Lucretius in *On the Nature of Things*, 1.927 and 4.2.

2.5.   *Hoc quoque, Tiresia, praeter narrata petenti*

In the eleventh Book of the *Odyssey*, lines 90–150, Odýsseus (whose name the Romans garbled
into "Ulysses") summons up the ghost of the prophet Tirésias to learn how his homeward
journey to Ithaca can be accomplished. The ghost foretells certain obstacles to that return,
including the suitors who are wasting Ulysses's substance back home while courting his
(faithful) wife Penélopē. Ulysses then asks one further question: what must he do to elicit
speech from the ghost of his mother, who is hovering near? With wry irony Horace makes
that "one further question" an inquiry about how to regain his lost wealth, prolonging the
interview as follows here.

Ulysses:
One further question, Tirésias: grant me yet one further answer!

By what devices and methods am I to recover my wealth and
Substance now lost to me? — Why do you laugh?
                              Tirésias: For the man of the many
Wiles mere return to his Ithaca is not enough? nor beholding
5   Gods of his hearth and his homeland again?
                              Ulysses: But you see, never-lying
Prophet, how destitute I shall return — you have said so yourself: no
Storehouse, no herd has been spared by those suitors; and valor and noble
Birth, unless backed with a fortune of money, are meaner than seaweed.
Tirésias:
Faced with such horror of poverty, let me, without any lengthy
10   Circumlocution, instruct you in how to get rich. If a present —
Such as a thrush — has been given to you for your own, let it fly at
Once to where fortune shines bright on an elderly owner. When first-fruits —
Say, the sweet apples — turn ripe on your farm, before Lars of you *own* hearth,
See that the Lars of the wealthy and worthier man first enjoy them.
15   Even if he is a perjuror, even if he is an upstart,
Even if he is a runaway slave, or has murdered his brother,
If he expects you to stroll with him, do so, and walk on the *out*side.
Ulysses:
I should go trailing some cheap little Dama around?! That was *not* my
Custom at Troy, where I always competed with men of the better
20   Class.
Tirésias:
        Very well, then: stay poor.
                              Ulysses: I'll compel my great spirit to bear it.
I have borne worse in my time. But continue, O prophet, and tell me
How to accumulate wealth and amass a great treasure of money.
Tirésias:
Once I have said and I now say again: go a-fishing for old men's
Wills, and if one or another of them is too sly for the angler,
25   Nibbling the bait off the hook but declining to bite, never mind: just
Do not abandon your hopes and the art after one disappointment.
When there's a case in the law courts of great — or of lesser — importance,
Find out which party is rich and without any children, and then, though
He is a scoundrel and brazen enough to bring suit against someone
30   Innocent, *you* defend *him*, disregarding one better reputed
But with a son or a healthy young wife, though his cause has more merit.
"Quintus," you call him, or "Publius," — delicate ears just adore first
Names, "your exemplary qualities make me your friend, and I do know
Something about our ambiguous laws, I can plead a defense case,
35   And I would sooner have someone pluck both of my eyes out than see you
Brought to disgrace or lose even the price of a nutshell. I really
Worry about your defeat and becoming a laughing-stock." Bid him
Simply go home and take care of himself: you are now his attorney.
Then you stick by him, no matter if "ember-red Dog Star is riving

Mute-standing statues in twain," or if Furius, with guts full of blubber,   40
Goes on "bespitting the peaks of the wintering Alps with his hoarfrost."
"Just look at *him!*", someone nudges his next-standing neighbor in court, "how
Tireless he is, how devoted in service to friends! And how forceful!"
Then watch the mackerel swimming and swarming right into your stockponds!
    Furthermore: not to expose your intentions by bachelor-stalking,   45
Look for a father, of outstanding wealth, with an invalid son who
Stands to inherit, and gently intrude yourself into his graces;
Get yourself named in his will as contingency heir, then if any
Unforeseen accident happens to take the lad down into Orcus
You will step into the vacuum. This is a ploy nearly foolproof.   50
If you are handed a will to read over, be sure to decline that
Honor, and also be sure that you motion the tablets aside, but
Not without stealing an eye-corner glance at the wording, page one and
Second line down: with the quickest of looks see if you stand alone there
Or if your name is but one in a list. A policeman reborn in   55
Second existence as clerk will outwit the old beak-gaping raven:
Fortune-pursuing Nasíca will only be mocked by Coránus.
Ulysses:
Are you insane? or deliberately fobbing me off with sheer nonsense?
Tirésias:
Son of Laértēs, what *I* foretell either will be — or it won't be.
Mighty Apollo endows me with vision and powers prophetic.   60
Ulysses:
Nevertheless, if you may, would you spell out the sense of this fable?
Tirésias:
Some future day, when a hero descended from noble Aenéas,
Terror-inspiring to Parthians, mighty by land and by sea shall
Stand, then Nasíca's high daughter, in lieu of her father's
Outstanding debts, will be given in marriage to doughty Coránus.   65
Then will the son-in-law fetch forth his will for his father-in-law and
Urge him to read it; Nasíca will, after a show of refusing,
Finally take it and read it in silence, but only to learn that
He and his child have inherited nothing except lamentation
Privileges. — Now for some further advice: if a freedman or crafty   70
Woman has charge of a senile old man, make alliance with them and
Praise them so roundly that they will sing praises of you in your absence.
This can be useful, but better by far is to get on the inside
Track with the oldster himself. If the silly old fool is a poet,
Praise his bad poetry; if he's a lecher, don't wait to be asked: send   75
Home for Penélopē, bidding her serve the superior man.
                         Ulysses: But
How do you think any woman so sober and chaste could be tempted
When she was never induced to misconduct by all of those suitors?
Tirésias:
Overly generous giving was never too common with those young

80   Fellows, and many came less for amour than because of the cooking.
Under conditions like those, your Penélopē *would* behave well, but
If she had one older man for her pleasure, and *you* shared the profits,
Nothing could get her away — like a dog with a greasy old deer-hide.
      Back in my own elder years an indecent old woman of Thebes so
85   Ordered her will that her corpse should be liberally coated with oil and
Carried to burial over her heir's naked shoulders, to see if
She could just once, even dead, slip away from him; he, I suppose, had
Pestered her more than a little while she was alive.
                                  Start your business
Cautiously; stick to the job, but avoid overdoing your efforts.
90   Talking too much may annoy the morose and the testy, but too much
Silence can also be bad. Like the Davus of comedy roles, stand
Hunching your head like a man who is ever profoundly respectful;
Ply him with flattery; warn him at any first sign of a breeze he
Ought to be cautious and cover his precious old head; shoulder passage
95   For him through crowds; if he runs to much talk, cup your ear as you listen.
If he adores being praised, lay it on till he flings up his hands to
Heaven, exclaiming "No more!" Then you lay it on thicker than ever;
Never let up with your talking so long as the windbag keeps swelling.
      Some day when he has released you at last from your service and care, and
100   You, with your wideawake senses, hear: "Of my estates the quarter
Share I bequeath to Ulysses," you then will exclaim: "Is my old friend
Dama no more? Where to find me another so staunch and so loyal!"
If you can manage it, shed a few tears with those words of affliction,
Though you may cover your face if it shows the delight you are feeling.
105   Spare no expense in erecting the monument left to your judgment:
Neighborhoods relish elaborate funerals. Then if it chances
One of your co-heirs is elderly, hacking perhaps with a nasty
Cough, you suggest an estate or a town house from *your* share — in case he
Has any purchase in mind — could be his for a trifle. — But here is
110   Tyrannous Próserpine dragging me back, so farewell. May you prosper!

    3–4   "Of the many/Wiles" = *doloso*, but Horace had in mind Homer's epithets for this
        hero: *polymēkhanos*, "of many resources," and *polýtropos*, "turning many ways."
   13   "Lars," like *penatis* (translated "Gods of his hearth and his homeland") in line 5, are
        Roman terms deliberately used for these "Greek" characters.
17–18   "On the *out*side," or, at the left, as military etiquette still requires. "Go trailing
        around" is literally "cover the side of . . ."
   32   "Quintus" and "Publius" were *Roman* names replacing such slave-names as "Dama,"
        "Syrus," and so on, which recalled the bearer's former slave status.
39–41   The bombastic quotations are from lost works of Marcus Furius Bibáculus of
        Cremona, who was still alive at the time of this Satire. He is the "Alpinus" of S.1.10.36
        and note. The unusually caustic "with guts full of blubber" = *pingui tentus omaso*,
        "crammed with fat tripe," which may have been meant for the poet or for the
        poem — or both.
52–54   "Tablets" were shallow wooden trays, hinged to open like a book, tied shut with a

cord or sealed shut. Each "tray" held smooth wax on which one wrote with a sharp "pen" (*stilus*); see the note to S.1.10.72 "Page one" = *prima cera*, "the first wax." The first line of a will gave the name of the testator, the second line that of his heir.

55–57   Tirésias "foretells" an event of the 30s B.C. From the expanded explanation of lines 64–70 we infer that Nasíca is a nobleman head-over-heels in debt who marries his daughter to the rich commoner Coránus, expecting him to pay his debts, or at least to enrich his daughter; after the marriage Coránus presents his will, according to which neither schemer will inherit anything "except lamentation privileges."

Coránus is "a policeman," *quinquevir*, "one of the Board of Five" (a minor police committee)," who has had a "second existence" as a clerk (*scriba*) by virtue of being *recoctus*, "recooked," or, killed, cut into pieces, and revived by being boiled in a magic cauldron, as Medea did with old Aeson. (In American slang he is a "retread.")

62–64   The "hero" descended from Aenéas is, of course, Octavius Caesar. Not until after his victory over Antony at Actium, September 2, 31 B.C., could he have been called "mighty by land *and by sea*," and only after that date was there talk of his making war on the Parthians (which Antony had tried and failed to win); hence the present poem must date from the winter of 31–30 B.C.

"Hero" = *iuvenis*, literally "a youth," but used for any male citizen between the ages of twenty and forty, and also applied to figures like Hercules. Octavius Caesar at Actium was three weeks short of his thirty-second birthday.

83   Like a dog with a greasy old deer-hide" translates a Greek saying.

91–92   "Davus" (Greek *Daos*, "a Dacian") was the "type name" for a confidential slave. Terence's comedy *Phormio*, of 161 B.C., has a slave named Davus, and an illustrated manuscript of that play shows him in the posture here indicated.

110   *Imperiosa Proserpina*, queen of the underworld, like an irate mother with a truant child, hauls the straying ghost back into "the house of the dead."

2.6.   *Hoc erat in votis: modus agri non ita magnus*

This I had asked for in prayers: a not overly large piece of farmland,
Space for a garden plot, close by the house-door a spring of clear water,
And, overlooking the rest, just a small patch of woodland. The gods so
Granted, in better and ampler degree than I asked. It is good. No
More, son of Maia, than this, save to keep these possessions securely.   5
If I have not sought a larger estate by some kind of sharp dealing,
And if in future I never am wastrel enough to reduce its
Size; if from folly I never implore: "Oh, if only that jog there,
Spoiling my property line as it does, could be somehow squared out," or
"Oh, if I only could chance on a pot full of gold like that other   10
Fellow, who then with the treasure proceeded to purchase the very
Fields he had plowed as a hireling, made wealthy by Hercules' friendship;"
If what is here is enough, let me utter this prayer in contentment:
"Fatten my livestock, and fatten all else save the master's own head, and
As in times past, so in times yet to come, be my highest protector!"   15
		Now, having moved to these mountains, — this citadel far from the City,
What can I praise without plodding my slow Muse's pace in these Satires?
Here, no distraction of errands exhausts me, no leaden sirocco
Stifles, no autumn weighs heavy, enriching the funeral parlors.

20   Father of morning — or Janus, if that is the name you like better,
      You with whom mortals initiate projects and start undertakings
      (As it best pleases the gods), you shall stand at the head of my poem.
            How you would whisk me away down in Rome to post bail-bond for someone,
      Bidding me: "Hurry! Another will meet the man's need before you do!"
25   Whether the northwind was sweeping earth bare, or the midwinter solstice
      Shortened the daylight with snow in the seasonal cycle, I *went*, and
      Then, after "loudly and clearly" declaring some things that I yet may
      Live to regret, there were crowds to be battled and slowpokes to bark at.
      "What are you up to, you idiot? Watch where you're going!", some foul-mouthed
30   Ruffian spits out, "Must you knock us all down because you have remembered
      All of a sudden that *your* destination is up with Maecenas?"
      That, I admit, I find sweeter than honey. But once up the gloomy
      Esquiline Hill, through my head and my heart run a hundred commitments
      Solely concerned with the business of others: "No later than seven
35   Roscius said you should be at the Puteal Curbing tomorrow";
      "Major new issues are up for discussion today at the Guild of
      Clerks, Quintus: try to be with us again for at least this one meeting";
      "Here is a document: do get it stamped with the seal of Maecenas";
      Tell him "I'll try," and he answers, "It needs but your wish for the doing."
40   Seven, yes, going on eight years ago now, Maecenas began to
      Count me as one of the circle of friends that frequented his household,
      Simply as someone to ride in his carriage and act as companion
      When he was traveling, someone to chat with and carry on small talk,
      Things like: "What time is it?" — "How will 'the Chicken' in Thracian equipment
45   Do against Syrus?" — "Unless you dress warmly, these mornings are nippy," —
      Things that are safely entrusted to unleaky ears. Not a day since
      Then, not an hour, but this "friend" has endured persecutions of envy.
      Whether I joined him at public performances, or on the Field of
      Mars played at sports with him, "Lady Luck's pet" was the usual comment.
50   If from the Rostra a chilling report trickles down to the byways,
      Every last person I meet will inquire of me: 'Excellent Sir, please
      Tell me — you surely must know, since you live up so close to the sky-gods —
      Haven't you heard some report of a Dacian attack?" — "Not a thing." — "Oh,
      How you enjoy making fun of us!" — "No, as the gods may torment me,
55   Nothing at all!" — "Will it be in the three-cornered island that Caesar
      Means to grant lands to his soldiers, or will they get farms on Italian
      Soil?" When I swear I know nothing about it they marvel that any
      Mortal can live in this world and so tightly keep secrets as I do.
            Daylight, I glumly perceive, has been wasted while I was thus busied;
60   Meanwhile I sigh: "O my countryside, when will I see you again? and
      When may I sleep at my leisure and read in the books of the ancients,
      Lulling the cares and vexations of life to delicious oblivion?
      When will the bean, old Pythágoras' cousin, be served at my table,
      Flanked by a salad of greens in a bacon-fat dressing?" Ah, those

Evenings and suppers befitting the gods! at which I and my guests may   65
Dine by the Lar of my very own hearth, while my unceremonious
House-slaves may feast from the platters of left-overs; each of us mixes
Water with wine in proportions to suit his own taste, without senseless
"Laws" to forbid him: a head that is stronger takes headier drinks, one
Happy to mellow on lesser admixtures may do so. Our talk is   70
Not about farmsteads and households of others, nor do we debate: does
Lepos dance well or dance badly? Discussion is rather of matters
More of concern to us, things it is wrong to be ignorant of, as:
Whether mankind is made happy by wealth or by virtuous conduct,
Or: what attracts us to friendship: advantage or goodness of persons?,   75
What is the nature of Good, and wherein lies its final perfection?
      Cervius, my neighbor, will sometimes regale us by telling a story
Gleaned from an old woman's stock of such stories. For instance, if someone
Praises Aréllius's wealth without knowing the problems of riches,
Cervius begins: — It is told of a country mouse long, long ago that   80
Once he played host to a city-mouse friend of his out at his mousehole,
Crude in his manners and mindful of how he'd acquired his possessions,
Yet with the grace for relaxing frugality. Not to go into
Too much detail, he begrudged him no part of his chickpea reserves or
Long-bearded oats; in his teeth he kept bringing him raisins and scraps of   85
Half-nibbled bacon rind, hoping so varied a menu would tempt his
Guest, who had hardly been touching the food with a finicky whisker.
Meanwhile the lord of the household, reclining on this-summer straw, was
Eating his darnel and spelt, taking none of the daintier viands.
"Friend," said the city mouse finally, "how can you find any pleasure   90
Living in hardship up here on this jagged old ridge of a forest?
Wouldn't you rather have people and city than woodland and wildlife?
Take my advice, come away with me now! Inasmuch as the earthly
Lot of all creatures that live is a mortal one, leaving no way past
Death for the great or the small, the conclusion, dear fellow, is surely   95
This: live in happiness, while there is time, under pleasant conditions;
Bear in mind always how brief is your span of existence." The words struck
Home with our rustic, who instantly sprang to his feet for departure.
Both of them traveled the journey proposed, with the object of creeping
Under the walls of the city by night. Now the center of heaven's   100
Regions lay deepest in darkness as first they set foot in a wealthy
Mansion, where coverlets dyed to a splendor of crimson were lying
Spread over ivory couches that shone with a luster of whiteness;
Numerous dishes still left from a sumptuous banquet that evening
Stood there collected and stacked to one side in some reed-woven baskets.   105
So, after showing his rustic a crimson-dyed cover to lie on,
City mouse, acting as host, with his tunic bloused short like a house-slave,
Bustled about serving course after course, not omitting a single
Function of waiters, and first licking bits of each dish as he served it.

110 Lying in comfort and charmed by his newly-found status, the guest was
Playing the role of contentment, when all of a sudden a mighty
Tumult of opening doors sent them hurtling right off of their couches.
Out they ran scampering wildly through room after room in their terror,
Frenzy increasing still more as the mansion reechoed Molossian
115 Hounds in a uproar of barking. "This kind of life," said the country
Mouse, "does not suit me at all, so I bid you farewell. In my woodland
Hole give me safety from perils and the plainest of vetch for my diet."

5 The god Mercury (Hermes) was the son of Zeus by the nymph, Maia.

10–12 Ancient editor Porphyrio supplies the folktale (*fabula*) alluded to here: prayers to Hercules obtained the favor, but locating the treasure itself required the help of Mercury, as the god of riches. Mercury's wry comment was that no treasure could make this man happy because he did the same work with it as without it. Since the entire passage, lines 5–15, is an address to Mercury, only Hercules is mentioned by name.

17 Here again, as in S.2.1.1, Horace himself uses the word "Satires" (*saturis*), as if he too thought of his *Sermones* as *Satirae*.
Compare S.1.4.41–42: ". . . you would not consider a 'poet' a man who/ Wrote about matters belonging in mere conversation, as I do." Line 17 hints that, as of the winter months of 31–30 B.C., Horace was casting about for a new mode of poetic composition—the *Odes*.

19 The deliberate Americanism "funeral parlors" is, in the text, simply Libitina, the goddess whose temple served as undertakers' offices and death registrations.

20 Roman prayers mentioned alternate names of a divinity, "leaving it up to him to select, as it were, the most acceptable." (Morris)

24 Furnishing security for someone in a law court was regarded as an act of friendship, even as an honor. Compare E.2.2.67.

27 In the crowded courtroom the judge called on persons to "speak up loud and clear."

32–33 Why the Esquiline Hill is "gloomy" is not clear, unless the allusion is to the large cemetery there, as in S.1.8.

35 The Puteal Curbing enclosed a "sacred" spot in the Forum where lightning once struck; it was near both the law courts and the banking booths.

36–37 Before being subsidized by Maecenas, Horace had worked as a government clerk; thus he was a member of the "Guild of Clerks" (*Ordo scribarum*). Here a former colleague calls him by his first name, Quintus, and urges him to come back (*reverti*), presumably from Maecenas's house, for "an important meeting." The text mentions "clerks," but "Guild of Clerks" is brought into the translation for the sake of clarity.

38 Maecenas was deputy chief-of-state from mid-31 until 29 B.C. while Octavius Caesar was at Actium, in Greece, in Egypt after the deaths of Antony and Cleopatra, and elsewhere in the Near East, hence Maecenas had the use of the official government seal.

41 Horace is reckoning backward "seven, yes, going on eight years ago now" from the winter of 31–30 B.C. This would place his *second* meeting with Maecenas (S.1.6.61–62) in 38 B.C.; "nine months" before that, in 39, he would first have been presented to Maecenas (S.1.6.56–61), but, as we say in the note to s.1.6.61, "nine months" need not be taken as more than "after quite some time."

44–45 "The Chicken" (*Gallina*) and Syrus (see S.1.6.38 and note) are gladiators. Thracian equipment was heavy armor and weapons.

50 The Rostra was the speakers' platform in the Forum. It was so called since 338 B.C., when the front of the platform was decorated with the ships' beaks (*rostra*) taken from enemy ships in a Roman sea battle.

53 The warlike Dacians (of modern Transylvania) were expected to attack Roman frontiers to the NE in 31 and did attack in 30. The circumstances are explained in the note to *Odes* 1.26.4.

55–57 "The three-cornered island" (*Triquetra*) is Sicily. Octavius Caesar's military operations from 31 (Actium) to 29 B.C. would once again require land confiscations in order to pay his soldiers.

61 "The ancients" are the Greeks; see S.2.3.11–12. Horace did not much like the early Roman authors, except for Lucílius and perhaps Ennius.

63 Pythágoras, the mathematician and philosopher of the 6th century B.C., believed in the transmigration of souls, hence an animal slain for its meat might contain the soul of a departed relative or friend. Why the same prohibition applied to beans is a matter of dispute, but in Horace's time the prohibition of beans had become a joke.

67 Guests ate what they wished from the huge serving platters at dinner, what was left—and sometimes that was a great deal—went to the slaves. From medieval banquets the platters were likewise carried "out" to persons of lesser degree, with the final scraps going to the beggars at the gates. In Wolfram of Eschenbach's *Willehalm* 276, 3–5 young Rennewart ate with such appetite that "no one was going to bow thanks for what *he* sent away from the table."

67–70 For the after-dinner drinking, guests elected a "drinking master" who set the "law" for all present: such and such proportions of wine and water, with no exceptions.

72 Lepos ("Charm") was an actual dancer, says an ancient commentator, and one much admired by Caesar.

74–76 The topics are those of Cicero's philosophical dialogues and essays, but Plato's philosophical dialogues also treated such topics. The Highest Good (*Summum Bonum*) was a point debated in all ancient philosophies.

77 *Neighbor* Cervius cannot = the Cervius of S.2.1.47. The name suggests *cervus*, "stag." His story of the city mouse and the country mouse is, of course, retold from Aesop.

2.7.   *Iamdudum ausculto, et cupiens tibi dicere servus*

Davus:
I have been listening to find you at leisure and speak a few words, but
Being a slave, I am hesitant.
                          Horace: Davus?
                                   Davus: Yes, Davus, his master's
Honest, devoted domestic, — enough so, that is, for your thinking
He will be long for this world.
                          Horace: Use the freedom of festive December
Granted by custom of old and say frankly whatever you wish to.   5
Davus:
Some men delight in their vices consistently and are determined
In the pursuit of them; others are drifters, now clutching at right things,
Now again passive to wrong ones. Take Priscus, for instance, with *three* rings
Flashing at times on his fingers, and then again not wearing any;
Never consistent, he often changed clothes on the hour, putting off his   10
Senator's toga on leaving some mansion and making his way to
Parts a respectable freedman could — decently — not be seen leaving.
Now he chose whoring in Rome, now the life of a scholar in Athens,
Destined from birth by Vertúmnus, the god of the multiple changes.
Take Volanérius, the funny-man dinner companion: when gout (quite   15

Fittingly) paralyzed him in the fingers, he hired an assistant,
Paying him so much a day, to retrieve his thrown dice and to put them
Back in the dice-cup. Persisting to such a degree in his vices,
He was the less to be pitied — and much better off than the person
20 Struggling with tether too taut or with tether too slackened.
Horace:
Come to the point of this rubbish! What *are* you referring to now, you
Scallywag?
    Davus: I am referring to you.
                Horace: In what way, rascal?
                        Davus: Well, you
Always are praising the manners and luck of the people of yore, and
Yet, if a god offered sudden return to them, you would refuse him,
25 Either because you are less than sincere in your claims of their goodness
Or because you do not care about decent behavior: your foot clings
Hopelessly fast in the muck, though you say you would like to withdraw it.
Rome makes you long for the country; once there, you're so fickle, the absent
City gets praised to the stars. If perchance no one asks you to dinner,
30 Vegetable supper at home is your utter delight — as if *you* went
Anywhere only when forced to; you claim that you like it that way, you
Hug yourself, having no cause to go drinking. But just let Maecenas
Send for you late, around lamp-lighting time, and say "Join me for supper":
Then it's "Won't *some*body bring me the oil!" and "Can't *any*one hear my
35 Orders!", and so you storm off amid din and a dither of babble —
Leaving guest Mulvius and jokesmen to find their way out — with some curses
I must refrain from repeating. As *he* would say: *I* am the fickle
Type that gets led by the stomach, a savory odor excites me,
I am complacent and lazy, and if you insist, I'm a cook-shop
40 Addict. But since you are everything *I* am and possibly worse, why
Need you abuse me, as if you were better, enfolding your own bad
Doings in fine terminology? What if you're shown up as being
Even more stupid than I, — who cost only five hundred in drachmas?
Glaring won't scare me! Just check your right hand and your temper while I set
45 Forth in good order the doctrines taught *me* by Crispínus's doorman.
    You fancy somebody's wife, while a nice little harlot suits Davus:
Which of us really deserves crucifixion? When vehement Nature
Gives me the urge, and the clear-shining lamplight has shown me the naked
Woman who took all the flailings and thrusts of my stiff-swollen prick and
50 Worked her lascivious thighs for the horse on his back underneath her,
She sends me forth undisgraced and without any worries about some
Richer or handsomer man's getting rid of his load on that very
Spot; but when *you* have discarded your badges of rank, both your Roman
Robe and equestrian ring, and from gentleman status step out as
55 Cheap little Dama, and muffle your perfume-drenched head in a cloak, then
Are you not just what you look like? You shiver with fear as they let you
In, and then alternate terror and lust make your bones fairly rattle.

What is the difference if you are a gladiator seared by the whip and
Put to the sword or merely shut up in some stinking old closet,
Stowed by the maid as her unscrupled mistress instructed, and hide there,   60
Knees doubled up to your chin? Is it not the provision of law that
Erring wives' husbands are justly empowered to deal with you both — with
Even more drastic authority over seducers? Such wives will
Never change garb or position, nor are they the primary sinners:
They are afraid of you, and, when you talk about love, they distrust you.   65
Yet you go putting your head in the noose, to the furious husband's
Mercies exposing your fortune, your life, and your life's reputation.
Say you escape, and I trust that the lesson has taught you some caution:
Off you go looking again to find terror, again to face ruin,
Slave that you are to the core! When a beast of the forest once slips its   70
Chain, is it ever wrongheaded enough to return to its bondage?
"*I*," you say, "am no adulterer." Nor can you say I'm a thief, by
Hercules!, since I do *not* steal your silver. Suspend your reprisals,
Then see the way uninhibited Nature runs wild without checkrein.
You are my *master*?!, controlled as you are by such great and so many   75
Persons and things?, when the magistrate three or four times has pronounced you
Free of your slavery, *still* without setting you free of your wretched
Fears? — And another thing, no less important than those I have mentioned:
Whether a slave in the hire of a slave is a sub-slave, as termed by
People like you, or a fellow-slave, what, pray, are we to each other?   80
True, you give orders to me, but in turn, sorry man, you must dance at
Orders from others, as if you were dangled on strings like a puppet.

  Who, then, is free? Why, the wise man, the man in control of himself, whom
Poverty, death, and imprisonment never can daunt with their terrors,
One with the will to defy his desires and disdain every honor,   85
One so complete in himself and so perfectly rounded and smooth that
Nothing outside of, or alien to, him can grip on his smoothness,
One against whom all assaults of Dame Fortune are futile. Of all these
Traits is there one you can claim as applying to *you*? Say a woman,
Asking five talents, torments you, and empties cold water upon you,   90
Driving you back from her door, then recalls you, — shake off her disgraceful
Yoke from your neck! Go and shout "I am free! I am free!" But you cannot.
It is no lenient master that governs your spirit, that jabs sharp
Spurs in your wearying flank, and that keeps you at wheeling and turning.
Or, take the case where you stare in a daze at a painting by Pausias: 95
Madman, are you any less of an idler than I when I tarry
Over the posters of Pacideiánus with tense-muscled thighs, or
Fulvius and Rútuba, lifelike in charcoal and red-colored chalk as
If they were really in action with weapons and dealing and dodging
Blows? But then Davus is shiftless, he dawdles along on his errands;   100
You they call "great connoisseur of the art of the ancients," the "expert."
I am a dunce if I thrill at a smoking-hot pancake: does *your* great
Spirit achieve its distinction from turning down sumptuous dinners?

Why is my belly-indulgence so wicked of *me*, will you tell me?

105 Granted, my back pays a price to the whip; but do you go unpunished
Any the less for your grabbing of dainties denied to inferiors?
Banquets pursued without let-up go stale in the end, and the feet you
Fooled for so long will refuse their support to your overweight body.
Is it so wrong for a slave to trade off, in the twilight, a stolen

110 Bath-scraper, say, for some grapes, when to sell off a farm for the sake of
Stuffing a gullet is *un*slavely? — Then add the fact that you cannot
Stand your own company even an hour or wisely make use of
Leisure, forever a runaway fleeing yourself and in search of
Some way, in wine or in sleep, to elude the distress that consumes you:

115 Never succeeding; that dismal companion keeps dogging your footsteps.

Horace:
Where can I find me a stone?
                              Davus: Why a stone?
                                                  Horace: Or a bow and some arrows!

Davus:
Either the man is insane or he's making up poetry lines.
                                                         Horace: Get
Out of here! Fast! Or it's off to my Sabine estate as my *ninth* slave!

1–4   "Davus," as in the note to S.2.5.91–92, is a "confidential" slave.

4–5   "Festive December" means the Saturnalia festival days, December 17–18–19 (see the note to S.2.3.5), when slaves were free to say anything they wished to their masters, in recollection of "Saturn's reign," before there was distinction of master and slave. Saturnalia feasting, gift-giving, and lighting of candles became Christmas practices.

6 ff.   "Using the freedom of festive December," Davus, the slave, launches into a sermon, the theme of which is eventually seen as the Stoic paradox that all men are slaves except the (Stoic) philosopher—just as S.2.3 consisted largely of a sermon by Damasíppus on the Stoic paradox that all men are insane except the (Stoic) philosopher.

8–9   "One ring was usual, two were conspicuous, three would be effeminate." (Morris) Rings were worn only on the left hand.

14   Vertúmnus (Vor-) was the god of all changes, but especially in the crops. He was the patron of orchards and the husband of Pomóna.

15   "Funny-man dinner companion" paraphrases *scurra*, a word translated as "jokesmen" in line 36 below, and as "parasites" in S.2.3.229. The same type of person is represented by the "extras" of S.2.8.21 and E.1.5.28.

24   Compare S.1.1.15–22.

37   "*He*" = Mulvius.

43   The price is cheap, but why the amount is given in Greek drachmas, rather than Roman *denarii*, is not evident.

45   Crispínus is the Stoic philosopher and bad poet of S.1.1.120 and note and the "silly Crispínus" of S.1.3.138. Note that the Stoic doctrines are transmitted from one slave to another.

50   Compare S.1.2.125. That this coital position was common is attested by vase paintings, Pompeian wall paintings, and other literary allusions.

55   "Cheap little Dama" (*Dama/turpis*), as in S.2.5.18 (*spurco Damae*); see also S.1.6.38 and note.

58   "Gladiator" is properly "sent to be a gladiator" (*auctoratus*), that is, as a disgraced man, in lieu of execution.

64   That is, they will never exchange the white garments of matrons for the dark garb of prostitutes; see the note to S.1.2.36

66   "In the noose" = *sub furcam*; misbehaving slaves had their outstretched hands tied to the ends of a forked pole worn over the back of the neck and the shoulders.

76–77   The text uses the legal phrase: *vindicta . . . imposita*, indicating the formal freeing (manumission) of a slave by having the magistrate (lictor) touch the person with his staff—somewhat like the ceremonial dubbing of a knight by tapping his shoulder with a sword.

83–88   The essential passage in the sermon: no one is free except the "wise man" (*sapiens*), that is, the Stoic philosopher; all others are "slaves."

89–92   The infatuated lover is another variety of slave. Again Horace seems to be thinking of Terence's comedy *Eunuchus*, as in S.2.3.260–265 and note.

             Five talents would represent several thousands of dollars.

95   Pausias was a famous Greek painter of the 4th century B.C.

97–100   "Posters" means wall drawings advertising coming attractions in the arena. Actual examples are known from Pompeii.

110   A bath-scraper (*strigilis*) was a curved instrument of horn or of metal used to scrape the skin after bathing.

118   We infer that Horace had a modest staff of eight slaves at his Sabine farm. Roman comedy often threatens slaves with a "transfer" from easy city duties to farm labor.

2.8.   *Ut Nasidieni iuvit te cena beati*

Horace:
What sort of time did you have at your dinner with rich Nasidiénus?
When I invited you yesterday, that was your prior commitment,
Drinking from midday, you said.
                    Fundánius: I enjoyed myself more than I ever
Hope to again in my life.
                    Horace: If it isn't too much of a bother,
Tell me what dish you began with to satisfy ravenous stomachs.   5
Fundánius:
Starting us off was Lucánian boar, which the host said was captured
Under the sigh of a southerly breeze, and around it, for tangy
Garnish, were turnips and lettuce and radishes, whetting the sluggish
Appetite, skirwort and fish-brine and wine-tartar crustings from Coan
Jars. On removal of platters a high-girdled slave with a purple   10
Cloth wiped the maplewood tabletop clean while another collected
Crumbs and such other superfluous items as might be offensive
Or an encumbrance to diners. Then out stepped Hydáspēs, a dusky
Hindu, supporting the Cáecuban wine the way Attican maidens
Balance the emblems of Ceres; then Álcon, with Chían unmixed with   15
Sea-salt. The host said, "There's Alban, Maecenas, — Falérnian too, if
One or the other is more to your taste; we have both in supply here."
Horace:
Wealth has its miseries! Tell me, Fundánius, who were the other
Guests in attendance that you should have found it so hugely amusing?

Fundánius:

20   I had the first couch, with Viscus of Thúrii next, and beyond him,
     If I remember, was Varius. Two extras had come with Maecenas,
     One was Vibídius, the other Servílius — the one they call "Jester."
     Up from the host Nomentánus was placed, while below him was Porcius, —
     Playing Ol' Porker by swallowing pastry-pies whole. Nomentánus
25   Had been assigned to the place which by custom the host should have taken
     So he could point with his finger to anything missing our notice.
     Meanwhile the rest of the crowd — meaning *us* — ate our fowl and our fish and
     Shellfish, each differently flavored from any we ever conceived of,
     As I discovered, in fact, at the start, when he passed me some fish roe
30   Such as I never had tasted before, from a turbot or flatfish.
     Musk-apples redden, he later informed me, for having been gathered
     During the wane of the moon. How that circumstance alters the matter
     You would do better to hear from the source. Then Vibídius turned to
     "Jester" and said, "If we don't drink him bankrupt, we'll die unavenged!" and
35   Asked to have bigger-size drinking-cups. Pallor came over our "steward,"
     Since there was nothing he dreaded so much as excessive imbibers,
     Either because they get going too freely with things that they say, or
     Else because heat of the wine mutes perception in delicate palates.
     Using their over-size goblets, Vibídius and "Jester" kept draining
40   Entire decanters of wine, and the others did likewise, except for
     Those on the low couches: *they* never once laid a hand on the flagons.
         Then came a fish called *muréna*, arranged on the platter to look as
     It it were floating in shrimps. "She was caught," said the host, "with the roe still
     In her, unspawned; after spawning, her meat would lose much of its flavor.
45   Here's what goes into the dressing: to olive oil — only Venáfran,
     Only first pressings! — add liquor from mackerel roe from the River
     Ebro and five-year-old wine, but domestic!, while heating the mixture;
     Once it is heated, the best kind of wine to be added is Chían;
     Season with pepper — the white kind, and vinegar — only the product
50   Yielded by ferment of grapes from Methýmnaean vineyards on Lesbos.
     Adding green rockets and bitters of elecampane in the cooking
     Process was something that *I* first discovered; Curtíllus takes unrinsed
     Sea-urchins, claiming their shells make a brine that is better than others."
         Just at that moment the canopy over the table collapsed and
55   Totally ruined the fish platter, raising a billowing dust cloud
     Blacker than any swept up from Campanian fields by the northwind.
     We were afraid that still worse was to come, but with imminent danger
     Past, we sat up again. There was our Rufus, his head on the table,
     Weeping as though for the death of a son in his prime. He might still be
60   Weeping, except Nomentánus, by talking philosophy to him,
     Offered this comfort: "Fortuna, alas!, was there ever a god more
     Cruel than you? How you love to make sport of the works of us mortals!"
     Varius had all he could do with a napkin to smother his laughter.
     "Jester" Servílius, whose habit is always to look down his nose, said:

"Such is the human condition, and by that same token, fame never   65
Yields a reward in proportion to efforts required to attain it.
Think of it! Just to show *me* all this nice hospitality, *you* must
Go to all sorts of annoyance and bother, — so bread won't be burned, so
Fish sauce will not be improperly made, and so we may have waiters
Properly garbed, with good grooming of hair, as they serve us at table.   70
Then take the mishaps like this one that happened: a canopy falls, or
Maybe some oaf of a stable boy stumbles and smashes a platter.
But, with a host or a General, it is the adverse events that
Bring out the genius in each, while prosperity tends to obscure it."
To these remarks Nasidiénus replied: "May the gods answer all your   75
Prayers, you are such a considerate person," and called for his slippers.
You should have heard what a buzzing arose after that, and the whispers
Secretly passing from person to person on this side and that side.
Horace:
This I would rather have seen than a theater spectacle! Tell me,
What, after that, could have happened to laugh at?   80
                              Fundánius: Well, while our Vibídius
Kept up inquiries to waiters to learn if the flagon was broken
Too, since he wanted more wine and was not being served, and while others
Thought of new jokes to excuse all the laughter, — abetted by "Jester,"
Back came our Nasidiénus, with countenance altered, and bent on
Mending his luck by the uses of art: in his wake came a group of   85
Waiters supporting a monstrous great bread-tray with portions of heron
Already carved and well dredged in a mixture of flour and salt, with
Liver of white-goose fed fat on a diet of succulent figs, and
Forelegs of hares, which make daintier eating if torn from the shoulders
Than if left whole and attached to the loins. Then we also saw breasts of   90
Blackbirds well roasted, together with pigeons with rump-parts removed, — all
Very good eating if only the host had not dwelt on the laws and
Characteristics of each. So we took our revenge by departing,
Simply refusing to taste any more of his foods, as if things bore
Taint of Canídia's breath more infectious than African serpents.   95

Fundánius is the comedy writer praised in S.1.10.40–42 and note, and he reports the banquet from the point of view of a comedy writer.

Nasidiénus, surnamed Rufus in line 58, is unkown. He can hardly be identical with Quintus Salvidiénus Rufus, Octavius Caesar's friend and army commander who defected and was sentenced to death, but it may be significant that neither name was genuinely Roman.

So odd are the details of this banquet—the roll call of the diners, the naming of the waiters, the silence of Maecenas—that we suggest it was an imaginary gathering, quite possibly one to which Horace assigned certain friends of his, for maximum comic effect, as witnesses of an event—the collapse of the canopy—which had actually occurred elsewhere.

Nine diners, the ideal number according to tradition, are disposed, either three to a dining couch on three couches or on nine individual couches, thus:

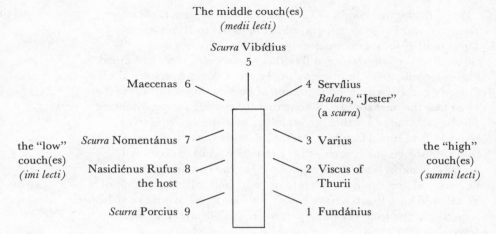

The middle couch(es)
(medii lecti)

Scurra Vibídius
5

Maecenas 6   4 Servílius
Balatro, "Jester"
(a *scurra*)

the "low"   *Scurra* Nomentánus 7   3 Varius   the "high"
couch(es)   couch(es)
(imi lecti)   Nasidiénus Rufus 8   2 Viscus of   *(summi lecti)*
the host   Thurii

Scurra Porcius 9   1 Fundánius

Scurra = "funny-man dinner companion," as in S.2.7.15 and note. Vibídius and Servílius the "Jester" are *scurrae* who have come with Maecenas as "extras" (line 21), literally "shadows" (*umbrae*); Nomentánus and Porcius are *scurrae* between whom the host has ensconced himself, as if afraid to take the host's proper position (7) next to Maecenas in the place of honor (6). The narrator reports only the speeches of the host, "Jester," and Nomentánus.

     Counterbalancing the four *scurrae* are the four distinguished guests: 1 Fundánius, the writer of comedies; 2 Viscus of Thurii, one of the two brothers mentioned in S.1.10.83 for their literary taste; 3 Horace's friend, the epic poet Lucius Varius Rufus; see S.1.5.40 and note; and 4 Maecenas.

6   That is, from the mountainous S-Italian province of Lucania; compare S.2.3.234.
10   The "cloth," of coarse wool, is a *gausapē*, a Balkan word borrowed through the Greek; it is purple for elegance. Fragment 598 of Lucílius reads: "Then he wiped the broad tables with a purple *gausapē*."
13–14   Hydáspēs is named for the river which Alexander the Great crossed in 326 B.C. to defeat Hindu King Porus; it is now the Jelum/Jhelum of N Pakistan; compare *Odes* 1.22. 7–8 and note. His pace is stately because he is balancing the wine jar on his head, perhaps steadying it with one hand; compare S.1.3.10–11: "... a pace such as Juno's/Cult-object bearers observe in processionals," and note.
       Alcon (Greek for "mighty") was the name of a companion of Hercules.
20   Thurii (pronounced TOOR-ee-ee) was a Greek colony founded in 443 B.C. in S Italy, across the bay from Taréntum. Its precise location has yet to be ascertained.
35   "Steward" is Fundánius's contemptuous word for the host as a mere purveyor of wine.
39   The text specifies that the goblets are from Allifae (now Alife), a mountain town some 60 km due N of Naples.
41   The host's two *scurrae* do only as the host does.
45   Compare S.2.4.69: "Olive oil pressed from the far-renowned orchards of Samnite Venáfrum," and note.
46–47   The River Ebro (*Hiberus/Iberus*) flows through NE Spain to the Mediterranean.
58   Chían (pronounced KYan) wine came from the Greek island of Chíos, now off W Turkey.
50   Methýmna was a town on the Greek island of Lesbos. The affectedly elaborate wording does not include the phrase "on Lesbos," though there was a second Methýmna on Crete.
51   Rockets (*eruca*) and elecampane (*inula campana*) are no longer used in cooking. See the note to S.2.2.44.

76 Wealthy Romans dined barefoot, while a slave kept an eye on the light leather slippers worn on some errand, such as the host's now going to the kitchen to supervise a replacement for the ruined fish platter.

86 Some joke may underlie this use (or misuse) of a bread-tray, (Greek) *mazonómus*, from *máza*, "(barley-) bread."

86–93 These gastronomic absurdities, like those in S.2.4, are mild compared to the ones in the "Trimalchio's Banquet" section of Petronius's *Satiricon* some ninety years later.

95 For Canídia, see S.1.8, Epodes 5 and 17, and the Note on Canídia on p. 122. "African," or at least Saharan, snakes must have been proverbially horrible even in Horace's time, but some ninety years later Lucan's catalogue of them (*Pharsalia*, late in Book IX) is flabbergasting: some fly, some leap out of trees, the bite of some causes the blood to boil, and a bite from the tiny *seps* causes the entire body, bones and all, to deliquesce on the spot and evaporate, leaving no trace of the victim.

The Book of Epodes
Epodon Liber
30 B.C.

Epodes

Besides his second Book of "Satires," Horace also published in 30 B.C. a Book of "Iambics" (*Iambi;* 17 poems; 615 lines), which by the latter first century A.D. had somehow acquired the title of *Book of Epodes (Epodon Liber),* which it has borne ever since. Greek *epōdós* was a technical term meaning a lyric poem in couplets—without rhyme, of course. We retain the traditional title of "Epodes" for lack of a better term. Some English writers have substituted the word "Refrains," which we find misleading, and Horace's own title, "Iambics," applies, strictly speaking, only to the first ten of the seventeen poems. Perhaps it may be helpful to see the entire collection as poems made up of alternating "lines" and "echo lines," but this definition leaves No. 17 as an exception.

Horace's primary model was now the Greek poet Archílochus from the island of Paros who, in the 650s and 640s B.C., composed lyric verse in many forms but who was particularly remembered for his "scorpion-tongued iambics." His extensive production is known to us only in a few fragments. About this Archílochus, son of a nobleman and a slave girl, tradition reported that a fellow citizen named Lycámbēs promised him his daugher Neobulē in marriage and then withdrew his promise; thereupon Archílochus directed such bitterly mocking poems against the two of them that both father and daughter hanged themselves for shame. Horace, at age forty-five (20 B.C.) was to state in *Epistles* 1.19.23–25:

> I was the first to show Latium
> Parian iambics that followed Archílochus' meters and spirit,
> *But* on such topics as did not occasion the death of Lycámbēs.

On the subject of meters, in *Epistles* 2.3.251–254, Horace states:

> Any long syllable after a short one produces an iamb,
> Lively of movement, and "trímeter" came to be used as the term for
> Verses in which six iambics proceeded in unbroken sequence,
> Each foot alike from the first to the last.

For a *six*-foot line we would expect the term "*hex*ameter," but for the six-foot iambic line in drama "trímeter" was the traditional term, and Horace happens to be discussing dramatic meters; hence there is no mention of "echo lines" or couplets, since these notions regarded lyric poetry only. In 1899 a chance find in Egypt

96

recovered thirteen lines of an Archílochus poem which patently served as the model for Epode 10. If the Greek inveighed against a betraying friend where the Latin is aimed "merely" at a bad contemporary writer, the prosodic forms are identical in the two works: six-foot iambic lines regularly alternating with "echo lines" of four iambic feet.

This "6/4" formula is followed in the first ten Epodes, several of which are plausibly Archílochan in spirit, though the Greek originals are lost. No. 4 is "scorpion-tongued" invective against a social upstart, No. 6 against a slanderer, No. 8 against a whorish female, and No. 3 is a tirade against garlic. Yet Epodes 1 and 9 are noninvective poems using the Archílochan "6/4" formula for personal messages to Maecenas.

On the other hand, Epodes 11 through 17 vary the metrical formula repeatedly, without achieving significant change. No. 12, against another whorish female, and No. 15, against a rival lover, may represent Archílochan invective, but others among the seven anticipate the gentler tone of the future Odes. No. 11, for instance, about a mistress's locked door, looks forward to *Odes* 3.10, and No. 13 is demonstrably patterned after a Greek poem of Alcáeus, not Archílochus at all, and it is demonstrably a "first version" of *Odes* 1.9.

In lines 5–8 of Epode 14 Horace laments to Maecenas that he cannot finish his book of "Iambics" because he is distracted by a love affair. Whether the excuse was genuine or a pretext, we suggest that Horace set out to compose a "Book" of poems in the manner of Archílochus, wearied of the project, and wound up by assembling a miscellany, into which he introduced even the much admired No. 16, datable to 41 B.C. and probably his earliest preserved poem.

Pieces that can be closely dated by reference to political events are: No. 1, to the preparations for war against Antony and Cleopatra in the summer of 31 B.C.; No. 7, to the outbreak of war with Sextus Pompey in 38; No. 9, to September of 31 upon hearing the news of victory at Actium; and No. 16, in all likelihood to the outbreak of the "Perusine war" between Mark Antony and Octavius Caesar in 41. We note the mixed chronological sequence of these four works of historical significance. Epode 1 "dedicates" the whole collection to Maecenas. The perennial favorite among the seventeen is No. 2, with its idyllic charm and its surprise ending in ironic wit. No. 16 strongly appeals to many by its urgent longing to escape civil turmoil by escape to "the Happy Isles." In the invective pieces the anger sometimes seems artificial and disproportionate. All in all, the "Book of Epodes" is Horace's weakest production.

1. *Ibis Liburnis inter alta navium,*
        amice, propugnacula

Meter: "iambics":   U _ U _ U _ U _ U _ U _
                  U _ U _ U _ U _ *

*See Publisher's Note, p. viii.

Over the winter of 32–31 B.C. Antony and Cleopatra, with headquarters at Patrae (now Patras) in western Greece, kept five hundred ships in readiness off the Cape of Actium (now Cape Pápas), facing NW toward the foot of Italy. Some of these were "fortress" vessels (*propugnacula*) with as many as nine banks of oars, and with such super-galleons Antony was super-confident of victory. At Brundísium (modern Bríndisi) on the heel of Italy lay Octavius Caesar's fleet of fast boats with two tiers of oars like those of the Liburnian pirates (of what is now the coast of Albania), hence "Liburnians." With the warm weather of 31 B.C. all Roman leaders, Maecenas among them, were summoned to Brundísium for the coming sea battle.

To Maecenas departing or already departed Horace expresses his wish to be at his patron's side, speaking diffidently in first person plural in lines 5–14 and then in the more intimate first person singular through the rest of the poem.

So you will really sail in our Liburnians,
    My friend, against those fortress ships,
Prepared to face the perils Caesar faces and,
    Maecenas, risk your own life too.
5   But what of us whose life is sweet if you survive,
    But in contrary case, is grim?
Shall we pursue our leisure as you bade us do
    And find without you no delight,
Or shall we bear the burden as we are prepared
10   To do, wherever brave men go?
We choose the burden, and through passes of the Alps
    Or over savage Caucasus,
Or to the furthest harbor of the setting sun
    We shall with staunch heart follow you.
15   And if you ask what help could I, unwarlike as
    I am and less than rugged, be,
I say that, with you, I feel less anxiety,
    As in your absence I feel more,
Just as a mother bird with fledglings in the nest
20   More fears the glide of serpents toward
Her brood while she is gone than when she folds them close,
    However futile her defense.
This battle and all others shall be gladly fought
    In hopes of favor in your sight,
25   Not so more plows will strain behind more oxen hitched
    To heave the furrows of my fields,
Not so my herds may leave Calábria before
    The Dog Star's heat for upland grass,
Nor yet so any villa's gleam may top the high
30   Circéan walls of Tusculum:
Enough and more of wealth have you bestowed on me
    With lavish hand; nor is my wish
To hoard, like miser Chremes, treasure in the ground,
    Or squander like a spendthrift heir.

6   "In contrary case" (*si contra*) avoids the word "die."
15–16   "Unwarlike" = *imbellis;* compare *Odes* 2.7.9–14. "Less than rugged" (*firmus parum*) may be merely self-deprecating, or it may suggest poor health—at age 35.
25–26   That is, at the Sabine farm, which Maecenas had given Horace about two years before.
27–28   The Roman province of Calabria, with its low pasture lands, was in the *heel,* not the toe, of Italy. In the heat of summer livestock was herded northwest into the mountain pastures of Lucania (which the text names); see *Odes* 1.31.5–6 and E.2.2.177–8.
          The text seems to suggest that Maecenas had also enabled Horace to repossess his father's confiscated lands around Venusia.
29–30   The fashionable resort town of Tusculum (modern Frascáti), SE of Rome in the Alban Hills, was said to have been founded by Telégonus, last born of the three sons of Odysseus/Ulysses by the enchantress Circē, hence "Circéan walls." See the note to *Odes* 3.29.8. As far as we know, Horace owned no villa at Tusculum, but Maecenas may have offered the gift of one.
33   "Miser Chremes" presumably figured in a comedy by Fundánius; see S.1.10.40–42.
34   Compare *Odes* 2.14.25–28.

2.   *Beatus ille qui procul negotiis,*
        ut prisca gens mortalium

Meter: "iambics":   U _ U _ U _ U _ U _ U _
                                  U _ U _ U _ U _

Happy the man who, far from business and affairs
    Like mortals of the early times,
May work his father's fields with oxen of his own,
    Exempt from profit, loss, and fee,
Not like the soldier roused by savage trumpet's blare,   5
    Not terrified by seas in rage,
Avoiding busy forums and the haughty doors
    Of influencial citizens.
And so he leads his grapevines' new-maturing shoots
    To wed with lofty poplar trees,   10
Or in a distant valley gazes out upon
    His flocks of sheep that bleat and browse,
Or with a sickle trims unbearing fruit-tree boughs
    And buds them for a better yield,
Or puts pressed honey up for storage in clean jars,   15
    Or shears the wool from tender lambs;
Or then again, when Autumn lifts his head adorned
    With ripened apples over fields,
Our man delights in harvesting his grafted pears
    And grapes that rival royal red,   20
With portions set for you, Priápus, and for you,
    Silvánus, guard of boundaries.

He loves to stretch at ease beneath an ancient oak
    Or on the densely matted grass,
25 With waters meanwhile flowing in the high-banked brook,
    And birds at murmur in the woods,
And trailing branches rustling in the moving stream
    With gentle, slumber-coaxing sound.
But when the wintry season comes and thundering Jove
30   Brings on the falls of rain and snow,
He either drives the fierce wild boar this way and that
    With dog-packs to the waiting snare,
Or with a smooth forked pole unfolds the coarse-meshed nets
    Where greedy thrushes will be caught,
35 Or else he traps the timid hare or migrant crane
    As game meat for a fine repast.
Who would not quite forget the fret of love intrigues
    Amid diversions such as these?
Then if a loyal wife would do her share to tend
40   Our lovely children and the house—
A Sabine woman, or perhaps the sunburnt wife
    Of some Apúlian countryman—
And light the seasoned wood upon the sacred hearth
    When home her weary husband came,
45 And, shutting healthy livestock in their wattled pens,
    Would drain their swollen teats of milk,
And, drawing new wine from the fragrant storage cask,
    Would serve a meal of home-grown foods,
I would not ask for oysters from the Lúcrine Lake
50   Or turbot any more, or scar,
Which winter, roaring in the eastern sea, drives west
    With waves until they reach these parts;
No Afric bird into my stomach would descend,
    Nor heathfowl from Ionia,
55 More tasty than the plumpest olives gathered from
    The branches of my orchard trees,
Or sorrel herb and healthful mallows that relieve
    Congestion and dyspepsia,
Or lamb fresh slaughtered at the Terminália,
60   Or goat meat wrested from the wolf.
Amid these feasts what fun it is to see the sheep
    Come skipping home from pasture lots,
To see the weary oxen come with upturned plows
    Laid crosswise on their sluggish necks,
65 And home-born slaves, the staff that serve a wealthy house,
    At supper by the household shrine.
Now with these words the money-lender Álfius,

> Soon, soon to be a country squire,
> Revoked all mid-month loans at interest,—
> But plans relending on the first.   70

2   That is, in the Golden Age, at the beginning of time.
1–3 Compare the opening stanza of the *Ode on Solitude*, which Alexander Pope claimed to
     have written "at about twelve years old," in 1700:

> Happy the man whose wish and care
> A few paternal acres bound,
> Content to breathe his native air
> In his own ground.

5–8 Without the hardships of soldiers (5), or sailors (6), and without the worries of
     businessmen (7) or *clientes* (7–8). These last were men otherwise employed or not, who
     reported daily at sunrise to their patron, received assignments for the day, presented
     petitions, obtained loans or repaid them, and so on.
9–10 Grapevines trained to climb elms or poplars were said to be "wedded" to those trees.
9–36 Spring-summer occupations of the gentleman farmer (9–16); autumn occupations
     (17–22); warm-weather pleasures (23–28); winter occupations (29–36): hunting,
     fowling, trapping.
21   Priápus, the garden god, as in S.1.8.2–7 and note.
22   Silvánus, "(he) of the forest," was an ancient Italian, i.e., non-Greek, divinity.
41–42 Sabines, from the mountains E of Rome, and Apúlians, from Horace's native
     S-Italian region, were proverbially rugged folk.
49   For the Lucrine Lake see S.2.4.31–32 and note; also the note to *Odes* 2.15.3–4.
49–54 Five luxury foods: 1. oysters; 2. turbot, a choice fish; 3. scar (*scari*), a still choicer,
     east-Mediterranean fish; 4. the "Afric bird" (*Afra avis*) was probably the guinea hen; 5.
     the *attagen Ionicus* was probably a kind of grouse from the Near East; Saint Jerome—
     echoing Horace?—wrote his friend Salvinus advising against it.
55–60 Five wholesome, native foods: 1. olives; 2. sour-leafed sorrel herb, and 3. the sticky-
     juiced mallow, both salad herbs; 4. and 5. fresh meat slaughtered at home for a holiday
     such as the Terminalia, February 23rd, in honor of Terminus, "Year's End"; the old
     Roman year began on March 1st. Proverbially, wolves killed the best goats.
66   Literally: "around the shining Lars," that is, polished images of the household gods.
67–70 Lines 1–66 have been a city man's wishful day dream, put into the mouth of
     money-lender Álfius, an actual person of Cicero's generation. Now Horace, in four lines,
     tells the sad truth of the matter.
     Money transactions were made on the Kalends (the 1st) of the month, on the Nones
     (the 5th or 7th), or on the Ides (the 13th or 15th). Álfius called in all his loans on the Ides,
     sincerely intending to set up his ideal farm, but got cold feet and decided to put all the
     moneys back out at interest at the next Kalends.

Dryden paraphrased Epode 2 in 102 rhymed lines in his 1685 collection called *Sylvae*.

3.   *Parentis olim si quis impia manu*
senile guttur fregerit

Meter: "iambics":   U _ U _ U _ U _ U _ U _
                             U _ U _ U _ U _

If ever any man is criminal enough
    To break his aged father's neck,
A death by garlic, not by hemlock, let him die.
    How tough our reapers' guts must be!
5   What poison could so twist the diaphragm in knots?
    Was viper venom added to
That salad dressing? Would Canidia have had
    A finger in that ghastly meal?
When over all the Argonauts Medea most
10   Admired the beauty of their chief
And Jason went to force a first yoke on those bulls,
    This must be what she smeared him with;
With this she smeared her gifts of vengeance to his whore,
    As wingèd dragons sped her flight.
15   No burning heat to equal this has ever parched
    The thirsting of Apúlia;
The poison-cloak on Hercules's back could not
    Have seared so hideously with fire.
If ever, prankish friend Maecenas, you should try
20   This sort of thing again, I pray
Your girl may meet your kiss with nothing but her hand
    From where she sleeps at bedstead's foot.

3   Hemlock (*cicuta*), a poisonous weed of the carrot family. Socrates died by drinking a potion made of it.
7   For Canidia see the Note at the end of the *Epodes*.
9–18   Three examples of all-consuming heat:
    · Medea's magic salve protected Jason against the fire-breathing bulls but it also burned Creusa, Medea's rival, to death; for the latter story see Epode 5, 61–66;
    · the heat of Horace's native Apulia in summer;
    · when Deianéira was deserted by Hercules she sent him a cloak impregnated with the poison-blood of Nessus, the Centaur, which burned Hercules to death.
19–20   "Prankish Maecenas" = *iocose Maecenas*. The "trick" may have been a gourmet experiment or a practical joke.

4.   *Lupis et agnis quanta sortito obtigit,*
       tecum mihi discordia est

Meter: "iambics":   ∪ _ ∪ _ ∪ _ ∪ _ ∪ _ ∪ _
                      ∪ _ ∪ _ ∪ _

As far apart as wolves and lambs by nature stand
    The two of us are opposites,—
You with the scars across your back from Spanish ropes

And shackle-goudges on your shins.
For all your strutting in your pride of money now,   5
    Your luck will never change your breed.
As you go pacing off the Sacred Way with six
    Full ells of cloth in toga folds,
Do you not see the utter indignation of
    The passers-by that blush for you?   10
"That fellow's had the whip so many times they're tired
    Of flogging him, and now he plows
His thousand acres and wears out the Appian Way
    With pleasure drives by pony cart
And lords it as a knight, in spite of Otho's Law,   15
    By sitting in reserved-row seats.
What use is there in building all these mighty ships
    With ramming beaks of bronze to mount
Attack against those convicts and those outlaw slaves,
    When this man holds a tribune's rank?!"   20

We infer that some pushy ex-slave had remarked that he and Horace were, after all, in much the same case in their lives. The present angry outburst should be compared with Horace's statements in a calmer moment in S.1.6.1–44.

11–12   In the text, the *praeco* is tired, that is, the crier who stood by during a public flogging, repeating to passers-by the reason for the punishment.

15–16   By the law of Lucius Roscius Otho (Otho's Law, the Roscian Law) of 67 B.C. fourteen rows of theater seats, behind the senators' seats, were reserved for knights.

17–19   For a decade Sextus Pompey had fought by land and sea to recoup his murdered father's political power, enlisting political fugitives and runaway slaves for his purpose. In 38 B.C. he disastrously defeated Octavius Caesar. In the winter of 37–36 the latter had the heavy, bronze-beaked ships built with which he defeated Sextus in a naval battle off Sicily, July 1–3, 36 B.C. Thus Epode 4 probably dates from the spring of 36 B.C.

5.   *At o deorum quicquid in caelo regit*
        terras et humanum genus

Meter: "iambics":   ∪ _ ∪ _ ∪ _ ∪ _ ∪ _ ∪ _
                        ∪ _ ∪ _ ∪ _ ∪ _

Canidia and three other witches have kidnapped a boy of noble birth, perhaps ten years old, and are about to murder him in order to obtain ingredients for a love philter.

"Now by whatever gods of upper air may rule
    The lands and race of human kind,
What is the meaning of this wild commotion? Why
    Are all eyes grimly fixed on me?
I beg you by your children—if you ever bore   5

A child yourself with prayer and pang—
And by this unavailing boyhood garb I wear,
     And by the stern revenge of Jove,
Why do you glare stepmother-like at me, or like
10   A wounded animal at bay?!"
As now the boy stood stripped of clothes and amulet
     And made this plea with trembling lip,
His smooth and hairless body such a sight as would
     Have softened savage Thracian hearts,
15   Canidia, with locks disheveled and entwined
     With little twisting vipers, calls
For barren wild-fig wood that sprouts from gravestone cracks,
     And cypress from a dead man's door,
And screech owl's eggs besmeared with gore of poison-toad
20   And feathers of that bird of night,
And herbs produced in Iólcos and Hibéria
     Abundant in the weeds of bane,
And bones snatched from the very jaws of starving dogs,—
     All these to feed the Colchian flames.
25   Sagána meanwhile, with her skirt bloused short, stalks through
     The house to sprinkle everything
With waters of Avérnus, every hair on end
     Like bristles on a charging boar
Or like sea-urchin spines. The conscienceless old hag
30   Named Veia hacks the ground with spades
And, groaning at her labor, hollows out a hole
     Sufficient to contain the boy
And where, in sight of food brought twice and thrice a day,
     The boy will starve by slow degrees
35   While buried to the chin, his head projecting up
     Like something floating on a pool,
So that his marrow and his liver, drawn and dried,
     May spice a philter-brew of love
As soon as he has gazed his last with staring eyes
40   Upon the food denied to him.
And present there as well, and lustful as a man,
     Was Folia of Rímini,—
So idle gossipers in Naples think, and all
     The neighbor towns report the same;
45   With her Thessalian witching spells she charms the moon
     And stars down from the very sky.

Now here, with untrimmed thumbnail clenched between her teeth,
     Up steps the fierce Canidia;
What are her spoken or unspoken thoughts? "O you
50   Staunch witnesses of my concerns,

Night and Diana, rulers of the silence when
 Dark rituals are carried out,
Be with me now! Now on the houses of my foes
 Direct the power of your rage!
Now while wild animals in fearsome forests hide   55
 Away in sweet and sluggish sleep,
Let mongrels in Subúra bark and raise the jeers
 Of all as my old lecher prowls;
He has an unguent smeared on him more powerful
 Than any I shall brew again.   60
—What noise was that?! . . . Why should my poison less avail
 Than when Medea used it once
Against that haughty whore, great Creon's daughter, in
 Revenge, and then escaped before
The robe, which was her death-dyed parting gift, burst forth 65
 In flames that killed that second bride?
I surely overlooked no herb, no root escaped
 My notice in the wilderness.
He falls asleep in any salve-anointed bed,
 Forgetting all his mistresses.   70
Ah, ah! he must be walking in the safety of
 Some other witch's stronger spell
No, Varus, not by common ordinary spells,
 O you who soon shall sorely weep,
Will you come back to me, nor will your heart return 75
 At summons of a Marsic charm:
I'll brew a stronger dose to pour into your cup
 For treating me with such disdain,
And sooner will the heavens sit below the sea
 With lands of earth above them spread   80
Than you shall not be racked with love of me until
 You blaze like pitch in smoky fire!"

The listening boy no longer uses soothing words
 To move these evil harridans
But recklessly breaks silence with the ghastly kind 85
 Of utterance Thyéstes used:
"Your poisons are not strong enough to change the laws
 Of right and wrong for humankind!
My curse upon you! And no prayer or sacrifice
 Shall expiate my curse of hate!   90
When I have perished at your murderous command
 I shall return here as a ghost
And claw your faces with my curved and spectral nails,—
 Such is the power of the dead—
And squatting as a nightmare on your heaving ribs 95

          I shall with fears destroy your sleep.
     From street to street the mob will pitch their stones at you
          To crush and kill such filthy hags;
     Your limbs unburied shall be torn by wolves and birds
100   Of prey that haunt the Esquiline;
     Nor will my parents, then surviving me, alas!,
          Avoid that satisfying sight!"

1–2   The *sky* gods are invoked, not the gods of the underworld who might favor the malignant kidnappers.

7 and 11   We paraphrase technical terms which indicate the toga of boyhood (*toga praetexta*) with a purple border signifying the class of nobles. The "amulet" (*bulla*) was a medallion, usually of gold and containing protective charms, which a noble Roman boy wore on a necklace from his ninth day of life until official manhood, around age seventeen.

14   "Thracian" here = "savage." See the notes to *Odes* 3.25.10 and 4.12.1.

21   Iólcos was Jason's city in Thessaly, the N-Greek province noted for witchcraft. Hiberia/Iberia (*not* Spain-Portugal) was an Asiatic land, now approximately the Soviet Republic of Georgia, in the Caucasus Mountains.

23–24   The "craving" of the starving dogs is "in" the bones and will pass to the philter. "Colchian" means Medea's witch-fires in her native land of Colchis, just W of Hiberia.

25   Sagána is Canídia's elder sister, as in S.1.8.24–25; Latin *saga* = "witch."

27   Lake Avérnus, W of Naples, was said to be the outlet for the rivers of hell.

30   "Veia" means "a woman from Veii" (now Veio), the once Etruscan town 18 km/11 m NNW of Rome.

41–46   The significance of "Folia of Rímini (*Aríminum*)" is lost to modern readers. Oddly, though she is "of Rímini" in NE Italy, she is reported by the people of S-Italian Naples—in a poem set in Rome.

47   Witches never cut their fingernails. Since iron nullifies witch powers, the nails must serve for cutting flesh, digging earth, and so on, though Veia does use a spade.

51   Diana in her aspect as Hécatē, the witch goddess.

57   Subúra was a slum quarter of ancient Rome, just E of the Forum and at the foot of the Esquiline Hill.

61–66   Apparently Canídia thinks her "old lecher" Varus (line 73) may be at the door. The rest recalls Medea's destruction of her rival, Creusa, as in Epode 3, 13–14.

73   "Varus" was a common *cognomen* among the upper classes, but in its meaning of "bandy-legged" or "knock-kneed" it may apply to Canidia's lover; see S.1.3.47 and note.

76   The Marsians were mountain folk E of Rome, credited with witch lore; compare Epode 17, 29 and note.

86   Thyéstes (uncle of Agamemnon) was tricked into eating the cooked flesh of his sons. His curse is quoted by Cicero from Ennius's lost tragedy *Thyéstes*.

6.   *Quid immerentis hospites vexas canis*
          ignavus adversum lupos

Meter: "iambics":   ∪ _ ∪ _ ∪ _ ∪ _ ∪ _ ∪ _
                          ∪ _ ∪ _ ∪ _ ∪ _

(Retort to a scandalmonger)

Why bother unoffending passers-by, you dog
    So cowardly when facing wolves?
Why not direct your ineffective threats at me
    And learn how I would bite right back?
Molossian, or the tawny Spartan, is my breed,   5
    The kind of dog that shepherds like:
Through depths of snow and with my ears pricked up I track
    Whatever game runs on ahead,
But when your fearful barking fills the woods it means
    You've only sniffed a tossed-out bone.   10
Watch out! Watch out! Against an evil-doer I
    Can turn a wicked pair of horns,
As did the son-in-law that false Lycámbes spurned,
    Or Búpalus's bitter foe.
If someone slanders me, you don't suppose that I   15
    Will stand there weeping like a boy?

5   "Molossian" and "Spartan" are breeds of dog. In *A Midsummer Night's Dream* IV,1
Theseus says: "My hounds are bred out of the *Spartan* kinde."
9–10   Apparently: "You amplify insinuations of others."
13–14   Archílochus wrote satirical "iambics" against Lycámbes after the latter reneged on
giving him his daughter Neobulē in marriage; see paragraph 2 of the foreward to the
Epodes.
     The sculptor Búpalus of Chios made a bust of the poet Hipponax and then
ridiculed it for its ugliness; Hipponax retorted with mocking poems against the sculptor.

7.   *Quo, quo scelesti ruitis? aut cur dexteris*
        aptantur enses conditi?

Meter: "iambics":   U _ U _ U _ U _ U _ U _
                          U _ U _ U _ U _

In August of 39 B.C. the ruling triumvirs: Octavius Caesar, Mark Antony, and Lepidus,
signed the Treaty of Misenum with Sextus Pompey, promising governorship of the
Peloponnesus and high offices in Rome beginning January 1, 38 in return for Sextus's
withdrawal of soldiers from southern Italy and of grain blockades from Sardinia and Sicily.
Noble fugitives with Sextus were to be pardoned, slave fugitives were to be set free, and all
men in his service were to be treated as Roman veterans.
    On the following day Sextus entertained the triumvirs on board his flagship. His
lieutenant commander, Menas, urged him to assassinate the whole party and seize control of
the Roman world, but Sextus declined such conduct as unbefitting a Roman aristocrat.
Shakespeare portrays this meeting in *Antony and Cleopatra* II,7.

Before New Year's of 38 the treaty had become "a scrap of paper." Resumption of warfare awaited only the coming of good weather. Epode 7 probably belongs to the spring of 38 B.C.

> What are you villains rushing into now? Why are
>   Your late-sheathed swords back in your hands?
> Across the fields and over Neptune has there been
>   So little Latin blood poured forth,—
> 5   Not so the Roman may burn jealous Carthage down
>   And fire her rival citadel,
> Nor so the Briton still unscathed may yet be marched
>   In fetters down the Sacred Way,
> But so this City, as the Parthians have prayed,
> 10   May perish by its own right hand?
> This is not wolves' or lions' way, who only kill
>   A species other than their own.
> Has some blind madness seized you? or a Higher Force?
>   Or retribution? Answer me!
> 15   They have no answer; ghastly pallor comes into
>   Their faces; they are thunderstruck.
> So this is how it is: harsh Fate drives Romans on
>   To kill their brothers,—and so has
> It always done since sinless Remus' blood became
> 20   A curse on all his lineage.

5–10   Three enemies of Rome, one past, one future, one present:
- Carthage was burned to the ground in 146 B.C. at the end of the Third Punic War;
- since Julius Caesar's raids into Britain in 55 and 54 B.C. the Romans had meditated conquest of the island, but the invasion was to come only in 43 A.D.;
- the Parthians— the new Persian Empire established in the late 200s B.C.—had defeated Roman armies in 53, in 40, and in 36 B.C., but the struggle was to continue for centuries.

19–20   The death of Remus at the hands of his twin brother Romulus (or by Romulus's men; Livy's History 1.6 gives both versions) was the Roman equivalent of "the blood of Abel."

8.   *Rogare longo putidam te saeculo*
     viris quid enervet meas

Meter: "iambics":   U _ U _ U _ U _ U _ U _
                U _ U _ U _ U _

> So, rotted out with length of years, you ask me what
>   Can have unstrung my manly strength,

When every tooth of yours is black, and ancient age
    Has creased your brow with wrinkle folds,
And in between your withered buttocks gapes a hole   5
    As raw and nasty as a cow's!
I am aroused, however, by your sagging breasts
    That hang like udders on a mare,
Your flabby belly, and your scrawny hams above
    The swollen thickness of your calves.   10
But bless you!, may the images of triumphs past
    Accompany your funeral,
And may no married woman walk abroad decked out
    In bigger, rounder pearls than yours.
What if the tracts and pamphlets of the Stoics lie   15
    About your silken cushions strewn?
Do unschooled muscles stiffen less on that account,
    Or does the penis hang less full,
Which, when you tease it from its haughty groin, requires
    A working over by your mouth?   20

15–16   The wealthy lady, ostentatiously perhaps, reads the tracts of the severely puritanical
    Stoic philosophers and leaves them lying about her quarters, but she is lusty enough for
    all of that.

9.   *Quando repostum Caecubum ad festas dapes*
victore laetus Caesare

Meter: "iambics":   U _ U _ U _ U _ U _ U _
                       U _ U _ U _ U _

On September 2, 31 B.C. the naval battle anticipated in the headnote to Epode 1 was fought
off the Cape of Actium to bring Octavius Caesar a victory which put him in control of the
entire Roman world. In this poem the news has reached Horace at a moment when the
fleeing Antony's destination is not yet known, and he writes to inquire when this triumph will
be celebrated in Maecenas's Roman mansion the way they had celebrated the defeat of
Sextus Pompey five years before, in 36 B.C. Where Horace wrote the poem and where
Maecenas received it are disputed points.

When shall the two of us, Maecenas, lucky man
    By Caesar's victory made glad,
Drink up the Cáecuban reserved for festive times
    In your high house,—as pleases Jove,
With flutes and lyres both sounding, lyres in Doric hymns   5
    And flutes in Asian revelry,

The way we did when "Neptune's son" was driven from
    The Straits with all his ships on fire,
The man who vowed to load this City with the chains
10   That he removed from traitor slaves?
A *Roman*—future times will not believe it!—at
    A woman's orders shoulders arms
And palisade stakes, and a *soldier*, at commands
    From wrinkled eunuchs, can obey,
15 While in among the battle flags the sun beholds
    The shame of a mosquito net.
Disgusted Gauls then turned two thousand horses back,
    Acclaiming Caesar with their shouts,
And ships that lay in port for enemy attack
20   Turned prows to leftwards and away.
Go, Triumph, fetch the victor's golden chariot now
    And untamed steers for sacrifice!
Oh, Triumph, you did not bring such a victor home
    In him who crushed Jugúrtha's war,
25 Nor in "the African" who over Carthage reared
    His manhood's lasting monument.
By land and sea defeated now, our foe has changed
    His purple for a cloak of grief,
And either sails to hundred-citied Crete on winds
30   That in his favor do not blow,
Or else by his uncertain course is headed for
    The sandbanks that the southwind churns.

Bring on the larger goblets, boy, and pour us wines:
    The Chian or the Lesbian,
35 Or better, since it checks the urge to vomit, bring
    Us cups of drier Cáecuban.
Our fears and cares for Caesar's sake are best released
    In the Releaser's gracious wines.

---

4 Maecenas's "high house" (*alta domus*) will be called (*Odes* 3.29.10): "Your mansion steeply vying with neighbor clouds"; see the note to that line.

7–10 On September 3, 36 B.C. Sextus Pompey, who termed himself "Neptune's son," had been defeated in the Straits of Messina by Agrippa—in the name of Octavius Caesar, of course. Sextus fled to Asia (modern Turkey), raised a private army of three legions, but was hunted down by Antony's generals. He was captured and slain by one Marcus Titius, whose life he had spared some years before.

    For the fugitive slaves in Sextus's service see the headnote to Epode 7.

11–20 Details of the Battle of Actium:

    · 11–16 Roman aversion to Cleopatra, her eunuch courtier-commanders, and the "Oriental luxury" of mosquito netting on her tent;

    · 17–18 Refusing to take orders from a woman and eunuchs, 2000 cavalrymen, allies of Antony, switched sides on the spot. These "Gauls" (*Galli*), led by their king, Amýntas, were the Galatians, or Kelts, who had forced their way southward from Danube regions after 300 B.C. and settled in what is now central Turkey, around Ankara.

Upon the death of King Amýntas in 25 B.C. Galatia became a Roman province. Some seventy years later St. Paul was to send his "Epistle to the Galatians" to the Christians of that province. Around 400 A.D. St. Jerome remarked that their language resembled the speech heard around Lyon (in France), for the Galatians were indeed related to the Gauls, the Britons, and the Irish.

19–20 "Turned . . . leftwards" (*sinistrorsum citae*) is usually explained as some naval maneuver; the present translator believes it means no more than that ships deserting Antony turned *left* and therefore *west* to join Caesar's fleet.

21–22 Horace "foresees" the triumphal procession (of August 13–15, 29 B.C.), with the victor riding in his golden chariot down the Sacred Way. Only unbroken cattle were permissible for sacrifice to the gods; see *Odes* 3.23.9–13 and note.

24 General Gaius Marius celebrated his triumph over Jugúrtha of Numidia (Tunisia and E Algeria) on January 1, 104 B.C. after seven years of warfare.

25–26 Scipio Aemilianus "Africanus," the Younger, destroyed Carthage in 146 B.C.

27–32 "Our foe" = Antony. His unknown destination might be "hundred-citied Crete" (Homer's *Krētē hekatómpolis*) or the *Syrtes*, the shallow gulfs E of Tunisia and N of Libya; see *Odes* 1.22.6 and note. Actually, Antony sailed, with 40 ships, to Alexandria, where Cleopatra had preceded him.

34–36 Chian and Lesbian were sweet wines which, in quantity, made one sick, as the drier Caecuban did not.

37–38 "The Releaser" (*Lyaeus*) is Bacchus. Horace puns on "released" (Latin *solvere*) and *Lyaeus*, from Greek *lúo*, "to release."

10.   *Mala soluta navis exit alite,*
ferens olentem Mevium:

Meter: "iambics":   U _ U _ U _ U _ U _ U _
                          U _ U _ U _ U _

An ironic *bon voyage* poem (*propemticon*) to the detested poet Mevius.

With evil omen now the ship sets sail that bears
    Our rancid-smelling Mevius.
Remember, Southwind, do not fail to lash this boat
    With savage waves on both its sides;
May black southeasters on a sea turned upside down   5
    Snap off its oars and scatter them;
And may the northwind rise as violent as when
    It rends the oaks on mountain crests;
And may the friendly star not shine in dismal night
    When, grim with storms, Oríon sets;   10
And may he ride no calmer seas than bore the Greeks
    As homing victors from the War
When Pallas turned her wrath away from burned-out Troy

Toward impious Ajax and his ship.

15   Oh, what a terror-sweat awaits your mariners,
What sickly pallor waits for you,
And what unmanly howls and gibberings of prayers
To an indifferent Jupiter
When under gusts of drenching rain the roaring Gulf

20   Ionian has split your hull!
If then a corpulent repast for coromants
Lies sprawled upon the curving shore,
A frisky goat, together with a lamb, shall die
In honor of the Weather Gods.

Vergil's Third Eclogue, 90–91, says: "Anyone who does not hate Bavius, let him love your poems, Maevius, and let him also harness foxes and milk he-goats." Beyond that and the present Epode nothing is known about poet Maevius/Mevius—or about Bavius. But see the last note to this poem.

11–14   In *Aeneid* 1.39–45 it is recalled that Pallas Athena sank Ajax's fleet, caught the hero himself up in a whirlwind, and hurled him down upon a spiky crag to die in agony for having violated Trojan princess Cassandra in Athena's temple.

19–20   The Ionian Gulf (or Sea) is that part of the Mediterranean S of Italy and W of Greece. Mevius must, then, be sailing to Greece.

23–24   The lamb would make the storm as gentle as a lamb. The goat may be for Mevius's rancid smell and "frisky" (*libidinosus*) character.

In 1899 a waste pit in Egypt yielded up a 13-line fragment of Archílochus which must have served as model for Epode 10, but it wishes ill to a treacherous friend, not to a bad poet. Moore translates:

... driven by the wave, and in Salmydessus may the tufted Thracians give him kindest welcome, naked, stiffened with cold,—there shall he suffer many woes to the full, eating the bread of slavery. And I pray that he may have over him (for his covering) deep weed of the surge, that his teeth may chatter as those of a dog that in its weakness lies on its belly on the edge of the strand near the waves. This is what I could wish to see (the man suffer) who has done me injustice and trampled on his pledges, though he was once my friend.

11.   *Petti, nihil me sicut antea iuvat*

Meter: in the odd-numbered lines: U _ U _ U _ U _ U _ U _
in the even-numbered lines: _ U U _ U U _   U _ U _ U _ U _

I find that versifying pleases me no more,
Pettius, as in the past,   now love has smitten me so hard,
A love that sets me, as it sets no other man,
Yearning for softness of lads   or for the tenderness of girls.

5   Since giving up my passion for Ináchia

Three times December has thus   despoiled the glory of the groves.
Alas, how through this City (I recall with shame!)
I was the talk of the town.   In company they frown upon
The listlessness and silence that identify
Someone in love and consumed   with passion to his very depths.   10
"Against competitors with money, what can mere
Innocent genius attain?",   (so ran my tearful plea to you
When once the reticence-dissolving god brought out
Secrets of mine to the light   as I grew heated with his wine),
"But if the anger seething in my vitals comes   15
Bursting from all its restraints   and tears away the poultices
That merely irritate and do not soothe my pain,
Pride may get thrown to the winds   and I will cry 'Enough of this!' "
With that portentous declaration made to you,
After you bade me go home   I used to trail my sorry way   20
To doors that held (alas!) no welcome, and (alas!)
Doorsteps so bruisingly hard   my back and ribs would ache from them.
The bonds of love Lycíscus now upon me holds;
No little lady on earth,   he boasts, can match his gentleness.
The frank advice of friends will not dissolve this bond,   25
Nor will severest rebukes   from him, nor any other thing
Except the passion for some other lovely girl
Or for as shapely a lad   who also ties his long hair back.

Names: Pettius is unknown. Ináchia and Lyciscus are Greek, by literary convention.
5–6   Horace is reckoning by his December 8th birthdays.
22   Hard-doorstep vigils occur elsewhere in classical poetry. See *Odes* 3.10 for a superior version of the theme.

12.   *Quid tibi vis, mulier nigris dignissima barris*

Meter: in the odd-numbered lines: dactylic hexameter as in the *Satires* and *Epistles*

    in the even-numbered lines: $\_ \cup \cup \_ \cup \cup \_ \cup \cup \_ \cup$

"What do you want with me, woman best suited for elephant mating?
Why must you send me these gifts and these letters
Better addressed to a rugged young man with no smell to his nostrils?
Nose-tumor odors, and whether a stinking
Goat is ensconced in the armpit, I notice more quickly than any   5
Hunting dog scents where the boar is in hiding."
Oh, what a rank perspiration all over her withered old body
Rises in stench when a disengaged penis

Puts her in frantic excitement to satisfy uncontrolled lust, till
10   Down streaks her make-up dissolved in that dew, and
Red-pigment tincture of crocodile dung, while her flailing reduces
          Bedsheets and canopy curtains to tatters.
Why, she will even abuse me most vilely for being too squeamish:
          "Oh, with Ináchia you're not so feeble!
15   Three times a night with Ináchia, always a one-time-around and
          Soft-headed business with me! And be damned to
Lesbia, sending a sluggardly bull like yourself when I asked her.
          Now, when Amýntas of Cos was around here,
He had a muscle that stood in his untiring groin with a stouter
20   Hold than a sapling has roots to a hillside.
Why did I rush to get fleeces of double-dyed Tyrian crimson?
          Was it for anyone's sake but your own, — so
There among equals at dinner no guest would be viewed by his wife with
          More admiration than you were. I seem to
25   Play in bad luck, since you panic and run at the sight of me, like a
          She-lamb from wolves, or like she-goats from lions."

15   For Ináchia see line 5 of the preceding ode.
21–24   She put magnificent drapes on *his* dining-couch only, to emphasize his distinction.

The names, by literary convention, are Greek. Cos is a Greek island off SW (modern) Turkey.

13.   *Horrida tempestas caelum contraxit, et imbres*

Meter: in the odd-numbered lines: dactylic hexameter as in the *Satires* and
                                                                                                Espistles
       in the even-numbered lines: ∪ _ ∪ _ ∪ _ ∪ _   _ ∪ ∪ _ ∪ ∪ _

Masses of stormclouds have narrowed the space between earth and the heavens,
          The sleeting rain has drawn Jove low;   hear how the forest and sea
Roar under blasts of the northwind: the day lets an hour be captured,
          So let us capture it, my friends   while we have strength in our knees
5   And, as behooves us, while brows are not clouded with wrinkles of aging.
          Go fetch my birth-year wines, the ones   pressed in Torquatus's term.
Let us not broach other topics: a god may perhaps in his kindness
          Restore these things as they should be.   Perfumes of Persia shall now
Yield us their fragrances, and, with the lyre-strings that Hermes invented,
10   It will be sweet to lift our hearts   free of the weight of their cares,
For, as the Centaur foretold to his pupil advanced into manhood:
          "Unconquered youth of mortal fate,   born though of Thetis divine,
Destiny waits for you off in the Ilian land interknit with
          Scamánder's icy stream and swift   Símois smooth in its flow,

Whence you will never return, for the thread that the Parcae have spun is   15
 Snapped short, nor will your corpse be brought   home to your mother's
                                                                      blue sea.
Therefore I counsel you: lift every sorrow with wine and with music,
 For these things solace all your griefs,   comfort and lull them away.

  6   Lucius Manlius Torquatus was consul in 65 B.C.; compare *Odes* 3.21.1 and note.
  7–8   The other topics are probably political.
  11   Chíron (Greek Kheíron) the centaur brought up Achilles from childhood.

Epode 13 is of particular interest as Horace's first known imitation of Alcáeus, who in the Odes will supplant Archílochus as model. From a waste pit in Egypt the opening lines of Alcíaeus's original have been recovered, making possible a threefold comparison of the original Greek, of Epode 13, and of the far more distinguished imitation in *Odes* 1.9; see the note to lines 1–8 of the later poem.

14.   *Mollis inertia cur tantam diffuderit imis*
oblivionem sensibus

Meter: in the odd-numbered lines: dactylic hexamater as in the *Satires* and
                                                                            Epistles
  in the even-numbered lines: $\cup \_ \cup \_ \cup \_ \cup \_$

Why should my softness of indolence so have imbued all my senses
 And lulled me into lethargy
Much as if I, in a parching of thirst, had been greedily drinking
 The waters of forgetfulness:
Honest Maecenas, you're killing me, asking that question so often.   5
 A god, I say, a god forbids
Finishing up my "Iambics," as promised a long time ago, so
 The total work could make a book.
I am in love, as Anácreon, poet of Teos, is said to
 Have been with his Bathýllus once,   10
He who lamented his love to his lyre in the simplest of meters
 And unelaborated forms.
You are yourself in a love-fire, and if no more beautiful flame once
 Brought siege-fire into Ilium
You may rejoice at your lot. As for me, it is freedwoman Phrynē   15
 Who wrings my heart — and not just mine.

  7–8   The "Iambics" are the *Epodes,* and noncompletion of them is due to Horace's being in
     love. It is temptng to speculate about details and reasons, but the poem tells no more.
  9–12   For lyric poet Anácreon see the notes to *Odes* 1.17.19 and 4.9.9. Between 539 and 522
     B.C. he was at some point on the island of Samos, S of Teos, and the text names his

beloved Bathýllus *of Samos*. None of his Bathýllus poems have survived, however.

Possibly the allusion carried extra meaning for Maecenas: The historian Tacitus, in *Annals* 1. 54, mentions that Maecenas had been passionately fond of a performer named Bathýllus, but we cannot be sure that the attachment antedated 30 B.C., when the *Epodes* were published.

15.   *Nox erat et caelo fulgebat luna sereno*
inter minora sidera

Meter: in the odd-numbered lines: dactylic hexameter as in the *Satires* and
Epistles

in the even-numbered lines: U _ U _ U _ U _

It was at night, and serenely the moon in a heaven of splendor
        Stood out among the lesser stars
When, without dread of affronting the almighty gods in their power,
        You swore the vow that I proposed,
5   Clinging more closely than ivy embracing the height of a holm oak
        With supple arms around me twined: —
Ever, while wolves attacked sheep, while Oríon struck terror in sailors
        By roiling up the winter sea,
While there were breezes to winnow the hair of the unshorn Apollo,
10   Our love would be reciprocal.
Oh, what Neáera shall suffer for any offense to my manhood!
        If Flaccus is a man at all
He will not stand for devotion of nights to a luckier rival,
        But find himself a constant love;
15   Nor will his flouted affection relent at the sight of your beauty
        If his distrust is proven true.
And as for you, lucky rival, whoever you are and wherever
        You strut at my discomfiture:
Though you have livestock and lands in abundance, and though the Pactólus
20   Flows golden at your Midas-touch,
Though you are master of re-born Pythágoras' mystical secrets,
        Though Níreus' beauty you surpass,
You shall not fail to have reason for ruing that alienation,
        And then the last laugh will be mine.

19–20   For the Pactólus River in Lydia (W-central Turkey) see Herodotus 5.101. Its silt contains gold dust ever since King Midas plunged his head into it in order to rid himself of his "golden touch."

21   Pythágoras, the philosopher of the 6th century B.C., taught the doctrine of the reincarnation of souls. See the note to *Odes* 1.28.9–13.

22   Níreus (*not* Nereus!) was "the most beautiful man who came beneath Ilion." (*Iliad* 2. 673–4) Compare *Odes* 3.20.15.

16. *Altera iam teritur bellis civilibus aetas*
     suis et ipsa Roma viribus ruit

Meter: in the odd-numbered lines: dactylic hexameter as in the *Satires* and
                                                                          Epistles
          in the even-numbered lines: U _ U _ U _ U _ U _ U _

Epode 16 may be Horace's earliest preserved poem, composed at the outbreak of the
"Perusine War" in 41 B.C.

The dismal year 41 B.C. brought the victorious Octavius Caesar home from Philippi,
physically ill, to face unpaid soldiers, near-mutinous provincial governors, disrupted
agriculture, a population close to famine, and a Rome crowded with landowners demon-
strating in the streets against the proposed confiscation of farms.

At this juncture Mark Antony's wife Fulvia and his brother Lucius Antonius attempted
to seize power by force of arms. With treason threatening on all sides and with the state on the
verge of collapse, Generals Agrippa and Salvidiénus headed off the forces of the provincial
governors and drove the army of Lucius Antonius to barricade themselves inside the city of
Perúsia (Perugia). The siege of that city was known as "the Perusine War." It continued until
February of 40 B.C. and ended with ghastly reprisals by Octavius Caesar. Meanwhile Mark
Antony remained in the East, lifting not a finger to help his brother. His failure to do so was
blamed on the Circē-spells of Cleopatra, but intervention would only have confronted him
with the same problems that Octavius Caesar faced. Like other prominent parties he too may
simply have been waiting to see what would happen.

It is noteworthy that Epode 16 says not a word about Horace's own desperate situation,
with his father dead, his land confiscated, and himself adrift in the distressed City.

Now comes a second affliction of civil disorders among us
     And Rome in all its strength is rushing toward its fall.
Rome, which our neighbors the Marsians could not succeed in destroying,
     As Pórsena's Etruscan menace also failed,
Rome, which survived rival Cápua's treachery, Spártacus' rebels,   5
     And in more recent times the faithless Állobrox,
Rome, unsubdued by assaults of the wild blue-eyed host of the Germans
     Or by that fiend of parents' terror, Hannibal,
Tainted in blood we ourselves shall destroy in our own generation
     And animals will claim its soil once more as theirs.   10
Over her ashes will stalk a barbarian conqueror, over
     The City cavalry with ringing hooves will ride,
Brutally scattering bones of Quirínus — improper to look on! —
     That long have lain without the touch of suns and winds.
All of you wonder perhaps, or the right-thinking persons among you   15
     At least, if there is some way out of such distress.
No way will serve quite so well as the way the Phocéans elected
     When with a vow against their city they went forth,
Leaving the farms of their fathers and leaving the shrines of their gods to
     Become a dwelling place for boars and savage wolves,   20
Following only as footsteps might take them, or only as southwinds
     Or gales from Africa might drive them on by sea.

Shall we so vote? Or can someone persuade us to better proposals?
    The omens favor: why delay to board our ships?
25   First, let us swear to this oath: "Until rocks that we raise from the deep will
    Remain afloat let all returning here be cursed;
Let a reversal of sails for our homeland be thought about only
    When northern Po flows past our southern mountain tops,
Or when the high-crested Apennines rush to the sea and plunge headlong,
30   Or if a mating urge unknown to nature breeds
Monsters and freaks, so the tigress accepts being covered by stags and
    The steadfast dove, grown lustful, wantons with the hawk,
Or until oxen have unlearned their terror at tawny-maned lions
    And slippery-hided goats delight in briny seas."
35   Swearing to this and to anything else that might hinder returning,
    Let all of us depart this City and its curse, —
Those of superior spirit, at least: let the sluggards and faint-hearts
    Remain behind to cumber evil-omened beds.
You who have manliness in you, desist from your womanish wailing
40   And set your sails for flight from these Etruscan shores.
Still the circúmfluent Ocean remains; let us go, then, and look for
    The blessèd fields of plenty in the Happy Isles,
Where there is never-plowed earth that brings Ceres to annual harvest,
    Where never-grafted vines bear grapes the year around,
45   Where there is never a failure of fruit on the boughs of the olive
    And where the darkly ripened figs adorn their trees,
Where from the hollows of oaks trickles honey, and where from the mountains
    The limpid waters downward dance with splashing feet.
There without herdsmen to herd them the she-goats assemble for milking
50   And friendly flocks with heavy udders homeward come.
Never is growl of a bear to be heard around sheepfolds at twilight,
    And deepest grass does not puff up with vipers' heads;
61   Cattle incur no contagions, and never a star of the summer
62   Afflicts the flock with torpor from the parching heat.
53   Many a marvel will cheer us, as neither the rainy southeasters
54   Strip fields of planted crops with raking swaths of storm
55   Nor as the succulent grain-ears are burnt to a dryness of stubble,
    According to which sky-god moderates extremes.
Never did oarsmen of Argo strain sinews to land on those islands,
    The shameless witch of Colchis did not there set foot,
Never have sailors from Sidon swung yard-arms to enter those harbors,
60   Nor did Ulysses' much enduring crew make port.
63   Jupiter set all those islands apart for a race of good people
64   When he debased the Golden Age with bronze alloy;
65   Ages he hardened with bronze, then with iron, and forth from the latter
66   My poet's vision now foretells good men's escape.

1 Rome had known civil disorders for a century, so that it is hard to know what Horace

means by "second"; Moore understands "a second generation from that of Marius and Sulla," or, since the period 100 to 80 B.C.

3–8   Near-disasters of the past:

- 91–88 B.C. the Marsians (E of Rome) led a revolt of the Italian allies to found a Republic of Italia, with capital in the Apennines, at Corfinium;
- 508 B.C. Lars Porsena captured Rome and briefly restored the banished Etruscan kings;
- 216 Capua deserted to Hannibal, hoping to become the capital of Italy;
- 73–71 B.C. ex-gladiator Spártacus led a slave revolt; see *Odes* 3.14.18–20 and note;
- 63 B.C. envoys of the Keltic Allobróges (singular Állobrox), from the Lyon-Grenoble area, were coaxed to support Catiline's *coup d'état* but "faithlessly" chose to betray the plot instead;
- 102 B.C. the Teutones and Cimbri, invading "Provence," were stopped by Marius;
- 218–201 B.C. the Second Punic War, when Hannibal invaded Italy.

11   Horace is thinking of the Parthians; compare Epode 7, 9–10.

13–14   Quirĭnus = Romulus, whose grave was said to be under "the black stone" behind the speakers' platform in the Forum. Excavations there in 1899–1900 revealed a stone inscription earlier than 500 B.C. and remnants of sacrifices, but no burial.

17–22   Herodotus (1. 162–7) tells how the Greeks of Phocéa (on the W coast of modern Turkey), abandoned their city under pressure from the Persian empire and settled in Corsica and elsewhere, ca. 600 B.C. Their curse is merely mentioned, but they did sink a mass of iron in the sea, vowing no return until the iron floated.

28   "Southern mountain tops," = *Matina . . . cacumina,* "Matine peaks"; see the note to *Odes* 1.28.3.

41   "Circúmfluent" .. *circumvagus,* a word apparently coined by Horace. For Homer Ōkeanós was a river that circled the perimeter of the disc-shaped earth.

42   Hesiod: *Works and Days* 171 located the "Islands of the Blest" near the shore of Ōkeanós; in later times they were "identified" as either the Madeiras or the Canaries. See Tennyson's *Ulysses* 63: "It may be we shall touch the Happy Isles."

48   This exquisite line reads: *levis crepante lympha desilit pede.*

61–62   Despite the manuscripts these lines require Moore's transposition. The star of summer is the Dog Star; see *Odes* 1.17.19 and 3.13.9 and notes.

66   "Poet" = *vates,* as regularly in Horace; see the note to *Odes* 2.6.24.

17.   *Iam iam efficaci do manus scientiae*

Meter: iambic "trimeter" (i.e. hexameter) throughout

$$\cup \_ \cup \_ \cup \_ \cup \_ \cup \_ \cup \_$$

but with numerous "substitutions," which, if imitated in English, would produce a kind of doggerel.

A "mock palinode" to Canidia, that is, an apology more insulting than the original insults.

> I do, I do surrender to your mighty lore
> And as a suppliant I beg, by Próserpine's
> And by Diana's wills that must not be opposed,
> And by your books of spells so powerful that you

5   Can summon down the stars firm-fixed in heaven's vault:
      Canidia, desist from incantations now
      And with all haste reverse, reverse your magic wheel!
      Old Néreus' grandson once relented in his wrath
      At haughty Télephus for leading Mýsians
10   In war against him and for sharpened missiles flung;
      Man-slaying Hector's corpse, the prey of birds and beasts,
      Was still prepared by Trojan dames for burial
      When once their king had journeyed from the city walls
      And begged it back at obstinate Achílles' feet;
15   Ulysses of the many labors saw his crew
      Divest themselves of bristly hides and shapes of hogs
      As Circē broke her evil spell: with sense and speech
      Their faces too regained the human dignity.
            For my offenses I have all too dearly paid,
20   You darling of the sailor and the peddler crowd: —
      My modest youth's complexion has deserted me,
      I'm wasted down to bones encased in sallow skin,
      My hair is white from scented unguents you have brewed;
      By no amount of rest is my distress relieved,
25   My nights cut short the days, my days the nights, nor can
      My gasping breath relax constriction in my chest;
      And so I woefully admit what I denied:
      That Sabine spells do cause a rattle in the lungs
      And Marsian chant does cause a splitting of the head.
30   What more, then, do you want? Oh, sea and earth!, but I
      Am all on fire, like Hercules when poison-gore
      Of Nessus touched his skin, like Etna seething with
      The ever-burning flames of Sicily; and you
      Will keep increasing heat there at your poison-hearth
35   Till I am ashes blowing on a noxious wind.
            If this is not enough, what more do you demand?
      Proclaim it! I will do whatever penance you
      Ordain for expiation, whether you require
      A hundred-bullock sacrifice, or whether you
40   Demand a lying poem saying "Thou art chaste,
      And as a golden star shalt move with other stars."
      Both Castor and his brother, stung by libel of
      Their sister Helen, still were by entreaties moved
      To give the poet's eyesight back who caused offense:
45   From madness, then, save *me,* since you too are divine!
      You are not base by birth from parentage debased,
      You are no hag to paw around in poor men's graves
      And spill and scatter ashes of the nine-days-dead;
      Your bosom welcomes one and all, your hands are pure,
50   And Páctuméius is your womb-child: every time

The midwife washes out your bedsheets red with blood
You jump up hale and hearty from confinement-bed.

    (Canidia replies:)

Why pour out these entreaties when my ears are shut?
To mariners in naked shipwreck rocks are not
More deaf when wintry Neptune pounds them with salt seas.   55
Shall you go free, when you divulged and ridiculed
Cotýtto's rites, unbridled Passion's mysteries?
When you played pontifex to poison-crafting on
The Esquiline and filled the City with my name?
Why did I lavish gold on those Paelígnian hags,   60
Or why obtain a swifter-acting poison brew?
A slower death awaits you than your pleas may crave:
In wretchedness your sorry life shall be prolonged
With new and endless torments that you shall endure.
The prayer of Tántalus, false Pélops' father, is   65
For respite from starvation in the sight of food,
Prométheus prays for respite from the vulture's beak,
And Sísyphus prays for his rock to lie at last
Atop the hill; but laws of Jupiter forbid.
Your wish will be a death-leap from some tower's height,   70
Or else to fend your heart with sword of Noric steel;
Or you will knot a noose — in vain — around your neck
In your despair and sickened weariness of life.
Then on your hated shoulders I shall mount and ride
So earth drops out of sight below my frenzied flight!   75
Shall I, who, as you know yourself from having snooped,
Possess the skill to make the waxen puppets live,
To make the moon come down to earth at my command,
To raise the dead although they were consumed in fire,
To mix the potions that constrain to seething lust, —   80
Shall I bewail my arts because they failed with you?

2–3   Próserpine as queen of the dead, Diana in her Hécatē aspect as in Epode 5.51.
7   The magic wheel is probably a bull-roarer: a flat piece of wood whirled by a long cord.
    The artificial thunder thus produced, says Jane Harrison (*Themis*, p. 64), "possesses in a
    high degree the quality of uncanniness. Heard in the open sunlight it sends a shudder
    through even modern nerves." The magic spell is broken by reversing the direction of the
    whirl.
8–18   Three relenting foes:
      · Achilles (grandson of Néreus, the sea god) forgave Télephus and gave him the
        secret cure for his incurable wound;
      · Achilles (in the final Book of the *Iliad*) allowed King Priam of Troy to claim
        Hector's corpse when that royal father pleaded for it at his enemy's feet;
      · Circē, after turning Ulysses's crew to swine, was induced to restore them to their
        human shapes. In *Odyssey* 10 the men retained their human wits even in hog
        shape.

19–35   All this is comic exaggeration; Horace is safe and sound, as Canidia admits in line 81. Line 22 must have raised a laugh when recited by the roly-poly poet.

      28–29   Eastward from Rome to the Adriatic coast the mountains were inhabited by three ancient Italic peoples: the Sabines, the Marsians, and the Paelignians (line 60), all of them reputed to be skilled in witchcraft (and all of them "Roman" since ca. 305 B.C.). Compare the "Marsic chant" of Epode 5, 75–76 and the Sabine fortune-teller in S.1.9.29.

      31–32   See Epode 3, 17–18 and note.

42–44   The poet Stesíchorus (see *Odes* 4.9.8 and note) was stricken blind by Castor and Pollux for slandering their sister, Helen of Troy, but his eyesight was restored after he apologized.

45–49   Comic exaggeration, as in 19–35: Canídia is precisely what Horace says she is *not*.

50–52   Canidia fakes a childbirth each time she kidnaps an infant, so she can keep the baby for her own dark purposes. "Páctuméius" may be "a genuine Roman name," as Moore says, but the statement is banal if *tuusque venter Pactumeius* means no more than that Canídia's unborn child is named Pactumeius. We suspect an obscene pun having to do with feminine hygiene: *venter* = "belly, womb" or "foetus"; *meio* = "to urinate," and *pactum* = either "marriage contract" or "manner, way, means."

53   Canídia's imaginary reply is, of course, spoken by the same person who recited the entire poem; no actress is involved.

57   Cotýtto was a goddess worshipped with orgiastic rites in far-off Thrace, but not in Rome. No preserved poem of Horace portrays "unbridled Passion's mysteries."

58–59   "Pontifex" (priest) in the sense of "supervisor (of religious rites)." It is not clear whether the charge of spying regards S.1.8 or Epode 5, or both; the former poem was definitely set "on the Esquiline," but we suspect that Canídia's house, the scene of Epode 5, was also on the Esquiline, or in the slum of Subúra at the foot of that hill.

65–69   Three unending punishments in the afterlife: Tántalus starving in sight of food, Prométheus with his liver forever torn by a vulture, and Sísyphus rolling a heavy stone uphill and always losing his grip on it just before the summit.

71   "Noric" is a "decorative adjective," as in *Odes* 1.16.10. Noricum, approximately modern Austria, was famous for its iron.

74   In children's games the winner got to ride piggyback on the loser. But see the final remarks under the "Note on Canídia."

Note on Canídia

In Horace's "Canídia pieces" there are to be found small motifs and verbal echoes of two earlier "witching" poems: lines 64–109 of Vergil's 8th *Eclogue* (ca. 39 B.C.) and the model for that poem, the second *Idyll* of Theocritus, from the 3rd century B.C. But these are gentle, sentimental works expressing the longings of lovers, whereas the "Canídia pieces" are harsh, lurid works suggestive of theatrical declamation, S.1.8 being calculated for scatological shock and Epodes 5 and 17 being intended to create effects of horror. Thus assignment of these pieces to the same literary tradition as those earlir poems is justified only in small degree.

    More significantly, ancient commentator Porphyrio states that the name Canídia stood for an actual person, one Gratidia of Naples, a perfume maker. This point, while readily believable, raises questions.

    In S.1.8 we are asked to believe that Canídia/Gratidia plundered graves with impunity in an old pauper cemetery recently (in 35 B.C.?) acquired by Maecenas for extending the "urban park" around his mansion on the Esquiline Hill. In Epodes 5 and 17, published in 30 B.C., we are asked to believe that this abominable woman practiced kidnapping, child-murder, and poison manufacture in her house which was apparently within easy walking distance of the mansion. This, in 30 B.C., the year when Maecenas was acting head of the Roman state during the absence of Octavius Caesar in the East, and in charge of all military and police powers, including the effective spy system. By this token, Maecenas, the "deputy emperor," so to speak, tolerated known crimes and known criminals almost at his doorstep.

The gratuitous quips about Canídia in Epode 3, 7–8 and in the final line of Book 2 of the *Satires*, also published in 30 B.C., may perhaps offer a clue to the riddle. They suggest that Canídia was the subject of a standing joke among Maecenas's associates: *any* bad thing could be attributed to her. The further implication is that *all* the "Canídia material" represents Horace's literary exploitation of a little myth founded and fostered within the Maecenas circle. Canídia/Gratidia had, of course, no recourse to libel laws, but we do wonder why the published poems did not themselves give rise to a general hue-and-cry against the woman. Had such been the case, commentators would surely have mentioned it. Our proposed explanation does not satisfy on all counts, but we tend to believe that the "Canídia pieces" are a joke, and not in the best of taste, and we are relieved to know that Canídia disappears from Horace's works after 30 B.C.

Further to be noted in the "Canídia pieces" is the conspicuous paralleling of Canídia with Medea in Epode 3, 6–14 and again in 5, 61–66, as if Horace had been deeply affected by either a reading of Euripides's drama *Medea* or by a performance of it. A third instance is, we believe, Canídia's "reply" in Epode 17, 53–81, which seems to reflect the final scene of Euripides's play. The piggyback ride in line 74 and note, takes on, in line 75, the quality of Medea's exultant escape from Corinth in a chariot drawn by flying dragons. In both cases there is a kind of apotheosis of hate and of fulfilled revenge, even if, with Canídia, the hate and the fulfilled revenge are ludicrous for being unrealized. Interestingly enough, Horace, afrer 30 B.C., does not recur to the topic of Medea, except for two passing allusions, wholly different in spirit, in E.2.3. 123 and 185.

Odes. Books 1, 2, and 3

Carmina. Libri I, II, III

23 B.C.

Odes. Books 1, 2, and 3

By general agreement, Horace's finest work is the collection of eighty-eight lyric poems composed between 30 and 23 B.C. and published in 23 as *Carmina* I, II, III (*Odes* 1, 2, 3).

Within this collection the eighty-eight pieces were arranged for pleasing variety and contrast of themes and meters, the compositional dates being only occasionally ascertainable, but certain procedures establish the unity of the total work. The first and last poems (1.1 and 3.30), for instance, are in "the lesser Asclepiadic meter" used nowhere else in the collection. Odes 1.1 and 3.29 "enclose" the collection within the name of Maecenas, Ode 3.30 being reserved for the poet's personal epilogue. Each Book opens with poems of particular address, three in Book 1, three in Book 2, and six in Book 3. Those in Book 1 are directed, respectively, to Maecenas, to the emperor, and, indirectly, to Vergil; those in Book 2 are directed to Caius Asinius Pollio, statesman and patron of poets, to the emperor's adviser Sallustius Crispus, and to the emperor's friend Quintus Dellius; the six "national odes" that open Book 3 are directed to the whole Roman people.

Freshness and variety are to be found throughout the collection, but nowhere in greater degree than in Book 1 (38 poems, 876 lines). The point of view is predominantly objective, and we note four hymns to divinities (poems 10, 17, 21, and 30), as well as a prayer to Apollo (poem 31).

Book 2 (20 poems, 572 lines) is shorter and more subjective in tone. Personal sympathies are more in evidence, and several pieces are addressed to friends.

Book 3 (30 poems, 1004 lines) opens with the solemn "national odes" and, in general, lies on a more exalted plane. New in manner are three "story poems" (Nos. 4, 7, and 9) and four poems containing grand "dramatic speeches": by the goddess Juno (3), by the patriot-martyr Regulus (5), and by the heroines Hypermnestra (11) and Europa (27). Quasi-dramatic movement also marks poems 19 and 28, as opposed to the perfection of tranquillity in the ode to the Bandusian spring (13). The gentle speech to the humble peasant woman (23) is also remarkable.

The themes of these eighty-eight poems include love and friendship, sardonic mockery, wine, patriotism, devotion to the gods, wit and humor, "philosphy," bits of autobiography, and reverence for the Muses, which is to say for the art of poetry itself.

Odes. Book 1

1.1.   *Maecenas atavis edite regibus*

Meter: "the Lesser Asclepiadic": $\_\ \cup\ \_\ \cup\ \cup\ \_\quad \_\ \cup\ \cup\ \_\ \cup\ \_$*

Yes, Maecenas, whose line   issued from ancient kings,
My protector and dear   ornament of my life:
Some there are who enjoy   chariots raced in dust
On Olympia's course,   wheels at a scorching heat
Barely grazing the turns,   glory of victor's palms   5
Lifting them to the gods,   rulers of earth's domain;
Fickle citizen crowds   gratify one man's will
By electing him up   through the official ranks,
Yet another is best   pleased with his storage bins
Stocked with Libyan grain   swept from the threshing floors.   10
Someone glad for a hoe   hacking ancestral fields
You would never persuade,   even on Áttalus'
Terms, to leave for a life   full of a sailor's fears
In a Cyprian boat   cleaving Myrtóic seas.
Yet the trader amid   howls of an Afric gale   15
On Icárian waves,   dream though he may of home
Deep in countryside peace,   soon has his battered ship
Back in trim, because lean   purses distress him most.
Someone else does not shun   cups of old Massic wine
Nor the passing of some   part of the livelong day   20
Stretched at ease in the shade   under a greenwood tree
Or where softly a brook   wells from a sacred spring.
Many people enjoy   camps and the din of curved
Trumpets in signal calls,   warfare itself, indeed,
By all mothers abhorred.   Hunters stay out all night   25
Under rigors of sky,   leaving young wives at home,
Once the sight of a deer   rouses the faithful dogs
Or a Marsian boar   breaks from the wide-spanned nets.

*See Publishers Note, p. viii.

> I, with ivy as prized   crown on my poet's brow,
> 30   Am made one with the gods;   coolness of groves and fleet
> Troops of nymphs in a dance,   joined with a Satyr throng,
> Take me far from the mob —   if but Eutérpē's breath
> Does not cease in the flutes   or Polyhýmnia's
> Lyre of Lesbos leave off   sounding its tuneful strings.
> 35   If you rank me among   poets of lyric fame,
> I shall find that my head   jostles the very stars.

This "Lesser Asclepiadic" meter is used here in 1.1 and in 3.30 to open and close the three-book collection of the *Odes*; thereafter only once again, in *Odes* 4.8.

1   Maecenas was descended from Etruscan "kings" of Arretium (Arezzo); see S.1.6.1–4 and *Odes* 3.29.1. Propertius opens the 9th poem of his Book III (or IV) with: "Maecenas, knight sprung from the blood of Tuscan kings."

4–6   Chariot racing was one of the events of the Olympic Games, instituted in 776 B.C., in Elis (NW Peloponnesus). From the time of Alexander the Great the prize was a palm branch, a custom adopted at Rome in 293 B.C.

8   The text specifies the "threefold" grades of public office. These were: curule aedile (in charge of public works), praetor (judge), and consul (chief of state).

10   "Libyan" = North African, primarily the grainfields of Tunisia and eastern Algeria.

12   Attalus III, King of Pergamum (the western third of Turkey), bequeathed his country to Rome in 133 B.C. "As rich as Attalus" was proverbial for great wealth.

14–16   The merely "decorative" adjectives locate the voyage SE of Greece. The Myrtóic Sea stretched from Athens S to Crete, with the Cyclades islands dividing it from that part of the Aegean Sea around the island of Icaria; see note to *Odes* 4.2.14. The large island of Cyprus lies further E. The "Afric gale" is the sirocco.

19   The *Mons Massicus* (now Monte Massico) looked SE over the famous Falernian wine area.

20–22   A glance at Epode 2.23–28 and E.1.14.35 will show that Horace is thinking here of himself.

     "A greenwood tree" = *arbutus*, "the wild strawberry tree," defined by Webster's dictionary as "a European evergreen with clusters of small, white flowers and red, strawberrylike fruit."

     The headwaters of any stream were considered the home of a water divinity and hence "sacred."

28   That is, a wild boar from the mountain country 100 km/60 m E of Rome.

29   Ivy, sacred to Bacchus, protected poets; compare E.1.3.25 and *Odes* 4.11.4–5.

32–33   Eutérpē ("charming, well-pleasing") and Polyhýmnia ("many hymns"), were, to the classical Greeks and to Horace, simply two of the nine Muses; in later Greek times Eutérpē became the Muse of music, Polyhýmnia the Muse of sacred song.

34   The "lyre of Lesbos" means poetry in the manner of Alcaeus and Sappho, both of whom lived on this island of Lesbos.

36   This famous line rewords a Greek saying: "to touch the sky with one's head." Moore cites imitations of Horace's phrasing by Ovid (*Metamorphoses* 7.61; published 7 A.D.) and by Ausonius (4th century A.D.), as well as the concluding line of Robert Herrick's poem beginning "Dull to my selfe, . . .": "Knock at a Starre with my exalted head," and from Tennyson's *Epilogue*: "Old Horace? 'I will strike,' said he,/The stars with head sublime.' "

1.2.   *Iam satis terris nivis atque dirae*

Meter: Sapphic stanza: lines 1, 2, and 3:   _ ∪ _ > _ ∪ ∪ _ ∪ _ ∪

line 4:　　＿ U U ＿ U

This poem, which offers difficulties on first reading, may be summarized as follows:

(1–4) These winter storms are warnings from heaven; (5–12) the floods seem like the beginning of a second Deluge; (13–20) even part of the Forum is under water from the overflowing Tiber.

(21–24) To the younger generation we can report nothing but the horrors of civil war. (25–28) To what god should prayers be offered to avert calamity? (29–30) To "whom" will Jupiter assign the task of making peace? — (31–32) to Apollo? — (33–34) to Venus (the mother of Aeneas and hence of the Roman race)? — (35–40) to Mars (father of Romulus and hence of the Roman race)? — or to *you*, Mercury (son of Maia)? (41)

The shift to "you" is followed by a series of qualifications culminating in the name of Caesar, so that lines 41–52 become a "prayer" to Caesar, as the earthly embodiment of the god Mercury, to save the state.

The time is likely to be the winter of 29 or of 28 B.C., after Octavius Caesar's return from the East (following the deaths of Antony and Cleopatra) but before January of 27, when the Senate voted him the title of "Augustus"; Horace would hardly have omitted the new title if it had been in existence.

> Now sufficient warnings by snows and hailstorms
> Have been sent by All-father, who with flaming
> Hand has pelted holiest temples, striking
> 　　　Fear in the City,
>
> Striking fear in nations as well, lest Pyrrha's　　　　　　　5
> Time might be returning with grisly monsters,
> As when Próteus herded his sea-calves up to
> 　　　Views over mountains,
>
> And when fish were stranded in tops of elm trees
> Once the perching places of pigeons only,　　　　　　　　10
> And when deer in panic swam open seas of
> 　　　Limitless deluge.
>
> We have seen the waters of tawny Tiber
> Shunted back with violence from the Tuscan
> Shore as if to topple both Vesta's shrine and　　　　　　　15
> 　　　Numa's old palace:
>
> Boasting over-much of his vengeance taken
> Once for wailing Ília, wife-devoted
> Tiber strayed — with Jove's disapproval — flooding
> 　　　Left-shore embankments.　　　　　　　　　　　　20
>
> Youth, with ranks depleted from crimes of sires, will
> Hear how steel, that might have destroyed oppressor
> Persians, was — by citizens! — whetted sharp for
> 　　　Fighting each other.
>
> To what god shall people appeal for aid when　　　　　　25
> Total ruin threatens? What supplications
> Shall the holy virgins address to Vesta,
> 　　　Deaf to their pleadings?

30   And to whom will Jupiter give the role of
                Expiation for the atrocious wrong? Oh,
                Come with clouds of splendor around your shoulders,
                    Augur Apollo;

                Or, if you so deign, merry Queen of Eryx,
                Come with Mirth and Cupid around you flitting;
35   Or, if you regard your neglected race and
                    Offspring, great Parent,

                Halt this cruel sport over-long protracted,
                Mars of gleaming helmets and shouts of battle,
                Fond of grim-faced foot-soldiers braving savage
40   Enemies' weapons;

                Or, if, wingèd son of sweet Maia, you have
                Changed your shape to that of a youthful hero
                And on earth agree to be designated
                    Caesar's avenger,

45   May you long delay your return to heaven,
                May you gladly stay with the Roman people,
                May you not in anger at our transgressions
                    Be in a sudden

                Whirlwind taken from us; abide yet greater
50   Triumphs here, rejoice in the names of "Prince" and
                "Father," let no Medes ride in raids unpunished,
                    Caesar, our leader.

1–4   Ancient commentator Porphyrio (3rd century A.D.) explains that the storms were "signs" (*portenta*) (from the gods) demanding vengeance for Julius Caesar's murder and threatening punishment for those "who would not desist from waging civil wars."

5–12   From Greek writers and from Ovid (*Metamorphoses* 1.260–415) we have the classical account of the Deluge, with Deucalion in the role of Noah. When Deucalion's boat came to rest atop Mount Parnassus (above Delphi, in Greece), he and his wife Pyrrha were the sole survivors. As directed by a representative from Zeus, they tossed stones over their shoulders, and the stones became, respectively, men and women for the restoration of the human race.

      Próteus was Neptune's herdsman of the sea-creatures, some of which were "monsters" (*monstra*), as in lines 17–20 of the next ode.

13–16   Etruscan/Tuscan territory began on the Tiber shore opposite Rome and stretched northward to beyond Florence.

      At the low, northern end of the Forum stood the shrine of Vesta and a structure commonly believed to have been the "palace" of King Numa Pompilius, 716–672 B.C.

      In December of 1900 the same area was under water from Tiber floods that washed in between the Capitoline and Palatine Hills.

16–20   The "wife-devoted Tiber" flooded from excitement of recollection of how he once rescued the Vestal Virgin Ilia when she was being drowned for illegitimately bearing the twins, Romulus and Remus, to the god Mars.

      Here, as in *Odes* 3.3.32 and 4.8.23, Horace takes Ilia to have been the daughter of Aeneas, following Ennius, so commentator Porphyrio states, and contradicting the account in Livy's *History* 1.4.

21   The civil wars of 48–31 B.C. had seriously depleted the population.

23   "Persians," like "Medes" in line 51, means "Parthians"; see under "Foreign Nations," p. 397.

29   "To whom" (*cui*) echoes the "To what god" of line 25, but the significance is not clear until the last line of the poem.

30   "The atrocious wrong" is the assassination of Julius Caesar, 15 or more years ago.

31–32   Apollo is invoked as "augur" (taker of omens from the behavior of birds), wearing a prophet's cloak of sun-struck clouds. Compare *Iliad* 5.186: "mantling in mist his shoulders." (Lattimore translation)

  Octavius Caesar regarded Apollo as his patron divinity. The statue of Apollo at the just-begun (29 B.C.) library-temple on the Palatine Hill was to have the facial features of the emperor. The poet Propertius (see note to E.2.2.91–101) was to claim (poem 6 of Book IV—or V) that Apollo hovered over Caesar's ship at Actium and directed the victory.

33–34   From prehistoric times, Eryx (now Monte Erice) in NW Sicily had been the site of a cult of "Venus of all nations" (*pandemica*).

  "Mirth (*Iocus*, translating Greek *Kōmos*, "revel") and Cupid hover like birds around the shoulders of Venus.

  In the Centennial Hymn 50, Augustus, as "the new Aeneas," is "Venus' and Anchises' exalted scion."

35–36   Mars, through his son Romulus, was the "Parent" of the Roman race.

37   "This cruel sport (*ludus*)" means the civil wars.

41–42   Mercury (Greek "Hermes") was the son of Zeus by the nymph Maia. By long tradition he was a shape-shifter—note English "mercurial" in the sense of "changeful"—and his Roman name has the same root as *merch*ant and *merch*andise. Thus Horace subtly alludes to the revival of economic prosperity since the end of the civil wars in 31.

  "Youthful hero" = *iuvenis*, meaning any man between the ages of 20 and 40, "in the prime of manhood." Octavius Caesar had his 32nd birthday three weeks after the victory at Actium and was now 34 or 35 years old.

49   Romulus (Livy's *History* 1.16) was swept up to the skies in a whirlwind to become "a god."

49–50   Octavius Caesar (writes Suetonius in his Life of Augustus, 22) "celebrated three full triumphs for his victories won in Dalmatia, off Actium, and at Alexandria"; that is, three occasions of solemn processional through the Forum, concluding with prayers and sacrifices at Jupiter's temple on the summit of the Capitoline Hill.

50–51   "Prince" = *princeps*, in the sense of "first citizen." "Father" may be merely the common term of respect (see the note to E.1.7.37), but more likely has the sense of "Father of his people,"—though not until 2 B.C. was the title "Father of the Fatherland" (*Pater patriae*) officially conferred upon Augustus.

1.3.   *Sic te diva potens Cypri*

Meter: in the odd-numbered lines: $\_ \cup \_ \cup \cup \_ \cup \_$
   in the even-numbered lines: $\_ \cup \_ \cup \cup \_ \; \_ \cup \cup \_ \cup \_$

  Thus: — be favored by Cyprus' queen,
    By the twin-shining stars   (brothers of Helen once),
  By the father of blowing winds —
    All winds stilled but the one   blowing from west-northwest, —
  Ship entrusted with Vergil's self,

On condition (I pray)   you will restore him safe
Home again from the Attic shores
      And, so doing, preserve   half of my very soul.

Staves of oak and of triple brass
10   Must have girded the heart   which to the savage sea
Ventured first in a fragile boat,
      Fearing neither the fierce   wind out of Africa
Headlong clashing with northern winds,
      Nor the Hýadēs' gloom   vying with Southwind's wrath:
15 Over wild Adriatic waves
      None more strictly commands   tumult or settled calm.
Who dreads any approach of Death
      Once dry eyes have beheld   monsters in ghastly pomp
Float on foam of the seething gulfs
20   Past the ill-omened Rocks   Acroceráunian?

All for nothing a prudent god
      Set the dry lands apart   by the estranging sea,
If in impious boats men still
      Probe the watery ways,   rating the ban as naught.
25 Brashly challenging every law,
      Mankind plunges ahead   into forbidden things;
Brashly Titan Iapétus' son
      Stole by trick or by fraud   fire for the use of men;
Once the household of upper air
30   Thus was robbed of its fire,   all about earth there lurked
Wan infections and fever chills,
      So that Death, who before   slothfully tarried far off,
Hastened up at a lively pace.
      It was Dáedalus who   first through the empty air
35 Flew on wings unallowed to man;
      Main force Hercules used   bursting the gates of hell.
Nothing towers beyond man's will;
      Sky itself in our fool-   hardiness we assail,
And our criminal acts allow
40   Jove no rest from enraged   use of his thunderbolts.

Summary: (1–8) A prayer to the ship carrying Vergil to Athens to bring him safely home again; (9–20) Horace meditates on the terrors of the sea; (21–40) "philosophical" remarks about man's proper limits, with rueful recall of three instances where those limits were overstepped: Prometheus, who stole fire from the gods; Daedalus, who made artificial wings and flew; Hercules, who stormed through the gates of the Afterworld.

1   "Thus" = *Sic*. Roman prayer was often "contractual" and began with this word; for example, "May you have fair sailing, ship, on this condition (line 6) . . ."
Compare the unobtrusive "So" in Tennyson's *In Memoriam* XVII (329–330):

      So may whatever tempest mars
         Mid-ocean spare thee, sacred bark, . . .

The influence of lines 1–8 is also felt in *In Memoriam* IX (157–160).

"Cyprus' queen" is *Venus marina*, "Venus-of-the-Sea," whose ancient shrine stood near Paphus, at the SW corner of the island of Cyprus.

2 Castor and Pollux, twin brothers of Helen of Troy in life, became after death the two brightest stars in the constellation Gemini (The Twins), faithful guides to sailors. Their "fire," now called "St. Elmo's fire," might descend protectively to the ship itself. Moore cites Macaulay's *Regillus*:

> Safe comes the ship to haven
>   Through billows and through gales,
> If once the great Twin Brethren
>   Sit shining on the sails.

3 Aeolus was the ruler ("Father") of the winds. Horace may well have had in mind the fine "Aeolus passage" in *Aeneid* 1.65–123.

4 The wind "blowing from west-northwest" paraphrases *Iapyx*, the wind blowing from Horace's native Apulia/Iapygia/Daunia. (The reverse wind would presumably be needed for the return journey.)

7 "Attic shores" = Athens, chief city of the region of Attica.

(This poem was published in 23 B.C., three years before the only *attested* voyage of Vergil to Greece, but the dedication of the first three odes, respectively, to Maecenas, to the emperor, and to Vergil, demand that this be the *poet* Vergil, then at the pinnacle of his fame, and not some otherwise unknown namesake of his.)

9 The admired formula is *robur et aes triplex*, "oak and triple brass."

12 The wind out of Africa is the sirocco.

14 Five stars in a V-shaped cluster, with the first-magnitude star Aldebaran at upper left, comprise (with about 150 lesser stars) the Hýadēs, whose rising betokens storms.

The word is from Greek *hýein*, "to rain"; Vergil (*Aeneid* 3.516) has *pluvias Hyadas*, which Tennyson translates literally as "the rainy Hyades" (in *Ulysses* 10). Latin poets usually avoided the native Italian name *Suculae*, "(litter of) piglets."

20 The Acroceráunian Rocks (almost synonymous with "shipwreck") still line the dangerous coast of SW Albania, from opposite the island of Corfu northward. To Horace this was the coast of Epírus and Illýria.

Paradise Lost 11. 491–2, after Adam beholds a panorama of the future diseases of mankind, says:

> Sight so deform what heart of Rock could long
> Drie-ey'd behold?

27–33 Prometheus, son of the Titan Iapétus, stole fire from the gods ("the household of upper air"), and the diminished sunlight caused diseases and early deaths. The notion is expressed by both Hesiod and Sappho, says the late-Roman commentator Servius, à *propos* of line 42 of Vergil's Sixth Eclogue, but we do not have those texts.

36 As his Twelfth Labor, Hercules broke through the gates of the Afterworld.

21–26 and 34–40 Compare Dante's disapproval of Ulysses' last voyage ("the mad flight"), *Inferno* XXVI, 125,—and the reversal of that judgment in Tennyson's *Ulysses*.

Note the structure of Ode 1.3: 8 + 12 + 20 lines, to a total of 40 lines.

Dryden, in his miscellaney of translations called *Sylvae* (1685), has a paraphrase of this Ode 1.3. in 55 tetrameter lines, chiefly couplets.

1.4. *Solvitur acris hiems grata vice veris et Favoni*

Meter: in the odd-numbered lines:

     _ U U   _ U U   _ U U   _ U U   _ U   _ U   _ U

in the even-numbered lines: U _ U _ U _ U _ U _ U

(This meter, called "the Fourth Archilochan strophe," is used only in this poem. In the odd-numbered lines the Latin allows either a spondee (_ _) or a dactyl (_ U U) in the first three feet. The fourth foot, however, must be a dactyl, and all the rest is as indicated.)

Harshness of winter relents at the welcome return of Spring and Westwind,
    The ships are hauled by windlass down from dry dock,
Oxen no longer are glad for their stables, nor plowman for his fireside,
    And pastures do not whiten under hoarfrost.
5   Now by the low-hanging moon start the dances of Cytheréan Venus,
    As nymphs of hers link hands with lovely Graces
Treading the earth in their alternate rhythms, and Vulcan, red at fire-glow,
    Inspects the Cyclops blacksmiths at their forges.
Now is the season when hair is perfúmed and entwined with glossy myrtle
10   Or flowers which the unlocked earth releases.
Now in the shadowy groves is the time for a sacrifice to Faunus —
    A she-lamb or a he-goat, as he chooses.
Ashen-pale Death comes a-knocking at mansions of kings and paupers' hovels
    With equal clamor. Lucky Sestius, our
15   Briefness of life-span forbids us to open a long-range hope's investment.
    To darkness and the fabled ghosts you soon shall
Pass, to the cramped little quarters of Pluto; and once you are ensconced there,
    The dice will not elect you banquet-master,
Nor will you marvel to gaze on young Lýcidas, over whom all young men
20   Wax ardent now, and girls will soon do likewise.

1   "Westwind" = *Favonius*, "the favoring (wind)," also called Zephyrus.
1–2 These two lines may paraphrase Poem 10, 15 of "The Greek Anthology,"—or the reverse may be the case, since the date of Poem 10, 15 is unknown; or both poems may imitate a lost Greek original.
5   Venus/Aphroditē was born of the sea foam near the island of Cythéra (Kýthēra), off the southernmost tip of mainland Greece: hence "Cytheréan."
6–7 The three Graces (*Gratiae*; Greek *Khárites*) were sister divinities personifying all that is charming, lovely, and elegant. See *Odes* 3.19.15; 3.21.22 and note; 4.7.5.
7–8 Vulcan/Hephaistos was the husband of Venus/Aphroditē. The Cyclops (plural) were giant blacksmiths, with forges usually located in the crater of Mount Etna in Sicily.
     Compare the passage early in Book 3 of the *Argonautika* (*The Voyage of Argo*) by Apollonius of Rhodes, ca. 250 B.C.: "(Hephaistos) had gone early to his forge and anvils in a vast cavern on a floating island, where he used to turn out all kinds of curious metalwork with the aid of fire and bellows." (E.V. Rieu translation, p. 110)
     The relevance of lines 7–8 is puzzling; presumably Vulcan's male "ardor" is the complement of the feminine figures who have eagerly responded to awakening springtime.
9–10 That is, for banquets and drinking parties.
11 Faunus was the old Italian divinity protective of animals and plants but later identified with the Greek god Pan. *Odes* 3.18. is addressed to him.
13–14 ". . . knocking . . . with equal clamor" = *aequo pulsat pede*, "kicks with equal foot." The Romans kicked at a door, rather than rapping with finger-knuckles.

14   Lucius Sestius Quirinus, interim consul July–December, 23 B.C., was probably a fel-
      low-soldier of Horace's in 42 B.C. We can only guess why he is called "lucky" (*beate*).
16–17 The "fabled ghosts" = the famous dead. "The cramped little quarters of Pluto,"
      literally "the tiny Plutonian house," = the grave.
18   At the after-dinner drinking, the proportions of wine and water were "legislated" by the
      magister bibendi, who was elected by a roll of the knucklebones.
18–20 Line 18 stands for "wine," lines 19–20 for "love." Milton may have borrowed the
      name "Lycidas" from this poem, or from Theocritus (the Seventh Idyll), or from Vergil's
      Eclogues 7 or 9. Line 20 implies that *this* Lycidas is pubescent, whereas the others are
      young adult "shepherds."

1.5.   *Quis multa gracilis te puer in rosa*

Meter: in lines 1 and 2:   _ > _ U U _ _ U U _ U _
          line 3:   _ > _ U U _ _
          line 4:   _ > _ U U _ U _

> What slim lad, in his fine   perfumes and scented oils,
> Couched on rose petals strewn   thick in a charming cave,
>   Now makes love to you, Pyrrha?
>   For whom now is your golden hair
>
> Dressed so artfully plain?   How many times shall *he*   5
> Mourn for vows and for gods   fickle and false, and stand
>   Dazed — the innocent! — when black
>   Wind-gusts darken your shining sea,
>
> Who so trustingly now   takes you as purest gold,
> Hopes you worthy of love   always, and his alone,   10
>   Unsuspecting that winds change.
>   Woe to any for whom you gleam
>
> Unadventured. A shrine   wall holds the picture still
> Which attested my vowed   gratitude there as I
>   Hung my dripping-wet clothes up   15
>   To the god whom the seas obey.

3–4   Pyrrha's name means "red" or "reddish" in Greek, but her hair is *flavam*, "golden" or
      "golden yellow." Color adjectives in the classical languages are, however, not precise.
      The coiffure is doubtless like Lydē's in *Odes* 2.11.24, or like that of the Venus de Milo.
13–16 "Votive pictures" are still hung in Catholic shrines—a miniature replica of a crutch
      discarded, if not the actual crutch itself, or a representation of any cured part of the
      body. Sailors escaping from shipwreck might hang up their garments to Neptune.
      Compare the dedicated chains of an ex-slave in S.1.5.65–66 and the dedicated weapons
      of the ex-gladiator in E.1.1.4–5.

One of several poems added to the 1673 reprint of Milton's *Minor Poems* (first published in
1645), and with the Latin text placed after it for purposes of comparison, was:

The Fifth Ode of Horace. Lib. I.

"*Quis multa gracilis te puer in Rosa*, Renderd almost word for word without Rhyme according to the Latin Measure, as near as the Language will permit."

> What slender Youth bedew'd with liquid odours
> Courts thee on Roses in some pleasant Cave,
> > *Pyrrha* for whom bind'st thou
> > In wreaths thy golden Hair,
>
> Plain in thy neatness; O how oft shall he
> On Faith and changed Gods complain: and Seas
> > Rough with black winds and storms
> > Unwonted shall admire:
>
> Who now enjoyes thee credulous, all Gold,
> Who always vacant, always amiable
> > Hopes thee; of flattering gales
> > Unmindfull. Hapless they
>
> To whom thou untry'd seem'st fair. Me in my vow'd
> Picture the sacred wall declares t' have hung
> > My dank and dropping weeds
> > To the stern God of Sea.

This famous and admirable translation by a great English poet may have been undertaken as an experiment in unrhymed verse—Milton's dislike of rhyme is well known. Quite another matter, however, is what Milton meant by "according to the Latin Measure," since his four stanzas consist of two regular English blank-verse lines followed by two trimeters, by no means following Horace's pattern as indicated at the head of our translation. While the pentameters are smooth, the trimeters have "hovering accents" and "hesitations" that uncannily create Latin-language "effects."

The Latinisms of grammar and vocabulary present problems: "vacant" means "committed to no other suitor"; "credulous" (line 9) goes with "who" and not with "thee"; and so forth. One needs *some* Latin even to read the translation.

1.6.　*Scriberis Vario fortis et hostium*

Meter: in lines 1, 2, and 3:　　$\_ > \_ \cup \cup \_ \quad \_ \cup \cup \_ \cup \_$
　　　　　　line 4:　　$\_ > \_ \cup \cup \_ \cup \_$

A poem of self-excuse for not writing the poem requested.

> Victor over our foes,　　brave in your every act:
> Thus shall Varius paint　　you in Maeónian verse
> In whatever campaigns　　either by land or sea
> 　　Brave men fought under your command.
>
> We, Agríppa, shall not　　even attempt such themes,
> (Nor Achilles in bile　　knowing no word for "yield,"
> Nor Ulysses the sly　　sailing about the sea,
> 　　Nor grim kinsfolk of Pelops' line)

5

Being feeble at grand   themes, and while modesty
And the Muse of this mild   lyre bid us not to mar   10
Praise of you — and thereby   eminent Caesar's self —
    With a talent that shows a flaw.

Who could rightly describe   Mars in his coat of steel?
Or Meríones ridged   black with the dust of Troy?
Or, with Pallas's help,   how Diomédes gained   15
    Skill to fight as a peer of gods?

Our whole art is a small   matter of banquet scenes,
Girls — with fingernails trimmed —   sharply at war with beaux,
Or, if *we* are in love,   singing away of love
    Like as not, and without a care.   20

1–4   Not Horace, but the *epic* poet, Lucius Varius Rufus, will celebrate your achievements,
Agrippa, in a poem as great as the *Iliad*.
    "Maeónian" = Homeric. Homer was sometimes said to have been born at Smyrna,
anciently called Maeonia, (now Izmir, on the W coast of Turkey); *Odes* 4.9.5 has
"Maeonian Homer."
    Varius, whose works are all lost, was mentioned with esteem in: S.1.5.40; S.1.6.55;
S.1.9.23; and S.2.8.21, his name being usually spoken in the same breath with that of
Vergil. In the Epistle (2.1.245–7) to Augustus, Horace will praise the emperor for having
cherished and financially rewarded "Vergil and Varius." See also E.2.3.55.
5   Throughout this poem Horace observes deference by referring to himself as "we" or
"our." Elsewhere in the Odes he will do so only in the odd instances of 2.17.32 and 3.28.9.
5–8   The theme of Agrippa's achievements exceeds Horace's poetic powers, as would an
Achilles poem like the *Iliad*, a Ulysses poem like the *Odyssey*, or Greek dramas about the
descendants of Pelops, for example, Aeschylus's *Agamemnon*.
13–16   Only Homer could adequately portray the god of war, i.e., Agrippa; or battlefield
scenes like the one in *Iliad* 13. 246–329 concerning the Cretan hero Idoménéus and his
charioteer Meríones; or the prowess of Greek hero Diomédes before Troy.

Marcus Vipsanius (63/62–12 b.c.), who called himself Agrippa (a genuinely ancient Roman
name) and who had no discoverable family, was, like Maecenas, "in college" with Octavius
Caesar at Apollonia, on the coast of Illyria (now Albania), when the news came of Julius
Caesar's murder. If he joined "the party of Octavius Caesar" immediately, there is no record
of his activities until the year 41. From that time, however, his rise was meteoric. As the chief
military man supporting Octavius, he won the naval battles against Sextus Pompey in 36 and
the naval battle at Actium against Antony and Cleopatra in 31, both times stepping back to
allow his master to receive all the glory. His command of land armies was no less successful. It
was he, for instance, who completed the long conquest of Spain in 20–19 b.c. To all intents
and purposes, he was Admiral, Chief General, and Minister of War.
    In 21 he married the emperor's only child, the recently widowed Julia, thereby becom-
ing essentially co-ruler of the Roman state, with the prospect of the empire's passing either to
him or to his sons. He died, aged about fifty, worn out from long and arduous service, and
neither of his sons lived to see the end of Augustus's reign. His surviving monument is the
Pantheon, built in 27; a fragment of his great map of the world can be traced; his autobiog-
raphy is lost.
    His great influence on the emperor had, from the beginning, to be shared with the
nonmilitary, finicky, esthetic, subtle, not to say devious, Maecenas, the very opposite of

Agrippa's rugged, soldierly, even brutal, personality. No great love was lost between these two, and Horace, we recall was the protégé and devoted friend of Maecenas.

    The date of the poem is likely to be 29 B.C., when Agrippa and Octavius Caesar had just returned from the conquest of Cleopatra's Egypt and Antony's Near Eastern lands. We can only wonder who requested Horace to write a poem in Agrippa's honor. Of the several excuses offered for not writing, the one beyond all challenge is the one in line 11—which is susceptible of ironic interpretation.

1.7.   *Laudabunt alii claram Rhodon aut Mytilenen*

Meter: in the odd-numbered lines: (hexameter, as in the Satires and Epistles)
          in the even-numbered lines: ‿ U U ‿ U U ‿ U U ‿ U

Some people may, of course, praise famous Rhodes, or perhaps Mytiléné,
    Ephesus possibly, two-harbored Corinth's
Bastions, or Delphi renowned in Apollo, or Thebes in old Bacchus,
    Or the delights of Thessalian Tempē.
5   And there are people whose sole occupation is singing the Maiden
    Goddess's city in praises unceasing,
Gathering branches of olive for coronals almost at random;
    Many a man out of honor to Juno
Sings about Argos, the land rich in horses, or wealthy Mycénae.
10   But as for me, neither hard Lacedáemon
Nor yet the lush fertile fields of Larísa have ever impressed me
    Like Albunéa's reechoing grotto
There by the Ánio's falls and the consecrate grove of Tibúrnus
    Close by the orchards with neat-channeled waters.
15   Just as the southwind may whitely at times sweep the sky clear of rain-clouds,
    Not blowing always for gathering storms, be
Wise and remember to limit the sorrow and struggles of living,
    Plancus, with mellowing wine, whether gleam of
Armor surrounds you in camp or you find yourself back in the densest
20   Shade of your well-beloved Tibur. When Teucer,
Starting for exile, was bidding farewell to his father and native
    City of Sálamis, then (so they say) he
Twined him a crown out of poplar leaves, placed it on brows well bedewed with
    Wine-the Releaser, and sadly addressed his
25   Fellows in exile: "Wherever a fortune more kind than my father
    Takes us, my comrades, we willingly follow.
Never despair while your leader is Teucer, while Teucer protects you,
    For the unfailing Apollo has promised
Sálamis new on new ground shall in fame be the match of the old one.
30   Oh, you brave men, who with me have so often
Lived through experiences direr than these, drown your worries in wine-cups:
    Ocean again is our way for tomorrow.

Even in the 3rd century A.D. commentator Porphyrio felt it necessary to state that these 32 lines constitute a single poem, not two poems inadvertently run together.

After listing 12 famous places in the Greek world (1–11), Horace says none of them has ever so impressed him as Tibur (modern Tivoli) (10–14). He advises Lucius Munatius Plancus to ease life's burdens with wine, whether he is on campaign or in Tibur (15–20); Porphyrio says Plancus was a native of Tibur. Teucer of old, when sentenced to exile, set the example of consoling grief with wine (20–32).

1–11   Twelve famous places in the Greek world: 1. the island of Rhodes; 2. Mytilenē, capital of the island of Lesbos and home of Alcaeus and Sappho; 3. Ephesus, capital of the Roman province of Asia (approximately modern Turkey); 4. luxurious Corinth, with its two harbors, 6 km/4 m apart, on either side of the Isthmus of Corinth; 5. Delphi, home of Apollo and his oracle; 6. Thebes, "a birthplace" of Dionysus/Bacchus; 7. the beautiful "Vale of Tempē," that is, the valley of the Peneus River, under the shadow of Mount Olympus, in the region of Thessaly; 8. Athens, "the university town" of Horace's time, the city of the virgin goddess Athena and of literary works as numerous as the olive trees sacred to the goddess; 9. Argos, which Homer calles "rich in horses," chief city of Argolis (NE Peloponnesus) and sacred to Hera/Juno; 10. Mycénae, which Homer calls "rich in gold," (but dwindled to a village in the 900 years since Agamemnon ruled there); 11. Lacedáemon, i.e., Sparta, once the dwelling of Menelaus and Helen of Troy; 12. Larísa/Laríssa, on the Peneus River, capital of Thessaly.

12–14   "Albunéa is a nymph who dwells in the falls of Albunéa . . . near Tibur," says T.E. Page (to *Aeneid* 7. 82–84). At Tibur (Tívoli) the Anio (now called the Aniéne) flows through a deep, wooded gorge and then descends in several picturesque waterfalls from the Sabine mountains to the *campagna* (plain) of Rome.

Tibúrnus, with his brothers Coras and Cátillus, was the legendary founder of Tibur.

18   Lucius Munátius Plancus (distinct from the Munatius of E.1.3.30) was an officer of Julius Caesar's; Governor of Gaul in 43 B.C.; founder of Lugdunum (Lyon, France) and of Augusta Rauracorum (Augst, near Basel, Switzerland) that same year; Governor of Asia (modern Turkey) and Syria for Mark Antony, until, from objections to Cleopatra, he joined Octavius Caesar for the battle of Actium in 31. In January of 27 B.C. he was the man who proposed the title of "Augustus" for Caesar to the Senate.

20–32   "Telamonian Teucer," illegitimate half-brother of "the Great Ajax" and a warrior at Troy (*Iliad* 8. 266–344), sailed home to Salamis, capital of the island of Salamis across the bay from Athens, only to find that his father, Telamon, forbade him to land because he had failed to save the life of Ajax. Pleading from shipdeck to his father on the shore, he received the command to sail the seas until he could find a new city of Salamis somewhere. (The new Salamis was established at the E end of the island of Cyprus, where excavations were begun in the 1960s.) Lines 20–32 are spoken by Teucer to his shipboard companions as he turns away sadly from the interview with his father.

24   "Wine-the-Releaser" (*Lyáeus*; Greek *Lúaios*, from *lúo*, "to release"). See Epode 9,38.

25–32   These lines may imitate *Aeneid* 1. 198 ff. If so, composition dates to after 29 B.C.

27   "Never despair" = *Nil desperandum*—Mr. Micawber's advice to David Copperfield.

1.8.   *Lydia, dic, per omnis*

Meter: in the odd-numbered lines: $\_ \cup \cup \_ \cup \_ \cup$
       in the even-numbered lines: $\_ \cup \_ \cup \_ \quad \cup \cup \_ \quad \_ \cup \cup \_ \cup \_ \cup$

Lydia, tell me now by
    All the gods: why rush   to destroy   Sýbaris with your loving?

Why should he hate the sunny
    Field of Mars, where once   he endured   sunglare and dust unflinching?
5   Why does he ride no more, like
    Other rugged lads   of his age,   using the wolf's-teeth bit for
Breaking his Gaulish pony?
    Why is he afraid   of a swim   out in the tawny Tiber?
Why does he shrink from athletes'
10   Oil as worse than blood   of the asp?   Why are his arms unmarked by
Bruises from weapons practice,
    Never winning fame   with a new   spear-throw or discus record?
Why does he stay in hiding,
    As they say the son   of divine   Thetis hid out when dismal
15   Ruin threatened Troy, for fear that
    Man's apparel might   be his death   under the hordes of Lycians?

1   "Lydia," meaning "a woman from Lydia" (now west-central Turkey), is a name further assigned in *Odes* 1.13., 1.25., and 3.9, and in its Greek form, Lydē, in *Odes* 2.11., 3.11., and 3.28. No two of these seven characters are identical.

2   "Sýbaris" means "an inhabitant of the luxurious Greek city of Sýbaris," in S Italy, across the Gulf of Táranto from the city of Taréntum (now called Táranto). The name carries the same sense as in English: "a Sybarite," "a voluptuary." "Lydia" and the adjective "Lydian" also connote voluptuousness.

4   The Field of Mars, or Mars Field (*Campus Martius*), was a large open area in the NW quadrant of ancient Rome, surrounded on three sides by a great bend of the Tiber. In remoter times a drill ground, it was, in Horace's time, an extensive park with athletics areas, space for racing horses, and with the Tiber close at hand for swimming. In 27 B.C. Agrippa built the Pantheon and other structures there. It is now a close-packed section of the modern city, with a main avenue leading to the bridge that approaches the Vatican.

6   Vergil, in *Georgics* 3. 179–208 also mentions the wolf's-teeth bit (*lupatis frenis*) used in breaking horses.

8   The Tiber was traditionally "tawny" (or "yellow"): *flavus*, as in *Odes* 1.2.13 and 2.3.18.

14–16   Post-Homeric legend had it that the boy Achilles was dressed as a girl by his sea-goddess mother, Thetis, and hidden among the daughters of Lycomédes, King of (the island of) Scyros, because she foreknew that her son would perish if he went to the Trojan War. Ulysses, disguised as a peddler, came to Scyros with women's wares and a few military weapons, and Achilles betrayed himself by his interest in the weapons. The oldest-known mention of this story is by the Greek pastoral poet Bion, third century B.C., and Ovid briefly relates it in *Metamorphoses* 13. 162–170.

    The Lycians (from what is now SW Turkey) were allies of the Trojans, but here they stand for the entire Trojan forces.

1.9.   *Vides ut alta stet nive candidum*

Meter: Alcaic stanza: in lines 1 and 2:   U _ U _ U _ U U _ U _
                       in line 3:   U _ U _ U _ U _ U
                       in line 4:   _ U U _ U U _ U _ U

You see Soráctē white where it stands in depths
Of snow, and forests straining beneath the weight,
    And rivers halted in their courses
        Under the sharpness of frost and winter.

Stand off the cold by heaping the hearth with new   5
Supplies of firewood; do not stint measures of
    The four-year wine, my Thaliárchus,
        Drawn from the two-handled Sabine seal-jar.

All else leave to the gods, who allay the winds
That clash in raging wars on the stormy sea,   10
    For neither cypresses nor mountain
        Ash are forever by wind tormented.

Cease asking what will happen tomorrow, and
Whatever Lady Luck puts before you, set
    It down to "Gain," and while you still have   15
        Youth, do not miss any chance for loving

Or dancing while your vigor still blooms ungrayed
By crabbèd age. And now is the time for trysts
    At nightfall on the Field of Mars and
        Whisperings under arcades; and now is   20

When laughter rippling low from a shadowed nook
Delightfully betrays that a girl is there,
    With bracelet yielded from an arm or
        Ring from a finger not quite reluctant.

---

1   Mount Soráctē (now Sorátte), at 691 meters (over 2,000'), is west of the Tiber and
visible, though not conspicuously so, some 30 km/20 m NW of Tibur.
1–8   Snow is rare on Soractē, and Horace may have intruded the Italian mountain into the
Greek landscape of a poem of Alcaeus, beginning:

> The Sky-God rains. From heaven comes a mighty storm, and the streams of waters
>   are frozen fast . . . (2 lines missing)

> Defy the storm, lay on the fire, mix the sweet wine unsparingly, put a soft pillow
>   about your temples.
>   (Denys Page translation, in *Sappho and Alcaeus*,
>   Oxford University Press, 1955, p. 309)

    Epode 13 was an earlier "study" after the same poem of Alcaeus. It would appear
that both Roman poems followed only the opening stanzas of the Greek and then
digressed in separate directions.
    Lines 1–8 also underlie Tennyson's *In Memoriam*, CVII, 2254 ff. (which regards a
February 1st):

>   Fiercely flies
>   The blast of North and East, and ice
> Makes daggers at the sharpen'd eaves,

>   But fetch the wine,

Arrange the board and brim the glass;

Bring in great logs and let them lie,
To make a solid core of heat;
Be cheerful-minded, talk and treat
Of all things e'en as he were by.

7–8   Four-year-old wine may have been a convention of poetry; see the 7th and 14th Idylls
of Theocritus.
"Thaliárchus," meaning "feast-ruler," is a name attested for actual persons.
11–12   Cypresses were "domestic" trees in gardens, ash trees grew wild in the mountains.
Two types of human life are implied.
13–18   Commonplaces of popular Epicureanism are expressed. "Lady Luck" = *fors*,
"chance." ". . . set/It down to 'Gain' " = *lucro adpone*, a bookkeeping term.
21–22   Highly inflected Latin permits the extraordinary word arrangement:

21	*nunc et*	*latentis*	*proditor*	*intimo*
	and now	(of a) hidden	betrayer	(from a)secret
22	*gratus*	*puellae*	*risus*	*ab angulo*
	pleasing	girl's	laughter	from (a) nook

Dryden's miscellany of translations, called *Sylvae* (1685), includes a 38-line paraphrase of this
ode.

1.10.   *Mercuri, facunde nepos Atlantis,*

Meter: Sapphic stanza: in lines 1, 2, and 3:   _ U _ > _ U U _ U _ U
in line 4:   _ U U _ U

Nimble-spoken Mercury, Atlas' grandson,
Who by speech astutely advanced mankind from
Brute and worked a comeliness into him by
Grace of gymnastics,

5   You I sing, great Jupiter's herald bearing
Words of gods, first founder of song and lyre-shell,
Deft, whenever anything took your eye, at
Impishly stealing.

As Apollo threatened your infant self in
10   Anger once unless you returned his oxen,
He perceived his quiver was missing too, and
Could not help laughing.

And, with you to guide him, rich Priam even
Fooled the haughty chiefs of the Greeks, when out from
15   Troy he passed Thessalian fires and war camps
Sworn to Troy's ruin.

You conduct good souls of the dead to happy
Dwellings, herding swarms of them with your golden
Wand, yourself as welcome to gods supernal
20   As to the nether.

Ancient editor Porphyrio terms this ode a reworking of a hymn to Hermes by Alcaeus: *hymnus est in Mercurium ab Alcaeo lyrico poeta*. Only the opening stanza of the Greek original is preserved, and it is in the *Sapphic* meter:

> Hail, ruler of Cyllene: of you it is my will to sing; whom on the hilltops
> ... Maia bore, having lain in love with the almighty son of Cronos ...
> (Denys Page translation, in *Sappho and Alcaeus*,
> Oxford University Press, 1955, p. 253)

1 Mercury/Hermes was the son of Zeus by the nymph Maia, daughter of the Titan, Atlas (who was transformed into the sky-supporting "Mount Atlas" in Morocco).

The ode is a hymn of praise, not a "contractual prayer" like 1.3. above, and lists several, but by no means all, of the complex aspects of the god:

1–2	Mercury as a master of language (*Hermes lógios*)
3–4	Mercury as god of athletics (*Hermes agōnios*)
5–6	Mercury as messenger of the gods (*Hermes diáktoros*)
6	Mercury as the inventor of the lyre (*Hermes mousikós*)
7–12	Mercury as clever thief (*Hermes kléptēs*)
13–16	Mercury as helper-in-need (*Hermes erioúnios*)
17–20	Mercury as "soul-sender" (*Hermes psychopómpos*)

No allusion is made to the god's specifically Roman name and function as the god of *merc*hants and *merc*handise, as in the last 3 stanzas of Ode 1.2. above.

2–4 The social evolution of mankind, described in S.1.3.99–104 as spontaneous, if slow, is here seen as directed by Mercury. Compare E.2.1.5–8, where the evolution is guided by "heroes."

6 Lines 24–61 of the "Homeric Hymn to Hermes" (before 500 B.C.) relate how Hermes/Mercury, a few hours after birth, invented the lyre by stretching seven strings of sheep-gut across the hollow of a tortoise shell; in lines 490 ff. of the same poem the young god made a gift of the lyre to Apollo.

Moore quotes Matthew Arnold's *Merope*, 1641–5:

> ... in the glens,
> The basking tortoises,
> Whose strip'd shell founded
> In the hand of Hermes
> The glory of the lyre.

7–10 The bulk of the 580-line "Homeric Hymn to Hermes," from line 68 on, is devoted to the story of how the one-day-old god stole fifty of Apollo's cattle, disguising their and his own footprints, and what came of that act of theft.

When Porphyrio says of line 9: "This fable, however, was invented by Alcaeus," he must have been thinking of the stanza as a whole, meaning primarily the theft of Apollo's quiver and Apollo's surprised laughter.

But there were many thievings by the young Mercury/Hermes, and Goethe's own "hymn to Hermes" in *Faust, Part II,* lines 9668–78, collects a number of them:

> ...
> Quickly from the lord of the sea
> He stole the trident; from Ares himself
> Slyly the sword from its sheath;
> Arrows and bow from Phoebus too,
> And from Hephaistos the tongs;
> Zeus the Father's very lightning
> He would have taken but for the fear of fire;
> Eros too he downed in a
> Leg-tripping boxing bout;

> Even from Cyrpis as she caressed him
> He stole her bosom's girdle.
> (Passage translation)

13–16 In *Iliad* 24, especially lines 349–694, Hermes guided old King Priam by night past enemy camps and to Achilles, where the king pleaded for and received the corpse of his son from the hands of Achilles, his son's slayer.

"Haughty chiefs" = *Atridas superbos,* that is, Agamemnon and Menelaus, sons of Atreus.

Achilles came from Phthía in S Thessaly.

17–19 Hermes soul-sender herded the ghosts of the dead to the underworld. *Odyssey* 24 begins: "Hermes the Cyllenian bade forth those ghosts . . . In his hand was the rod of pure gold with which at will he charms men's eyes to rest or stirs them from sleep. By a wave of it he had them afoot and following him with such thin cries as bats use . . . So they flocked after, weakly piping, while gentle Hermes led them down the dank, dark passage . . . till soon they entered the asphodel meadows where harbour the shadowy ghosts of those that have passed away." (T. E. Lawrence translation)

The "rod (*rhabdos*) of pure gold" is a kind of enchanter's wand, not the messenger's staff (*kērýkeion*) with its two white ribbons (which later became the *cadúceus* with its two symmetrically twining serpents).

19–20 Mercury is welcome among the named sky-gods and among the nameless, usually multiple, under-earth divinities: that is, he freely visits heaven, earth, and hell.

1.11.   *Tu ne quaesieris, scire nefas, quem mihi, quem tibi*

Meter: _ U _ U U _   _ U U _   _ U U _ U _

> Give up trying to learn —   knowing is wrong!—   what span of life the gods
> Plan for me or for you,   Leuconoē;   draw up no more of these
> Babylonian charts.   Simply accept   all that the future brings,
> Whether Jupiter means   we are to know   many a winter more
> 5 Or makes this one the last,   now dashing waves   over the porous rocks
> Of Tyrrhénian shores.   Show yourself wise: strain the wine clear, and trim
> Lengthy hope to the short   space of our lives.   Envious time escapes
> Even now as we talk.   Harvest this day,   discount tomorrow's gains.

2 "Leuconoē" is based on Greek *leukós,* "white," or of fair complexion.

3 "Babylonian charts" (*Babylonios numeros*) means "horoscopes." Still preserved astronomical data covering at least 800 years before the Christian era show that the Babylonians sought "to discover all that is periodic in celestial phenomena, and to reduce it to a numerical expression in such a manner as to be able to *predict* its repetition in the future." (F. Cumont: *Astrology and Religion among the Greeks and Romans,* Dover, 1912, p. 13.)

As early as 139 B.C. astrologers were banished from Rome by law; clearly, they still persisted there.

6 The Tyrrhénian Sea is that part of the Mediterranean west of Italy and "enclosed" by Italy, Sicily, Sardinia, and Corsica.

Wine was strained from the storage jar through a fine cloth or sieve to remove sediment.

8   "Harvest this day" = *Carpe diem,* a phrase so famous as to be sometimes quoted even in
present times in Horace's own Latin words. Ancient commentator Porphyrio says that
the metaphor is from picking (*carpere*) fruit.

1.12.   *Quem virum aut heroa lyra vel acri*

Meter: Sapphic stanza: in lines 1, 2, and 3: $-\,\cup\,-\,>\,-\,\cup\,\cup\,-\,\cup\,-\,\cup$
in line 4: $-\,\cup\,\cup\,-\,\cup$

Come, what man or demigod shall you choose to
Hymn with lyre or high-shrilling pipe, Muse Clio,
Or what god? Whose name shall be lifted up and
  Sportively echoed

Down the shaded glens of Mount Hélicon or   5
On the slopes of Pindus or snow-capped Haemus?
There the forests crowded to follow singing
  Orpheus, whose music

(Taught him by his mother) made rushing rivers
Cease their flow and blustering winds be silent,   10
All so sweetly sounding to strings of lyre that
  Ears grew on oak trees.

Whom shall I address with accustomed praises
Sooner than our Parent, whose varied seasons
Temper works of men and of gods, and seas and   15
  Lands and the heavens?

Sprung from him and greater than he, is nothing,
Nor is any like him or closely second:
Yet the highest honors next after his are
  Pallas Athena's,   20

Bold in battle; nor shall I pass in silence
Over Father Liber; or you, great virgin
Foe of savage monsters, or you, dread Phoebus
  Deadly of arrow.

Hercules I praise, and the sons of Leda,   25
One renowned with horses, the other famed for
Boxing; once their star flashes whitely forth at
  Sailors' entreaties,

Back the foaming breakers recede from cliffs, and
Mighty gales subside, and the stormclouds scatter,   30
And where ocean horribly tossed, the billows
  Sink to the sea-bed.

Shall I next praise Rómulus? or the peaceful
Reign of King Pompílius? Or shall Tarquin's
35   Haughty rods-and-axes be praised? or Cato's
        Death as a martyr?

Régulus, both Scauri, and Paullus grandly
Wasteful of his life at the Punic triumph,
And Fabrícius too, I shall praise in poems
40   Such as grant glory.

He, and Curius of the unshorn hair, and
Old Camillus useful in times of war, came
Out of starkest poverty, from ancestral
        Farms no less humble.

45   Like a tree that steadily grows unnoticed,
Grows Marcellus' fame, while amid the lesser
Fires the Julian star is a moon outshining
        All of the others.

Father, high protector of humankind, born
50   Son of Saturn, yours from the Fates is mighty
Caesar's charge: be rulership yours, with none but
        Caesar as second.

Whether he hauls Parthians (threats to Latium)
Captive at his chariot wheels in triumph,
55   Or the conquered men from the lands of sunrise,
        Seres and Hindus,

He will rule the world — under you — in justice;
You will ride in thunder to shake Olympus,
And upon pollution of sacred places
60   You will hurl lightnings.

Essaying the grand rhapsodic manner of Pindar (518 to after 446 B.C.), but in trim stanza form, Horace begins with a 12-line prologue asking the Muse Clio for a suitable theme and recalling all the Muses as well as the exalted song of Orpheus. The rest of the poem (13–60) is a sequence of praises of gods and heroes, culminating in praise of the emperor:

13–18   Jupiter ("our Parent")
19–24   other deities: Pallas Athena, Father Liber (Bacchus), Diana, Phoebus Apollo
25–32   demigods: Hercules; Castor and Pollux
33–35   three early kings of Rome: Romulus, the deified warrior-founder of Rome, ruled 753–716 B.C.; Numa Pompílius, ruled in unbroken peace, 716–672 B.C.; and Tarquin the Haughty (*superbus*), 7th and last king, ruled 534–509 B.C.
35–44   heroes of the Roman Republic (in mixed sequence): Cato the Younger, Regulus, the two Scauri, Paullus, Fabrícius, Curius, and Camíllus
45–48   Marcellus, the youthful heir-apparent of the new empire
49–60   the Emperor Augustus

Lines 1–2 deliberately echo the opening of Pindar's 2nd Olympian ode (for Theron, winner in the four-horse-chariot race):

> My songs, lords of the lyre,
> which of the gods, what hero, what mortal shall we celebrate?
>
> (Lattimore translation)

Lines 13–14, beginning the ode proper, echo Pindar's 2nd Neméan ode, lines 1–3:

> Even as the Homeridai,
> the rhapsode singers of stories, for the greater part
> begin with a prelude to Zeus, . . .
>
> (Lattimore translation)

5–6   Three traditional haunts of the Muses:

- Mount Hélicon in Boeótia, between Thebes and the Gulf of Corinth
- the Pindus mountain chain in northern Greece, separating Thessaly from Epirus
- the Haemus mountain chain of ancient Thrace, now the (Great) Balkan Mountains (or the Stara Planina) extending east-west to divide modern Bulgaria into northern and southern halves

7–12   Orpheus was Thracian and associated with the Haemus mountains. His mother was the Muse Callíopē.

14   "Parent" (*parentis*) here = Jupiter. (In 1.2.36 *auctor,* translated "Parent," = Romulus.)

19–24   The four deities named—"great virgin/ Foe of savage monsters" = Diana/ Artemis—all contributed to making the earth a place habitable for man.

25   "Hercules" = *Alcídes,* that is, *grand*son of Alkaios, often so called because his father, ambiguously, might be either Amphitryon or Zeus.

25–32   The sons of Leda (and brothers of Helen, as in *Odes* 1.3.2.) were the twins, Castor the horse-tamer and Pollux the boxer. Deified, they were the twin stars, Gemini, that guided ships on stormy seas, as in the note to *Odes* 1.3.2. and in 4.8.31–32.

Moore points out that the storm-at-sea lines imitate the opening of the 22nd Idyll of Theocritus (3rd century B.C.).

35–36   Marcus Porcius Cato, "the Younger," called *Uticénsis* ("of Utica"), great grandson of "Cato the Elder," reassembled the army of the murdered Pompey the Great after its defeat at Pharsalus in 48 B.C., transported it to North Africa, and made Utica (the port city of Carthage) his headquarters for a last stand against Julius Caesar. By 46 B.C. he saw that his cause was hopeless and committed suicide.

As the selfless martyr dying voluntarily to protest "Caesarism" he appears in an extraordinary series of literary works:

1. Cicero's (lost) panegyric, delivered before the senate in 46 B.C.
2. Julius Caesar's own (lost) *Anticato*
3. Lucan heroizes Cato in Book IX of his poem *Pharsalia* (left unfinished at his death in 65 A.D.) in order to denigrate Julius Caesar, ancestor of Nero.
4. Dante, in the opening canto of the *Purgatorio,* accepts Cato as an "ideal of pagan virtue, the hero and martyr of liberty" (J. D. Sinclair), and makes him the watchman on the lonely shore of the island of Purgatory.
5. Joseph Addison's classicizing drama, *Cato,* enjoyed success in 1713 because it expressed Whig political doctrines.
6. J. G. Gottsched, seeking to found German drama, composed, as the model for a serious play, *Der sterbende Cato* (*The Dying Cato*) in 1742, based on Addison's already antiquated play of 30 years before.

37   Marcus Atilius Regulus led a Roman expedition against Carthage in 256 B.C., was defeated and captured (as a result of overconfidence), and held prisoner for six years. In 250 the Carthaginians, having suffered reverses, sent him to Rome to coax a favorable treaty out of the senate, swearing him to return to Carthage if negotiations failed. He urged the senate to defeat Carthage at any cost, but he honored his oath and went back

to Carthage, where he was allegedly tortured to death. *Odes* 3.5.13–40 presents his speech to the senate, as Horace imagined it.

37   In an Alpine campaign of 101 B.C. a Roman army was defeated but a young man named Scaurus escaped; on receipt of a letter from his father, saying the father would rather see his son dead than defeated, the son committed suicide.

37–38   Lucius Aemilius Paullus, commander against Hannibal at the battle of Cannae in 216 B.C., refused to escape from the midst of the Roman defeat and died with his men.

39–40   Caius Fabrícius Luscínus, ambassador to King Pyrrhus of Epírus in the winter of 280–279 B.C., resisted all the king's bribes to betray Rome and the following season led the expedition against him. (In *Aeneid* 6. 844 Vergil calls him "poor but mighty.")

41   Manius Curius Dentatus, consul in 290, 275, and 274 B.C., refused all bribes of the Samnites, whom he defeated when they allied themselves with King Pyrrhus. At the end of the war he declined all booty and retired to his farm.

Romans wore long hair and beards until around 300 B.C., when the first barbers appeared, and many continued the custom for a long time thereafter.

42   Marcus Furius Camillus, five times dictator (army commander in time of crisis), captured Veii from the Etruscans in 392 B.C. and drove off the invading Gauls in 386. One of Plutarch's "Lives" is devoted to him.

45–46   In 25 B.C. the 18-year-old son of the emperor's sister Octavia, Marcellus, was married to the emperor's daughter and only child, Julia, and simultaneously adopted as the emperor's son and future heir of the empire. But in 23 B.C., at age 20, the young man died. (In 21 B.C. Agrippa married the widowed Julia; see the final note to *Odes* 1.6.) Famous lines of the *Aeneid* (6. 860–885) comprise Vergil's tribute to the recently deceased Marcellus.

The present poem, therefore, dates probably to 25, in any case to the years 25–23.

46–48   The "Julian star" (*Iulium sidus*) has the astrological sense of the high destiny of Julius Caesar's family, but more specifically it means "Augustus."

In Horace's time the most advanced thought held that the stars were, quite literally, burning fires. (See pp. 79–80 in the chapter "Astral Mysticism" in F. Cumont's *Astrology and Religion* . . . , 1912)

49–60   The ode concludes as a prayer to the "Father of gods and men," Jupiter, son of (the Titan) Saturn, (Greek: Zeus, son of (the Titan) Cronos). Jupiter rules the skies and Augustus is his regent on earth.

53   For "Parthians," see under "Foreign Nations," p. 397.

56   For the "Seres" ("Chinese") and Hindus, see under "Foreign Nations," p. 397.

59   "Places," in the text, is "groves."

1.13.   *Cum tu, Lydia, Telephi*

Meter: in the odd-numbered lines: _ U _ U U _ U _
             even-numbered lines: _ U _ U U _   _ U U _ U _

Touting Telephus' rosy throat,
      Touting Telephus' arms,   Lydia, white as wax,
And to *me*! . . . why, it makes my gorge
      Rise and gives me the hot   heartburn of bilious rage.
5   Then my thoughts, like my face, will not
      Keep their color and form;   down over both my cheeks
Steal the tears that betray what slow

Fires inside of me burn,   eating my heart away.
Oh, I rage, if in heat of wine
    He belabors those white   shoulders of yours with blows,   10
Or the crazy, unthinking boy
    Leaves the mark of his teeth   cut in your rosy lips.
If you listen to me, you will
    Not forever desire   someone who makes a sweet
Kiss outrageously hurt, not when   15
    Venus' self has instilled   nectar in any kiss.
Triple blessing and more is theirs
    Whom unbreakable bonds   hold and conjoin, and whose
Love, from grievous dissent intact,
    Will not end till their own   lifetimes' concluding days,   20

1–2   This is the second of 4 "Lydias"; see the note to *Odes* 1.8.1. "Telephus" here is a random-assigned masculine name, as in *Odes* 3.19.23 and 4.11.21. The mythological Telephus is mentioned in Epode 17,8 and E.2.3.95.
4   Literally: my burning liver swells with surly bile ("bile" being the "humor" of anger).
16   Literally: (kisses which) Venus imbues with *quinta parte* of her own nectar. The phrase echoes Pythágoras's (6th century B.C.) *hē pémptē ousía* (or *tò pémpton ón*), which became the medieval *quinta essentia* ("quintessence"), that is, "the fifth substance"—beyond earth, air, fire, and water—of which the heavenly bodies were composed.

1.14.   *O navis, referent in mare te novi*

Meter: in lines 1 and 2:   _ > _ U U _   _ U U _ U _
    in line 3:   _ > _ U U _ _
    in line 4:   _ > _ U U _ U _

On such billows as these   you will again be swept
Out to sea, O my ship!   What are you doing! Make
    Utmost effort to reach port!
    On your one side your oars are lost;

See, your mast has been split   under the Southwind's gusts,   5
Yard-arms groan with the strain,   and, with its cables burst,
    Not for long will the keel stand
    This implacably hurtling sea's

Force. Your sails are in shreds,   battered and broken off
Stand the after-deck gods   heedless of cries for help.   10
    Pontic pine though you are, still,
    Famous daughter of forests green,

It will do you no good   boasting your race and name;
Daunted sailors do not   pluck up their courage from

15   Painted prows. Have a care *your*
                      Fate is not to be gale-winds' toy.

                 Once my anxious concern   and my most heartsick care,
                 Now the theme of my thoughts,   O my belovèd ship,
                      Shun the sea lanes where thick strewn
20   Lie the glittering Cýcladēs.

6–9   Cables were girded round and round midship of ancient vessels to withstand rough
      seas (or ramming by enemy warships). From *Acts of the Apostles* 27:17 Moore cites the
      words: "they used helps, undergirding the ship."
9–10 Small "protective" images—brightly painted, according to Ovid (*Heroides* 16.114).
11   Excellent ship timber came fom Pontus, the mountainous region along the SE coast of
      the Black Sea, (Roman-controlled since 65 B.C.; now NE Turkey). In Catullus's poem
      No. 4, lines 9–16, the poet's boat was built from timber of this region.
17–18 "Once" (*nuper*) may refer to the Perusine War of 41 B.C. and Epode 16, which was
      inspired by it; but *nuper*, "recently, not long ago," suggests rather the anxieties before the
      battle of Actium (September 2, 31 B.C.). "Now" (*nunc*) would presumably refer to a time
      soon after that battle, but the immediate occasion for the poem is unknown.
20   The Cýcladēs islands, which separate the Aegean Sea from the Mediterranean proper,
      are noted for sudden and treacherous squalls. Compare the parallel but nonmenacing
      phrase in *Odes* 3.28.15.

The "Ship of State" was a frequent figure with the Greek poets, and Quintilian, about a
century after Horace, cites this poem as a prime example of allegory.
      Longfellow's *The Buildilng of the Ship* (1849), particularly its last 22 lines: "Thou, too, sail
on, O ship of State!", etc., reflects Horace's ode only in a general way.
      The present poem is, at least in part, "a study after" a Greek original by Alcaeus—which
may or may not have been "an allegory"—which began:

            I cannot tell where the wind lies; one wave rolls from this side, one from
                  that, and we in their midst are borne along with our black vessel
            Toiling in a tempest passing great. The bilge is up over the masthold, all
                  the sail lets the daylight through already,and there are great rents
                  along it,
            All the wooldings are slackening, the rudders . . . .
                              (Denys Page translation, in *Sappho and Alcaeus,* p. 184)

1.15.   *Pastor cum traheret per freta navibus*

Meter: in lines 1, 2, and 3:   _ U _ U U _ _ U U _ U _
          in line 4:   _ U _ U U _ U _

                 When that shepherd of old   in his Idáean ships
                 Was abducting the fair   Helen across the seas,
                 Néreus halted the swift   winds with unwelcome calm,
                      Prophesying the woeful things

Yet to come of the deed.   "Under an evil sign   5
You now voyage with her   who will but be reclaimed
By the armies of Greece,   swearing your wedlock's end
   And an end to the kingdom long

Ruled by Priam. Ah, *then*   horses and men shall sweat!
What disasters shall fall   on the Dardánian race!   10
Pallas' helmet and dread   aegis are donned, her rage
   Mounts, her chariot is at hand.

Bold enough while you have   Venus as your support,
You will vainly go on   combing your splendid hair,
Charming women with songs   to the unwarlike lyre;   15
   All in vain on the nuptial couch

You will seek to avoid   man-crushing spears and sharp
Stings of Cnóssian darts,   and, amid battle's din,
Ajax swift in pursuit: you in the end will dredge
   Your adulterer's hair in dust.   20

Does Laértes's son,   seal of your country's doom,
Not loom up where you flee?   Nestor of Pylos too?
And the dauntlessly brave   hero of Sálamis,
   Teucer? Sthénelus, battle-shrewd,

Wise in skills of the horse,   charioteer of no   25
Slight abilities? There   surely you recognize
Swift Meríones? There   fierce Diomédes, that
   'Better man than his father was,'

Stalking you in his rage?   Then like a stag that leaves
Grass at sight of a wolf   off at the valley side,   30
You, with upward-tossed head,   gasping for breath, will flee —
   Not as lady-fair heard you boast.

True: Achilles's fleet,   sulking, will yet protract
Phrygian women's and great   Ilium's day of doom;
But, when winters of known   count will have passed, in Greek   35
   Fires shall Ilian houses burn."

---

1 "That shepherd" is Paris, son of Trojan King Priam. Because it was foretold at his birth
that he would grow up to be the ruin of his country, he was taken as an infant to "Mount
Ida"—a range of mountains SE of Troy—and left to die. But the herdsman entrusted
with the deed chose to bring the child up as a shepherd on Mount Ida.
  "Idáean" here means "Trojan."

3 Nereus was the prophetic Old Man of the Sea, a shape-shifter like Proteus and often
confused with him. His children by the nymph Doris were the fifty Nereids (mermaids).
His halting of the winds in order to deliver the present prophecy is doubtless Horace's
invention.

9 In echo of *Iliad* 2. 388–390:

> There will be a man's sweat on the shield-strap . . . .
> There will be sweat on a man's horse straining at the smoothed chariot.
>
> (Lattimore translation)

10   "Dardanian" = "Trojan" (from Dardanus, founder or "second founder" of Troy).

11–12   In echo of *Iliad* 5. 733–747, about Athenē's self-arming, especially 738–741:

> And across her shoulders she threw the betasseled, terrible
> aegis, all about which Terror hangs like a garland,
> and Hatred is there, and Battle Strength, and heart-freezing Onslaught,
> and thereon is set the head of the grim gigantic Gorgon . . .
>
> (Lattimore translation)

By Horace's time, art represented the aegis as a metal breastplate with a fringe of snakes and with Medusa's head in the center. But the word itself meant "goat-skin" (Greek *aigís,* from *aix, aigós,* "goat"), and Robert Graves (*The Greek Myths* 8.1) claims it was originally "a magical goat-skin bag containing a serpent and protected by a Gorgon mask"; Graves also believes it was Athenē's before it was Zeus's—the reverse of the usual assumption. A. R. Benner (pp. xxix–xxx of the Introduction to his *Iliad* edition, 1903) says the aegis was the divine counterpart of the *laisēion* worn by human warriors, an animal skin serving as shield for shoulders and arms, and reproduces a painting of one from a late 6th-century B.C. vase.

13–20   Underlying these lines is the extensive episode in *Iliad* 3. 380–454, where Paris withdraws from battle to make love to Helen in his "perfumed bedchamber."

The "splendid hair" will again be mentioned with contempt in *Odes* 4.9.13–16.

Cnossian darts" means "arrows from the famous Cretan archers," Cnossos being the capital of Crete.

21–29   Nereus foretells how Paris will flee from various opponents, all from the *Iliad:*

19   "the Great Ajax"

21   Odysseus/Ulysses, son of Laértes, stole the Palladium, the magical preserving statue in Troy, thereby dooming the city.

22   Nestor of Pylos, according to *Odyssey* 24. 51 ff., rallied the Greeks to continue the war after the death of Achilles.

23–24   Teucer of Salamis is the "Telamonian Teucer" of *Odes* 1.7.20–32 and note.

24–26   Sthénelus was Diomédes' charioteer and co-leader of the men of Argos. (*Iliad* 2. 563–4; 5, 108 ff.)

27   Meríones was the heroic charioteer of Idomonéus of Crete, as in *Odes* 1.6.14 and note.

27–29   Diomédes (in the text *Týdides,* i.e., son of Týdeus). In *Iliad* 4. 405, Sthénelus, speaking about himself and Diomédes, says to Agamemnon:

> We two claim we are better men by far than our fathers.

32   In the "perfumed bedchamber" episode of the *Iliad* Helen says bitterly to Paris (430–1):

> There was a time before now you boasted that you were better
> than warlike Menelaos, in spear and hand and your own strength.
>
> (Lattimore translation)

33–36   Nereus foreknows the fall of Troy, which is not told in the *Iliad.*

Ancient commentator Porphyrio says that Ode 15 was modelled on a (lost) poem of Bacchýlides in which Cassandra prophesied the disasters of the Trojan War.

Scholars consider Ode 15 to be one of Horace's early imitation of Greek models: (a) a metrical flaw in line 36 (three short syllables in succession); (b) the repetition of "Ilium"/"Ilian" in the final stanza; (c) the awkward, and apparently invented, device of having Nereus stop the ship on the high seas in order to deliver his prophecy.

1.16. *O matre pulchra filia pulchrior,*

Meter: Alcaic stanza: in lines 1 and 2:   U _ U _ > _ U U _ U _
               in line 3:   U _ U _ U _ U _ U
               in line 4:   _ U U _ U U _ U _ U

O daughter yet more beautiful than your own
  Fair mother: on those nasty iambics of mine
    Inflict what penalty you will; go
      Burn them or drown them in Adriatic.

The Pytho-dweller never so addles thoughts   5
  Of sanctuary priestesses; neither does
    Dindýmenē, or Liber; nor do
      Corybants' ear-splitting cymbals shatter

Our calm of mind, so much as a fit of rage,
  Which is not fazed by Nórican swords, nor all-   10
    Consuming fire, nor wrecking seas, nor
      Jupiter's self in convulsive uproar.

They say Prometheus, shaping mankind from clay
  And forced to borrow random component parts
    From other creatures, put the lion's   15
      Frenzy of temper inside our bosoms.

From wrath Thyéstes' ghastly undoing came,
  And in the final count it was wrath by which
    Great cities suffered total wreck and
      Over their ruins of walls and towers   20

The hateful plow of insolent foes was drawn.
  Subdue your anger! Back in my tender youth
    My heart endured its fevers also,
      Rushing in fury to write iambics

Of rapid movement; now it is kindly words   25
  I wish to speak, and not those abusive ones,
    — Provided this retraction makes us
      Friends and restores me to your good graces.

2   The term "iambics," both as a meter and in the extended sense of "a poem of abuse," is
   explained in the introduction to the *Epodes,* p. 96 above.
5–21 With elaborate indirectness Horace says that a fit of rage upsets one's mind worse
   than an oracle's frenzy, a religious orgy, or drunken madness (5–8); rage is not daunted
   by swords, fire, stormy seas, or tempest (9–12); Prometheus, when creating human
   beings, put the lion's temper in them ((13–16); rage was the cause of the hideous things
   that befell Thyéstes (17), and rage has caused the destruction of cities (18–21).
5–6 Apollo dwelt at Delphi, formerly called Pytho; his priestess delivered his oracles while
   in a state of frenzy inspired by him.

7   Dindýmenē, or, the Lady of Mount Dindymus in Phrygia (west-central Turkey), was also known as Cybelē, Rhea, and *Magna Mater* (the Great Mother). Her orgiastic worship was introduced into Rome in 204 B.C. from its original shrine at Pessinus, near Mount Dindymus. The complex circumstances of this action are explained by F. Cumont in *Oriental Religions in Roman Paganism,* New York: Dover Publications, 1956; pp. 46 ff.

7   (Father) Liber = Bacchus/Dionysus.

7–9   Corybants were the priests of "Dindýmenē" who danced themselves to a frenzy, slashing their own bodies with knives, and sometimes castrating themselves as they danced. See the note on "Berecynthian horns" in *Odes* 1.18.14, the note on "Berecynthian flutes" in 3.19.19; also 4.1.22–24.

10   "Norican" (a decorative adjective) means "from Nóricum" (approximately modern Austria), famous for its iron.

13–16   The creation of human beings from clay is mentioned by Ovid (*Metamorphoses* 1. 78–88), by Pausanias (10.4.3), and by other late writers, but not by Hesiod's *Theogony* (before 600 B.C.). See also Goethe's drama fragment of 1773, called *Prometheus,* which includes the famous ode of the same title.

   The inclusion of "the lion's temper" seems to be Horace's invention.

17   Two sons of Thyéstes were murdered by their uncle, Atreus, who served their flesh as food for their father's dinner.

   Horace's friend, Lucius Varius Rufus (see the note to *Odes* 1.6.2.), presented his tragic drama *Thyestes* in 29 B.C. Possibly that (lost) work was fresh in Horace's mind when the present ode was composed.

18–21   The obliteration of Carthage by the victorious Romans in 146 B.C. must have been in Horace's mind, though Moore suggests the wrathful curse of Oedipus upon Thebes.

Ancient commentator Acro stated that Ode 16 "imitated Stesíchorus" (a Sicilian-Greek lyric poet of ca. 640 to ca. 555 B.C).

Ode 16 is a palinode (like Epode 17), that is, a poem of mock recantation. In the 26 (or 28) books of poems by Stesíchorus, of which only tiny fragments survive, there may well have been *a* palinode, if not a particular palinode, which served as Horace's model.

1.17.   *Velox amoenum saepe Lucretilem*

Meter: Alcaic stanza: in lines 1 and 2: $\cup\,\_\,\cup\,\_\,>\,\_\,\cup\,\cup\,\_\,\cup\,\_$
                         in line 3: $\cup\,\_\,\cup\,\_\,\cup\,\_\,\cup\,\_\,\cup$
                         in line 4: $\_\,\cup\,\cup\,\_\,\cup\,\cup\,\_\,\cup\,\_\,\cup$

Swift Faunus often leaves his Lycáean height
For glades of gracious Mount Lucretílis, where
    He always shields my goats from fiery
        Heat of the summer and gusting rainstorms.

5   My placid nannies, brides of the smelly buck,
    Seek out the fruits of strawberry trees and crop
        Wild thyme while straying through the woodlands,
            Nor do my kidlets have cause for fearing

    Green vipers or the warrior clan of wolves,
10   My Týndaris, as long as his dulcet pipes

Are heard along the smooth-worn rocks on
Ústica's slope and along the valleys.

The gods protect me, holding my reverence dear
And my poetic muse. And on you the horn
    Of brimming plenty here shall lavish   15
        Uttermost fullness of rural riches;

Remote within this valley, you will escape
The Dog Star's heat and sing to the Teian lyre
    About Penélopē and wave-bright
        Circē at strife over one man's favor;   20

And here beneath the shade you shall drink full cups
Of wine of Lesbos, all without ill effects:
    No ecstasies of Bacchus starting
        Quarrels, and free from the fear that hasty,

Mistrustful Cyrus, — hardly a match for you —   25
May yet burst in with violent hands to grab
    The garland from your hair and rip your
        Innocent party garb off your shoulders.

1   Horace assumes the exact identity of Faunus, the old Italian god of agriculture and of cattle (see the note to *Odes* 1.4.11.), with the Greek god Pan. The latter had his native shrine in SW Arcadia, on Mount Lycáeus (Greek *Lykaîon*, from *Lýkos*, "wolf"; see Pausanias 8. 37–38).

2   Mount Lucretílis, now Colle Rotondo, is a spur of Monte Gennaro and the highest elevation to the W of Horace's Sabine farm; it overlooks the lower Tiber valley. This, and other identifications relative ot the present ode, are taken from E.K. Rand, *A Walk to Horace's Farm*, Cambridge, Mass., 1930; see p. 32.

      Of two sites, both identified as that of Horace's villa, Rand prefers "site A," at 384 meters elevation, about a mile from "site B," at 650 meters elevation.

6   The (wild) strawberry tree (*arbutus*) is an evergreen described in the note to *Odes* 1.1.21.

8   "Kidlets" — *haediliae* (from *haedus*, "goat"), a word apparently coined by Horace and occurring only here.

10 The feminine name Týndaris would ordinarily mean "daughter of Týndarus"; in a different context it might be a paraphrase for Helen (of Troy). (In *Odes* 4.8.31 *Tyndaridae* means "Castor and Pollux," the brothers of Helen.)

12 Ancient editor Porphyrio says merely that Ústica was one of the Sabine mountains. Rand (p. 34) interprets the name as "sun-burnt" and identifies it as the rounded hill, consisting chiefly of bare rocks amid sparse vegetation, diagonally across the stream of the Digentia (now the Licenza) from the Colle Rotondo that Horace calls Lucretílis. Thus, as Faunus played his pipes on Lucretílis, the sounds would drift *across* the poet's villa to Ústica.

      The "dulcet pipes" of Faunus/Pan are the soft summer-sounds of nature imagined as tones of the Panspipes (or syrinx); the tones are an enchantment against harm. Alternately, the tones are produced by an actual but unseen goat-herd whom the poet is pleased to identify with Faunus/Pan.

19 The Dog Star (*Canícula*) is Sírius (Greek *Seírios*, "scorching"), which rises and sets with the sun during the "dog days" of July and August.

      "The Teian lyre" means song in the light and graceful manner of Anácreon of

Teos (Teus), on the coast of Lydia (now west-central Turkey). For Anácreon see the note to *Odes* 4.9.9.

20–21   Týndaris will not recite the *Odyssey*, but will sing (and possibly invent) lyric songs about faithful wife Penélopē and sorceress Circē vying for the affections of Odysseus/Ulysses.

21–22   Here one may recall "A Jug of Wine, a Loaf of Bread — and Thou/Beside me singing in the Wilderness," but Horace's resemblance to Omar Khayyám (or Edward FitzGerald) is commonly exaggerated.

23–25   ". . . all . . . Quarrels" paraphrases "nor will Semélius Thyóneus start up battles with Mars." The mother of Bacchus/Dionysus was Semelē, who was sometimes called Thyónē, from Greek *thýō*, "to rush (in wild excitement)."

1.18   *Nullam, Vare, sacra vite prius severis arborem*

Meter: $\_ \cup \_ \cup \cup \_ \quad \_ \cup \cup \_ \quad \_ \cup \cup \_ \cup \_$

Set out, Varus, no tree,   set out no shrub,   other than holy grape
There in Tibur's rich soil   outside the walls   Cátilus founded long,
Long ago. For a god   seems to have wished   all of life's miseries
On teetotalers; no   other relief   is there for nagging cares.
5   Who talks soldiering woes,   who talks of want,   once he has had his wine,
Failing, Bacchus, to praise   you, and to praise   Venus the fair as well?
But the brawl to the death   fought by the wild   Centaurs and Lapiths once
Over wine is a stern   warning against   making too free with gifts
Liber grants us, and so   too is the god's   fierceness of hand in Thrace,
10   When, from greed, right and wrong   come to be judged   only by appetite's
Narrow will. Nor shall I,   fair Bassaréus,   rouse your reluctant might,
Nor go telling what things   lie under leaves   inside the baskets which
Your initiates see.   Silence your mad   drums and your frenzied horns
Berecýnthian then: they but incite   blind love of self, inane
15   Boasts and touting of things   lacking all sense   up to the very skies,
And a trust that reveals   secrets contained,   clearer than glass itself.

Ode 1.18. probably imitates a poem of Alcaeus, of which we have one line preserved:

Plant no other tree rather than the grapevine . . .

1   For the identity of the Varus here addressed see the note to *Odes* 1.24.5. He is not to be confused with the Lucius Varius Rufus of *Odes* 1.6.2.

2   Tibur (now Tívoli) was said to have been founded (*Odes* 2.6.5 "Tibur, which the exile from Argos founded") by three brothers: Tibúrnus, for whom the town was named (see the note to *Odes* 1.7.13.), Coras (whom Horace nowhere mentions), and Catíllus, whose name passed to the *Mons Catíllus*, (now Monte Catillo), just E of the town. For metrical reasons "Catíllus" (long-long-short) here becomes "Cátilus" (long-short-long).

7–8   Robert Graves (*The Greek Myths* 102) sees the Centaurs and Lapiths as primitive mountain tribes to the north of Greece, remembered in legend as traditional enemies of the Greeks and of each other. When both groups were at a wedding feast, the rustic Centaurs got drunk on the unfamiliar wine and began an orgy which turned into a ferocious battle with the Lapiths. The metopes of the Parthenon depict this battle.

9   "... the god's fierceness of hand in Thrace" paraphrases "Euhius not gentle with the Sithonians." "Euhius" is the personified cry of the bacchanals, in Greek *euoi!*, in Latin (and English) *evoé*! For resisting the advance of Dionysus-worship, the Thracian king Lycurgus (like Pentheus of Thebes) was torn to pieces and his land made barren. The story is alluded to in *Iliad* 6. 130–140.

11   "Bassaréus" is still another name for Bacchus, from Greek *bassára*, said to have been the Thracian word for "fox"; bacchanals were also sometimes called "foxes."

      "Fair" (*candide*) means "youthfully beautiful." Bacchus was frequently portrayed as a youth beautiful almost to effeminacy.

12–13 In the rituals of various divinities "secret" cult objects were presented, in baskets or in chests, to be "handled" by the worshippers. The objects were often nestled in grape leaves, ivy leaves, or the like. The celebrant was forbidden to say what the objects were, but see Jane Harrison, *Prolegomena* . . . , pp. 157–8. (In the 26th Idyll of Theócritus the objects are merely specially baked cakes.)

      The words "inside the baskets which/ Your initiates see" are supplied by the translator, since Horace is deliberately mysterious and discreetly stops with the word "leaves."

      The cult objects of Juno in S.1.3.10–11 were such baskets, and the slave Hydáspes in S.2.8.13–15 walks balancing the wine jar on his head as if he were carrying such baskets.

14   "Berecýnthian horns" (named for Mount Berecýnthus) summoned to "Asiatic" frenzy and orgy in the rites of "the Great Mother," who is called Dindýmenē in *Odes* 1.16.7.

1.19. *Mater saeva cupidinum*

Meter: in the odd-numbered lines: _ U _ U U _ U _
        in the even-numbered lines: _ U _ U U _ _ U U _ U _

Savage mother of Cupids all,
      Theban Semelē's boy,   wantoning Unrestraint,
All together command me thus:
      Into love believed dead   breathe a restoring breath!
I for Glýcera's beauty burn,   5
      Beauty whiter than pure   Parian marble's sheen;
Dainty impudence feeds that fire,
      And a face that is too   dazzling to look upon.
Venus, rushing at me full force,
      Leaves all Cyprus behind,   bans me all song of Scyths   10
Or of Parthians' rearward darts
      Shot while shamming retreat, —   bans even neutral themes.
Bring me sods, boys, of living turf,
      Build an altar with green   branches bedecked, and fetch
Incense, saucer, and two-year wine: 15
      After sacrifice done   she may abate her force.

1   In Hellenistic and Roman poetry "Cupids" (Desires) are often plural.

2 Semelē, princess of Thebes, was the mother of Dionysus/Bacchus; as her "boy" (*puer*) he is mischievous, like the Cupids. "Unrestraint" = *Licentia* (self-permissiveness).

5 The name "Glýcera" depends on Greek *glykerós*, "sweet." Conceivably, *this* Glýcera could be identical with the one in *Odes* 1.30 and even with the one in *Odes* 3.19. The one in *Odes* 1.33 is presumably distinct. The reader will do best to imagine all four separately, like the various Chloēs, and so forth.

6 "Shining whiter than Parian stone" is Lattimore's version of a phrase in Pindar's 4th Neméan ode, line 81, though it refers to the splendor of a *poem*. Some of the finest Greek marble came from the island of Paros, just S of Delos. Ancient marble in public places was meant to dazzle; under the noon sun even whitewashed walls make tourists resort to dark glasses in our own time.

10 The primary "residence" of Aphroditē/Venus was at Paphus, on the SW coast of the island of Cyprus, as in the note to *Odes* 1.3.1. Here, the goddess comes rushing from Cyprus to harry the poet.

10-11 For Scyths and Parthians, see under "Foreign Nations," p. 397. Horace will mention this Parthian cavalry maneuver several times.

13-15 "Boys" means "slaves," without reference to age, as usual.

Altars of turf would be rustic, archaic, and built for a single occasion. The scene, by implication, is at the Sabine farm.

"Green branches" = *verbanas*, as in *Odes* 4.11.6-7; the term meant fresh greenery from almost any plant used to deck an altar. English "verbena" and its derivative "vervain" now bear specialized botanical meanings.

The "saucer" (*patera*) is for ritual pouring out of the sacrificial wine, *merum*, that is, wine undiluted with water.

1.20.   *Vile potabis modicis Sabinum*

Meter: Sapphic stanza: in lines 1, 2, and 3:   _ U _ > _ U U _ U _ U
                     in line 4:   _ U U _ U

> Common Sabine served in my homely goblets
> You shall have to drink; in a jar from Greece I
> Sealed it up myself in the very year when
>   You were applauded,
>
> 5 Dear Maecenas, Knight, in the theater
> So that from your ancestors' River jolly
> Echo bore the tribute redoubled, and from
>   Mount Vaticanus.
>
> Grape of Cáecubum or the Cálēs presses
> 10 You may drink at home: but Falérnian vineyards
> Do not flavor *my* cups, nor vine-clad slopes of
>   Formiae either.

1-3 "Common Sabine," the lightest of the ancient Italian wines, would take on some aroma of high-quality Greek wine by being stored in the imported container. S.1.10.24

speaks of flavoring "Falernian wine with a tinge of the Chían," that is, from the Greek island of Chios. The practice is recommended by Columella in his treatise *De Re rustica*, ca. 65 A.D. E.1.2.69 says: "Earliest use of the wine jar imparts the bouquet that is longest/ Lasting."

3–8   In 30 B.C., after a severe illness, Maecenas had been given an ovation at his first public appearance, at the theater.

Maecenas held the rank of Knight (*eques*) and declined promotion to the higher senatorial rank.

Rome's only stone theater at this time was the Theater of Pompey, built in 55–52 B.C. for 12,000 spectators, in the Campus Martius (the Field of Mars, as in *Odes* 1.8.4. and note) a few hundred feet W of the Pantheon. For two centuries dramas had been presented, at certain annual festivals, on temporary wooden stages which were also set up in the Campus Martius.

The Tiber, in S.2.2.33, is "the Tuscan (i.e., Etruscan) River" of Maecenas's Etruscan ancestors, but it was the traditional eastern boundary of Etruscan territory, not *in* that territory. The *Mons Vaticanus* ("Seer's Hill") was due W across the Tiber.

9–12   Four of the very best Italian wine areas, all just NW of Capua.

1.21.   *Dianam tenerae dicite vigines*

Meter: in lines 1 and 2:   _ U _ U U _ _ U U _ U _
                  in line 3:   _ U _ U U _ _
                  in line 4:   _ U _ U U _ U _

Raise your hymn, tender girls,   sing of Diana now,
Hymn the Cynthian, lads,   god of the unshorn locks,
    Sing Latóna as well, most
        Deeply loved by the heart of Jove.

Tell her fondness for streams,   girls, and for woodland boughs   5
Such as spread above cold   Algidus ridge, above
    Forest-dark Erymánthus
        Or Mount Gragus of lighter green;

No less praised be the fair   Valley of Tempē, lads,
Praised be Delos no less,   place of Apollo's birth,   10
    Quiver-shouldered and famed god,
        Famed as well for his brother's lyre.

Dismal warfare and bleak   famine and plague he will
Send, on hearing your plea,   far from our people, far
    Too from Caesar, our prime lord,   15
        Off where Persians and Britons dwell.

The bad harvest of 24 B.C., a serious illness of Augustus in 24–23, and other adverse events led to plans for a public ceremony of entreaty to Apollo—Augustus's patron deity since the battle of Actium (see the note to *Odes* 1.2.31–32)—and to Diana to avert further harm, but for reasons unknown the planned rites were abandoned. Ode 21 seems to have been composed for the ceremony that did not take place.

1–4   Apollo, son of Zeus/Jupiter by Latóna (Greek: Leto), was called "the Cynthian" (*Cynthius*) from his birth on the north side of low Mount Cynthus on the island of Delos. His twin sister, Diana/Artemis, though she was born shortly before and not on the island of Delos, was nevertheless called "Cynthia," "the Cynthian," "Delia," and "the Delian."

       Tradition had it that Apollo was *intonsus*, "with hair never cut," but classical statuary (e.g., the Apollo Belvedere) sometimes temporized in this matter.

5–8   Pindar's 2nd Pythian ode, line 6, calls the goddess "river-Artemis."

       The great Roman shrine to Diana-of-the-woods was on the Álgidus ridge ("Algidus" itself means "cold") of the Alban Hills which begin some 25 km/15 m SE of Rome. See the opening pages of Frazer's *The Golden Bough*. *Odes* 3.23.9. calls the ridge "snowy," and goes on to speak of the woods and pastures there, where animals were specially raised by the priests for use in sacrifices. See also *Odes* 4.4.57–60, *Centennial Hymn* 69, and *Odes* 4.1.19–28

       Odyssey 6.102 names Mount Erymánthus (in the northern Peloponnesus) as a favorite hunting area of Artemis/Diana.

       Mount Gragus (or Cragus) in Lycia (SW Turkey) was sacred to Latóna/Leto.

9   For the famous "Vale of Tempē," at the foot of Mount Olympus in N Greece, see the note to *Odes* 1.7.4. Apollo's particular association with Tempē is obscure.

12   Hermes/Mercury, "first founder of song and lyre-shell" (*Odes* 1.10.6.), made a gift of his newly invented lyre to his half-brother, Apollo, as explained in the note to that line. Hermes was the son of Zeus by the nymph Maia; Apollo was Zeus's son by Latona.

13   "Famine and plague" translate the Greek formula: *limòs kaì loimós*.

16   "Persians" (*Persas*) = "Parthians," as often; see under "Foreign Nations," p. 397. The "Persians" lived outside the Roman empire to the east, the Britons outside the empire to the west. (Julius Caesar conducted raids into Britain in 55 and 54 B.C., but the conquest of the island was not undertaken until 43 A.D., under the emperor Claudius.)

Ode 21 should be compared with *Odes* 4.6. and with the *Centennial Hymn*. There are also unexpected parallels with Poem 34 of Catullus, *Dianae sumus in fide*, composed a generation earlier.

1.22.   *Integer vitae scelerisque purus*

Meter: Sapphic stanza: in lines 1, 2, and 3: $\_ \cup \_ > \_ \cup \cup \_ \cup \_ \cup$
                         in line 4: $\_ \cup \cup \_ \cup$

One whose life is clean and by crimes unblemished
Needs no Moorish javelins, needs no bow and
Load of poisoned arrows to carry, Fuscus,
     Crammed in his quiver,

5   Travel though he may over burning sands of
Syrtes, or through Caucasus ever savage,
Or to regions washed by the far and fabled
     River Hydáspes.

For, as I was strolling about the Sabine
10   Woods beyond my property's edge, no worries

On my mind, and singing of Lálagē, a
    Wolf, when he saw me,

Fled, though I was weaponless, — such a monster
As the oaken forests of warlike Daunia
Never bred, or African Juba's kingdom,   15
    Dry nurse of lions.

Put me down in tracts of the bleakest fields where
Not a single tree is refreshed by summer
Breezes, — wastelands muffled in mists, and sullen
    Jupiter glowering;   20

Put me down too close to the sun-god's flaming
Wheels, in lands prohibiting habitation:
I shall still love Lálagē sweetly laughing,
    Prattling so sweetly.

2   "Moorish" is a "decorative" adjective.

3   Aristius Fuscus was the friend who chose not to rescue Horace from the bore in S.1.9. 61–74; he was cited for his literary taste in S.1.10.82; and in E.1.10, which is addressed to him, lines 1–3 say he and Horace are almost twins, save that Fuscus likes city life while Horace prefers the country.

5–8   Here, *Syrtes* means Saharan sands. (In Epode 9, 32 they were "The sandbanks that the southwind churns" in shallow waters E of Tunisia and N of Libya, as they are also in *Aeneid* 1. 102 ff. and Acts of the Apostles 27:17.)

    The Caucasus Mountains, between the Black and Caspian Seas and higher than the Alps, lay outside Roman control, though "Greater Armenia" had been a Roman protectorate since 63 B.C. But Horace may be referring to the Hindu Kush, which, as Arrian explains (*Anabasis of Alexander* 5. iii), was renamed the Caucasus so Alexander could claim to have gone over Caucasus.

    The Hydáspes, now the Jhelum, is a tributary of the Indus, in N Pakistan; Alexander defeated Hindu King Porus on its further shore in 326 B.C. Compare the slave named Hydáspes, "a dusky/Hindu" in S.2.10.13–14.

11   "Lálagē" is coined from Greek *lalagéō*, "to prattle, babble," or, of birds, "to chirp."

12–13   A real wolf was entirely possible.

14   "Daunia" = Horace's native Apulia, so called from a legendary King Daunus (*Odes* 3.30.11. and 4.14.25), whom Vergil makes the father of Aeneas's opponent, Turnus.

15   The boy-Prince Juba was brought up in Rome under the emperor's protection, married to Cleopratra Selēnē ("the Moon"), daughter of Antony and Cleopatra, and in 25 B.C. established as Rome's puppet-king in his native Maurentania (Morrocco and NW and N-central Algeria); his capital was Iol, later called Caesarea, and in more recent times Cherchell, some 110 km/70 m W of Algiers on the coast. In his long reign, 25 B.C. to 23 A.D., King Juba II of Mauretania wrote numerous scholarly books, all of which are lost. His son, Ptolemy, ruled from 23 to 40 A.D., when he was murdered at the orders of the emperor Caligula (Suetonius: Life of Gaius Caligula, 35).

    Allusion to him here would have been most natural in 25–24 B.C., when he was "in the news."

In this light poem lines 1–8 are tongue-in-cheek, but that fact has not prevented their being taken solemnly. *The Golden Book of Favorite Songs*, 1915, p.23, prints lines 1–8 in Latin and in an English translation to be sung as a hymn to the tune of *Praise for Peace*, which appears on the same page: "Using the Latin words, the song is a very effective number for male voices."

1.23. *Vitas inuleo me similis, Chloe*

Meter: in lines 1 and 2: $\_ \cup \_ \cup \cup \_ \quad \_ \cup \cup \_ \cup \_$
in line 3: $\_ \cup \_ \cup \cup \_ \_$
in line 4: $\_ \cup \_ \cup \cup \_ \cup \_$

You keep fleeing from me,   Chloē, the way a lost
Fawn darts off to the wilds   seeking his timid dam
    Scared for nothing at each slight
        Breath of air in the forest trees;

5   If the coming of spring   rustles the leaves for one
Instant, or if the green   lizards go whisking through
    Tangled briars, he stops dead,
        Terror-stricken in heart and knees.

I protest I am no   ravening tiger, no
10   Lion stalking your path,   bent on devouring you;
    Trail your mother no more, time:
        Suits you now to receive a mate.

Ode 23 probably imitates a lost poem of Anácreon (ca. 572 to ca. 488 B.C.), the preserved fragment of which Moore translates as:

Gently as a new-born fawn unweaned, which quivers from terror when left in the wood by its antlered mother. . . .

1   "Chloē" = Greek *khloē*, "a tender shoot of a plant; a new blade of grass; early leaves."
    Three more Chloēs, all distinct from each other, will be named in *Odes* 3.7., 3.9., and 3.26.
10   The text specifies "Gaetulian lion," the Gaetulians being inhabitants of ancient Morocco.

1.24. *Quis desiderio sit pudor aut modus*

Meter: in lines 1, 2, and 3: $\_ > \_ \cup \cup \_ \quad \_ \cup \cup \_ \cup \_$
in line 4: $\_ > \_ \cup \cup \_ \cup \_$

Could shy reticence set   limits to grief for so
Fondly cherished a head?   Teach me your saddest strains,
Muse Melpómenē, whom   All-father blessed with pure
    Voice along with the lyre he gave.

5   So Quintílius lies   lost in eternal sleep:
When will modest Restraint,   when will unsullied Trust
(Which is Justice's twin),   when, too, will naked Truth
    Find his equal or like again?

Mourned by many good men,   he now has passed to death,
But by none to be mourned,   Vergil, as you shall mourn;   10
Where you wished him the gods'   keeping — but not like this! —
    You implore his return in vain.

Say you drew from the lyre   lovelier tones than did
Thracian Orpheus when trees   harkened to hear him play
Would blood surge once again   into the hollow ghost   15
    Now by Mercury's dreaded wand

Forced to huddle along   gathered with somber flocks
Whence no plea for return   ever is granted ear?
Hard it is: yet a thing   not to be changed becomes,
    By acceptance, less hard to bear.   20

3   Melpómenē, "Songstress," from Greek *mélos*, "melody," and *mélpein*, "to sing," is probably not specifically the Muse of Tragedy but simply one of the nine Muses.
4   For 24 B.C. Saint Jerome's Chronology (ca. 400 A.D.) lists: "Quintilius of Cremona, close friend (*familiaris*) of Vergil and Horace, died." He is the (Quintilius) Varus of *Odes* 1.18.1., who was bidden to plan only grapevines at Tibur; E.2.3.438–441 will cite him posthumously as an astute critic of poetry.
13 For Orpheus's enchantment of the trees see *Odes* 1.12.7–12 and note.
15–18 See *Odes* 1.10.17–19 for Mercury as soul-sender herding the dead with his *rhabdos*.

1.25. *Parcius iunctas quatiunt fenestras*

Meter: Sapphic stanza: in lines 1, 2, and 3:   _ U _ > _ U U _ U _ U
                    in line 4:   _ U U _ U

Lively lads less often besiege your bolted
Windows now with fistfuls of high-flung pebbles,
Rob you less of sleep, and the entrance door finds
    Rest on its threshold,

Where before it readily swung upon its   5
Hinges; less and less do you hear them calling:
"Must I perish, Lydia, through the nights while
    You go on sleeping?"

Now, old crone, it's *your* turn to sit alone on
Back stairs, grieved by lovers that will not take you,   10
Raising louder rumpus than Thracian gales that
    Bluster at new-moon

While a searing lust and tormenting passion
Such as drives a mother of horses frantic
Rages through your heart where the love-wounds fester,   15
    Railing for spite that

> All the lusty partners-in-bed delight in
> Gloss of verdant ivy and dusky myrtle, —
> Withered boughs consigning to fellowship with
> 20   Winds of the winter.

2   Not glass windows but apertures closed by shutters; a crossbar "locked" the shutters.
14   That is, Lydia craves a stallionlike partner.

1.26   *Musis amicus tristitiam et metus*

Meter: Alcaic stanza: in lines 1 and 2:   U _ U _ > _ U U _ U _
            in line 3:   U _ U _ U _ U _ U
            in line 4:   _ U U _ U U _ U _ U

> In favor with the Muses, I give my gloom
> And fears for saucy winds to disperse across
>   The Sea of Crete, without a thought for
>   Kings that by terror may rule cold northlands,
>
> 5   Or what it is that scares Tiridátes so.
> O you who most delight in a fountain-source
>   Untainted, weave a garland for my
>   Lamia, weave it of sunny flowers,
>
> O sweet Pimpléa. Praises of mine avail
> 10   But little. Celebration of him in new
>   Poetic forms and Lesbic tones is
>   Seemly in you and your sister Muses.

Worried as I am about a possible Dacian invasion and about the turmoil in Iran, I shall nevertheless write a poem of congratulations to young Lucius Aelius Lamia, —using a new poetic form.

4–5   These two political allusions suggest a compositional date of 30–29 B.C. for Ode 26: (a) Cotiso, King of the Dacians and a supporter of Mark Antony, threatened to invade westward prior to the battle of Actium (September 2, 31 B.C.). He was defeated in campaigns of 30–28 B.C., but Dacia—now Rumania Transylvania—was not subdued until the Emperor Trajan's campaigns of 101–6 A.D. "Cold northlands" (*sub Arcto!*) betray a geographical naiveté.

After the disaster had been averted, *Odes* 3.6.14 will speak of how Rome "was brought to ruin's brink by the Dacian," and *Odes* 3.8.18 will mention how "Hosts of Dacian Cootiso have been scattered."

(b) In 31 B.C. Tiridates, the Parthian sub-king of Media (NW Iran) and ally since 36 B.C. of Mark Antony, drove his overlord, Parthian King Phraátes IV, into exile among the nomad Sakas (Scythians of Asia) E of the Caspian sea. With Saka support, Phraátes regained his throne, whereupon Tiridates fled as a suppliant to Octavius Caesar, who, at that point, was in Egypt; this was in the months following the suicides of Antony and Cleopatra on approximately August 1, 30 B.C..

Tiridates fled to Augustus a second time in 26 B.C.; see "Parthia" under "Foreign Nations," p. 397.

6–9 Horace begs inspiration from the Muse of the Pimpléan spring, near Mount Olympus, in making a "garland of praises" for young Lucius Aelius Lamia.

Odes 3.17 will jocularly address Lamia, and Odes 1.36.1–10 will imply that his age, as of that poem, is a few years more than 17 (when the toga of manhood was customarily adopted). He was consul in 3 A.D., city prefect (mayor) in 32 A.D., and died in 33 A. D., sixty-three years after the present poem—assuming 30 B.C. as the compositional date.

Under the date of 33 A.D. the Annals (6.27) of Tacitus says: "The last days of the year witnessed the death and State funeral of Lucius Aelius Lamia, who, finally released from his fictitious imperial governorship of Syria, had become City Prefect. Nobly born, vigorous in old age, he had gained prestige by not being allowed to take up his governorship." (Michael Grant translation, in Penguin Classics) Similar praise is given by the historian Velleius Paterculus (ca. 30 A. D.): "a man of the most ancient morals, and always tempering his olden severity with humanity" (2.116.3).

The occasion for Ode 26 is unknown; perhaps it was a coming-of-age celebration: see the note to Odes 1.36.3. The youth's father, of the same name, was a friend of Cicero's and in 43 B.C. held the office of praetor (judge). Horace himself was thirty-five years old in 30 B.C.

10–12 The words "new/Poetic forms and Lesbic tones" paraphase "with new lyres and with Lesbic plectrum," meaning the use of the stanza form of Alcáeus (Alkaios), whose home was the island of Lesbos. It has been inferred that Ode 26 is an early experiment in the Alcaic stanza form. The Muse's delight "in a fountain-source/Untainted" (line 9) would imply the same. Such early experimentation would also fit well with a compositional date of 30 B.C.

1.27. *Natis in usum laetitiae scyphis*

Meter: Alcaic stanza: in lines 1 and 2:   ∪ _ ∪ _ _ > _ ∪ ∪ _ ∪ _
                                 in line 3:   ∪ _ ∪ _ ∪ _ ∪ _ ∪ _ ∪
                                 in line 4:   _ ∪ ∪ _ ∪ ∪ _ ∪ _ ∪

      The Thracians, over cups that were meant for joy,
      Start brawls: let those barbarian ways be banned!
            Let us observe a seemly Bacchus
                  Here by desisting from strife with bloodshed.

      With wine and lamplight Median saber blades   5
      Are monstrously ill-suited: so quiet this
            Unholy din and uproar, comrades;
                  All of you keep to your dining couches!

      You say you want me with you to drink my share
      Of strongest-grade Falernian? Let me ask   10
            Megilla's brother, then, to say whose
                  Arrow has dealt him a wound so blissful.

      His courage fails him? These are my only terms
      To get me back to drinking. "No matter what
            Amour possesses you, it is no   15
                  Passion to blush for; your weakness always

Preferred the free-born. Be it whoever, come!,
My ears can hold a secret." — Alas, poor lad!
What effort spent for *that* Charýbdis;
20   You are deserving of something better!

What witch can save you now? or what mage with spells
And philter-brews of Thessaly? or what god?
Not even Pégasus could save you
Now from this three-shape Chiméra's tangles.

Ancient editor Porphyrio says that Ode 27 imitates a poem by Anácreon (see the note to
Epode 14, 9–12), probably the poem from which Athenáeus, around 200 A.D., quotes five
lines; Moore translates:

Come, now, let us no longer with din and shout practice Scythian drinking
at our wine, but sip it while we blithely sing. . . .

5   "Saber blades" = *acinaces*, said to be a Persian word for "short swords." (Did Horace
find the Greek form *akīnákés* in Anácreon's poem?)
10   Pliny's *Natural History* 14.8.6. (before 79 A.D.) distinguishes "strong," "sweet," and
"light" Falernain wines.
11   Megilla is unknown. The text calls her "Opuntian," that is, from Opūs, a town in
E-central Greece mentioned casually by Thucýdides (2.32) and as "Opoeis" or "Opous"
in *Iliad* 2.531. (*Odes* 3.9.14. Offers a parallel phrase: "Ornýtus's son, Thurian Cálaïs.")
Perhaps Megilla's *brother*, who is present at this drinking party (*comissatio*), takes his
distinction from his sister's beauty.
14–18   The words "No matter. . . hold a secret" are whispered by Horace, who has either
walked around to "Megilla's brother" or perhaps reoccupied his own dining couch next
to him.
18–24   The dash indicates Horace's withdrawal, and all the rest is best taken as his unspo-
ken thoughts.
19   "Charýbdis," the ship-engulfing whirlpool of *Odyssey* 12, acquired the meaning of
"any insatiably greedy person."
22   The north-Greek area of Thessaly was, by tradition, the land of witches, spells, and
magic portions.
23–24   The Chiméra (Greek *Khímaira*), according to both *Iliad* 6.181 and Lucretius's *On the
Nature of Things* 5.905, was a monster "lion-fronted and snake behind, a goat in the
middle." The hero Bellerophon flew through the air on the winged horse Pégasus in
order to slay the Chiméra from above. See the notes to *Odes* 4.2.15–16 and 4.11.26–28.

1.28   *Te maris et terrae numeroque carentis harenae*

Meter:
in the odd-numbered lines: $\_$ U U $\_$ U U $\_$ U U $\_$ U U $\_$ U U $\_$ U
in the even-numbered lines: $\_$ U U $\_$ U U $\_$ U U $\_$ U

On the Adriatic coast, some 90 km/60 m NE of Horace's native town of Venusia, the ghost of
a drowned man washed ashore addresses the grave of the scientist-philosopher Archýtas
(lines 1–22) and then (lines 23–36) begs a passing sailor to perform the ritual act of burial by
casting three handfuls of earth upon his unburied corpse.

You, who had measured the sea and the earth, who had reckoned the sum of
    Grains in the sands without number, Archýtas,
Now are retained by a tiny allotment of dust on this Matine
    Shore, nor is any advantage now yours for
Having made bold to explore with your mind the expanses of sky and   5
    Houses of heaven, though destined to perish.
Equally dead is the father of Pelops, the guest of the gods, and
    So is Tithónus who dwindled to whispers,
Likewise great Minos who shared in the secrets of Jove; and the realm of
    Death holds Euphórbus who twice was compelled to   10
Go there, although by removing his shield from the temple he showed that
    Only his sinews and skin had that first time
Passed to the gloom of the afterlife, — he (you admit) having no slight
    Lore of how nature had ordered the total
Universe. Yet there is one single night for all creatures, and late or   15
    Soon they must follow the path to oblivion.
Some by the Furies are given to staring-eyed Mars for his war-shows;
    Ravening seas bring destruction to sailors;
Funerals jumble the old and the young in confusion together;
    Cruel Prosérpina misses no mortal.   20
My death came likewise from waves of Illýrian seas driven on by
    Southwinds companion to setting Oríon.

Sailor now passing, begrudge not from churlishness some bit of drifting
    Sand to be strewn by your hand on these bones and
Head: for which deed may southeasters, whenever they offer you peril,   25
    Heaping Hesperian billows to drown you,
Wear out their gales on Venúsian forests while you are left safe, and
    May you be equally blessed by the lavish
Bounties of Jove and of Neptune, the patron of sacred Taréntum.
    Will you commit, from indifference, a crime which   30
May work to harm of your innocent children hereafter? It may be
    Duty undone will bring fearful requital
On your own head: my unanswered entreaty shall hound you forever,
    No expiational rite will acquit you.
You are in haste, but the briefest delay will suffice for the triple   35
    Handfuls of dust, then be off on your errand.

The meter is "the Alcmanian strophe," used only here and in Epode 12. The long lines are strictly dactylic—not the "standard" hexameter—but with a specifically short 6th foot; the short lines are likewise dactylic, save for the shortened final foot. One feels that this poem belongs with the *Epodes* rather than among the *Odes*.
1–6 Archýtas of Taréntum (now Táranto), between 400 and 350 B.C., was his city's successful military commander, inventor of the pulley and the screw, discoverer of musical enharmonics, writer on geometrical theory, and the most distinguished mathematician-philosopher of the "school" of Pythágoras; tradition claimed he was a friend of Plato's.

There is no evidence earlier than this poem for Archýtas's having been drowned at sea. Since line 3 indicates a particular spot, we infer that his body was washed ashore and properly buried there, or else that a duly consecrated cenotaph was erected there.

3   "Mátine" (*Matínum*), according to ancient editor Porphyrio, was either a mountain or a promontory of Apulia; the text requires that it be by the edge of the sea; a town of Matinum stood—at some time in classical antiquity—on the south coast of Mount Gargánus (now the Promontorio del Gargano; see the note to *Odes* 2.9.6–8); and in *Odes* 4.2.27–28 Horace whimsically describes his compositional methods as those of a Matine bee (our translation omits that adjective), which presumably means that he came from the area in question. Yet the distinguished German editor Kiessling insists that the place is unidentified but probably in the vicinity of Taréntum. Epode 17,28 speaks of "Matine peaks."

6   "Houses of heaven" (*aerias domos*) are the twelve zodiacal regions of the sky.

7–15 Four illustrious dead men—who are just as dead as if they had never been illustrious at all:

   1. Tántalus, father of Pelops, dined with the gods.
   2. Tithónus, for whom the dawn goddess obtained immortality but not eternal youth, so that he wasted away to a mere voice—some say to a chirping cicada.
   3. "Minos, who from his ninth year talked familiarly with great Zeus." (*Odyssey* 9.178; T. E. Lawrence translation)
   4. Euphórbus, son of Panthus (hence the Panthoides of the text), slew Patroclus at the close of *Iliad* 16 and was himself directly slain by Menelaus, at the opening of *Iliad* 17.

Pythágoras, the historical mathematician-philosopher of the 6th century B.C., believed in the reincarnation of souls and claimed to be himself the reincarnation of Euphórbus; to demonstrate his claim he took possession of the shield of Euphorbus which ever since the Trojan War had hung on the wall of Hera's temple at Argos. Archýtas, as a Pythagorean, would know that Euphorbus died twice, once under the name of Euphorbus and once under the name of Pythágoras.

20 Prosérpina, as queen of the land of death, here is death itself.

21 Illyria, of imprecise boundaries, is now Albania and part of Yugoslavia.

22 The constellation of Oríon sets in the stormy month of November.

26 "Hesperian," from Greek *hespéra*, "west," here means "westward (toward Italy)."

27 The SE wind (*Eurus*), driving NW up the Adriatic, should be deflected toward the wooded ridges near Horace's native Venusia.

29 "They say that the hero Taras was a son of Poseidon by a nymph of the district (of Taréntum), and the city and the river were named after him: city and river both having the same name." Pausanias: *Guide to Greece* 10.10.4., after 150 A.D.; Peter Levi translation, in Penguin Classics, 1971.

Scholars are not agreed on an interpretation of Ode 1.28. Possibly lines 1–22 represent Horace's adaptation of a lost poem by a Greek poet of southern Italy after 350 B.C., and possibly lines 23–36 represent Horace's reworking of a different Greek poem, also lost. We attribute the entire poem to one speaker, but some readers have thought that lines 7–23 are a reply by Archýtas to lines 1–6, ghost answering ghost.

1.29.   *Icci, beatis nunc Arabum invides*

Meter: Alcaic stanza: in lines 1 and 2:   U _ U _ > _ U U _ U _

                     in line 3:   U _ U _ U _ U _ U

                     in line 4:   _ U U _ U U _ U _ U

Are you so greedy, Íccius, for the wealth
Of Araby the Blest as to join campaigns
    Against the yet unconquered kings of
        Saba and gather supplies of chains for

Ferocious Medes? So what Oriental girl   5
With husband slain will act as your serving maid?
    What royal page with perfumed hair will
        Ladle your wine into drinking goblets,

Though Chinese arrows shot with his father's bow
Were all his training? Can it be now denied   10
    That downhill streams can run their courses
        Uphill and Tiber reverse direction,

When you announce your carefully gathered books
Are all for sale — Panáetius's noted works
    The whole Socratic school — to purchase   15
        Armor? You seemed to show better promise.

1–2   In 26 B.C., which must be the date of the present poem, a Roman expedition started on a conquest of "Araby the Blest" (*Arabia Felix*), the fertile coast of modern Saudi Arabia across the Red Sea from newly conquered (30 B.C.) Egypt. Command was assigned to Aelius Gallus, the emperor himself being in Spain through 27–26–25 B.C. directing campaigns against the Cantabrians and Asturians, but for some reason the expedition was called off.
      In E.1.12., composed six years later, in 20 B.C., Iccius will be found still pursuing philosophical studies while managing Agrippa's estates in Sicily, apparently discontented with his lot.

4   Saba = Biblical Sheba, famous for frankincense (Jeremiah 6:20) and as the land of the rich queen who visited Solomon (1 Kings 10); note also the Sabaeans of Job 1:15. Saba/Sheba was more specifically the Yemen, in the SW corner of the Arabian peninsula, perhaps extending to the frankincense country of the Hadramawt inland from the southern coast of Arabia.

5   "Medes" here means "Orientals" in a general sense. The historical Medes had been assimilated to the Persians four centuries ago and their territory was some 1400 miles NE of "Saba."

9   "Chinese" (*Sericas*) is humorous exaggeration by way of teasing Iccius. See under "Seres" in "Foreign Nations," p. 397.

14   Panáetius of Cos, ca. 185 to 109 B.C., was a Stoic philosopher of importance to Roman thinkers, especially Cicero.

1.30.   *O Venus, regina Cnidi Paphique,*

Meter: Sapphic stanza: in lines 1, 2, and 3:   _ U _ > _ U U _ U _ U
                   in line 4:   _ U U _ U

Venus, queen of Cnidus and Paphus, leave your
Cherished Cyprus: here in the pretty shrine where
Incense-burning Glýcera now invokes you
    Set up your dwelling!

5   With you bring your boy of the fervent ardors,
Bring the Graces too, with their robes loose-flowing,
Nymphs,and Youth — too bashful with you not by — and
    Mercury also.

1–2   A famous temple of Venus/Aphroditē stood at Cnidus (Greek *Knidos*), a now unin-
habited site at the tip of the southernmost peninsula of SW Turkey; her "primary"
temple was at Paphus (Greek *Pafos* now) at the SW corner of the island of Cyprus;
compare *Odes* 1.3.1 and 1.19.10 and notes.
3   Possibly this Glýcera is identical with the one in *Odes* 1.19.
5   "Boy" (*puer*) = Cupid/Eros.
6   For the Graces see the note to *Odes* 1.4.6–7. "Loose-flowing" — (literally) "with girdles
loosened," that is, for lively dancing.
7–8   "Youth" — (*Iuventas*), meaning both "youthfulness" and actual youths to dance with
the "nymphs," i.e., girls, as in *Odes* 4.1.26.
    Mercury is he of the nimble tongue and of athletic grace, as in *Odes* 1.10.1–4. and
note.

1.31.   *Quid dedicatum poscit Apollinem*

Meter: Alcaic stanza: in lines 1 and 2:   U _ U _ > _ U U _ U _
                 in line 3:   U _ U _ U _ U _ U
                 in line 4:   _ U U _ U U _ U _ U

What shall the poet ask of Apollo now
Enshrined? With new wine poured from the saucer, what
    Shall he entreat? Not teeming harvests
        Reaped from Sardinia's fertile acres,

5   Nor herds that thrive in sun-flooded pastures of
Calabria, not ivory of Ind or gold,
    Nor lands the gently flowing Liris
        River erodes with its quiet waters.

Let those with vineyards granted by Lady Luck
10   Prune vines with Cáles sickles, and let the wines
    He got in near-East trade be drained from
        Vessels of gold by the wealthy merchant, —

The gods themselves must love him: he sees the far
Atlantic waters three or four times a year

Unharmed, while *I* subsist on olives,   15
   Endive, and lightly digesting mallows.

The use of my possessions and sturdy health,
Latóna-born, are what I entreat of you,
   Sound mind, and not to spend old age in
      Shame or deprived of the lyre to cheer me.   20

1–2   The new library-temple of Apollo, begun in 29 B.C. (see the note to *Odes* 1.2.31–32), was dedicated on October 24, 28 B.C.

2–3   Horace represents himself in the act of pouring out a libation from the shallow ritual saucer—*patera*, as in *Odes* 1.19.15 and note—and making his prayer before the newly emplaced cult statue. The prayer itself would seem to be rather too personal to have been recited, as Moore thinks it was, at the dedication ceremony.

4   Cicero, in an oration of 66 B.C., had named Sardinia, Sicily, and "Africa" (Tunisia and eastern Algeria) as the three major grain-producing areas for Rome; in 30 B.C. Augustus added Egypt as a fourth.

6   Calabria = modern Apulia, lowland pasture country in the *heel* of Italy during the winter season, as explained in the note to Epode 1, 27–28. (Modern Calabria, in the *toe* of Italy, was ancient Bruttium.)

7–8   The southward-flowing River Liris, now the Liri and a tributary of the Garigliano, flowed through good vineyard country. *Odes* 3.17.8–9 speaks of its floods.

9–10   The town of Cáles, now Calvi just N of Capua, overlooked the famous Falernian wine fields (as in *Odes* 1.20.9.). "Lady Luck" = *Fortuna*.

14   To the Romans the Atlantic coast of Europe was the western edge of the known world.

15–16   Compare the menu in S.1.6.115: "scallions and chickpeas and flour-and-oil pancakes."

18   "Latóna-born" (*Latoë*) = Apollo, whose mother was Latóna/Leto, as in *Odes* 1.21.3 and note.

19–20   Moore quotes Austin Dobson's lines to Longfellow, beginning: "Not to be tuneless in old age! . . . "

1.32.   *Poscimur. Si quid vacui sub umbra*

Meter: Sapphic stanza: in lines 1, 2, and 3:   _ U _ > _ U U _ U _ U
                                    in line 4:   _ U U _ U

By request, then. — If, in the shade and carefree,
You and I, my lyre, have created what will
Last for this and many a future year, come
   Sing something Latin,

Using modes that citizen first in Lesbos   5
Fashioned, who, while nonetheless fighting his wars, or
On his storm-tossed ship at a wavy shore, would
   Still go on singing

Liber and the Muses, and Venus with that
Boy of hers that follows her everywhere, and   10

Black-haired Lycus too, with his eyes of matching
  Blackness, and handsome.

Shell of tortoise wrought to a lyre, adorning
Phoebus' godhood, gracing the feasts of Jove, and
15   Lovely solace after distress: I hail you,
  Prompt at my summons.

1   "By request" (*Poscimur*), Horace will compose a poem with Roman subject matter but in
the Alcaic meter. (He uses the Sapphic meter to make this statement!)

5–8   Alcáeus (Alkaios), ca. 620 to ca. 580 B.C., was a contemporary of Sappho and, like her,
a native of Mytiléně, capital city of the island of Lesbos. As a citizen (*civis*), that is, not as
a professional soldier, he fought strenuously in political wars (6), over a period of years,
to make himself ruler of Lesbos, and for a time was forced into exile (7). When his ally,
Píttacus, went over to a victorious rival, Alcáeus seems to have been left in exile, and
around 590 B.C. Píttacus was elected ruler of Lesbos. Much of the biography is obscure,
especially the final years. Presumably he invented (as Horace says he did) the stanza
form that goes by his name, but the surviving fragments of his poems are in various
meters, including the Sapphic.

9–12   Even amid warfare, even in exile, Alcáeus composed poems in praise of wine
("Liber" = Bacchus), poetry (the Muses), love (Venus and Cupid/Eros), and of his own
black-eyed lover, Lycus.

13–14   The note to line 6 of *Odes* 1.10 explained how Mercury, when a few hours old,
invented the lyre by stretching strings over an empty tortoise shell and how, that same
day, he made a gift of the instrument to his half-brother Apollo.

Ode 32 gives the impression of a prelude to some group of poems, but we know it only as a
separate work.

1.33.   *Albi, ne doleas plus nimio memor*

Meter: in lines 1, 2, and 3:   _ > _ U U _   _ U U _ U _
        in line 4:   _ > _ U U _ U _

No more grieve to excess,   Albius, for your lost
Heartless Glýcera; cease   harping on doleful thoughts
In your elegies, where   someone more youthful now
   Triumphs over her pledge of faith,

5   Where Lycóris with famed   beauty of narrow brow
Burns for Cyrus's love, —   Cyrus avoiding *her*
For hard Phóloě; yet   sooner will she-goats mate
   With Apulian wolves than that

Ever Phóloě stoops   basely to base-born love.
10   Such is Venus's way: coupling a pair ill-matched
Both in looks and in mind,   fitting a yoke of bronze
   To their necks as a cruel joke.

I myself, when I sought   love of a higher sort,
Clung fast caught in the chains   freedwoman Mýtalē
Held, and fiercer she was,   too, than the sea that grinds   15
     At Calabria's hollowed shores.

1   This Albius, like the one in E.1.4, was, as early as the first century A.D., believed to be the
poet Albius Tibullus, whose unknown birth year was probably close to Horace's own 65
B.C. and who died in 19 B.C. His love poems address mistresses named Delia and Nemesis,
nowhere does he mention a Glýcera or a Lycóris, and a Phóloē is addressed only once, in
1.8.69. Almost all of his poems are elegies, that is, composed in alternating hexameters
and pentameters; for this poetic form see the note to E.2.2.91 and E.2.3.75–78.
5   The narrow forehead, oddly, is an admired feature. Petronius, before 65 A.D., praises
such a "minimal brow" (frons minima; in Satyricon 126), but Horace, in E. 1.7.26, deplores
his own receding hairline—not, we assume, in a parallel case.
13–14   "Love of a higher sort" (melior Venus) apparently means love for a freedwoman rather
than for a slave. In Odes 1.27.14–17 Megilla's brother's "weakness always/Preferred the
free-born." See also S.1.2.47–49 and note.
16   Calabria — modern Apulia, Horace's home province in the heel of Italy, as in the note to
line 6 of the foregoing ode.

1.34.   *Parcus deorum cultor et infrequens,*

Meter: Alcaic stanza: in lines 1 and 2:   U _ U _ > _ U U _ U _
                 in line 3:   U _ U _ U _ U _ U
                 in line 4:   _ U U _ U U _ U _ U

Infrequently and never too much concerned
About the gods, and ever pursuing mad
     Philosophies, I see I now must
         Turn my sails back and revert to courses

Abandoned. For Diéspiter, splitting clouds   5
Asunder with his glittering lightning-fires,
     Has driven thunder steeds and rushing
         Chariot over the open heavens

So stolid earth and wandering streams alike,
So Styx and ghastly Táenarus' fearsome depths,   10
     The Atlantéan shore itself, are
         Rattled and shaken. For godhead still can

Change lowest things to highest, abase the great,
And bring the hidden forth; on a gust of wings
     Fortúna sometimes swoops to shatter   15
         Crowns, — yet bestowing them too delights her.

2–3   "Mad philosophies" (*insanientis sapientiae*, literally "foolish wisdom") may signify the Epicuréan doctrine which, while granting the gods' existence, directed man's serious study to science.

5   *Diéspiter* ("Day-father, Sky-father) was the archaic form of "Jupiter," as Horace's contemporary Varro stated. It is cognate with Greek *Zeus Patēr* and Sanskrit *Dyaus pita*, while the first component is cognate with Germanic *Zio* and Anglo-Saxon *Tiw*, as in *Tiwes daeg*, "Tuesday."

10–11   The Styx, a river at the border of the land-after-death, here stands for the land-after-death itself.

   Táenarus (Greek Taínaros) promontory (English: Cape Matapan) at the southernmost point of mainland Greece, had a cave which was said to be one of the entrances to the underworld. There Orpheus descended, according to line 467 of Vergil's 4th Georgic.

   "Atlantéan" is Horace's own unusual form of "Atlantic."

1.35.   *O diva, gratum quae regis Antium,*

Meter: Alcaic stanza: in lines 1 and 2:   U _ U _ > _ U U _ U _
                         in line 3:   U _ U _ U _ U _ U
                         in line 4:   _ U U _ U U _ U _ U

Fortúna, goddess-queen of fair Ántium,
Who can indeed lift man in his mortal clay
   From pit to pinnacle or turn his
      Haughtiest triumphs to utter ruin:

5   Poor farmers court your favor with anxious prayers;
As mistress over waves you are pleaded to
   By all who brave Carpáthus' waters
      In a Bithýnian sailing vessel;

The Dacian savage, like the nomadic Scyths,
10   As well as ordered cities and nations, our
   Fierce Latium, mothers of barbarian
      Monarchs, and tyrants in purple, fear you,

Lest you should overthrow with a scornful kick
The column standing tall, and the mob in arms
15   Incite to arms the idle others
      To the destruction of law and power.

Before you strides Necessity ever grim,
With spikes and wedges grasped in her iron hand,
   Nor does she lack supplies of rigid
20   Clamps, or of thick molten lead to seal them.

By Hope and rare Fidelity — veiled in white —

You are esteemed, — the latter abandons no
Man, even when with altered raiment
    You turn away from exalted houses;

But fickle mobs and mistresses take their false   25
Oaths back, and when the wine jars are emptied to
    The lees, friends have a way of fleeing,
        Far too deceitful to share a burden.

Keep Caesar safe, we pray, as he moves against
The Britons at the edge of the world; protect   30
    The forces newly formed for striking
        Fear in the Eastern and Red Sea regions.

Alas, the shame of scars, and alas, the crime
Of brothers fighting brothers! When has our time
    Recoiled from acts of savagery? What   35
        Wrongs have we left uncommitted? When have

The hands of men, from fear of the gods, been stayed?
What altars have they spared? I had rather far
    You forged our blunted swords anew and
        Turned them on Arabs and Massagétae.   40

1   At Ántium (now Anzio), on the coast some 55 km/35 m S of Rome, there stood until late classical times an oracle-shrine to Fortuna (Lady Luck), or more precisely to "the fortunes of Ántium" (*Fortunae Antiátes*).

7–8   The geography is merely decorative. Carpáthus is the Greek island between Crete and Rhodes. Bithýnia (now NW Turkey, along the S coast of the Black Sea), adjoining Pontus to the E, may mean here "good ship timber country"; Pontus was mentioned in this sense in *Odes* 1.14.11 and note. (In 74 B.C. the king of Bithynia bequeathed his kingdom to Rome, and in 65–62 B.C. Pompey the Great organized Bithynia-Pontus as a Roman province.)

    Lines 7–8, however, merely exemplify dangerous voyaging.

9   The Dacians inhabited Transylvania (now western Rumania); see the note to lines 4–5 of *Odes* 1.26. The Scyths lived N of the Black Sea. For both peoples see under "Foreign Nations," p. 397.

11   Latium (pronounce: LAY-shum) was Rome's home province, now called Lazio.

17–20   "Necessity" ("what-must-be") walks ahead of Fortuna carrying symbols of "what-cannot-be-changed," just as Roman lictors, carrying instruments of punishment—"the *fasces*," walked ahead of a Roman chief of state. Compare *Odes* 3.24.5–8.

21–22   The "goddesses" Hope (*Spes*) and Fidelity (*Fides*) had shrines in Rome, the latter allegedly dating from the reign of pious King Numa Pompilius, 716–672 B.C.

    "Veiled in white" stands for the over-condensed *albo . . . velata panno*, which refers to the custom whereby the priest offered sacrifices to Fidelity with his right hand swathed in a white cloth.

29–32   Since Julius Caesar's raids of 55 and 54 B.C. the Romans had meditated a conquest of the island of Britain, and Augustus twice, in 27 and in 26 B.C., prepared invasions, only to be detained both times by uprisings in northern Spain; see *Odes* 1.21.16 and note.

    Lines 31–32 refer to the abortive campaign of 26 B.C. against "Araby the Blest," as in the note to *Odes* 1.29.12.

    The present poem, therefore, dates to 26 B.C.

33–38   With genuine anguish (reminiscent of Epode 16) Horace recalls the grimmest years
of the civil wars, 44 to 31 B.C., when Octavius Caesar was striving for supreme power.

40   Here Arabs inhabit Araby; in *Odes* 1.29.5 they were "Medes." The Massagetae,
frequently mentioned by Herodotus, were a warlike people of northern Iran, W of the
Caspian Sea, 400 years before Horace's time.

The opening stanza of Ode 35 distinctly echoes Pindar's 12th Olympian Ode, which is also
addressed to Fortuna (Greek: *Týkhē*), but the two poems are otherwise without parallels.

Thomas Gray's *Hymn to Adversity* (1742) had Ode 35 as its model, and Wordsworth had
Gray's Hymn in mind when he composed his *Ode to Duty* (1805).

1.36.   *Et ture et fidibus iuvat*

Meter: in the odd-numbered lines: _ > _ U U _ U _
in the even-numbered lines: _ > _ U U _ _ U U _ U _

Now approaches the happy time
   When, with incense and lyres   and with the slaughtered calf
Vowed to Númida's saving gods,
   We shall welcome him home   safe from far-distant Spain,
5   Bringing kisses to many friends,
   But with heartier share   waiting no other than
Dear old Lamia: he recalls
   Boyhood's games that were played   under no other chief
And their togas of manhood donned
10   Simultaneously.   Chalk up the day in white,
Set no limit on wine jars broached,
   Give no respite to feet   treading the Salic dance,
Let not toperess Dámalis
   Out-drink Bassus in cups   drained in a single breath,
15   Be there roses to deck the feast,
   Long-lived parsley for crowns,   brief-lasting lilies too.
Every wine-mellowed eye shall dwell
   Long on Dámalis, but   from her new lover here
She will never withdraw her gaze:
20   Ivy thick on a tree   does not more closely cling.

3   Númida is unknown except for what this poem conveys. Augustus returned from Spain
in the spring of 24 B.C., and *if* Númida came home at the same time, Ode 36 would date
to 24 B.C. As the close contemporary (lines 7–10) of the Lucius Aelius Lamia addressed in
Odes 1.26, the age of both young men may be guessed as about 23, according to the
following, purely conjectural, chronology:

   47 B.C.   Lamia and Númida born.
   30 B.C.   *Odes* 1.26 addressed to Lamia on the occasion of his coming of age. The
           toga of manhood (*toga virilis*) was customarily donned when the youth was

16 or 17 years old, amid a great family celebration. Horace himself was then age 35.

24 B.C.   Augustus returned (in the spring) from Spain, and *if* Númida came home at the same time, both young men would now be about 23. Horace would now have been age 41.

33 A.D.   Known date of Lamia's death (? at age 80).

8   "Chief" stands for "king" (*rege*). Compare E.1.1.59–60: "But boys at their play have a jingle:/ "You shall be king (*rex*) if you play the game fair."

10   The equivalent of our "red-letter day."

12   The *Salii* were priests of Mars who danced in three-quarter time through the streets in the annual month-of-March festival of that god. Compare *Odes* 4.1.28 and see the note to E.2.1.86–87.

13   "Dámalis" is Greek for "heifer calf." One of the Empress Livia's *freedwomen* attendants had this name. "Toperess" renders *multi meri,* "of much wine," which in turn renders Greek *polýoinos.*

14   "Bassus" was an actual family name, but we know nothing of this individual. The phrase "cups drained in a single breath" is expressed in a single word: *amystis,* and in the text it is qualified by "Thracian fashion."

18   Her new lover is, presumably, Númida.

1.37.   *Nunc est bibendum, nunc pede libero*

Meter: Alcaic stanza: in lines 1 and 2:   U _ U _ > _ U U _ U _
in line 3:   U _ U _ U _ U _ U
in line 4:   _ U U _ U U _ U _ U

Rome, September of 30 *B.C.*, on receiving the news of Cleopatra's suicide.

Now comes a time for drinking, my friends, a time
For feet to leap up dancing, a time to deck
        Resplendent places for the gods who
                Honor our Salian banquet couches.

It would have been amiss, until now, to fetch   5
Ancestral stocks of Cáecuban forth as long
        As that demented queen was plotting
                Ruin to Capitol and to empire,

Conspiring with a herd of the basest men
That lust depraves, so foolishly blind herself   10
        That any venture offered hope, and
                Drunk with good luck. But her madness lessened

With hardly one ship saved out of battle flames,
And then her mind, that swirled from her Eastern wines,
        Was forced to know real fears by Caesar   15
                Making all speed with his oars to drive her

From our Italian coasts, as a hawk pursues
The softly wanton dove, or a hunter swift
    To pounce upon a hare in snowy
20   Fields of Haemónia, fetters ready

To chain the deadly monster. But she, who sought
To die a nobler death, neither shrank from swords
    In woman's fashion nor repaired with
        Speed of a fleet to remotest regions;

25   She even dared to gaze with serenity
Upon her ruined palace and bravely take
    The savage serpents up to let her
        Body drink deep of their livid venom,

The more intensely fierce when resolved to die,
30   And doubtless scorning transport by victor's ship
    To trail, unqueened, behind his haughty
        Triumph, — for she was no humble woman.

2–4   For Salian priests see the note to line 12 of the foregoing ode. The wealth of such priesthoods and the lavishness of their banquets were proverbial; see *Odes* 2.14.25–28.
      At thanksgiving celebrations images of the gods were placed on special dining couches and food was set before them; the priests dined separately.

7–8   One rumor had it that Antony had promised Cleopatra the Roman empire as a wedding gift and that the queen had vowed to rule from the sacred Capitol.

9–10   Horace probably means the "corrupt, Oriental" court at Alexandria, but the underlying notion must be that of Circē the enchantress with her men transformed into swine.

13–17   Horace exaggerates Cleopatra's (and Antony's) ship losses at Actium, though Octavius Caesar's account claimed as many as 300 of them destroyed. The swiftness of pursuit is also exaggerated: Caesar spent the entire winter of 31–30 B.C. in Greece and Asia (Turkey) and did not advance against Egypt until the summer of 30. The approximate date for the suicide of Cleopatra is August 1, 30 B.C.

14   "Eastern" paraphrases *Mareotico*, that is, wine from around the large, shallow Lake Mariout—which the Romans called "the Mareotic swamp—immediately S and SE of Alexandria.

20   Haemónia = The N-Greek region of Thessaly, by tradition, winter hunting country.

22–24   Plutarch, who wrote a century or more after these events, says, in his "Life of Antony" (79), that Cleopatra tried to stab herself upon seeing that a Roman emissary from Caesar had gained access to the "tomb" (or "monument") where she had barricaded herself. The same "Life" (69) reports that Cleopatra contemplated having her remaining ships hauled overland from the Mediterranean to the Red Sea and sailing away with all her wealth to found a new kingdom somewhere along the Indian Ocean.

30   "By victor's ship" replaces "in Liburnians," that is, the small, quick craft that had made the victory at Actium possible. The term is explained in the headnote to Epode 1.

31–32   At Octavius Caesar's formal triumph in Rome in August of 29 B.C. an effigy of Cleopatra was paraded.

Ode 37, as a whole, was probably modeled on an ode of Alcáeus upon the death of the tyrant Myrsilus (ca. 590 B.C.), from which two lines are preserved in quotation by a late writer; Denys Page translates in *Sappho and Alcaeus,* 1955, p. 238:

Now must a man get drunk, aye, drink with might and main, for Myrsilus has died.

To the translator's notion, Epode 9 has the excited immediacy of September 31 B.C., when the news of the victory at Actium reached Rome, whereas Ode 37 reflects a deliberateness that would be possible only some time after the excitement of September of 30 B.C. had abated. The intricate workmanship so suggests, as does the imitation of a model by Alcáeus.

Note that, like Epode 9, Ode 37 avoids any mention of the defeated *Roman,* Mark Antony.

1.38. *Persicos odi, puer, apparatus i*

Meter: Sapphic stanza: in lines 1, 2, and 3:   _ U _ > _ U U _ U _ U
                    in line 4:   _ U U _ U

Persian frills I hate, boy; those showy chaplets
Twined with linden strip-bark I find distasteful;
Hunt no more for nooks where the roses linger
        Last in the season.

Do not try improving on simple myrtle,   5
Over-conscientious! For you, the server,
Myrtle answers well, — and for me, in checkered
        Arbor shade drinking.

1   "Persian" (*Persicos*) here means simply "Oriental." "Boy" (*puer*) means "slave," as usual;
    lines 6–8 show him as a waiter, pouring the master's wine of a summer afternoon.
2   Strips of the inner bark of linden trees were used for holding garlands together.

Odes. Book 2

2.1. *Motum ex Metello consule civicum*

Meter: Alcaic stanze: in lines 1 and 2:   ∪ _ ∪ _ > _ ∪ ∪ _ ∪ _
in line 3:   ∪ _ ∪ _ ∪ _ ∪ _ ∪
in line 4:   _ ∪ ∪ _ ∪ ∪ _ ∪ _ ∪

In praise of Caius Asínius Pollip: warrior, jurist, statesman, tragic dramatist, and historian, and in particular of his still unfinished "History of the Civil Wars."

The civil broils that date from Metéllus' term
Of consulship, the causes of war, its wrongs,
   Its phases, Fortune's tricks of malice,
      Solemn alliance of leaders, weapons

5   Imbued with blood — and no expiation done:
In short, the dice-game's perils in full account
   Comprise your theme, and you proceed through
      Fires beneath treacherous crust of ashes.

Your sterner Muse of tragedy must a while
10   Be missed upon our stages; but soon, when this
   Historic work is well in order,
      You will resume your Cecrópic buskin,

Preëminent defender of those accused
At law and of the Senate in grave debates,
15   And wearer of eternal laurels,
      Pollio, since your Dalmatian triumph.

At times you deafen ears with the din and threat
Of trumpet blasts, the bugles at times shrill forth,
   And then again the flash of weapons
20   Dazzles both rider and horse with terror.

I seem to hear the shouts of the battle chiefs

180

And see them — to their honor — befouled with grime,
   And everything on earth brought low, save
      Cato's resisting and stubborn spirit.

There Juno and the other divinities   25
   Once forced to leave the African towns they loved
      Slew grandsons of their former victors,
         Sending them down for Jugúrtha's vengeance.

Where lies a field unfattened by Latin blood
But what attests with graves these unholy wars?   30
   Or whence the Medes have not rejoiced at
      Hearing Hespéria's sounds of ruin?

What gulfs or flowing streams are unversed in sights
Of dismal war? What sea has been left unstained
   By slaughter of Italian brothers?   35
      Where is the shore by our blood uncolored?

And yet, pert Muse, you must not abandon jest
And love-song for the grief of a Céan dirge:
   Together in Dióně's grotto
      Let us seek music of lighter poems.   40

1–2   Pollio's (lost) history must have begun the civil wars at 60 B.C., in the consulship of Quintus Caecilius Metellus Celer and Lucius Afranius (when Horace was 5 years old).

4   The "solemn alliance" was the First Triumvirate (60 B.C.), when Julius Caesar, Pompey the Great, and Crassus (the richest man in Rome) took control of the Roman state.

7–8   This memorable line suggests a compositional date of 30-to-28 B.C. for this Ode 1.

9–10   All of Pollio's works are lost. Vergil, in Eclogue 8.10, terms Pollio's tragedies the only ones worthy of the buskin of Sophocles; and Horace, in S.1.10.42, said that "in tragical trimeter Pollio sings of the feats of/ Kings."

12   "Cecrópic" = "Athenian," that is, of the classical Greek tragedies. Cecrops was a legendary king of Athens.

16   In 39 B.C. Pollio had subdued the Parthini, a tribe in Dalmatia (now Yugoslavia). With the booty from that conquest he established the first public library in Rome.

24   Cato (as in *Odes* 1.12.35–36 and note) is Marcus Porcius Cato, "the Younger," "Uticensis," who fought a last stand for the republican cause against Julius Caesar and, when he saw the cause was lost, committed suicide at Utica (in present-day Tunisia) in 46 B.C.

     Pollio's "History," starting at 60 B.C., must, then, have been brought down to 46 B.C., but we do not know whether it was ever completed or not—or even what terminal date he had selected.

25–28   Other "African" memories of the Romans:

   · Juno, in the *Aeneid,* was the patron goddess of Carthage and the foe of Rome. No city could be captured until its protecting gods abandoned it; Roman armies had a rite called *evocatio* to entice the deities away.

   · Cato determined upon suicide after learning that 10,000 republicans had been slain in April of 46 by Julius Caesar's army at Thapsus (now Ras Dimas on the E coast of Tunisia). The republican commander was Metellus Scipio, grandson of the Metellus Numidicus who fought against Jugúrtha in 109–8 B.C.

   · In 111 B.C. the native (Berber) prince Jugúrtha seized the kingship of Numidia (Tunisia and E Algeria) and baffled Roman attempts to dislodge him from power until 105, when he was captured through a relative's treachery. He was paraded in chains—see *Odes* 1.37.21–22 and 31–32—in General Marius's triumph, imprisoned, and killed. Horace sees the 10,000 slain at Thapsus as propitiatory victims to Jugúrtha's ghost.

31   "Medes" = Parthians, as usual.

32   "Hesperia," Greek for "western land," here means Italy. (In *Odes* 1.36.4 it meant Spain.)

35   "Italian" = Horace's "Daunian," that is, Apulian, an odd word in this context. (See *Odes* 1.22.14 and note.)

38   The "Céan" was Simónides of Ceos, 556–467 B.C., famous for his sad elegies. Compare Catullus 38.8 "sadder than the tears of Simonides."

39   Diónē was the mother of Venus; here the phrase means "in a grotto (*antro*) of love"; compare the "cave" (*antro*) of the lovers in *Odes* 1.5.2.

Caius Asínius Pollio, 76 B.C. to 4 (or 5) A.D., was mentioned, as of age 16, by Catullus (Poem 12) as "a lad skillful at things witty and amusing." He was with Julius Caesar as an officer at the crossing of the Rubicon on the night of January 10–11, 49 B.C., he supported Caesar in the defeat of Pompey at Pharsalia and in other campaigns down to 45, and in 44 he commanded forces against Sextus Pompey. After Julius Caesar's assassination he joined Mark Antony, who made him Governor of Cisalpine Gaul (northern Italy), with seven legions under his command. From "the Perusine War" of 41–40 he managed to hold aloof, though at several points he was on the verge of intervening. As consul in 40, he represented Antony in the meeting with Maecenas, who represented Octavius Caesar, to negotiate that "Treaty of Brundisium" which divided the Roman world between those two leaders. In 39 he conquered the Parthini of Dalmatia, but then saw that he could not loyally serve both Antony and Octavius and so withdrew from public life. For 35 years thereafter he remained apart, a respected statesman known to be loyal to the old republican ideals but in no way interfering with the new order of things under Augustus.

Three letters of Pollio to Cicero are preserved, and from their stylistic stiffness one would not guess that he was either a tragic poet or a vivid historian.

It was to Pollio as Governor of Cisalpine Gaul that young Vergil, living in that jurisdiction, turned for assistance in saving his father's farm, which had been marked for confiscation in order to pay the soldiers who defeated Brutus and Cassius at Philippi in 42. Presumably Pollio's attention had already been caught by early poems of Vergil's. Eclogue 4 (11–12) promises glory to Pollio's consulship in 40; Eclogue 8 (6–13) salutes Pollio the poet-General not yet arrived home from his Dalmatian victory in 39. Through Pollio's sponsorship Vergil gained access to Maecenas and to the emperor, who successively became his patrons. Posterity remembers Pollio as the man who launched Vergil's career.

S.1.10.85 lists Pollio among the persons of sound literary judgment. Horace probably *heard* readings from the "History of the Civil War," since it was Pollio who instituted the custom of oral readings by authors.

2.2.   *Nullus argento color est avaris*

Meter: Sapphic stanza: in lines 1, 2, and 3:   _ ∪ _ > _ ∪ ∪ _ ∪ _ ∪
                           in line 4:   _ ∪ ∪ _ ∪

Lines 1–8 cite two men known for their generosity; lines 99–16 condemn "greed," the oppposite of generosity; lines 17–24 generalize the theme.

Silver has no gleam when concealed in greedy
Earth, and you, my Crispus Sallústius, feel
Only scorn for bars of the metal not yet
    Shiny from usage.

Proculéius' fame will endure forever   5
For the father's love that he showed his brothers;
Over him shall hover with wings unflagging
    Posthumous glory.

You will rule an empire more vast by taming
Greed than by combining the breadth of Afric   10
Lands with furthest Gadès till both the Punic
    Kingdoms obey you.

Dropsy grows more virulent with indulgence,
Nor is thirst allayed till the cause of illness
Quits the system, freeing the body from its   15
    Watery languor.

To Phraátes gaining the throne of Cyrus
Once again, right Judgment, in sharp dissention
From the mob's opinon, denies the name of
    "Fortunate," urging   20

People rather not to apply untruthful
Terms, reserving praises for diadem's and
Kingship's safety solely for one not squinting
    Sideways for treasure.

2 Of Gaius Sallústius Crispus—Horace inverts the name—the historian Tacitus, a century
    later, wrote (*Annals* 3.30):

      He took his name from his grandmother's brother, the eminent historian Sallust,
who had adopted him. So he had easy access to an official career. But he followed the
example of Maecenas and, without senatorial rank, exceeded in power many ex-consuls
and winners of Triumphs. Elegant and refined—the antithesis of traditional sim-
plicity—he carried elaborate opulence almost to the point of decadence. Yet underneath
was a vigorous mind fit for great affairs, all the keener for its indolent, sleepy mask. So, as
a repository of imperial secrets, he was second only to Maecenas during the latter's
lifetime, and thereafter second to none.

                      (Michael Grant translation, in *Penguin Classics*, p. 131)
      A poem by Crinágoras in the Greek Anthology (16. 40) also praises his generosity.

5–8 Caius Proculéius Varro, intimate friend of the emperor and from 23 B.C. Maecenas's
    brother-in-law (see *Odes* 2.10.1 and note), divided his wealth with his two brothers when
    the latter found themselves ruined by the civil wars. (As one of the last persons to see
    Cleopatra alive, he has a small role in Shakespeare's *Antony and Cleopatra*, V.)

10–12 "Gadès" = the *city* of Cadiz in SW Spain. Horace sees, in terms of 200 years before,
    two Punic (Phoenecian, Carthaginian) kingdoms: North Africa, ruled from Carthage,
    and Spain, ruled from New Carthage (now Cartagena) on Spain's Mediterranean coast.

17–18 In 30 B.C. the Parthian king, Phraátes IV, regained the Persian throne once held by
    Cyrus II, the Great, from 559 to 530 B.C.; see note (b) to *Odes* 1.26.5. But confused

accounts seem to show Phraátes deposed and restored a second time in 27–26 B.C., so that the dating of the present ode must remain uncertain.

18–24 These lines express the Stoic doctrine that "Only the wise man (philosopher) is a king." But see the next-following ode.

2.3. *Aequam memento rebus in arduis*

Meter: Alcaic stanza: in lines 1 and 2: ∪ _ ∪ _ > _ ∪ ∪ _ ∪ _
in line 3: ∪ _ ∪ _ ∪ _ ∪ _ ∪
in line 4: _ ∪ ∪ _ ∪ ∪ _ ∪ _ ∪

Remember in adversity to maintain
A calm and even mind, and when times are good
    To guard no less against excessive
        Happiness, Déllius, who are destined

5   To die no less if you are forever sad
Than if on every holiday you enjoyed
    Secluded picnics with Falernian
        Out of the storeroom's remotest corner.

Why else should these white poplars and lofty pines
10   So love to interweave their congenial shade?
    Why else should trembling waters scurry
        Down through the windings of brooklet courses?

Bid servants fetch us wines here, and scented oils,
And blossoms of the lovely if short-lived rose,
15   While age and fortunes still permit such
        Things, and the threads of the three grim Sisters.

Your upland pastures you shall abandon, and
Your town house and your villa that Tiber laves,
    You shall abandon wealth you hoarded
20   High, and your heir will be its possessor.

Born wealthy and descended from Ínachus
The ancient king, or born of the humblest folk
    And poor, you dwell beneath the daylight,
        Victim of Orcus, who knows no pity.

25   A single destination awaits us all,
And soon or late one lot from the shaken urn
    Will send each man to board the vessel
        Carrying him to eternal exile.

Ode 3 expresses the Epicurean principles of "Live for today" and "Nothing too much," in contrast to the Stoic principles of the foregoing ode.

4   Quintus Déllius was another of the emperor's circle of friends. Once known as "the acrobat of the civil wars" for his repeated changing of sides, he came over to Octavius Caesar on the eve of the showdown battle of Actium (31 B.C.) and remained there ever afterwards.

16   "The three grim Sisters" are the Fates who, respectively, spin, guide, and cut the thread of life.

21   Ínachus was a legendary king of Argos.

24   Orcus is both the land-after-death and the king of that land.

25   Literally: "We are all herded to the same place" (*Omnes eodem cogimur*), by Hermes/Mercury, "soul-sender." See the opening of *Odyssey* 24 as quoted in the note to *Odes* 1.10.17–19.

27–28   The figure of Charon's boat that ferries souls cross the Styx to the land of the dead is combined with the realistic picture of a Roman statesman, disgraced or merely out of favor, boarding ship for exile; for example, Cicero in 58 B.C., and Regulus in 250 B.C. See the note to *Odes* 1.12.37 and 3.5.13–56 and note.

2.4   *Ne sit ancillae tibi amor pudori,*

Meter: Sapphic stanza: in lines 1, 2, and 3:   _ U _ > _ U U _ U _ U
                                    in line 4:   _ U U _ U

Do not blush for loving a pretty slave-girl,
Xánthias of Phocis! Achilles, haughty
As he was, felt love for the slave Briséis'
         Snowy-white beauty;

Loveliness of captive Tecméssa troubled   5
Ajax son of Télamon as her master;
For a kidnapped girl Agamemnon languished
         Even in triumph —

After he of Thessaly slew such droves of
Enemies, and after the loss of Hector   10
Left the Trojan ramparts an easy prey for
         War-weary Grecians.

And — who knows? — your golden-haired Phyllis' parents
May prove rich and famous and do you honor;
She is doubtless grieving for royal forebears   15
         Woefully fallen.

Never dream you chose a belovèd born of
Wicked people, or that a girl so faithful,
So averse to money, *could* have a mother
         One is ashamed of.   20

Oh, I praise her features, her arms, her shapely
Ankles, — quite objectively! Stop suspecting

> One whose years have hurried along to bring their
>   Total to forty.

2   The identity behind "Xanthias of Phocis" is unknown. It was probably unknown outside the inner circle of Horace's friends. "Xanthias" means "golden-haired," and Phocis was a region of central Greece that included Delphi.

2–7   Three heroes who loved slave-girls:
· Achilles had a captive Trojan concubine, Briséis. (*Iliad* 1. 184 and 19. 282–300)
· "The Greater Ajax" had a beloved concubine named Tecméssa, who appears as a charcter in Sophocles's *Ajax,* but the early part of her story is obscure.
· Cassandra, a captured Trojan princess and a prophetess, became Agamemnon's concubine; she appears in the *Agamemnon* of Aeschylus.

9   "He of Thessaly" is Achilles, who came from Phthía in the north-Greek region of Thessaly.

22   "Ankles" = *suras,* "calves (of the legs)."

23–24   Horace turned 40 on December 8, 25 B.C. The text says "to close their eighth *lustrum,*—a *lustrum* being a period of five years.

2.5.   *Nondum subacta ferre iugum valet*

Meter: Alcaic stanza: in lines 1 and 2:   U _ U _ > _ U U _ U _
in line 3:   U _ U _ U _ U _ U
in line 4:   _ U U _ U U _ U _ U

> She does not yet have strength to endure a yoke
> Across her neck, in team work she cannot yet
>   Perform her proper share, nor can she
>   Bear the full weight of the bull in rutting.
>
> 5   Your heifer's thoughts are all for the verdant grass
> Of meadows, sometimes finding the cool relief
>   Of streams from summer's heat, and sometimes
>   Down with the calves at their frisking antics
>
> Beneath the humid willows. Give up your taste
> 10 For unripe grapes; the many-hued autumn soon
>   Will set the gray-green clusters off with
>   Crimsoning flushes of early color.
>
> She soon will follow *you,* for relentless time
> Speeds on, subtracting years from your own account
> 15   To add to hers. With wanton glances
>   Lálagē soon will seek *you* as lover,
>
> More dear to you than ever coy Phóloē,
> Or Chloris with the shoulders of whiter gleam

Than sheen of moonlight on nocturnal
    Seas, or than Cnídian Gyges, who, if   20

Concealed among a bevy of girls, might well
Deceive the shrewdest strangers in search of him,
    So far would he belie his sex by
        Exquisite features and unshorn tresses.

1–9   Compare the girl's name "Dámalis," Greek for "heifer calf," in *Odes* 1.36.

9–12   A common metaphor in Greek poetry after 300 B.C. was that of ripe versus unripe grapes.

13–16   The transition from the metaphorical heifer calf to the actul girl is abrupt. The name "Lálagē," ("sweetly prattling") suits poorly with the metaphor, and the girl can hardly be identical with the Lálagē of *Odes* 1.22.11 and 23.

17   This "coy" (*fugax*) Phóloē can hardly be identical with the "hard" (*asperam*) Phóloē of *Odes* 1.33.7. Besides the Phóloē in Tibullus 1.8.69, there is a slave woman named Phóloē in *Aeneid* 5. 285; otherwise, "Phóloē" is the name of a mountain chain dividing Arcadia from Elis in the western Peloponnesus.

18   The name "Chloris" is from Greek *khlōrós*, "having the freshness of springtime green." Compare "Chloē" in *Odes* 1.23.1 and note.

20   The Greek masculine name "Gyges" means "earth-born," according to Robert Graves. The famous Gyges of Herodotus's History 1. 8–15 is irrelevant here, but we note that the present erotic figure is "Cnídian," that is, from Aphroditē/Venus's town of Cnídus, as in *Odes* 1.30.1 and note. It is likely that Gyges, Lálagē, Phóloē, and Chloris are all Greek slaves.

20–24   "Cnídian Gyges" is explicitly paralleled with the young Achilles concealed in a girl's costume and hidden among the girls, as explained in the note to *Odes* 1.8.14–16.

2.6.   *Septimi, Gadis aditure mecum et*

Meter: Sapphic stanza: in lines 1, 2, and 3:   _ U _ > _ U U _ U _ U
                      in line 4:   _ U U _ U

Off with me, Septímius? Off to Gadès?
Off to where Cantábrians have not learned our
Rule? and sail the barbarous Syrtès ever
    Seething with storm-waves?

Rather, let me live my declining years at   5
Tibur, which the exile from Argos founded;
I have had enough of the sea, and roads, and
    Service with armies.

But, if adverse Fates disallow my wishes,
I shall seek the lovely Galáesus valley,   10
Where the sheep wear raincoats in lands Phalánthus
    Settled from Sparta.

That spot charms me more than all other earthly
Places; there the honey is not surpassed by
15   Mount Hyméttus' product, and olives vie with
Those of Venáfrum;

Springtime there in Jupiter's sky is long, and
Winters mild, and Aulon, that loves a fruitful
Bacchus, bears Falernian grapes the fewest
20   Grudges in envy.

There for you and me is a home and happy
Citadel, and there you may shed the tear you
Owe the yet-warm funeral ashes of your
Friend and your poet.

1   Septímius is doubtless the friend whom Horace, in E.1.9, will recommend for service on
the staff of Tiberius (the future emperor).
    Gadès, the city of Cadiz in SW Spain, stands for the whole Iberian peninsula, as in
Odes 2.2.11 and note.
2   In 26–25 B.C. Augustus took personal charge of the campaigns against the Cantabrians
of northwest Spain. His departure for Spain in 27 may be the time when Septímius
proposed going there with Horace.
3–4 Here, "Syrtès" may mean no more than "dangerously shallow seas with sandbanks."
The actual *Syrtes* lie E of Tunisia and N of Libya, whereas line 4 has them "seething with
Moorish waves." Compare *Odes* 1.22.6 and Epode 9, 32 and the respective notes.
5   In 27–26–25 B.C. Horace was, respectively, 38, 39, and 40 years old.
6   Tibur (now Tívoli) was praised in *Odes* 1.7.1–14 above many famous places in Greece. Its
founders were the three exiled brothers from Argos: Tibúrnus, Coras, and Catíllus; see
the note to *Odes* 1.18.2.
10–12 The Galáesus River (now the Sinni; ancient Greek: Sírios) flows E through the
"foot" of Italy into the gulf of Táranto at a point opposite Taréntum. Pausánias: *Guide to
Greece* 10.10.4, after 150 A.D., tells how Phalánthus of Sparta captured the city of
Taréntum from barbarians, in 708 B.C.
    The encyclopedist Varro, contemporary with Horace, reports that blankets of hides
were attached to the sheep of the Taréntum region to safeguard their fine fleeces.
15–16 The whitest and sweetest honey came from Mount Hyméttus just SE of Athens, the
finest olive oil from Venáfrum (now Venáfro) ca. 70 km/45 m NNW of Naples.
18–20 The unidentified Aulon was probably a hill near Taréntum. The true Falernian wine
was produced N of Naples, 250 km/160 m NW of the Galáesus valley.
24 "Poet" = *vates*, the old word for "prophet," revived in classical Rome in contrast to
Greek *poietēs*, Latinized as *poēta*. (The "inspired" *vates* of old "sang" his "wisdom": *vati*- +
can-.)

2.7.   *O saepe mecum tempus in ultimum*

Meter: Alcaic stanza: in lines 1 and 2:   U _ U _ > _ U U _ U _
                in line 3:   U _ U _ U _ U _ U
                in line 4:   _ U U _ U U _ U _ U

My friend that often shared in the worst of times
With me when, under Brutus, we followed war,
    Who is it that restores your civic
        Rights under skies of Italian homelands?

Pompeius, first of comrades I ever knew,   5
How often we once shortened the length of day
    With wine, while garlands decked our hair all
        Gleaming from Syrian oil of laurel!

With you I shared the headlong retreat and rout
At Philippi, my neat little shield thrown down,   10
    When valor broke and loud-mouthed boasters
        Bit the inglorious dust and perished.

But me through foes swift Mercury swept away
In all my terror, cloaked in a thickened cloud,
    Whereas the seething tides of warfare   15
        Carried you back into further battles.

So pay to Jove the banquet you vowed to him,
Find rest from long campaigns on a dining couch
    Beneath my laurel tree, — not sparing
        Wine jars selected for your enjoyment.   20

Brim polished cups with Massic that lets a man
Forget, and pour out deep-bellied conch-shells full
    Of scented oils. — Won't someone kindly
        Hurry and braid us some wreaths of myrtle

And moistened parsley! — Who, by the Venus-throw,   25
Will be the drinking-master? — I'll carry on
    More madly than a Thracian: it is
        Nice to go wild at a friend's returning.

1–2   After the assassination of Julius Caesar on March 15, 44 B.C. Brutus tarried in Rome until July. He then went, not to his governorship of Crete as assigned by the senate, but to Athens, where he recruited Roman university students for his army, Horace among them, and probably the present Pompeius, of whom nothing is known beyond what this poem says. Campaigns in "wild" Thrace followed, while conspirator Cassius was raising his own army in Syria and Asia (Turkey). The two armies joined in September of 42 B.C. See S.1.6.48 and note.

3–4   In 29 B.C., the date of Ode 2.7, Octavius Caesar granted amnesty to all Romans who had fought against him. He, therefore, has brought Pompeius home again.

8   "Oil of laurel" = *Malobathrum*, which Moore says is Hindu *tamalapattram*, "the leaf of the *tamala* tree. "Syria" is merely the transshipment port for Oriental wares.

9–12   Actually, there were two battles at Philippi. On October 23rd Mark Antony defeated Cassius, who then committed suicide. Octavius Caesar was present, but ill, and he abandoned his camp before Brutus captured it. On November 16th, 42 B.C. the combined forces of Antony and Octavius Caesar routed the army of Brutus, who escaped but committed suicide the following day. Thus it is 13 years since Horace has seen Pompeius.

Recruited at Athens, Horace may well have carried the Greek *pármē,* "a small round shield used by light infantry," but there is whimsicality in the Latin diminutive form *parmula,* hence our "neat little shield." And Horace may well have jettisoned his *parmula — non bene,* "not as one should"; but since both Alcáeus and Archílochus speak of shields *they* threw away when fleeing from battle, the detail may be more poetic tradition than autobiography. Compare Epode 1, 16, where Horace called himself "unwarlike . . . and less than rugged."

13–14   Mercury is the protector of poets, as in *Odes* 2.17.29 below. The lines echo *Iliad* 3. 380–382 (as did *Odes* 1.15.13–20):

> But Aphroditē caught up Paris
> easily, since she was divine, and wrapped him in a thick mist
> and set him down again in his own perfumed bedchamber.

> (Lattimore translation)

15–16   We infer that Pompeius remained with Antony's forces, perhaps right down to the final defeat in the summer of 30 B.C. (whereas Horace had been "home" since 41 B.C.).

19   A laurel tree, sacred to Apollo and to poetry, probably did grace the patio of the Sabine farm.

21   The *Mons Massicus* (now Monte Massico) was near the famous wine region N of Capua.

25   The "Venus-throw" was the highest throw at dice, or at knuckle-bones (*tali*), when each bone (of four) landed with a different side uppermost.

27   The text days *Edoni,* a particular tribe of Thracians; compare *Odes* 1.27.1–2. Horace recalls more than one impression of Thrace from his campaigning days with Brutus.

2.8.   *Ulla si iuris tibi peierati*

Meter: Sapphic stanza: in lines 1, 2, and 3:   _ U _ > _ U U _ U _ U

                in line 4:   _ U U _ U

> If a single one of your perjured vows had
> Ever brought you punishment, Barinē, if
> You had been disfigured by one black tooth or
>   Fingernail blemish,

5
> I would now believe you; but just as soon as
> You forswear your head, the effect is beauty
> Flashing brighter still, so our young men's heads are
>   Fairly distracted.

> Oaths you falsely swear by your mother's ashes

10
> Work to your advantage, and those by total
> Skies of spangling stars, and by gods who know not
>   Death's chilling terror.

> Venus laughs to hear them, I say; the guileless
> Nymphs laugh also; pitiless Cupid laughs — and

15
> Goes on whetting arrows of torment at his
>   Blood-bedashed grindstone.

What is more, a whole generation, growing
Up is now augmenting your corps of slaves, while
    Old ones do not quit your disloyal roof as
        Threatened so often.   20

You are feared by mothers of sons maturing,
You are feared by oldsters of frugal ways, and
    Young brides live in dread that a breath of yours may
        Charm away husbands.

1–4   "Barinē" is Greek for "a girl from Barium," that is, modern Bari on the SE coast of
Italy, a place which *was* Greek-speaking.
      Telling lies was supposed to cause white spots on fingernails.
13–14   Plato (*Symposium* 183, speech of Pausanias) says: ". . . strangest of all, (a lover) may
swear and forswear himself (so men say), and the gods will forgive his transgression, for
there is no such thing as a lover's oath." (Jowett translation)
      From a poem (3.6.49–50) that goes under the name of Tibullus: "Jupiter laughs at
the false oaths of lovers and bids the winds carry them off without fulfillment." (Postgate
translation in Loeb Classical Library)
      Juliet (in II,2) reminds Romeo that: ". . . at Lovers perjuries/ They say Jove
laught." (Parallels cited by Moore)
21   The text rather surprisingly says: "Mothers fear you for the sake of their young bullocks"
(*iuvencis*). Compare Lalagē as a heifer calf in *Odes* 2.5 and the fond name of Dámalis,
meaning "heifer calf," in *Odes* 1.36.

2.9.   *Non semper imbres nubibus hispidos*

Meter: Alcaic stanza: in lines 1 and 2:   U _ U _ > _ U U _ U _
                  in line 3:   U _ U _ U _ U _ U
                  in line 4:   _ U U _ U U _ U _ U

The clouds do not forever pour murky rain
On sodden fields, the Caspian Sea is not
    Whipped up in gusting squalls forever,
        Nor, in Armenian mountain regions,

Do tracts of ice, friend Valgius, lie inert   5
Through all the seasons; high on Gargánus' crest
    The oaks are not by northwinds bent or
        Ash-trees bewidowed of leaves forever,

But you persist in uninterrupted grief
For Mystes lost in death; at the evening star   10
    Your poems do not cease lamenting,
        Nor do they cease under fleeting sunlight.

As fair lost son, Antílochus was not mourned
Throughout his father's kingship of triple length,
15   Nor did the parents or the Phrygian
Sisters of Tróilus go on weeping

That boy forever. End this unmanliness
Of protestations once and for all, and let
Augustus Caesar's newest triumphs
20   Serve as our subjects: — Niphátes ice-bound;

The river of the Medes now compelled to roll
Less haughty waves for peoples subdued to law;
And in restricted bounds Gelóni
Riding their raids of a narrowed compass.

5   Caius Valgius Rufus was fellow poet of Horace's in the Maecenas circle, cited in S.1.10.82 for his respected literary judgment. All his writings are lost: elegies (*amores*; see the note to E. 2.3.75–78), rhetorical and medical works, even an epic on an unknown subject. "None other comes nearer to immortal Homer," says a pseudo-Tibullus poem, 3.7 (or 4.1).179–180. In 12 B.C. he was *consul suffectus*, that is, he filled a consular vacancy.

6–8   Gargánus (now the Promontorio del Gargáno) is the mountainous "spur" on the "boot" of Italy, NE of Horace's birthplace.

10   The Greek name "Mystes" means "an initiate into the religious mysteries." Comparison with Antílochus and Tróilus indicates an *ephebus* aged 16 to 20. He is likely to have been a Greek slave or freedman.

13–14   Antílochus, son of Nestor, was too young to join the Greek forces at the beginning of the ten-year Trojan War, but he came later. In *Odyssey* 3.112 ff. Nestor says: "And there too died my lovely son, the strong, clean Antílochus, who was surpassingly swift-footed and a fighter." (T.E. Lawrence translation)

Iliad 1.250–2 tells how Nestor was king of Pylos over three generations of men.

15–17   Of Tróilus, son of Priam, it was prophesied that Troy could not fall if he lived to age 20. Moore says that vase painters frequently represented Achilles killing Tróilus near a spring and that, in art, his was the "type" of premature death.

Iliad 24.257 barely mentions his death, *Aeneid* 1.474–8 says hardly more, but "Dares the Phrygian" (? 1st century A.D.) supplies a few non-Homeric details, which Benoit de Sainte-Maure, ca. 1160, will expand on; from Benoit the medieval "Troilus story" is further developed by Boccaccio, Chaucer, and Shakespeare.

19   The title of "Augustus" was conferred upon Octavius Caesar in January of 27 B.C. The full phrase "Augustus Caesar," which occurs only here, suggests that the present poem was composed when the title was still new.

20   Horace addresses Valgius as fellow poet in Maecenas's household.

20–24   Niphátes was probably a mountain in Armenia, though some ancient writers considered it a river.

"The river of the Medes" is the Euphrates.

"The Gelóni were a Scythian tribe along the Tanaïs (now the Don) River in S Russia.

All three names are "west-Asian." But Augustus was directing the campaigns in NW Spain in 26–25 B.C., and the expedition to "Araby the Blest" (note to lines 1–2 of *Odes* 1.29) was called off. Perhaps the "newest triumphs" (*nova tropaea*) were diplomatic and had to do with that *second* mission of deposed Parthian King Phraátes IV to Augustus in 27–26 B.C. (note to *Odes* 2.2.17), or with the Scythian embassy that came to Augustus at Tarraco (Tarragona), Spain, mentioned in *Monumentum Ancyrum* 5.51.

2.10   *Rectius vives, Licini, neque altum*

Meter: Sapphic stanza: in lines 1, 2, and 3:   _ ∪ _ > _ ∪ ∪ _ ∪ _ ∪
                           in line 4:   _ ∪ ∪ _ ∪

Seek to live, Licínius, life more fitly,
Neither pressing always to open seas nor
So afraid of storms that you steer too close to
          Treacherous shorelines.

Any man that prizes the golden mean will   5
Live secure from ramshackle roof and squalor
And, in wisdom, equally safe from mansions
          Subject to envy.

Mighty pines most often endure the brunt of
Gales, and more disastrously falls the lofty   10
Tower when it falls, and the lightnings ravage
          Summits of mountains.

Any heart well fortified hopes in times of
Trouble, and, when fortune is showing favor
Most, will fear the opposite fate. Bleak winters   15
          Jupiter sends, and

Takes away again; and if things are adverse
Now, they will not stay so; Apollo sometimes
Wakes the silent Muse with his lyre and does not
          Always speed arrows.   20

When the pinch most hurts, it is time for strength and
Staunchness; wisdom counsels no less a cautious
Taking in of sail when the wind too strongly
          Swells them with favor.

1   Licínius was Aulus Licínius Muréna, commonly known as "Varro Murena" from
having been adopted by the famous scholar and encyclopedist, Marcus Teréntius Varro.
Thus he was the brother-in-law of the Caius Proculéius Varro of *Odes* 2.2.5–8 and note,
and brother-by-adoption of the beautiful but petulant Teréntia whom the middle-aged
Maecenas took to wife in 23 B.C. As co-consul with Augustus in 23 B.C., "Varro Muréna"
challenged the emperor's authority to overrule the senate and suffered rebuff, with the
result that he entered into a conspiracy to assassinate Augustus. The plot was discovered
and "Varro Muréna" was put to death.
     Maecenas, aware of the impending arrest, warned Teréntia, who in turn warned
her brother-by-adoption, but too late to save him. Maecenas's breach of
confidence—and to a woman!—gravely offended Augustus, so that there was ill-will for
some time between the two friends.
     With these subsequent events in mind, we read the present poem with more
poignant attention.
5   After *carpe diem* (*Odes* 1.11.8), "the golden mean," *aurea mediocritas*, is Horace's best-known
phrase.

18–20   Apollo with his lyre was the patron of music and poetry; with his bow, he was a god
        of death, disease, and vengeance.

2.11.   *Quid bellicosus Cantaber et Scythes,*

Meter: Alcaic stanza: in lines 1 and 2:   U _ U _ > _ U U _ U _
                               in line 3:   U _ U _ U _ U _ U
                               in line 4:   _ U U _ U U _ U _ U

          Cease fretting how Cantábrians may proceed
          In war, Hirpínus Quinctius, or the Scyths
                Across the Adriatic there, and
                      Cease being anxious about requirements

5   When life demands but little. Our beardless cheeks
          And beauty swiftly fall to the rear of time;
                Gray hair and withered age deny us
                      Frolicsome loves and an easy slumber.

          Spring's loveliness of flowers does not endure
10   Unchanged, the blushing moon does not always shine
                In single aspect: why, then, vex your
                      Mind with eternal and hopeless problems?

          Why don't we both go lie at our ease beneath
          That lofty plane tree there, or beneath this pine,
15   With roses round our gray hair, scented—
                      While there is time — with Assyrian perfumes,

          And drink at leisure? Bacchus dispels the cares
          That gnaw our gizzards. — Where is a lad to run
                For water from the passing brook to
20   Cool this Falerian fire in wine cups?

          Won't someone go fetch Lýdē, the easy wench
          From down the path? And tell her to hurry up,
                And bring her ivory lyre, and wear her
                      Hair in a bun like a Spartan woman.

1–3   The allusions suggest the years 26–25 B.C., when Augustus was directing the cam-
      paigns against the Cantabrians of NW Spain and when the Scythian embassy came to
      him at Tarraco (Tarragona), as mentioned in the note to *Odes* 2.9.20–24. The Scyths of
      south Russia were considerably farther off than "Across the Adriatic there": we infer
      that Quinctius was geographically naive and that Horace is teasing him.
7–8   In 26–25 B.C. Horace was 39–40 years of age.
16   "Assyrian" and "Syrian" meant much the same thing. "Perfumes" is "nard" in the text;
      Moore says "nard" is the same as the "Syrian oil of laurel" in *Odes* 2.7.8.

17   "Bacchus" is *Euhius*, the personified cry of the bacchanals, as in *Odes* 1.18.9 and note.
21–22   "Lýdē" is the Greek form of "Lydia"; see the note to *Odes* 1.8.1. The text calls her a
"whore" (*scortum*) outright, while "From down the path" stands for the single word
devium, modifying *scortum*; it seems to mean one who lives "off the main road" (*via*),
presumably in a cottage by herself. (Compare *Odes* 3.14.21–24.)

The poem is addressed to Quínctius Hirpínus—Horace inverts the name (as in *Odes* 2.2.2.);
"Quinctius" is a variant of "Quintus"; the Hirpini were a Samnite tribe from southern Italy.
    If this man is identical with the Quinctius addressed five or six years later in E.1.16,
Horace speaks to him in an utterly different manner there. He also describes the Sabine farm
as if Quinctius had never seen it, whereas here the setting *is* the Sabine farm: where else
would Horace make himself so completely at home as in lines 13–24?

2.12.   *Nolis longa ferae bella Numantiae*

Meter: in lines 1, 2, and 3:   _ > _ U U _ _ U U _ U _
                    in line 4:   _ > _ U U _ U _

Not long warfare and fierce   siege of Numántia,
Not grim Hannibal's work,   nor the Sicilian sea
Red with blood of the men   Carthage sent forth, — all themes
    Suiting ill with the tender lyre;

Not brute Lapiths against   centaur Hyláeus wine-   5
Crazed, nor Earth Mother's wild   giants whom Hercules
Tamed in combat that shook   Saturn's primeval house
    Where in glory it shone above

Sky and cloudbanks; besides,   *you* shall relate in prose
Works, Maecenas, the wars   Caesar has won, with more   10
Skill than I can command,   telling of tyrant kings
    Led in chains through triumphal streets.

My sweet Muse bids me sing   lady Licýmnia's
Praise, describing the fair   light of her lustrous eyes
And the mutual trust   holding her heart and yours   15
    In the bonds of devoted love.

Stiff constraint does not keep   her from the choral dance,
Nor from light repartee,   nor from entwining arms
With the maidens attired   grandly before the throngs
    On Diana's most holy day.   20

Would you take the entire   wealth of Acháemenēs
Or the treasure of King   Mýgdon of Phrygia
In exchange for but one   lock of Licýmnia's hair?
    Or all Araby's precious stores

25   When she stretches her neck   up for the ardent kiss
             You have waiting, or when,   feigning austerity,
             She refuses, and while   wishing it might be forced
                  From her, steals one herself from you?

Horace declines to write poems, or an epic, about the wars of Roman history (1–4), or about
mythological wars (5–8), and he will leave it to Maecenas to write a prose history of the wars
won by Caesar Augustus (9–12); rather, he will write in praise of Maecenas's bride.

1–4   Three Roman wars suitable for epic poetry:
        · Ten years of war, 143–133 B.C., ending with the capture of Numantia, a now
          uninhabited mountain site W of Saragossa, had brought all of Spain and Por-
          tugal under Roman control, except for the NW region of the Cantabrians and
          Asturians.
        · Hannibal, the great Carthaginian General, was defeated in the Second Punic
          War, 218–201 B.C.
        · Roman annihilation of the Carthaginian fleet off the W coast of Sicily ended the
          First Punic War, 264–241 B.C.
5–9   Two mythological wars:
        · The battle of the Lapiths and Centaurs: see *Odes* 1.18.7–8 and note. "Hyláeus"
          means "of the woods," in the sense of "backwoodsman."
        · Hercules rescued the gods when the giants—earth-born creatures with human
          bodies but with serpent-tails in lieu of feet—stormed the very sky. This was
          already in Zeus/Jupiter's time, but Horace puts it further back, in the time of
          Saturn (Jupiter's father). (On this point Horace will contradict himself when he
          tells the story of the battle in *Odes* 3.4.49–64, but mythology may have two
          versions of the event.)
9–12   As far as is known, Maecenas never undertook such a prose history.
13   Classical antiquity understood "Licýmnia" as a poetic cover-name for Teréntia, whom
       Maecenas married in 23 B.C., when he was in his latter forties. The two names are
       metrical equivalents, like Catullus's "Lesbia" for an actual Clodia and Tibullus's
       "Delia" for an actual Plania. For more about Teréntia see *Odes* 2.10.1 and note. The
       stormy marriage ended in separation, and Teréntia seems to have become a mistress of
       the emperor.
21–24 Acháemenēs was the alleged ancestor of the Persian "Great Kings" whose line
       extended from 559 B.C. until Alexander the Great's conquest of 330 B.C.
            Mygdon, like Midas of the golden touch, was a half-legendary king of Phrygia (NW
       Turkey).
            Araby = Biblical Sheba, as in *Odes* 1.29.4 and note.

2.13.   *Ille et nefasto te posuit die*

Meter: Alcaic stanza: in lines 1 and 2:   U _ U _ > _ U U _ U _
                          in line 3:   U _ U _ U _ U _ U
                          in line 4:   _ U U _ U U _ U _ U

             Whoever set you out in the first place, tree,
             He chose an evil day, and he nurtured you

With evil hands, to bring the district's
    Future inhabitants bane and mischief;

A strangler of his father, as like as not,   5
A man that likely murdered a guest by night
    And splashed the victim's gore on shrines of
        Household divinities; Colchis poisons

Were stock in trade to him; every sort of crime
He practiced, he that planted you on my land,   10
    You sorry stick that, in your falling,
        Aimed at the life of your harmless master.

For all precautions taken, from hour to hour
No man is safe. The Tyrian sailor dreads
    The Bosporus in storms but fears no   15
        Fate that may strike from another quarter;

The soldier dreads the Parthian's arrows shot
From swift retreats, the Parthian, dungeon chains
    In Rome; yet death has come to men in
        Forms unforeseen and will ever come so.   20

How close I was to seeing the gloomy realm
Of Próserpine, Aeácus's judgment seat,
    The homes assigned the good, and Sappho
        In her Aeólian strains complaining

About the girls that lived in her native land,   25
And you, with golden plectrum, Alcáeus, in
    Full song of hardships known at sea, and
        Hardships of exile, and warfare's hardships.

The shades with awe are silent, as at a rite,
To hear them both, but shoulder-to-shoulder dense   30
    The crowd most stands there drinking air at
        Songs about battles and ousted tyrants.

No wonder, then, that, hearing those songs, the beast
Lays back the swarthy ears on his hundred heads
    And in the Furies' hair the coiling   35
        Snakes come to rest from their ceaseless writhing.

Prométheus, even Tántalus, turn away
From dooms of torment, hearing that lovely sound;
    Oríon, hearing, cares no more for
        Starting of lions and coward lynxes.   40

1–2 One day on his farm Horace narrowly escaped death from a falling tree. How the
  near-accident came to happen is not disclosed, but from the anniversary poem, *Odes* 3.8,

the day can be determined as March 1, 30 B.C. Horace will allude to the event again in *Odes* 2.17.27 and 3.4.27.

8   Colchis, at the E end of the Black Sea, was the homeland of Medea and of poisons.

17–18   The famous Parthian cavalry maneuver, as in *Odes* 1.19.11–12 and note.

21–23   Horace now proceeds to speak as if he had, in very fact, descended to the land of after-death; the journey's stages are:

1. *into* Hades, where Próserpine is queen over the dead;
2. *past* the judgment seat of Aeácus, who, like his brothers Minos and Rhadamánthys, is a judge of the dead;
3. and *on to* the Elysian Fields where the good have their dwellings and where Sappho and Alcaeus are.

23–28   Both poets spoke and wrote in the Aeólic/Aeólian dialect of Greek. Sappho's complaint is that the girls evade her love. A few fragments survive from the poems Alcaeus composed on the themes mentioned here.

29–30   The phrase "as at a rite" seeks to clarify *sacro digna silentio* for the modern reader; Milton, in *Paradise Lost* 5.555, closely follows the Latin: "Worthy of Sacred silence to be heard."

33–34   Cerberus, the watchdog of hell, usually has three heads; Horace gives him a hundred; Robert Graves (*The Greek Myths* 31.3 claims the original number was fifty.

37   Prometheus is nowhere else said to be in the underworld. Horace may be echoing the lost prose work, *Prometheus*, by Maecenas.

39–40   Oríon is not the constellation, as in *Odes* 1.28.22, but the ghost of the mighty hunter whom Ulysses/Odysseus saw still hunting wild beasts in the afterlife in *Odyssey* 11. 572 ff. A few lines further, *Odyssey* 11 describes the punishment of Tantalus.

2.14. *Eheu fugaces, Postume, Postume*

Meter: Alcaic stanza: in lines 1 and 2:   U _ U _ > _ U U _ U _
in line 3:   U _ U _ U _ U _ U
in line 4:   _ U U _ U U _ U _ U

Alas, the swift years, Postumus, Postumus,
Slip by us, nor does piety toward the gods
    Delay relentless age and wrinkles,
        Nor will it save us from Death Unconquered,

5   Not if on every day of your life, my friend,
You slay three hundred oxen in sacrifice
    To tearless Pluto, in whose kingdom
        Three-torsoed Géryon lies enclosed by

A dismal stream, and Títyus too, — a stream
10 Enclosing all who feed on the fruits of earth,
    And none of us escape it, neither
        Monarchs nor poverty-stricken farmers.

In vain we seek avoidance of cruel Mars
And shattered waves of hoarse Adriatic seas,

In vain we fear our bodies' harm from   15
　　Southwinds that waft us autumnal poisons.

We must and shall behold, in its sluggish flow,
Cocýtus' stream, and Dánaüs' evil brood
　　Of daughters, and the everlasting
　　　　Torments of Sísyphus, son of Áeolus.   20

The earth, your house, the wife that you love so well,
Must be abandoned, and, of these trees you tend
　　So fondly, none except the hated
　　　　Cypress will follow its short-lived master.

Your heir will drink the Cáecuban hoarded up   25
Behind a hudnred keys — and deserve it more:
　　The haughty wine will stain bright floors at
　　　　Suppers more lavish than pontiffs' banquets.

1　Postumus is unknown.
6　*One* hundred oxen (a "hecatomb") was already a very expensive offering.
7　Pluto/Hades/Orcus was the god who ruled the land of the dead.
8　Three-headed Géryon was a monster slain by Hercules.
9　For attempted rape of Leto/Latona, mother of Apollo and Artemis/Diana, as she came
　　to Delphi, the giant Títyus was pegged down over nine acres of hell forever, with a vulture
　　to eat continuously at his liver. More will be told of him in *Odes* 3.4.77–79 and note. See
　　also the note to line 20 of the present poem.
9–10　The enclosing stream is named in line 18 below as Cocýtus: Greek: *kōkȳtós*, "wailing,
　　lamentation"; *Aeneid* 6. 132 says it surrounds (*circumvenit*) the land of the dead.
18–19　The fifty daughters of King Danaüs of Argos, at their father's bidding, murdered
　　their bridegrooms on one and the same bridal night, for which crime they carry water in
　　leaky jars forever in the land-after-death. One daughter disobeyed her father and
　　rescued her bridegroom, as Horace tells in *Odes* 3.11.22–52.
20　For betraying secrets of Zeus/Jupiter, Sísyphus forever rolls a great stone uphill in the
　　afterlife, only to have it slip from his hands just before the crest. The "dooms" of Oríon
　　and Tántalus (in the preceding ode) and of Títyus and Sísyphus are all described in a
　　continuous passage, *Odyssey* 11. 572 ff.
23–24　Cypress trees were planted in cemeteries.
28　The wealth of "pontiffs" (priests) and the lavishness of their banquets were proverbial,
　　as the note to *Odes* 1.37.2–4 remarked *à propos* of the *Salii*. These nongovernmental
　　organizations of priests corresponded to modern "benevolent orders" like the Masons,
　　Knights of Columbus, and so on, and, in imperial times at least, the banqueters dined in
　　the temple of their particular god, as the god's guests for the occasion.

2.15　*Iam pauca aratro iugera regiae*

Meter: Alcaic stanza:　in lines 1 and 2:　　U _ U _ > _ U U _ U _
　　　　　　　　　in line 3:　　U _ U _ U _ U _ U
　　　　　　　　　in line 4:　　_ U U _ U U _ U _ U

With all these lordly mansions, there soon will be
Few acres left to plow; we will everywhere:
    See fish-weirs broader than the Lucrine
        Lake, and the vine-wedded elms displaced by

5   The bachelor plane tree; violet beds, and stands
Of myrtle then, and nose-tickling flower scents,
    Will waft their odors over olive
        Groves that bore fruit for their former owners,

And matted laurel branches will wall away
10   The burning sun-darts. Romulus did not so
    Ordain things, nor was this the rule when
        Long-bearded Cato announced the omens.

The lists of private riches were short ones then,
The state's accounts were long; with no ten-foot rod
15   Were private colonnades laid out to
        Capture the shade and the northern breezes,

The laws forbade disdaining of random sods
For thatch, directing rather that public funds
    Be used for this new stone adornment
20   Only in temples and public structures.

3–4   The Lucrine Lake, near Baiae, furnished oysters (Epode 2, 49) and "jumbo-size mussels" (S.2.4.32). The narrow neck of land dividing it from the sea had been pierced by Agrippa's engineers in 37 B.C. to make a storm-safe harbor for the war fleet.

4–5   Grapevines were trained up elms and poplars (as in Epode 2, 9–10 and note), but the broad leaves of the plane trees would not allow the grapes to ripen; hence the plane tree is a "bachelor"—or a "widow"—in Martial's poem 3.58.3 a century later.

5–6   The myrtle is a 9-foot-high aromatic *shrub* with pink and white flowers; at Baiae there were myrtle *groves* (E.1.15.6). Ground-cover "myrtle" is properly the periwinkle.

12   "Announced the omens" as officiating augur; see the note to *Odes* 1.2.32 about "Augur Apollo." Marcus Porcius Cato, the "Elder," 234–149 B.C., was the model of plain living and stern morality.

19   "This new stone adornment" is the very white Carrara marble (from ancient Luna, N of Pisa) first used in 28 B.C. in the new library temple of Apollo (*Odes* 1.31.1–2 and note).

2.16   *Otium divos rogat in patenti*

Meter: Sapphic stanza: in lines 1, 2, and 3:   _ U _ > _ U U _ U _ U
                    in line 4:   _ U U _ U

Peace is what is asked of the gods when one is
Caught amid the open Aegéan Sea as

Stormclouds hide the moon and the stars no longer
    Shine for the sailors;

Peace is what the war-crazy Thracians want, and   5
Peace the Medes desire, with their fancy quivers,
Grosphus, — peace unboughten with gems or gold or
    Garments of purple.

Neither wealth nor magistrate's escort guard can
Clear a path through worries that fret our minds or   10
Drive off cares that over our paneled ceilings
    Circle and circle.

Living well on little is he whose father's
Silver salt-dish gleams on a frugal table:
Neither fear nor covetous greed prevents his   15
    Lightness of slumber.

Why, in life's brief span, do we bravely fight for
Many things? Why move to another land and
Sunlight? What expatriate once escaped him-
    self in his exile?   20

Bronze-beaked ships are never without grim Care on
Board, she rides with cavalry squadrons ever,
Swifter than the stag she is, swifter too than
    Cloud-driving southwinds.

If the present moment contents you, never   25
Mind the future, temper unpleasant things with
Quiet smiles: no happiness ever yet was
    Total and perfect.

Sudden death befell the renowned Achilles,
Endless aging wasted Tithónus' body,   30
And perhaps an hour disallowed to you, to
    Me will be granted.

Your Sicilian flocks and a hundred herds of
Lowing cows surround you, your jaunty driving
Mare sings out in whinnies, and, double-dyed in   35
    African purple,

Woolen garments clothe you: a little farm and
Gentle promptings breathed by the Grecian Muse are
Mine from trusty Fate, — and the gift of scorning
    Ill-wishing people.   40

6 Medes = Parthians, as usual.
7 Grosphus must be the Pompeius Grosphus whom Horace will recommend for his

high-principled character to Íccius in E.1.12.21–24. Both men are connected with Sicily, Grosphus in line 33 of this poem and Íccius in line 2 of the Epistle.

14   A salt-dish (*salinum*) and a plate (*patella*) for offerings to the gods were traditionally the only items of luxury in poor households. Both were usually of silver and were kept brightly polished.

19–20   A more famous formulation of the same thought will come in E.1.11.27. No word division occurs here between lines in the Latin text, but the word *ve-nale* (represented by "unboughten") *is* divided between lines 7 and 8 above. Similar divisions occur in *Odes* in 1.2.19–20 (*u-xorius*) and 1.25.11–12 (*inter-lunia*), all cases being in the 3rd and 4th lines of the Sapphic meter, and with "authorization" from Sappho herself. Evidently the 3rd and 4th lines of the Sapphic stanza were taken as a single long unit of verse.

30   Tithónus had immortality but not eternal youth; see the note to *Odes* 1.28.8.

35–37   "Double-dyed" = *bis tinctae* (Greek *díbapha*), a trade word. (Epode 12, 21 *iteratae* has the same sense.) African *murex* was almost as highly prized as the Tyrian *murex*. Roman clothing was chiefly woolen, though linen was also used.

2.17.   *Cur me querellis exanimas tuis?*

Meter: Alcaic stanza: in lines 1 and 2:   U _ U _ > _ U U _ U _
                              in line 3:   U _ U _ U _ U _ U
                              in line 4:   _ U U _ U U _ U _ U

Why must you so torment me with your complaints?
The thought that *I* should die before *you* shocks both
    The gods and me, Maecenas, staying
        Pillar and glory of my existence.

5   Ah, if some force untimely should wrench away
One portion of my soul, would the rest of me,
    Less dearly prized and incomplete, go
        Lingering on by itself? That day would

Pull both parts down in ruin. I did not swear
10   An oath of false allegiance: we shall, we shall,
    If you precede me, make that final
        Journey together as furnished comrades.

Chiméra's breath of fire will not part us, nor
Will hundred-handed Gyas, if from the ground
15   He rises up with force: almighty
        Justice so wills, and the Fates eternal.

No matter whether Libra or Scorpio
In all his wrath was in the ascendency
    When I was born, or whether it was
20   Capricorn, lord of the western ocean,

Our guiding stars — incredibly — do maintain
One common course: Jove's guardianship flashed out
    Resistance to the bane of Saturn,
        Checking the wings of the bird of death as

It sped to you, — and theater crowds burst forth   25
In three hurrahs of joy at your health restored;
    The tree that fell upon my head would
        Surely have killed me, except that Faunus,

Who watches over Mercury's men, restrained
The mortal blow. Remember the shrine and all   30
    Your votive sacrifices promised;
        I will give merely a humble she-lamb.

10–12   Horace died on November 27, 8 B.C., just short of his 57th birthday; Maecenas died some months before, J.-M. André (in *Mécène,* Paris, 1967) says in September.

13   The Chiméra, as in the note to *Odes* 1.27.24, was the monster with lion's head, she-goat's body, and serpent's tail, but here she also breathes fire; see *Odes* 4.2.14–15.

14–15   Gyas is obscure. *Iliad* 1. 402–3 speaks of a hundred-handed Briareus, who is elsewhere said to have a brother Gyges, of simlar shape; perhaps "Gyas" = "Gyges," though in *Aeneid* 10. 318 Aeneas slays a *human* enemy, "enormous" Gyas.

16   "Justice" (*Iustitia*) = Themis, the Titaness older and more powerful than Zeus himself and personification of Law, Justice, Right. See Jane Harrison; *Themis,* pp. 480–535.

17–23   The allusions are all astrological. Jove (Jupiter) and Saturn are planets of opposing influences. The zodiacal signs also controlled territories; Capricorn's domain included Spain and what is now France.

25–27   Maecenas received the ovation in the theater in 30 B.C. (*Odes* 1.20.3–8 and note); Horace narrowly escaped death from the falling tree on March 1, 30 B.C. (*Odes* 2.13. 1–12 and note).

28   Roman Faunus/Greek Pan, as in the note to *Odes* 1.17.1.; as forest god, he would control a falling tree. (But see our suggestion in the note to *Odes* 3.18.1–4.)

29   Mercury/Hermes, as "first founder of song and lyre-shell" *Odes* 1.10.6), is a protector of poets; see also *Odes* 3.11.1–2. Still, "Mercury's men" (*Mercurialium virorum*) would usually suggest someone successful in business, as in S.2.3.26, and it is not clear why Faunus should be interested in such persons.

32   In the text, "I" = "we" (*nos*), though the entire poem up to line 32 speaks in first person singular. The plural indicates humble deference; compare *Odes* 1.6.5 and note.

2.18.   *Non ebur neque aureum*

Meter: in the odd-numbered lines: _ U _ U _ U _
       in the even-numbered lines: U _ U _ U _ U _ U _ U

On the ceiling of my house
    No gold or polished ivory gleams in splendor,
    Nor do marble beams from Mount

           Hyméttus burden columns hewn in furthest

5   Africa; no unknown heir

           Of Áttalus am I to take his palace

Over, nor do client dames

           From Sparta give me gifts of purple dye-stuffs;

But a vein of honesty

10   And talent brings me rich men's visits, poor as

I am: and I importune

           The gods for nothing more, I do not press my

Influential friend for more,

           Enriched enough with just my Sabine farmstead.

15   But, while day crowds after day

           And new moons swiftly grow and perish,

You, with one foot in your grave,

           Keep letting contracts out for sawing marble,

Building houses but no tomb,

20   And pushing back the sounding seas of Báiae

From their normal shores because

           You find the present coastline unattractive.

Will it be too long before

           You rip up corner markers of your neighbor's

25   Property and jump wth greed

           The bounds of clients' rights? Your prey, evicted,

Household gods in toga-fold,

           With wife and ragged children goes to exile.

But no hall more certainly

30   Awaits proprietors of wealth than greedy

Orcus and the destined goal

           Of Death. Why seek more treasure? Equal plots of

Earth contain the sons of kings

           And poor men's sons, and Orcus' boatman would not

35   Ferry shrewd Prométheus back

           For bribes of gold. The haughty Tántalus and

All the race of Tántalus

           Death holds in his constraint, and he releases

Toilworn drudges from their toil

40   When they invoke him — or do not invoke him.

3–5   The crossbeams (architraves) are of the bluish white marble fom Mount Hyméttus just SE of Athens ((whence came also the prized honey in *Odes* 2.6.14–15), while the columns are of the "antique yellow" (*giallo antico*) marble of Numidia (Tunisia-Algeria).

5–7   The proverbially wealthy Áttalus III, King of Pergamum, bequeathed his kingdom and treasure to Rome in 133 B.C., as mentioned in *Odes* 1.1.12 and note. In Horace's time this was felt by many to be the beginning of Rome's "corruption by luxury"; thus ancient commentators understood lines 5–7 as Horace's reproach to his countrymen.

7–8   The allusion is not entirely clear but bribes are surely meant. From the pointed "you" (*tu*) of line 17 we infer that the entire poem addresses an elderly lawyer who has amassed a fortune by sharp practices.

13   The "influential friend" is patently Maecenas, donor of the poet's Sabine farmstead.

20–22   Offshore villa foundations may still be seen when the water is calm in the Bay of Báiae (now Baia, about 16 km/10 m W of Naples). *Odes* 3.1.33–37 imply that there was a veritable rush to build such mansions out over the water. More will be said about those structures in E.1.1.83–85 and note.

23–28   By Roman standards, two extremely grave crimes: removing boundary markers and a lawyer's cheating of clients. Moore compares Deuteronomy 27:17: "Cursed be he that removeth his neighbor's landmark." Pitiless foreclosure of mortgages seems to have been this man's specialty.

34   Orcus' boatman—in the text, "henchman" (*satelles*)—is Charon, who rowed souls of the dead across the Styx to the land-after-death.

35–36   Contrary to all authorities (as in *Odes* 2.13.37 and note), Horace places Prometheus in the underworld; he may again be echoing the lost prose *Prometheus* by Maecenas.

39–40   In Aesop's fable, *Death and the Old Man,* a "toilworn drudge" begs Death to deliver him, but, when Death appears, is horrified and drives him away. La Fontaine's fable I, 15 (*La Mort et le malheureux*) paraphrases Aesop, while I, 16 (*La Mort et le bucheron*) freely reworks the same theme.

2.19.   *Bacchum in remotis carmina rupibus*

Meter: Alcaic stanza: in lines 1 and 2:   U _ U _ > _ U U _ U _
in line 3:   U _ U _ U _ U _ U
in line 4:   _ U U _ U U _ U _ U

> I did see Bacchus, high in a mountain glen —
> Believe me, future hearers! — instructing nymphs
>   In dithyrambs of his, and goat-foot
>   Satyrs all cocking their ears to learn them.
>
> Evoé! My mind still reels from that recent dread   5
> And in my heart, by Bacchus possessed, I feel
>   Wild joy. Evoé! But spare me, Liber,
>   Spare me the goad of your painful thyrsus!
>
> I feel a strong compulsion to sing in praise
> Of dancers dancing tirelessly, fountain jets   10
>   Of wine and milk, abounding brooks, and
>   Honey that drips from the hollow reed-wands;
>
> I feel compelled to sing of the blessèd spouse
> Immortalized in stars, and the palace hall
>   Of Péntheus toppled to a ruin,   15
>   And of the Thracian Lycúrgus' downfall.
>
> You shunt aside the rivers and eastern seas,
> And drunken on the furthest mountain crests

You tie the hair of Thracian maenads
20   Harmlessly back with a knot of vipers.

And when the wicked gang of the Giants braved
The steep ascent approaching your Father's seat,
In lion-aspect you used claws and
Hideous teeth to send Rhóetus plunging, —

25   Although they said that dances and jesting play
More suited with your nature and rumored you
Unfit for fighting; yet in midst of
Warfare and peace you showed equal prowess.

At sight of your resplendently golden horns
30   Wild Cerberus grew tame, so he softly wagged
His tail, and then with three tongues fondly
Licked at your shins and retreating footsteps.

3–4   Horace makes the Satyrs goat-footed, as did Lucretius: *On the Nature of Things* 4. 580.
The "Pans" were goat-footed, but satyrs were human backwoodsmen with human feet.

5   *Evoé* (*Euhoe,* Greek *euoî,* pronounced approximately "oo-WAY!") was the bacchanal cry.
In *Odes* 1.18.9 it was personified as "Euhius" (translated as "Liber"), also in 2.11.17
(translated as "Bacchus"), meaning "the god of that cry."

5–8   "Evoé!" in ecstasy in line 5, in terror in line 7. The thyrsus, carried by both the god
and his worshippers, was a long reed tipped with a pine cone and sometimes twined with
ivy or vine leaves.
The terror is of literary origin, from that most appalling of all scenes in drama,
when, toward the close of Euripides's *The Bacchae* (ca. 405 B.C.), Queen Agávē appears, in
still-tipsy exaltation, carrying on the tip of her thyrsus what she believes to be the head of
a lion that she tore limb from limb at the height of the night's ecstatic orgy; as her reason
returns to her under the morning's sunlight she comes gradually to realize that the
"lion" was her own son and king, Pentheus.

9–12   Recollections from the Herdsman's speech (lines 706 ff. of *The Bacchae*), describing
how fountains of milk and of wine sprang up for the bacchanals at a thrust of the thyrsus
into soil or rock, how earth was clawed with fingernails, and how honey dripped from the
hollow thyrsi ("reed-wands") themselves.
"Dancers dancing tirelessly" paraphrases "tireless Thyiades," a word formed from
Greek *thúō,* to rush wildly"; see the note to *Odes* 1.17.23–25.
By comparing E.1.16.73–79 one can see how deeply Horace was impressed by *The
Bacchae.*

13–17   Other prodigies of Bacchus/Dionysus:
• He found Ariádnē abandoned on the island of Naxos, married her, and set her
bridal crown as a constellation in the skies; see the finale of Richard Strauss's
opera, *Ariadne auf Naxos.*
• In Thrace, King Lycúrgus of the Edonian tribe (see the note to *Odes* 2.7.27) drove
the god away and imprisoned his followers, for which deed the god struck him
with madness. In what is clearly a variant to the Theban story about Queen
Agávē and her son Pentheus, Lycúrgus in his "ecstasy" axed his son Dryas to
death under the impression that he was cutting down a vine and then regained his
senses while in the act of pruning the corpse of its nose, ears, fingers, and toes. *Iliad*
6. 130–140 says Zeus blinded him for that action and that he died soon afterward,
but others report that his people had him torn to pieces by wild horses.

· In his Asiatic progress Bacchus/Dionysus had merely to touch the rivers Oróntēs (now the Nahr el 'Asi in Syria) and Hydáspēs (now the Jhelum in Pakistan) with his thyrsus and the waters parted to let him cross dry-shod; "eastern seas" = *mare barbarum,* vaguely the Persian Gulf and parts of the Indian Ocean.

18–20   "Thracian maenads" = *Bistonides,* that is, (women) members of the Bistones tribe. Maenads (Greek for "raving ones") were depicted in vase paintings as wearing snakes in their hair. The "furthermost mountain crests," to judge by *Odes* 3.25.8–12, may be those of the Rodopi Mountains along the modern Greek-Bulgarian frontier.

21–24   Here, as in *Odes* 3.4.42–64, Horace follows a version of the Giants' revolt against the sky-gods in which Bacchus and other divinities—even Eros!—fought for Zeus ("your Father," 22). In *Odes* 2.12.6–9 Hercules fought the giants who attacked Saturn.

The "lion-aspect" may be Horace's invention, though Bacchus/Dionysus assumed many animal shapes, especially bull-shape, and though in *The Bacchae* he was mistakenly hunted as a lion.

Giant Rhóetus (pronounce ROY-tus) is obscure.

25–27   Bacchus is regularly beautiful to effeminacy. When he is brought before King Pentheus in *The Bacchae* the king mocks his curls, roseate complexion, and unrugged physique—features derived from the young tendrils and vineleaves.

29–32   The scene is the land-after-death, whither the god has descended in order to bring up the shade of his mortal mother, Semelē. (She was accepted as a goddess on Olympus, but under the name of Thyónē—from Greek *thúō,* as in line 10 above—so as not to offend the other deities.)

Here Cerberus has his usual three heads, not a hundred, as in *Odes* 2.13.33–34.

Bacchus is often "the horned god," commonly with bull's horns, as the half-hypnotized Pentheus fancies he sees him, but sometimes with ram's horns. Here, golden ram's horns curve back from his forehead, we believe, though *aureo cornu* is singular. Moore takes him to be carrying a golden drinking horn.

2.20.   *Non usitata nec tenui ferar*

Meter: Alcaic stanza: in lines 1 and 2:   U _ U _ > _ U U _ U _
                           in line 3:   U _ U _ U _ U _ U
                           in line 4:   _ U U _ U U _ U _ U

On neither weak nor commonplace pinions I
Shall soar aloft, a poet in double shape,
    Through limpid air; I will not longer
       Tarry on earth but, outranging envy,

Will leave the towns behind me. From humble,folk   5
Derived, and yet, belovèd Maecenas, your
    Invited friend, I shall not die, nor
       Shall I be prisoned by Stygian waters.

Upon my legs already the scaly hide
Of birds is forming, upwards my body turns   10
    White-swan-shaped, while from fingers and from
       Shoulders the lightest of feathers lengthen.

> In fame surpassing Ícarus, I shall view
> The shores of moaning Bosporus in my flight,
> 15   And Afric gulfs, and be the singing
>   Swan on the Hyperboréan meadows.
>
> The Colchian shall know me, the Dacian too,
> Who hides his dread of Marsian cohorts, and
>   Remote Gelóni; learnèd Spaniards,
> 20   Rhone-drinkers likewise, will be my scholars.
>
> Beside my empty grave let there be no dirge,
> No gross displays of grief or lamenting wails;
>   Refrain from crying out my name, and
>   Cease and desist from unneeded honors.

1-2   Allegorically: by virtue of my poems, which are neither poor-quality nor in forms trite from much usage by others before me (in Latin). "In double shape" (*biformis*) means "of bird and man," though ancient editor Porphyrio understood the two types of Horace's poems, hexameter and lyric. "Poet" = *vates,* as in *Odes* 2.6.24 and note.

4   With the phrase "outranging envy" (literally "bigger than envy") compare *Odes* 2.16.39–40: "scorning/ Ill-wishing people" (*malignum/ spernere volgus*), but the tone is remote from the protest in S.1.6.46 ff.

7-8   Horace's *fame* will survive, he will not be one of the *nameless* dead beyond the Styx. The meaning, like the meaning of line 1, will be more clearly expressed in *Odes* 3.30.

9   Ícarus fell to his death in "the Icarian Sea": ". . . and a sea shall keep his/ Name and his body," as *Odes* 4.2.3–4 will put it.

14-20   "My works shall be known 'everywhere'." The "Hyperboréan meadows" lie "beyond the northwind (*Boreas*)." The Gelóni were a tribe of Scythians in what is now S Russia.

21-23   Hired women mourners chanted the funeral dirge (*nenia*) and "portrayed" grief by tearing their hair, scratching their cheeks, and beating their breasts. The *conclamatio* was a formalized last crying out of the name of the deceased.

Odes. Book 3

3.1. *Odi profanum volgus et arceo*

Meter: Alcaic stanza: in lines 1 and 2:   U _ U _ > _ U U _ U _
                 in line 3:   U _ U _ U _ U _ U
                 in line 4:   _ U U _ U U _ U _ U

I loathe the mob impure and forbid it place.
Let tongues be silent! Songs hitherto unheard,
    As priestly spokesman of the Muses
        I shall now sing for our youths and maidens.

*

If nations are the charges of mighty kings,   5
The kings themselves are under control of Jove,
    Jove famed in triumph over Giants,
        Moving all things by a flex of eyebrow.

True, one man spaces wider his furrowed rows
For vineyards than another; and this one may   10
    With nobler name on Mars Field canvas
        Votes, with superior reputation

Another may compete, while a third counts more
Supporters: even-handed Necessity
    Allots the fates of high and low, her   15
        Urn being ample to hold all ballots.

Sicilian banquets rouse no desire for food
In someone with a naked suspended sword
    Above his wicked head, and neither
        Music of lyres nor of singing birds will   20

Restore his sleep; yet sleep of the tranquil kind
Does not shun humble houses of rustic men
    Or shady places by a brookside,
        Nor is a valley disturbed by breezes.

25   The man desiring only *enough* will not
            Be worried by the tumult of storms at sea,
                    Or gusting onsets of Arctúrus
                        Setting, or stars of the Haedi rising,

            Or when the hail is lashing his vineyard rows,
30   Or when his farm plays false and the olive tree
                    Blames now the rains and now the burning
                        Heat and again the excessive winters.

            Fish feel their native waters constricted by
            Foundation piers invading the deep, as more
35   Contractors' workmen sink their loads of
                        Stone for support of a rich man's villa

            Who scorns to build on shore. Apprehensive fears
            Go nonetheless wherever the master goes,
                    His private yacht takes Care aboard, and
40   Care sits in saddle behind the horseman.

            And so, if Phrygian marble will not relieve
            Distress, nor wearing purples more lustrous than
                    A star, nor fine Falérnum wine, nor
                        Spices and perfumes of Persian monarchs,

45   Why should I rear up towering palace halls
            In this new style, with envy-arousing gates?
                    Why give my Sabine valley up for
                        Riches entailing more strain and effort?

1–4   The opening stanza regards all six odes that follow, and which ancient commentator
       Porphyrio considered a six-part poem of variations on a theme.
             Line 1 is a priestly injunction before the solemn moment, with parallels in *Aeneid*
       6.258 and in the hymn to Apollo by Callímachus (ca. 260 B.C., in Alexandria), not an
       expression of personal antipathies of the poet.
             "Let tongues be silent!" (*Favete linguis!*, literally: "Favor your tongues!"), is likewise
       a priestly call for solemn silence.
             "For our youths and maidens" (*virginibus puerisque*) means "for our young adults."
       R. L. Stevenson used the Latin phrase as the title for a set of early essays, taking the
       words in an arch sense not intended by Horace.
5–8   The political sense of 5–6 seems made-to-order for the west-European centuries from
       Charlemagne to Napoleon, while the religious sense of 7–8 seems rather more heno-
       theistic than polytheistic.
11   Elections were held on Mars Field (*Campus Martius*); see the note to *Odes* 1.8.4.
14–16 Here "Necessity" = Fate.
17–19 Damocles was enjoying a banquet given by the famous 4th century B.C. Dionysius,
       tyrant of Syracuse, Sicily, until he noticed a sword suspended by a single horsehair over
       his head.
20   Wealthy Romans had aviaries of singing birds in their mansions.
21–24 Horace is thinking of himself and his Sabine farm, as lines 47–48 make clear.
27–28 Arctúrus sets in stormy October; the Haedi ("the Kids") are two stars in the hand of
       "the Charioteer," that is, the constellation Auriga (pronounce oh-RY-guh), whose rising
       betokens rain.
33–36 Another allusion to the villas being built out over the Bay of Báiae, as in *Odes*

2.18.20–22 and note.
41 A costly, purple-veined marble from Synnada, in what is now W-central Turkey.
44 Literally: "the *costum* (an Oriental aromatic shrub) of the Achaeménians," that is, the
    Persian kings claiming descent from Acháemenes, as in *Odes* 2.12.21 and note.

3.2.   *Angustam amice pauperiem pati*

Meter: Alcaic stanza: in lines 1 and 2:   ∪ _ ∪ _ > _ ∪ ∪ _ ∪ _
                        in line 3:   ∪ _ ∪ _ ∪ _ ∪ _ ∪
                        in line 4:   _ ∪ ∪ _ ∪ ∪ _ ∪ _ ∪

In army service toughened, let any boy
Learn how to welcome want like a bosom friend,
    And how to ride with dreaded spear and
        Harry the Parthians bent on battle,

And how to manage life under open skies,   5
In perils' midst: from enemy ramparts then
    The warring tyrant's wife will watch him;
        For him her daughter, of age to marry,

Will sigh — alas! — for fear her betrothèd prince,
Inept at war, may chance to invite the wrath   10
    Of this ferocious lion in his
        Ravening course through the blood and carnage.

To die for country offers a grace, a joy;
Death also overtakes any man that flees,
    Nor does it spare the young who lack for   15
        Spirit, or knees of a running coward.

True manliness, an alien to vile defeat,
Forever shines with honors untarnished, not
    Assuming office or resigning
        Office at wind-shifts of mob opinion;   20

True manhood opens heaven for those too great
To die and tries a path where the ways were barred,
    Abandoning the common herd and
        Dankness of earth on upsurging pinions.

Reward is likewise due for a secret kept;   25
I would forbid a man who divulged the rites
    Of Ceres' sacred mysteries to
        Stand under rafters where *I* stood, or to

Put out to sea with me, for Diéspiter,
Once slighted, often lumps the defiled and pure   30
    Together; Retribution limps but
        Seldom gives up on an evil-doer.

1-6   From the "negatives" of the foregoing poem Horace now turns to the "positives":
       sturdiness of body and of character, self-sacrifice, self-reliance.

6-12   The scene is imaginary—with possibly an echo of *Iliad* 19. 291-2.

13   This famous line reads: *Dulce et decorum est pro patria mori.*

25   Paraphrase of a line by the lyric poet Simónides of Ceos (556 to ca. 467 B.C.), often
       quoted by Augustus in the original Greek.

26-29 The "Eleusínian mysteries" in honor of Ceres/Deméter at Eléusis, a few miles NW of
       Athens, were kept so secret that modern scholars can only partially reconstruct
       them—chiefly from Christian denunciations of them.

          Augustus—himself an initiate—once was judge in "a case in which the privileges of
       Deméter's priests were questioned. Since certain religious secrets had to be quoted in the
       evidence, he cleared the court, dismissed his legal advisers and settled the dispute *in
       camera.*" (Suetonius: *Augustus* 93; Robert Graves translation)

3.3.   *Iustum et tenacem propositi virum*

Meter: Alcaic stanza: in lines 1 and 2:   U _ U _ > _ U U _ U _
                         in line 3:   U _ U _ U _ U _ U
                         in line 4:   _ U U _ U U _ U _ U

         The upright man and staunch in resolve will not
         At howling mobs' demands for an evil act
              Or at a raging tyrant's threats, be
                   Shaken in purpose, or by the Southwind,

5   The Adriatic's turbulent lord, or by
         The lightningbolts from Jupiter's mighty hand;
              And if the very sky collapses,
                   Ruin will fell him untouched by terror.

         By upward striving Pollux and Hercules
10   Attained the fiery stars and the heights of sky,
              With whom Augustus now reclines at
                   Banquets and, crimson of lip, drinks nectar;

         And you too, Father Bacchus, were swept aloft,
         For merit, by your tigers, their restless necks
15   Submitted to your yoke; Quirínus
                   Too escaped Ácheron, borne on horses

         Of Mars, when Juno nobly declared before
         The gods in council: "Ilion, Ilion,
              A foul and ruin-bringing judge it
20   Was, and an alien woman, turned you

         To dust; but you were doomed by Minerva and
         By me the day Laómedon failed to pay
              The gods who built his walls, and with your
                   Fraudulent leader and all your people.

25   No longer does the Spartan adulteress

Stand dazzled by her guest, and the perjured house
   Of Priam drives the fighting Argives
      Backward no longer with feats of Hector,

The war, by our divisions so long drawn out,
Has now subsided: as of this moment I   30
   Renounce my bitter rage; that hated
      Son of his, born of the Trojan priestess,

I now restore to Mars; I hereby permit
His entrance to these starry domains, to learn
   The taste of nectar and be numbered   35
      One of the gods amid tranquil order.

So long as broad seas surge between Ilion
And Rome, the exiles may, as they find a place,
   Be prosperous in rule; so long as
      Priam's and Paris's graves are trampled   40

Upon by frisking cattle, and savage beasts
Dig dens for whelping there, let the Capitol
   In glory stand, and over Medes let
      Rome in its triumph pass warlike judgment;

To furthest shores of earth let its name extend,   45
Inspiring fear, where watery straits divide
   The land of Africa from Europe
      As in the region where fields drink Nile-floods.

And stronger too, for leaving undug the gold
That earth keeps better hidden in proper place,   50
   And not with greedy hands profaning
      Everything sacred for human uses,

Let Rome attain by arms every furthest end
And terminus of earth, at the sight of lands
   Exulting where the torrid suns hold   55
      Revel, or lands of the mists and rainfalls.

But to the warlike Romans I grant this fate
On one condition only: that in success,
   From reverence of ancestral homes, they
      Seek no rebuilding of Troy from ruins.   60

Troy's fortunes born anew under evil signs
Would finish like the first ones, in dismal death,
   And I would lead the host of victors,
      I, who am Jupiter's spouse and sister.

And if those walls a third time arise — in bronze! —   65
At Phoebus' will, they shall, yet a third time, fall
   Before my Argives, and a third time
      Captives shall mourn for their mates and children."

But these are hardly themes for a sportive lyre.
70   What path have you been taking, my Muse? Desist
From speaking speeches of the gods: you
Only make matters of greatness trivial.

1–3   Horace may have in mind Plato's *Apology*, section 32, (compare S.2.4.3), where Socrates, speaking in self-defense at his trial, recounts how he once risked death by refusing to carry out a government order which he deemed both illegal and unjust. Moore compares Robert Herrick's 6-line poem beginning "No wrath of Men, or rage of Seas."

9–15   Five mortal heroes who attained godhood: Pollux, Hercules, Augustus (!), Bacchus, and Quirínus, (i.e., the deified Romulus).

Ácheron, the River of Sorrow in the afterworld, here = death.

The use of the term "Augustus" dates the poem later than January of 27 B.C. There will be a second "deification" of Augustus in *Odes* 3.25.5–6.

Bacchus/Dionysus in his Oriental progress tamed tigers and was portrayed in art as driving a team of tigers, as here, or as riding on a tiger's back.

15–17   Livy's History 1.16 says that Romulus vanished mysteriously from an assembly during a sudden, violent storm, but that certain senators standing near him declared he had been swept up to heaven in a whirlwind. Here, Romulus is carried aloft on horses of his father, the god Mars, at the very moment when Juno, in the council of the gods, gives her permission for his deification.

18   Greek "Ilion" = Latin "Ilium" = Troy (Troia).

199–20   Paris offended Juno/Hera and Minerva/Athenē by awarding the apple of beauty ("to the fairest") to Venus/Aphroditē. The "alien woman" and the "Spartan adulteress" of line 25 are both Helen of Troy. Horace (like Euripides) cannot mention Paris or Helen without angry disgust.

22–23   King Laómedon of Troy hired Poséidon/Neptune to build his city's walls and Apollo to tend his cattle for a year, then insolently refused to pay either one of them, as Poseidon angrily declares in a council of the gods, *Iliad* 21. 441–460.

32–33   Juno hatefully avoids speaking the names of the "son," Romulus, and of the "Trojan priestess," Ília; the latter, as in the note to *Odes* 1.2.16–20, is usually called 'a Vestal Virgin," daughter of Aeneas, and illegitimately the mother of Romulus by the god Mars. See also *Odes* 4.8.22–24 and note.

42–56   Roman dominion shall extend: to the "Medes" (Parthians), that is, to the Himalayas (43–44); to North Africa from the Strait of Gibraltar to the Nile (45–48); and from the "torrid zone"—presumably the Sahara—to "unknown lands" of northern Europe (53–56)—always without mining the gold that corrupts everything (49–52).

57–60   Some ancient commentators interpreted these lines as warning against "Asiatic luxury," others pointed to the "persistent rumour that Caesar intended to move the seat of government to Troy or Alexandria . . ." (Suetonius: *Life of Julius Caesar* 79; Robert Graves translation).

64   "I, who am Jupiter's spouse and sister" repeats Juno's words in *Aeneid* 1.46–47, but the concept was Greek, and from prehistoric times.

3.4.   *Descende caelo et dic age tibia*

Meter: Alcaic stanza: in lines 1 and 2:   U _ U _ > _ U U _ U _

in line 3:   U _ U _ U _ U _ U

in line 4:   _ U U _ U U _ U _ U

Callíopē, descend from the skies, O queen,
And sing your flute a lingering melody,
   Or lift your lovely voice alone, or
      Sing to the lyre or the harp of Phoebus.

Hark! Is illusion sweetly deceiving me?   5
I seem to hear those strains, as I seem myself
   A stroller in the sacred groves where
      Waters and breezes are softly stirring.

I wandered far from home as a boy one time
And, past Apúlia's borders, on Vóltur's slope,   10
   Tired out from play, I fell asleep, while,
      As in the fable, the ring-doves fetched me

Young leafy boughs for cover: "A miracle!,"
Cried everyone that lived from the eagle's-nest
   Of Acheróntia and down through   15
      Bantia's woodlands as far as lowland

Foréntum's fertile meadows, that I should sleep
Unharmed by deadly vipers or bears and be
   With sacred laurel heaped, and myrtle:
      Not without gods such a lad of mettle!   20

Yours am I, Muses, yours, when I climb the steep
Ascents of Sabine hills, or at times when cool
   Praenéstē has delighted me, or
      Hillslopes of Tibur, or shining Baiae.

Devoted to your fonts and your singing choirs,   25
I was not killed at Philippi when the lines
   Of battle broke, or by that cursèd
      Tree, or in voyage like Palinúrus.

With you beside me, I, as a mariner,
Will freely brave the gales of the Bosporus,   30
   Or as a traveler, the burning
      Sands of Assyrian wildernesses;

Among the Britons, savage to visitors,
Among the horse-blood drinkers, the Cóncani,
   No harm will come to me, or at the   35
      Scythian river among Gelóni.

Exalted Caesar, once he has quartered all
His weary cohorts safely in villages
   And seeks repose himself from labors,
      Finds your Piérian recreations.   40

You counsel mildness, Sisters benign, and then
You foster counsels given. We know indeed

How brutal hordes of monstrous Titans
　　Perished in sudden-descending lightning

45　From him who gives brute earth and the windy sea
　　Their harmony of order, and rules the realms
　　　　Of gloom, and cities, gods, and mortals,
　　　　　　Reigning alone in his perfect justice.

A mighty terror they had inspired in Jove,
50　That brash young band of warriors hairy-armed,
　　　　Those brothers at their toil to hoist Mount
　　　　　　Pélion onto Olympus' summit.

But what avails Typhóeus' and Mimas' strength,
Or what avails Porphýrion's scowling brow,
55　　　Or Rhóetus, or Encéladus, that
　　　　　　Impudent hurler of torn-up tree-trunks

Against the clanging aegis of Pallas, wild
In onset? Vulcan, lusting for battle, stands,
　　　　And lady Juno too, and he who
60　　　　　　Never will lower his bow from shoulder,

Who laves his flowing locks in Castálian fonts,
Who rules the bramble-thickets of Lycia
　　　　And rules his native woodlands also,
　　　　　　Delos' and Pátara's lord, Apollo.

65　Brute force and blind revolt, of their own weight, fail:
A tempered force the gods will themselves exalt
　　　　To higher ends; they loathe, however,
　　　　　　Force that attempts to accomplish evil.

Let hundred-handed Gyas attest this claim,
70　Notorious Oríon be witness too,
　　　　Who once assailed the chaste Diana,
　　　　　　Only to fall by her virgin arrow.

Earth suffers from the monsters she must contain
And mourns her creatures sent by the lightningbolt
75　　　To grisly Orcus; but spurting fire has
　　　　　　Yet to escape from the weight of Etna,

Nor has the lustful Títyus' liver been
Abandoned by the guardian vulture sent
　　　　To rend that criminal; three hundred
80　　　　　　Chains check Piríthoüs' lewd advances.

1–8　Horace invokes one of the Muses, Callíopē ("beautiful-voiced") for poetic inspiration
　　(1–4), and directly he is transported to "sacred groves," where the inspiration is granted
　　him.

9-20   A boyhood adventure, which may be compared with Wordsworth's story about himself at age ten, in *The Prelude* 1. 305–325. Lost all night in a dangerous forest, he was covered with the laurel of poets and the myrtle of Venus, and thus was consecrated a "love poet."

Vóltur (now Monte Vúlture), some 16 km/10 m due W of his native Venúsia (now Venósa), was on the border between the ancient provinces Apulia and Lucania.

Acheróntia (now Acerénza, 833 meters up), Bantia (now Banzi), and Foréntum (now Forenza) form a triangle some 10 miles S and SE of Venúsia, Acheróntia being farthest S.

21-24   The climb is up from Rome to the Sabine farm; Praenéstē (now Palestrina, about 30 km/20 m ESE of Rome) was, like Tibur (Tívoli) and Baiae (Baia), a resort town.

26-28   For the battle of Philippi see *Odes* 2.7 and notes; for the accident with the falling tree, *Odes* 2.13.1–12 and note. Death at sea is added for good measure; Palinúrus was Aeneas's helmsman who was swept overboard in a storm (*Aeneid* 6. 337–383).

32   "Assyrian" = "Syrian," as in *Odes* 2.11.16.

34   The Cóncani were a tribe of Cantabrians in NW Spain.

36   The "Scythian river" is the Tanaïs, now the Don, in S Russia; the Gelóni tribe lived near that river; see *Odes* 2.9.23 and 2.20.19; also under "Scytha" in "Foreign Nations," pp. 397 below.

37-39   Not only was Augustus interested in literature, but, on his way home in 29 B.C., after the deaths of Antony and Cleopatra, he rested, as Moore says, "some time at Atella in Campania (N of Napels), where on four successive days the *Georgics,* which Vergil had just finished, were read to him by Vergil and Maecenas."

40   Piéria was a region in Macedonia (N Greece) sacred to the Muses. Springs were often sacred to the Muses. See Alexander Pope's famous couplet:

> A *little learning* is a dang'rous thing;
> Drink deep, or taste not the Pierian spring.

> (*Essay on Criticism* 215–6)

41-42   The Muses were nine sisters. The sense is that the study of literature results in compassionate behavior, and that further study of literature shows the rightness of compassionate behavior.

41 ff.   The story of the "Revolt of the Giants" (against Jupiter) is now told at length *as an allegory* of what would happen to any armed revolt against Augustus. Allusions to this story occurred in *Odes* 2.12.6–9; 2.19.21–24; and 3.1.7.

46-47   "The realms of gloom" are the land-after-death, where Pluto/Hades/Orcus is usually said to be king. The theologically problematical claim is that Jupiter rules *all.*

51-56   The brothers Ephiáltes and Otus instigated the revolt. The giants' names are culled from various sources, Vergil, Euripides, Pindar, et al.; Rhóetus, as in *Odes* 2.19.24. Vergil's *Georgics* 1. 281–2 has the more familiar piling of Pélion on top of Ossa.

57   Here the aegis is clearly a metal breastplate, but see *Odes* 1.15.11 and note.

60-64   Apollo as the patron of Augustus (see the notes to *Odes* 1.2.31–32 and 1.21.1–4) is especially praised. He was born on the island of Delos (*Odes* 1.21.10); the Castálian Spring (of his inspiration) still flows from the side of Mount Parnassus at Delphi; time was when he spent half of every year in Lycia (now SW Turkey), the port city of which was Pátara; his "native woodlands" (*natalem silvam*) were hardly more than a grove on the small island of Delos.

69-80   Cases of punishment for violence (three out of five being sexual assaults on goddesses):

- Gyas (69), as in *Odes* 2.17.14–15, is obscure; his punishment is unspecified.
- Oríon (70), as in *Odes* 2.13.39–40, forever hunts wild beasts in the afterlife; his crime was an affront to Diana, as Horace tells it, but Oríon's story is beset by contradictory variants.
- Encéladus (55 and 75–76), according to *Aeneid* 3. 578–582, was pinned under Mount Etna, the Sicilian volcano (but Aeschylus and Pindar both say that the giant so pinned was the Typhóeus of line 53).

- Títyus (76), for attempted rape of Latóna (see the note to *Odes* 2.14.9), was, according to both *Odyssey* 11. 572 ff. and *Aeneid* 6. 595–600, pegged down over nine acres of hell, with a vulture to gnaw his continuously self-renewing liver—or, as we would say, his heart.
- Piríthoüs (Greek: Peir-) (80), for attempted seduction of Perséphonē/Proserpine, queen of the underworld, was seated in a chair into which his flesh grew, so that he could not get free; in *Odes* 4.7.27–28 Horace will refer to "Proserpine's fettering chains" as holding Piríthoüs.

3.5.   *Caelo tonantem credidimus Iovem*

Meter: Alcaic stanza: in lines 1 and 2:   ∪ _ ∪ _ > _ ∪ ∪ _ ∪ _
in line 3:   ∪ _ ∪ _ ∪ _ ∪ _ ∪
in line 4:   _ ∪ ∪ _ ∪ ∪ _ ∪ _ ∪

When once the Britons "on the western edge of the world" and the "Persians" (the Parthians) "on the eastern edge" have been brought under Roman control, Augustus will be "a god on earth," enjoying universal dominion (1–4). But these objectives cannot be realized with soldiers who surrender! In 53 B.C. 10,000 Roman soldiers were captured by the Parthians—and they are still in the East (5–12). Regulus, of old, set the proper example; lines 13–56 recount the story of Regulus, the martyr-patriot.

That Jove in thunder rules in the skies above,
We know: a god on earth will Augustus be
    When once the Britons and the vexing
        Persians are gathered within his empire.

5   Can any soldier Crassus commanded once
Have lived with some barbarian wife — (Disgrace
    Upon the Senate!) — growing old with
        Enemy brothers-in-law for comrades?

A Marsian soldier under a king of Medes,
10   Forgetting name and toga, the shield of Mars,
    The never-dying flame of Vesta, —
        Jupiter's Rome being still in power!

This Régulus foresaw, and against it warned,
When he rejected terms of surrender which
15   Would set a precedent for shameful
        Mischief to follow forever after

Unless the captives were, without pity, left
To perish. "I," he said, "have seen Punic shrines
    With trophies on their walls, and weapons
20   Taken from soldiers without resistance,

And free-born Roman citizens held as slaves

With twisted arms in fetters behind their backs,
   And city gates unclosed, and planted
      Fields where our armies had once wrought havoc.

Will any soldier ransomed with gold come back   25
The braver for it? Payment for shame incurred!
   No woolen treated with a dye will
      Ever come back to its one-time color,

True manliness, when once it is truly lost,
Will hardly be restored in a coward's breast.   30
   When deer escape from tangled nets to
      Fight again, then there will still be spirit

In men who trusted enemies' blandishments,
And when a second battle is fiercely fought
   By men who tamely took the Punic   35
      Lash and who feared for their lives while captive.

Not knowing how they ever will save their skins,
Such men have peace confused with the aims of war.
   O mighty Carthage, thus to tower
      Over Italian disgrace and ruin!"   40

And yet they say he turned from his chaste wife's kiss
And from his little boys, like a slave that has
   No civil rights, and bowed his manly
      Head to the ground and remained so, grimly,

Until he had the wavering senate nerved   45
To vote a course of action unknown before
   And he might hasten past his grieving
      Friends to his grandeur of doom in exile.

He knew barbaric tortures awaited him,
And yet he brushed his kinsmen aside and made   50
   Himself a path through crowds of people
      Bent on preventing his going back there,

Proceeding much as if, after handing down
His verdict in a long and distressing case,
   His destination were the pleasant   55
      Fields of Venáfrum or sweet Taréntum.

1–4   Expeditions against the Britons and "Persians" were planned in 27–26 B.C., as in *Odes* 1.35.29–34 and note, and the term "Augustus" could not have been used before January of 27 B.C.

5–9   Parthians defeated a Roman army under Marcus Licinius Crassus in 53 B.C. at Carrhae, (= Haran, Abraham's resting place in Genesis 11:31), now in SE Turkey just N of the Syrian border. Crassus died in battle, 10,000 captives were taken, and the Roman standards were kept as trophies. (E.1.18.56–57 and note and the headnote to E.1.3 will regard the recovery of those trophy-standards in 20 B.C.)

    The Italic Marsians from the mountains E of Rome were proverbially rugged soldiers. The text says "a Marsian and an Apulian."

10–12   A list of things most sacred to a Roman. The shield of Mars fell from heaven in the reign of pious King Numa Pompilius (716–672 B.C.), and was kept by the Salian priests (for whom, see *Odes* 1.36.12; 4.1.28; E.2.1.86–87; and notes).

13   As was said in the note to *Odes* 1.12.37, Regulus was defeated by Carthaginians in 256 B.C., held prisoner for six years, and then sent, under oath, to Rome to coax a favorable treaty out of the senate. The circumstances of that visit were devoutly believed by all Roman patriots, but the historian Polybius, who wrote a century later, says nothing of the matter.

18–40   The speech of Regulus to the Roman senate is as Horace imagined it to have been.

41–56   This justly famous dramatic close approaches Euripides in grandeur, and the final stanza has about it the majestic calm of the finest Greek tragedies.

3.6. *Delicta maiorum immeritus lues,*

Meter: Alcaic stanza: in lines 1 and 2:   U _ U _ > _ U U _ U _
                in line 3:   U _ U _ U _ U _ U
                in line 4:   _ U U _ U U _ U _ U

You shall continue paying for forebears' crimes,
Though innocent, O Roman, yourself, until
    The shabby temples of your gods and
        Grime-covered statues have been refurbished.

5   Because you act as less than the gods, you rule:
From them was all beginning, in them all ends.
    From gods neglected came the many
        Woes of Hesperia's grievous sorrow.

Monáeses first, then Pácorus, strong of hands,
10   Have twice now crushed unlucky attacks of ours,
    So that, besides their paltry torques of
        Honor, they beam over captured treasure.

Our City, with dissentions preoccupied,
Was brought to ruin's brink by the Dacian and
15   The Ethiope, the latter with his
        Ships, and the former with dreaded arrows.

The guilt-infested age first defiled the bed
Of marriage, then the household, the very breed,
    And from that fountainhead corruption
20   Flooded the nation and all its people.

The girl past childhood age is agog to learn

Iónic dances now, she affects coy ways,
　　And love affairs engross her thoughts till
　　　　She to her fingertips fairly tingles;

Soon, while her husband tarries at wine, she seeks   25
　　More youthful paramours; she does not select
　　　　The one on whom she will bestow her
　　　　　　Illicit favors at lamps' removal,

But from her husband's side (who is well aware)
　　She rises at the call of some peddlar man   30
　　　　Or captain of some Spanish freighter,
　　　　　　Liberal rewarder of such dishonors.

Of no such parents ever were born the men
　　Who stained the sea-waves crimson with Punic blood,
　　　　Who beat the Great Antíochus, and   35
　　　　　　Pyrrhus, and Hannibal's grisly armies;

No, those were rugged scions of rural folk
　　And soldiers' sons, who knew how to hack a turf
　　　　With Sabine mattocks, as they also
　　　　　　Knew how to carry and split the firewood   40

At mothers' strict commands, when the sun would shift
　　The shadows of the mountains and lift the yokes
　　　　From weary oxen, bringing day's best
　　　　　　Hour at his chariotwheels' departure.

What *has* not been corrupted by passing time?   45
　　Our parents' era, worse than the one before,
　　　　Produced our own more wicked selves, who
　　　　　　Soon will see offspring still worse corrupted.

9–10　The unidentified Monáeses must have been the victor of 53 B.C. at Carrhae; see the note to lines 5–9 of the foregoing ode. In 40 B.C. Parthians under Pácorus defeated a Roman army under Decidius Saxa in Syria.

　　　Horace says "twice," omitting Mark Antony's defeat in 36 B.C. As in Epode 9 and *Odes* 1.37 Antony's very existence is ignored.

11　Torques were ornamental collars of twisted metal which, along with bracelets for the upper arm, were the most prized gifts a Parthian king could bestow.

13–16　The threat from Dacian King Cotiso is explained in the note to *Odes* 1.26.4–5. The "Ethiope" = the sailors manning Cleopatra's ships at Actium.

17–32　These strictures are addressed only to "the ruling class" and primarily in Rome; for Horace's notions about adultery see S.1.2.47–49 and note.

21–22　Ionia (now W-central Turkey) was a Greek area under some Oriental influences. For Horace's notions about dancing see: S.1.9.24; S.2.1.24–25; and *Odes* 2.12.17–20, and notes.

33–36　The naval victory over Carthage is doubtless that of 241 B.C., which ended the First Punic War; see *Odes* 2.12.2–3 and note.

　　　The Romans defeated Antíochus III, the Great, of Syria in a three-year war, 192–189 B.C.

Pyrrhus, King of Epirus (now Albania-Yugoslavia), invaded S Italy, trying to prevent Roman expansion, and was finally defeated in 275 B.C. (His "Pyrrhic victory"—"Another such victory, and we are lost"—was won at Áusculum (now Áscoli Satriáno) some 35 km/20 m NW of Horace's native Venusia, in 279 B.C.)

Hannibal's Carthaginians ravaged Italy 218–207 B.C., during the Second Punic War.

3.7.   *Quid fles, Asterie, quem tibi candidi*

Meter: in lines 1 and 2:   _ > _ U U _ _ U U _ U _
              in line 3:   _ > _ U U _ _
              in line 4:   _ > _ U U _ U _

Why, then, weep for your lad   Gyges, Astérie?
Not till spring with its bright   breezes can he return,
        From Bithýnian wares grown
              Rich, but steadfastly true to you

5   Meanwhile. Gales from the south   keep him at Óricum
     Since the setting of mad   Capra, the she-goat star;
        There he passes the cold nights
              Sleepless, not without many tears.

     Yet his landlady's sly   go-between tells him how
10   Chloë sighs with distress,   wretched amid the same
        Fires of love as you too feel,
              Craftily tempting a thousand ways.

     Once (this creature reports)   there was a king whose wife,
     Falsely claiming affront,   urged him to speed the young
15   Man's death, namely, that far-too-
              chastely-minded Bellérophon;

     And she tells him of how   Péleus was almost slain,
     Though he modestly fled   wanton Hippólytē; —
        Always up to some tale meant
20   As example of how to sin.

     Wasted effort! He is heart-   whole, and to tales like these,
     Cliffs of Ícarus Isle   stand not more deaf. Take care
        You are meanwhile not too charmed
              By your neighbor Enípeus,

25   Though no other can so   skillfully wheel a horse
     While the onlookers watch   out on the Field of Mars,
        Nor can anyone else match
              Him in swimming the Tiber's waves.

Let the night find your doors   locked when the plaintive flute
Starts its song, and avoid   watching the street below;   30
      Plead your name as he will, stand
            Firm, unyielding in fixed resolve.

1   "Astérië" is from Greek *astēr*, "star."

2–5   The rich area of Bithýnia is now N Turkey, along the Black Sea coast. Óricum, in
      Epírus, now Albanian Vlorë/Vlonë, was the port opposite Italian Brundisium; the
      crossing at that point offered the shortest possible sea travel.

6   Capra (or Capella) is a bright triple star in the constellation Auriga; it sets in stormy
      mid-December. (Compare "the Haedi" in *Odes* 3.1.28 and note.)

13–16 Bellérophon, while a guest of King Proétus of Tiryns, was falsely accused of advances
      to Queen Antéia (or Sthenebóea), as Joseph was accused by Potiphar's wife in Genesis
      39. The king, shrinking from outright murder, sent him to Antéia's father with a sealed
      letter of instructions to kill him; but that king, likewise shrinking from murder, sent
      Bellérophon on dangerous adventures instead.

17–18 Of Péleus (later to become the father of Achilles) Pindar's Fifth Neméan Ode, 26 ff.,
      tells how wanton Queen Hippolyta of the Magnesians (of W-central Turkey)

            . . . fabricated a story that was a lie,
            how Peleus had sought to be with
            her, a wife, in the bridal bed of Akastos.
                        (Lattimore translation)

22   "Icarus Isle"—a merely decorative detail—is the Aegean island of Icaria.

24–28 Enípeus takes his name from a tributary stream to the Peneus, in Thessaly. He is an
      aristocrat who displays horsemanship on the Field of Mars and swims in the Tiber,
      whereas Gyges is a trader.

29–30 Serenades in classical Rome! Moore compares Shylock's warning to Jessica in *Merchant of Venice* 2.5:

            Lock up my doores, and when you heare the drum
            And the vile squealing of the wry-neckt Fife,
            Clamber not you up to the casements then,
            Nor thrust your head into the publique streete. . .

3.8.   *Martiis caelebs quid agam Kalendis*

Meter: Sapphic stanza: in lines 1, 2, and 3: $\_ \cup \_ > \_ \cup \cup \_ \cup \_ \cup$
                                    in line 4: $\_ \cup \cup \_ \cup$

      Why am I, a bachelor, celebrating
      Married Women's Day on the first of March, with
      Flowers on an altar of fresh-cut turf and
            Coals burning incense,

      You may wonder, erudite friend in either   5
      Language. On surviving that falling tree I

> Vowed a white goat slain and a tasty feast in
>> Honor of Liber.
>
> Now at year's full circle, today's rejoicing
> Shall remove the cork from the pitch-sealed wine jar
> Set among the rafters to get the smoke when
>> Tullus was consul.
>
> Drink a hundred toasts to your friend who came off
> Safe that time, Maecenas, and keep the night-lamps
> Burning till the dawn — but without a hint of
>> Brawling or quarrels.
>
> Put aside your worries about the City:
> Hosts of Dacian Cótiso have been scattered
> And the Medes that threatened have turned to feuding
>> Now with each other;
>
> Off in Spain Cantábrian foes of old have
> Been reduced at last and now wear our fetters;
> Scyths, with slackened bowstrings, are entertaining
>> Thoughts of surrender.
>
> Unconcerned lest something befall the nation,
> As a private citizen drop your worries.
> Here! Enjoy the gifts of the present hour;
>> Banish all strictness.

10

15

20

25

A poem for a March 1st celebration (line 2), the anniversary of the falling tree incident (9), during the period: summer (or autumn) 31 to the summer of 29 B.C., when Maecenas was acting head of state (17; 25–26), and after a major defeat of Dacian King Cótiso (18). The date, therefore, is March 1, 29 B.C., and Horace's narrow escape from the falling tree occurred on March 1, 30 B.C. The tree incident was the subject of *Odes* 2.13.1–12; allusion to the incident in *Odes* 2.17.27–30 was made in the good-weather months of 30 B.C., while the allusion in *Odes* 3.4.27–28 belongs probably to 26 B.C.

2   At the *Matronalia,* March 1st, married women carried offerings to the temple of Juno Lucina, goddess of childbirth, on the Esquiline Hill, not far from Maecenas's mansion.

3–4   Compare the improvised altar of *Odes* 1.19.13–15. A hollowed spot in the green turf may have contained the fire. To give Maecenas time for the journey out to the Sabine farm, the poem must have been prepared in advance; or possibly the scene is at Horace's town house.

5   Educated Romans knew the literatures of "both languages," that is, Greek and Latin. It never occurred to them to *study* any other.

7–8   The celebration is in honor of Liber (Bacchus), yet it was Faunus who saved the poet's life, according to *Odes* 2.17.27–30.

11–12   Probably the Tullus who was consul in 33 B.C., but a Lucius Volcacius Tullus was consul in 66 B.C., the year before Horace was born. (*Odes* 3.21 is an address to a wine jar put up in 65 B.C.) Such jars were regularly stored under the roof, in the belief that smoke helped to "ripen" the wine.

18   For Cótiso's Dacian invasion see the note to *Odes* 1.26.4; also *Odes* 3.6.14.

19–20 For the dynastic feuds among the Parthians ("Medes") involving Tiridátes and Phraátes IV, see the note to *Odes* 1.26.5; also *Odes* 2.2.17–18 and note, and under "Foreign Nations," p. 397.

21–22 Horace is overoptimistic: as of 29 B.C. the last and hardest decade in the Roman conquest of the Cantabrians of NW Spain lay still in the future.

3.9. *Donec gratus eram tibi*

Meter: in the odd-numbered lines: _ > _ U U _ U _
          in the even-numbered lines: _ > _ U U _ _ U U _ U _

(*He*)   While your favor was all for me,
             While your preference shunned   having your lovely self
         Clasped in other embrace than mine,
             I could glory in life   more than a Persian king.

(*She*)   While your wildfire of love did not   5
             Rush to Chloë and leave   Lydia second place,
         Spurning Lydia's far renown,
             I knew glory beyond   Ília, queen of Rome.

(*He*)   Thracian Chloë is now my queen,
             Skilled at melodies drawn   sweetly from strings of lyre,   10
         And for her I would gladly die,
             If the Fates would but spare   life in that soul of mine.

(*She*)   Love's torch mutually flames for me
             And Ornýtus's son,   Thurian Cálaïs,
         And for him I would perish twice,   15
             If the Fates would but spare   life in that splendid boy.

(*He*)   What if previous love revives,
             Yoking us, who are now   sundered, with yoke of bronze?
         What if now I cast Chloë off
             And to Lydia scorned   open the door again?   20

(*She*)   Though more fair than a star is he,
             And though *you* bob about   lighter than cork, with worse
         Temper squalls than the untamed sea,
             Life with you is my choice,   and to face death with you.

8   Ília was the mother of Romulus, Rome's first king; see *Odes* 1.2.16–20 and 3.3.32–33.

14 Cálaïs (Greek *kálaïs*, "topaz") is the "son of" someone, hence noble, as the present lover presumably is not. For the S-Italian city of Thurii see the note to S.2.8.20.

Besides the obvious symmetries, the past, present, and future tenses are accorded two stanzas each.

3.10. *Extremum Tanain si biberes, Lyce,*

Meter: in lines 1, 2, and 3:   _ >   ∪ ∪ _ _ ∪ ∪ _ ∪ _
                    in line 4:   _ > _ ∪ ∪ _ ∪ _

> Even out by the world's   edge, by the Tanaïs,
> With some savage as mate,   Lýcē, you yet would weep
> At beholding me here   huddled against your door,
>   Freezing under these northern gales.
>
> 5   Hear the clattering gate,   hear how the planted trees
> Moan in answer beneath   winds in the inner court!
> See how Jupiter's sky,   cloudless in majesty,
>   Crusts the late-fallen snow with ice.
>
> Cease this lofty disdain —   Venus abhors it — cease,
> 10   Lest the taut-girding rope   snap from the whirling wheel;
> You, Tyrrhénian born,   never were meant to play
>   Suitor-scorning Penélopē.
>
> Ah, though you are umoved   either by gifts or prayers,
> Or the sallow and wan   lover's complexion, or
> 15   Husband love-sick for some   Macedon concubine,
>   Show some mercy to suppliants
>
> Who entreat you, — a bit   softer than rock-hard oak,
> Somewhat gentler than fierce   serpents of Africa:
> This poor body of mine   will not forever bear
> 20   Threshold stone or the heavens' rains.

1   Along the lower course of the Tanaïs (now the Don), where it empties into the Sea of Azóv, lived the Scythian tribe of the Gelóni (*Odes* 3.4.36 and note); beyond it was unknown territory.

2   Attic Greek *lykê* means "wolf's skin" or a helmet made of wolf's skin. Compare *Odes* 4.12, which is also addressed to a "Lýkē."

5–6 Roman mansions had planted trees in the inner courtyard (*peristylium*).

10 The figure is probably that of a windlass, used in hoisting huge building stones. Compare *Odes* 1.4.2 and E.2.2.73.

11 "Tyrrhénian" = Etruscan, and Etruscans were proverbially sensual.

14 "Sallow and wan" paraphrases "paleness of the (*yellow*) violet."

18 For "serpents of Africa" see the note to S.2.8.95.

19–20 The hinted threat was made explicit in Epode 11, 15–22: If you won't love me, I'll find someone who will.

3.11. *Mercuri, nam te docilis magistro*

Meter: Sapphic stanza: in lines 1, 2, and 3:   _ ∪ _ > _ ∪ ∪ _ ∪ _ ∪
                            in line 4:   _ ∪ ∪ _ ∪

Grant me music, Mercury, as you did when
Stones moved into place for Amphíon singing;
Bear my song, O tortoise-shell deftly strung with
    Seven strings sounding,

Once a lifeless object unpleasing, welcome   5
Now at rich men's tables as in the temples:
Sing such strains that even the stubborn ears of
    Lýdē will listen:

She now gambols over the breadth of meadows
Like a three-year filly that shies at being   10
Touched, unmated yet, and not ripened for a
    Wantoning husband.

Trees and tigers walk in your train, O lyre, and
You can halt the currents of rapid rivers;
At the gate of Horror the very watchdog,   15
    Cerberus, yielded

Once before your ravishment, though a hundred
Snakes bedeck his hideous head and though his
Triple gullet reeks with a fetid breath and
    Blood-dripping slaver;   20

In their torments Títyus and Ixíon
Smiled despite themselves, and for just a little
Time the jar stood dry while your song enchanted
    Dánaüs' daughters.

Oh, let Lýdē hear of those maidens' crime and   25
Far-known punishment: how their jar is always
Empty as the water leaks out the bottom;
    Tell her how tardy

Fate still finds the guilty in depths of Orcus.
Wicked — (Was there ever a deed more heinous?) —   30
Wicked girls, resorting to ruthless swords to
    Murder their bridegrooms.

Out of all their number, one worthy of her
Nuptial torch sublimely deceived her crafty
Father, thus becoming a maiden known to   35
    Fame through the ages.

"Rise," said she, addressing her youthful husband,
"Rise, and sleep no more, lest you sleep forever!
Dupe your trickster father-in-law, and dupe my
    Criminal sisters: 40

Each one like a lioness chancing on young

Bullocks, means to tear them — alas! — to pieces
One by one. But *I* will not murder *you* or
Hold you in prison.

45   Let my father load me with chains for mercy
Shown a helpless man in his mortal peril;
Off to far Numidians' lands and exile
Let him transport me,

But, as feet or winds may conduct — wherever —
52   Now, while night and Venus are in your favor, —
Go! May omens prosper! And on my gravestone
Carve my sad story."

1   Mercury/Hermes, as "first founder of song and lyre-shell" (*Odes* 1.10.6), grants "music" to poets, and Horace is one of "Mercury's men" (*Odes* 2.17.29 and note).
2   To Amphíon the god himself made the gift of a lyre, and taught him music as well. E.2.3.394–6 will say:

> And of Amphíon, the founder of Thebes, it is told that he moved great
> Stones by the sounds of his tortoise-shell lyre and emplaced them at will by
> Sweetest entreaties of singing.

3–5   The invention of the lyre from a scooped-out tortoise-shell is described in detail by the "Homeric Hymn to Hermes," lines 31–61, to which passage Horace alludes in *Odes* 1.10.6; see the note to that line.
8–12   Greek "Lýdē" = Latin "Lydia"; see the note to *Odes* 1.8.1. As a three-year-old filly she is much like the young heifer in *Odes* 2.5.5–9.
13–24   The lyre's enchantment is described in terms close to *Odes* 1.12.7–12, about Orpheus, and 15–17 allude to Orpheus's quest for Eurydicē, but the allusion to Cerberus also recalls *Odes* 2.19.29–32, about Bacchus's descent to the land-after-death to bring up the shade of his mother Semelē, as well as the Cerberus description in *Odes* 2.13.33–36. In other words, there is here a recombination of Horatian motifs.
   Títyus, pegged to the ground of hell and with a vulture to eat his liver, is described in *Odes* 2.14.9 and 3.4.77–79 and notes.
   Ixíon, king of the Lapiths (*Odes* 1.18.7 and note), for attempted rape of Hera/Juno, queen of the gods, was bound forever to a revolving wheel of fire.
22–32   "Dánaüs' evil brood/Of daughters" were mentioned in *Odes* 2.14.18–19, and statues of them stood between the portico columns of the new library temple to Apollo; see *Odes* 1.2.31–32 and 1.31.1 and notes.
   The fifty daughters of King Dánaüs of Argos were to conclude the strife between their father and King Aegyptus by marrying the latter's fifty sons in a single ceremony, but Dánaüs ordered them to murder the fifty bridegrooms on the common bridal night. For this crime the daughters are doomed in the afterworld to carry water in sieves to fill a huge jar—which leaks. The "jar" may be imagined as a terracotta *pithos* twice the height of a man and perhaps sunk to the brim in the ground, i.e., a common type of storage receptacle for grain, oil, and other commodities.
33–38   One daughter (Hypermnéstra) out of the fifty, however, disobeyed her father and gave her young husband (whose name was Lynceus) warning in time to escape. She did so from love—as Lýdē should note.
   "Sublimely deceived" (line 34) = the admired phase *splendide mendax,* "magnificently false."
41–43   The compressed metaphor plays on the double meaning: "young bullocks (*vitulos*)": "young men," parallel to the word *iuvencis* in *Odes* 2.8.21; see the note to that line.

47   In the remote time of the story the Numidians were *Numidae,* "nomads," but in Horace's
      day Numidia was an organized Roman province (Tunisia and E-Algeria).
51–52   Around 100 A.D. a Roman woman tourist carved a lament for her lost brother on the
      Pyramid of Gizeh, paraphrasing Horace's words.

3.12.   *Miserarum est neque amori dare ludum neque dulci mala vino*
         lavere, aut exanimari metuentis patruae verbera linguae.

The above is *line 1* of a *four*-line poem in "the Ionic meter," which Horace uses only here. We
describe the meter in a last note below and meanwhile offer a translation in blank verse.

> Unhappy girls! They may not show their love   1
> Or drown their cares in wine for fear of uncle's
> Tongue-lashing. Cytheréa's wingèd boy   2
> Makes off, Neobulē, with loom and wool-basket
> And all industrious Minerva's work,
> Once Liparéan Hebrus' shining beauty
> Splashes well-oiled shoulders in the waves   3
> Of Tiber; better than Bellérophon
> At horsemanship, not slow of foot in races,
> In boxing matches always unsurpassed;
> He deftly spears the fleeing stag in open   4
> Country while the herd is in confusion;
> He pounces on the boar concealed in thickets.

1   The adjective *patruae* applies to paternal uncles only. In Roman folk traditions harsh
     uncles and harsh stepmothers were parallel figures.
2   For "Cytheréan Venus" see *Odes* 1.4.5 and note; her wingèd boy is Cupid. "Neobulē"
     repeats to name of the real-life girl loved by the poet Archílochus; see the Introduction to
     the *Epodes,* p. 96 above. The handsome athlete comes from the island of Lípara, off the
     northern coast of Sicily, yet he is named for the Hebrus River of Thrace (now the
     Maritsa of Bulgaria and Turkey-in-Europe; see E.1.3.3 and E.1.16.13 and notes). Com-
     pare the river-name of young Enípeus in *Odes* 3.7.24 and note.
3   The scene is the Field of Mars (*Campus Martius*); see the note to *Odes* 1.8.4. With the
     athlete Hebrus compare the Sýbaris of *Odes* 1.8.3–12, the Enípeus of 3.7.25–28, and the
     Ligurínus of 4.1.37–40.
        The hero Bellérophon (*Odes* 3.7.13–16) rode the winged horse Pégasus (*Odes*
     1.27.23–24 and 4.11.27 and notes).

In *Sappho and Alcaeus,* pp. 291–4, Denys Page discusses the fragment of a poem by Alcaeus
which undoubtedly served Horace as the model for *Odes* 3.12. The Greek poem is in the same
odd "Ionic meter," it provides the earliest known example of a lyric that is entirely a
"spoken" monologue, and, in Page's translation, reads:
    "Me, a woman pitiable, me, who am spared no misery . . . destiny of shame . . .
        For upon me comes grievous injury.
    The belling of the deer grows . . . in the timid heart . . . maddened . . . infatuations . . ."

To the same poem probably belongs: "I fell by the arts of the Cyprian goddess . . ."

If *Odes* 3.12 is indeed to be taken as a soliloquy, the girl Neobulē calls herself by name in line 2. Into that same line 2 Horace seems to have introduced a motif not in Alcaeus's poem (so far as we have it), but from a poem of Sappho's of which the following fragment is preserved:

> Mother darling, I cannot work the loom
> for sweet Kypris has almost crushed me,
> broken me with love for a slender boy.
>
> > (translation by Willis Barnstone, in
> > *Sappho*, Doubleday Anchor, 1965,
> > p. 30)

In the Ionic meter each poetic foot consists of two "shorts" followed by two "longs" (∪ ∪ _ _). In *Odes* 3.12 there are 10 such feet to a line, through 4 lines. In English imitation the effect would be bizarre:

> Oh, to think girls/ may not show love,/ may not drown cares/ in the sweet wine/ lest they face cru-/ elest tongue-lash-/ings from harsh un-/ cles . . .

3.13.   *O fons Bandusiae, splendidior vitro,*

Meter: in lines 1 and 2:   _ > _ ∪ ∪ _   _ ∪ ∪ _ ∪ _
        in line 3:   _ > _ ∪ ∪ _ _
        in line 4:   _ > _ ∪ ∪ _ ∪ _

The occasion for the poem is the October 13th *Fontinalia* (festival of springs), when offerings of wine and flowers were thrown into the waters. The goat sacrifice implies a banquet celebration.

> O Bandúsian spring,   limpid as crystal light,
> Fair, sweet wine you shall have,   mingled with flower sprays;
> > In your honor a young goat
> > Shall tomorrow be offered you,
>
> By his now-sprouting horns   destined for love and war —
> Quite in vain: for your cold   runnels and fonts shall then
> > Take the stain of his red blood
> > From that scion of sportive herds.
>
> Dog Star season can not   touch you with savage heat:
> At the oxen's return   weary from yoke and plow
> > Cool refreshment is your gift,
> > As to cattle that stray and graze.
>
> You with other renowned   fountains shall rank in fame
> From my poem that sings   holm-oak and hollow rocks
> > Whence you merrily gush forth
> > Lightly babbling in liquid speech.

5

10

15

---

1   *Bandusia* is unexplained, unless it is a form of Greek *Pandosía,* "all giving."

The location of the spring is unknown. Readers have often assumed, without evidence, that it was an actual spring on or near the Sabine farm, perhaps the one near the house; E.1.16.12–13 says: "I have a spring of such force that the stream might be named for it — Hebrus/Never flowed colder or purer. . . " E.K. Rand (*A Walk to Horace's Farm*, 1930) reports his explorations in pp. 50–68, but without offering much hope to further seekers. A document of 1103 A.D. is doubtless wrong in locating a *fons Bandusinus* near Horace's native Venusia in S Italy yet the bilingual Venusian area was the one most likely to garble "Pandosía" into "Bandúsia."

9   For the Dog Star (*Canicula*) see *Odes* 1.17.19 and note.

13 Other renowned springs were: Castalia, at Delphi, on the side of Mount Parnassus (*Odes* 3.4.61 and note); Hippocrene ("spring of the horse," because it was created by Pegasus's stamping his hoof), W of Thebes; Dircē, on Mount Cithaeron, S of Thebes (*Odes* 4.2.25 and note); and others still. All were sacred to the Muses, and all conferred poetic inspiration upon those who drank their waters.

3.14.   *Herculis ritu modo dictus, o plebs*

Meter: Sapphic stanza: in lines 1, 2, and 3:   _ U _ > _ U U _ U _ U
                                       in line 4:   _ U U _ U

He who sought the laurel of deadly cost, good
People, now like Hercules has returned to
His ancestral hearth from the shores of Spain: our
    Caesar triumphant.

Let the wife rejoicing in this dear husband   5
Honor gods of justice with sacrifices,
And his noble sister, and matrons wearing
    Suppliant headbands,

Mothers, too, of safely returning heroes
And of those men's brides; have a care, you lads and   10
Girls not knowing wedlock, to avoid pronouncing
    Words of ill omen.

On this truly festive occasion all my
Cares can be dismissed: I fear neither civil
Strife nor death by violence, now that lands are   15
    Safe under Caesar.

Go, boy, bring me perfumes, and crowns of flowers,
Fetch a jar from times of the Marsian War — if
Any such by chance eluded the hands of
    Spartacus' vagrants.   20

Bid that clear soprano Neáera hurry
Here, with chestnut hair in a simple bun, but
If that churlish doorman of hers gives trouble,
    Cancel your errand.

25   Graying hair now softens a temper once too
                           Quick at disputation and reckless quarrels;
                           I would not have stood for it in my youth, when
                                Plancus was consul.

1–4   Augustus returned to Rome in the spring of 24 B.C. after directing the war against the
       Cantabrians of NW Spain for almost three years. His propaganda claimed victory, but
       the war was to drag on until 19 B.C.
            Even as Commander-in-chief he risked death, to be sure, but there may be a hint of
       the grave illness that kept him at Tarraco (Tarragona) through the winter of 25–24 B.C.
            Augustus is associated with Hercules in *Odes* 3.3.9 and 4.5.36.

5   "Wife" = Livia Drusilla, married to Augustus since January 17, 38 B.C. and surviving
       him by fifteen years, dying in 29 A.D. By her previous husband she was the mother of the
       next emperor, Tiberius.

7   "Sister" = Octavia. By her first husband she was the mother of Marcellus, whom
       Augustus adopted as heir to the empire but who died at age nineteen in 23 B.C.; see *Odes*
       1.12. 45–46 and note, also the famous scene in *Aeneid* 6. 855–886. Married in 40 B.C., for
       political reasons, to Mark Antony, she bore him two daughers (one of them the grand-
       mother of the future emperor Nero), before he abandoned her in 37. Living thereafter in
       her brother's household, she devoted herself to bringing up children: her own two
       daughters (both named Marcella) from her first marriage; her two daughters (both
       named Antonia) by Antony; Antony's daughters by Fulvia (his first wife) and his son by
       Fulvia, that Iullus Antonius to whom Horace addresses *Odes* 4.2; Antony's daughter by
       Cleopatra, Cleopatra Selēnē ("the Moon"); and the young captive king of Mauretania,
       Juba II (see *Odes* 1.22.15 and note), who married Cleopatra Selēnē.

5–12   The scene is a public ceremony of thanksgiving (*supplicatio*), at which women wore
       elaborate headbands. (The senate had proposed a formal "Triumph," but Augustus
       declined.)
            Of line 6, ancient commentaror Porphyrio says the gods were "just" because they
       brought Augustus safely home, as he deserved.
            Lines 10–12 call for reverent silence on the part of young unmarrieds, lest they mar
       the blessing on the Roman breed.

18–20 The Marsian War of 90–88 B.C. was usually called "the Social War," that is, the
       revolt of the Italian allies (*socii*) against Rome.
            The third "Servile War" (slave revolt) raged 73–71 B.C. under the leadership of the
       Thracian gladiator Spártacus.
            Both grim allusions are meant to contrast with the present peace, but Horace
       avoids referring to the *civil* wars.

21–24 Compare *Odes* 2.11.21–24.

25–28 Horace was "graying" at age forty-one in 24 B.C., and, past his forty-fourth birthday,
       some time in 20 B.C., he will describe himself as prematurely gray. In the same passage
       (E.1.20.24–25) he will speak of his "quick-flaring temper, yet soon reinduced to compo-
       sure." Compare also *Odes* 1.16.22–25.
            Plancus was consul in 42 B.C., when Horace was in his twenty-third year and in
       military service under Brutus.

                         3.15.   *Uxor pauperis Ibyci*

Meter: in the odd-numbered lines: _ > _ U U _ U _
         in the even-numbered lines: _ > _ U U _ _ U U _ U _

Wife of penniless Íbycus,
    It is time you gave up   once and for all these lewd
Ways that make you notorious.
    Ripe for death as you are,   no more cavort among
Girls still young: all you do is cast   5
    Haze and dimness of cloud   over the shining stars.
Things becoming in Phóloē
    Suit ill, Chloris, with you, —   granting your daughter does
Take the homes of young men by storm,
    Like a frenzied bacchante   banging a tambourine: 10
Love for Monkeyface drives her wild
    So she sports like a mad   nanny goat at her pranks.
You need some of that famous wool
    From Lucéria, all   ready to spin, — not lyres,
Not red roses of dancing girls,   15
    Not your wine jars, old hag,   drained to the very dregs.

1   "Íbycus" is a random-chosen Greek name. Plato's *Parmenides* recalls the lyric poet Íbycus
    (of the 5th century B.C.) as falling in love, against his will, in his old age.
       Schiller's famous ballad, *Die Kraniche des Ibykus,* retells a late legend about him.
11 "Monkeyface" paraphrases *Nothus,* which = Greek *nóthos,* "mongrel, bastard," (though
    Moore says inscriptions attest the name for actual persons). For Romans who could not
    pronounce Greek *theta* (*th*) the name might come out as *Nŏtus* (Greek *Nŏtos*), "the
    (oppressive) southwind"; Latin *nŏtus* meant either "famous" or "notorious." Thus a
    multiple pun may be involved.
14 Lucéria (now Lucera) was a town some 70 km/45 m NW of Horace's native Venúsia and
    noted for its excellent wool.
       In theory, all Roman women spun wool and wove it into garments. The empress
    Livia kept a staff of 18 slaves busy at such tasks, and Augustus customarily wore only
    homespuns produced by his wife, sister, daughter, and granddaughter. Many senators
    imitated his practice.

3.16.   *Inclusam Danaen turris aenea*

Meter: in lines 1, 2, and 3:   _ > _ U U _ _ U U _ U _
            in line 4:   _ > _ U U _ U _

Danaë in a bronze   tower immured, behind
Oaken doors, and with dogs   posted outside by night,
Should have had quite enough   safeguards to ward against
    All nocturnal adulteries,

Had anxiety not   fretted her father so   5
That both Venus and Jove   fooled him with laughing ease:
Access ready and safe   opens before a god
    Who takes shape as a golden rain.

Straight past sentinels' lines   gold without effort goes,
10   Gold with mightier might   splits through a rocky cliff
Than a thunderbolt's force;   witness the Argive seer's
House undone and in ruin left

By a bribe; witness too   Philip of Macedon
Bribing cities to yield,   witness how rival kings
15   Conquer thrones with their bribes: bribes are the traps that catch
Grim commanders of ships and fleets.

Worries follow as more   money accumulates;
So does hunger for more.   Rightly I shrank with dread
From excessively high   place, as, Maecenas, you
20   Grace the ranks of the knightly class.

In denying oneself   many a thing, one gains
That much more from the gods.   I have the urge to flee
Empty-handed from wealth's   faction and seek the camp
Where desire is for nothing more,

25   Standing higher as lord   over a state despised
Than if I had entire   granaries crammed with what
Hard Apulian toil   reaps from the fields, and stood
Destitute amid opulence.

Water pure from a brook,   some little stand of woods,
30   And the harvests that I   count on unfailingly
Make for happiness not   even imagined by
Grand proconsuls of provinces.

Though my honey is not   brought by Calabrian bees,
And though Bacchus does not   mellow for me in jars
35   Laestrygónián, and   though I do not have fine
Wools from pastures in Gaul,

I am also without   worries of poverty, —
Nor, if more were my wish,   would you refuse the gift.
By retrenching my wants   I can make income stretch
40   Further than by possessing all

Rich King Mýgdon's domains   with the domains of rich
King Alyáttes combined.   Cravers of many things
Go without many things;   he is well off on whom
Stinting gods bestow just enough.

1–8   Danaë's father, Acrisius (whom the text names), had an oracle's warning that he
would have no sons but yet would die by the hand of a grandson. Accordingly, he locked
Danaë up, but Jupiter-in-love came in the form of a shower of gold and begot upon her
the hero Perseus. Horace arbitrarily interprets the shower of gold as a liberal bribe.
(Robert Graves: *The Greek Myths* 73.4 proposes two possible interpretations of this
strange story.)

11–16   Three examples of what bribes can accomplish:
   · the wife of Amphiaraus, the Argive seer, took a bribe to persuade her husband to join the expedition of the Seven Against Thebes, though he foreknew he would perish in the course of it;
   · King Philip II of Macedon, father of Alexander the Great, was said to have bribed his way into more cities than he ever conquered;
   · this unclear allusion may regard Menas, Sextus Pompey's admiral, who switched sides four times between Sextus Pompey and Octavius Caesar in the years 38 to 36 B.C. (Menas appears as a character in Shakespeare's *Antony and Cleopatra*.)

19–20   Maecenas declined senatorial rank and chose to remain a knight (*eques*).

33   That is, the honey from around Taréntum, as praised in *Odes* 2.6.14–15.

34–35   "Bacchus ... in jars/Laestrygónian" means "first-rate wine put up near Formiae." The Laestrygónians were the cannibal giants of *Odyssey* 10, whom the classical Greeks "located" near Leontini on the E coast of Sicily, but whom Cicero (in letter 2.30 to Atticus) "located" near Formiae (modern Formia) in the heart of the best wine district; see *Odes* 1.20.12 and note.

41–42   Mýgdon (as in *Odes* 2.12.22 and note) was a half-legendary king of Phrygia. King Alyáttes of Lydia was the father of proverbially wealthy Croesus but a real personage mentioned by Herodotus (1.6 and numerous other places). Phrygia and Lydia were adjacent kingdoms in what is now W Turkey.

3.17.   *Aeli vetusto nobilis ab Lamo*

Meter: Alcaic stanza: in lines 1 and 2:   U _ U _ > _ U U _ U _
                            in line 3:   U _ U _ U _ U _ U
                            in line 4:   _ U U _ U U _ U _ U

> Distinguished son of Lamus of old, — since all
> The Lamias before you derive their name
>   From him, with all descendants written
>   Down in the family tree, you also
>
> From him must take your origin, Aelius;   5
> He ruled the walls of Formiae once, they say,
>   And Liris River's overflowing
>   Channels in goddess Maríca's district, —
>
> Tomorrow shall the Eastwind in storm bestrew
> The woods with many leaves, and along the shore   10
>   Wash useless seaweed up, if *I* have
>   Not been deceived by that rain-foreteller,
>
> The long-lived crow. So, while you can do so, lay
> A stock of firewood in: you shall treat yourself
>   To wine tomorrow and, with servants   15
>   Off for the day, to a two-month piglet.

1–5   To the Lucius Aelius Lamia addressed in *Odes* 1.26, and whose age we guessed as about twenty-three in the note to line 3 of *Odes* 1.36, Horace explains that the whole Lamia family is descended from Lamus of old, that is, from the king (or the king-ancestor) of the cannibal giants called Laestrygónians, from whom Odysseus/Ulysses escapes with only his own ship and his own crew in *Odyssey* 10.

   In the note to lines 34–35 of the foregoing ode (3.16) it was explained that, to the Romans, at least since Cicero's time, the mythical Laestrygónians of the *Odyssey* had been "located" near Formiae (modern Formia) on the Italian coast (and also on the Appian Way) some 120 km/75 m SE of Rome. (Perhaps the long presence of the Lamia family there led to the identification in the first place.) Lines 10–11 below indicate that the present Lamia's home is by the seacoast.

   (Horace does not play on the common Greek *and* Latin sense of *lamia* as "witch, sorceress, vampire," but such is the meaning in E.2.3.340–1.)

7–8   For the Liris River, near Formiae, see *Odes* 1.31.7–8 and note, where flood marshes are also indicated. Maríca was an ancient Italian goddess worshipped in that region.

9–13   Horace affects solemnity, like an augur—*aquae . . . augur* = our "foreteller of rain"—in predicting tomorrow's weather by the crow.

   Moore cites a fragment of Hesiod's which says crows live nine times as long as man. Seaweed was proverbially useless; compare "meaner than seaweed" in S.2.5.8.

14   "Treat yourself" is actually "treat your *genius*," that is, the spirit-double that lives with any man from birth to death. See Horace's own definition of this *genius* in E.2.2.187–9.

3.18.   *Faune, nympharum fugientum amator*

Meter: Sapphic stanza: in lines 1, 2, and 3: $\_ \cup \_ > \_ \cup \cup \_ \cup \_ \cup$

in line 4: $\_ \cup \cup \_ \cup$

Faunus, ardent wooer of nymphs that flee you,
Gently may you enter my lands and sunning
Fields, and with my weanlings again deal gently
     In your departing:

5   Thus at year's conclusion I pray, and offer
This young goat, abundance of wines for Venus'
Friendly mixing-bowl, and this ancient altar
     Smoking with incense.

All the flocks and herds are at play on grassy
10   Meadows for your Nones-of-December feast-day;
Countryside and oxen alike relax in
     Holiday leisure;

Lambs grown bold ignore that a wolf strays with them,
Wildwood strews its branches to smooth your pathway,
15   Toilsome earth gets stomped in our gleeful rustics'
     Three-quarter dances.

1–4   Faunus, the old Italian god of Agriculture and cattle, was described in *Odes* 1.4.1–12 as if he were the exact equivalent of the Greek god Pan, and such may be the case here as well, but his arrival and departure suggest that there may be truth in Robert Graves's guess, made tentatively in the index to *The Greek Myths*, that *Faunus* is a form of *Favonius*, "the favoring (wind)," usually understood as the Westwind. This suggestion casts a different light on the Faunus of *Odes* 2.17.28–30, who stayed the falling tree from killing Horace.

5–8   The prayer is of the "contractual" sort, lines 1–4 stating what the asker asks and lines 5–8 what the asker offers in return.

10   The Nones of December = December 5th, the date of the *rural* festival of Faunus; the *urban* festival of the *Lupercalia* fell on February 15th (as in the second scene of Shakespeare's *Julius Caesar*). But see *Odes* 1.4.11–12 where springtime is said to be the proper season for sacrificing to Faunus.

3.19.   *Quantum distet ab Inacho*

Meter: in the odd-numbered lines: $\_ > \_ \cup \cup \_ \cup \_$
           in the even-numbered lines: $\_ > \_ \cup \cup \_ \ \_ \cup \cup \_ \cup \_$

On a chilly afternoon some gentlemen have lingered over an out-of-doors discussion of certain abstruse details of ancient history, until Horace abruptly protests.

How long Ínachus ruled before
   Codrus lived (who by death   rescued his fatherland),
Who Aeácus' descendants were,
   And what wars assailed Troy,   you have told us at length:
What a jar of good Chian costs,   5
   Who will offer his house,   who gets the water hot,
And how long I must stand out here
   In Paelígnian frost,   you have not yet proposed.

Quick! A toast to the new month's moon!
   And a second — (Pour wine,   boy!) — to the midnight hours!   10
To Muréna the Augur, third!
   Mix the water and wine   three parts or nine, to taste:
Out of love for the Muses nine
   Here the poet inspired   opts for the three-times-three,
While the Graces who lock their arms   15
   As a trio of nude   sisters, bid others take
Only three — from their fear of brawls.
   Revel's utter most now!   Why at this moment must
Berecýnthian flutes lack breath?
   Why do reed-pipes and lyre   hang on the wall, untouched?   20
Skimping hands are a thing I hate:
   Come, strew roses around!   Lycus shall hear our mad
Sport — and Lycus shall envy us,
   Agèd Lycus and that   ill-suited mate of his.

25   Thick-haired Télephus, you who shine
                Pure as the Evening Star: Rhódē with youth in bloom
            Looks to you in her heart's desire;
                I feel Glýcera's love   burning as with slow fire.

1   The river god Ínachus became the first king of Argos in remotest Greek times.
2   The probably historical Codrus was the last king of Athens before the Dorian invasion,
    around 1,000 B.C. He provoked his own death because an oracle had said that Athens
    would be defeated if its ruler remained alive.
3   Aeácus, son of Zeus, was the father of Péleus and Télamon and grandfather of Achilles
    and Ajax.
        Antiquarian lore commanded much respect among Roman gentlemen. The future
    emperor Tiberius used to test professors of Greek literature, Suetonius reports in his *Life
    of Tiberius* 70, with such questions as: "Who was Hecuba's mother?", "What name did
    Achilles assume when he disguised himself as a girl . . . ?", "What song did the Sirens
    sing?" and so forth.
8   The "decorative adjective" Paelígnian refers to the cold mountain country of the Italic
    Paelígni about 125 km/90 m ENE of Rome; see Epode 17, 60 and the note to Epode 17,
    28–29.
9   At line 9 it is to be assumed that the party has moved to someone's house, perhaps
    Horace's (? on the slope of the Esquiline Hill), since he now assumes the office of
    Drinking Master, proposing the toasts and "legislating" the mixing of the wine.
        For Horace (13–14) as poet (*vates*) and devotee of the nine Muses, the mixture shall
    be nine ladles of wine to three of water; for the others (15–17), who are to be guided by
    the three Graces, that is, by seemly behavior, the mixture shall be the reverse: three
    ladles of wine to nine ladles of water.
11 Muréna must be the Aulus Licínius Muréna addressed in *Odes* 2.10; see the note to line
    1 of that poem. Only here is it said that he was Augur (official taker of bird omens).
18 "Revel's uttermost now!" paraphrases *Insanire iuvat,* "it pleases (me) to rave."
19 "Berecýnthian" = "orgiastic," as in the rites of Dindýmenē (*Odes* 1.16.7–9 and note).
    The *music* is to be "wild," the *instruments* may be horns (*Odes* 1.18.14), flutes (as here), or
    flutes and lyres (*Odes* 4.1.22–23).
22–28 Though the poem's setting is in Rome, the names, by the usual poetic convention,
    are Greek: Lycus ("wolf"), Rhódē ("rose" or "Rhodian"), Glýcera ("sweet"), Télephus
    (a mythological name said by Robert Graves to mean "suckled by a doe").

3.20.   *Non vides quanto moveas periclo*

Meter: Sapphic stanza: in lines 1, 2, and 3: $\_ \cup \_ > \_ \cup \cup \_ \cup \_ \cup$
                            in line 4: $\_ \cup \cup \_ \cup$

            Don't you see the peril in meddling, Pyrrhus,
            With the cubs of African lionesses?
            You will soon abandon so rough a contest,
                Daunted abductor,

5   When, through hosts of heroes opposing, on she
            Comes to take him back, her superb Neárchus:

Mighty combat then must decide the issue:
    Which of you wins him.

But, while you are speeding your flights of arrows
And while she is whetting her teeth in fury,   10
There the battle's arbiter rested one bare
    Foot on the palm-branch

Prize (they say), allowing the gentle breeze to
Fan his scented hair where it draped his shoulders,
Like a second Níreus, or lad from fountained   15
    Ida abducted.

1–10   The excellent conclusion (lines 11–16) is made to depend on the woefully mixed metaphors of the first ten lines. If we overlook the fact that Neárchus is hardly parallel to a lion *cub*, it is harder to accept the parallel of lioness *mother* and the girl who is Pyrrhus's rival. That the girl must fight against "hosts of heroes" is worse. Nor do lionesses whet their teeth. All becomes clear, however, when we see that the true picture is that of a wild boar's charge against a hunter and the hunter's party. A merging of two, perhaps three, passages from the *Iliad* probably accounts for the confusion.

    Iliad 18.318–322 has the image of a hunter's theft of lion cubs; *Iliad* 11. 413–416 and 13. 471–5 both describe the fury of a wild boar's charge; we quote the first of these (in the Lattimore translation):

    . . . . as when
    closing about a wild boar the hounds and the lusty young men
    rush him, and he comes out of his lair in the deep of a thicket
    grinding to an edge the white fangs in the crook of the jawbones . . .

15   Níreus (as in Epode 15, 22) is *not* Néreus, the sea god, but "Nireus, the most beautiful man who came beneath Ilion . . . after perfect Achilles." (*Iliad* 2. 673–4)

15–16   South of Troy, Mount Ida of-the-many-fountains (springs), Homer's *Ídē polypîdax*, was the home of Ganymedes,

    who was the loveliest born of the race of mortals, and therefore
    the gods caught him away to themselves, to be Zeus' wine-pourer,
    for the sake of his beauty, so he might be among the immortals.
                          (*Iliad* 20. 233–5)

Aeneid 5. 254–5 has him caught away by Zeus's eagle; Ovid: *Metamorphoses* 10. 155–161 has him caught away by Zeus in the form of an eagle, because the king of the gods "burned with love for the lad."

3.21.   *O nata mecum consule Manlio*

Meter: Alcaic stanza: in lines 1 and 2:   U _ U _ > _ U U _ U _
                       in line 3:   U _ U _ U _ U _ U
                       in line 4:   _ U U _ U U _ U _ U

Twin-born with me in Manlius' consulship,
    With tribulation in you, or jolly jest,

Contentions, crazy love adventures,
Or, dear old wine jar, untroubled slumber,

5   Your Massic vintage be for whichever cause
Preserved, but worthy of a red-letter day,
Come down from storage at Corvínus'
Bidding and furnish us wine well mellowed.

For all that he is steeped in Socratic books,
10   He is not one to turn up his nose at you;
They say that even stern old Cato
Warmed to his wine when occasion offered.

To genius all too often recalcitrant
You give a gentle spur; what philosophers
15   Long pondered, and obscure decisions
Too, you reveal through the Glad Releaser;

You put new hope in minds overwrought with cares,
On poor men's stooping heads you set horns of strength,
Who then no longer fear the rage of
20   High-turbaned kings or the swords of soldiers.

May Liber, joyous Venus (if present), and
The Graces who but slowly disjoin their arms,
And wakeful lamps, prolong your course till
Phoebus returns and the stars are banished.

1   The wine was made in 65 B.C., the year when Horace was born and when Lucius Manlius
Torquatus was consul. (Epode 13,6 says: "Bring out my birth-year wines, the ones
pressed in Torquatus's term.")

5   The superior vintage from near Monte Massico, as in the note to *Odes* 1.1.19.

7   "Come down from storage," because wine jars were "Set among the rafters to get the
smoke"; (*Odes* 3.8.11 and note).

The distinguished lawyer and patron of letters, Marcus Valerius Messala Corvínus,
had been Horace's fellow-student in Athens and his fellow-soldier under Brutus in 42
B.C. He was consul in 31, and in 27 he celebrated a military triumph over the Aqui-
tanians (of what is now SW France). S.1.6.42 alluded to the prominent family of the
Messalas; S.1.10.28 spoke of Corvínus's oratorical skill, and line 85 of the same poem
listed "Messala" as one of the persons approving of Horace's works as of 35 B.C. His
literary group, which held aloof from the imperial court, included the poet Tibullus; see
Odes 1.33.1 and E.1.4.1 and notes.

9   The Socratic "books" ("conversations," in the text) are the dialogues of Plato in which
Socrates appears as a speaking personage.

11   That is, Marcus Porcius Cato, the Elder, 234–149 B.C., as in the note to *Odes* 2.15.12.

16   "The Glad Releaser" — *iocoso ... Lyáeo*; compare Epode 9, 38 and *Odes* 1.7.24 and notes.

18   Horn, as a symbol of strength, was Latin, but also Hebrew: 1 Samuel 2:1: "mine horn is
exalted in the Lord," and 1 Samuel 2:10: "(the Lord) shall give strength unto his king,
and exalt the horn of his Anointed." Ernest Weekley, under "horn," suggests that in the
Semitic languages the figure was "apparently taken from horned head-dress."

20   The kings are Persian; their "high turbans" are properly tall, pointed caps: *apices*
(singular *apex*); the same word was translated as "crowns" in *Odes* 1.34.16.
Lines 13–18 will be phrase-by-phrase reworded in E.1.5.16–20.

22   The three sister Graces (as in the note to *Odes* 1.4.6) personified what we would now call the "social graces"; in the plastic arts, as in *Odes* 3.19.15–16, they might appear with locked arms "As a trio of nude   sisters," and here they "but slowly disjoin their arms," meaning, apparently, that one does not come without the other two. Hesiod (*Theogony* 911) first gave them names: Aglaia ("bright"), Euphrósynē ("good cheer"), and Thalia ("festive"). We will not go far astray in thinking of them as Charm, Wit, and Courtesy. In *Faust, Part II*, 5299–5304, Goethe introduces them as allegories of gracious giving, gracious receiving, and gracious thanking. In any case their presence banishes all that is gross or boorish.

3.22.   *Montium custos nemorumque virgo,*

Meter: Sapphic stanza: in lines 1, 2, and 3:   _ U _ > _ U U _ U _ U
                                    in line 4:   _ U U _ U

> Virgin goddess guarding these woods and mountains,
> You who aid young women in childbirth when they
> Three times call your name and avert their deaths,
>   Triple in aspect:
>
> May this pine tree shading my house to you be   5
> Sacred: each year's end it shall taste wild-boar's blood, —
> One just forming notions of how his tusks might
>   Slash a foe sideways.

1–4   The virgin goddess is Artemis/Diana, the huntress and protectress of wild things, so that dedication of a pine tree is unexpected.
    As goddess aiding childbirth her name might be Ílithýia (Greek *Eileíthuia*), Lucína ("she who brings to light"), or Genitális; see the *Centennial Hymn* 13–16 and note.
    The goddess is "Triple in aspect," being Luna (the Moon) in the sky, Diana on earth, and Hecatē in the underworld.
    W. K. C. Guthrie explains much of the goddess's complex character in *The Greeks and their Gods*, pp. 99–106.
    By coincidence or otherwise, lines 1–4 resemble lines 9–16 of the Hymn to Diana (Poem 34) by Catullus, a poet to whom Horace seems unsympathetic; see S.1.10.19 and note.
5   The same pine tree as in *Odes* 2.11.14?
8   The sideways slash is zoologically correct (in contrast to *Odes* 3.20.10), perhaps because recalled from *Odyssey* 19.449–451: " . . . the boar struck first with a sideways lift of the head that drove in his tusk above (Odysseus's) knee . . . " (T.E. Lawrence translation)

3.23.   *Caelo supinas si tuleris manus*

Meter: Alcaic stanza: in lines 1 and 2:   U _ U _ > _ U U _ U _
                                  in line 3:   U _ U _ U _ U _ U
                                  in line 4:   _ U U _ U U _ U _ U

If at the new moon's rising you lift your hands
Palms upward to the sky, rustic Phídylē,
    And treat your household gods to incense,
        First-garnered fruits, and a greedy piglet,

5   No pestilent Sirocco will parch your grapes
Just rounding to their fullness, no blight will rot
    Your grain, nor will your tender lambs be
        Harmed by foul weather at fruiting season.

At pasture out on Álgidus' snowy ridge,
10   Among the oaks and holm-oaks, there may be herds,
    As on the Alban grasslands there are
        Flocks, that will die under pontiffs' axes

As sacrificial victims, but *you* need not
Cajole your homely little divinities
15   With many sheep, nor need you deck their
        Statues with rosemary or with myrtle.

The guiltless hand that touches an altar, not
The more acceptable for expense incurred,
    Has moved indifferent household gods with
20   Patties of spelt-mash and crackling salt-grains.

1–2   In classical times prayer was uttered while standing and with arms extended forward and up, palms upward.
      "Phídylē" = Greek *Pheidýlē*, from *pheídomai*, "to use sparingly, thriftily."
4   The "greedy piglet" (like the one in *Odes* 3.17.16) is doubtless two months old, the earliest permissible age for sacrifice.
5   The sirocco (*Africum*) carries untold billions of tiny sand particles from the Sahara, and, if blowing violently, embeds these in each individual grape, ruining the crop.
6–7   "Blight" (or "rust"), *robigo*, is a plant disease occurring in an early, wet spring.
9–13   For the Álgidus Ridge of the Alban Hills SE of Rome see the note to *Odes* 1.21.6. The land there was the property of the pontiffs (priests), who used it to raise animals exclusively for sacrifices to the gods; necessarily these animals brought high prices.
16   Rosemary (older English "rosmarine," translating Latin *ros marina*, "sea dew") is an aromatic shrub of the mint family, with light blue flowers. For the myrtle *shrub*, with its pink and white flowers, see the note to *Odes* 2.15.5–6.
19   "Household gods" in line 3 was *Laris*, here it is *Penatis*. The former were benign ancestral spirits, the latter were spirits of the place and of the family order.
20   A very ancient type of offering to the gods consisted of salted patties ("cakes") made of ground spelt, a primitive variety of hard-grained wheat. While these burned on the hearth, the fire was made to crackle by strewing salt upon it.

3.24.   *Intactis opulentior*

Meter: in the odd-numbered lines: _ > _ ∪ ∪ _ ∪ _

in the even-numbered lines: $\_ > \_ \cup \cup \_ \ \_ \cup \cup \_ \cup \_$

You, with treasure surpassing all
  Ind, or Araby's still undespoiled wealth, can build
Stone foundations usurping both
  Seas enclosing our shores, western and eastern too,
But Necessity, driving nails   5
  Adamantine, may build rafters and roof, and then
You will hardly escape from fear,
  Hardly rescue your head out of the snares of death.
Nomad Scyths have a better life
  With their wagons that haul movable houses across   10
Open steppes, or the Getae, whose
  Unsurveyed and unmarked stretches of common lands
Yield the fruits and the grain for all;
  Not for longer than one year do they till and plant,
Then the worked-over site is left   15
  For an alternate tract which will in turn be sown;
There the stepsons with mother lost
  Find a father's new wife steadfastly kind and good;
There no rich-dowered women rule
  Husbands, nor do they take any sleek paramours;   20
Parents' worthiness makes the most
  Valued dowry, and chaste conduct is there assured
By avoidance of other wives'
  Spouses: lapse from that rule brings the offender's death.
Oh, if anyone seeks to end   25
  Civil strife and insane slaughter of citizens,
Or aspires to a statue styled
  "Patron lord of the state," let him attempt the brave
Feat of curbing licentiousness, —
  Winning posthumus fame, since we abhor, alas!,   30
Any excellence while it lives,
  Yet, when once it is gone, grievously mourn its loss.
What is gained by protesting if
  Evil's causes are not ruthlessly pruned away?
What can powerless laws achieve,   35
  Failing moral restraint, seeing that neither earth's
Torrid zone of forbidding heat
  Nor the region that lies nearest the Northwind's source
Frozen under a crust of snow
  Keeps the merchant away, nor do the savage seas   40
Baffle mariners' cunning skill,
  While from shame at itself poverty goads a man
Into doing no matter what,
  Even if he deserts strenuous virtue's path?

45   Let us either go up, amid
            Cheers of crowds, and commit   all of our useless gold,
        All our jewels and gems, to Jove
            In the Capitol's shrine,   or in the nearest sea
        Throw the mischievous stuff, this prime
50   Source of evil, if we   truly repent our ways.
        We most need to eradicate
            Seeds of greedy desire,   bring the too softly reared
        Minds of young people under some
            Sterner governance. Why,   nowadays free-born youths
55   Hardly know how to sit a horse;
            Hunting scares them, but games   find them adept at play,
        Such as rolling a hoop like Greeks,
            Or at rolling the dice   (which is against the law),
        While their fraudulent fathers cheat
60   Partners out of their just   dues, and cheat guests besides, —
        Always thrusting their money on
            Toward their unworthy heirs.   Nevertheless their wealth
        Keeps increasing, of course; and yet
            Always some little thing   seems to be lacking still.

1–2   With Araby's wealth still "undespoiled" (*intactis*), we infer a date after that abortive
        expedition of 26 B.C. mentioned in connection with *Odes* 1.29. A line of Propertius
        (2.10.16), mentioning "intact Arabia," is probably contemporary with the present
        poem.
2–4   Horace imagines Italy's entire coastline as ringed with villas built out into the water,
        like the ones at Baiae (*Odes* 2.18.20–22 and 3.1.33–37 and notes).
5–8   "Necessity" = "what-must-be," as in *Odes* 1.35.17–20: the rich man begins his fine
        villa but the finishing work is done by Fate.
9–11   The crude houses-on-wheels of the nomad Scyths of the S Russian plains were
        mentioned by Aeschylus in *Prometheus Bound* 709–710, around 460 B.C., but the same
        custom was observed by their kinsmen and successors, the Sarmatians, of Horace's time.
11–24   Julius Caesar had reported (in *The Gallic War* 4.1) that the Germanic Suebi, E of the
        lower Rhine, held croplands in common and cultivated them for one year only before
        moving to a new location. Tacitus (in *Germania* 26), more than a century after Horace,
        will claim the same custom for all Germanic tribes.
            Strictest monogamy and ferocious punishment of adultery will likewise be reported
        of the Germanic tribes by Tacitus (*Germania* 19).
            Dr. Johnson and Rousseau and many another believed, in different ways, in sinless
        primitives, and the myth was not exploded until the twentieth century. Horace, like all
        the others, is using the myth to correct home vices.
25–29   "Anyone" clearly means Augustus, who *had* ended the civil wars, but not until 18 B.C.
        did the emperor promulgate the laws making adultery a public crime and penalizing
        unmarried persons. The *Centennial Hymn* 17–18 and *Odes* 4.5.21–24 will allude to those
        measures; meanwhile Horace is speaking in the tone of the six "national odes" that open
        Book III. Again it is wise to remind ourselves that only "the Romans," that is, the ruling
        class, are concerned.
30–32   Compare E.2.1.5–14, where living and dead authors are the subject.
57   A ceramic oil jar (*lēkythos*) in the National Museum at Athens shows an adolescent youth
        (ca. 450–400 B.C.) rolling a large hoop. Romans found this sport less than masculine.
        Compare the note to S.2.2.10–12 and also E.2.3. 380.

3.25.   *Quo me, Bacche, rapis tui*

Meter: in the odd-numbered lines: $\_ > \_ \cup \cup \_ \cup \_$
          in the even-numbered lines: $\_ > \_ \cup \cup \_ \ \_ \cup \cup \_ \cup \_$

Whither, Bacchus, am I swept on,
      Thus possessed by your wine?   What are the groves and caves
This new self of mine must behold?
      By what grottoes shall I,   singing, be heard to tell
Caesar's eminent glory set   5
      High in Jupiter's hall   up with eternal stars?
Fame-conferring, unheard-of song,
      New and strange, shall be mine.   As a bacchante might stand,
Roused from trance on a mountain ridge,
      Wonder-struck to behold   snow-covered Thrace below,   10
Hebrus River, and Rhódopē's
      Slopes by alien feet   trodden: so I, astray,
Gaze bewildered at streams that wind
      Through untenanted groves.   Lord of the Naiads, lord
Of bacchántes with their human hands   15
      Wrenching ash trees full grown   up from the forest floor,
Nothing common shall I compose,
      Nothing destined to die.   Sweet is the peril braved,
Wine-press god, in your footsteps' wake,
      While with tendrils of green   grapevine my brows are crowned.   20

5–6   Compare the similar "deification" of Augustus in *Odes* 3.3.9–12.

8–12   "Bacchánte" = *Euhias,* "she who cries the cry of Evoé!"; see the note to *Odes* 2.19.5.
      Ancient Thrace is now divided among Bulgaria, Greece, and Turkey-in-Europe, with the lower Hebrus River (now the Maritsa) separating the latter two. The NW-SE stretch of the Rhódopē (modern Rodopi) mountain chain is within Bulgaria but sloping down to the modern Greek border. These mountains are no great distance E of Philippi, where Horace was in the autumn of 42 B.C., and quite possibly the scenery is recalled from the time when, at age 23, he was campaigning in this area with Brutus.
      (The Haemus mountains associated with Orpheus in *Odes* 1.12.6–12 are far to the N and NW, yet it was down the River Hebrus that Orpheus's severed head floated to the sea.)

14   Naiads are water nymphs (from Greek *náein,* "to flow"). The god is addressed as "ruler over Naiads and Bacchae" in Hymn 53.6 of the 80-odd songs in the ancient Orphic hymnal.

15–16   The long Messenger's speech in Euripides's *The Bacchae* (after line 1100) reports how the bacchantes, with no more than their human hands, uprooted a high tree in which King Pentheus was hiding to spy on their rituals. (Compare *Odes* 2.19.9–12, where parts of the Herdsman's speech, lines 706 ff., were paraphrased from the same drama.)
      Euripides's *The Bacchae* is set in Thebes, with events reported from Mount Cithae-ron just S of the city, and Thrace is some 500 km/300 m NE of there; hence the lost bacchante of the present poem must have wandered from some *Thracian* ritual site to recover her senses on "Mount Rhódopē."

19   "Wine-press god" = *Lenáee,* from Greek *lēnós,* "wine press."

Though this poem is not a hymn *to* Bacchus, like *Odes* 2.19, it is hard to say whether its primary concern is with Caesar, as Moore thinks, or with a subjective experience of Horace's. Though it sounds like a prelude to a series of poems, it stands as an independent work. It may even be a fragment, salvaged for its hauntingly beautiful lines 8–14.

3.26. *Vixi puellis nuper idoneus*

Meter: Alcaic stanza: in lines 1 and 2:   U _ U _ > _ U U _ U _
in line 3:   U _ U _ U _ U _ U
in line 4:   _ U U _ U U _ U _ U

> I always lived, till lately, to suit the girls
> And soldiered with some glory on those campaigns,
>   But I shall now hang up my war-worn
>   Lyre and my weapons upon this shrine-wall

5
> Where Venus-of-the-Sea at her left-hand side
> Will guard them. Here deposit your torches, here
>   Your crowbars, here your bows for sieges
>   Brought against gateways denying entry.

> O goddess-queen of fortunate Cyprus Isle
10
> And Memphis never whitened by Thracian snows,
>   Lift up your whip and give a single
>   Flick of the lash to this haughty Chloē.

3–4   That is, the lyre and the "weapons" will be dedicated in token of service completed, as the gladiator in E.1.1.4–6 hangs up his fighting gear, and somewhat as the shipwrecked sailor hangs up his dripping-wet clothes in the shrine of the sea god in *Odes* 1.5.13–16.
5   "Venus-of-the-Sea" = *Venus marina*. Hesiod (*Theógony* 195–8) calls Aphroditē "the foam-born goddess . . . because she grew amid the foam (*aphrós*.)."
9   Venus/Aphroditē, after birth in the seafoam, came to land at the island of Cythéra (*Odes* 1.4.5 and note), but she established her principal shrine on the large island of Cyprus (*Odes* 1.3.1, 19.10; and 30.2). She was also said to be "Cyprus-born," and Hesiod himself is unclear on this point (*Theógony* 198–9).
10   Herodotus (2.112) says there was a temple to Aphroditē the Stranger at Memphis, the ancient capital of Lower (northern) Egypt, which was situated a short distance S of Cairo and on the opposite (west) bank of the Nile.
   "Thracian" = "Sithonian" (for a particular tribe of Thracians) in the text, as in *Odes* 1.18.9. Horace more than once connects Thrace with snow and ice, for example, in lines 9–12 of the foregoing ode.

3.27   *Impios parrae recinentis omen*

Meter: Sapphic stanza: in lines 1, 2, and 3:   _ U _ > _ U U _ U _ U
in line 4:   _ U U _ U

May the wicked travel with evil omens —
Hoot-owl's echoed call and a pregnant bitch, or
She-wolf on Lanúvian slopes, or vixen
    Close to her whelping;

May their journeys have to be started over   5
As a snake goes darting across the road and
Scares the ponies: *I,* for a friend, will act as
    Provident augur,

And, before the crow, that foretells impending
Rains, flies back again to his stagnant marshes,   10
Will entreat that prophet, from sunrise-side, for
    Prospering signals.

So: I wish you happiness, Galatéa,
Anywhere you go — and remember me! — with
No unlucky woodpecker or no vagrant   15
    Raven preventing.

Notice, though, how setting Oríon wavers
Under tempest. *I* know what Adriatic
Storms are like, and how the Apulian wind plays
    Havoc when cloudless.   20

Leave to wives and children of foes the blinding
Squalls and sudden storms of the rising southwind,
Seas of roaring darkness, and surf that lashes
    Shuddering coastlines.

Thus Európa also once trusted both her   25
Life and snow-white self to the trickster bull, with
Valor changed to terror at sight of sea waves
    Teeming with monsters:

Just that morning she had been picking meadow
Flowers for the Nymphs as a promised garland: 30
Nothing now but glimmering night and stars and
    Waters around her.

Once at mighty Crete with its hundred cities,
"Father!", she exclaimed, "I have lost a daughter's
Claim to be a daughter by leaving home while   35
    Madness possessed me.

Where and whence now am I? One death is little
For a lapse like mine. Am I now awake and
Weeping for the deed of my shame, or only
    Mocked by a hollow   40

Dream that rushes up from the ivory gate as

Sleep conducts its passage? I now ask which was
Better: crossing over those endless waves or
    Gathering flowers?

45   Give me for my fury that graceless bull-calf
Now, and I will muster the strength to lop those
Horns which only yesterday I so loved while
    Fondling that monster.

          Shameless, I abandoned my native gods, and
50   Shameless now, I tarry this side of Orcus.
Oh, if gods can hear me, conduct me forth where
    Lions will eat me!

Now, before my cheeks in their comely prime have
Turned to haggard hollows, before the vital
55   Sap has all been drained from their prey, let tigers
    Feast on my beauty.

'Base Európa!' mutters my distant father.
Why delay your death? From that mountain ash tree
You can hang yourself by the maiden girdle
60   You are still wearing.

Or, if cliffs invite you to die on sharpened
Rocks, go hurl yourself to the wafting winds, or
Else obey a mistress who sets you days of
    Carding and spinning, —

65   You, a princess, concubine, under orders
From a brute barbarian's wife!" — Here Venus,
Slyly smiling, comes, and that son of hers with
    Bowstring now slackened;

After making fun of her woe,"Refrain," said
70   She, "from scenes and angry recriminations
When your hated bull reappears and offers
    Horns for the lopping.

Jove Unconquered makes you his wife without your
Knowledge. Hush your sobs and discover how to
75   Bear exalted fortune: your name will pass to
    Half the earth's surface."

  3 Lanúvium (now Lanuvio) was a town some 30 km/20 m SE of Rome, on the right of one
     southbound on the Appian Way. The slopes were those of an outer spur of the Alban
     Hills on which the town stood.
  7 "Ponies" = *mannos*, the Gaulish breed of driving horse, as in Epode 4,14 and E.1.7.77.
  9–10 The rain-foretelling crow is also in *Odes* 3.17.11–13.
 11 The "sunrise side" was the good-luck side of the omens-taker, who always faced south.
     Compare the note to E.1.16.5–7.

13   "Galatéa" is Greek for "milk-white." There is no allusion to Pygmalion's statue-come-to-life.

15   Woodpeckers are also "rain-foretellers."

17–18   The constellation of Oríon sets in stormy November; compare *Odes* 1.28.22: "Southwinds companion to setting Oríon." The constellation "wavers" (*trepidet*) because it is so low (*pronus*) on the horizon that the sea-swells keep obscuring it from viewers on shipboard. (The *hero* Oríon of *Odes* 2.13.39 and 3.4.70 is not concerned here.)

18–20   Horace had made the Adriatic crossing to Greece around age 20 and back around age 23–24, but from boyhood in Apulia he would have heard much about Adriatic seafaring.

Galatéa's journey started from Rome, went S past Lanúvium on the Appian Way, doubtless to Brundisium along much the same route covered by Horace in *S*.1.5, and across the Adriatic to Greece, with no specific destination named.

In warning her against the Adriatic crossing Horace is reminded of another heedless girl, Európa, who once made a regretted "voyage." (Was a lover involved in both cases?)

25–26   Zeus/Jupiter, in the form of a handsome young bull, lured Tyrian princess Európa onto his back and swam with her to Crete. Tyre and Sidon were the chief cities of Phoenicia (now Saïdâ and Sûr in Lebanon).

As Ovid, after Horace's time, relates the abduction scene at the close of Book II of the *Metamorphoses,* the god came as a young, snow-white bull of demurely affectionate behavior among the herd at pasture by the seaside; the princess was gathering flowers nearby. After accepting her garlands upon his dainty horns, he lured the girl to the water's edge and onto his back, then boldly swam away with her. The myth may reflect prehistoric Greek sea-raids to Crete and Phoenicia.

27–28   Compare *Odes* 1.3.18–19: " . . . monsters in ghastly pomp/ Float on foam of the seething gulfs . . . "; also *Odes* 1.2.5–8.

33   Homer's "hundred-citied Crete" (*Krḗtē hekatómpolis*). Coins from Gortyna in S-central Crete suggest that the landing "occurred" on the shore S of Gortyna.

All the rest of the poem takes place during a temporary absence of the bull, as line 71 indicates.

40–42   In *Odyssey* 19. 562 ff. Penélopē says: "Twin are the gates to the impalpable land of dreams, these made from horn and those of ivory. Dreams that pass by the pale carven ivory are irony, cheats with a burden of vain hope: but every dream which comes to man through the gate of horn forecasts the future truth." (T.E. Lawrence translation)

In *Aeneid* 6.893–6 Anchises says:

> These are two gates of Sleep: one, they say, is of horn,
> through which an easy way is given to the true shades;
> by the other, which shines with the gleam of ivory,
> the Manes send false dreams into the world above.
>
> (Mantinband translation)

42–44   "*Now* ask," that is, in self-irony.

45   "Bull-calf" (*iuvencum*) is to be taken literally, since that was the shape which Jupiter had assumed (note to lines 25–26 above), but the Latin word also carried the sense of "young man," as in *Odes* 2.8.21 and note, and even in 3.11.41–42 and note. Freud would doubtless have had an extra comment to make on lines 45–48.

50   "Orcus" = "death."

63–64   " . . . days of/ Carding and spinning" paraphrases *pensum*, literally "weight," that is, a day's "weight" of wool that a slave girl had to card, spin, or weave. (See French *le pensum* and German *das Pensum,* both in the sense of a punitive "task" for schoolboys.)

65–66   Compare *Odes* 3.10.15: "Husband love-sick for some   Macedon concubine." For other fates of noble captives see *Odes* 1.29.5–10.

67–68   Cupid's bowstring is slack because he has already shot his arrow of love.

75–76   In listing some 40 land nymphs, daughters of Ocean, Hesiod's *Theógony* names Eurṓpē (line 357) and also Asíē (Asia), but the earliest known occurrence of "Europe" in its geographical sense is in lines 251 and 291 of the "Homeric Hymn" to Apollo, before 600 B.C. Horace's contemporary, Varro, and also the later Pliny took Europe and Africa together as "Half of the earth's surface," equivalent in size to Asia, though ancient geographers more commonly divided the world into *three* parts: Asia, Africa, and Europe.

Greek *Eurōpē* (the form Horace uses here) and Latin *Europa* were used for both the heroine and the continent; English uses "Európa" for the heroine. Robert Graves debates the etymology in *The Greek Myths* 58.2: either *eur-opē*, "broad face" and "a synonym for the full moon" or *eu-ropē*, "good for willows," that is, "well-watered."

3.28.   *Festo quid potius die*

Meter: in the odd-numbered lines: ∪ > _ ∪ ∪ _ ∪ _
          in the even-numbered lines: _ > _ ∪ ∪ _ _ ∪ ∪ _ ∪ _

On the July 23rd *Neptunalia* (the Feast of Neptune) Horace suddenly realizes he has made no preparations for celebrating the holiday.

Let me think of a way to show
    Neptune honor today: hurry and broach some wine,
Lýdē, — Cáecuban, long reserved —
    And for once let your strict   habits be set aside.
5   Noonday's tilt to the west you see,
    Yet, as if in its bird's   swiftness the day stood still,
You delay bringing down the jar
    Which has waited there since   Bíbulus' consulship.

I shall start with a song about
10   Neptune's might and his nymphs   green-haired within the sea;
You shall then take the lyre and sing
    Of Latóna and swift   Cynthia's whetted darts;
Hers my song who with swan-yoked car
    Visits Paphus and rules   Cnidus and all the isles
15   Of the glittering Cyclades;
    Lastly, we will salute   Night with a lullaby.

3–4 Lýdē is clearly a domestic, at her master's orders. Moore sees her as an elderly housekeeper. The scene is surely the Sabine farm.

Lýdē, we infer, rarely drinks wine. Line 4, literally, says: "Put up opposing force to fortified wisdom"; the C.T. Lewis dictionary suggests: "Storm the defences of wisdom"; Moore suggests: " . . . your well fortified (and stern) philosophy."

7 "Bringing down," that is, from where it has been "Set among the rafters to get the smoke," as in *Odes* 3.8.11; see also 3.21.7.

8 Marcus Calpurnius Bíbulus was consul in 59 B.C., when Horace was six years old. Compare the wine jar of Horace's birth year, 65 B.C., in Epode 13,6 and *Odes* 3.21.1–8.

9 At this point the scene doubtless shifts to an out-of-doors booth made of branches; such *umbrae* ("shadows") were temporarily set up for the Feast of Neptune. A similar "scene change" occurs between lines 8 and 9 of *Odes* 3.19.

"I" = *nos*, literally "we," as in *Odes* 1.6.5 and note, and in 2.17.32 and note. Possibly *nos* signifies the master's self-dignity before a servant.

10 Neptune is honored by being praised first, but deities take pleasure in hearing other deities praised as well.

12 Latóna/Leto was the mother of Cynthius (Apollo) and Cynthia (Artemis/Diana), as in *Odes* 1.21.1–4 and note. Lýdē is to sing in praise of the two *chaste* female divinities.

13–15 Horace, in turn, will then sing in praise of Venus. See *Odes* 1.30.1: "Venus, queen of Cnidus and Paphus," and note.

20 The wistfully comic poem ends with a lullaby (*nenia*) as night falls.

3.29. *Tyrrhena regum progenies, tibi*

Meter: Alcaic stanza: in lines 1 and 2:   U _ U _ > _ U U _ U _
in line 3:   U _ U _ U _ U _ U
in line 4:   _ U U _ U U _ U _ U

Descendant of Tyrrhénian kings: for you
A mellow wine is waiting, Maecenas, here
    At my house, never yet decanted,
        Roses as well, and some oil of ben-nut

As perfume for your hair: you should tear yourself   5
Away and not forever be glued to scenes
    Of Tibur's lushness, Áefula, or
        Télegon Parricide's mountain ridges.

Come, leave your cloying superabundance and
Your mansion steeply vying with neighbor clouds,   10
    Stop gazing wonder-struck at blessèd
        Rome with its riches and din and smoke-fumes.

Wealthy people often are charmed by change,
While simple suppers under a modest roof,
    Without grand purple drapes, have sometimes   15
        Smoothed out the wrinkles on brows of poor men.

Andrómeda's illustrious father now
Reveals his hidden fire, and the days of drought
    Return with raging Prócyon and
        Under the star of the maddened Lion: 20

And now both weary shepherd and listless flock
Find shady spots like shaggy Silvánus' lair
    Amid the briars, or a brook with
        Banks never ruffled by passing breezes,

But your concern is all with affairs of state,   25

And, fearful for the City, you dwell on what
The Seres may have planned, or Cyrus'
　　　Bactrians, or the contentious Scythians.

30 With providential wisdom divinity
　　Conceals the future from us in deepest night
　　　And laughs if mortals falter past their
　　　　Limits. Remember with constant mind to

　　Direct things now existing, since all the rest
　　Is swept along as if by a river's force
35　　　Now flowing smoothly in its channel
　　　　Down to Etrúrian seas, but sometimes

　　With smooth-worn stones caught up in its roily tide,
　　And tree-trunks, livestock, houses as well, it rolls
　　　With mountain cries and cries of near-by
40　　　　Forests when floods have enraged its quiet

　　Composure. Self-control is the happy lot
　　Of any man who can, at the close of day,
　　　Declare: "My life is lived: tomorrow
　　　　All-father's will may becloud the skies or

45　Bestow pure sunlight; what he can never do
　　Is render non-existent what *has* been done
　　　Or seize what once a fleeting hour
　　　　Brought and demolish its one-time being."

　　Fortuna, working harm with malicious glee,
50　Persistent at the game of her hateful tricks,
　　　Today may kindly grant me shaky
　　　　Honors, tomorrow confer them elsewhere.

　　I praise her when she keeps to her post: but once
　　She flaps her sudden wings, I return her gifts,
55　　　Don virtue's cloak, and go a-wooing
　　　　Dowerless Poverty, who is honest.

　　If masts are groaning under an Afric gale,
　　It's not my way to grovel in abject prayer
　　　Or drive a bargain made with vows lest
60　　　　Cyprian and Tyrian wares in shipment

　　Contribute further wealth to the greedy sea:
　　A two-oared lifeboat then will be all I need,
　　　And safely through Aegéan tumult
　　　　Castor and Pollux will lightly speed me.

1 "Tyrrhénian" = "Etruscan." The Three-Book collection of *Odes* began with the line:

" . . . Maecenas, whose line   issued from ancient kings," so that the total work begins and ends (except for the personal epilogue of *Odes* 3.30) in the name of Maecenas.

The Etruscans/Tyrrhénians, whose name for themselves was Rasenna, seem to have immigrated from Asia Minor around 900 B.C. and settled the area between the Tiber River and the Mediterranean Sea, from the river bank opposite Rome to well north of Florence. This region was known to the Romans as Etruria (line 36), and a large portion of it became, in 1569, the Grand Duchy of Tuscany (Toscana), the name being a modified form of "Etruscan." The last three of Rome's early kings were Etruscans, ruling from 616 to 509 B.C., after which date Etruscan power declined; as a military force opposing Rome it was last heard of in 294 B.C. See the note to S.1.6.1–2.

4   Costly "oil of ben" was pressed from the nut of the ben (Arabic *bān*) tree and imported from Egypt and Arabia. Compare *malobathrum* (translated as "oil of laurel") in *Odes* 2.7.8 and "Assyrian perfumes (*nardus*)" in 2.11.16.

7–8   Three resort towns, all within easy distance from Rome:

- Tibur (Tívoli), 24 km/15 m NEE of Rome; see the note to *Odes* 1.7.12–14;
- Áefula, a mountain town just SE of Tibur (? now Casape);
- Túsculum (now Frascáti), 22 km/14 m SE of Rome near the N edge of the Alban Hills, was said to have been founded by Telégonus (whom we call Télegon for metrical reasons), son of Circē and Odysseus/Ulysses. As a young man he journeyed in search of his father, raided Ithaca under the mistaken impression that it was Corcýra (Corfu), and slew Ulysses with his own hand; hence "Parricide."

10–12   Maecenas's mansion on the summit of the Esquiline Hill, on the E edge of ancient Rome, was called "the high house" (*alta domus*) in Epode 9,4 not only for its site but also for its tower, the *Turris Maecenatiana*, the highest point of elevation in the city. Lines 11–12 suggest the westward panorama viewed from that height. From the top of that tower Nero was to watch the great fire of Rome in 64 A.D. (Suetonius' "Life of Nero" 38). Compare Tennyson's *In Memoriam* 89,8: "The dust and din and steam of town."

17–20   Three July star-signs indicating midsummer heat ("the Dog Days"):

- July 9: rising of the five-star constellation of Cépheus, its apex close to the Pole Star. In myth, Cépheus was the Ethiopian (Egyptian) king of Joppa (Jaffa) on the coast of Palestine. Andrómeda was his daughter by Queen Cassiopéa, and the constellations of Andrómeda and Cassiopéa adjoin that of Cépheus.
- July 15: rising of Prócyon (pronounced PRO-see-on), "the Little Dog Star," just before the rising of the Dog Star (Canicula, Sirius; see *Odes* 1.17.19 and note, and 3.13.9). "Prócyon" = Greek: *pro-* + *kyōn*, "ahead of the dog."
- July 30: rising of Régulus, the brightest star in the constellation of the Lion (*Leo*).

22–23   Silvánus ("he of the forest") was a woodland god, called "guard of boundaries" in Epode 2,22; in E.2.1.143 he is honored with gifts of milk at the old harvest festivals.

25–28   Maecenas was acting chief of state during Augustus's absences of 31–29 B.C. (Actium, Egypt, the East) and of 27 to the spring of 24 B.C. (Spain). A similar invitation to Maecenas in *Odes* 3.8.17 and 25–28 can be dated with certainty to the spring of 29 B.C., so that the present poem is more plausibly dated to the period of Maecenas's second deputyship, namely to the midsummer season of either 26 or 25 B.C.

Three enemy peoples are named, each so remote as to give no true cause for concern:

- The Seres ("Chinese"); see under "Foreign Nations," p. 397.
- The E-Iranian Bactrians of what is now Afghanistan were conquered by Cyrus II, the Great, 559–530 B.C. (see the note to *Odes* 2.2.17), and organized as the 12th satrapy (province) of the first Persian Empire.

  Alexander the Great conquered Bactria in 329 B.C., and after his death in 323 the area was ruled by a line of Bactrian Greek kings until 139 B.C., when Scythians of Asia seized power; a small area around Kabul held out until 40 B.C. or so. But Horace is referring to a political situation of 500 years before his own time.

· The Scythians—that is, the Sarmatians of S Russia. The text says: "the contentious Tanaïs," that is, the Scythians who live near the Tanaïs (Don) River and who quarrel among themselves."

54   The Roman Fortuna was always winged; see *Odes* 1.34.14–16: ". . . on a gust of wings/Fortuna sometimes swoops to shatter/ Crowns . . . "

64   Castor and Pollux, as in the note to *Odes* 1.3.2, were the twin stars that guided sailors; see also *Odes* 4.8.31–32 and note.

In his collection called *Sylvae* (1685), Dryden included *Odes* 3.29 "paraphras'd in Pindaric verse," to a total of 104 lines grouped in 10 strophes of irregular form.

3.30.   *Exegi monumentum aere perennius*

Meter: "the lesser Asclepiádic," as in *Odes* 1.1. $\_ > \_ \cup \cup \_ \; \_ \cup \cup \_ \cup \_$

> This, my monument, stands,   destined to outlast bronze
> And to tower above   pyramids reared by kings,
> Neither toppled by gales,   nor by eroding rains
> Washed away, nor undone   through the recurrent years
> 5 Yet — past counting — to come   over the range of time.
> I shall not wholly die: rather, my greater part
> Will live free of the grave;   I shall increase and grow,
> Ever fresh in renown.   While to the Capitol
> Silent Vestal and priest   solemnly still ascend,
> 10 Men shall say of me, by   Áufidus' roaring stream
> And where Daunus once ruled   over a rustic folk:
> Risen high in a parched   land from obscure degree,
> This man first wove a song   of the Aeólic kind
> In Italian designs.   Take, then, the honors won
> 15 As your own, and with pride,   gracious Melpómenē,
> Wreathe my head with the twined   Delphian laurel crown.

8–9   Vestal virgin and priest (*pontifex*) would ascend the long stairs up from the Forum to the temple of Capitoline Jupiter to perform their religious offices. The summit of the Capitoline Hill was Rome's most sacred point, and it was in Horace's time that Rome was beginning to be called "the eternal city."

10–12   Unexpectedly Horace speaks as an Apulian rather than as a Roman.

The Áufidus (Ofánto) River begins as a mountain stream W of Horace's native Venúsia. *Odes* 4.9.2 and 4.14.26 will mention its "roaring;" S.1.1.58 mentioned its floodings in its lower courses. Epode 3,16 spoke of the "thirst" of Apulia.

Legendary King Daunus (*not* Danaüs!) founded "Daunia," that is, Apulia; see the note to *Odes* 1.2.14.

13–14   That is, Horace first in Latin poetry used the meters and themes of Alcáeus and Sappho, who composed in the Aeólic dialect of the island of Lesbos. Compare "lyre of Lesbos" in *Odes* 1.1.34 and note.

Our "wove" and "designs" reflect Moore's interpretation of *deduxisse* as " 'composed,' apparently a metaphor taken from spinning."

In E.1.19.32–34 Horace will repeat his claim with regard to Alcáeus only. Perhaps someone in the meantime had reminded him that Catullus used the Sapphic meter thirty years earlier in two poems, 11 and 51. (Horace's apparent antipathy for Catullus was mentioned in the note to S.1.10.19, yet *Odes* 3.22.1–4 seem to echo lines 9–16 of Catullus's Hymn to Diana (poem 34).

15   Melpómenē, the "songstress" Muse, as in *Odes* 1.24.3–4 and note.

The unabashed confidence of Horace's claim startles the modern reader. It seems to be a "first" in literature, though with so much of Alcáeus's work lost, and other Greek poets as well, we cannot be sure. Moore suggests a possible model in Pindar's 6th Pythian Ode, lines 5ff.:

> There stands builded . . .
> A treasure house of song . . .
>   . . . .
> Neither rain driven from afar on the storm,
> nor the merciless armies
> of the crying cloud, no wind shall sweep it, caught
> and stricken with the blown debris into the corners
> of the sea.

(Lattimore translation)

Be that claim as it may, Ovid's 9-hexameter epilogue to the *Metamorphoses*, published in 7 A.D., thirty years after *Odes* 3.30, frankly paraphrases lines 1–8. Echoes of those same eight lines may also be heard in *The Pillar of Fame*, the concluding poem of Robert Herrick's *Hesperides*, 1648.

Epistles. Book I
Epistulae. Liber Primus
20 B.C

Epistles. Book I

With the presentation copy of the *Odes* to Augustus in 23 B.C. Horace included the amusing nineteen-line poem that figures as No. 13 in the collection of letters in verse that he published three years later. Possibly the notion of composing poems in the form of letters, a wholly new idea in literature, originated with this No. 13. At any rate, the three-year period produced twenty such poems, to a total of 1,006 lines, which were issued as a volume of *Epistles* (*Epistulae*) in 20 B.C. Editors later added "Book I" to the title. All twenty poems are in dactylic hexameters, the meter of the earlier "Satires."

Some items, like Nos. 6, 16, and 17, are meditative essays, letter-like only by grace of perfunctory salutations, in these three cases to unknown persons. Others, like No. 2, 10, and 11 are half letter, half essay. Others, again appear to be genuine letters and may actually have been sent to their addressees. No. 9, for instance, in its mere thirteen lines recommends friend Septimius for a position on Tiberius's expeditionary staff, and rarely has a letter of recommendation been so deftly turned, or so persuasively. No. 5 is a dinner invitation; No. 3 asks for news of absent friends; and No. 12 replies to a letter received from a friend in Sicily and concludes with "all the news from home."

Three pieces (Nos. 1, 7, and 19) are addressed to Maecenas. No. 19 concerns literary matters. No. 1, doubtless written last or second-last as the "dedication poem," complains of "the tedious and profitless flowing of time" and expresses the desire to retire "deep in the countryside." The vivid No. 7, with its lively story-insets, is the most memorable item in the collection, but we are startled by its main theme, a sharp disagreement with Maecenas on the point of the poet's personal independence. "Rebellion" is far too strong a term here, but we marvel that so delicate a subject should be broached in a poem intended for publication. The spiritual malaise carries over, without mention of Maecenas, into No. 8, a strangely confessional letter to a young officer off on campaign.

Since eight of the twenty pieces (Nos. 1, 3, 8, 9, 18, 19, 20) can be dated to the publication year itself, we infer that the idea of a volume of verse letters came belatedly. Philosophical ruminations mark the majority of these poems. The predominant mood is mellow, even tame, with little of the pungent wit of the

"Satires" or of the exuberance of the *Odes*. The final piece, No. 20, wistfully sends
Epistles. Book I forth into the world as if it were a bright slaveboy eager to escape his
old master and discover a new life of his own.

1.1. *Prima dicte mihi, summa dicende Camena*

Sung in my earliest, and to be sung in the last of my poems,
You now, Maecenas, behold me retired and rewarded with trophies,
Yet you would have me return to the scenes of my former encounters.
Neither the times nor my mind are the same. I exist like Veiánius,
Deep in the countryside, weapons of Hercules hung on a pillar,   5
No more entreating for favor from down below spectators' loges.
Over and over a voice in my fully cleansed ear keeps repeating:
"Wisely withdraw the old race horse in time and release him to pasture,
Lest he come in broken-winded at last and be jeered as a failure."
Therefore I now put aside all my poems and other diversions;   10
None but things noble and true hold my interest, but they hold it fully.
I am now storing and ordering things for my use in the future.
And, if you ask me what teacher, what doctrinal school I am sworn to,
I bear allegiance to none, I have taken no master at all, but
Rather, wherever the winds of the tempest impel me, I follow.   15
Sometimes I dive in the torrent of civic affairs and am "active,"
Rigidly standing my sentinel's watch as true Virtue's adherent;
Sometimes I softly steal back to the teachings of good Aristíppus,
Seeking to subjugate things to myself, not myself unto things. As
Night seems unending to someone whose mistress has told him a lie, and   20
Day seems unending to laborers bonded to toil, and the slow year
Drags for a fatherless boy under galling restraint from his mother:
So too for me is the tedious and profitless flowing of time which
Hinders my hopes and intentions of speeding some project I know will
Benefit equally those who are wealthy and those who are poor, and   25
Which, if left *un*done, will bring detrimental effects upon old and
Young. So I cling to these simple ideas for guidance and comfort:
Though you may not have the far-ranging vision of Lýnceus, you still would
Not, for that reason, disdain to use salve for your eye inflammation;
Nor, in despair from not having the prowess of unconquered Glýcon,   30
Would you refuse to be treated for cure of your knotted arthritis.
Up to a point there is progress, if further than that is denied us.
If in the heart there is turmoil of greed and a miserable craving,
Magical sayings and words are available which can allay your
Torment and even eliminate major distress altogether.   35
Or, if ambition distends you with bloat, there are recipes which, if
Three times read over with purified mind, can relieve and restore you.
Envious, violent, indolent, drunken, in lust never sated:

No one is any of these to the point where he cannot be treated
40 If he but lends and accustoms his ear to philosophy's mandates.
Virtue begins with avoidance of vice, and the first rule of wisdom
Is to abstain from one's folly. You see how the ills you considered
Greatest and direst — the lack of a fortune and social rejection —
Goad you to shun them with anguish of mind and at risk of your life, so
45 Off you go, business-obsessed, as a trader to farthermost Hindus,
Fleeing from poverty ever by sea and through fire and at cliff's brink.
Why will you rather not listen and learn and believe with a better
Man not to care for the things that you crave and admire in your folly?
Is there a roughneck performing at countryside hamlets and crossroads
50 Who would disdain the Olympic contender's award if he only
Had the assurance the palm could be his without dust or exertion?
Silver is baser than gold, which in turn is yet baser than virtue.
    "Citizens, citizens! Money comes first, any virtues come second!"
That is the cry, high and low, of the bankers by Janus's archway,
55 That is the dictated chant and response of the children and oldsters
"Each with a bookbag and tablet slung leftwards and over his shoulder."
Brains you may have, and good character, loyalty, talent for speaking,
Yet, being six-seven thousand this side of the magic four hundred
Thousand, you stay a plebeian. But boys at their play have a jingle:
60 "You shall be king if you play the game fair." Let our rampart of bronze be
This: to have consciences clear, to turn pale over no guilty action.
Tell me now which is the better: the Róscian Law or the children's
Jingle that promises kingship to persons of proper behavior —
And which the manly Camíllus and Curius chanted in boyhood?
65 Is it superior wisdom that urges: "Make money! Make money
Honestly if you can do it, but somehow or other, make money!" —
So you can sit up in front at the tear-jerking dramas of Pupius;
Or is the wisdom with someone who bids you defy haughty Fortune,
Wisdom unfailingly there to sustain your firm stance amid freedom?
70 Thus, if the great Roman people should happen to ask me the question:
Why, since I stroll in their porticos, do I not share their opinions,
Prizing what *they* prize and shunning whatever they hate?, my reply would
Be, in the words that the fox once returned to the invalid lion
Long, long ago in the fable: "Because I am scared by the many
75 Footprints that lead to your den and not one of them ever returning."
They are the beast with the multiple heads. Whom or what can I follow?
Some men are eager for government contracts, while others again go
Hunting for greedy old widows, with apples and pastries for bait, and
Some cast their drag-nets for elderly men to impound in their fish-weirs, and
80 Many have capital gathering interest from secret investments.
Various things may preoccupy various persons, we grant; but
Can those same persons put up with those things for an hour's duration?
"Nothing on earth," let a rich man remark, "like the exquisite Bay of
Baiae for light," and directly the sea and the salt pools feel thrusting

Villa walls down to their depths as a mark of his love; but capricious   85
Impulse may seize him, and then it's: "Tomorrow you move your equipment
Inland, my men, to Teánum." With conjugal bed by the household
Shrine, he exclaims, "What is finer or better than bachelor life!", but
Lacking a conjugal bed, he declares only married men happy.
How can I fasten a knot that will hold such a shape-shifting Próteus?   90
— Maybe a fellow is poor? — Then the joke is, he too is forever
Changing apartments and barbers and bath houses, and in his rented
Boat suffers seasickness just like the rich man on *his* private trireme.
    Say I run into you after a barber has botched up my haircut:
That sets you laughing. My undershirt happens to show, with the nap worn   95
Thin, at the edge of my tunic, or maybe my toga drapes badly:
That sets you laughing. But what if my mind is at odds with itself and
Spurns what it chooses, returns to its yesterday's discards, all ebb and
Flow like the tide, inconsistent with life's every order and system,
Builds and tears down, changes circles to squares and then back into circles?   100
Then you consider me mad in the usual sense, and you *don't* laugh;
Nor do you think that I need a physician or guardian such as
Judges appoint, since you watch over all my existence yourself and
Fuss if so much as a fingernail looks not quite properly trimmed on
Me, who am ever devotedly yours, with esteem and affection.   105
    Summing the matter, the wise man stands second to Jupiter only;
He is the rich man, the free man, the honored, the handsome, the king of
Kings. Above all, he is clear in the head — save when nursing a head-cold.

2–6   Veiánius (known only from these lines) was a successful gladiator who had
      "dedicated" his weapons and retired to rural tranquillity. Other "dedications" are: a
      slave-chain in S.1.5.65–66, "dripping-wet clothes" in *Odes* 1.5.13–16, Horace's own lyre
      and "weapons" in *Odes* 3.26.3–6; see also S.2.1.33. and note.
7   "Cleansed" (*purgatam*) in the sense of "licked clean by the serpent of widom," as in the
      note to S.1.3.27. Robert Graves cites other cases in *The Greek Myths*: 105 g (Tirésias); 72
      c (Melámpus); 119.2 (Heracles); 158 p (Cassandra).
11–19 That is, I am now solely concerned with philosophy, though I follow no one
      "school" of philosophy. Sometimes I act like a Stoic (16–17)—the Stoics urged their
      "morally perfected" members to be "active" in civic affairs—and sometimes I am an
      Epicurean with Aristíppus (S.2.3.100–102 and note).
28–29 Lýnceus, the "lynx-eyed" Argonaut, as in S.1.2.91 and note. For Horace's eye-
      trouble see S.1.5.30 and ibid. 49 and note.
30   Glýcon was a never-defeated athlete celebrated in poem 7, 692 of the "Greek
      Anthology."
31   "Knotted   arthritis" — *nodosa . . . cheragra,*—"hand-gout,"   as opposed to *podagra*,
      "foot-gout."
34   "Magical sayings and words are available" translates line 478 of Euripides's *Hippolytus*,
      (the Nurse to Phaedra), but, as with "recipes" in line 36, Horace means "philosophy."
36   "Ambition" — *laudis amore*, "greed for praise."
47–48   "A better/ Man" means "a philosopher."
49   Suetonius (Augustus 45) mentions that the emperor delighted in boxing matches,
      including "slogging matches between untrained roughs in narrow City alleys." (Graves
      translation)

54   The text says only: "Janus proclaims"; see the note to S.2.3.18. The American
     equivalent would be: "Wall Street proclaims."
56   Either Horace quotes himself as of S.1.6.74 or some early scribe's cross-referencing was
     incorporated into the text.
57–67 · "Talent for speaking" (57) was a necessary accomplishment for a public career.
       · 400,000 sesterces was the minimum fortune required of Knights (*Equites*).
       · "The Roscian Law"—"Otho's Law" in Epode 4,15 and note—had, since 67 B.C.,
         reserved the 14 rows of theater seats, just behind the senators, for the Knights.
         See also S.1.6.40–41 and note.
       · An ancient commentator cited the actual jingle of line 60 as: *Réx erit qui récte
         faciet, quí non faciet nón erit*. The meter is accentual and preclassical.
       · *Odes* 1.12.41–42 and note: " . . . Curius of the unshorn hair, and/ Old Camillus
         useful in times of war." The text generalizes: "(all) the Camilli and Curii," that
         is, all the grand old-timers.
       · Pupius (67) and his tear-jerking dramas (*lacrimosa poemata*) are unknown.
71   Porticos were roofed colonnades, or porches, where people strolled and talked.
73–75 In one of Aesop's fables an old and weak lion pretended illness so as to kill and eat
     his visitors without exerting himself; the fox declined to step in.
76   The "beast with the multiple heads" is the public with its many discordant opinions.
     The notion was proverbial before Horace worded it: *Belua multorum est capitum*.
77   Government contracts constituted "one of the chief uses of large capital in Rome."
     (Morris)
83–85 Baiae (now Baia) looked S across what we now call the Bay of Naples; the "salt
     pools" (*lacus*) = the nearby Lucrine Lake (whence came the jumbo-size mussels of
     S.2.4.31–32). Construction of villas out into the water was mentioned in *Odes*
     2.18.20–22 and note; *Odes* 3.1.33–36; and even *Odes* 3.24.2–4. See also Shelley: *Ode to the
     West Wind* 32–34:

> . . .
> Beside a pumice isle in Baiae's bay,
> And saw in sleep old palaces and towers
> Quivering within the wave's intenser day, . . .

87   Teánum (now Teáno), a mountain town about 15 km/10 m NW of Capua, looked S
     over the plain of Campania.
          The conjugal bed was called *lectus genialis* because it stood by the *genius*
     ("household spirit") and the shrine of the other household gods (*Lares et Penates*).
90   The shape-shifting sea-god Próteus is described in the note to S.2.3.71–73.
93   A trireme was a large craft rowed by three tiers of oarsmen. We would say "private
     yacht."
106–108 With elaborate irony Horace restates some basic claims of the Stoics; see
     S.1.3.124–5 and note. "Clear in the head" = *sanus*, which means both "healthy" and
     "sane," recurring to the Stoic paradox that all men are mad except the Stoic
     philosopher.

1.2.   *Troiani belli scriptorem, Maxime Lolli*

While you are busy in Rome with your speeches on themes out of Homer,
Maximus Lollius, I've been rereading him here at Praenéstē,
Noticing how he defines what is noble or base, what can be — or
Not be — of profit, in much clearer ways than Chrysíppus and Crantor.
5   Let me explain why I think so, if leisure permits your attention.

(Human follies depicted in the Iliad)

Paris's love affair having occasioned the long-drawn-out war where
Greece threw its forces against the barbarians, here is a story
Dealing with passions of monarchs and people beset with unwisdom.
Ántenor moves they get rid of the *cause* of the war; what does Paris'
Answer amount to but "no one can *force* him to govern in safety   10
Or to live happily?" Nestor makes haste to compose the disputes of
King Agamemnon and mightly Achilles, but neither will listen:
One is still seething with love and the other still burning with anger.
Thus, with their leaders in frenzy, the Argives must suffer reverses.
Trickery, treason, depravity, anger, and wantonness, all are   15
Recklessly practiced both inside and outside the Ilian ramparts.

(The corrective example of the Odyssey)

Yet, in display of what courage and wisdom can also accomplish,
Homer has offered a useful example for us in Ulysses,
Tamer of Troy, who with shrewdness of eye made inspection of many
Cities and customs of men, who while voyaging far in his quest for   20
Homeward return for himself and his crew endured hardships aplenty,
Ever undrowned by the waves of adversity driving against him.
Songs of the Sirens you know of, you know of the potions of Círcē:
How, had he greedily drunk them in folly, as did his companions,
He would have languished, a slave to a slut, in a brutish existence,   25
Foul as a dog and rejoicing in filth like a pig in a quagmire.

We are mere ciphers in life, mere consumers of fruits of the earth, mere
Idlers pursuing Penélopē, or like the youths at Alcínous'
Court who excessively labored at tending their health and complexions,
Finding the crown of all Good to be sleeping till noon and then coaxing   30
Reticent slumber at nighttime with lyres in mellifluous music.
Bandits get up in the hours of darkness to strangle a man: will
You not bestir yourself then for the sake of your self-preservation?
Exercise healthy, or else you will do so from dropsy; unless you
Call for your book and a lamp before daylight, unless you exert your   35
Mind in the study of noble and serious matters, your sleepless
Nights will be tortured by cravings of envy or amorous passion.
Why do you rush to remove any objects offensive to eyesight
When you delay for a year taking care of what troubles your spirit?
Starting a task is as good as accomplishing half of it. Dare to   40
Know. Begin working. Postponing the time for right living is only
Aping the rustic who waits for the river to finish its flow, but
Onward the river now flowing will flow for the mutable ages.

Always the quest is for money, for getting of sons by a wealthy
Wife, and the plow is forever subduing the wilderness. Any   45
Man who is lucky in having enough should not want to seek further.
Never did house or estate, nor the silver and gold of a treasure
Draw off the fever tormenting the frame of their invalid owner,

Nor have they ever purged cares from his mind; the possessor must first have

50   Health if he hopes to make suitable use of collected possessions.
Someone who craves or is worried delights in his mansion and fortune
Much as sore eyes are delighted by pictures, or gout by a foot-muff,
Or as the eardrums impacted with wax by the twanging of lyre strings.
Jars left uncleanly will carry their taint to what contents soever.

55   Spurn all delights; any joy that is purchased with pain will be harmful.
Greed is forever unsatisfied: vow to keep definite limits.
Envy grows lean on the fatness of others' good fortune; Sicilian
Tyrants could never invent any torture more ghastly then envy.
Anyone not curbing anger shall long for the chance of undoing

60   All that his fury at injury led him to do in the first place;
Evil effects come the swifter for violence coupled with hatred.
Rage is but madness in shorter duration; your temper must either
Bend to your will or bend *you*, so control it with chain or with bridle.
Only a colt that is tender of neck can be broken to follow

65   Courses the rider decides to pursue, and the puppy that early
Barked at the buckskin you stuffed and set up in the barnyard will later
Hunt as a hound in the woods. While your heart is still youthful and wholesome
Drink up instruction. Drink now, and to higher things open your senses.
Earliest use of the wine jar imparts the bouquet that is longest

70   Lasting. But whether you tarry or whether you briskly push forward,
I shall not wait for the laggard nor rush to keep up with the leader.

1   Rhetorical training stressed composing and delivering speeches based on situations in the Homeric poems, for example, Priam's entreaty to Achilles for the return of Hector's corpse. Thus line 1 says actually: "While you are declaiming the writer of the Trojan War."

2   Lollius Maximus—Horace inverts names occasionally—is further advised in E.1.18, and the two poems comprise all that we know of him. But see the note to *Odes* 4.9.33. Praenéstē (now Palestrina) was a mountain resort town some 40 km/25 m ESE of Rome.

4   Chrysíppus was the apostle of Stoicism, as in S.2.3.44 and note. Crantor was a prominent Platonist of the late 300s B.C.

9–12   Ántenor's speech to the Trojan council, *Iliad* 7.347–353; Paris's reply, ibid. 354–364; Nestor's speech to the Greek council, *Iliad* 1.247 ff.

17–26   Ulysses as "tamer (*domitor*) of Troy" reflects a Roman, rather than a Greek, opinion. Lines 19–22 freely paraphrase part of Homer's invocation to his Muse at the opening of the *Odyssey,* as does E.2.3.141–2 also. Compare Tennyson's *Ulysses* 13–14:

> Much have I seen and known, — cities of men
> And manners, climates, councils, governments, . . .

The Sirens are in *Odyssey* 12, Círcē in *Odyssey* 10.

28   With "Idlers pursuing Penélopē" compare S.2.5.76–80. *Odyssey* 8.248 ff. tells about Alcínous, King of Phaeácia, and his court, but the details are of Horace's invention and in the Roman tradition, which considered the Phaeácians as mere voluptuaries.

40–41   Dare to/ Know" = *sapere aude*, often quoted as having profounder meaning than the present context would seem to justify, for example, "Dare to know dangerous and forbidden things."

57–58   The Sicilian Greek "tyrants" of the 5th and 4th centuries B.C. had become proverbial for the cruelty and ingenuity of their torture devices.

69–70   In *Odes* 1.20.1–3 Horace proposes to serve local Sabine wine which he himself had
stored "in a jar from Greece" to improve its flavor.

1.3.   *Iuli Flore, quibus terrarum militet oris*

In 20 B.C., while Augustus was in the East negotiating peace with the Parthians, a show of
Roman force was being made by an army marching across northern Greece, through the
Roman province of "Asia" (now Turkey), and on into the large region then called Armenia,
almost to the Caspian Sea. Without fighting a battle, the expedition had the desired effect on
the Parthian negotiations. The expedition commander was the emperor's stepson, aged
twenty-one at the time and still going by the name of Tiberius Claudius Nero; thirty-four
years later, as the designated successor of Augustus, he was to become the Emperor Tiberius,
reigning from 14 A.D. to 37 A.D. The Julius Florus addressed here (and in E.2.2.) was one of the
young men on Tiberius's staff.

Let me, dear Julius Florus, begin with a question: please tell me
Where on this earth has the march taken Claudius, the emperor's stepson?
Are you detained up in Thrace where the Hebrus lies shackled in ice, or
Out where the Hellespont narrows its current between the two towers,
Or in the meadows and hills of luxuriant Asia? And tell me   5
What sort of works may the erudite staff be composing at present?
Who may have ventured to write an account of the feats of Augustus?
Who is reporting his wars and his peace for the times of the future?
What about Títius, soon to be famous in Rome for his poems?
Has he not faltered in terror from drinking the fountains Pindaric   10
After so boldly disdaining accessible rivers and wellsprings?
Is he in health? He remembers me? Does he rely on his Muse to
Make those high cadences sound in accord with the rhythms of Latin,
Or is he ranting to heaven and booming with tragedy-thunder?
What may my Celsus be up to? I warned him, and warn him again, to   15
Seek out the treasures within him and not to be taking from works of
Authors Apollo has stored in his Palatine library-temple,
Else, when the birds all come back and demand the return of their stolen
Plumage, he may, like the drab little crow, be the object of laughter,
Standing there stripped of his colors. And what of your own undertakings?   20
Over what thyme fields do *you* skim in searches for honey? Your no small
Talent is neither untilled nor abandoned to rankness of brambles.
Whetting your eloquence for the debates of the courtroom, or giving
Citizens counsel at law, or composing fine poems, you cannot
Fail to achieve the victorious ivy crown. Now if you ceased your   25
Sopping of cold-water compresses over your worries and fretting
You would directly advance at celestial philosophy's guidance.
This is, for eminent men and obscure ones, the goal and objective,
If our desire is to live and be friends to ourselves and our country.

30   Also, be sure, when you write me, to say if you now bear Munátius
     All the esteem he deserves. Has the wound to that friendship, so poorly
     Mended, been knit back together, or has it reopened? But whether
     You are hot-blooded, or whether the mere inexperience at living
     Galls your two necks both resistant to harness, your brotherly bond ought
35   Not to be severed — wherever you are at this moment. A heifer
     Pasturing here is reserved for you both at your homecoming dinner.

    2   Here, as elsewhere, Horace avoids the regular but metrically awkward name "Tiberius," with its four short vowels in succession.

  3–5   Ancient Thrace (*Thraca,* later *Thracia*) is now divided among Bulgaria, modern Greece, and Turkey-in-Europe; the River Hebrus is now the Maritsa (Turkish: Meriç), and its lower course separates Greece from Turkey-in-Europe.

      The two towers associated with Hero and Leander, and in ancient times called Sestos and Abýdos, stood on the European and Asiatic shores, respectively, of the Hellespont (Dardanelles), where the very swift current flows in a channel less than a mile wide.

      Western "Asia" (Turkey) was proverbially wealthy. Catullus, in Poem 46.4–6, praises its agricultural richness and its famous cities.

  9–14   Apparently the fame of Títius did not materialize: he is "unknown." For the difficulties in matching the grandiose sweep of Pindar's poems, see *Odes* 4.2 and Horace's own not entirely successful attempt at imitation in *Odes* 4.4.

  15   Celsus must be the Albinovánus Celsus, "the scribe and companion of Nero" (that is, of Tiberius), to whom E.1.8 is addressed.

  17   The great library-temple, of which a few foundation stones now remain on the Palatine Hill, was dedicated to Apollo on October 24, 28 B.C., Apollo being Octavius Caesar's patron divinity; see the note to *Odes* 1.2.31–32; also *Odes* 1.31.1–3 and note. Statuary groups adorning its porticos were mentioned, of the daughters of Danaüs; note to *Odes* 3.11.22–32, and of the slaying of Niobē's children: note to *Odes* 4.6.1–4. Further details and allusions occur in the headnote to the *Centennial Hymn,* in E.2.1.216–8 and 229–231 and notes, and in E.2.2.92–95 and note.

      The library-temple was constructed as part of the imperial palace. Its walls were faced with the very white Carrara marble, here used for the first time in Rome, the doors were of ivory, and the portico columns were composed of colored marble from Africa. Two wings of the building housed, respectively, Greek books and Latin books. The Sibylline Books, newly edited by the emperor himself, were deposited, says Suetonius (*Augustus* 31), "in two gilded cases under the pedestal of Palatine Apollo's image." Suetonius also says (29) that Augustus, in his later years, held meetings of the Senate in the nave, or revised jury lists there.

      Apart from the architectural splendor, which exemplified Rome's grandeur and power for both Romans and foreigners, the libraries were meant to vie with the library at Alexandria, the largest collection of books in the classical world, and, more particularly, to establish Rome as a principal cultural center.

 18–20   "The drab little crow" = *cornicula,* an ornithologically disputed word. Aesop has a fable about a jackdaw who, in a beauty contest of the birds, arrayed himself in the moulted plumes of other birds and almost won the prize, until his competitors indignantly stripped him naked; but Morris feels that Horace was following Fable 1.3 of his contemporary Phaedrus.

 23–25   That is, as a trial lawyer, as a legal consultant (like Trebatius in S.2.1), or as a lyric poet. The ivy crown was bestowed only on poets.

  30   Munátius is unknown. He must be young, perhaps in his early twenties, and perhaps a relative of the Lucius Munátius Plancus described in the note to *Odes* 1.7.18.

1.4.   *Albi, nostrorum sermonum candide iudex,*

Albius, fair and appreciative critic in judging my Satires,
What shall I make of your now being here in the region of Pedum?
Writing, perhaps, to surpass the small pieces of Cassius of Parma?
Or are you silently haunting the wholesome retreats of the woodlands,
Pondering matters befitting a lover of wisdom and goodness?   5
Never were you any shell of a man with no heart: from the gods you
Did receive beauty and wealth and the knack of enjoying those blessings.
Where is a nurse who could wish any more for her nurseling than being
Able to realize and to express what he feels, having also
Charm, reputation, abundance of physical health and of every   10
Comfort in life, all sustained by a purse that is never found wanting?
So, amid hopes and depression, with rages and fear to contend with,
Welcome each dawning of day as if never another would brighten:
Then you will find your delight in another one's rising unhoped for.
     Visiting me, you will see I am fatted and sleek and well tended,   15
And, for your glee, like a pig Epicúrus could herd with his porkers.

1   For consistency, we translate *Sermones* as "Satires"; see the Introduction to the *Satires,*
     paragraph 1, p. 12.
          As said in the note to *Odes* 1.33.1, Albius is identified as the melancholy love-poet
     Albius Tibúllus, who had an estate at Pedum, near modern Frascáti, on the edge of the
     Alban Hills ESE of Rome.
          One infers a long separation of the two poets, since the *Satires* had been published 15
     and 10 years, respectively, before this present poem, which was published in 20 B.C. The
     separation is usually explained, without evidence, by saying that Tibúllus was away
     with his patron, Marcus Valerius Messalla "Corvínus" (see the notes to S.1.10.28 and
     Odes 3.21.7), on the latter's campaign, after 27 B.C., against the Aquitanians in what is
     now SW France. In that case, *Odes* 1.33 must have been addressed from afar to "Albius."
3   Cassius of Parma, as *one* of the assassins of Julius Caesar, was executed after the battle of
     Actium on orders from Octavius Caesar; the famous *chief* conspirator was Cassius
     Longinus. The "small pieces" (*opuscula*) of the former are lost.
10   Despite this statement Tibúllus died within a year (19 B.C.), aged less than fifty.
16   A happy pig was the popular Roman notion of an Epicuréan.

1.5.   *Si potes Archiacis conviva recumbere lectis*

If you can bear to put up with my Archian couches, and if you
Feel no dismay at a vegetable menu on crockery service,
I shall expect you, Torquatus, at *my* house for dinner at sundown.
You shall have wine that was bottled when Taurus was second-term consul,
Marsh-grown between Sinuéssan Petrínum and Latian Mintúrnae.   5
If you have better at home, send it up, or else drink as I bid you.

Hearthfire and kitchenware both are already agleam for your coming.
Leave all your high aspirations behind, and the struggle for wealth, and
Moschus's case in the law courts: tomorrow we celebrate Caesar's
10   Birthday with sleep and remission of labors, and thus conversation
May be prolonged at our leisure on into the summery night. What
Good is my having a fortune if never permitted to use it?
Stinting oneself for the sake of an heir and just doing without things
Borders on madness, and so I shall start strewing flowers and drinking,
15   Ready, if need be, to face admonitions for frivolous conduct.
What is not settled by wine's exaltation? It opens things hidden,
Marshals our hopes to their realization, drives cowards to battle,
Lightens the burden on spirits oppressed, and induces new learning.
Is there a man whom abundance of cups has not rendered more fluent:
20   Or is there one whom it never delivered from poverty's clutches?
I undertake all appropriate functions as host very gladly:
Seeing no noses are wrinkled at couch-cover stains or at dirty
Napkins; have platters and two-handled cups polished up to a brilliance
Where they reflect you like mirrors; no word between friends to be carried
25   Over the dining-room threshold; put only congenials together.
I am inviting Septícius and Butra for you, and Sabínus
Also, unless he is bound by a prior engagement for dinner —
Or by a girl. I can further accommodate several extras,
Though overcrowding results in distress from the odor of she-goats.
30   Write back how many of you there will be; then with business forgotten,
Fool all the clients lined up in your hall and duck out by the *back* door.

1   "Árchias built short couches," explains an ancient commentator. The point of the verb *recumbere,* instead of the usual *accumbere,* may mean: If you are able to get comfortable by stretching out full length . . .

2   Meat was sold only fresh-slaughtered and might not be available on short notice. We can only wonder whether Horace would serve guests with "a bowlful of scallions and chickpeas and flour-and-oil pancakes" (S.1.6.115 and ff.).

3   Torquatus is the prominent lawyer of *Odes* 4.7.23 and note. Mid-afternoon was a more usual time for dinner, but the next day's holiday (lines 9–12) permits a later start.

4   Taurus was consul for the second time in 26 B.C. (Augustus himself was his fellow consul.) Thus the unexceptional wine was aged from one to six years, the poem being published in 20 B.C.

    "Bottled" meant pouring off the wine from the fermentation vat into earthenware storage jars and "sealing" it with a thin layer of olive oil.

5   The marshy vineyard was between Mintúrnae (now Mintúrno) in the province of Latium (pronounce: LAY-shum) and the Petrínum estate at Sinuéssa (see S.1.5.40 and note); in other words, near, but not actually in, the famous "Falernian Field," where the best wines were produced.

6   "Drink as I bid you" = *imperium fer,* literally "bear my command (as drinking master)." See the note to S.2.6.67–70.

9   The rhetorician Moschus was on trial for poisoning; his defense attorneys were Torquatus and the lawyer-statesman Asinius Pollio; for the latter see the note to S.1.10.42 and the final note to *Odes* 2.1.

9–10   Augustus Caesar's birthday was September 23rd; hence the present invitation is for sundown on September 22nd, of some year between 26 and 20 B.C.

15   "Admonitions for frivolous conduct" paraphrases *inconsultus,* and Torquatus is a *iuris consultus,* ("counselor-at-law").

16–20   Phrase by phrase, these lines reword *Odes* 3.21.13–18.

26   "For you" (*tibi*), doubtless means: to occupy adjoining couches (or share your couch). As of the diagram following S.2.8, Torquatus would occupy place 6, Septícius and Butra places 4 and 5, that is, on the "middle" couch (or couches). The "extras" of line 28 are *umbris* ("shadows"), as in the diagram-note to S.2.8.

30   The slave delivering the dinner invitation is to wait for a reply. The haste implied throughout the poem indicates that the dinner is to be at Horace's house in Rome, not at the Sabine farm thirty miles away.

1.6.   *Nil admirari prope res est una, Numici,*

Not to be awed to a stupor, Numícius, is almost the only
Notion conducive to winning and holding mankind to a happy
State of existence. This sun, and the stars, and the seasons in cyclic
Changes: there *are* people who, in the face of these things, are not stricken
Speechless with terror. What value, then, ought to be placed on the wealth of   5
Earth, on the sea that enriches the farthermost Arabs and Hindus,
Or on the ludicrous games of applause and support of the voters?
How do you feel we should look on such things and how ought we to treat them?
Anyone dreading their opposites fares very nearly the same as
One who is greedy to get them; his fear is distressful in either   10
Case, and abrupt confrontation with either is vastly dismaying.
Happy or sorrowing, dreading or coveting, what does it matter,
If, upon seeing things better or worse than he hoped, he just hangs his
Head and does nothing but stand there dumbfounded in mind and in body?
Even a wise man is really insane, and the just man is unjust,   15
Seeking for goodness and wisdom in quantities more than sufficient.

Go, then, and dote on your silver, your marbles and bronzes from ancient
Times, and your artifacts; marvel at Tyrian colors in jewels;
Gloat at the thousands of eyes bent upon you when making your speeches;
Bustle at dawn to the Forum and never come home before evening;   20
Mutus's farm (that he got from his wife) mustn't yield in excess of
Yours, — to your shame it would be, since he comes of inferior folk, and
Keep him deferring to *you,* and see *you* never do the deferring.
Everything time ever brings out of earth into brightness, time also
Buries, for all of its splendor, and takes it back down to the darkness.   25
Known you may be on the Appian Way, at the Porch of Agrippa,
Yet you shall also go down where King Numa descended, and Ancus.

If you are suffering a painful disease of the chest or the kidneys,
Seek out a remedy for the disease; if your object is proper

30   Living — Whose isn't? — and virtue alone can provide it, be strong in
     Giving up pleasures. But if you think virtue is nonsense, and sacred
     Groves merely firewood, be watchful that nobody beats you to ports so
     You lose the trade from Cibýra or miss the Bithýnian commerce;
     Round out those talents to make them a neat even thousand, then double
35   That, then increase it to three, then go on for a pile that is four-square.
     Then, as you know, come the gifts from Queen Money; a wife with a dowry,
     Credit in business, and friends, and good looks, and a roster of forebears,
     Nor are the wealthy unhonored by gracious Persuasion and Venus.
          Slaves in abundance, but no ready cash, Cappadócia's monarch
40   Has: he should *not* be your model. They say that Lucúllus, when asked if
     He could contribute a hundred fine mantles as theater costumes,
     Said: "Who am *I* to have *that* many? But, let me look, and I'll send you
     Down what I have." Very shortly he wrote that he had some five thousand
     Mantles at home, and the praetor was welcome to all or to any.
45   Meager the household must be where a lot of superfluous items
     Do not lie stored out of sight of the master and handy for stealing.
     So, then, if nothing but gaining and keeping of wealth makes you happy,
     Make it the first job you tackle and make it the last job neglected.
          If influential position and favor best serve to content you,
50   Let's hire a slave to remind you of names when a greeting is wanted,
     Elbow your ribs when it's time to extend a good handshake, and whisper:
     "This one is strong in the Fabian ward, in Velína the other;
     He over there will be handing out magistracies, and if crossed, he
     Also takes ivory chairs from incumbents quite ruthlessly." Call them
55   "Brother" or "Father," in tactful adoption befitting their ages.
          Or, if it's "Lives best who dines best," it's time to go shopping, and off we
     Go with our gullets to guide us; we'll fish, and we'll hunt — like Gargílius,
     Who of a morning would order his slaves to proceed through the Forum
     Carrying draw-nets and spears for the hunt past the masses of people
60   Just so the masses of people could watch the return of a single
     Mule with a boar he had bought at the butcher's; — then stuffed full of food we'll
     Rush to the bath house, forgetful of what may be seemly or not, and
     Meriting disenfranchisement, a low-living crew of Ulysses
     Choosing forbidden delights over any return to their homeland.
65   If, as Mimnérmus opined, there is nothing in life to enjoy but
     Love and amusements, go live for enjoyment of love and amusements.
          Thrive and farewell! If you know any rules that improve on these mentioned,
     Kindly inform me; if not, then observe the ones listed, as I do.

---

1   Numícius is probably an imaginary person, with a name coined from the Numícus River
    S of Rome, draining from the Alban Hills SW to the sea.
         The whole poem is more of an essay (or "Satire") than a letter and for this reason it
    has been suspected of being a first experiment with the "Epistle" form.
         The often-quoted *nil admirari* translates the *tò mèdèn thaumàzein* of Pythágoras, the
    mathematician-philosopher of the 6th century B.C. Of it, Morris very rightly remarks:

"Horace is not preaching indifferentism; the words stand for that self-control and inward composure which . . . was the end sought after in all Greek systems of philosophy."

9   Their opposites are poverty and obscurity.

26 Compare Epode 4,13–14:". . . wears out the Appian Way / With pleasure drives by pony cart." The *Porticus Agrippae,* built around three sides of a rectangular reflecting pool, was one of those porticos where people strolled and talked (E.1.1.71 and note). Both the Porch (25 B.C). and the nearby Pantheon (27 B.C). were the creations of Agrippa—for whom see the final note to *Odes* 1.6.

27 Two of the seven early kings of Rome: Numa Pompílius (716–672 B.C.) and Ancus Marcius (640–616 B.C.).

33 Cibýra was an inland (!) city of Caria (SW Turkey). Bithynia (now NW Turkey) had been a wealthy Roman province since 65–62 B.C.; see the note to *Odes* 1.35.8.

39–40 The sense is: Don't be half-rich like the king of Cappadocia, be all-the-way rich like Lucúllus. The thought connection lies with the name "Cappadocia," as Horace's contemporaries would have understood immediately.

Cappadocia (now NE Turkey), since 96 B.C. had had kings installed at Roman dictation and Lucius Licínius Lucúllus was the Roman General who repeatedly intervened in support of those native kings. The now-reigning King Archelaus was like his predecessors: rich in slaves but "with no ready cash." He died in 17 A.D. in Rome, whither he had been summoned by the Emperor Tiberius, who then made Cappadocia a Roman province.

Lucúllus's name had come to stand for boundless wealth. His "life," as recounted by Plutarch a century after Horace's time, reports in section 39:

". . . there was a praetor of Rome that, making plays to show the people pastime, sent unto Lucullus to borrow certain purple cloaks to set forth his players. Lucullus made him answer that he would cause his folks to look if he had any. And the next morning, demanding of him how many he should need, the other answered that a hundred would serve his turn. Whereupon Lucullus told him again he would furnish him with two hundred, if his case so required. And therefore the poet Horace, writing this story, addeth to a notable exclamation against superfluity, saying that men think that a poor house, where there is no more riches than necessary, and where there is not more than appeareth in sight, and that the master knoweth of."

(Sir Thomas North translation, 1579)

49–55 The life of the politician. In line 51, "when it's time to extend a good handshake" guesses at the sense of the Latin, which has been much debated. In 52, *Fabia* and *Velina* represent "clan" names which had acquired the sense of "voting districts." In 53, "magistracies" = *fasces* (whence "fascist"), bundles of whipping rods tied around an executioner's ax and carried as symbols of authority. "Ivory chairs" (54) were the curule chairs, shaped like a camp stool, on which officiating magistrates sat. For "Father" (55) as a respectful term of address, compare S.2.1.12, where Horace addresses the elderly lawyer Trebátius as "excellent father"; see also lines 37–38 of the next *Epistle,* and note.

56–64 The life of those "who live to eat." Morris paraphrases 61–62 as: "Let us go at once from a gluttonous meal to a hot bath, from one indulgence to another."

"Disenfranchisement" (63) paraphrases *Caerite cera,* "wax (tablets) of Caere." In Caere (now Cervéteri, just NNW of Rome) Roman citizens without voting rights were so listed, and the Censor was empowered to degrade others, for cause, to that status.

63–64 show the *crew* living as Ulysses himself would have lived (E.1.2.25–26) had he drunk Círcē's potions: ". . . a slave to a slut, in a brutish existence/ Foul as a dog and rejoicing in filth like a pig in a quagmire."

65 Mimnérmus of Colophon (in Ionia, now W. Turkey) was a 7th-century B.C. love poet.

1.7.   *Quinque dies tibi pollicitus me rure futurum*

"Five days at most" was my promise to you when I left for the country:
False to my word through the whole month of August, I still keep you waiting.
And, if your wish is to have me continue to live and be healthy,
Then the indulgence you grant me in illness must also be granted
5   Now as I fear to *become* ill, Maecenas, when ripening figs and
Late-summer heat surround funeral directors with black-suited escorts, —
Also when fathers and fond little mothers grow pale over sons in
Sickbed, and paying of courtesy calls and attendance at functions
Bring on the fevers that end in the breaking of seals on our wills. But
10   Once come the midwinter solstice, when snow streaks the slopes of the Alban
Meadows, your bard will descend to the seaside and look to his comfort,
Snugly ensconced with his books; and to you, cherished friend, he will come, if
You so permit, with the first of the swallows and wafting of westwinds.
        Riches you gave me, but not in the way the Calábrian urges
15   Pears on a guest: "Help yourself to these pears!" — "Oh, no thanks, I've already
Eaten enough." — "Go ahead and take all you would like!" — "Oh, no thank you."
— "Take a few home to your boys as a present, I'm sure they'd enjoy them."
— "I'm as obliged for the offer as if I went home with a cartload."
— "All up to you, but the pigs will be getting what's left yet tomorrow."
20   Anyone wasteful and foolish makes presents of what he despises;
That sort of planting yields crops of ingratitude now and forever.
        Good men of wisdom will always stand ready to give to the worthy,
Not without knowing what difference there is between money and lupine
Beans. And I hope I show worthiness matching the honor accorded.
25   But, if you never allow me to leave you, you need to restore my
Stoutness of lungs and my glossy-black hair — on a narrower forehead,
Give me again to speak graciously, give me again to laugh lightly,
And among wines to mourn wantoning Cínara's flight and desertion.
        Once it befell that a slim little fox squeezed his way through a narrow
30   Opening into a granary, and, after eating his fill, was
Squirming with full-bellied bulk to get out by the same little cranny.
Not far away was a weasel, who said: "To get out through a chink as
Narrow as that, you will need to be thin as you were when you entered."
If I applied this analogy, I would return all you gave me;
35   Laborers' slumbers shall not be my theme while I feed upon dainties,
Nor will I ever take Araby's treasures in trade for my freedom.
Often enough you have praised me for deference; "Father" and "King" you
Hear me address you, and out of your presence I still use those titles.
Try me and see if I — cheerfully — will not return what you gave me.
40   Not at all bad was that answer Telémachus gave Meneláus:
"*My* land of Ithaca cannot accommodate horses for lack of
Open and level expanses and grasslands for pasture, O son of
Átreus: I therefore shall leave your gift here in more suitable country."

Small things befit a small man: royal Rome does not charm me at present;
Rather, the quiet of Tibur attracts me, or peaceful Taréntum.   45
     Tough, old Philíppus, renowned for his able defenses in law courts,
Once was returning, they say, around mid-afternoon from his office,
Voicing complaint as he came that, for one of his age, the Carínae
Quarter was really too far from the Forum, when, glancing about, he
Sighted a man in the shade of a barber-booth awning, already   50
Shaven and quietly cleaning his nails with a knifeblade. "Go over
To him, Demétrius," he said to his slave (who was clever at errands),
"Ask and report to me who he may be, of what household he is, of
What sort of fortune and standing, and who is his father or patron."
Over and back with the answer: he calls himself Mena Voltéius: —   55
Limited means, auctioneer, a clean record, reputed as one who
Works and who plays at appropriate times, makes his money and spends it,
Pleased with quite common companions, of sober, respectable household,
Theater-going, and — once he has finished his workday — athletics.
"What you report I would like to hear over again from the man, so   60
Tell him to join me for supper." But Mena, not quite comprehending,
Puzzled in silence. No need to go into details: his reply was
"Thanks just the same." — "He refuses?" — "The rascal refuses! He's either
Bashful or impudent." Next day Philíppus surprised this Voltéius
Busy conducting his auction of secondhand junk for some riffraff   65
Clad in their tunics, stepped over, and offered first greetings. Voltéius
Pleaded his work and imperative business engagements for having
Failed to appear at his house for a courtesy visit that morning
And for not seeing him first at his present arrival. "Consider
That as excused — if you join me for dinner today." — "At your service."   70
— "Come in the late afternoon. Now go back to increasing your fortune."
     Over the dinner he easily chatted of this and of that, in
Wisdom and folly, till bedtime. And so he continued his visits,
Swimming right up like a fish to the well-hidden bait, paying morning
Calls and becoming a regular dinner companion, till Latin   75
Festival time brought a bid to Philíppus's house in the country.
Riding along in the pony-cart, he was ecstatic at Sabine
Landscape and sky, as Philíppus observed with enormous amusement.
Since what Philíppus most wanted was restful diversion, and since he
Made him a gift of a round seven thousand, with promise of seven   80
More, he persuaded his man to the purchase of some little farmstead.
     Purchased it was. Not to hold up my story with rambling digressions,
Here was our neatly groomed man from the city transformed to a rustic
Chattering on about vineyards and plowshares, preparing his elm trees,
Working his head off and rapidly aging from zeal to be wealthy.   85
But, what with sheep being stolen, and goats dying off with disease, and
Crops disappointing his hopes, and his ox dropping dead at the plowing,
Irked past endurance, he got on his horse in the middle of night and

Furiously headed straight down to Philíppus's house in the City.
90   There at first glimpse of him haggard, unkempt, and unshaven, Philíppus
Cried, "Why, Voltéius! You look overworked and distraught by the strain of
Worry." — "By Pollux, that isn't the half of it, patron!" he answered,
"No other word can describe my condition but 'Misery' — outright.
So, in the name of your honor, your guardian spirit, your household
95   Gods, I here beg and implore: put me back in my former existence!"
Once we perceive how the things we abandoned were better than those we
Strove for, we ought not to lose any time going back to reclaim them.
Each man must gauge things himself by his own proper standard and measure.

2   "August" = *Sextilis,* "the sixth month" (from the old usage of beginning the year on
March 1st); Augustus did not name that month for himself until 8 B.C., the year Horace
died.

5   Early-ripe figs were considered unhealthy.

6   "Black-suited escorts" were officials with authority to move funerals through traffic.

10–13   The present Epistle was written around September 1st (line 2) of an unidentified
year presumably between 23 (when *Odes* 1, 2, and 3 were published) and 20, when this
poem was published. It addresses Maecenas, who is clearly in Rome (where the dis-
tractions of line 8 are to be found).

On the basis of line 45 below, we suggest that Horace wrote the Epistle in Tibur
(Tívoli), that he planned to be in the region of Taréntum (Táranto), in the extreme
South of Italy, by December, and in Rome by, say, March. *Odes* 2.6 named Tibur and
the region of Taréntum as favorite places, and lines 9–20 of the Ode surely signify that
Horace had been in the latter region at least once before 23 B.C. See also the geographical
implications of the following Epistle (E.1.8.)

14   "Riches" is surely a compliment to Maecenas; nowhere else does Horace call himself
"rich."

23–24   Lupine beans served as stage money: "good men of wisdom" are clearly aware of
values.

25–28   Horace, approaching 45, is feeling old, though loss of his former "stoutness of lungs"
(*forte latus*) need not imply any actual lung disease or heart disease. The receding hair
line (26) is not mentioned in E.1.20.24 below. His real ailment would seem to be a
certain spiritual malaise, and E.1.8 reinforces that impression.

Line 28 contains the first allusion to an early mistress named Cínara. The rough
outlines of her "story" may be inferred from this line and from E.1.14.33; *Odes* 4.1.4;
4.13.21–24; and notes.

29–33   Variant versions among Aesop's *Fables* have the fox crawl into a hollow oak (or into a
herdsman's hut) to eat bread and meat, and the advice comes from a second fox, not
from a weasel.

Since foxes do not eat grain, Richard Bentley (1662–1742) proposed to read *nitédula,*
"shrew-mouse," for Horace's *vulpécula,* but the zoology of fables is often fanciful.

37   For "Father" as a term of respectful address see E.1.6.55 and S.2.1.12, and notes.
"King" = *rex;* see E.1.17.43 and note.

From a preserved letter of 43 B.C. by Brutus we learn that young Octavius Caesar
was at that point addressing Cicero as "Father," but six months later he assented to
Mark Antony's murder of Cicero.

40–45   In *Odyssey* 4.601 ff. Telémachus so declines the gift of three horses and a two-seated
chariot offered by his host, King Meneláus of Sparta; the king substitutes a silver-and-
gold bowl—as a portable gift. From Maecenas Horace wants no "kingly" gifts but only
the liberty to "be off on his own" for a while.

46 The famous lawyer Philíppus was consul in 91 B.C.; Cicero, then 15 years old, later described him in *The Orator (46* B.C.).

Historical or not, this fourth story occupying lines 46–95 of the poem contains several parallels to the Horace-Maecenas relationship.

47; 71 "Mid-afternoon" = "around the 8th hour" (2 P.M.); "late afternoon" = "after the 9th hour" (3 P.M.).

48 The Carínae ("Keels") Quarter was a wealthy residential district not too far from the Forum. Notable residents included Pompey the Great and Cicero's brother Quintus and, after Horace's death, the future emperor Tiberius.

50 A tiny booth just large enough for the barber and his client, with the front wall hinged and swung up and held by a pole. Such may still be seen in Moslem souqs (markets).

52 The slave attendant (*pedisequus*), as in S.1.9.10 and note.

55 He is a Greek freedman named Mena, with a patron named Voltéius.

56 "Auctioneer" = *praeco,* as in S.1.6.86 and note. But compare line 65.

66 "In their tunics" because togas were too cumbersome for active work.

68; 74–75 The "client's" daily courtesy call at dawn, as in S.1.1.10 and elsewhere.

75–76 The *Feriae Latinae* were a national holiday period falling in April or May.

84 That is, training grapevines to the elm trees, as in Epode 2, 9–10 and note.

88–89 He rode after midnight so as to arrive by dawn and courtesy-call time.

1.8. *Celso gaudere et bene rem gerere Albinováno*

A letter to Albinovánus Celsus who is on the expedition led by Tiberius Claudius *Nero* in 20 B.C. to make a Roman show of force during negotiations with the Parthians, as in E.1.3.

Muse, I invoke you to carry my greetings to Albinovánus
Celsus, the scribe and companion of Nero, with all my good wishes.
If he inquires of my doings, report that I plan many splendid
Projects by live neither wisely nor happily. Not that the hail has
Battered my grapevines, and not that hot weather has shriveled my olives,   5
Nor that my cattle are plagued with distemper in far mountain pastures:
It's that my mind, which is somewhat less strong than the rest of my body,
Simply refuses to listen and learn what might cure it of illness;
Trustworthy doctors annoy me, and even my friends try my patience,
Eagerly rushing to rescue me out of my dreary indifference;   10
Things proven harmful I do, and avoid doing those that might help me;
Tibur I love when in Rome, but in Tibur I crave, as my fickle
Way is, for Rome. Then inquire how he is, how his lot and his life are
Managed, and whether his prince and his fellows regard him with favor.
If "Very well" is his answer, remember to say "I am glad," but   15
This little precept should also be dropped in his ear: "By the way you
Handle your fortunes we'll know how to think of you, Celsus, and treat you."

1–2 Albinovánus Celsus must be the Celsus of E.1.3.15–19 whom Horace there advised (through Julius Florus) against composing literary works too closely imitative of established authors. "Scribe" = (scriba, "(private) secretary,"—an English word unusable in English dactylic meter. "Companion" = *cómes, cómitis,* the word which, centuries later, became "Count," or, the ruler's "companion."

6 Livestock was regularly herded to mountain pastures in the Dog-star heat of summer.

9 "Doctors," of the spirit, that is, philosophers; compare E.1.1.33–48 and the wording of 47.

12–13 At least 10 years earlier Horace had the slave Davus say, in S.2.7.28–29: "Rome makes you long for the country; once there, you're so fickle, the absent/City gets praised to the stars."

Lines 4–6 suggest the farm as the place of composition for this Epistle, while line 12 suggests Tibur; *both* are possible, since the two places were only 10–12 miles apart. The time of composition is during the summer heat, most probably August (lines 4–6 again), and the year must be 20 B.C. We infer that E.1.8 preceded E.1.7 by a couple of weeks (and that E.1.9 preceded both of them), the reasons for the reversed order being obscure. The spiritual malaise of 7 and 8 must regard a single period, but we can only wonder why Horace chose to broach so delicate a subject to young Celsus, not to mention the whole reading public.

1.9.   *Septimius, Claudi, nimirum intellegit unus,*

A letter of recommendation on behalf of a friend desiring appointment to the staff of Tiberius Claudius Nero for the expeditionary show of force in the East in 20 B.C.

Claudius, no one, it seems, is aware of how much you esteem me,
Save for Septímius: *he* keeps imploring my recommendation
Of him to you as a person of caliber worthy of Nero's
Standards and intellect and of the staff now assembling
5 Under your orders, presuming that I am your intimate friend and
Placing more trust in my powers than I would myself ever dream of.
I have objected good reasons aplenty for being excused, but
Still I am fearful of seeming to pretext mere inconsequentials,
Hiding my own capabilities, seeking my private convenience
10 Only. And so, to avoid that more heinous offense, I am stooping
Now to an urban man's brashness in courting the honor requested:
If you can countenance decency dropped for the sake of a friendship,
Enter this man on your staff and feel sure he is hardy and loyal.

2 Septímius is presumably identical with the travel-eager Septímius addressed in *Odes* 2.6 around 26 B.C. and with the person mentioned as "our Septímius" by the emperor in a letter quoted by Suetonius in his *Vita* of Horace. The name is a *nomen,* "family name," neither given name nor *cognomen* being known.

3 Tiberius Claudius Nero, now aged 22, was still going by his own name, though he was "the emperor's stepson" (E.1.3.2); not until 4 A.D., when Augustus formally adopted him as son and heir, did he acquire the extra name of "Caesar."

   The ancient family of the Claudii was of Sabine origin, and Suetonius states (in *Tiberius* 1) that "Nero" was a Sabine word meaning "strong and energetic."

10   The more heinous offense is avoidance of responsibility for a friend. Yet E.1.18.76–81
     below urges caution in recommending people.
11   "Urban man's brashness" is the opposite of rural man's modesty. Horace considers
     himself "rural," and possibly the recommendation letter was composed at the Sabine
     farm.

1.10.   *Urbis amatorem Fuscum salvere iubemus*

Greetings to Fuscus, the lover of city life, greetings from me who
Cherish the country life! This is the one count, you know, where we differ
Greatly; in other respects we are almost like twins. With out kindred
Spirits, a "No" from the one is a "No" from us both, and we also
Nod our approvals as one, like a pair of old doves that are cronies.   5
You are for keeping the nest, whereas *I* sing in praise of the lovely
Countryside's brooks, and its rocks overpainted with moss, and its woodlands.
        Need I say more? Here I live and I reign from the minute I leave those
Things "that you praise to the skies amid clamor of shouted approval."
I, like a runaway slave from a priest's house, have lost my desire for   10
Cakes: it is bread that I want, and not honeyed confections of sweetcake.
If it is fitting and proper to live in accordance with Nature,
And, if the place to establish a house is the first of our problems,
Where is a better location than out in the glorious country?
Is there a place where the winters are milder, where breezes more gently   15
Temper the rage of the Dog Star and curb the wild leaps of the Lion
When he is stung to a fury and maddened by Sol's burning arrows?
Is there a place where invidious worries less trouble our slumbers?
Or are the grasses less fragrant and dew-bright than Libyan mosaics?
Or does the water gush purer in towns out of conduits of lead than   20
Water that pours on its murmuring way between steep-sloping brooksides?
Even your courtyards are planted to trees between multi-hued marble
Columns, and houses are also admired for a far-ranging vista.
Drive Nature out with a pitchfork, and back it will come every time, in
Ways unexpected, to foil your disdain and to win the last battle.   25
        Yet, if an expert imagines he knows how to tell the Sidonian
Purple from wool that is dyed with the rock-lichen-red of Aquínum,
He is as sure to be quite as heart-breakingly swindled as someone
Never perceptive enough to distinguish a truth from a falsehood.
Anyone who has enjoyed an excess of prosperity suffers   30
Worst from reverses of fortune. If something enthralls you, be strong and
Put it away. Avoid grandness. A life can be lived in a poor man's
Cottage surpassing the lives of a monarch or friends of a monarch.
        Fighting for grasslands, the stag long ago drove the horse from their common
Pastures, until in defeat the less powerful animal came and   35

Pleaded for help from mankind — and was given the rein and the bridle.
But, after winning his violent struggle, the horse had the rider
Still on his back and the bit in his mouth. So it is with the man who,
Fearful of poverty rather than fearful of riches, must forfeit
40 Liberty, and in his greed must forever be serving a master
Simply because he could *not* see his way to make do with a little.
Dissatisfaction with what one possesses is much like a shoe: too
Big for the foot, it may trip you, too small, it may chafe up a blister.
  May you live happy, Arístius, and wisely accept your position;
45 Meanwhile do not let me go unrebuked if I ever seem bent on
Gathering more than I need and not taking the time for relaxing
Properly. Money amassed can be master or slave to a man, and
Surely it ought to unwind from the pulley, not tighten around it.
  This I am writing you out past the moldering shrine of Vacúna,
50 Happy in every respect of my life save that you are not with me.

1 Arístius (line 44) Fuscus was the friend who waggishly declined to rescue Horace from the bore in S.1.9.60–74; he was cited in S.1.10.82 for his literary taste; and to him was addressed the whimsical *Integer vitae* poem (*Odes* 1.22).

9 A free rendition of a line from Ennius (*Annals* 260). Other quotations from Ennius were made in S.1.2.37 and S.1.4.61–62.

10–11 A priest's house would have abundant supplies of sacrificial cakes (*liba*), roughly equivalent to a supply of Communion wafers. Horace, we infer, found the sumptuousness of Maecenas's household cloying, hence the metaphor, like 32–33 below, offers a clue to his spiritual malaise expressed in E.1.7 and 8.

15 Surely the winters were not milder at the Sabine farm than at Rome. Morris suggests Horace was thinking of the S-Italian region of Taréntum, as in *Odes* 2.6.17 ff.: "Springtime there in Jupiter's sky is long, and/ Winters mild. . . ," pointing out that all Italy outside of Rome was "country" (*rus*), regardless of what cities might be there. Yet the present poem was surely written at the Sabine farm, as line 49 shows, and the statement is confusing.

16 "The Lion" is the zodiacal sign of Leo, ascendant from July 21 to August 22, when the Dog Star (Sirius) rises and sets with the sun.

19 The metaphor is not inexact: mosaic floors were sprinkled with perfumes. Libya (Greek Libuē) might mean any N-African area W of Egypt.

22–23 For "trees" the text says "a forest" (*silva*). Compare the winter scene in *Odes* 3.10.6–7, where ". . . the planted trees/ Moan in answer beneath winds in the inner court."

24 This line became a proverb.

26–29 The genuine and expensive "Tyrian purple" was made from mollusks off the shore of Tyre and Sidon (now Sūr and Saïdâ, respectively, in Lebanon). The cheaper substitute came from Aquínum (now Aquíno) two-thirds of the distance S from Rome to Naples.
  The antiques dealer who misjudges is like someone who "picks up" philosophical ideas without knowing much about philosophy.

34–38 The fable is apparently No. 4.4 in the collection of Horace's contemporary Phaedrus, yet Stesíchorus, ca. 640–555 B.C. (see *Odes* 4.9.8 and note), mentioned *some* form of the story in a public speech against the "tyrant" of Agrigentum.

48 We guess at the meaning of a line which says literally: "(money is) worthy of following the twisted rope rather than guiding it."

49 Morris (1909) has no explanation of "Vacuna," though the C. T. Lewis dictionary (1890) confidently says "a goddess of fertility, the ancestral divinity of the Sabines." E. K. Rand: *A Walk to Horace's Farm*, 1930, p. 12, cites an inscription from Rocca Giovane (S

of the Sabine farm): "The Emperor . . . Vespasian . . . restored at his own expense the temple of Victoria, which had crumbled through," and concludes that "Vacuna" was the Sabine-language equivalent of "Victoria." The stone containing the inscription is now incorporated into the wall of a medieval castle, but the original shrine is likely to have stood on or near Horace's own land, and the present poem was surely composed "at the Sabine farm."

1.11.   *Quid tibi visa Chios, Bullati, notaque Lesbos,*

What did you think about Chíos, Bullátius, and Lesbos the far-famed?
What about elegant Samos, and Croesus's grandiose Sardis?
What about Smyrna and Cólophon? Greater or less than reported?
Were they all shabby, compared to Mars' Field and the stream of the Tiber?
Or was it one of King Áttalus' cities that utterly charmed you?   5
Or are your praises for Lébedus, out of sheer boredom with seas and
Highways? You realize Lébedus numbers less people than hamlets
Like our Fidénae or Gábii? *I* would, however, choose these to
Live in, forgetting acquaintance and by my acquaintance forgotten,
Gazing from shore over distances wrought to a fury by Neptune.   10
     But, if you're rain-drenched and mud-splattered coming from Capua up to
Rome and you stop at an inn, you don't stay there the rest of your life; nor
If you are chilled to the bone and get warm at a bath house or baker's
Shop, do you claim that such places afford the ideal existence;
Nor, after having been tossed on the deep by a powerful southwind,   15
Do you dispose of your ship on the coast of the further Aegéan.
Rhodes, to a sensible person, and fair Mityléné, are quite as
Useful as woolens at midsummer solstice or loin-cloths in blizzards,
Or as the midwinter Tiber, or fireplaces roaring in August.
While I am still so allowed and Fortuna keeps smiling, I'll do my   20
Praising of Samos and Chios and Rhodes here in Rome — without visits.
     When from a god you are granted an hour of happiness, take it
Gratefully, never postponing enjoyable things, and of any
Place where you ever have happened to be, may you say that you lived there
Cheerfully. What relieves troubles is reason and prudent behavior,   25
Not some location commanding the sea in a far-distant prospect;
Landscapes, but never our minds, may be altered by overseas travel.
Strenuous idleness keeps us distraught; we go hunting the happy
State in our ships and with four-in-hand teams, but the goal of our search is
Here: if your mind is at peace, little Ulubrae offers contentment.   30

1   Bullatius is likely to be an imaginary person with a name appropriately coined from *bulla,* "bubble"; the alternate meaning of "one wearing an amulet (*bulla*)" would carry no appropriate sense for this bustling tourist.

Where *Odes* 1.7 named 12 famous places in Greece as being less attractive than Tibur, the present Epistle subordinates 10 Greek places to certain hamlets in Italy.

Lesbos, Chios, Samos, and Rhodes were, from N to S, tourist islands off the W coast of "Asia" (Turkey).

Mityléné was the capital city of Lesbos.

Inland Sardis (near modern Salihli) was the capital of Lydia under the fabulously wealthy King Croesus in the 6th century B.C. and a cosmopolitan center for 1200 years thereafter; since 1964 American archaeologists have been excavating the site.

Coastal Smyrna/Zmyrna (now Izmír) has a 5,000-year history; in Horace's time it was a dependency of Pergamum.

Colophon, now an abandoned site, was a coastal town near Smyrna.

"One of King Áttalus' cities" is likely to be Pérgamum, most splendid of the cities of "Asia" in Horace's time, opposite Lesbian Mityléné and somewhat inland, adjoining Turkish Bergama. It was the capital of a kingdom, also called Pérgamum, ruled by three kings named Áttalus (and others of the same family) from 269 to 133 B.C., when, for reasons not entirely clear, Áttalus III (see *Odes* 1.1.12 and 2.18.6) bequeathed his country and treasure to the Roman state.

Lébedus, now an abandoned site, was a coastal village of "Asia" facing due S toward the island of Samos.

4   "Mars' Field" (*Campus Martius*) is an allusion, not to the athletic grounds as usual, but to the impressive new buildings erected on its eastern edge by Agrippa: the (still standing) Pantheon (27 B.C.), baths, and the Porch of Agrippa (25 B.C.); (see E.1.6.26 and note).

8-10 The inland villages of Fidénae (now Castel Giubileo) 5-6 km/4 m N of Rome and Gabii 15 km/10 m E of Rome had once been enemy strongholds 500–600 years in the past; (see Book I of Livy's *History of Rome*). The seashore image of line 10 is a reminiscence of the opening lines of Lucretius's *On the Nature of Things*, Book II:

> How sweet, when on the sea the winds whip up the waters,
> To watch another's troubles, while you are safe on shore . . .
>   (Mantinband translation)

19   August = *Sextilis,* as in E.1.7.2 and note.

27   This line became a proverb: *caelum, non animum, mutant qui trans mare currunt.*

30   Úlubrae was a village overlooking the Pontine marshes, about 60 km/40m SE of Rome. The American equivalent would be "Podunk."

1.12. *Fructibus Agrippae Siculis, quos colligis, Icci,*

If, in collecting the revenues from the estates of Agrippa
Down there in Sicily, Íccius, you put them to suitable uses,
Jupiter's very own hand could not offer more generous bounty.
Cease your complaints: no one ever is poor if his needs are supplied, and
5   Once all is well with your stomach, your chest, and your feet, there is nothing
More that the treasure of monarchs could possibly add to your riches.
If you, by chance, are avoiding the usual items of food to
Eat only nettles and herbs, you will never abandon that diet,
Not if the River of Fortune should instantly grant you the golden
10   Touch, just because it is not in the power of money to alter
Nature, or else because nothing, with you, has the value of virtue.

We are amazed how Demócritus' cattle devoured his planted
Fields while his mind, disencumbered of body, went soaring in distant
Flights, but no less at how you, amid itch and contagion of riches,
Are not affected by that but continue your loftier studies: —   15
What keeps the sea at one level? What orders the cycle of seasons?
Should we see planets as self-moved or governed by laws in their motions?
Why does the moon have a shadow, and how is the full orb rebrightened?
What is the sense and effect of harmonious discord in Nature?
Whether Stertínius or whether Empédocles preaches sheer madness?   20
     Anyway: whether it's fish that you slaughter or leeks and green onions,
Cultivate Grósphus Pompéius, and if he should ask you a favor,
Grant it without second thought: only honest requests come from Grósphus.
Friends are a bargain when persons of character need some assistance.
     So you may know how things stand with our Roman affairs: the Cantábrian   25
Spanish have bowed to Agrippa, and Claudius Nero has triumphed
Over Armenia; Phraátes, less tall on his knees, has acknowledged
Caesar's control and authority. Meanwhile the goddess of Plenty
Pours out her horn over Italy, shedding down gold of the harvest.

1   For Agrippa, General and Admiral and, in 21 B.C., all but co-emperor, see the final note
to *Odes* 1.6.

2   All that is known about Íccius must be inferred from this poem and from *Odes* 1.29,
where he was selling his philosophical books in order to buy armor for the expedition of
26 B.C. against Arabia. Now, six years later, he is making a living at the uninspiring job of
bailiff for Agrippa's estates in Sicily and busy over scientific books.

9–10   Actually, King Midas cured himself of the curse of the "golden touch" by washing in
the River Pactólus.

12   Demócritus (5th century B.C.), as one of the first teachers of "the atomic theory," was a
forerunner of Epicurus. Horace here gives one of the variant stories about "the absent-
minded philosopher": his own cattle ruined his farm while he was absorbed in scientific
speculations.

20   Stertínius (see S.2.3.33 and note) represents the Stoics, Empédocles (see also E.2.3. 464–6
and note) represents the Epicureans. As of line 17, the Stoics held that the planets were
divine beings who moved of their own accord, while the Epicureans saw the planets as
objects moved according to the laws of physics.

22–23   Of Pompéius Grósphus — for reasons of English metrics we invert the name, as
Horace himself sometimes did—we know only what these two lines convey and what is
implied by *Odes* 2.16. Lines 33–37 of that ode show him as a wealthy landowner in Sicily.
"Grósphus" is Greek for "a kind of javelin."

25–29   Horace summarizes the news of the autumn of 20 B.C. for his Sicilian correspondent,
who may not yet have heard that

- the Roman conquest of Spain (which had been going on for two centuries) had
been completed by Agrippa; the brutal final campaign had reduced the
Cantábrians and Astúrians in the mountainous NW of the peninsula;
- Tiberius Claudius Nero's expeditionary show of force had won an "accom-
modation" to Roman power on the part of the Parthian king Phraátes IV (who
ruled 38 to 2 B.C.); see *Odes* 2.2.17–18 and note.
- the harvest was bountiful (in contrast to a disastrously bad harvest two years
before).

1.13.   *Ut proficiscentem docui te saepe diuque,*

A note of 23 B.C. accompanying a presentation copy of Books 1, 2, and 3 of the *Odes* to Augustus, ostensibly addressed to the messenger but meant for the emperor. We are to understand that the note is dispatched by a *second* messenger who overtakes the actual messenger, Vinnius Ásina, *en route* and delivers it to the latter.

As I explained in detail and at length when you left on this errand,
Vinnius, deliver these volumes, with unbroken seals, to Augustus
Only in case he is well, in good mood, and he *asks* to receive them.
See that you give no offense by a blundering haste and excessive
5   Eagerness so that the books are disliked for the bearer's ineptness.
If you, by chance, become galled by the weight of the packet, just drop it
Anywhere rather than plod right along to the end and then bolt it,
Saddle and all, like a donkey in temper, until your paternal
Surname of "Ásina" makes you the butt of an asinine joke. Put
10   Forth every effort of manhood up hills, over rivers, through sinkholes.
Then, when your mission is crowned with success and you reach destination,
Hold out the package like *this:* don't go standing there hugging the bundle
Under your armpit the way that a rustic holds onto a lamb, or
Tipsy old Pýrrhia clutches the threadballs of yarn she has pilfered,
15   Or, like a humble relation at dinner, his cap and his slippers.
Do not explain to the public at large, furthermore, that your sweat of
Toil is from carrying poems that *may* claim the eye and the ear of
Caesar. With all these injunctions in mind, now get on with your journey.
Go. Fare you well. And don't stumble and ruin both package and mission.

> 2   Vinnius Ásina, surely a person of rank, is known only from this poem; *ásina* means "donkey, ass," and some manuscripts have *aséllus,* "little donkey." This *cognomen* is recorded of actual persons.
> 3   Augustus, often ill and under doctors' care, was so seriously ill in 23 B.C. that he was not expected to live. The note to E.1.15.2 below mentions his cure by the doctor Antonius Musa on this occasion. He is apparently convalescing, probably at some cold-water spa in the country, to judge by line 10, since cold baths were prescribed by the doctor.
> 6   The three Books of the *Odes* would make a light parcel, but Horace is building up his word play on the messenger's name in line 9.
> 14 An ancient commentator says Pýrrhia is a character in a play by Titínius.
> 15 The "humble relation" holds his own cap and slippers because he has no slave to hold them for him; see the note to S.2.8.76.

1.14.   *Vilice silvarum et mihi me reddentis agelli,*

Foreman in charge of the woods and the fields that refresh me and give me
Back to myself, which you scorn for supporting five homesteads and sending
Upstanding heads of five households to market in Varia, I challenge

You to debate with me: do I more stoutly clear brush from my mind, or
You, from my land? Is the farm, or is Horace, in better condition?   5
    I, it is true, am detained here by Lamia's grief and affliction
Mourning his brother, distraught inconsolably over his brother's
Untimely death, but in mind and in spirit I long to be there, I
Champ like a race horse to burst from the starting gate into the running.
Lucky the rural man, *I* say, and *you* say the man of the city;   10
Hate of one's own lot, of course, goes with envying somebody else's.
Folly in men puts the blame for their troubles on innocent places:
It is the mind, which can never escape from itself, that is guilty.
You, as a house drudge, kept silently praying to be in the country;
Now, as a foreman, you pine for the shows and the baths of the ctiy.   15
I am consistent, you have to admit: I leave sadly whenever
Unwelcome errands oblige me to travel to Rome. We are quite at
Odds in the things we admire, hence we cherish divergent opinions.
Scenes that you look on as dreary and desolate wilds are considered
Places of charm by a person who feels the way I do, and those that   20
You think are beautiful, he deems detestable. Brothels and greasy
Cook-shops incite your desire for the city, I see, while that nook of
Mine will produce, you feel, pepper and frankincense sooner than vineyards,
Nor is there any good tavern around to provide you with decent
Wine or a flute-playing harlot to furnish a tune you can dance to,   25
Stomping the ground to the beat of her music. And yet you keep working,
Hacking at fields long untouched by a pick or a mattock, attending
Needs of the unharnessed ox and untying his fodder-bales for him;
Then, too, the stream bank makes work for your laziness: after a downpour
Earthworks must bolster it back and compel it to spare the fair meadow,   30
    Let me now come to the matter of prime disagreement between us.
I, who you know once rejoiced in a fine-woven toga and glossy
Hair, who could satisfy Cínara's greed without giving her presents,
Who in my day could begin a Falérnian bout with the noontide,
Relish a simple meal now — and a snooze in the grass by the brookside.   35
There was no shame in all that, — but continuing *would* have been shameful.
Out there where *you* are, no eye looks askance at my innocent comforts,
Nor am I stung by anonymous fangs darting venom of envy:
Neighbors goodnaturedly smile at my moving of stones and of turf-clods.
    You prefer rations my city slaves gnaw on and hope to be numbered   40
One of them; meanwhile my groom speaks in eloquent envy of you for
Access to firewood and dairy and herd and the yields of the garden.
Ox wants the saddle, while lazy old riding horse longs to go plowing;
Each should be happy, as *I* see it, doing the things he is good at.

1–3   This unnamed foreman would be in charge of the eight slaves (S.2.7.118) who
    maintained Horace's farm and farmhouse. Horace leased the largest part of his estate to
    five *coloni,* independent citizen farmers, who did their trading in nearby Varia, now
    Vicováro ("Varus' town").

6 Lamia is doubtless the Lucius Aelius Lamia of whom Horace speaks so warmly in *Odes* 1.26; 1.36; and 3.17. In the note to *Odes* 1.36.3 we guessed his birth year as 47 B.C.; accordingly he would have been aged 25 to 27 at the time when he was bereaved of his brother. He became consul in 3 A.D. and died in 33 A.D.

12–13 A rephrasing of E.1.11.27.

19 "Wilds" = *tesqua/tesca* (a neuter plural), which an ancient commentator identifies as a Sabine word, and therefore a touch of "local color."

23 Pepper and frankincense were costly imports from the tropical East.

24–26 The 38-line *Copa* (said to be an early poem of Vergil's) describes such a tavern.

28 "Fodder" = *frondibus*, "leafy branches" (tied in bundles).

32–33 With "glossy/ Hair," compare E.1.7.26: "my glossy-black hair."

33 E.1.7.28 spoke of "wantoning Cínara's flight and desertion"; see the note to that line.

34 Drinking before sundown was a sign of "fast living"; compare S.1.4.51–52 and *Odes* 2.7. 6–7.

35 But Horace praised such brookside snoozes as long ago as Epode 2,23–28, as well as in *Odes* 1.1.20–22.

44 Paraphrase of a Greek proverb, which Cicero identified as such and paraphrased a little differently in his *Tusculan Disputations* (1.18.41) of 45 B.C.

1.15. *Quae sit hiems Veliae, quod caelum, Vala, Salerni,*

How is the winter at Velia, how is the sky at Salérnum,
Vala, and how are the roads and the people? (Antonius Musa
Says that the hot springs of Baiae are useless to me, and he even
Makes me resented down there for requesting to bathe in cold water

5 Right in the middle of winter. The town, nor surprisingly, moans at
Seeing its myrtle groves empty and patients avoiding the sulphur
Springs which are said to drive lingering ache out of muscles, — the patients
Off, what is more, to duck bellies in Clúsium's icy cold springs, or
Gabii's maybe, or other such chilly resorts in the country.

10 I must go elsewhere, it seems, and my horse must avoid once-familiar,
Hostelries: "Where are you going!" his rider rebukes him, "My way is
Neither to Cumae or Baiae," and peevishly jerks at the left-hand
Rein, — as if horses knew words, when their hearing is all in the bridle.)
Which of these places enjoys a more plentiful grain supply? Are they

15 Forced to drink rainwater, or are there wells running fresh at all seasons?
(Wines of your region I do not much care for; when I'm at my country
Place I can manage to suffer along with whatever I have, but
When at the seaside I need a good-quality wine, something smooth that
Drives away cares and infuses abundance of hope and good promise

20 Into my spirits and veins and supplies me with words when I need them,
Something that gives me the air of a youth to Lucánian girlfriends.)
Which of the two districts mentioned produces more hares? and more boars? and
Which one has waters that harbor more fish and more sea urchins, so that
I can go home again fattened and plump like a well-fed Phaeácian?

Kindly advise me in writing, and I shall rely on your guidance.   25
       Maenius, once both his father's and mother's estates had been squandered
Gallantly, took up the role of a man-about-town and a jokesman,
Cadging a hand-to-mouth living without any definite manger;
Till he had dined he would make no distinction of friend or of foe but
Savagely make up his insults at random to any and sundry;   30
He would descend like a storm, a consuming disaster, a walking
Butcher-shop refuse pit, stowing whatever he got in his belly.
Reaching the stage where his patrons grew wary and nothing or little
More could be wheedled from *them,* he made suppers of nothing but tripe and
Poor grades of lamb, but devouring enough for three bears, thus creating   35
Chances for comments — like Bestius after reforming, you know — like:
"Squandering money on food calls for branding of bellies with irons."
Yet, if this very same man rediscovered a major supplier,
All of this turned into ashes and smoke, and "By Hercules!" he would
Say, "I don't wonder that people spend total estates on a dinner: 40
Nothing so good as a thrush, nothing nicer than ample-size sow's womb!"
       Doubtless I stand in a similar case: cozy havens I praise when
Money is scarce, and I hardily bear with inferior food; but
Let something better turn up that is seasoned more richly to taste, and
I will admit that the only right livers are people like you, whose   45
Villas shine forth from afar on their solid foundations of money.

1 Horace inquires about possible wintering places: Salérnum (now the city of Salérno) 24
   km/15 m S of Naples, and Velia some 70 km/45 m still further S. The latter was Greek
   Elea, founded more than 500 years in the past, and the home of the "Eleatic school" of
   philosophers: Parménides, Xenóphanes, and Zeno (*not* the Stoic Zeno).
2 Vala is one Numónius Vala, known only from this poem, though the family of the
   Numónii are known from inscriptions and coins as wealthy inhabitants of Lucania
   province.
      Antonius Musa, the private physician of Augustus, saved the emperor's life in 23
   B.C. by a regimen of cold-water baths. Suetonius (in Augustus 81) says the malady was
   abscesses on the liver. Compare E.1.13.3 and note.
3 Baiae, as in E.1.1.83–85 and note. With Antonius Musa's cold baths suddenly fashion-
   able, its hot baths are deserted.
      The town was famous for its groves of aromatic myrtle *shrubs,* sacred to Venus,
   growing some three meters tall, and having glossy leaves and small pink or white flowers.
   To Americans, myrtle is a ground vine bearing blue flowers; more properly it is the
   periwinkle (*Vinca minor*). See *Odes* 2.15.5–6 and 3.23.16 and notes.
8–9 Clusium (now Chiusi), about 120 km/75 m NNW of Rome in mountain country.
   Gabii, as in E.1.11.8 and note, was 15 km/10 m ESE of Rome.
10–14 Cumae (now Cuma) adjoined Baiae. Going S from Rome, one turned right (west) to
   reach these places; by pulling on the left rein, Horace keeps his horse headed south.
22–23 Hares make choice eating according to S.2.4.44 and S.2.8.89. Lucánian boars are
   prized in S.2.3.234–5 and elsewhere, and sea urchins in S.2.4.33.
24 To the Romans the Phaeácians of *Odyssey* 8.248 ff. were voluptuaries; they are the youths
   of King Alcínous's court in E.1.2.27–31 and note.
26–27 Abruptly Horace begins a story about Maenius, who is not necessarily identical with
   the Maenius of S. 1.3.21–23. See also the Maenius in Lucílius's Fragment 1136–7.

"Jokesman" = *scurra*, as in S.2.7.36 and note.

46   Compare the gleam of the Tusculan villa in Epode 1,29, and "the precipice crowned
     with the far-gleaming city of Ánxur" in S.1.5.26.

1.16.   *Ne perconteris, fundus meus, optime Quincti,*

Rather than ask, esteemed Quínctius, whether my farm can support its
Owner from plowlands or lead him to riches by olive production
Or by its apples and pastures and vines strung to branches of elm trees,
Let me explain at some length its location and general layout.
5   Mountains extend in an unbroken series except for a single
Well-shaded valley, with morning sun lighting the side to my right and
Warmed on the left by the sun in its swift-wheeling course of departure.
Note the fine balance. — And is there abundance of thornbushes red with
Cornels? And sloes? Do the oaks and the holm-oaks yield plenty of acorns
10   Dear to the cattle while furnishing plenty of shade for the master?
Why, you would think that Taréntum had migrated here with its verdure!
I have a spring of such force that the stream might be named for it — Hebrus
Never flows colder or purer in winding its way across Thrace, and
Useful it is for an unsteady head, and no less for the bowels.
15   These are delightful retreats, — even (if you believe me) beloved
Ones, which amid the dire heat of September afford me protection.
      You, if you really live up to reports of you, surely are living
Wisely; at Rome we have long since agreed in pronouncing you lucky.
Yet I have fears you may trust, not your own, but opinions of others,
20   Reckoning other than good men and wise ones as fortunate fellows,
Or, in case people insist you are healthy and sound, that you may be
Hiding a fever within you until, in the presence of guests at
Dinner, your hands, with the food-grease upon them, betray you by trembling.
Fools in their falseness of shame make a secret of untreated ulcers.
25   If a man lauded your battles by land and by sea, or if people
Tickled your eagerly listening ear with their flatteries, saying:
"Whether the nation more longs for your safety or you for the nation's:
Let that be left as a question unsettled for Jupiter, who is
Mindful of you and the City," you'd know that they spoke of Augustus;
30   But, if you countenance tributes like "wise" and "in virtue perfected,"
Do you, pray tell me, reply with your name in accepting those tributes?
— "But I *enjoy* being called a good man, and a wise one, — as *you* do!"
— One who so hails you today, will tomorrow recant if he chooses,
Just as the emblems of office are voted and later rescinded.
35   Someone shouts: "Drop that! It's mine!" I comply, and retire disappointed.
But, if the very same person should call me a thief, or asserted
I was a lecherous rascal, or maybe had strangled my father,
Should I put up with this false defamation and start turning all colors?

Who but a villain or liar is charmed by an undeserved honor?
Who but the same is upset by a slander? Then who is the *good* man? 40
"Why, (they say) one who abides by the laws and our forefathers' judgments,
One who will serve as a judge and make many a weighty decision,
One on whose bail and whose word as a witness whole cases are settled."
Yet by his household and neighbors that very same man may be seen as
Inwardly rotten, resplendently cloaked in a hide that is borrowed. 45
Let a slave say to me: "*I* never stole, nor have *I* tried escaping;"
My answer is: "Your reward is a back never seared with a flogging."
— "*I* never killed a man!" — Then you won't rot on a cross and feed vultures."
— "*I* am a good man, a worthy man!" — "Don't be so sure," says the Sabine,
"Even a wolf can be wary of pitfalls, and even a falcon 50
Dodges what looks like a snare, or the kite-fish a well-hidden fish-hook."
    Good men abominate evil because of their fondness for virtue;
Never let fear of reprisals determine the course of your actions.
Any intention of cheating confuses profane things with sacred,
And, in removing one bean from a measure that numbered a thousand, 55
I suffer loss of a trifle, but *your* guilty act was no trifle.
Someone who passes for honest in every tribunal and forum
May, when he honors the gods with a sacrificed pig or a bullock,
Loudly cry out: "Father Janus!", or loudly: "Apollo!", and still may
Mutter in undertones: "Lovely Laverna, thou goddess of filchers, 60
Grant me the knack of deceiving, and grant me an honest and saintly
Semblance, and over my frauds and misdealings cast mantles of darkness!"
    How is the greedy man any more free than a slave, or more noble,
When he will stoop for a penny that street boys have glued to the pavement?
I see no difference. A man who is greedy is also in fear, and 65
Any man living in fear I will never regard as a free man.
Someone forever in haste and obsessed with increasing his fortune
Stands with his weapons all lost and the post of his valor deserted:
Captured, you may as well auction him off, but don't bother to kill him;
He can be useful: install him as shepherd or set him to plowing, 70
Let him go sailing the mid-winter waves selling goods as a merchant,
Put him in charge of the shipments of grain and commodity imports.
    As for the good man and wise, he will dare to speak up and say: "Pentheus,
Ruler of Thebes, what indignity will you compel me to suffer
Or to perform?" — "I will seize all your goods." — "I have property, livestock, 75
Furnishings, fine silver plate: help yourself, take it all." — "I will hold you
Shackled by hand and by foot, with a brute for a jailer." — "Whenever
I so desire it, my god will release me." — His meaning, I fancy,
Was: "I shall die when I choose to die." Death is the ultimate goal-line.

---

1   Quinctius is unknown. Lines 17–34 imply that he was a public official in some place
    remote from Rome, possibly even a provincial governor, since Livy's *History* (1.30)
    mentions the Quinctii/Quintii as Alban aristocrats as far back as ca. 650 B.C. He may or
    may not be identical with the Quinctius Hirpinus whom *Odes* 2.11 invited to a jolly *al*

fresco drinking bout at the Sabine farm. "Hirpinus" regards an ethnic group, the Hirpini, who inhabited the central mountains of Samnium province, due E of Naples. One would not think of the present Quinctius as either a close or an old friend if he had never seen Horace's Sabine farm.

4   "At some length" (*loquaciter*) is said in jest.

5-7   The mountains extend east-west, interrupted by one north-south valley. Horace, facing south, like a priest taking omens, sees the morning sunlight strike the "right" or western side of his valley, and the setting sun strike the "left" or eastern side.

12-13   The stream is the Digéntia (now the Licénza), to be mentioned by name in E.1.18. 104 below; it flows due S to empty into the Anio (now the Aniéné) just above Varia (now Vicováro; see E.1.14.3 and note). The Anio, in turn, flows SWW through Tibur (Tívoli), dropping in picturesque cascades (*Odes* 1.7.13 and note) to traverse the plain called the *campagna di Roma* and empty into the Tiber just N of Rome.

Upon no evidence at all, the spring is often misidentified with the Bandúsian Spring of *Odes* 3.13. The wording of line 12 does not necessarily mean that the spring is the actual source of the Digéntia/Licenza, as Morris thinks. E.K. Rand: *A Walk to Horace's Farm*, 1930, points out (pp. 13-14) that the Digéntia/Licenza does not gain great force until after receiving three tributary brooks.

The Hebrus River of ancient Thrace is now the Maritsa flowing east and southeast through Bulgaria and then S to divide modern Greece from Turkey-in-Europe; see *Odes* 3.25.11 and note; E.1.3.3 and note.

16   Oppressive September heat, as in E.1.7.5-9.

23   People ate with their fingers. (One Tom Coryat recorded his surprise in 1608-9 at the new invention of table forks in Italy; see *Shakespeare's England*, Oxford University Press, 1916; 1932, vol. 1, pp. 16-17 and vol. 2, p. 133.)

25-29   An ancient commentator identifies the quotation as being from the panegyric to Augustus by Lucius Varius Rufus; see S.1.5.40 and note; *Odes* 1.6.2 and note.

Battles fought "by land and by sea" (*terra . . . marique*) can refer only to Augustus after the battle of Actium in 31 B.C., as the identical phrase is used in Epode 9,27. The words are really part of the quotation from Varius and surely do not mean, as Morris thinks, that *Quinctius* had won battles by land and by sea.

The whole passage, 25-31, means that Quinctius would not dream of accepting flatteries he knew to be suited only to the emperor but might eagerly assent to tributes like "wise" and "in virtue perfected"—Stoic terms—and exclaim: "That's *me*, Quinctius!"

40-45   The manner of arguing recalls Plato's *Republic* 1. 331-332.

45   Another allusion to Aesop's fable about the donkey that imposed on people by draping a lion's skin around him, as in S.1.6.22 and S.2.1.63-65.

46-51   The rapid-fire question-and-answer procedure resembles S.2.3.159-162, and both manner and matter are thoroughly Stoic, as Morris points out. Indeed, the rest of the present Epistle is earnestly Stoic in attitude, without a trace of irony, and yet the following poem (E.1.17), not to mention other poems of the collection, is rather in opposition to the stern morality of the Stoics.

The "Sabine" (49) is the type of the stern moralist; just possibly it is Horace himself assuming the moralist stance for the moment, since he too was a "a Sabine farmer."

64   An ancient commentator on Persius's poem 5.111 explains how prankish boys would solder a penny to the pavement with melted lead and then watch passers-by try to pick up the coin. Compare the note to S.2.3.53 about attaching an animal's tail to the back of an unsuspecting person.

73-79   Taking considerable liberty with the second scene of Euripides's *The Bacchae*, especially lines 492-8, Horace turns the disguised god Dionysus into a nameless Stoic martyr standing at the mercy of King Pentheus of Thebes. When Dionysus says: "The god himself will set me free whenever I wish," he is himself that god, in disguise, and he surely means something more complex and mysterious than "I can always escape you by committing suicide." The shorter *Bacchae* allusion in S.2.3.303-4 is truer to Euripides, but there are other Horatian passages attesting the profound impression made by the Greek tragedy of ca. 405 B.C. upon our poet, for example, *Odes* 2.19 and 3.25.

1.17.   *Quamvis, Scaeva, satis per te tibi consulis, et scis*

Though you are perfectly capable, Scaeva, of managing matters
Quite on your own when the problem is dealing with high-ranking persons,
Hear what a friend thinks — himself having much yet to learn. His opinions
May be no more than a blind man's attempts as a road-guide, but glance at
What I suggest and see whether my policy merits adopting.   5
    If it is undisturbed quiet you like and your sleep in the morning,
And if you have an aversion to dust and a vehicle's clatter,
Not to say overnight inns, then you really should try Ferentínum.
Pleasant experiences do not exclusively come from great riches,
Nor is a life badly spent that from birth until death goes unnoticed.   10
But, if you want to be helpful to friends and a bit more indulgent
Too in regard to yourself, you will need to come fasting to banquets.
    "If Aristíppus could bear to eat potherbs for lunch, he would have no
Need to court kings." — "My reprover would scorn to eat potherbs for lunch if
He but knew *how* to court kings." Of these two ways of thinking and living   15
Tell me which one you subscribe to, or else (as my junior) give ear to
My demonstration of why Aristíppus's notion is better.
This (so they tell us) was how he then parried the snarl of the Cynic:
"*I* please myself as a courtier: *you* play the role for the rabble;
My way is best. For a horse I can ride and a king to support me   20
I perform services: *you* beg for handouts, demeaning yourself to
Less then the givers, and yet you insist there is nothing you lack for."
All of life's stages and states and conditions beseemed Aristíppus,
Whether aspiring to heights or content with existing arrangements.
Conversely, it would surprise me if someone enduring "the double   25
Layer of rags" could successfully live any other existence.
Here (let us say) is a man who does *not* have to wait for his purple
Cloak, but in any old clothes will appear in most eminent places,
Never inept at assuming the role that befits the occasion;
There (let us say) is a man who avoids a Milesian-wool cloak as   30
Worse than a dog or a snake and will die of exposure unless his
Rags are returned to him: give him his rags, let him live in his folly!
    Ruling a state and exhibiting enemy captives to crowds is
Close to attaining Jove's throne and to scaling the summits of heaven;
Pleasing the men who so govern is not the most trivial achievement;   35
Not every man that puts forth on the sea reaches harbor at Corinth.
    Someone afraid to risk failure sat still, without joining the stuggle:
All very well, but then what of the man who succeeded? the one who
Manfully acted? Right there is a crux of our question — or nowhere.

40 One man shirks tasks as beyond his poor spirit and body, the other
Enters the contest and wins. Either vigor is only a word, or
Else the experiencing man has the claim to the honors and trophies.
    Not pleading poverty while with one's "king" gets a better result than
Whining and wheedling; a modest acceptance of gifts is a very
45 Different affair from exploiting. And that is the point I was making.
One who says, "Mother's in want, there's no dowry for sister, my farm won't
Yield me enough of an income, yet nobody's willing to buy it,"
Simply is wailing "Give help to the needy!" Another chimes in, "Me
Too!" — so the loaf is divided in fractions, each smaller and smaller.
50 If, when he chances on food, Master Crow would just eat without squawking,
He would have more of a feast and decidedly less competition.
    Taken for company's sake to Brundísium or lovely Surréntum,
One may complain of the miserable cold and the rain and the potholes,
Or he may mourn for a money-chest shattered and theft of his luggage,
55 Much like a whore as she artfully clamors and sobs for a necklace
Lost or an ankle-chain stolen, till genuine sympathy fails him
When he sustains a significant loss or a real-life disaster.
Once made a fool of, one does not lift up the impostor with broken
Leg at the crossroads, no matter what tears he may shed and no matter
60 How many times he may call upon holy Osíris as witness:
"I am not fooling, believe me! Have pity and help the poor cripple!"
Neighbors are hoarse from repeating their answer, "Go tell that to strangers!"

---

 1 After perfunctory address to an unknown "Scaeva," this "letter" proceeds as an essay.
 6 "In the morning" — until the first hour," (approximately 7 A.M.).
 8 Ferentínum (now Ferentíno) was a mountain town about 65 km/40 m SE of Rome on
    the Via Latina, large enough at a later date to have a stone theater, hence probably a
    shade less "quiet" and "restful" than the obscure little Úlubrae of E.1.11.30.
13–26 Aristíppus of Cyréné (ca. 435 to 356 B.C.) was praised in S.2.3.100–102 for aban-
    doning a treasure in the desert because it impeded a march, and in E.1.1.18–19 for his
    doctrine of "Seeking to subjugate things to myself, not myself unto things." Morris
    suggests that, to Horace, he struck an ideal compromise between Stoic and Epicurean
    philosophies.
        The first speaker (line 13) is the famous Diógenes the Cynic (ca. 412 to 323 B.C.), and
    the dialogue is adapted from the 10-Book *Lives and Opinions of Eminent Philosophers* (2.8.68)
    by Diógenes Laertius (3rd century B.C.).
        The Cynic philosophers were forerunners of the Stoics by half a century or more,
    but they had neither an organization nor a fixed body of teachings. As "professional
    beggars," they wore "the double layer of rags" (lines 25–26)—*duplici panno,* expanded
    from Greek *diplois,* which served them by day as a cloak and by night as a blanket. They
    carried walking sticks and a wallet for storing the alms they received. Through eight
    centuries Cynics were familiar figures in the classical world, eliciting admiration from
    the early Christians and setting a pattern for ascetic Christian monks. In the Middle
    Ages their role was represented by the mendicant friars.
        Greek *Kynikós,* whatever its origin, surely has to do with *kyōn, kynós,* "dog," hence
    "snarl" (line 18) and "dog" (line 31)—"snake" (line 31) being thrown in for good
    measure.
27–29 "Here . . . is a man" = Aristíppus, as tradition reported him.
30–32 "There . . . is a man" = Diógenes, whom tradition reported as refusing a fine

cloak—Horace uses the Greek word, *chlamys*—which Aristíppus offered him. Milesian woolens, that is, from Milétus, now an abandoned site on the SW coast of Turkey, were especially fine.

33–34   Clearly Augustus is meant. Line 35, then, must be Horace's heartfelt opinion.

36   Paraphrase of a Greek proverb, with "Corinth" as "the city of one's aspirations."

43   "King," as in E.1.7.37, used (like "Father") in address to one's patron, though the context here is sardonic. Indeed, the sardonic humor extends through the rest of the poem. But Aristíppus served an actual king, Dionysus I, "tyrant" of Syracuse, Sicily, from 405 to 367 B.C.

50   "Master Crow" is borrowed, with apologies, from LaFontaine's *maître corbeau*.

52   Surréntum is modern Sorrénto, opposite the Isle of Cápri.

60   The fake cripple who calls on Osíris must be an Egyptian. Horace had an aversion to Oriental religious cults; compare S.2.3.288–295.

1.18.   *Si bene te novi, metues, liberrime Lolli,*

If I know *you* and your forthrightness, Lollius, you will avoid, with
Dread, any sort of obsequious fawning when showing your friendship;
But, as a matron will always be unlike a prostitute both in
Kind and in color, a friend is distinct from a treacherous upstart.
There is an opposite vice, nonetheless, almost worse than this first one,   5
Namely, a brusque, disagreeable, grating uncouthness of manner
Offering candor with close-shaven head and display of bad teeth and
Claiming the title of manly directness and truth-telling virtue.
Virtue, however, is located midway between these two vices.
    One man will overdo deference at dinner by playing the toady;   10
Placed with the host, he keeps hanging with awe on the nod of the rich man,
Seconding statements and catching remarks that might pass without notice
Till you would think him a schoolboy reciting his lesson to teacher
Or in the role of a foil playing up to a comic performer.
Then there's the man that will wrangle about whether goat-hair is wool, and,   15
Armed to the teeth, will do battle for trifles: "You doubt for one instant
Anything *I* say or anything *I* have approved, and expect me
Not to start barking? Two lifetimes would not be enough to appease me!"
What do they argue about? — Whether Castor or Dócilis knows more,
Roads to Brundísium: Minúcian or Áppian, which is the better?   20
    Anyone ruined by desperate dice or a Venus too costly,
Grandly exceeding his limits in outlays for clothing and perfumes,
Anyone gripped by a thirst and ungovernable craving for money,
Fleeing from poverty as a disgrace, will be loathed by his wealthy
Friend, who quite often has vices himself ten times greater in number,   25
Or, short of loathing, will rule you and govern you, like a devoted
Mother expecting that you will be wiser and better than *he* was,
Telling you home-truths like "If I have follies — don't tell me I haven't! —
I can afford them, while yours is a trifling estate; a less ample
Toga would be more befitting a sensible client-companion;   30

Do stop competing with me!" —When Eutrápelus wanted to ruin
Someone, he made him a gift of expensive attire, for no sooner
Decked in magnificent tunics than up will go hopes and pretensions,
Sleeping till well after daybreak, postponing his real obligations
35   All for a whore, putting debts out to grass and grow fat, till he winds up
Dueling arena performers or driving a cart for a peddlar.
        Nor must you ever go snooping in private affairs of your patron;
Secrets of his you will keep when in wine or a fit of resentment.
Do not boast interests of yours or belittle the interests of others.
40   When he is set to go hunting do *not* stay at home to write poems:
That was how concord between the twin brothers Amphíon and Zethus
Came to a rift, till the lyre that offended the stern-minded brother
Lapsed into silence: Amphíon, they say, gave it up and conformed to
Zethus's tastes. You should likewise defer to your powerful patron's
45   Gentle demands, and whenever he wishes to start for the country,
Taking his mules with Aetólian nets on their backs and his dog-packs,
Rise and abandon the unsocial gloom of the Muse that eludes you
So you may share as an equal the supper attained through exertions.
        Custom ordained that pursuit as best fitted to Romans and good for
50   Honor and virile well-being, especially when you have strength to
Outrun a dog on the trail or outstay a wild boar in your prowess.
Further consider that no one so brilliantly manages manly
Weapons as you. And you know very well to what plaudits of viewers
You have performed in the mock-battles held on Mars' Field. What is more, you
55   Fought as a youth and endured the campaigns in Cantábrian Spain, with
Him as commander who now has unfastened the emblems of Rome from
Parthian temples and given Italian dominion to lands yet
Lacking it. Lest you demur, I remind you of one fine occasion, —
Though you are ever at pains to avoid breaking cadence with what is
60   Seemly — when out on your father's estate you arranged entertainment:
Choosing up sides, you sailed squadrons of boats so the Battle of Actium
Under your orders was mimicked by slaveboys, the enemy captained
By your own brother, the farm-pond in lieu of the broad Adriatic,
Fighting till Victory sped with her crown to whichever was winner.
65   He who has reason to think you approve of his aims and objectives
Cannot but heartily cheer you for putting on war-games of that sort.
        First of my warnings (in case you have need of a person to warn you):
Watch what you say at all times, and about whom and to whom you say it.
Shun any person who quizzes you: *that* kind is given to talk, and
70   Wide-open ears do not faithfully keep every confidence trusted
To them; a word once released is in flight beyond ever recalling.
See that your heart never suffers a love-wound from slavegirl or slaveboy
Over your reverenced friend's marble threshold: you *might* find the master
Making you happy by giving the dear little girl or the handsome
75   Lad as a minimal gift of farewell — or annoyed by the bother.
Anyone you recommend you should scrutinize over and over
So you may have no occasion to blush for his shortcomings later.

Sometimes we do make an error and sponsor an unworthy party;
Once you perceive your mistake, discontinue support of the culprit;
Then, when a tested acquaintance comes under attack, you can save him,   80
Shielding not only the person you trust but your own reputation,
For, when the slanderous fang of a Theon is gnawing away at
Him, be assured that you will yourself very soon be imperilled.
You are in danger whenever the house of a neighbor is burning,
And, if the fire is not checked, its intensity only increases.   85
　　　Courting a powerful friend has a charm for the still-inexperienced:
For the experienced it terrifies. You who are sailing deep waters,
Heed my directions before any shift of the wind drives you backwards.
Staid folk abominate jolly ones, witty ones those who are somber,
Lively ones hate the sedate, and the languid the constantly active;   90
[Drinkers enjoying Falernian bouts in the midst of the nighttime]
Hate any man who refuses the goblets they offer, no matter
How many oaths you may swear that nocturnal carousing upsets you.
Clear up that cloud on your brow; the retiring are often misjudged as
Secretive, just as the quiet are often presumed to be crabbèd.   95
Through the mutations of life you should read and inquire of the sages
How to proceed in the matter of making existence flow smoothly:—
Is an insatiable craving forever to vex and torment you
Or shall your worries and hopes concern things of a lesser importance?;
Whether true Virtue is taught by a System or grows out of Nature;   100
What can alleviate problems and make you a friend to yourself once
More?; is serenity found amid honors and neat little profits
Or does it wait on the untraveled road and the out-of-sight byway?
　　　Often as I am refreshed by Digéntia's icy-cold waters,
Drunk by the folk of Mandéla in countryside stark under winter,   105
What do you fancy, my friend, are my feelings? and what do I pray for?
Grant me the things I now have, or still less, and allow me to live my
Life for such time as remains — if the gods are reserving me *any*.
Grant me an ample provision of books and supplies for a year, so
I do not dangle in air like a leaf with my hopes all uncertain.   110
It is sufficient to pray for what Jove gives or takes; may he grant me
Life and my needs: I myself will provide the sereneness of spirit.

1　Lollius is the Lollius Maximus addressed in E.1.2 while studying rhetoric in Rome. He is still young, in his early twenties we would guess; see the note to line 55 below. His "forthrightness" is perhaps to be related to the caution against uncontrolled temper in lines 59–63 of the earlier poem.

4　"Color": matrons dressed in white, prostitutes in dark colors, as in S.1.2.36 and note.

11　"Placed with the host" paraphrases "a scoffer on the low couch(es)," that is, occupying position 8 or 9 in the diagram following S.2.8.

19　Despite "knows" (*sciat*), Morris thinks these unidentified persons were well-known gladiators or actors: public lecturers would seem likelier.

20　The Appian Way (495 km/310 m from Rome, via Taréntum, to Brundísium) was the route followed by Horace in S.1.5 for about two thirds of the journey. The Minúcian Way must be the secondary road followed in the last third of that journey.

29-30   Compare Epode 4, 7-8: " . . . six/ Full ells of cloth in toga folds."

31-32   "Eutrápelus," Greek for "witty" or "ribald," is probably a name coined by Horace on the basis of a letter of Cicero's to the knight Publius Voluminus in which Cicero speaks of the latter's *eutrapelía*.

     A malign extension of the idea is to be found in the famous Chapter 6 of Huysmans' novel *À Rebours* (1884). It would be a profound irony if the idea for that "outrageous" chapter derived from the present lines, since Huysmans affected to despise Horace.

36   That is, "sent for a gladiator" as punishment for licentious conduct and bankruptcy, as in S.2.7.58 and note.

41-44   Mythological Amphíon, the artistic man, and Zethus, the man of action, were twin sons of *Antíopē* by Zeus (or another), and their fraternal conflict figured in the (lost) Greek tragedy *Antíopē* by Euripides (before 406 B.C.) and of the (lost) Latin tragedy *Antiopa* by Pacúvius (before 130 B.C.); note also Goethe's unfinished *Elpenor* of 1781. Moderns have to piece the story together from various sources, primarily Pausánias's *Guide to Greece* (2nd century A.D.). Morris adds that, in art, Amphíon is depicted in the act of hiding his lyre under his cloak.

46   An ancient commentator believed that "Aetólian" was an allusion to the mythological hunting of the Calydonian boar in Aetolia (W-central Greece).

49-50   Hunting (and military-type sports) were *Roman*, as opposed to Greek gymnastics; see S.2.2.9-13.

55   Lollius must have been in Cantábrian Spain while Augustus was in personal command there in 27-26-25 B.C. "As a youth" = simply *puer* ("boy") in the text, so that he may have been with the emperor as a page-attendant and not an actual soldier.

56-57   Horace represents Augustus as unfastening with his own two hands the Roman army standards which the Parthians had kept mounted on their temple walls since capturing them from Crassus in 53 B.C. Actually the emblems were surrendered to Tiberius Claudius Nero; see the headnote to E.1.3. Thus the present poem dates itself to late in 20 B.C.

     Horace also assumes that "Parthian temples" were much like Roman temples. The fire-temples of the Parthians were merely four columns supporting a canopy, but other cults were tolerated, and about the temples of those cults very little is known, as indeed very little is known about the whole five centuries of Parthian rule, down to ca. 225 A.D.

66   We paraphrase this line rather than engage in the disputed interpretations of the "thumbs up" and "thumbs down" gesture mentioned in it.

82   Not even the ancient commentator could identify Theon.

91   Good manuscripts of Horace do not include this line. Quite obviously some scholar, at an unknown point in history, found the grammatical shift to line 92 so distastefully abrupt that he invented a transition line based on E.1.14.34:

> *quem bibulum liquidi media de luce Falerni*
> (the present line is:) *potores bibuli media de nocte Falerni.*

100   "Virtue," as often in Latin, means "human excellence." Whether it is inculcated by a "System" (*doctrina*), that is, by "training" according to a set of religious or philosophical rules, or whether it is "innate" is still in dispute. In Christian terms it is the problem of Grace.

104   The Digéntia (now the Licénza) is "the stream" of E.1.16.12 and note.

105   The village of Mandéla, E of the Digéntia and opposite Varia/Viccustomers (E.1.14.3 and note) on the W bank, officially became Mandéla once again in the 1880s, in Horace's honor, but in the intervening centuries it seems to have been variously known as Cantalupo in Bardella (or Bardella-Cantalupo) and Massa Mandelana. See E.K. Rand: *A Walk to Horace's Farm*, pp. 10-12.

107-112   Compare Horace's prayer to Apollo in *Odes* 1.31, especially 17-20:

> The use of my possessions and sturdy health,

Latóna-born, are what I entreat of you,
　　Sound mind, and not to spend old age in
　　　　Shame or deprived of the lyre to cheer me.

1.19.　　*Prisco si credis, Maecenas docte, Cratino,*

If you believe what Old-Comedy master Cratínus asserted,
Learnèd Maecenas, no poems can live or find favor too long if
Drinkers of water compose them. Once Bacchus had reckoned the frantic
Poets as kin to his Fauns and his Satyrs, the mornings have often
Found the adorable Muses themselves reeking strongly of wine fumes.   5
Recommendations of wine are discovered in bibulous Homer;
Good Father Énnius himself never sprang into war-song except when
Drunk; I myself once declared: "I consign both the Forum and Libo's
Wall to the drys and enjoin the dour fellows from poetry writing."
That proclamation no sooner was issued than poets would never   10
More be dissuaded from tippling by night and from stinking by day. But
Just because someone goes barefoot, forever with scowls on his brow, and
Wearing a toga like Cato's — the skimpiest made by the weaver,
Does he embody the virtue and loftier morals of Cato?
Iárbitas ruined himself by attempting Timágenes' scathing   15
Sarcasms, strive as he might for a style that was cogent and polished.
Models misguide when their faults can be copied. If chance were to turn my
Skin to a fairness, they'd bleach their complexions with caraway tonic.
Oh, how the toadyish pack of you copycats time and again have
Stirred me to fury and moved me to laughter with some of your antics!   20
　　　　I was the first to set footprints unguided on ground never trodden,
I have not walked in the traces of others. By trust in oneself one
Comes to be swarm-leader. I was the first to compose and show Latium
Parian iambics that followed Archílochus' meter and spirit
But on such topics as did not occasion the death of Lycámbes.   25
Nor should you deck me with scantier laurels by way of reproach for
Being too timid to alter his verse-form and manner in lyrics:
Male-minded Sappho adjusted her Muse to Archílochus' measures,
As did Alcáeus, yet both of them varied the subjects and patterns —
All without savage remarks toward a father-in-law's defamation,   30
All without making satiric abuse a girl's reason for dying.
No other poet before me in Latin had used the Alcáic
Strophe, and *my* pride it is to have offered that never-yet-uttered
Form to be scanned and perused by all readers of fair-minded judgment.
　　　　Would you be curious to know why the ungracious reader admires and   35
Loves my small pieces at home, yet maligns them unfairly in public?
I never *was* any hand to go hunting for votes from the fickle
Mob, with great outlays for dinners and secondhand-clothing donations;

"Authors' recitals" I shun, both as listener and as avenger;
40   Nor do I visit the tribes of professors and critics on platforms.
Hence all the wailing. If *I* say: "I shrink from reciting unworthy
Works before lecture-hall crowds, giving trifles an undue importance,"
Back comes the answer: "You're joking! You keep all your things for the ear of
Jove. You imagine that no one but you can distill the poetic
45   Honey. You're stuck on yourself!" At remarks of this nature I very
Nearly stop breathing, and sooner than face into claws that this fellow
Uses to fight, I cry "Foul!" and "Time out!" and demand intermission.
That kind of sport leads to heated dispute and to anger, and anger
Only leads on to hostilities followed by blood-letting warfare.

1–3   For Cratínus and "Old Comedy" see S.1.4.1–5 and note. Horace may be paraphrasing a line from Cratínus's *The Wine-Flask* (*Pytíně*) of 423 B.C.: ". . . but if he drinks water he can create nothing wise." See Gilbert Norwood: *Greek Comedy*, New York: Hill and Wang, 1931; 1963, p. 116.

3   Bacchus (Liber in the text) would have done this in remotest antiquity. "Frantic" = *male sanos*, "hardly sane."

6   Homer praises wine only occasionally and in conventional terms.

7–8   A preserved line of Énnius's says: "I never write poetry unless I have the gout," and Horace may be whimsically distorting the old poet's words, as he did in S.1.2.37.

8–9   The sense is: "I once said businessmen and judges should neither drink wine nor write poetry." No preserved poem by Horace contains such a line.

The "Forum" is the business district; an ancient commentator explains that the *praetor* (judge) held court near "Libo's Wall" (*puteal Libonis*), a landmark near the north (low) end of the Forum. This is the "Puteal Curbing" of S.2.6.35 and note, with the enclosing wall rebuilt by Scribonius Libo (who would become consul in 16 B.C.).

12–16   Copying mannerisms of Cato the Elder (S.1.2.32 and note) will not make you Cato, any more than Iárbitas's copying one mannerism of Timágenes made *him* Timágenes.

Timágenes was a professor of public speaking who, in 39 B.C., had offended Octavius Caesar. The statesman Caius Asínius Pollio (see the final note to *Odes* 2.1) simply took him into his house, where no one ventured to harm him.

Non-Latin "Iárbitas" must be a cover name for some antagonist of Horace's. Compare Dido's African wooer Iárbas in *Aeneid* 4.196. Line 15 says literally: "The tongue emulating Timágenes burst Iárbitas," in echo of Vergil's Eclogue 7.26: "so that Codrus's sides may split with envy"; in both cases the "burst/split" verb alludes to the fable of the mother frog who puffed herself up (as in S.2.3.314–320). "Codrus" was a cover name for a poet named *Cordus*, who was hostile to Vergil.

The abstruse cross-referencing implies that "Iárbitas" and "Codrus"/Cordus were one and the same enemy of the Vergil-Horace "faction."

21–32   The sense is: My *Epodes* were the first poems in Latin to adapt the iambic-couplet form used by Archílochus of (the island of) Paros, but I adapted freely, as did Sappho and Alcáeus in *their* adaptations of Archílochan forms.

Repeating from our Introduction to the *Epodes*—see also Epode 6,13: a fellow Parian named Lycámbes promised his daughter Neobulē in marriage to Archílochus, then retracted his promise, whereupon the poet directed such savage satires against both of them that father and daughter both committed suicide.

33–34   Beginning with *Odes* 1.9 Horace used the Alcáic strophe in 37 of his odes. No mention is made here of 26 odes in the Sapphic stanza form, which Catullus had used before Horace; see the note to *Odes* 3.30.13–14.

36   "My small pieces" must be *Odes* 1, 2, and 3. The curiously self-deprecating term is *opuscula*, the same word used in E.1.4.3.: "the small pieces of Cassius of Parma."

39 "Avenger" (*ultor*), that is, by reading his own poems in turn.
44 "Jove" = Augustus, "as the supreme representative of the inner circle of cultivated readers." (Morris)

1.20.   *Vertumnum Ianumque, liber, spectare videris,*

In this epilogue poem Horace addresses *Epistles. Book I* itself, now about to be released from the privacy of a circle of friends to the general reading public. With elaborate ambiguities, especially in lines 1 through 18, he speaks to the book as if it were a young slave-boy eager to leave his old master so as to be put up for auction and go forth to a new life.

So, then, my book, you look forward to seeing Vertúmnus and Janus,
Eager to loiter fresh-pumiced, no doubt, by the Sosii bookstalls.
Keys and their locks you detest, and the seals that the modest are glad for;
Known to the few, you complain; what you praise is a wider acquaintance,
Though you lack training for such. Hurry down to the place of your choosing!   5
But — there can be no returning, you know. When your fancier's fondness
Wanes and you meet with ill usage, your cry will be "Why did I ever
Do it, alas!" as you feel yourself tightly rolled up and discarded.
Yet, if my guess is not wrong (from embitterment at your desertion),
You will find favor in Rome while the blush of your youth is upon you;   10
Once you begin to look shopworn from being too often pawed over,
You will be silently eaten by slow-feeding bookworms, or else take
Refuge in Utica or be deported in chains to Ilérda.
Then your unheeded old counselor-guardian will laugh, like the man who
Angrily shoved his recalcitrant donkey on over the cliffside   15
Where it persisted in straying: why try to hold back the unwilling?
And you may further expect in your doting old age to be used for
Teaching small boys elementary reading in hinterland hamlets.
       While you still bask in the warmth and the sunshine of audience favor
You must report me as born of a freedman of limited means but   20
Afterwards gaining a wing-spread more broad than my nest, — so the value
You must subtract for my birth is made good by the weight of my virtues.
Say that I pleased the best men of the City at home and in wartime;
Say I was little in stature, with hair early gray, very fond of
Sunshine, quick-flaring in temper, yet soon reinduced to composure.   25
And, if by chance someone asks you how old I may be, go ahead and
Say I completed my four-times-eleven Decembers the year when
Lollius ruled and brought Lépidus in as his partner in office.

1–2 In the *Vicus Tuscus* (the "Tuscan Street" of S.2.3.228), which ran from the Forum to
    the Tiber, there were bookstores, such as the store of the Sosii (to be mentioned again in
    E.2.3.345), and "stations" for prostitutes, as well as a shrine to Vertúmnus (the god of
    changes; see S.2.7.14 and note), and "Janus." Given the context, this last is likely to be
    the Janus Brothel (*Fornix Janus*), but Morris takes the word in the sense of arch(way),

either as an arch over the Vicus Tuscus itself or as one of the arches in the Forum. The note to S.2.3.18 identified the "middle Janus" of the Forum as the center of the banking district, and E.1.1.54 mentioned the same structure; perhaps the Vicus Tuscus debouched into the Forum just opposite this "Janus" of the bankers. (The topography of the Forum area underwent many changes between 20 B.C. and the final ruin at the end of the classical era, so that archæologists often see only the last stage of the process.)

"Loiter" = *prostes,* literally "stand forward," that is, offer oneself for sale at a prostitute's "station" (*prostibulum*). Perhaps a display copy of a new book was suspended on a pillar in front of the bookstore.

For "fresh-pumiced" see the final note below about book manufacture.

5   "Down" is expressed in *descendere,* that is, to the low-lying Forum area from the residential quarters on the hillsides. Horace's own house in Rome (see S.2.7.32–33) was, we imagine, on the lower slope of the Esquiline Hill E of the Forum.

8   The translator could not find English words to convey the double meaning of *in breve te cogi;* of the book it means that the papyrus (or parchment) roll is rolled up tight before being discarded; of the slaveboy it means, as Morris puts it, "driven to poverty and hardship."

13   Morris thinks Utica and Ilérda are random-named provincial towns "where books no longer salable in Rome might find purchasers."

Utica, in Horace's time, was a thousand-year-old city and a busy port; it is now an abandoned site 20 miles NW of ancient Carthage and modern Tunis.

Ilérda (now Lérida) in NE Spain had witnessed a lightning victory of Julius Caesar's over Pompey's supporters in 49 B.C.

20   Compare S.1.6.71: "Poor, with his few meager acres," and other remarks about the poet's father in the same poem, lines 6, 45–46, 76, 83–88.

24   Compare "short and stout" (*brevis atque obesus*) in Suetonius's *Vita.* E.1.19.18 implies that Horace was dark-complexioned. E.1.7.26 indicates that the formerly "glossy-black hair" had receded. See also *Odes* 3.14.25–28 for graying hair and mellowing temper at age 41.

27–28   That is, I had my 44th birthday last December 8th, in 21 B.C. when Lollius served alone as consul until he belatedly "brought in" Lépidus as second consul. Compare Epode 11,7: "Three times December has (passed) . . . ."

There is a graceful version of E.1.20 by Austin Dobson (1840–1921) in 23 tetrameter couplets, beginning: "For mart and street you seem to pine/ With restless glances, book of mine," and concluding: "Add (if they ask) I'm forty-four,/ Or was the year that over us/ Both Lollius ruled and Lepidus."

A Note on Book Manufacture

From the author, a manuscript went to a scriptorium, where multiple copies were produced simultaneously by scribes at dictation from a single "reader." The text appeared in successive vertical columns of handwriting on a long, horizontal band of papyrus or sheepskin. Wooden rods were then glued, parallel to the handwriting columns, to either end of the strip, and the book (*liber*) was rolled up from right to left, that is, from the end to the beginning, to be unrolled from left to right in the course of reading. The reader exposed one column of text at a time, rolling up each completed section from left to right so that, on finishing the book, the roll was "backwards"; to reread, the entire book had to be "rewound."

Before the book was ready for sale the outer surface of the roll and the top and bottom edges were *rubbed smooth with pumice stone.* The identifying title might appear on the outer surface or on a tag attached to the projecting end of one of the roller-rods. The roll might then be fitted into a slipcase. E.2.3.332 will mention deluxe editions on cedar-oil paper and contained in cypress-wood cases, both *bookworm-resistant.* Multiple-volume works were placed in a *capsa,* a kind of bucket with lid and handle; see S.1.4.21 and note and S.1.10.63–64.

Centennial Hymn (*Carmen saeculare*)

Performed June 3, 17 B.C.

The Centennial Hymn

In 17 B.C. five completed centuries of Roman power were celebrated in continuous religious exercises from the night of May 31st to the afternoon of June 3rd, with seven further days and nights given over to secular entertainments. At the climax of the solemn rites of June 3rd a double chorus of twenty-seven (3 x 3 x 3) unmarried youths and twenty-seven unmarried girls sang the *Centennial Hymn* which Horace, at the emperor's request, had composed for the occasion.

The ceremonies had been conducted at various points in the city, but the concluding ritual, with the performance of the *Hymn,* took place on the Palatine Hill in front of the library-temple of Apollo as immense crowds gazed up from the Forum below. Augustus himself presided, standing before the cult statue of Apollo whose features had been modeled on his own. The god was represented as holding his poetic lyre but with his mighty bow of vengeance and of death laid aside, perhaps at his feet.

The *Hymn,* addressed to Apollo and Diana, implores those divinities for continuance of their past favor to the Roman state. Some stanzas were sung by the male chorus only, some by the female chorus only, and others again by all fifty-four voices together, but it is not possible to be sure of the distribution in all cases.

Meter:: Sapphic Stanza: in lines 1, 2, and 3: $\_\,\cup\,\_\,>\,\_\,\cup\,\cup\,\_\,\cup\,\_\,\cup$

in line 4: $\_\,\cup\,\cup\,\_\,\cup$ *

> Phoebus, and Diana in woodlands regent,
> Glories of the sky, to be held in future
> Honor as in past: we entreat you on this
>   Sacred occasion

5

> When the Sibyl's chanted instructions call for
> Chosen maidens chaste and unwedded youths to
> Sing this hymn to gods in whose sight our seven
>   Hills have known favor.

10

> Sun of bounty who, with your shining chariot,
> Bring and close the day, ever new yet changeless,
> May no greater thing than this Rome, our City,
>   Rise in your prospect.

* See Publisher's Note, p. viii.

Duly open wombs at their proper season,
Ílithýia, gently attending mothers,
Or, with your approval, be named Lucína   15
    Or Genitális.

Goddess, rear our children, uphold the laws our
Leaders have enacted to govern wedlock,
Laws we pray may yield generations also
    Fruitful in offspring,   20

So that through eleven recurrent future
Decades there may be, without fail, repeated
Hymns and games of holiday thrice by daylight,
    Thrice after nightfall.

Destinies you uttered proved true, O Parcae;   25
What you so ordained, may the fixed and changeless
End of time preserve, and let blessings past be
    Ever continued.

May our Earth, abundant in fruits and cattle,
Yield the headed grain as a crown for Ceres;   30
May our crops be nurtured with wholesome rains and
    Jupiter's breezes.

With your bow laid down, and benignly lending
Ear to boys entreating you, hear, Apollo!
Harken, queen of stars and the two-horned crescent,   35
    Luna, to maidens!

If the gods willed Rome into being when they
Bade the walls of Troy win Etruscan shores and
Bade the nation's remnant transplant its hearths by
    Rescuing voyage;   40

If unscathed from Ilian flames, Aeneas,
Blameless chief survivor of perished homeland,
Led the way, predestined to found a city
    Greater than ever:

Then, O gods, give young people taintless morals,   45
And, O gods, to tranquil old men give peace, and
To the race of Romulus give all glory,
    Riches, and offspring;

Grant the pleas submitted with votive bulls by
Venus' and Anchíses' exalted scion,   50
He who first wars enemies down, then lets them
    Live in his mercy.

Sea and land acknowledge his hand of power,
By the Alban axes the Medes are daunted,

55   Scyths and Hindus, haughty not long ago, now
                    Seek his pronouncements.

                Trust and Peace and Honor and ancient Manners
                Venture back among us, and long-neglected
                Upright Conduct; Plenty comes too, and brings her
60   Horn of abundance.

                Prophet god resplendent with bow of silver,
                Phoebus, welcome chief of the ninefold Muses,
                Master of the skills that relieve the human
                    Body of sickness,

65   If you find our Palatine altars pleasing,
                Prosper Roman power and Latium's fortunes,
                Five years more extend them, and thence forever
                    Down through the ages.

                Áventine and Álgidus Ridge, Diana,
70   Hold your shrines: the Board of Fifteen implore you:
                Hear their prayers and harken with gracious ear to
                    Prayers of these children.

                                         *

                Homewards now I carry my trust that Jove and
                All the gods have heard these entreaties: I am
75   Phoebus' and Diana's instructed chorus,
                    Hymning their praises.

1–2 The twin deities, god of the sun, goddess of the moon. "Diana in woodlands regent"
(*silvarum . . . potens*) paraphrases *Diana Nemorensis*, "Diana-of-the-woods." See the note
to *Odes* 4.1.19–28 and the opening pages of Frazer's *The Golden Bough;* compare also *Odes*
1.21.5 and 3.22.1.
5   "Sibyl" = "prophetess"; from Doric dialect *siobólla,* "divine wish," (Attic Greek *theo-
boúlē*), says Ernest Weekley. Antiquity counted up to 12 Sibyls in various parts of the
classical world.
        One Sibyl allegedly came before Rome's last king, Tarquin the Proud, (534–509
B.C.), offering, for a price, nine "books" of prophecies written in Greek hexameter lines;
after twice refusing to purchase, and after six of the books had been burned before his
eyes, the king paid the original price for the three remaining books. These were kept in a
stone chest at the temple of Jupiter on the Capitol and consulted in times of peril. When
they were nevertheless destroyed by fire in 82 B.C., the collection was "recomposed."
Occasionally new items were added, one of which was the detailed instructions for the
procedures followed in the festival of 17 B.C., and this item, in Greek hexameter lines, is
preserved in part, as quoted by the historian Zosimus after 450 A.D.; see the Extra Note
below.
        All Greek and Roman "sibylline books" are lost, but Jewish and Judeo-Christian
specimens have been preserved from the period ca. 80 to ca. 300 A.D.; see Henry
Chadwick: *The Early Church,* 1967, p. 78. Wolfram of Eschenbach (before 1225) makes
"Plato and the Sibyl" foretell the Redemption (*Parzival* 465) and attest the fall of Adam
(*Willehalm* 218). In the great hymn, *Dies irae* (ca. 1250), King David and the Sibyl
guarantee the future events of Judgment Day. Michelangelo painted five Sibyls on the
walls of the Sistine Chapel.

13–16   Horace here identifies Diana with Ílithýia: Greek *Eileíthuia,* "she who comes to aid (in childbirth)."

        "Lucina" (Latin, "light-bringing") was usually a name, not for Diana, but for Juno in her childbirth-assisting character.

        "Genitalis" seems to be Horace's own adaptation of Greek *Genetyllís,* " goddess of one's birth hour."

        Invocation by alternate names was a regular feature of pagan prayer.

17–18   The allusion here, as in line 45, is to the two laws sponsored by Augustus and passed the previous year (18 B.C): the *lex Iulia de adulteriis coercendis,* which made adultery a pu⊦lic crime, and the *lex Iulia de maritandis ordinibus,* which rewarded marriage and parenthood and penalized unmarried persons. See *Odes* 4.5.21–24 and note; 4.15.9–16; and E.2.1.1–3.

21–24   Horace reckons 110 years (eleven decades) to a century, following the procedures of the Board of Fifteen (line 70) who computed the centennial. See the Extra Note below.

25–28   The Fates (*Parcae*), who had been honored on the night of May 31st, *foreknew* Roman greatness, and *willed* it; the Sibyl, inspired by them, *foretold* it. The Fates are now implored to continue that greatness.,

29   "Earth" = *Tellus,* a feminine noun, hence *Mother* Earth. Sacrifice to Tellus had been made the previous night, June 2nd.

33–36   A transition passage sung, two lines each, by the divided chorus. Lines 13–32 honored three dark and mysterious powers: the womb of woman, the hidden Fates, and the food-producing Earth. "Daylight matters" will now be broached.

37–44   The "If" of line 37, as in lines 41 and 65, means "As surely as" and constitutes the basis for a prayer.

        The allusions are to the *Aeneid,* recently published after Vergil's death on September 22, 19 B.C. by his literary executors, Plotius Tucca and Lucius Varius Rufus; see S.1.5.40 and note. The emperor himself had ordered the publication.

49–50   The *son* of mortal Anchíses and the goddess was Aeneas, the *scion* is Augustus, "the new Aeneas." The "votive bulls" had been sacrificed to Jupiter on June 1st by Augustus and Agrippa.

51–52   A paraphrase of *Aeneid* 6. 853: *parcere subiectis et debellare superbos,* "to show leniency to the conquered and to 'war down' the haughty."

54–56   "Sea and land" had become a set formula since the victory at Actium in 31 B.C.; see Epode 9, 27 and note.

        "The axes of Alba" stand for Roman military might, Alba Longa (in the Alban Hills SE of Rome) having been "proto-Rome" during the "three" centuries from Aeneas down to the founding of the City by Romulus in 753 B.C.

        "Seek his pronouncements" (*responsa petunt*), that is, as from a god.

56–60   The time is primarily the ten years, 27 to 17 B.C., since the title of "the August One" was conferred upon Octavius Caesar.

61–64   Apollo as god of prophecy (*augur,* as in *Odes* 1.2.32 and note), as patron of all the arts, and as god of medicine.

67   The Romans counted longer periods of time by five-year periods (*lustra*).

69   The Áventine Hill, in the SW corner of ancient Rome, was first included within the city limits by King Servius Tullius (587–534 B.C.), who, around 550 B.C., built a temple to Diana there, copying the plan of the famous temple of Artemis/Diana at Ephesus. See Livy's History. 1, 44–45.

        For the Álgidus Ridge in the Alban Hills see *Odes* 1.21.6; 3.23.9; 4.4.58, and notes; also the note to 4.1.19–28.

70   The Board of Fifteen (*quindecim . . . virorum*) had charge of the Sibylline Books. At the behest of Augustus they planned the entire festival, computing the year and composing the written "oracle" in Greek hexameter lines. See the Extra Note below.

73–76   Like the chorus (of fifteen) in Athenian tragedy of the 5th century B.C., the present chorus speaks in first-person-singular. Compare *Odes* 4.6.31–44, which depict a rehearsal of the festival chorus, especially the epilogue stanza.

Extra Note About the Centennial

Origins. In the Field of Mars, in the NW quadrant of ancient Rome, there was a spot known as Terentum or Tarentum, at which, from times remote, the Valerii family performed rites in honor of the dark and nameless gods of the underworld. When, in 249 B.C., a Roman fleet was destroyed by Carthaginians off NW Sicily, an oracle was discovered in the Sibylline Books directing the celebration of "Terentine Games" then and on every hundredth anniversary thereafter. Thus the family rites came to be a responsibility of the state. The outbreak of the Third Punic War forced postponement of the first centennial from 149 to 146 B.C. The second centennial could not be held in 49 B.C. because in January of that year Julius Caesar's crossing of the Rubicon had plunged the whole Roman world into civil war. A belated observance of the festival was intended for 23 B.C. and again postponed. The actual celebration of 17 B.C was therefore thirty-two years behind schedule, but Augustus wished it to mark his ten-year rule amid peace and prosperity. At that point the Board of Fifteen, in charge of the Sibylline Books, found evidence for centennials going back to 456 B.C., and, by reckoning a century as 110 years—as was sometimes done, they were able to make a fifth centennial fall in 16 B.C. Thus the observances of 17 B.C. were 499, not 500, years after a postulated event of 556 B.C.

Schedule. With Augustus presiding over all ceremonies, and with Agrippa as his assistant, the celebration of 17 B.C. opened with nocturnal rites at the spot called Terentum or Tarentum. On the night of May 31st nine black ewe lambs and nine she-goats were offered "in holocaust" to the Fates (*Parcae*), that is, the sacrificial animals were totally consumed by fire and the participants ate none of their flesh. On the night of June 1st, again at Terentum, consecrated "cakes" were offered to Ílithýia, goddess of childbirth, and on the night of June 2nd, still at Terentum, a pregnant sow was offered to *Tellus* (Mother Earth). Lines 13–32 of Horace's *Hymn* allude, in mixed sequence, to these rites.

In the daytime sacrifices of June 1st Augustus and Agrippa each slew a white bull on the Capitol in honor of Jupiter. At the same spot on June 2nd each slew a white heifer in honor of Juno. On the third day each presented consecrated "cakes" to Apollo and Diana in front of the library-temple of Apollo on the Palatine, that temple being quite close to the imperial residence. Performance of Horace's *Hymn* in that place followed next, and in final conclusion of the formal ceremonies the chorus moved to the Capitoline Hill for a second performance of the *Hymn* before the temple of Jupiter.

After the nocturnal rites of May 31st at the spot called Terentum in the Field of Mars, spectators moved a short distance over to the Tiber's edge, where performances began on a temporary stage of wood, but with no seats provided for the audiences. These performances continued without interruption for the duration of the festival. In the daytime hours a committee if 110 matrons held religious banquets (*sellesternia*) in honor of Juno and Diana. Through the seven days, June 4th to June 11th, following the festival proper there were banquets of honor and entertainments of the amphitheater.

Evidence. Subsequently there were erected at the spot called Terentum two columns, one of bronze and one of marble, each inscribed with the particulars of the celebration. In 1890 shattered fragments of the marble pillar were discovered *in situ* and later removed to the Museo delle Terme, where they still are; the partially reconstructed inscription ends with the words: *Carmen composuit Q. Horatius Flaccus.* The bronze pillar, however, has vanished without a trace, thus justifying with a literalness not intended by *Odes* 3.30.1 Horace's claim to have constructed a poetic monument "destined to outlast bronze."

Five hundred years later, between 450 and 500 A.D., a Greek-language "History of Rome" (down to about 410 A.D.) was published in four Books by an imperial official named Zosimus. Chapter 5 of Book II contains an extended account of the centennial celebration of 17 B.C., including quotations from the Sibyl's oracle, in Greek hexameters, that directed the ritual procedures. It is thought that these verses were composed *after* the festival.

Subsequent Centennials. A mere sixty-four years after Augustus's festival of 17 B.C. the Emperor Claudius celebrated *800* years of Roman power in 47 A.D., reckoning centuries of 100, not 110, years and beginning with 753, the traditional date for the founding of Rome.

Suetonius, in his "Life of Claudius" 21, mentions the embarrassments of arithmetic and of nonexistent records, adding that living persons could remember the previous celebration and therefore laughed when the herald proclaimed rites never seen before by anyone alive. In 88 A.D. the Emperor Domitian found both Augustus and Claudius guilty of errors in arithmetic and so held his own "centennial." Variant formulas account for the centennials celebrated by Antoninus Pius in 147 (900 years after 753), by Septimius Severus in 204, and by Philip in 248 (1001 years after 753). Emperors Gallienus and Maximian seem to have held centennial festivals in 257 and 304. Amid the decline of the Empire the custom lapsed.

In 1300 Pope Boniface VIII may have looked back to pagan tradition when he proclaimed a papal jubilee year. With successive popes the jubilee years were proclaimed at intervals of fifty years; the interval now observed is twenty-five years.

Odes. Book 4
Carmina. Liber Qvartvs
ca. 13 B.C.

Odes. Book 4

Carmina IV (*Odes* 4: 15 poems, 582 lines) was probably published in 13 B.C. It probably owes its very existence to the emperor's request that the nation's greatest living poet celebrate the momentous Roman victories north of the Alps in 15 B.C. Accordingly, the companion odes 4 and 14 praise Drusus and Tiberius, the emperor's stepsons and his commanders in those campaigns, but in both cases Horace is at pains to say that the victories were properly the emperor's own, his stepsons being only his executive hands. To make that point doubly sure, separate odes 5 and 15 exalt the emperor himself. Poem No. 2 also praises the emperor's success in a campaign of 16 B.C. Readers need not disdain these five pieces as having no more than a historical interest: even as official works written to order, they are esthetically valid.

Horace apparently came out of semiretirement to compose these poems in the years 16–15–14 B.C. Poem 9 is also likely to date to those years. Poem 6 portrays a rehearsal of the chorus that performed the *Centennial Hymn* on June 3, 17 B.C. and must itself, therefore, be of 17 B.C. Poem 1, to the youth Ligurinus, dates itself to "around" the poet's fiftieth birthday, December 8, 15 B.C., and No. 10, likewise to Ligurinus, must be of that period.

The seven remaining pieces are of uncertain dates. Maecenas's April 13th birthday is the occasion for No. 11, but the year is unknown. No. 12, a jolly dinner invitation to Vergil, who was six years dead in 13 B.C., was probably composed in the years 23 to 20 B.C.; see our final note to that poem. Poems 3 (the poet to his lyre), 7 (springtime), 13 (mockery of a faded beauty), and 8 (the immortalizing power of poetry), could be of any time; all repeat themes from *Odes* 1–2–3. Poem 8 is in "the lesser Asclepiadic meter" which conspicuously marked only the first and last pieces of the earlier lyric collection, so that one wonders whether it was a metrical exercise in preparation for *Odes* 1.1 and 3.30 salvaged from earlier days and perhaps adapted for a later occasion. If so, its mediocre quality would be understandable, as would a tiny flaw in the metrics of line 17 and a startlingly garbled, or else overcondensed, historical allusion in lines 15–20.

The patriotic pieces constitute the core of *Odes* 4, the rest is a miscellany. Except for poem 8, poetic assurance is everywhere, poem 1 is remarkable for its poetic intensity, but no themes are new.

4.1. *Intermissa, Venus, diu*
      rursus bella moves?   *Parce, precor, precor.*

Meter: in the odd-numbered lines: _ ∪ _ ∪ ∪ _ ∪ _
          in the even-numbered lines: _ ∪ _ ∪ ∪ _   _ ∪ ∪ _ ∪ _

Must this warfare so long left off,
        Venus, now be resumed?   Spare me, I plead, I plead!
I am not what I was in dear
        Days of Cínara's rule.   Tenderest Cupids' harsh
Mother, do not coerce the man   5
        Ten-times-five years in age,   awkwardly stiff before
Your so supple commands. Be off,
        Answer blandishing youth   begging for you to come.
Much more fitting would be descent,
        Winged by roseate swans,   bearing your revels to   10
Paulus Maximus' household, if
        You are seeking a heart   suited to ardent love.
He is noble, and handsome too,
        And, in cases at law,   never too slow with words;
With his hundredfold talents graced,   15
        He will carry your flag   forward from battle's edge,
And, whenever your gifts allow
        Him a gleeful success   over a rival in wealth,
He will set you in marble shape
        Under a cedarwood roof   out by the Alban lakes.   20
There your nostriis will breathe the sweet
        Wafted incense in clouds,   there Berecýnthian
Flutes and lyres will afford delight
        Intermingled with hymns,   not without reedy pipes;
There twice daily your goddess-self   25
        Shall in dances be praised,   dances of lads and girls
Treading three-quarter measures like
        Those of Salian priests,   nimbly on gleaming feet.
Neither woman nor boy delights
        Me now, nor do I feel   hope for response in love,   30
Toasts in wine hold no charm for me,
        Nor do flowers of spring   twined as a banquet crown.
Yet, alas!, Ligurínus, why,
        Why, then, is there a tear   slowly coursing my check?
Why do words often fail my prompt   35
        Tongue, with silence instead   awkwardly catching me?
I dream dreams in the night when I
        Hold you captured and close,   or you may seem a bird
I pursue over grass of Mars
        Field, or (harsh one!) through waves   weltering as you swim.   40

1   In the eight years (23 to 15 B.C.) since publishing *Odes* 1–2–3 Horace has engaged in no "warfare" (*bella*), that is, no "struggles," with love, and he is now (line 6) fiftyish.

4   Those "dear/ Days of Cínara's rule" were five or more years in the past: E.1.7.28, published in 20 B.C., already mourned "wantoning Cínara's flight and desertion."

Ernest Dowson's poem of 1896, with its refrain: "I have been faithful to thee, Cynara! in my fashion," borrows from Horace only the name of "Cynara" and the title: *Non sum qualis eram bonae/ sub regno Cinarae,* lines 3–4 of the present poem.

4–5 All impulses of love are "Cupids," and hence "sons of Venus." The common noun *cupido* meant "desire, passion."

6   Horace turned fifty on December 8, 15 B.C. The text says *"around* ten-times-five years."

11 The aristocratic Paulus Maximus was a confidant of the emperor, a friend of the poet Ovid (who was born in 43 B.C.), and consul in 11 B.C. At a guess, he was half Horace's age, or a little less.

19–28 In Horace's fancy, Paulus Maximus will erect a statue to Venus and institute a cult for her in an imaginary temple *like* the temple of Diana-of-the-woods in the Alban Hills SE of Rome. The two lakes there, both nearly circular because they occupy craters of extinct volcanos, are the Alban Lake (now *Lago Albano*) and the Lake of Nemi (*Lago di Nemi*), the latter being known to the Romans as "Diana's Mirror" (*Speculum Dianae*). See the note about "Álgidus ridge," *Odes* 1.21.6.

22 "Berecýnthian" implies "Asiatic, wild, voluptuous"; see the notes to *Odes* 1.18.13 and 3.19.19.

28 The *Salii* were the dancing priests of Mars, as in the notes to *Odes* 1.36.12 and E.2.1. 86–87.

33 "Ligurínus" means "little Ligurian," but he cannot be a slave or foreigner if he plays sports on the Field of Mars. He is addressed again in *Odes* 4.10.

The Ligurians were a prehistoric population of what is now the Italian and French Rivieras and inland from there. The district around Genoa is still called Liguria.

40 "Waves" (*aquas*), that is, of the Tiber, which curved around three sides of the *Campus Martius.* "Liparéan Hebrus" swam there (*Odes* 3.12.2), as did all the sports players—though Sýbaris, in *Odes* 1.8.8, avoided doing so.

"Weltering as you swim" paraphrases the subtle final word *volubilis* with its multiple meaning: "turning," "rolling (like waves)," "twisting (like a snake,)" and its secondary sense of "fickle"; these must be "distributed" to the water, to the swimmer's movements, and to the youth's attitudes toward the poet.

4.2.   *Pindarum quisquis studet aemulari*

Meter: Sapphic stanza: in lines 1, 2, and 3:   _ ∪ _ > _ ∪ ∪ _ ∪ _ ∪
                                             in line 4:   _ ∪ ∪ _ ∪

In 16 B.C. a Roman army under Marcus Lollius was defeated by the Germanic Sygambri, but with the arrival of Augustus "at the front" they retreated. Iullus Antonius, the son of Mark Antony and himself a published poet, has suggested that Horace compose a victory ode in the manner of Pindar to celebrate the occasion. Horace replies as follows:

> Any poet seeking to rival Pindar,
> Iullus, puts on Dáedalus' wings of wax to
> Rise in soaring flight, and a sea shall keep his
>   Name and his body.

Like a river headlong from mountains pouring   5
Forth to drown its banks with the glut of rainfalls,
Pindar's language, seething with boundless power,
    Bursts like a torrent,

Every work deserving Apollo's laurels,
Whether his invented expressions roll in   10
Waves of daring dithyrambs or in measures
    Formed without pattern,

Whether gods or kings are his theme, or heroes
Born of blood divine, at whose hand the Centaurs
Met a death deserved, or who quenched the flame of   15
    Grisly Chiméra,

Whether he reports how the palms of Elis
Bring the horse or pugilist home in glory,
Granting each an honor a hundred statues
    Never could equal,   20

Or if in lament to a widow grieving
For her youthful spouse he extols his golden
Virtues to the stars, thus defying gloom of
    Orcus to claim him.

Mighty gales, Antonius, lift up Dírcē's   25
Swan in flight and sweep him beyond the furthest
Range of cloudy pinnacles: I am merely
    Bee-like and busy,

Culling honeyed thyme with prodigious effort
Through the groves and well-watered glens of Tibur,   30
Working up my poems from little substance
    Crafted with labor.

Poet of a mightier strain, the hymn to
Caesar shall be yours, when he rides the Sacred
Way with fierce Sygámbri in tow and wearing   35
    Merited laurels;

Greater, better ruler to earth was never
Granted by the Fates, nor will gods in kindness
Send his like again, not though time regains its
    Golden beginning.   40

Yours shall be the hymn for the joyous days and
Public celebration throughout the City
When the brave Augustus returns and every
    Law court is emptied.

Then, if *I* have any command of words worth   45

Hearing, I shall also cry "O thou sun of
Splendor, hail to thee!" At his coming I am
    Blessèd in Caesar.

As thou movest, Triumph, across the Forum
50   We shall all be shouting our "Hail to Triumph!",
Sending up to bounteous gods the praise of
    Thanksgiving incense.

Bulls and cows, ten each, you shall sacrifice, while
I fulfill my vow with a single, tender
55   Weanling calf now gaining his growth in verdant
    Meadows at pasture, —

One with horns resembling the crescent fires of
Luna on the night of her third-time rising,
Snowy white of blaze on his brow, but coated
60   Otherwise russet.

1–4   Wearing the wings that his father Dáedalus fitted together with wax, Ícarus plunged to his death in that small section of the Aegéan Sea which, from him, was called Icárian. Its central island is still called Ikária and its eastern shore was ancient Caria (now SW Turkey).

    Iullus Antonius (lines 2 and 25) was the son of Mark Antony by his third wife, the redoubtable Fulvia (d. 40 B.C.; see the first two scenes of Shakespeare's *Antony and Cleopatra*). When, in that same year, 40 B.C., Antony, for political reasons, married Octavia, the sister of the future Augustus, this fourth wife took Iullus and Antony's other children under her care; for her increasing brood of foster-children see the note to *Odes* 3.14.7. Upon Antony's "repudiation" of Octavia in the summer of 37 B.C. (see *Antony and Cleopatra* III,6) she and the children became part of her brother's imperial household, where Iullus was well treated.

    At the time of the present poem Iullus was aged about 30 and had composed a 12-Book epic poem called the *Diomedea* (which is lost). A year or so later he was Praetor of the City, and subsequently Consul, but in 2 B.C. he was convicted of adultery with Augustus's daughter Julia and put to death. (Julia and four other paramours were sent to separate exiles.)

5–27   Forty-five victory odes of Pindar (518 to some date after 446 B.C.) have all the grandeur described by Horace. His dithyrambs (hymns to Dionysus) are lost, as are his funeral eulogies (*Thrênoi*), lines 21–24. His free rhythms have something in common with Walt Whitman, and Moore quotes a passage from Saint Jerome's *Preface to Job* in which the style of that Biblical book is described in terms almost identical to lines 11–12 of the present poem.

    13–15   Heroes Theseus and Pirithoüs slew the wild Centaurs; see the note to *Odes* 1.18.7.

    15–16   In Pindar's 13th Olympian Ode hero Bellérophon slew the flame-breathing monster, the Chiméra; see the note to *Odes* 1.27.23–24.

    17–18   Fourteen of Pindar's odes celebrate winning athletes and horses of the Olympian Games held, in honor of Zeus, at Elis (also called Pisa) in the NW Peloponnesus.

    25–26   "Dírcē's swan" is Pindar. The Muses' spring called Dírcē (see the note to *Odes* 3.13.13) was just S of Thebes, Pindar's birthplace. For the equivalency "poet = swan" see Horace's own anticipated transformation into a swan in *Odes* 2.20.1–16.

27–30   The text specifies "a bee of Matina," raising anew the question of identification of Matina discussed in the note to *Odes* 1.28.3. The translator suggests, with no strong conviction: "I am a south-Italian bee, now gathering honey *at Tibur.*"

34–35   The Sacred Way (*Via Sacra*), sloping NWW through the Forum to the foot of the Capitoline Hill, was the route followed by triumphal processions. The text says "sacred slope." The law courts (line 44) were clustered near the foot of the Capitoline Hill.

39–40   Time's "golden beginning" = "the Golden Age," "the reign of Saturn," parallel to "the Garden of Eden."

53–56   Compare *Odes* 2.17.30–32, where Maecenas was to make expensive sacrifices, while Horace was to offer "merely a humble she-lamb"; also E.1.3.36: "I have a heifer at pasture, reserved for your homecoming dinner."

4.3.   *Quem tu, Melpomene, semel*
nascentem placido lumine videris

Meter: in the odd-numbered lines: _ U _ U U _ U _
in the even-numbered lines: _ U _ U U _ _ U U _ U _

One on whom, in his hour of birth,
    You, Melpómenē, once   gaze with your quiet eyes
Will not win any boxer's crown
    At the Ísthmian Games,   nor will a tireless horse
Bring his chariot in for first   5
    Prize, nor will his superb   prowess in war attain
Triumph's chaplet of laurel leaves
    For kings' insolence crushed   when, in his glory, crowds
Hail him victor on Capitol;
    Yet, from waters that cool   Tibur and from the dense   10
Shade of bowers on Tibur's hill,
    His Aeólian song   shall be accorded fame.
By the race of the Romans, earth's
    Greatest, I have been deemed   worthy of rank among
Noble choirs of its singing bards;   15
    Thus I now am the less   hounded by Envy's fang.
O my Muse of the golden shell,
    You who modulate sweet   sounding of harmonies,
Who could grant even toneless fish
    Gifts of song like the swan's,   were you so willed to do,   20
All of this is a gift from you:
    Having passers-by point   fingers at me as Rome's
Lyric singer; if what I write
    Pleases, yours were the thoughts,   yours was the pleasure's source.

1–12   Any newborn infant gazed upon by the Muse (like a gift-bestowing good fairy) is not destined to fame as an athlete in the Greek games (3–6) or as a Roman General in triumph (7–9), but he *is* destined to fame as a poet (10–12).

2   Melpómenē, the "songstress" Muse, as in *Odes* 1.24.3 and note, and in 3.30.15.

3–6   Of the 45 victory odes by Pindar (see the note to lines 5–27 of the foregoing ode), 8 are "Isthmian," celebrating winning athletes or horses in the games held at the city of Corinth on the narrow (6 km/4 m wide) Isthmus of Corinth in honor of the sea god Poseidon (Roman Neptune).

6–9   Horace has Augustus in mind; compare lines 43–52 of the foregoing ode. "For kings' insolence crushed" again echoes Vergil's *debellare superbos,* as in the *Centennial Hymn* 51–52 and note.

10–12   Two distinct notions seem to be, somewhat unclearly, combined: 1 the beauty of Tibur's streams and groves inspired the poet to compose in the first place, and 2 the notion of Tibur as "a hill of the Muses" where the acknowledged poet is received into "poets' heaven." E.2.1.27 will hint at making "the Alban Mount" a hill of the Muses, "an Italian Helicon."

12   "Aeólian," as in *Odes* 3.30.13, means the dialect, and therefore the works, of Alcáeus and Sappho.

17   "Shell" is a lyre made from an empty tortoise shell, as in *Odes* 1.10.6 and note, but "golden" probably echoes the opening words ("Golden lyre") of Pindar's first Pythian Ode—that is, an ode celebrating victors in the games held at Pytho/Delphi in honor of Apollo,

21–24   As in *Odes* 3.30.14–15: "Take, then, the honors won/ As your own, . . . gracious Melpómenē," Horace credits his poetic gifts to a "higher source."

Odes 4.3 is a skillful and pleasing poem: 12 lines general, 12 lines personal, the latter group of 12 being further ordered as 4 lines of personal "assertion," followed by 8 lines of humble reverence, yet it contains hardly a thought or a poetic turn which is not better expressed somewhere in earlier odes.

4.4.   *Qualem ministrum fulminis alitem*

Meter: Alcaic stanza: in lines 1 and 2:   U _ U _ > _ U U _ U _
                      in line 3:   U _ U _ U _ U _ U
                      in line 4:   _ U U _ U U _ U _ U

Once Gaul had been conquered from the Atlantic to the Rhine by Julius Caesar, 58 to 50 B.C., it was apparent that a great wedge of hostile territory—Switzerland-Austria-Germany—divided the Roman Empire north of the Mediterranean into two parts. The wedge was all the more dangerous in that its pointed end thrust down through the Alps into northern Italy itself. The campaigns of 16 B.C. against the Germanic Sygambri, mentioned in the headnote to *Odes* 4.2, were already part of Augustus's master plan for subduing that great wedge of territory. In 15 B.C., with Augustus personally directing operations from Lugdunum (Lyon) on the Rhone, a double offensive was launched, one moving eastward from Lugdunum under the command of the emperor's 27-year-old stepson Tiberius Claudius Nero (the future emperor), the other moving northward from what is now northern Italy under the command of the emperor's second stepson, 23-year-old Drusus Claudius Nero.

Upon command from Augustus, so Suetonius's "Life of Horace" reports, our poet composed the present ode in honor of Drusus's victory and *Odes* 4.14 in honor of Tiberius's victory.

Pindar was his model for the rhetorical sweep of the opening stanzas, for the "digression" in lines 18–22, for the approximation to "myth" in lines 38–72, and for the reflective conclusion in lines 73–76.

Much like that mighty, thunderbolt-bearing bird
Assigned dominion over all birds of air
  For proven loyalty in fetching
    Golden-haired Ganymede for the god-king,

Once youth and innate vigor expel him from   5
The nest, of strife and perils still unaware,
  The rain-storms being done, the winds of
    Springtime now teach him some startling lessons

In terror; then his natural impulse drives
Him down on sheepfolds enemy-fashion; soon   10
  Against resisting dragons he has
    Gone, out of lust for both feast and battle;

Or as the fawn at pasture in lovely grass
Espies the lion weaned only lately from
  Its tawny dam and realizes   15
    Danger and death in a single instant:

So Drusus waging war in the Rhaetian Alps
Was sighted by Vindélici — (why from times
  Remote it was their custom still to
    Use Amazonian battleaxes   20

As chosen weapon, I have yet failed to learn:
No use in knowing everything) — but those hordes
  So long unvanquished, being vanquished
    Now by our youthful commanders' shrewdness,

Have seen what inborn nature and mind well trained 25
Within a house of loftiest auspices
  Can do, and what Augustus has in
    View as a father to sons of Nero.

From strong and good men issue the strong and good;
In cattle and in horses the sire's good strain   30
  In seen, and fiercely warlike eagles
    Never have peaceable doves as offspring;

And yet an inborn vigor requires a guide;
From right things nurtured, hearts gain an oaken strength;
  As soon as right behavior lapses   35
    Natural excellence grows disfigured.

How great a debt you owe to the Neros, Rome!
Recall Metáurus River, and Hasdrubal

Destroyed, and how the wondrous sunlight
40   Burst from the darkness across all Latium

When first the sign of victory smiled on us
Since through Italian cities grim Hannibal
           Began to rage like fire in pitchpine
               Or, over Sicily's waves, the southwind.

45 But then as efforts throve, and our Roman youth
Were gaining strength, and temples in ruins from
           The godless Punic devastation
               Offered our gods once again some shelter,

Then up spoke that perfidious Hannibal
50 Anew: "We are but deer and the prey of wolves,
           Pursuing foes whom we would conquer
               Better by cheating and sheer avoidance.

This is the race that bravely from burned-out Troy,
By Tuscan storm-waves buffeted, brought its gods,
55   Its children, and its aged fathers
               On to Ausónian shores and cities,

As tough as holm-oaks hacked with the double ax,
Of boughs dark green on Álgidus' fertile ridge,
           That from the very hands of damage
60   Gather new impluse to life and vigor.

No fiercer grew that Hydra with severed head
Against contending Hercules, to his grief;
           No greater monster bred in Colchis
               Or in the Thebes of Echíon's era.

65 Try drowning them, and out they come cleaner washed,
Wrestle them down, and up they rebound unharmed
           With every sort of glory covered,
               Waging such battles as women tell of.

I shall dispatch no trumpeting envoys back
70 To Carthage with these tidings: all hope is dead,
           All fortunes of our name have died with
               Hasdrubal murdered and taken from us."

No feat can fail the Claudian strength of hand,
Which is sustained by Jupiter's will divine
75   And guided by the wisest counsels
               Ever accorded, through bitter warfare.

1–12   Like a young eagle, prompted by instinct alone, Drusus has pounced on the enemy. "Proven loyalty" defines Drusus's role as army commander, while "Assigned" conveys the political "fact" that the command itself is at the will of "the supreme one," Augustus, who is equal to Jupiter. In Christian terms Jehovah sends the Archangel Michael. In terms of the note to *Odes* 3.20.15–16, the eagle's role agrees with Vergil but contradicts Homer and Ovid.

5–12   The eagle's development is in three stages: first flight in spring, attack on *un*dangerous sheep, attack on dangerous dragons (*dracones*), that is, snakes. Moore remarks: "The fact that young eagles do not fly until late summer need not disturb us."

Vividly described eagle-snake struggles occur in *Aeneid* 11. 751–6 and *Iliad* 12. 201–7.

"Resisting dragons" = *reluctantis dracones*; compare Kenneth Grahame's story for children, *The Reluctant Dragon* (1898).

13–16   *Or* (from the viewpoint opposite to 1–12), like an unwary fawn seized by a lion, the enemy have been surprised by Drusus.

18   The enemy are the Vindélici: Thracians, says Porphyrio in commenting on this line in the 200s A.D.; Liburnians (from N of Venice), says Servius, commenting, around 350 A.D., on *Aeneid* 1. 243; definitely Kelts, says Joshua Whatmough, 1970 (*The Dialects of Ancient Gaul*, p. 1156), on the basis of proper names associated with them

18–22   The "Pindaric digression" is so inept that some Horatian enthusiasts have wished to see it as an impertinent meddling with the text on the part of some editor or copyist.

22–24   Drusus's initial victory of 15 B.C. was won near Tridentum (Trent), after which he proceeded northward along the River Átagis (Italian *Ádige,* German *Etsch*) and through the Brenner Pass to effect a junction with the army of his elder brother Tiberius. Further victories were won in the valley of the River Aenus (Inn), in the Tyrol.

The Roman Province of Rhaetia/Raetia, as subsequently organized, included the easternmost Swiss canton of the Grisons (German *Graubünden*), the Tyrol (now divided between Austria and Italy), and southern Bavaria to the Danube. Bavarian Augsburg was founded as *Augusta Vindelicum,* "Augusta (for Augustus) of the Vindélici."

27–28   Tiberius and Drusus, sons of the Empress Livia Drusilla, were brought up in the imperial household, Tiberius having been four years old at his mother's marriage to Octavius Caesar on January 17, 38 B.C. and Drusus having been born a short time after that date. The boys were 19 and 15 respectively when, in 23 B.C., the emperor's nephew and heir, young Marcellus, died; see the note to *Odes* 3.14.7. Thereupon these stepsons became contingent heirs to the empire, depending, of course, on what might come of the offspring from Julia, the emperor's daughter and only child (from his first marriage).

Drusus married the second of Mark Antony's daughters by Octavia—both daughters being named Antonia, and by this "Antonia II" became the grandfather of the emperor Caligula (Gaius Claudius Nero Caesar Germanicus, commonly called Caligula, "Little Boot," ruled 37 to 41 A.D.) and the father of the emperor Claudius (Tiberius Claudius Nero Caesar Drusus, ruled 41 to 54 A.D.). After the victory of 15 B.C. Drusus held public offices and simultaneously pursued a military career in Germany, but, as consul in 9 B.C., he died, at age 29 of natural causes, in his German command post. He was buried in the Mausoleum of Augustus, the ruined hulk of which still stands where the emperor built it near the Tiber bank in the extreme NW corner of the ancient city, and where young Marcellus had been buried in 23 B.C., Agrippa in 12, and Octavia in 11.

37–44   At a point where Pindar might introduce mythological matter appropriate to his theme Horace pays tribute to the ancestor of Drusus (and Tiberius) who was the hero of the battle of Metaurus River in 207 B.C.

Hannibal was then at Canusium in Apulia (see S.1.5.91) facing an army under consul Marcus Claudius Nero, but inactive until his brother Hasdrubal, who had already crossed the Alps, could bring strong reenforcements down from northern Italy. Meanwhile, at the Metáurus (now the Metauro) River, which empties into the Adriatic 250 miles north of Canusium, Hasdrubal was facing a not too numerous army under co-consul Marcus Livius. Nero took 7,000 picked men, made a forced march of six days, combined the two Roman armies under cover darkness, and in the ensuing battle defeated the enemy and killed Hasdrubal. On the very next night he started the return march of 250 miles, reaching his own seriously depleted forces at Canusium without Hannibal's ever being aware of his absence. There he had Hasdrubal's severed head thrown over in front of Hannibal's outposts. Livy's "History of Rome" 27. 43–51 recounts the exploit at length.

The name "Nero" was Sabine for "strong and energetic," Suetonius explained for Roman readers in his "Life of Tiberius" 1.

49–72   This historically impossible speech of Hannibal represents Horace's patriotic invention. Lines 53–56, for instance, reflect the opening of the recently published *Aeneid*.

49   "Perfidious" (*perfidus*)was the regular Roman term for any Carthaginian.

56   "Ausonian" originally identified an area of S Italy; poets used it as equivalent of "Italian."

58   Álgidus ridge was venerated by Romans for its shrine to Diana-of-the-woods and its sacred pasture lands; see the note to *Odes* 1.21.5–8.

61–62   Whenever Hercules, in his battle against the water-monster Hydra, lopped off one of its serpent heads, two or three new heads quickly grew in place of the lost one.

63–64   In Colchis a dragon guarded the famous golden fleece. At Thebes, Echíon was one of the men who grew from the planted teeth of a slain dragon.

75–76   The "wisest counsels" are provided, of course, by Augustus. Horace astutely qualifies his praise of Drusus (and Tiberius).

4.5.   *Divis orte bonis, optume Romulae*

Meter: in lines 1, 2, and 3: $\_ > \_ \cup \cup \_ \ \_ \cup \cup \_ \cup \_$
            in line 4: $\_ > \_ \cup \cup \_ \cup \_$

Born when gods were benign,   noblest and best of wards
Over Romulus' race,   you are too long away;
In the Senate's august   conclave you pledged your word,
   Vowing early return: come home!

5   Gracious leader, restore   light to our fatherland;
When your countenance shines   down on this nation like
Springtime's brightness itself,   days are more sweetly spent,
   More resplendently shows the sun.

Like a mother whose son   southwinds with hateful breath
10   Keep detaining beyond   waves of Carpáthus' seas,
Wasting more than a year's   time in prolonged delays
   From his dearly beloved home,

Saying all of her prayers,   making her every vow,
Never letting her eyes   stray from the curving shore,
15   So this country of ours,   faithful in yearning hope,
   Pleads for Caesar's return to her.

Safely cattle now roam   over the pasturelands

Ceres nourishes fields,   Blessing provides increase,
By the sea lanes at peace   mariners safely sail,
   Trust most dreads being found remiss,   20

No defilement now stains   households of chastity,
Law and usage have banned   every offensive taint,
Fathers' features are now   welcomed in newborn babes,
   Guilt and punishment walk as one.

Who fears Parthians now,   who fears the icy Scyths,   25
Who fears shaggy-haired broods   Germany may have bred,
While our Caesar is safe?   Who is in much concern
   Over war in Iberia?

Each man settles his day's   work in his native hills
And to widower trees   marries his growing vines,   30
Then contentedly comes   home to his wine and bids
   Your divinity be his guest;

You are honored with prayers,   wine is poured out to you,
And your Spirit enshrined   nearest his hearthside Lars
Is revered, the way Greece   steadfastly bears in mind   35
   Castor's Spirit, and Hercules'.

"Blessèd leader, vouchsafe   times of extended peace
To Hesperian lands!"   Such is the prayer we pray,
Dry of throat at the dawn,   slaked with our evening wine
   When the sun is below the sea.   40

3–4   At his hurried departure in 16 B.C. Augustus intended only a brief absence, but
direction of the campaigns of Tiberius and Drusus kept him more than three years (16 to
13 B.C.) at Lugdunum in Gaul (Lyon, France). The present poem probably dates to 14
B.C.

10   Carpáthus Island, between Crete and Rhodes, is a decorative detail, as in *Odes* 1.35.7.

14   "Curving shore" (*Curvo litore*) repeats the stock phrase of Epode 10, 22.

18   "Blessing" (personified) is *Faustitas,* a word occuring only here.

19   The sea lanes were cleared of pirates after the defeat of Sextus Pompey in 36 B.C.

21–24   Horace claims that the laws of 18 B.C. concerning marriage and adultery have been
totally effective; see the *Centennial Hymn* 17–18 and note. But in the 9-volume Roman
History written by Dio Cassius between 211 and 222 A.D. Augustus is said to have stayed
away from Rome those three years, 16 to 13 B.C., to avoid the unpopularity incurred by
those reforms.

25–28   Horace overstates Roman conquests, as usual. The Parthian "submission" of 20 B.C.
was unofficial and unlasting; defeat of the "Scyths" was largely fanciful; "Germania"
was never to be more than partially conquered; only the Spanish peace of 19 B.C. was
real and durable.

30   See Epode 2, 10 and note.

32–35   "Your divinity" (32) = *te . . . deum;* "your Spirit" (34) = *tuum . . . numen.* People had
indeed, and of their own accord, begun placing a little bust or figurine of Augustus
among their household gods to whom they offered ritual food and drink before starting
their own meal, but the little icon represented, not Augustus the man, but his "Spirit"

(*Genius*). Horace himself will define this "Spirit" in E.2.2.187–9. Before 1917 Russian peasants included an icon of the Tsar among the holy pictures in the "icon corner" of their huts.

38 "Hesperian lands" = Italy; see the note to *Odes* 2.1.32.

4.6. *Dive, quem proles Niobea magnae*

Meter: Sapphic stanza: in lines 1, 2, and 3: $\_ \cup \_ > \_ \cup \cup \_ \cup \_ \cup$
in line 4: $\_ \cup \cup \_ \cup$

God, whose vengeance Níobē's children suffered
For their mother's blasphemy, Títyus for
Rape, and he who all but undid Troy's greatness,
    Phthian Achilles,

5   Who, outranking all except you in prowess,
Though he was of Thetis the sea-nymph born and
Smote Dardánus' ramparts until they wavered
    Under his spearshaft, —

Like a pine, however, by axes bitten,
10   He — or like a cypress by southwinds battered —
Fell, and in the Teucrian dust was measured
    Mighty of stature;

(He would not have hidden within Minerva's
Horse, misleading Trojans to ill-starred revel
15   Or the court of Priam to show their joy in
    Holiday dances,

But in open warfare — oh, horror! — would have
Grimly sent male infants to die in Grecian
Flames, not sparing even the ones enclosed in
20   Wombs of their mothers,

Had the Father God, at your own and lovely
Venus' plea, not nodded Aenéas favor
For his future walls to be founded under
    Happier omens);

25   Clear-voiced Thalia's teacher and lyric singer,
You whose hair is laved in the stream of Xanthus,
Phoebus: guard the Dáunian Muse's glory,
    Beardless Agýieus!

Phoebus has inspired me, and Phoebus gave me
30   Technic skill in song and the name of poet.

High-born maiden daughters and scions nobly
    Born of your fathers,

Wards of chaste Diana whose bow is flexed to
Drop the stags and lynxes that flee her hunting,
Keep the Lesbic rhythm and mark my thumbstroke   35
    Setting the cadence,

Duly hymn the son of Latóna-mother,
Duly hymn the waxing of Noctiluca
Prospering the harvest and swift in sending
    Months in their sequence.   40

As a wedded woman you shall say proudly:
"At the glad centennial celebration
I performed the hymn for the gods, as taught by
    Horace the Poet."

"God," in line 1, goes with "Phoebus" in line 27, everything in between being a series of observations, first about Phoebus Apollo, then about Achilles, all in grammatical suspension. See E.1.15.1–25 and note for a comparable tour de force of grammatical structure.

1–4   Where the *Centennial Hymn* recalls only the benign aspects of Phoebus Apollo, these lines recall his fearsome aspects:

- Níobē boasted that she had borne seven sons and seven daughters (to Amphíon of Thebes; *Odes* 3.11.2; E.1.18;41–44; E.2.3.394–6), whereas Leto/Latóna was mother only to the twins Apollo and Artemis/Diana. For her presumption Apollo slew the seven sons, Artemis/Diana the seven daughters, with arrows. A statuary group representing the slayings stood in the portico of Augustus's new library-temple to Apollo of 28 B.C.; see the note to E.1.3.17.
- Apollo and Artemis also slew Títyus with arrows for attempted rape of their mother at her arrival in Delphi. *Odes* 2.14.9;3.4.77–79; and 3.11.21, and notes, speak of Títyus's everlasting punishment but do not mention how he died.
- The dying Hector warns Achilles that Apollo may some day slay him (*Iliad* 22. 359–360), but that event is not related by Homer; it *is* related by Ovid (*Metamorphoses* 12. 580–606) and elsewhere, and in lines 9–13 of the present poem, where it is to be understood that Apollo's arrow brought Achilles down in the Teucrian (Trojan) dust.

5–24   The poem devotes excessive attention to Achilles:

- who came from the region of Phthia, in southern Thessaly (4);
- whose prowess was surpassed only by Apollo (5);
- who was half divine as the son of the sea nymph Thetis (and mortal Peleus) (6);
- who mightily battered the walls of Troy, the city "co-founded" by Dardánus (7–8); see the note to *Odes* 1.15.10;
- who was slain by Apollo's arrow before Troy (9–12);
- who was too forthright to participate in the trick of the Trojan Horse (13–16); the story of the hollow wooden horse filled with armed Greek soldiers is not in the *Iliad,* but is briefly summarized late in *Odyssey* 8 and reported by other writers. Horace surely has in mind Vergil's version in *Aeneid* 2.13–249.
- who would, however, have perpetrated atrocities in *open* warfare, such as Agamemnon urged Menelaus to commit in *Iliad* 6. 57–60; (lines 17–20);

all this so that Horace can say that Apollo (together with Venus and Jupiter) agreed to the re-founding of Troy as Rome; again Horace is thinking in terms of the *Aeneid.*

25–28   Horace comes back to Apollo:

- as *Mousagétēs* (leader of the Muses), Apollo taught poetry to Thalia, "the flowering Muse" (who later became the Muse of Comedy) (25);
- who laves his golden (*xanthós*) hair in either the Xanthus River of Lycia (SW Turkey) or "the river/ who is called Xanthos by the gods, but by mortals Skamandros," (*Iliad* 20. 74), that is, the Scamánder, near Troy (line 26);
- who is implored to "guard"—the verb at last!—"the Dáunian (Apulian) Muse's glory," that is, Horace as poet (27);
- "Agýieus," from Greek *aguía,* "road, street, public place," or "(guardian) of streets and public places." Moore says the term is common in Greek poetry but occurs only here in Latin poetry.

31–32   Horace now addresses the 27 youths and 27 girls who are to sing his Centennial Hymn on June 3, 17 B.C. and who had to be nobly born, unmarried, and with both parents living.

35–38   The double chorus of 54 is to "Keep the Lesbic rhythm," that is, the meter of the Sapphic stanza form; Horace, with his lyre, sets the cadence. The hymn is addressed to Apollo, Diana, and their mother Latóna.

     Belatedly we perceive that the poem depicts a rehearsal for the actual performance of June 3, 17 B.C.

     "Noctiluca" ("night-shining") was an archaic term for Diana as moon goddess. There was a shrine to Noctiluca on the Palatine Hill.

41–44   In the final stanza of the *Centennial Hymn* all 54 voices spoke in first-person-singular, as Greek tragic choruses did; here Horace addresses only the 27 girls, and he speaks to them in the singular and quotes their future words in the singular.

     "Poet" = *vates;* see the note to *Odes* 2.6.24.

4.7.   *Diffugere nives, redeunt iam gramina campis*

Meter:

in the odd-numbered lines: _ U U _U U _U U _U U _U U _U

in the even-numbered lines: _ U U _U U _

     Gone are the snows; over meadows the green of the grass is revived and
          Trees shake out foliage hair;
     Earth is renewing her changes, and rivers, abating their freshets,
          Bide by their channels once more;

5   Nymphs now attend on the three sister-Graces who lead them all naked
          Forth to their dances and songs.
     "Cherish no hope to be deathless," the seasons remind us, and speeding
          Hours of day say the same:
     Ice under westwinds is softened, the summer treads roughshod on springtime,

10   Apple-decked autumn pours forth
     Fruits that are destined to perish together and soon, and the dead of
          Midwinter stillness returns.
     Losses sustained in the skies are, however, made good by the rapid
          Moons, whereas we, when we die,

15   Are, with Aenéas the good and with opulent Tullus and Ancus,

Nothing but dust and a shade.
Who can say whether the gods will add times of tomorrow to sums of
    Time we have lived till today?
What you expend on the Spirit existing beside you through life will
    Not serve the greed of your heir.   20
Once you are dead and illustrious judgment upon you is passed by
    Minos in final decree,
Nothing, Torquatus, — not birth, not your orator's gifts, not your ways of
    Duty, — can bring you to life.
Nor can Diana deliver Hippólytus, chaste though he was, from   25
    Ghosts of the netherworld dark;
Théseus himself cannot wrench his belovèd Piríthoüs free from
    Próserpine's fettering chains.

1–6   These opening lines resemble the beginning of *Odes* 1.4.1–6, but then the present mood turns somber.

12–13   The constellations regularly disappear and return, "restored" by the months in cycle.

15   Three illustrious Romans long deceased: Aenéas, the founding father, and early kings Tullus Hostilius (672–640 B.C.) and Ancus Martius (640–616 B.C.).

19   The "Spirit existing beside you through life" means "yourself," as in *Odes* 3.17.14. The present line is paraphrased in terms of Horace's own definition of the "Spirit" in E.2.2.187–9. Compare also *Odes* 4.5.32–35 and note.

21   Minos, son of Zeus by Európa (*Odes* 3.27.25–76) and ruler of Crete, was seen as a ghost by Odysseus/Ulysses, who says, late in *Odyssey* 11: ". . . I saw Minos, Zeus's illustrious son, with his golden sceptre, enthroned in the broad gate of the house of Hades to judge the dead, who sat or stood before his seat enquiring of the King upon their sentences."
                                           (T. E. Lawrence translation)
    In *Aeneid* 6. 432 Minos is still at the gates of hell as a judge, but his special task is investigation of persons innocently condemned to death. Dante (*Inferno* 5. 4–15) makes him a snarling demon penetrating the guilt of sinners at the gate of hell and dispatching each of them downward to appropriate "circles" according to the number of times he winds his tail around himself.

23   Torquatus is the lawyer to whom Horace sent E.1.5. as a jocular invitation to a September 22nd dinner. He was doubtless of the lawyer family of the Manlii Torquati.

25–28   In Italian myth, as opposed to Greek, Diana *was* able to have her votary Hippólytus revived from death and brought, under the name of Virbius, to her sacred grove by Lake Nemi in the Alban Hills. See the opening pages of Frazer's *The Golden Bough.*
    Théseus and his boon companion—some say his twin brother—Piríthoüs (Greek *Peir-*) ventured to Hades to get Próserpine as a bride for Piríthoüs (see *Odes* 3.4.79–80 and note), but both were held captive by the irate lord of the dead. Four years later, Hercules, on his descent into hell, managed to release Théseus but not Piríthoüs. Horace may have in mind a variant form of the story: to some degree mythology confused Théseus with Hercules.

4.8.   *Donarem pateras grataque commodus,*

Meter: "the lesser Asclepiadic," as in *Odes* 1.1 and 3.30.
          _ U _ U U _   _ U U _ U _

Gifts of ritual bowls   I would bestow, and bronze
Vases suiting each friend's   taste, Censorínus, yes,
Tripods such as the Greek   victors received, and your
Gift would not be the least   precious of all the lot,
5   *If*, that is, I but owned   works of the different arts
Such as Scopas produced   or as Parrhásius,
One creating from stone,   one from his liquid paints,
Experts both at the shaped   likeness of man and god.
No such power is mine,   nor, with your wealth and taste,
10   Have you needed to go   hankering for such toys.
You find poems a joy,   poems I *can* bestow,
And, what's more, can explain   poetry's value too.
      Marble likeness and name   carved at the state's behest
Bring no leader's achieved   fame or his spirit back
15   Once he passes to death;   nor do retreat and rout,
Threats of Hannibal hurled   backwards upon himself,
Devastation that burned   impious Carthage down,
Give that man, who from tamed   Africa won a name
But no other reward,   glory to equal what
20   Fair Calabria's Muse   won for him later; nor
Will you profit at all   from an accomplishment
If no book tells the tale.   What would the son of Mars
Be?, or Ília?, had   envious silence then
Stifled impulse to sing   merits of Romulus?
25   Deeds, acclaim, and the great   power of poets' tongues
Bring Aeácus to life   back from the waves of Styx
And in Isles of the Blest   set him immortalized.
Muses will not permit   praiseworthy men to die:
Muses grant them the skies.   Laboring Hercules,
30   Thanks to poetry, now   banquets on high with Jove;
Poets' art makes the twins,   Castor and Pollux, bright
Stars who rescue the ships   riding the gale at sea;
Liber also, with green   vine tendrils round his brow,
Guides entreaties to fair   outcomes desired in prayer.

1   The occasion for gift-giving is unknown.
2   Gaius Marcius Censorínus was consul in 8 B.C., the year of Horace's death; see the
     concluding lines of Suetonius's *Vita Horatii,* p. 384.
6   Painter Parrhásius flourished 450–400 B.C., sculptor Scopas of Paros, 400–350 B.C.
11   In the text, "*I* can" is "we can" (*possumus*), perhaps for a certain degree of formality.
12 ff.   Horace "explains poetry's value" through the rest of the poem. It "keeps history
     alive," as statues and inscriptions fail to do, it makes Aeácus immortal, it defies Romulus
     and Hercules, and sets Castor and Pollux as everlasting stars in the sky.
15–20   In 202 B.C. Publius Cornelius Scipio (the Younger) ended the Second Punic War by
     annihilating a Carthaginian army at Zama, SW of modern Tunis, thereby acquiring the
     added name of "Africanus," but, as he said, no money.
     The victory was celebrated in the *Annals* of the poet Ennius, who died in 169 B.C.

and who, from his birthplace at Rudiae in Calabria, was known as "Calabria's Muse." That Horace studied the *Annals* in school is shown by quotations in S.1.2.37, S.1.4.61–62, and E.1.10.9.

In 146 B.C. Scipio Aemilianus "burned impious Carthage down" at the end of the Third Punic War (when the early Scipio was 37 years dead and Ennius was 23 years dead).

Perhaps because both Scipios were surnamed "Africanus" Horace treats them as a single person. The apparent blunder is unexplained. But see the note to E.2.1.162.

22–24   For Ília see the note to *Odes* 1.2.16–20. Romulus founded Rome and ruled 753–716 B.C., and Ília, as his mother, was earlier still. Latin poetry is close to nonexistent before 240 B.C. Thus Horace is either imagining early, lost poets or else he is speaking loosely of more recent poets who inherited and carried on a tradition.

25–27   The Isles of the Blest = "the Happy Isles" of Epode 16, 42. In *Odes* 2.13.22 Aeácus was a judge of the dead in the subterranean realm, his usual role, along with his two brothers Minos and Rhadamánthys; see the note to line 21 of the foregoing ode.

Aeácus was the son of Zeus and Európa (*Odes* 3.27.25–76), the father of Péleus, and the grandfather of Achilles.

29–33   Three cases of mortal heroes who became gods: Hercules, Castor and Pollux, and Liber/Bacchus. (In *Odes* 3.3.9–15 five such heroes were named: Pollux, Hercules, Augustus (!), Bacchus, and Quirínus/Romulus.) The accounts of deification are often obscure and complex.

33–34   Reduced to prose, these last two lines mean simply: And Liber too is a god.

4.9.   *Ne forte credas interitura quae*

Meter: Alcaic stanza: in lines 1 and 2:   U _ U _ > _ U U _ U _
                          in line 3:   U _ U _ U _ U _ U
                          in line 4:   _ U U _ U U _ U _ U

You have no cause to think that the words which I,
By far-resounding Áufidus born, compose
    For singing to the lyre, in meters
        All but unknown before mine, will perish:

Though highest place Maeónian Homer holds,   5
Yet Pindar's works are not overwhelmed by death,
    The Céan's and Alcáeus' are not
        Lost, nor Stesíchorus' stately Muses,

Nor are the sportive squibs of Anácreon
Destroyed by time; and still there is breath of love   10
    And passions live that were entrusted
        By the Aeólian girl to poems.

To blaze in lust for hair a seducer wears
In comely trim, for raiment of garish gold
    On him and on his vassals, was not   15
        Helen of Sparta's unique experience;

The first of arrows sped from Cydónian bow
Was not dispatched by Teucer; and Troy's was not
    The first of sieges; nor was giant
        Idomonéus the only fighter

To venture single combat that Muses vaunt;
Fierce Hector dared not first, nor Deíphobus,
    To suffer painful blows defending
        Virtuous spouse and belovèd children.

Before great Agamemnon there lived a host
Of heroes, now submerged in the endless night
    Without our tears and nameless all, for
        Lack of a consecrate poet's praises.

There is but little difference between mere sloth
And manly worth deprived of its true report.
    I shall not leave you unadorned in
        Writings of mine, nor permit your many

Accomplished labors, Lollius, such a doom
In bleak oblivion. Yours is a soul possessed
    Of prudent foresight, steadfast both in
        Times of good fortune and times that waver,

To cheats and frauds a foe, but yourself aloof
From money's self-assertion above all things,
    A consul not for one year only,
        Rather a judge for as many years as

A good and faithful man who maintains the rule
Of upright conduct over expediency,
    Declining bribes of wicked men and
        Fighting their hordes to prevail against them.

A man of vast possessions does not, by rights,
Deserve the name of fortunate: we reserve
    That term as more befitting one who
        Uses the gifts of the gods with wisdom,

Enduring all the harshness of poverty
And worse than Lethe dreading dishonor, one
    Who for the sake of cherished friends or
        Fatherland feels unafraid of dying.

20

25

30

35

40

45

50

---

2   The Áufidus (Ofánto) River near Horace's birthplace, as in *Odes* 3.30.10 and note.

4   "All but unknown" = *non ante volgatas*, "not previously made common (among the multitude)," a curiously hedging phrase after *Odes* 3.30.13–14.

5   "Maeónian," as in *Odes* 1.6.2 and note, = "of Smyrna" (modern Izmír), Homer's birthplace.

5–12   Though Homeric epic is the greatest poetry, immortality is also granted to such
serious lyric poets as:
- Pindar (as described in *Odes* 4.2.1–27 and notes);
- Simónides of (the island of) Céos, as in the note to *Odes* 2.1.38;
- Alcáeus of Lesbos, Horace's model in many of the Odes;
- Stesíchorus (ca. 640–555 B.C.) of Himéra (Roman Thermae Himeráeae, now
  Termini Imerése), E of Palermo on the N coast of Sicily. His stately (*graves*) poems
  sometimes included narrative matter, and one of them contains the earliest
  known version of Aenéas's voyage to the west:

and to such lighter lyric poets as:
- Anácreon of Teos (ca. 572 to ca. 487 B.C.); see Epode 14,9 and *Odes* 1.17.19 and
  note. Only fragments survive of his charming, small poems, but some 60 imita-
  tions called "Anacreontics" are preserved from Hellenistic times, and these were
  much admired in the 18th century by poets of western Europe. In the 17th
  century Robert Herrick often composed "Anacreontics" of his own.
- Sappho of Lesbos, who composed in Aeólic dialect.

13–30   Many human experiences are common enough, but we remember only the cases
reported by the poets,—a variation on the thought of lines 13–34 of the foregoing ode.
        "Helen of Troy" was Menelaus's queen in Sparta before going off with Paris.
Compare *Odes* 1.15.13–20 about Paris's hair.
        Other examples, all from the *Iliad*:
- Teucer (of Sálamis, as in *Odes* 1.7.20 and 1.15.24) was the best bowman among the
  Greeks at Troy (*Iliad* 13. 313). (The Trojans were called Teucrians from a
  different Teucer whom Horace nowhere mentions, but see the notes about
  Dardánus in *Odes* 1.5.10 and 4.6.7.)
- "Cydónian" = "Cretan," from a city of Cydónia (now Khania) in NW Crete.
- Idomonéus of Crete was the spear-famed leader of Cretan forces at Troy.
- Hector and Deíphobus (pronounce: day-IF-obus) were princes of Troy.
- Agamemnon was supreme commander of the Greeks at Troy. The beginning of
  this admired stanza (25–28) is semiproverbial: *Vixere fortes ante Agamemnona / multi.*
- Line 28 "Poet" = *vates*; see the note to *Odes* 2.6.24.

33   Marcus Lollius (probably an older relative of the young Lollius Maximus of E.1.2) was
the General defeated by the Germanic Sygambri in 16 B.C. (see the headnote to *Odes*
4.2.), and the present poem may have been composed for his consolation. See below.

40–44   Even ancient editor Porphyrio found these lines grammatically troublesome. The
present translator has done what he could with them.

Marcus Lollius arranged, in 25 B.C., the Roman annexation of Galatia (now the middle
portion of Turkey, centered on Ankara) following the death of the last Galatian king,
Amýntas; see the note to Epode 9, 17–18. In 21 B.C. he was consul, in 19 and 18 proconsul of
Macedonia, and in 17 and 16 deputy for Augustus in northern Gaul. His defeat by the
Sygambri in 16 had to be made good by the campaigns of Tiberius and Drusus in 15 (see *Odes*
4.4 and 4.14), and then for a time he was little heard of.
        With the death of Drusus in 9 B.C. (see the note to *Odes* 4.4.27–28), Tiberius seemed likely
to succeed his stepfather as emperor. By his marriage to Vipsania, daughter of Agrippa and
the emperor's daughter Julia, he came the closer to succession, but Augustus had begun to
look with favoring eye on his blood-grandsons by Julia, Gaius Caesar (born 20 B.C.) and
Lucius Caesar (born 17 B.C.), who were Tiberius's young brothers-in-law. But when Agrippa
died in 12, Tiberius received imperial command to divorce Vipsania (whom he dearly loved)
in order to marry Julia, his mother-in-law! Therewith young Gaius and Lucius became his
stepsons and his rivals for the succession.
        In 2 B.C. Marcus Lollius was appointed personal counsellor to 19-year-old Gaius Caesar
while the latter toured the Near East, patently as preparation for becoming emperor. Some

disagreement arising, Lollius died—or committed suicide—in 2 A.D. amid accusations of taking bribes from Asiatic rulers. Twenty years later Tiberius repeated the charges in a funeral speech for Lollius's successor as Governor of Syria.

Thus the man grandly praised for honesty and integrity in *Odes* 4.9 was officially declared a scoundrel at his death, and when he was twenty years in his grave the ruling emperor was at pains to repeat that declaration formally and publicly. Something here does not ring true, and there is at least the possiblity that Lollius was the scapegoat amid sinister intrigues of the imperial family.

4.10.   *O crudelis adhuc et Veneris muneribus potens,*

Meter: _ U _ U U _ _ U U _ _ U U _ U _

Ah, how cruel you are   while you are still   master of Venus' gifts!
When your cheek of disdain   comes to be plumed   with an unwelcome down,
When cascades of your hair,   falling in full   waves to your shoulders now,
Start to thin and to shed,   when into rose-   damask of fleshly tint
5 Harshness comes and a changed   roughness of face,   then, Ligurínus, then,
As your mirror reflects   someone unknown,   you will protest: "Alas!,
What I now understand,   why did I not   see as a lad? Or else,
May I not have again   cheeks unimpaired,   suiting what I know now?"

5   For Ligurínus, see *Odes* 4.1.33–40 and notes.

In its external form the poem imitates epigrams of "the Greek anthology" (or "Palatine Anthology"); Moore suggests 12,35 and 11,37.

4.11.   *Est mihi nonum superantis annum*

Meter: Sapphic stanza: in lines 1,2, and 3:   _ U _ > _ U U _ U _ U
                                    in line 4:   _ U U _ U

Let me see, now: here is the jar of Alban
More than nine years old; in the garden, Phyllis,
There is parsley ready for weaving crowns, and
        Ivy aplenty, —

5   You are always radiant with it in your
Hair; the silver gleams; and with boughs of sacred
Green bedecked, the altar delights in lamb's blood
        Votively sprinkled;

All the hands are busy, the serving lads and
Serving maids are rushing in all directions;   10
Spurting flames send smoke in a twisted column
    Murkily upwards.

What it is we celebrate, asking you to
Join our revel here, is the Ides dividing
Sea-born Venus' month into halves this thirteenth   15
    Morning of April,

Which I rightly reverence and keep with almost
Greater joy than birthdays of mine, since from this
Date my own Maecenas began the counted
    Years of his lifetime.   20

Télephus, the lad you are looking for, is
Taken by a girl of a higher station,
Rich, and frisky too, and she holds him fettered
    Sweetly in bondage.

Hopes too high, from Pháëthon burnt, take warning;   25
And a bitter lesson Bellérophon was
Taught when wingèd Pégasus balked at bearing
    Skyward an earthling:

These examples bid you pursue befitting
Objects only and to renounce improper   30
Hopes as thoughts unthinkable. Come along, then,
    Last of my loves, (for

I shall not feel ardor again for any
Woman), learn the harmonies I will teach your
Loving voice to sing: by a song our dreary   35
    Troubles are lightened.

---

1   Alban was the third-best wine, after Cáecuban and Falernian, says Pliny the Elder (23 to
79 A.D.) in his *Natural History* 14.64.

2   About Phyllis we know only what the present poem conveys.

3   Parsley crowns for dinner guests, as in *Odes* 1.36.16 and 2.7.24.

4   Ivy crowns for the after-dinner drinking. Bacchus, as Jane Harrison explains
(*Prolegómena* . . . , p. 428), favored "every tree and plant and natural product" except the
olive, his preference for vine leaves being a late development. "Ivy especially was sacred
to him; his Maenads chewed ivy leaves for inspiration, as the Delphic prophetess chewed
the bay."

6–7   "With boughs of sacred green" = *castis verbenis, verbena* meaning any fresh greenery,
even grass; see the note to *Odes* 1.19.14.

7–8   The blood of the freshly slaughtered lamb is sprinkled on the altar, but the diners will
feast on the meat.

14–16   *Venus marina,* as in *Odes* 3.26.5 and note. The Ides (*Idūs,* a plural) was the 13th day of
all months except March, May, July, and October, when it was the 15th. The word came

from Etruscan *iduare*, "to divide," according to Macrobius: *Saturnalia* 1.15.17, around 400 A.D.

18–20   April 13th, we learn here, was Maecenas's birth*day*; J.—M. André (in *Mécène*, 1967) estimates the birth *year* as between 74 and 70 B.C., thus making Maecenas 5 to 9 years older than Horace. The present poem regards an April 13th of some year between 23 and 13, possibly 15 or 14 B.C., if lines 31–34 below stand parallel to *Odes* 4.1.29–30.

In this fourth Book of Odes, which is oriented primarily toward the emperor, this is the only mention of Maecenas; it is also the last mention of him in Horace's works, though the *Vita Horatii* shows there was no abatement of the old friendship.

21   "Télephus" is a random fictional name, as in *Odes* 1.13.1 and note and 3.19.26.

25   Pháëthon (Greek: "the shining one"), son of Helios, the sun god, persuaded his father to let him drive the sun-chariot one day, but drove it so erratically that humans were either wintry cold or scorched with heat. Zeus "burned" him with a thunderbolt so he fell into the River Eridanus (the Po).

26–28   Bellérophon, riding the winged horse Pégasus, 'quenched the flame of/ Grisly Chiméra" (*Odes* 4.2.15–16); see also 3.12.3 and 3.7.13–16. But here Horace alludes to Pindar's 7th Isthmian Ode, 44, ff.:

> . . . Yet Pegasos,
> the wingèd, cast down
> Bellerophon, his lord, when he strove to reach
> the houses of the sky and the fellowship
> of Zeus.
>   (Lattimore translation)

4.12.   *Iam veris comites, quae mare temperant*

Meter: in lines 1, 2, and 3: $\_ > \_ \cup \cup \_ \ \_ \cup \cup \_ \cup \_$
                   line 4: $\_ > \_ \cup \cup \_ \cup \_$

Now blow breezes of Thrace   tempering waves and seas,
Comrade escorts of Spring,   driving the linen sails;
Meadows now are in thaw,   rivers no longer roar
    Densely swollen with winter's snows.

5   Back the swallow returns,   building her nest anew,
That unfortunate bird   grieving for Ítys slain,
Ever bearing the foul   name of a wife who took
    Evil vengeance on lusting kings.

Shepherds lie in the young   grass as they tend their plump
10   Sheep and sing to the reed   pipes that delight the god —
Pan, that is, who is well   pleased by the flocks that rove
    Over Arcady's dark-green hills.

Now the season of year,   Vergil, induces thirst;
But in case you crave wine   pressed from the Cáles grape,
15   Then, my client of high   heroes, you need to bring
    Equal value in oil of nard.

One small onyx of nard   gets us a jar of wine
Now reposing in stock   down in Sulpícius' sheds,
Such a drink as expands   hopes in the heart and works
   Wonders washing our cares away.   20

If these prospects for fun   tempt you at all, come up!
Bring the merchandise, though!   I do not plan on your
Scot-free use of my cups,   wetting your whistle here
   As in houses of wealthy men.

But in earnest: dismiss   thoughts of delay and cost,   25
And, remembering bleak   doom, while the time permits,
Intermingle some brief   folly with wisdom's ways:
   Nonsense properly timed is sweet.

1   Readers have puzzled to know why springtime breezes should blow from the northeast, out of Thrace, a region Horace associates either with snow and cold (*Odes* 3.25.10; 3.26.10) or with wild and primitive peoples. We suggest that he *began* his poem with the Thracian story of lines 5–8 in mind.

5–8   In these lines only the name of Ítys gives the clue that a *Thracian* story is being recalled about a particular *swallow*. Literally the lines say:

> She builds her nest, piteously lamenting Itys,
> (she) the ill-fortuned *bird* (*avis*) and the everlasting disgrace
> of the Cecropian House, because she took evil vengeance
>   on the barbarous lusts of kings.

The story is this: Tereus, King of Thrace, married Procnē, a princess of the Cecrópian dynasty of early Athens (compare *Odes* 2.1.12 and note), who bore him a son, Ítys. Then, falling in love with her younger sister, the king sequestered Procnē, cut out her tongue to keep her from divulging his secret, and married Philoméla. But Procnē wove the secret into her sister's bridal robe, and when Philoméla read the message she rescued her sister, who in frenzy then slew her own son Ítys and served his boiled flesh to his father at dinner. The gods intervened to prevent further horrors, changing Procnē into a swallow, Philoméla ("melody loving") into a nightingale, and Tereus into a hoopoe (a European bird with a whooping cry). For an interpretation of this complex myth see Robert Graves: *The Greek Myths* 46. See also T. S. Eliot: *The Waste Land*, 99–103; 203–6.

11–12   The text leaves Pan unnamed. "Arcady"/Arcadia, the landlocked central region of the Peloponnésus, was Pan's native country. On Mount Lycáeus in the SW corner of Arcadia stood the ancient shrine to Pan; see *Odes* 1.17.1 and note. The "Golden Age" of early mankind was traditionally localized in the rustic simplicity of Arcadia.

13   "Vergil": see the concluding note below.

14   The town of Cálēs, NW of Capua (as in *Odes* 1.20.9 and 1.31.10), overlooked the famous Falernian wine district; hence "wine pressed from the Cálēs grape" means "first-rate wine."

15   For "my client of high heroes" see under "Vergil" in the concluding note below.

16   "Oil of nard" (or spikenard) was an expensive Oriental perfume for the hair. The word here is *nardus*. Compare *Odes* 2.7.7–8: ". . . our hair all/ Gleaming from Syrian oil of laurel" (*malobathro Syrio*) and note; also "conch-shells full/ Of scented oils" in line 22–23 of the same poem; also *Odes* 2.11.16: ". . . hair scented . . . with Assyrian perfumes" (*Assyria . . . nardo*).

17   "Onyx," that is, a perfume bottle made of onyx, a semiprecious stone resembling agate.

Moore compares Mark 14:3, where an alabaster jar of "ointment of spikenard very costly" is "broken"—presumably the *seal* is broken—to pour the contents on Jesus's head.

18   The storage sheds (warehouses) of the Sulpícii (? brothers) were on the Tiber's edge in the SW corner of ancient Rome, at the foot of the Aventine Hill.

26   "Remembering bleak doom" paraphrases "mindful of black fires" (*nigrorum . . . memor . . . ignium*), suggestive of some grim scene in the land-after-death.

28   This famous line reads: *dulce est desipere in loco* (pronounce: *dúlc' ést désĭpĕr' ín lŏcó*), where *in loco* means "in proper (time and) place," and where *desipere*, "to act foolishly, to be silly," = *de* + *sapere*, "to un-wise oneself," "to descend from wisdom." Alternate translations might be: "Timely foolishness can be sweet"; "Acting silly at times is good."

Vergil. This jocular poem invites Vergil, who usually resided at Naples, to come and visit Horace, probably at the Sabine farm. Purchase of wine from a dealer in Rome (17–18) does not preclude drinking the wine at the farm.

Only to an old and trusted friend would anyone write and say, without offense, "Come visit me, but bring something that will pay for first-rate wine; you can't have free drinks at *my* house the way you do in the homes of your wealthy friends" (21–24).

Horace may have met Vergil, five years his senior, in 41 or 40 B.C., when both young men had lost paternal estates through land confiscations and when Vergil had already gained the protection and favor of his first patron, Caius Asínius Pollio, consul in 40; see the last note to *Odes* 2.1. It was "Vergil,/ Noblest of men" (S.1.6.55) who first recommended Horace to Maecenas, his own second patron, in 39. Both poets were in Maecenas's party for the "journey to Brundisium" in the autumn of 38 (S.1.5.40–42 and 48), and, as pensioners of Maecenas through the 30s, the two must often have met in their common patron's house and dined in the mansion on the Esquiline Hill. In *Odes* 1.3.8 Horace terms Vergil "half of my very soul," and *Odes* 1.24 is a poem of condolence to Vergil upon the death of a mutual friend. The friendship of the two poets lasted twenty years.

The indirect recall of the Procnē story in lines 5–8 would not only be perfectly clear to Vergil, but in this very personal poem may even have been intended to remind Vergil of how he had alluded, no less obliquely, to that story in his own works: *Eclogue* 6.78–81 and *Gerogics* 4.15.

Vergil's wealthy friends (24) are readily identified as: Pollio, Maecenas, and the emperor; beyond those three we need hardly inquire.

Line 15   As for the phrase "my client of high heroes" (*iuvenum nobilium cliens*), which puzzled Moore, we understand a whimsically grandiose paraphrase of "client (i.e., pensioner) of his Majesty," for, through the 20s, when the *Aeneid* was in composition, Vergil was indeed in the paid service of Augustus. "Heroes" (*iuvenum*) is a "poetic" plural-for-a-singular, like "kings" (*regum*) in line 8: Procnē, after all, took vengeance on one lusting king only, Tereus. The "my" before "client" is idiomatic English, as in "my fine-feathered friend."

The word *iuvenis*, "young (man)," meant commonly "one in the flower of manhood, between the ages of 20 and 40," but it also meant "hero," in the sense of a man exalted beyond the ordinary range of human beings and quite possibly destined for godhood. In S.2.5.62–63 it clearly signifies the future emperor:

> Some future day, when a hero (*iuvenis*) descended from noble Aeneas,
> One who strikes terror in Parthians, shall over earth and the sea rule
> Mightily . . .

And in E.1.8.14 the same word, translated as "prince," is used for Tiberius on his show-of-force expedition to the East, when Horace inquires of Albinovanus Celsus ". . . whether his prince and his fellows regard him with favor."

Only to Vergil the poet can *Odes* 4.12 be addressed. It is unthinkable that the poem was intended for some other intimate friend by coincidence named Vergil (a family name), to whom all the above-listed characteristics would apply but who is nowhere mentioned by any ancient editor or commentator, or indeed by any other ancient writer whatsoever.

The problem occasioning these remarks is this: Book 4 of the *Odes* was published in (approximately) 13 B.C. when the poet Vergil had been six years dead. Ode No. 12 cannot possibly have been written to a man six years in his grave. It must, then, have been written earlier and included in the published collection of 13 B.C. When?

Since it was not included in *Odes* 1-2-3, published in 23, it is likely to have been composed after 23. It cannot postdate Vergil's death on September 22, 19 B.C., at Brundisium on the way home from a journey to Greece, or even Vergil's departure for Greece in 20. As a "lyric epistle," it would plausibly fall betwwen the lyric *Odes* and first Book of *Epistles* published in 20. The period 23 to 20 B.C., rather than before 23, is further suggested by line 26, which may well hint at Vergil's chronic bad health.

Moreover, *Odes* 4.12 reads like an actual letter of invitation actually sent to its destination. Fancifully no doubt, but possibly, Horace could have recovered it from the papers of the deceased after 19 B.C.

4.13.   *Audivere, Lyce, di mea vota, di*

Meter: in lines 1 and 2: $\_ > \_ \cup \cup \_ \_ \cup \cup \_ \cup \_$
          in line 3: $\_ > \_ \cup \cup \_ \cup$
          in line 4: $\_ > \_ \cup \cup \_ \cup \_$

Gods have granted my wish,   Lýcē, the gods have seen
Fit to grant me my wish: you have beome an old
    Woman. Yet you claim beauty
        Still, cavorting and drinking still,

Still with quavering voice   drunkenly coaxing dulled   5
Cupid's listless approach.   Cupid prefers the fair
    Cheek of Chía in flower
        Singing songs to her skillful lyre;

Brusquely scornful he soars   over the withered oak,
Taking refuge in flight   from your unsightly teeth,   10
    From the web of your wrinkles,
        From the snows of your whitened head.

Not diaphanous red   silks from the isle of Cos,
Not the costliest gems,   nothing recaptures past
    Times once swift-winging days have   15
        Put them down in the chronicle.

Where, alas!, is love gone?   What has become of fair
Flesh and movements of grace?   What now remains of *her*,
    Her whose breathing was loving,
        Stealing me from my very self,   20

> Save for Cínara, most   lovely of face and form
> And most winsome of ways?   Years all too brief the Fates
>   Granted Cínara, meanwhile
>   Letting Lýcē continue on,

25
> Like the little old crow   living its lifetimes nine,
> Thus affording our hot-   blooded young men a sight
>   Fit for gales of their laughter,
>   How to ashes a torch may burn.

1   Whether this Lýcē is identical with the Lýcē of *Odes* 3.10 is left to the reader's judgment; Moore thinks not. Compare *Odes* 1.25 (to a Lydia) and Epode 8.

7   "Chía" (pronounced Kýa) means "a girl from (the island of) Chíos," S of Lesbos. She would be a Greek slave or ex-slave (freedwoman); Moore says that inscriptions attest actual freedwomen of this name.

9   *Winged* Cupid flies, like a bird or a butterfly, over the oak.

12   The text says merely "snows of your head." A century later, the critic Quintilian complained that this was one of Horace's harsh and far-fetched metaphors, a statement which implies that Horace was the first to use it.

13   The Greek island of Cos (SW of modern Turkey) was famous its "see-through" silks, as in S.1.2.101-2 and note.

15   Compare *Odes* 3.28.6: ". . . as if in its bird's   swiftness the day . . . ," the Latin in both cases being *volucris dies*. Compare also *Odes* 4.7.7-8.

21–23 In two passages of lamentation for his lost youth Horace mourns "wantoning Cínara's flight and desertion" (E.1.7.28) and a time when he "could satisfy Cínara's greed without giving her presents" (E.1.14.33). Both poems were published in 20 B.C., when Horace was forty-five, yet no earlier poem mentions Cínara,—at least not under that name.

     In *Odes* 4.1.3–4 he says: "I am not what I was in dear/ Days of Cínara's rule," with no hint as to when those days were. Now we are told that Cínara died young.

25   "Like the little old crow" = *parem/ cornicis vetulae*, parallel to the "long-lived crow" (*annosa cornix*) of *Odes* 3.17.13. To convey Horace's intention we add "living its lifetimes nine," on the basis of the Hesiodic fragment mentioned in the note to 3.17.13. Moore cites the Greek of *Hesiod* Fragment 193, but the Loeb Library Hesiod does not contain this fragment.

Louis Untermeyer (1885–1977) made a graceful, if extremely free, translation of *Odes* 4.13 in eight 5-line stanzas. Stanza 5 (lines 13–16) reads:

> No silks, no purple gauzes
> Can hide the lines that last.
> Time, with his iron laws, is
> Implacable and fast.
> You cannot cheat the past.

4.14.   *Quae cura patrum quaeve Quiritum*

Meter: Alcaic stanza: in lines 1 and 2: $\cup \_ \cup \_ > \_ \cup \cup \_ \cup \_$
                   in line 3: $\cup \_ \cup \_ \cup \_ \cup \_ \cup$
                   in line 4: $\_ \cup \cup \_ \cup \cup \_ \cup \_ \cup$

What act of conscript fathers or citizens,
Augustus, shall memorialize your high
    Accomplishments with fitting tribute
        Either on stone or in written annals,

O greatest Prince wherever the sun proceeds   5
Across the world's inhabited lands and realms?
    Vindélici, unschooled in Roman
        Justice, have recently learned what power

You wield as Mars in warfare. With armies you
Provided, Drusus battered the savage folk   10
    Geráuni, and the swift-foot Breuni,
        Hurling their forts down the fearsome chasms

Of Alps, with fierce requital of more than man
For man. The elder Nero gave battle then
    Against the gruesome Raetians and with   15
        Favoring auspices drove them headlong,

Himself an awesome sight in the clash of war
As he delivered blow upon deadly blow
    To hearts accepting death quite freely,
        Almost the way that the southwind hurtles   20

Across the sea's invincible waves when through
The riven cloud the Pléiades shine in storm,
    And as he rode his frenzied horse to
        Harry the foe over tracts of wildfire.

As when the River Áufidus, rolling past   25
The borders of Apulian Dáunus' land
    And raging like a bull, roars threats of
        Drowning the fields in horrendous deluge,

In such an onset Claudius overwhelmed
The armor-clad barbarian lines and mowed   30
    Them down, from front to rearmost, strewing
        Windrows of slain, but no loss sustaining,

With forces you had furnished, advised by you,
With gods of yours presiding; for since the day
    When Alexandria surrendered   35
        Harbor and tenantless royal palace

Fortuna has consistently prospered you
And granted happy outcome to all yours wars,
    Conferring glory and a hoped-for
        Honor upon your achieved dominion.   40

The hitherto unmastered Cantabrian,
The Mede, the Hindu, even the nomad Scyth,

> Defers to you, O shielding presence
> Over our Rome and the land Italian;

45
> The Nile, of sources hidden in mystery,
> The Danube, and the Tigris of rapid flow,
> The monster-teeming waves of Ocean
> Bursting in thunder to far-off Britons,

> The Gallic nation fearless in face of death,
50
> The rugged earth of Spain, all attend your word;
> Sygámbri who rejoice in slaughter
> Venerate you and put down their weapons.

This companion piece to *Odes* 4.4 celebrates Tiberius's role in the victory of 15 B.C.

1   "Conscript fathers," the regular term of address for the Senate, together with "citizens" (*Quirites*), makes the line a paraphrase for the official *Senatus Populusque Romanus*, the "SPQR" of inscriptions.

7–14   These lines add to the praise of Drusus in *Odes* 4.4. The Brenner Pass takes its name from the Breuni.

14   "The elder Nero" here, like "Claudius" in line 29, is Tiberius Claudius Nero (the future emperor). Six times in the *Epistles* similar paraphrases were used for the name "Tiberius," which could, with difficulty, be accommodated in a hexameter line; in the Alcaic stanza used here the name is impossible.

15   The Greek writer Strabo corroborates "gruesome" (*immanis*) Raetians and Sygambrians "who rejoice in slaughter" (line 51), but equivalent terms were used in the closely parallel case of the American Indians.

20   Moore rightly cites "Almost" (*prope*) as unpoetic and detrimental to the simile.

22   The seven clustered stars called the Pléiadēs are a constellation of stormy winter.

24   The text says "through the midst of fires" (*medios per ignis*); Moore suggests "burning villages," but extensive brushfires and grassfires are equally possible.

25–28   For the Áufidus (Ofánto) River near Horace's birthplace see the note to *Odes* 3.30.10 See the same note for King Daunus, legendary founder of Apulia.

30   "Armor-clad . . . lines" (*agmina ferrata*) may signify iron shields overlapped to make a continuous wall, since body armor is unlikely among Keltic or Germanic tribes in 15 B.C. A century later, Tacitus (*Annals* 3.43.3), writing of the Keltic Aedui (of E France) as of 21 A.D., mentions their being cased in iron "in the national fashion," but gives no details.

32   The historian Velleius, ca. 30 A.D., mentions the slight Roman losses in this campaign.

33–34   As with Drusus in lines 9–10, Horace stresses that Tiberius was a passive instrument in the hand of Augustus.

34–36   That is the day of Cleopatra's suicide, approximately August 1, 30 B.C. (No anniversary is implied.)

41–52   As in *Odes* 4.5.25–28, Horace overstates Roman conquests. Actually conquered were: the Cantabrians (19 B.C.), "the Nile" (= Egypt (30 B.C.), Gaul from the Atlantic to the Rhine (58-50 B.C. by Julius Caesar), and Spain-Portugal (over two centuries' time); the rest were "expected in the future," but did not always materialize.

49   Druidical doctrines of reincarnation were thought to make the Gauls indifferent to death.

47   Compare the sea monsters in *Odes* 1.3.18–19 and 3.27.27–28.

51–52   The Germanic Sygámbri retreated northward and settled on the E bank of the Rhine between Coblentz and Xanten, where they were under Roman "influence" but not control.

Only 19 lines (14–32) of this 52-lines tribute to Tiberius are devoted to Tiberius. The ode *addresses* the emperor, and the emperor is the focus of the two opening stanzas as of the five concluding stanzas, with praise of Drusus wedged into lines 10–14. The skimped praise for Tiberius and the placing of *Odes* 4.4 well ahead of 4.14, some readers have felt, reflect Horace's awareness of the emperor's marked preference for Drusus over Tiberius, but the point is moot.

4.15. *Phoebus volentem proelia me loqui*

Meter: Alcaic stanza: in lines 1 and 2:   U _ U _ > _ U U _ U _
                          in line 3:   U _ U _ U _ U _ U
                          in line 4:   _ U U _ U U _ U _ U

As I considered making a song of war
And conquered cities, Phoebus with sounded lyre
   Gave warning not to hoist my little
      Sails on Tyrrhénian seas. Your era

Has reestablished, Caesar, our fields in wealth,   5
And to our native Jove on the Capitol
   Restored the standards torn from haughty
      Parthian gateways, and closed the Temple

Of War, and laid a curb on licentiousness
That was exceeding proper restraints, and purged   10
   The faults and blemishes among us,
      And reinstated the olden manners

By which the Latin name and Italian strength
Grew great and throve and from which the majesty
   And fame of empire now proceed from   15
      Sunset's Hesperian bed to sunrise.

With Caesar watching over the state, no rage
Of civil strife, no force can expel the peace,
   Nor quarrels forging swords and setting
      Cities at odds of insane contention.   20

No tribe that drinks the waters of Danube deeps
Now breaks the Julian edicts, no Seres, Gett,
   Or faithless Persian, nor the folk who
      Issue from Tanaïs River regions.

But here at home on workdays and holidays,   25
Amid the sportive gifts of the god of wine,
   Together with our wives and children,
      After the gods have been duly honored,

Let us by ancient custom recall great men

30   In song sustained by Lydian flutes: let us
                            Of Troy and of Anchíses sing, and
                          Bountiful Venus's high descendants.

1–4   Phoebus Apollo, god of poetry, either by plucking a single string of his lyre or, perhaps, by a single stroke of his thumb across all the strings, warns Horace away from themes unsuited to his genius. Compare Vergil's *Eclogue* 6.3–4: "As I was about to sing of kings and battle, the Cynthian (Apollo) tweaked my ear and warned (me to keep to subjects appropriate to me)."

      The Tyrrhénian Sea W of Italy is treacherous; witness Shelley's drowning there in 1822.

4   The disconcertingly abrupt transition suggests that Horace may have deleted, as prosaic, the god's direction to hymn Caesar's praises.

5–32 The remainder of the poem parallels and partially overlaps lines 17–40 of the *other* "hymn to Augustus," *Odes* 4.5.

      5   Restoration of agriculture after the ruinous civil wars, as in *Odes* 4.5.17–18.

      6–8   The Roman army standards lost to the Parthians in 53 B.C. and recovered by Tiberius in 20 B.C.; as in E.1.18.56–58 Augustus is imagined as personally wrenching those trophies down from the walls (or gates) of a Parthian "temple".

      8–9   The gates of the Temple of Janus were open in times of war and closed in times of peace. Suetonius, in his "Life of Augustus" 22, says' "The gates of the Temple of Janus on the Quirinal, which had been closed no more than twice — (in the reign of King Numa, 716–672 B.C., and in 235, after the First Punic War) — since the foundation of Rome, he (Augustus) closed three times during a far shorter period, as a sign that the Empire was at peace on land and at sea."   (Robert Graves translation)

      9–16   Allusion to the laws of 18 B.C. governing marriage and adultery, as in *Odes* 4.5.21–24; *Centennial Hymn* 17–18; and E.2.1.2–3.

      21   "Danube" here is *Danuvius,* which is Latinized Keltic; in line 46 of the preceding ode it was the *Hister/Ister* traditional with the Greeks but avoided by Roman writers.

      22   The edicts of Augustus are "Julian" because he was the "son" of Julius Caesar.

      21–24 As in *Odes* 4.5.25–28 and in the last three stanzas of the foregoing ode Horace overstates Roman conquests—or, rather, overconfidently anticipates future conquests.

             For the "Danube drinkers" (of what is now S Bavaria) see the note to *Odes* 4.4.22–24.

             With "faithless Persian," that is, Parthian, compare E.2.1.112 "a Parthian liar," and *Odes* 4.4.49 "that perfidious Hannibal," and note.

             "Gett" is the translator's *ad hoc* invention for metrical convenience; it stands for *Getae,* a term left as *Getae* in *Odes* 3.24.11, where Horace goes on to tell something of this primitive Thracian tribe inhabiting around the Danube mouth. For this and other names in these lines see under "Foreign Nations," p. 397.

      30   The tunes, not the flutes, were in the pleasant Lydian "mode" (musical scale). Compare Milton: *L'Allegro* 136: "Lap me in soft *Lydian* Aires."

      31–32 Echoes of the *Aeneid:* Aeneas was the son of mortal Anchises by the goddess Venus, hence all Romans are descendants of Venus.

Epistles. Book II

Epistulae. Liber Secundus

ca. 13 B.C.

Introduction

Three long poems, to a total of 926 lines, comprise *Epistles. Book II,* published probably in 13 B.C. at about the same time as *Odes* 4. By ancient editorial tradition this Book is placed last in the collected works of Horace, though the second and third pieces had each circulated separately at ealier dates. The opening poem, by being addressed to the emperor, "dedicates" the whole three-poem collection to him, and E.2 is the only Horatian Book that does not mention the name of Maecenas.

E.2.2 explains to young Julius Florus that no new lyric poems have been sent to him and that Horace is resigning from poetry. The reasons given so resemble those in E.1.1, itself composed in 20, that this epistle is most plausibly dated to 19 or 18 B.C.

E.2.3 is the famous "Art of Poetry" (*Ars poetica*), a title acquired in the decades following Horace's death. When first composed and circulated in some unascertainable year between 20 and 17 B.C. it may have been called "A Letter to the Pisos," since it is addressed to a father and two sons with the *cognomen* "Piso" who had apparently requested from Horace some words of guidance for literary creations of their own; see the headnote to the present translation. Through most of this fascinating poem we hear Horace's own voice speaking with charm and cogency, but we have the word of ancient commentator Porphyrio that portions of the work paraphrase a Greek handbook of rhetoric by one Neoptólemus of the third century B.C., and in those "Neoptólemus sections," particularly lines 179–284, the modern reader may feel puzzlement and some lapse of interest. It was the fate of this "Art of Poetry" to be taken, with awe, as the very Law of literature in the European centuries between 1500 and 1800, but lingering vexation over that rigidly applied Law should not prevent moderns from enjoying the poem on its intrinsic merits.

E.2.1 is identified in the *Vita Horatii* (p. 385 below) as the piece written especially for the emperor who had complained at finding no mention of himself in certain other *sermones*—which can only be E.2.2 and E.2.3. Its subject is a plea for wider support for living authors and their works as opposed to enshrined classics. The Swiss Alpine scenery evoked in lines 252–3 corresponds to *Odes* 4.14.12, so that both poems must be dated after the Alpine victories of Drusus in 15, doubtless to 14 B.C. Horace may have worked simultaneously on E.2.1 and on the several patriotic pieces in *Odes* 4, with the result that his "last poem" cannot be cited.

2.1.   *Cum tot sustineas et tanta negotia solus,*

Knowing how great and how many affairs you sustain single-handed,
Giving the state its defenses, providing us moral example,
Mending the laws for our welfare, I might disrupt government business
If this extensive epistle impinged on your schedule, Caesar.
      Heroes of old: Father Liber and Romulus, Castor and Pollux   5
Though they attained to the skies of the gods after mighty achievements —
Fostering races and lands of mankind, making peace after savage
Warfare, assigning the limits of regions, establishing cities —
Always had cause to lament that the gratitude they had expected
Proved to be less than their merits. The hero who crushed the dread hydra   10
And in his Fate-imposed labors subdued the notorious monsters
Never discovered a means short of death to prevail over envy.
One overbearing inferior talents around him and dazzling
All by the fire of his lightnings must wait till he dies to be cherished.
You in your lifetime, however, we fully acknowledge and honor,   15
Setting up altars where vows may be made by invoking your godhood,
Sure that your equal will never arise nor has ever yet risen.
      Nevertheless, though this people of yours shows its wisdom and judgment
In its supreme estimation of you over all of our Roman
Leaders and over all Greeks, it by no means appreciates other   20
Things, since it holds in contempt and aversion whatever has not yet
Vanished from off of the face of the earth and departed this era,
Feeling such awe for the ancients that no works of theirs can be marred by
Faults, not the Tables of Laws that the Decemvirs drafted, nor treaties
Ratified either with Gabii or with the hard-headed Sabines,   25
Nor the old books of the pontiffs, nor soothsayers' oracle volumes,
Which they consider the Muses inspired from the heights of Mount Alba.
      If, because works of the Greeks which were written the longest ago are
Also the best, it must follow that anything Romans have written
Has to be weighed in the very same scale, then discussion is futile: 30
Olives are soft on the inside and nutmeats are hard on the outside.
We, having come to the summit of power, excel over Greeks in
Painting, in music, as also in body-anointing athletics.
      If it is argued that poems, like wines, become better with age, my
Question is: how many years does it take for a work to gain value?   35
Name any writer a hundred years dead: is his rank by that token
Up with the perfect and ancient or down with the new and the worthless?
Let some definitive term be agreed on to settle this matter!
— "Anyone dead for a century passes for ancient and worthy."
How about one that falls short by a month or a year of the limit?   40
How do you classify him: with the poets of old who are worthy
Or with the ones that our own and the ages to come should look down on?
— "Oh, it is perfectly proper and right to include with the ancients
Someone who died a mere month, or a year even, under the limit."
— Using your principle, let me start pulling out hairs from a horse's   45

Tail; I pull one hair, a second, and so on, until there is nothing
Left. By the rule of diminishing grain-heaps you see how he fails, your
Man who goes only by calendar records and feels no esteem for
Anything save as the goddess of funerals renders it sacred.

(*A brief survey and critique of the "old" Roman writers.*)

50   Énnius the wise and the warlike, our "Homer the Second," as critics
Sometimes have claimed, does not seem to be over-concerned about how his
Reincarnation worked out or what came of those famous predictions.
Náevius too: is he not in all hands and as fresh as a recent
Author among us? Indeed, every poem of old is held sacred.

55   If we debate where the one or the other is greatest, Pacúvius
Wins his renown by the wisdom of age, and by loftiness, Áccius;
Comic Afránius's toga, they say, would have suited Menánder;
Plautus can match Epichármus of Sicily's liveliest paces;
Terence excels for his style, and for dignity look to Caecílius.

60   These are the authors committed to memory, these are the plays that
Powerful Rome flocks to see in the densely packed theaters, these are
Reckoned our poets from Livius Andrónicus down to the present.
        Sometimes the public shows excellent sense, then again it makes blunders;
If it admires and so praises these poets of old as to know of

65   None to surpass them, or even compare with them, it is in error.
If it finds some of their pieces too stiff and old-fashioned and often
Clumsily worded, and many a thing over-bald in the statement,
Then it is wise and agrees with my own and with Jupiter's judgment.
I am by no means condemning or urging destruction of works by

70   Livius, which I remember from having them dictated to me
Back in my schooldays by cane-wielding master Orbílius, but I
Marvel to hear them called wonderful works little short of perfection.
If it so happens a word flashes out here and there in a glory
And if a line here and there is more pleasingly turned than another,

75   Still that is hardly enough to support the whole poem and sell it.
        I am impatient when something is criticized, not because someone
Thinks it is crudely composed or inelegant, but for its newness, —
Or when the ancients are honored and praised intead of forgiven.
If I expressed any doubt as to whether the dramas of Atta

80   Merit a staging with saffron and flowers, most oldsters would shriek that
Decency surely was dead, now that I was abusing the dramas
Graced by the stately Aesópus and acted by Róscius the learnèd,
Either because they consider that nothing is right but what *they* liked
Or from a sense of disgrace at conceding to juniors how things they

85   Learned in their unbearded youth must in now-advanced years be discarded.
Someone who praises King Numa's old Salian Chant and pretends to
Know what it means, when the rest of us have not the slightest idea,
Is not bestowing his praises on poets long buried, but rather
He is impugning the living, from hatred of us and our writings.

If innovation had been so abhorred by the Greeks as by some of   90
Us, would there *be* any ancients today? And what books would exist for
Man after man of our public to read and wear out with their thumbing?

> *(From a historical viewpoint the Greeks were of playful and inventive*
> *temperament, . . .)*

Once her great wars had been fought to a settlement, Greece began lightly
Turning to pleasures and drifting with favoring fortune toward vices,
Fired by a passion for athletes or fired by a passion for horses,   95
Doting on skills of the craftsmen in ivory, in bronze, or in marble,
Hanging with rapture of eye and of mind on a picture just painted,
Charmed with the music of flute-boys, entranced by tragedians' dramas,
All very much like some wee little girl in the care of her nursemaid
Eager for toys and rejecting them later when womanhood ripened.   100
Such was the upshot of ages of peace and those favoring breezes.

> *(. . . whereas the Romans were sober and steady, . . .)*

Meanwhile in Rome it was long the agreeable custom to open
House-doors at dawn, give advice to a client on legal procedures,
Cautiously count out the money for loans to the sober-reputed,
Listen to old fellows tell, and explain to the younger men, how to   105
Make one's reources increase and how ruinous waste can be lessened.

> *(. . . but Rome is now full of amateur poets.)*

Is there, however, a good thing or evil not subject to change?
Fickle and changeable, people now think about nothing but writing;
Lads and their stern-visaged fathers alike will now come to a dinner
Sporting their ivy-leaf crowns and with slaves to receive their dictations.   110
I am as bad as the rest: if I say that I never write poems
I come off worse than a Parthian liar; I'm up before daybreak
Calling to slaves for my papers, my pens, and my manuscript boxes.
No one sails ships without study of seafaring, no one gives even
Boneset to patients unless he has studied the dosage: let doctors   115
Handle all medical matters, leave tools to the competent workman;
Yet we write poems at will, whether trained or without any training.

> *(The value of poets in society.)*

There are advantages, nevertheless, to this mild sort of madness;
Let me enumerate some of these blessings. A poet is only
Rarely addicted to greed; he loves poetry; nothing else matters;   120
House-fires and losses and runaway slaves are disasters to smile at;
Fraud with a partner in business or cheating an orphan would never
Enter his mind; he exists on the bread made of chaff and the seconds;
Misfit and sluggard in warfare, he graces the City in peace time —
If you will grant me that little details can enhance things much greater.   125
Youth's incoherence and stammer take shape from the speech of a poet,

Ears of the young are diverted from raw and uncouth conversation;
Presently even the heart is directed by friendlier precepts
As he imposes correction on rudeness and envy and temper
130   By his portrayal of things done aright; through the stages of life he
Guides by instructive examples; he comforts the poor and the poorly.
Where would a pure-hearted lad or a girl who has not known a husband
Learn about prayers if the Muse did not send them a poet to teach them?
Choruses plead for assistance, aware of divinity's presence:
135   Trained in sweet parlance of prayer, they implore the celestials for rainfall,
Pestilence they can avert, or the perils that strike us with terror;
Peace they may also obtain, or a season of harvest abundance;
Poems are honored by gods of the sky and by gods of the ghost-realm.

(*The evolution of Roman drama.*)

Farmers of old, in their sturdy existence contented with little,
140   After the harvest was in, had the habit of festival-making,
Granting their minds and their bodies relief after worry and labor;
Workmen joined in, and the sons, and the stout-hearted wife, and a pig was
Slaughtered to Earth-mother Tellus, Silvánus was honored with milk, with
Flowers and wine for the Guardian Spirit who thinks of life's shortness.
145   Here was the origin, then, of Fescénnine abuse and the taunting
Verses of insult that bantering rustics exchange with each other.
That was a liberty welcomed in year after year as good-natured
Frolicsome play, till the jesting grew vicious and took on the form of
Open attack — the more harmful for being exempt from reproof — on
150   Old and respectable houses. The bite of those teeth was a painful
Matter, and others, escaping unscathed in the process, were also
Gravely disturbed for the general welfare. A penalty-bearing
Law had indeed to be passed, which forbade composition of hateful
Songs about persons or parties: on threat of a death under cudgels
155   Poets were forced to be civil and even to be entertaining.

Greece in its capture then captured its rough-mannered conqueror, thereby
Bringing the arts into countrified Latium. The clumsy old meter
Known as "Saturnian" vanished from poetry then, and refinement
Cleared the congestion befuddling our literature, — leaving persistent
160   Traces of crudeness, however, as blemishes down to the present.
Slowly the Romans directed their wits to the works of the Greeks and,
During the leisure that followed the struggles with Carthage, began to
Ask whether Sophocles, Thespis, and Aeschylus might not be useful.
Tests at translation to see if those works could be properly rendered
165   Brought them sucess with the subjects of high exaltation; yet Romans,
Breathing the tragical spirit and often expressing it grandly,
Still feel ashamed if they have to erase and rewrite any passage.

Comedy, drawing on everyday life for its subjects, is thought to
Need only minimum effort to write, when it needs all the greater
170   Pains because audiences judge it less leniently. Notice how Plautus
Plays up the roles of a love-smitten youth, of a no-nonsense father,

And of a treacherous pimp; what a thorough Dossénus he is in
Picturing ravenous parasites; notice the slackness with which he
Laces the comedy-shoe on such characters treading his stages;
Nothing much mattered to him but the money he made on his plays, and   175
Once he was paid, his creation might stand up erect or fall over.

He whom Ambition conveys to the stage in her breeze-fickle car is
Wilted by audience listlessness, given new breath at their laughter.
That is how little it takes to tear down or build up any spirit
Lusting at all costs for fame. They can keep their whole comedy business   180
If, as the palms are bestowed, I must either grow fatter or leaner.
Even a poet of courage is daunted and often scared off when
Faced with an audience mostly consisting of underlings lacking
Training and taste but prepared to insist on a point — if some haughty
Gentleman happens to say so — by calling for boxers or bear fights   185
Right in the midst of the play: there's the taste of the populace for you.

   (*Recent drama.*)

   Nowadays gentlemen's pleasure is not of the ear any more, but
All of the eye, with these gaudy spectaculars, dazzling and empty.
Four or more hours the fore-drop stays open for pageant-displays of
Squadrons of cavalry fleeing and infantry companies routed;   190
Then come the kings with their hands tied behind them, deserted by Fortune,
Captured equipment paraded, with chariots, carriages, carts, and
Ships' beaks, and ivory loot, and a Corinth of bronzes in booty.
Laughing Democritus, were he on earth, would find plenty to laugh at,
Seeing the people agape at a panther crossbred with a camel   195
Or a white elephant holding the gaze of the populace spellbound.
Our entertainments themselves he would view less attentively than he
Would all those spectators furnishing spectacles far more diverting;
Authors, he well might imagine, concocted their stories to tell to
Donkeys, and deaf ones at that. Have there ever been voices of human   200
Beings to cope with our theaters' uproar? You think you are hearing
Howling of winds through the woods of Gargánus or over the Tuscan
Sea. Amid that kind of racket our plays are performed — with their gorgeous
Loads of exotic apparel. The actor has only to step on
Stage in such trappings and right hands begin to clap left hands in frenzy: 205
"Has he said *any*thing yet?" — "Not a word." — "Then what *are* they applauding?"
— "Costume the color of violets, woolens of Tárentine purple."

   But, lest you think I begrudge recognition of excellent work that
Others have done in a form I myself have not even attempted,
I say a poet has really accomplished a tight-rope performance   210
When he has conjured illusions that grip my emotions, that rouse my
Anger, that stir me to pity, that fill me with fanciful terrors,
And, like a wizard, transports me at will, now to Thebes, now to Athens.

   (*Non-dramatic writers.*)

   But to the authors who choose to write only for readers in private

215   Rather than bear with the play-goer's captiousness, grant some attention,
       Caesar, if books are to fill up Apollo's new library-temple
       Such as will honor the god and provide an incentive to greater
       Efforts by poets in search of the Muses and Hélicon's verdure.
       Sometimes we poets admittedly act to our own disadvantage,
220   As when I hack my own vineyards to pieces by sending a book to
       You at a moment when you may be worried or weary, or when we
       Take it to heart and feel hurt if a friend says a line needs improving,
       Or in rereading a passage when no one has aked for an encore,
       Or by complaining that listeners fail to perceive what tremendous
225   Labor went into a work and how subtle a thread it was spun from,
       Or when we hope for results that will have you immediately sending
       For us the instant you hear we have poems in progress, declaring
       Poverty must not afflict us and bidding us write in your service.
       Still, it might not be amiss to investigate what sort of temple-
230   Guardians serve your high purposes tested at home and in warfare:
       Yours is a merit that must not be left to an unworthy writer.

       (*Though Alexander the Great rewarded a sincere but bad poet, . . .*)

       King Alexander the Great showed magnanimous favor to poet
       Chóerilus, who had accorded him praise in some very bad verses,
       Showering Philip-coins on him — which Chóerilus duly accepted.
235   But, as the handling of inks may leave blotches and stains on the fingers,
       Writers may often disfigure exalted achievements in poems
       Barren of talent or training. That very same monarch who squandered
       Money so rashly in purchasing such a ridiculous poem
       Issued an edict forbidding all painters except for Apélles,
240   Likewise all sculptors except for Lysíppus, to paint or cast bronzes
       Bearing the likeness of Great Alexander. Suppose now, however,
       Such sensitivity felt for the visual arts were transferred to
       Books and applied to the poems that come as the gifts of the Muses:
       Why, you would swear Alexander was born in the dark of Boeótia!

       (*. . . you, Caesar, have great poets to honor you, though I myself am of inadequate
       talents.*)

245   But no discredit reflects upon you for your having selected
       Vergil and Varius as poets to cherish and love, no discredit
       Clings to the gifts they received from your hand with the praise of the giver.
       Statues of well-molded bronze do not better show features of face than
       Works of the poets portray what illustrious men may be like in
250   Mind and in character. As for myself, I would sooner not write these
       Low-creeping essays, but willingly chronicle mighty achievements,
       Locating countries and rivers, and telling of citadels perched on
       Precipice summits and kingdoms barbarian, telling of wars and
       Battles well won to the ends of the earth with yourself as their leader,
255   Telling of Janus as guard over Peace within walls of containment;

And of how Rome in your principate terrifies Parthians, — all if
Only my talents but matched my desires. But a work of small compass
Cannot accommodate majesty equal to yours, and my sense of
Proper procedure forbids me to try where my powers would fail me.
Someone officious may only embarrass the person he seeks to   260
Honor, especially when he would tender his homage in verse, and
For the good reason that people more quickly pick up and remember
Something that strikes them as silly than something esteemed and commended.
I have no use for a nuisance, nor have I the slightest desire to
Have an inferior artist take waxen impress of my features   265
Or to be touted and praised in a wretchedly miswritten poem,
Lest I should blush for so stupid a present, and lest I should end by
Finding that I and my eulogist both had been put in a single
Book-box and carried on down to the street selling incense and spice and
Pepper — or anything else they do up in a wastepaper wrapper.   270

2–3   Augustus had laws passed—to little effect—to curb bribery of officials and to reduce
luxury spending, as well as his marriage and divorce laws, for which see the notes to
Centennial Hymn 17–18 and *Odes* 4.5.21–24.

5   Here Father Liber is not the wine god (Bacchus) but the patron of agricultural life.

7–8   This "evolution of civilization" was guided by the four heroes mentioned, as well as
Hercules (line 10), that is, by mortal men whose high achievements won them god-
hood. But compare the slow, spontaneous evolution of S.1.3.99–104 and Mercury's
guidance of evolving man in *Odes* 1.10.2–4.

10–11   The second of the Twelve Labors of Hercules was the slaying of the Hydra of Lerna,
a dog with multiple snake-heads. Ridding the earth of monsters was part of
"civilization."

16   The altars were not to Augustus but to his Guardian Spirit (*Genius*); see E.2.2.187–189
and note; though in Egypt he automatically inherited the "living godhood" of the
Pharaohs after the death of Cleopatra (30 B.C.). His official "deification" came after his
death. In life he aspired to be no more than the "chief Roman" with all the Roman
people as his "clients."

24–27   In 451 B.C. Rome's first written laws were engraved on *ten* bronze tablets at orders
from the elected Board of Ten (*Decemviri*) and put on view in the Forum; additions of
the following year created the "Twelve Tables of the Law," and when the invading
Gauls destroyed these in 390 B.C. they were recomposed. They are known to us only in
fragments as quoted by later writers from the version of ca. 198 B.C., where the crabbèd
and archaic language is only semi-archaic.

A treaty of ca. 520 B.C. with the enemy town of Gabii (E.1.11.8 and note), written
in archaic letters on bull's hide, was still to be seen in Horace's time, as were certain
treaties with the Sabines.

The books of the pontiffs were manuals of religious ritual and annals.

The oracles would include the Sybilline Books; see the note to E.1.3.17.

Patriotic awe might claim that Roman Muses inspired the oracles on the Mount
of Alba (in the Alban Hills SE of Rome, where tradition located Roman history prior
to 753 B.C.), as the Greek Muses gave inspiration on Mount Helicon in Greece. The
American equivalent of line 27 would perhaps be "Which they consider as angel-
delivered at Plymouth Rock."

49   The "goddess of funerals" = *Libitina,* as in S.2.6.19 and note.

50–52   The *Annals* of Énnius began with the account of a dream in which Homer appeared
and announced that he had been reincarnated as Énnius by the Pythagorean doctrine

of the transmigration of souls. Horace means that Énnius won fame on his own merits, not as Homer reincarnate.

50–62   Horace lists the "old Latin" writers (and traditional opinions about them) as a basis for comment in lines 63–92. In chronological order these writers are:

- Livius Andronicus (ca. 275–204 B.C.): tragedies and a translation of the *Odyssey* into "Saturnians" (line 158 below, and note). The Romans dated their literature from a performance, in 240 B.C., of a play by this captive of war, who was proficient in Greek, Oscan, and Latin.
- Naevius (ca. 270–199 B.C.): comedies and an epic poem on the (First) Punic War, in "Saturnians."
- Plautus (ca. 254–184 B.C.): comedies. Horace sets him parallel to Epichármus, the earliest of the Greek "Old Comedy" writers (ca. 530 to ca. 440 B.C.); see the note to S.1.4.1–5.
- "Father" Ennius (239–169 B.C.): tragedies and the *Annals* (Roman history in 18 Books of Hexameters).
- Pacúvius (220–ca.130 B.C.): tragedies; see S.2.3.60–62 and note.
- Caecílius (ca. 219–166 B.C.): comedies.
- Terence (*Teréntius*) (ca. 190–159 B.C.): six comedies before his early death.
- Afránius, a younger contemporary of Áccius: comedies on Roman subjects, though with plots derived from Menánder (342–291 B.C.; see the note to S.1.4.1–5).

More commonly, Roman comedy presented Greek characters in Greek settings.

Except for 20 comedies of Plautus (out of a much larger total) and all six comedies by Terence, only fragments of these authors now survive—less than 100 lines of Livius Andronicus, less than 200 lines of Naevius, and so on.

Unexplainably Horace omits all mention of his admired Lucílius (? 180–ca. 103 B.C.).

79–80   Titus Quinctius Atta died as recently as 78 B.C. (missing the hundred-years-old mark by about 35 years!). His comedies were staged in Roman costume.

It was not unusual to sprinkle the stage with sweet-smelling saffron, but the use of flowers is mentioned only here.

82   Aesópus (as in S.2.3.239) and Roscius were famous actors of Cicero's time. (In 80 B.C. Cicero was defense attorney for Roscius in a lawsuit.)

86–87   Numa Pompílius, Rome's second king, ruled 716–672 B.C. The "Salian Chant" (*Carmen Saliare*) was sung by the "leaping priests" of Mars, mentioned in the note to *Odes* 1.36.12; see also *Odes* 1.37.1–4.

If the "Salian Chant" survives only in fragments, Horace's point may well be judged from a similar "chant" dated from the 6th century B.C. but preserved on a marble tablet from the astonishingly late year of 218 A.D. The inscription, recording an actual performance of that year, says that the priests, known as the Twelve Arval Brethren, bloused their tunics up short, "took the books," "divided up," danced, and sang the *Carmen Arvale,* repeating each line three times:

> *Enos Lases iuvate!*
> *Neve lue Marmar sins incurrere in pleores.*
> *Satur fu, fere Mars, limen sali! Sta! Berber!*
> *Semunis alternei advocapit conctos.*
> *Enos Marmor iuvato!*
> *Triumpe! Triumpe! Triumpe triumpe triumpe!*

To Romans of Horace's time this was about as intellible as a stanza of *Sir Gawain and the Green Knight* might be to us. In the Loeb Classical Library *Remains of Old Latin,* iv, 250–253 E. H. Warmington translates (with some uncertainties):

> Oh! Help us, ye Household Gods!
> And let not bane and bale, O Marmar, assail more folk.

> Be full satisfied, fierce Mars. Leap the threshold! Halt! Beat the ground!
> By turns address ye all the Gods of Sowing!
> Oh! Help us, Marmor!
> Bound, bound, and bound again, bound and bound again!

93–102   The "great wars" are the Persian invasions of Greece in 490 and in 480–479. Horace's horizon of history is determined by Herodotus; before ca. 600 B.C. all is vague.

   The impressionistic view of Greek history from 490 to the Roman conquest may have been general Roman opinion, but we see it as shockingly distorted.

110   Poets wore crowns of ivy leaves, diners usually wore a chaplet of flowers.

112   "A Parthian liar" is a gratuitous slur on an enemy nation.

114–115   A simple household remedy is intended. The translator has substituted "boneset" for "southernwood" (abrotonum).

124   Horace alludes to his own inept soldiering in 42 B.C.; see Odes 2.7.9–14 and note.

138   "Gods of the sky" (di superi) were named divinities inhabiting Olympus or upper air; their worship was by day, with burnt offerings that produced rising smoke.

   "Gods of the ghost-realm" were nameless troops of spirits, worshipped by night and without use of fire, with offerings of animal blood or animal carcasses, black sheep and "earth-loving" pigs being the commonest victims scarificed. Compare Odes 1.10.19–20 and note.

139–144   Such rustic family idylls had their real-life counterparts in Horace's time.

   "Silvánus, guard of boundaries" in Epode 2,22 and note.

   For Horace's own definition of "the Guardian Spirit" see E.2.2.187–9 and note.

145–155   From the rustic family idyll of lines 139–144, the poet turns to a picturesquely raucous community festival which featured abusive and obscene songs in "Fescennine verses," putting both celebrations back at the beginnings of the national literature, presumably well before 240 B.C.

   Allegedly, "Fescennine verses" originated in the small, once Etruscan, town of Fescennia/-ium some 40 km/25 m up the Tiber from Rome, but Latin fascino and Greek baskaínō both meant "to abuse (verbally)" and "to bewitch," and Latin fascinum meant both "a charm" and "penis." Such verses were still in use in Horace's time for brides' homecoming, military victories, and so forth, and they were explained as a means of averting evil from lucky persons. Catullus's "Wedding Song" (Poem 61, lines 126–140) contains a mild version of such verses at a bride's threshold-crossing.

   148–150   Around 205 B.C. the comedy writer Naevius was jailed and then exiled to North Africa for saying that members of the Metélli family had achieved high office "by Fate."

   152–155   Cicero quotes "the Twelve Tables of the Law" (line 24 above) as assigning the death penalty for composing or singing a slanderous or insulting "song" (magic spell); see S.2.1.81–84 and note.

156   This famous and accurate line (Graecia capta ferum victorem cepit . . .) refers to the Roman conquest of Greece in 146 B.C., yet by Horace's own statements in lines 50–62 above Greek influence on literature began in 240 B.C. with Livius Andronicus.

157–158   The "Saturnian" meter was so ancient that it was said to have been used "in Saturn's reign," that is, the Golden Age at the beginning of time. It counted accents, as English poetry does, not "longs" and "shorts" as Vergil and Horace did; it was without rhyme, and resembled the cadence of

> The King was in his counting-house/ counting out his money,
> The Queen was in the parlor, eating bread and honey . . .

Compare the children's jingle in E.1.1.59–60 and note. See also under Livius Andronicus and Naevius in the note to lines 50–62 above.

162   "The struggles with Carthage" were the three Punic Wars: 264–241; 218–201; and 149–146 B.C. As with line 156 above, there is a time descrepancy, perhaps because Horace was using a false chronology, traces of which are to be discerned in other writers. See Odes 4.8.15–20 and the last note there.

163 Thespis (see the note to E.2.3.275–277) is named because "Euripides" will not fit the hexameter verse pattern. Note the very Roman adjective "useful" (*utile*).

167 Compare S.1.10.72: "Do not neglect your eraser if works are to merit a second/ Reading," and E.2.3. about "the labor of the file."

170–176 Horace was temperamentally alien to Plautus and to farce comedy, where stock clown-roles were acted with bravura within the flimsiest of plots. Dossénus was a stock clown in the "Atéllan farces," which may have been the lineal ancestor of the Italian Commedia dell'arte of fifteen centuries later; compare "Messius Roostercomb" in S.1.5.51–70 and note.

For Plautus's mercenary-mindedness we have only Horace's word. In the note to E.2.3. 270–274 we collect Horace's anti-Plautus remarks.

182–186 Clearly Horace has in mind the audience disruption of Terence's comedy *Hekyrá* (*The Stepmother*) in 165 B.C. at the instigation of "some haughty/Gentleman," —doubtless the disappointed poet Luscius Lanuvinus who headed a persistent cabal against Terence in the 160s.

187–193 Horace expects drama to be an oral art (*Sprechkunst*), admirable for what it says and how it says it, not a four-hour pageant "with a cast of thousands." Reading between the lines of 170–186 we see that he dislikes Plautine farce and approves of Terence's comedies of character and well-constructed plots.

189 The Roman theater curtain rolled *down* into a trough at the front edge of the stage, where it remained until it was rolled *up* to conclude the performance.

190 A cavalry squadron (*turma*) numbered 30 mounted riders.

192 The text uses Latinized Gaulish words: "chariots" = the (two-wheeled) *esseda*; *pilenta* were light carriages for ladies; "carts" = *petorrita*, from Gaulish *petvar*, "four," + *rith*, "wheel," perhaps something like a "lumber wagon."

193 Corinth, renowned for its bronzes; compare the note to S.2.3.21. The Romans burned and looted the actual city of Corinth in 146 B.C.

194 Demócritus is mentioned simply because he was known as "the laughing philosopher"; compare the story of his absent-mindedness in E.1.12.12–14 and note.

195 The animal is the giraffe, or camelopard: necked like a camel and spotted like a leopard/ panther. In his Alexandrian triumph of 46 B.C. Julius Caesar exhibited the first giraffe in Rome.

196 The "white elephant" (*elephas albus*) may have been an albino specimen of the now extinct North African elephant, such as Hannibal used in the second Punic War.

199–200 Horace combines: 1. a Greek saying: "A man told a story to a donkey; the donkey only shook its ears," and 2. "telling a story to a deaf man," line 222 of Terence's *The Self-tormentor*, which had become proverbial.

202 Gargánus (now the Promontorio del Gargáno) is the rugged peninsula of SE Italy mentioned in the note to *Odes* 2.9.6–8; also in the note to *Odes* 1.28.3.

The Tuscan/Etruscan/Tyrrhenian Sea is W of Italy; see the note to *Odes* 1.11.6.

207 The gorgeous costume was made of wool from around Taréntum, perhaps from "the lovely Galáesus valley,/Where the sheep wear raincoats" (*Odes* 2.6.10–11 and note), dyed royal crimson.

213 "Thebes" = "tragedy," "Athens" = "comedy," as the most frequent locales of each genre.

216–218 For the library-temple to Apollo see the note to E.1.3.17. Mount Hélicon, in Greece, was the home of the Muses.

220–221 "Hacking one's own vineyard to pieces" must have been a popular phrase close to slang. E.1.13.3 and note urged caution in delivering a book to Augustus.

232–244 The Chóerilus anecdote is apocryphal, or at least garbled, history. Variant versions are told by other Roman writers, and in Pliny's *Natural History* 35.10 and 85 Alexander's indifference (or ignorance) regards painting, not poetry.

234 "Philip-coins" (*Philippos*) were mintings of Alexander's father, King Philip of Macedon, 359–336 B.C.

239–240 Apélles and Lysíppus were the foremost artists of Alexander's time.

244 The Greek province of Boeótia, centered on Thebes, was proverbially a region of dullards—though it contained Mount Hélicon, home of the Muses.

245–247 In 14–13 B.C., when this poem was composed, Vergil had been dead since September 22, 19 B.C. and Varius was also probably deceased, though his death year is unknown. Both poets had been lavishly rewarded by the emperor.

250–251 "These/ Low-creeping essays" = *sermones . . . repentes per humum* (literally "creeping along the ground"), with *sermones* referring to all of Horace's nonlyric works, not just the "Satires" (*Sermones*). Similarly low estimates of his nonlyric poems may be found in S.2.6.17 (". . . plodding my slow Muse's pace in these Satires") and, more emphatically in S.1.4.39–44.

252–253 ". . . Telling of citadels perched on/ Precipice summits" closely resembles *Odes* 4.14.12, where Drusus is praised for his defeat of the Geráuni and Breuni, "Hurling their forts down the fearsome chasms/ Of Alps . . ." in the Brenner Pass during the campaign of 15 B.C. See the headnote to *Odes* 4.4 and the cluster of three poems, *Odes* 4.4, 4.14, and 4.15.

255 The whole elaborate line means simply "Telling of peace (after warfare)." As explained in the note to *Odes* 4.15.8–9, the doors of the Temple of Janus were open in times of war and closed in times of peace.

269 The "book-box" (*capsa*) is metaphorically a coffin for dead-letter authors. For (*capsa*) see the notes to S.1.4.21 and S.1.10.63.

"The street selling incense" = *in vicum vendentem tus*, punning on *tus*, "incense" and the *Vicus Tuscus*, that short street running from the Forum to the Tiber, as in S.2.3.228 (". . . the rabble frequenting the Tuscan Street quarter") and note; see also the note to E.1.20.1–2.

2.2.   *Flore, bono claroque fidelis amice Neroni,*

Florus, devoted companion to good and illustrious Nero,
What if perchance someone trying to sell you a slave who was born in
Tibur or Gabii made you an offer like this? "Here's a fellow
Fair of complexion and handsomely built from his head to his heels and
He can be yours on the spot for the nominal sum of eight thousand: 5
Suited for indoors assignment and prompt at a nod from his master,
Knowing a lick-and-a-promise of Greek, can be trained and is apt for
Just about anything, fit as a mass of wet clay for the molding,
Even can sing — without lessons — to please you while quietly drinking.
Too many promises undermine purchaser confidence, I will   10
Grant you, — if dumping of wares is the fast-talking seller's objective.
Don't think I'm out to raise cash! I'm not rich, but I do have some money.
This is an offer no regular dealer would make, and I wouldn't
Make it myself to just anyone. Once he played hookey from work — as
Sometimes they will — and hid out, below stairs, from the strap that was waiting." 15
    Then, if you buy, disregarding the truancy formally cited,
He will be safe in the eyes of the law from misrepresentation.
I say you knowingly made a bad bargain; he met the requirement,
Yet you are suing him anyway, knowing your case is ill-founded.
    Back when you started your journey I made it quite clear I was lazy,   20
Downright delinquent, I said, in performing the duties of friendship,

So as to head off your anger with me for not writing a letter.
What was the use of my issuing any such warning, if after
All you now heap your reproaches upon me? You even complain that
25 I have not honored my promise to send you the odes you expected.
            One of Lucúllus's soldiers, while snoring the sleep of the weary,
Lost to a thief every penny of savings amassed in a life of
Hardship, and therewith became like a ravening wolf in his fury,
Raging alike at himself and the enemy, till on a certain
30 Day, he dislodged a defense of the King's from a summit defying
Capture, they say, and containing the utmost of riches and treasure.
Fame of that feat won him all sorts of honors and special citations
And, in addition, some thousands of sesterces cash were awarded.
Not too much later his officer wanted some citadel taken —
35 I don't remember just where — and began to exhort him to take it,
Using such eloquent terms as might even put spunk in a coward:
"Up, my good fellow, your manhood is challenged! Go up there! Your foot is
Guided, and you shall collect the rewards you deserve! — You're not budging?"
To which the cagey, if countrified, fellow replied: "To take that one,
40 That one up there, you need someone that's just had his money-belt stolen."
            I was brought up, as it happens, in Rome, and in Rome I was taught how
Great was the harm that the Greeks had to bear from the rage of Achilles.
Then, good old Athens put gloss on my earlier training, my purpose
Being, of course, to distinguish a straight line from one that was crookèd
45 And to go questing for truth in the groves that Acádemus planted.
Very bad times then obliged me to leave that delightful location;
Civil disorders compelled me, unskilled as I was, to use weapons —
Weapons by no means a match for the sinews of Caesar Augustus.
After Philíppi my service was over, but I was in want; my
50 Wings had been clipped, I was destitute, left without home and deprived of
Land that my father had owned, until poverty gave me sufficient
Boldness to start writing poems. But once a man's needs are supplied, what
Doses of hemlock could possibly cure such a feverish madness
Short of deciding that comfortable drowsing is better than writing?
55   Years in their steady succession deprive us and rob us of one thing
After another; amusements and dinners and love they have taken
From me, and now they are trying to take away poetry also.
What can I do? And not everyone's taste is identical either.
You may like lyrical poems, another delights in iambics,
60 Somebody else is for satire as brackish and salty as Bion's.
Three persons in for a dinner are almost enough for a quarrel,
Each of them asking for something quite different by way of a menu.
What should I serve them and what should I not? You reject what the second
Orders; what *you* like, the other two dislike and say it's too sour.
65   More than all else, do you really expect me to write any poems
Down here in Rome in the midst of so many distractions and worries?
One needs a co-signer, one holds a reading and wants me to cancel

All my appointments; one up on the Quirinal Hill is in sickbed,
One is in sickbed way out on the Áventine: both must be called on, —
Distances highly convenient, you notice. You fancy the streets are   70
Open and clear and with nothing to hinder a man's meditations?
Here is a contractor bustling along with his mules and his porters,
There some enormous machine lifts a block or a timber by pulley,
Funeral processions and lumbering wagons get tangled in traffic,
Here's a mad dog on the loose, over there is a pig in the gutter   75
Wallowing. *So* much for making melodious poems while strolling.
Writers in general are fond of a forest and unfond of cities,
Given, with Bacchus, to pleasure in slumber and shadowy places;
Yet in this turmoil and uproar by night and by day you would have me
Sing as I thread my way up through the difficult pathways of poets?   80
Someone of genius who chose to inhabit in leisurely Athens,
Giving philosophy seven long years of devotion and growing
Old over problems and books, may come out talking less than a statue,
Serving more often than not for arousing derision in people, but
Here in the midst of the billows and blustering storms of this City   85
How could I ever compose any words fit to waken the lyrestring?
      There were two brothers, both lawyers, in Rome, one a jury-case man and
One a consultant, who never spoke words save in praise of each other,
One like a Gracchus, the other a Mucius in mutual tributes.
Why should a less intense fervor be shown between clear-throated poets?   90

      (*An afternoon's poetry reading.*)

I write my odes, and the next man writes elegies. — "Marvelous! Simply
Marvelous! Wrought by all nine of the Muses!" But first you should notice
All the self-satisfied pride and importance we show as we view this
Library-temple that stands here now open and waiting for Roman
Poets; then — if you're not busy — come in for the reading and hear what   95
Things are produced and how each of us weaves his own garland of praises.
There we trade compliment-blows till we both are completely exhausted,
Doggedly fighting like Samnites till lamplighting time ends the duel.
I come out *his* new "Alcáeus," but who, then, shall *he* be in *my* vote?
Who but "Callímachus!" If he holds out for additional honors,   100
I will allow him "Mimnérmus," an epithet he may rejoice in.
      I endure much to appease the excitable tribe of the poets
While I am writing myself and on canvassing rounds for supporters,
But, with my writing renounced and my mind repossessed, I am free to
Close up my ears with impunity now when they hold recitations.   105

      (*What is more, good poetry demands strenuous labor; advice to serious poets.*)

      Poets composing bad poems are ridiculed, yet they delight in
Nothing so much as composing; they awe-strike themselves, and if *you* keep
Silent, they gladly supply commendations of what they have written.
Anyone bent on creating a poem of recognized pattern

110   Will, when he picks up his tablets to write, bear in mind how a critic
Fairly might view it, deleting all words and expressions that lack for
Luster, that may be too vague or too bland, or that fall below standard
Dignity, even though everyday use makes it hard to reject them
And though till now they have even been heard in the sanctum of Vesta.

115   Poets do well to dig out certain words that have all but gone out of
General usage and bring to the fore what is vivid and forceful,
Words the Cethéguses sounded of old and the speech of the Catos
Which for their dirt of neglect and their tarnish of age are forsaken:
Grant a new franchise and life to those words of our forefathers' minting.

120   Any good poet will surge like a river in crystalline current
Lavishing wealth upon Latium and bearing us richness of language;
Over-luxuriant growths he will prune, he will smooth off excessive
Harshness with sensible care and remove what is lacking in vigor,
He will create the appearance of effortless ease, like the dancer

125   Miming the alternate steps of the faun and the clodhopping Cyclops.
     I would much rather be one of those crazy, self-satisfied writers
Charmed by my sorry productions and happy to have them delude me
Than to see clearly and suffer. — There was a prominent man of
Argos who had the illusion of listening to marvelous tragic

130   Dramas enacted for no one's applause but his own in an empty
Theater; other than that, he discharged all the functions of living
Perfectly well: a good neighbor, a host of agreeable ways, and
Kind to his wife; with his slaves he might just overlook an offense and
Not get excited if someone had tampered with seals on a wine jar;

135   Nor did he walk over cliffsides or fall into uncovered well-pits.
After great cost to his kinsmen in efforts to cure him, and after
Powerful doses of hellebore drove the infection away and
He was himself once agian, he cried: *"You* call it rescue, my friends, but
What you have done is to murder me! You have destroyed my delight and

140   Forcibly swept from my mind the most gloriously sweet of illusions!"

     (*Poetry is for the young, philosophy for the mature.*)

     Clear understanding enjoins resignation from playful amusements
Suited to boyhood and putting aside all these lyrical trifles,
Fitting my words to the lyres of the Romans no longer, but rather
Learning the modes and the measures of actual human existence.

145   Therefore I say to myself as I silently ponder these matters:

     (*Horace's inner monologue occupies the remainder of the poem, lines 146–216.*)

     If you were troubled by thirst that no water could quench, you would tell your
Doctor about it; then if, with possessions amassed, you feel only
Craving for more, would you fail to take counsel with someone about it?
And if a wound did not heal with the root and the herb that the doctor

150   Told you to use, would you not give up using the root or the herb that
Had no effect on the wound? Or perhaps you had heard that a man made

Rich by the gods was forever thereafter relieved of all wicked
Folly, and now that you see you are *not* any wiser for being
Wealthier, will you persist in relying upon those informants?
Yet, if your riches resulted in wisdom, reducing your greed for   155
More and your worry of losing the already-gained, you would blush to
Think there was someone on earth who was even more greedy than you are.

(*Use constitutes the only possession.*)

If what is purchased by measure and weight is to be a possession,
Only the use of it makes it so — if you agree with the lawyers.
Yours is the field that provides you with food, and the steward of Orbius,   160
Plowing and dragging the acres that later will bring you their harvest,
Looks upon you as his lord; for the money you pay you receive your
Grapes, and your pullets and eggs, and your jarful of mead; in so doing
Little by little you purchase the farm, in the long run perhaps at
Three hundred thousand in cash, if not more, and thus *you* are the owner.   165
Prepay expenses or pay as you go: does it really much matter?
Once having purchased a farm at Arícia or Véii, the buyer
Pays for the produce he eats, though he likes to think otherwise, and, in
Heating his cold copper kettle at nightfall, he pays for the firewood.

Someone may claim that he owns as far out as the row of those poplars   170
Planted to settle the line and prevent any quarrels with neighbors,
Just as if something could really be owned which within a mere hour,
Either by gift or by purchase, by force or by ultimate death, may
See an exchanging of masters and pass to a new jurisdiction.
Thus, since perpetual ownership does not exist, and possessor   175
Follows possessor like wave after wave in unending succession,
What is the good of estates or of granaries? What is the good of
Joining Lucánian lands to Calábrian pastures, if Orcus
Levels the great with the small and if gold cannot move him to pity?

Marble and ivory and gems, figurines from Etrúria, paintings,   180
Grand silver platters, apparel imbued with Gaetúlian crimson:
Some people may not possess these, and *one* man declines to possess them.
Why, of two brothers, the one prizes idling and pleasures and perfumes
More than the palm groves of Herod abounding in dates, while the other,
Wealthy and churlish, will drudge on his farm from the dawn to the twilight   185
Trying by fire and by sword to make arable fields out of woodland,
Only that Spirit can know, who adjusts the effects of our birth-star,
Mortal yet lord over natures of men as he walks at our side and
At his caprice makes particular characters cheerful or gloomy.

I am for using, for taking whatever is needed from modest   190
Stores, and not worrying how my inheritor thinks of me later
When he discovers no more than there is. Yet I mean to distinguish
Clearly the open and blithe-hearted type as opposed to the wastrel,
Just as I mean to distinguish the person of thrift from the miser.
There is a difference in whether you squander your money or pay it   195

Quite without grudging for meeting expenses, in whether you scrimp and
Save to accumulate further and further or make all you can of
Limited time, as you did in your boyhood with springtime vacation.

> (*An assessment of his own life.*)

        Short of affliction by squalor and want, I will sail in a little
200 Ship or a big one, so long as I still remain me and am carried.
      I do not voyage with sails bellied full by a favoring northwind,
      Nor is my life a continuous struggle with southwinds against me;
      Rather, in body and mind, personality, looks, and position,
      I may be seen as the last of the winners, but leading the losers.

> (*An "examination of conscience."*)

205   You are not greedy, you say. Very good! But have all of your other
      Vices been banished as well? Is your heart without futile ambition?
      Is it quite free of the terror of death and the turmoil of anger?
      Portents, and dreams, and the horrors of magic, and tellers of fortunes,
      Ghosts in the dark and Thessalian prodigies: can you now laugh at
210 Things of that sort? Do you number your birthdays with gratitude? Do you
      Overlook faults in your friends? Are you gentler and better for aging?
      What is the good of extracting one thorn if so many still prick you?
      If you are ignorant still of how life should be lived, then defer to
      Guidance by those who have learned. You have had enough fun, enough food and
215 Drink; it is time to depart, before *young* men, more gracefully sportive,
      Mock you for overindulgence and chase you away from the banquet.

---

1   Florus is the same Julius Florus who, in 20 B.C., went to the East as a member of the staff
        of Tiberius Claudius Nero, Augustus's stepson and the future Emperor Tiberius; see
        E.1.3. The present poem dates probably to 19 or 18 B.C., Florus is still with Tiberius,
        and lines 20–22 indicate that he has not been back to Rome in the interim.

2–3   The slave is Italian-born, not a captive of war or a purchased import, and from near
        Rome—from Tibur (Tívoli) 24 km/15 m E of Rome, or from Gabii, 15 km/10 m E, as
        in E.1.11.8 and note, and hence easier to train.

5   8,000 sesterces is a moderate but not suspiciously low price. In S.2.7.43 the slave Davus
        says he was bought cheap at 500 drachmas. As of 1909 Morris estimated the two prices
        as $400 and $100, respectively.

14–19 The dealer mentions the slave's major fault only casually, seemingly as an after-
        thought of no importance; failure to mention it would invalidate the sale.

20–25 Like the dealer, Horace gave fair warning that he was a poor correspondent. The
        promised odes were most likely promised in a vague and general way.

26–40 The anecdote of the soldier relates to campaigns led, between 74 and 67 B.C. in
        various parts of "Asia" (Turkey), by Lucius Licínius Lucullus (E.1.6.40 and note)
        against "the King" (line 30) Mithradates VI of Pontus.

        33   The text specifies "twice ten (thousand) sesterces;" Morris, in 1909, estimated
        "a little less than $1,000."

41–54 The autobiographical remarks establish parallels with the anecdote about the
        soldier: I had *my* money-belt stolen in the land confiscations after the Battle of Philippi;
        I stormed the citadel of poetry-writing and gained a rich reward; but one feat is
        enough, and, like the soldier, I beg to be excused from further exploits.

        41–42   As a schoolboy in Rome I studied the *Iliad* (in Greek).

43–45   In my "college days" in Athens I studied philosophy. Whimsically, moral philosophy is made to sound as if it were geometry. "Groves" probably stands for several "schools" of philosophy in Athens in the 40s B.C.

Around 387 B.C. Plato began teaching philosophy in a gymnasium and adjoining grove dedicated to the demigod Akádēmos, allegedly the planter of the grove long ago. Under a sucession of elected leaders and with varying fortunes, "Plato's Academy" endured for some 900 years until its closing by Christian Emperor Justinian shortly after 527 A.D. But, since Horace shows no trace of Platonic doctrines, he is likely to have studied at one of the other "groves."

46–49   The "very bad times" were the civil wars between the assassins of Julius Caesar (Brutus and Cassius) and the "Caesarians" (Mark Antony and the young Octavius), 44–42 B.C.; see the headnote to S.1.7.

49   For the two-phase battle of Philippi see *Odes* 2.7.9–12 and note.

49–52   A month after Philippi, Horace turned 23, but on his return to Italy he found his father's land confiscated as part of the payment of 28 legions of Philippi soldiers. For some part of the three years, 41 to 38 B.C., he worked in a government office (S.2.6.36–37 and note), but here he omits to say anything about his means of economic survival during those years before he became a pensioner of Maecenas.

53   *Small* doses of hemlock were used to reduce fever.

55–57   In 19 and 18 B.C., when this poem was probably composed, Horace was 46–47 years old.

55–105   I am resigning from poetry, because: (a) my health is declining (55–57); (b) no one is satisfied with what I compose (58–64); (c) composition is impossible in this madhouse called Rome (65–87); and (d) these poetry readings disgust and distract me (87–105). Besides, (e) poetry is for the young, and at my age only "philosophy" is a proper pursuit (141–145).

59–60   "Lyrical poems" (*carmina*) are *Odes* 1, 2, and 3; "iambics" are the *Epodes*. Bion was a philosopher of the 3rd century B.C. whose satires (*sermonibus* in the text!) were famous for their caustic sarcasm.

67   "One needs a co-signer" is the same as S.2.6.23: "to post bail-bond for someone."

68–69   The Quírinal and Áventine Hills were at the N and S ends of the ancient city and about equidistant from the Esquiline Hill, where Horace is likely to have had his Roman residence.

74   S.1.6.42–44 mentioned ". . . two hundred wagons/ Stalled by three funerals crossing the Forum" and the din of their horns.

89   Gaius Semprónius Gracchus (153–121 B.C.) and his older brother Tiberius (163–133 B.C.) were famous lawyer-statesmen-reformers. Three memorable jurists named Mucius Scáevola held consulships in 133, 117, and 95 B.C. respectively.

91   "Odes" = *carmina* as usual. "Elegy" (Greek *élegos, elegeía*) was originally a song of lamentation, meter unspecified; see Shelley's *Adonais* and Gray's *Elegy in a Country Churchyard*. A later development was the form with alternating hexameters and so-called pentameters, called "elegiac verses" (Greek *élegoi*, Latin *elegi*, always plural, as here). Love was the commonest theme in such poems, and Ovid (in *Tristia* 4.10.51–54) lists the Roman elegists as: Gallus (whose works are lost), Tibullus (see *Odes* 1.33.1 and note and E.1.4.1 and note), Propertius, and himself. Horace wrote no "elegiacs."

91–101   "Marvelous! . . ." is one poet's compliment on a rival poet's work.

92-95   Horace interrupts himself to say that "we poets" all have our eyes on the "Hall of Fame," that is, the new library-temple to Apollo (E.1.3.17 and note; also E.2.1.215-218).

95–101   At the poetry reading the rival poets trade compliments like Samnite gladiators who fought in heavy armor all day long until nightfall forced them to quit, and at the close of the session the rival poets elect each other "the new so-and-so" and "so-and-so the second."

That Horace should be "elected" as "the new Alcáeus" for his odes, is understandable.

Kallímakhos was the 3rd-century B.C. master of elegiacs in Alexandria.

Mimnérmos, around 600 B.C., was considered the inventor of elegiacs; see E.1.6. 65–66 and note.

The unnamed rival poet of lines 99–101 is thought to be Propértius, who in his last Book of elegiacs, ca. 16 B.C., (4.1.64, or, with some editors, 5.1.64) styled himself "the Roman Callímachus."

Almost everything about Sextus Propértius is beset with uncertainties. His full name is unknown; he was born at Asísium (Assisi), probably in 50, 49, or 48 B.C. His published works seem to begin with 26 B.C. and to end with 16 B.C., after which date no more is heard of him; he was surely deceased by 2 A.D. Later writers seldom mention him. The text of his works is marred by serious scribal corruptions. He has always appealed to a descriminating minority of readers. See Ezra Pound's long poem, *Homage to Sextus Propertius.*

As a fellow pensioner of Maecenas he must often have encountered Horace, but Horace never mentions him by name, and the present allusion is hostile.

117   Revered statesmen of the past were: Cethégus, consul in 204 B.C., and Marcus Porcius Cato, the Elder, 234–149 B.C., the model of puritanical morality in S.1.2.32; *Odes* 2.15.12; E.1.19.12–14; etc.

In the latter 40s B.C. the historian Sallust was not universally praised for his use of obsolete words and forms.

125   The mime-dancer alternately imitates the graceful faun (or satyr) and the clumsy Cyclops (one-eyed ogre) Polyphémus in their respective love-suits to the nymph Galatéa; compare S.1.5.63.

128–140   Several ancient writers tell the story of the pleasantly insane man from Argos.

133–134   That is, he stole some of the master's wine; compare S.1.3.80–83.

135   Similar "signs of madness" are mentioned in S.2.3.56–63.

137   For the plant hellebore as a remedy for madness see S.2.3.82–83 and note.

141   "Clear understanding" repeats the "see clearly and suffer" of line 128 and continues the line of thought interrupted by the anecdote of 128–140, the Latin word being, in both cases, simply *sapere,* "to know." Compare the *sapere aude* of E.1.2.40: "dare to know."

144   That is, studying philosophy.

158   "By measure and weight" = *libra . . . et aere,* "balance and brass (counterweight)."

158–169   The whole passage is conducted in pseudo-legal fashion, as if Horace were a theorist at law. The "jarful of mead" (fermented honey) is probably an ancient term used in agricultural tradition, rather than actual payment.

167   The place names imply a city man's "supplies farm" not too remote from Rome. Arícia (as in S.1.5.1), now Ariccia, was 32 km/20 m SE of Rome; Véii, now called Veio but an uninhabited site, 16 km/10 m NW of Rome, was taken from the Etruscans in 396 B.C. after a 10-year siege.

178–179   The alternation of summer pasture lands in mountainous Lucania and winter pasture in lowland Calábria was mentioned in Epode 1, 27–28 and note.

Orcus (or Pluto) = "death," as in *Odes* 2.3.24 and note.

180   Etrúria = the land of the Etruscans, between the Mediterranean and the Tiber.

181   "Gaetulian," from the name of a Berber tribe in ancient Morocco, here indicates a west-Mediterranean *murex* dye.

182   "*One* man" stands for Horace, of course.

183–189   A brief digression; the thought resumes from 182 at 190.

184   Herod is the King Herod of Matthew 2:1–15; the palm groves are doubtless those of Jericho.

After the Roman conquest of Palestine in 63 B.C. by Pompey the Great, an Idumean (south Judean) called Antípater was installed as ruler of Galilee, assisted by his sons Phasael and Herod. In the strife of 63 to 40 B.C. Herod survived his father and brother to become sole ruler; in 30 B.C. the Romans recognized him as "the king of the Jews," with jurisdiction over Galilee, Samária, Judea, and part of Trans-Jordan. During his kingship, 30 to 4 B.C., he renamed Samária City "Sebáste" in honor of Augustus, Greek *sebaste* being the equivalent of Latin *augusta.*

After 4 B.C. he was succeeded, in Galilee only, by his son Herod Antípas, who ruled from 4 B.C. to 39 A.D. This son is the "Herod the tetrarch" of Matthew 14:1–12 and of Luke 9:7–9, and, by error, the "*King* Herod" of Mark 6:14–29, who had John the Baptist executed. See the note on the generic term "tetrarchs" in S.1.3.13.

187–189   This "Spirit" (*Genius*), identical with "the Guardian Spirit who thinks of life's shortness" in E.2.1.144, is an invisible second self, a god and yet subject to death, who walks at each man's side from the hour when both were born until the hour when both die; it is he who determines temperaments of individuals, even to making two brothers antithetical. In *Odes* 4.5.32–35 it is the *Genius* of Augustus—not the *man* Augustus—who is worshipped among the household gods. See also *Odes* 3.17.14 and note. In Christianity this "Spirit" became the Guardian Angel.

189   "Cheerful or gloomy" is literally "white and dark" (*albus et ater*), a set phrase used by Catullus in Poem 93.

198   "Springtime vacation" (*festis quinquatribus*) annually honored Minerva, March 19th to 23rd.

208–210   That is, do you scorn all superstitious terrors?

- "The horrors of magic" (*terrores magicos*), such as Canidia's torturing of the wax image in S.1.8.29–33.
- "Ghosts in the dark" (*nocturnos lemures*) are explained by an ancient commentator as "wandering shades of men prematurely dead and therefore to be feared." (Compare the *Lemuren* who dig Faust's grave in Goethe's *Faust*, 11511–11611.)
- The N-Greek area of Thessaly was witch-country *par excellence*. See Epode 5, 45–46:

> With her Thessalian witching spells she charms the moon
> And stars down from the very sky.

215   "It is time to depart" means withdrawal from the banquet of life to await death in good time; it does not mean suicide. Compare S.1.1.119: "Willingly goes from this life like a diner replete from a banquet."

2.3.   *Humano capiti cervicem pictor equinam*

The Pisos (*Pisónes*) addressed in lines 6 and 235 of this poem were a father and two sons (line 24) who had apparently asked Horace to furnish them with some statement of literary principles as guides to their own creative efforts, though lines 365–6 seem to single out the elder of the two sons as the primary aspirant to poetic composition. The *cognomen* "Piso" was often borne by members of the Calpúrnii family, who traced their origin to one Calpes, a son of King Numa Pompílius (716–672 B.C.), hence the address in lines 291–2: "You scions of royal/ Numa Pompílius." Among more than two dozen recorded persons named Calpúrnius Piso, Morris identifies the present father with Gnaeus Calpúrnius Piso, veteran of the Battle of Philippi (as was Horace), consul in 23 B.C., and with an elder son who was to become consul in 7 B.C., a few weeks after Horace's death. The Charleton T. Lewis dictionary, however, identifies the father with Lucius Calpúrnius Piso Caesonínus, long Prefect (Mayor) of Rome and consul in 15 B.C. Precise identification is wholly incidental to the understanding of E.2.3, which for centuries has gone by its non-Horatian title of

"The Art of Poetry" (*Ars poetica*)

Say that a painter's caprice joins the neck of a horse to a human
Head, and adds plumage of multiple hues to the random-assembled

Bodily parts, till the woman of beautiful features above ends
Up as a fish and disgustingly ugly below: on admission
5   Into the studio, friends, could you manage to stifle your laughter?
Pisos, believe me: a book would be just like that painting if, in it,
Unreal conceptions, like dreams of a sick person's mind, were presented,
Neither the head nor the foot being properly suited to any
Single, particular figure. — "But painters and poets alike have
10   Always been freely allowed to create at the promptings of fancy!"
— True! And we poets both plead that excuse and allow it to painters, —
Not for the joining of savage and gentle, however, and not so
Serpents may couple with birds and the lamb be the mate of the tiger.

(I   *The component parts of a work of art need to be
consistent with each other and with the totality.*)

Poems beginning quite grandly, and promising much, may have one or
15   Two purple patches sewn on them as eye-catchers seen from a distance, —
Striking effects, like "the altar and grove of Diana," for instance,
"Waters in hurrying course through the beauteous meadows and fields," or
Maybe a view of the Rhine, or a rainbow, — but there was no cause for
Mentioning any of these in the first place. Perhaps you are skilled at
20   Drawing a cypress tree: how will that help you to paint, say, a person
Frantically swimming away from a shipwreck — who paid you to paint him
Swimming? A vat was intended: then why does the potter's wheel, spinning,
Turn out a cruet? Create what you will, but you must be consistent.
Many a poet, O father and sons who deserve such a father,
25   Errs in attempting one aspect of excellence: I may seek terseness
Only to wind up obscure; one who tries for a lightness of touch may
Sacrifice sinew and spirit; the grandiose strays into bombast;
One crawls along on the ground, over-cautious of stormwinds; another,
Lavishing ornament on a monotonous theme, paints a dolphin
30   Deep in a forest, or maybe a boar-pig bestriding the sea-waves.
Dodging defects leads to trouble unless there is skill in the craftsman.
Near the Aemílian gymnasium the bronze-smith last-down from the Forum
Imitates fingernails well in the metal, and soft-waving hair, but
Fails in the primary task since he lacks all control of the total
35   Figure. If I were composing a work, I would no more desire to
Be like that craftsman than I would enjoy being highly esteemed for
Blackness of eyes and of hair when I knew that my nose remained crookèd.

(II   *Order and style.*)

You who are writers, select the material components that you are
Able to cope with, and test them at length to determine how much your
40   Shoulders will carry or not carry. Once in control of your subject,
Excellent wordings will come, as will clearness of organization.
Order's prime charm and advantage, unless I am greatly mistaken,
Lies in expressing right now what right now is in need of expression

And in postponing a number of matters not needed at present.
    Deftly selecting and carefully placing his words, let an author   45
Fondly put one in his poem and scornfully banish another.
You would get splendid effects if adroit combination should freshen
Common old words so they seem as if new. If a topic untreated
Previously forces the usage, perchance, of some terms that are novel,
You may appropriately coin some expressions unheard in the days of   50
Wrap-loined Cethéguses, but without going too far with the practice.
Usable likewise are newly created expressions as may be
Drawn from the Greek, if you do not distort them. For why should the Roman
Grant to Caecílius and Plautus precisely what he has denied to
Vergil and Varius? Should I be begrudged the addition of *my* few   55
Words of new coinage, when Cato and Énnius so greatly enriched our
Forefathers' language and brought into general usage so many
Words for new things? From of old there was freedom, and freedom shall always
Be, to bring forth any word with the stamp of the present upon it.
Just as the leaves of the forest are shed with the annual change and   60
New ones are formed, so the old generations of words perish likewise
And, in the manner of mortals, the newer ones youthfully flourish.
We and our works are both destined for death, — whether Neptune, admitted
Into the heart of the land, shelters sea-faring fleets from the northwind
— *There* was a feat for a king!, — whether marshes long sterile and suited   65
Only for rowboats now suffer the plowshare and furnish the near-by
Cities with food, or the stream that brought ruin to crops is diverted
To a beneficent course, — and as handwork of mortals will perish,
Habits of speech will not hold in their charm and their glory forever.
Many a word which at present lies dead will revive in new birth, and   70
Many now cherished in honor will wither, if usage will have it
So, for in usage is law and the rule and the standard of language.

    (III   *Meters have been established for each sort of poetry.*)

    Deeds of great leaders and kings and the dismal befallments of warfare:
Homer has shown in what meter such subjects as these can be treated.
    Lines of dissimilar length first conveyed the expression of sorrow;   75
Later their use was expression of joy when one's wish had been granted;
Still, rhetoricians have never agreed as to who was the first to
Write in this delicate form, and the point remains quite undecided.
    Rage made Archílochus fashion iambics to serve as his weapon,
Which both the comedy sock and the tragedy buskin adopted   80
Later for dialogue purposes, finding that meter the best for
Drowning out audience noise and advancing a quick-moving action.
    Meters were set by the Muse for the praising of gods and of heroes,
Or of a champion pugilist or of a prize-winning race horse;
Also for lovers' distress and for wines that release us from sorrows.   85
Each of the genres should keep to the preassigned place that befits it.   92
Failing to go by these forms and thematic divisions from lack of   86

Knowledge or competence, how would I merit the name of a poet?
Why should false shame misdirect me to ignorance rather than knowledge?

(IV   *Drama*; 1. *The language of drama*.)

Comedy subjects refuse to be treated in tragedy's language.
90   Likewise such themes as Thyéstes's banquet rebel at portrayals
91   Couched in an everyday idiom or stated in comedy's language.
93   Sometimes, however, the tone of a comedy may be exalted,
As when the furious Chrémes expostulates loudly in outrage.
95   Tragedy likewise will sometimes let Péleus or Télephus mourn in
Commonplace language when each, in his exile and poverty, drops his
Booming and bellowing rant and his sesquipedalian words in
Hopes that his listeners' hearts may be touched by the tale of his sorrows.
Dramas that merely are beautiful will not suffice: they must also
100 Win us and carry our minds to wherever they seek to transport them.
Laughter begets other laughter, compassion depends on the sight of
Weeping. If I am to weep, you must first display sorrow yourselves, and
Then, O my Péleus or Télephus, *your* woes will cause me to suffer
With you; but if you go reeling off lines that were bad in the first place,
105 I shall be either asleep or else quaking with laughter. Sad looks must
Go with a sadness of words, and a threat requires looks full of menace,
Playful words call for a playful expression, and grim ones for grimness.
Nature disposes us inwardly first to all manner of fortunes,
Prompting our joys and our pleasures and goading us into our angers,
110 Bowing us down to the ground with our sadness and choking us on it,
Then, through the medium of speech, she releases our inward emotions.
If any character's speech does not fit his position and fortune
He will encounter the Roman guffaw, both from knights and from footmen.
Whether a god or a hero is speaking will make quite a difference,
115 Whether an old and mature sort of man or a passionate one with
Youth still aflowering, dignified matron or nurse full of duties,
Wandering trader or farmer of green-growing fields, man of savage
Colchis or perfumed Assyrian, scion of Thebes or an Argive.
Stick to tradition or else be consistent about your inventions.
120 If you perchance treat anew of the much-honored hero Achilles,
Show him as doughty, hot-tempered, implacable, ruthless, denying
Any adherence to law, and resorting on all points to weapons.
Let a Medéa be fierce and undaunted, an Íno to set us
Weeping, Ixíon perfidious, Ío astray, and Oréstes
125 Wretched. But if you attempt innovation on stage, with a hero
Wholly invented by you, then make sure that this character, from his
Entering line to the final conclusion, is fully consistent.
General experience is hard to depict in original terms, and
You might be safer recasting the Ilian epic as drama
130 Than in presenting a subject that no one before you has treated.
Themes in the public domain can be given your personal stamp, if

You do not dally along on the usual well-trodden treadmill
Circuit, or try to be overly literal with your translations;
Nor, as you imitate, should you get caught in a corner so tight that
There is no graceful way out short of breaking the rules of your story.   135

    (*A digression about narrative poetry; the* Odyssey *as model.*)

    Nor shall you start your work off, like a cyclical poet of old, with
"Priam's misfortune I sing, and the warfare so famous in story."
What can the promiser offer in keeping with any such mouthful?
Mountains in labor, and birth pangs produce a ridiculous mouse! How
Vastly superior is he who shapes nothing amiss in his works, with: 140
"Sing to me, Muse, of the man who, in times after Troy had been captured,
Witnessed the ways of mankind in his travels to many far cities."
His aim is *not* to make smoke follow blaze but to kindle a brilliance
Out of the smoke, so he then may present his astonishing monsters:
Ogre Antíphates, Scylla, the Cyclops himself, and Charýbdis.   145
He does not start Diomédes's home-coming story by telling
How Meleáger got killed, or the Troy tale with Helen's conception:
Right to the heart of his story he plunges and keeps pressing forward,
Sweeping the listener on as if all he reports were familiar,
Leaving out only what does not redound to his narrative's splendor.   150
Thus he invents by combining the true and the untrue until his
Tale is unflawed from the start to the middle, from middle to ending.

    (*The subject of drama is resumed, . . .*)

Let me now speak of what I, and what people in general, look for.—
If you want those in attendance to stay in their seats till the final
Curtain is drawn and the singer says "Now let us hear you applauding!",   155
You must observe the behavior that goes with the various ages,
Giving appropriate attitudes to them as years bring their changes.

    (*. . . only to be interrupted by a description of the four "Ages of Man."*)

    First is the boy just beginning to talk and to keep his feet steady
Eager to play with his peers, flaring angrily up over nothing,
Cooling again just as quickly, and changeful from hour to hour.   160
    Next comes the unbearded youth, at last rid of his guardian tutor,
Joying in horses and dogs and the grass of the bright open meadow,
Wax-like in taking the imprints of folly, rebellious to counsel,
Slow in providing what serves his best interest, lavish with money,
Lofty-aspiring and passionate, quick to abandon a fancy.   165
    Shifting of plans comes with manhood's estate and the outlook of manhood;
Now he seeks wealth and alliances, offices claim his devotion,
Now he avoids doing things which he soon might find need for undoing.
    With his advancement in years many troubles beset him; amassing
Still, he is either afraid to make use of the wealth he has gathered   170
Or he treats everything warily, frigidly, always postponing,

Slow to take hope, ineffectual, grasping for longer existence,
Querulous, testy, with praises for nothing but bygones and times when
He was a boy, a reprover and censor of all who are younger.

175   Many agreeable things are conferred by the on-coming years, and
Many are taken away by the years in retreat, so we must not
Misassign roles of the agèd to youth, or of manhood to boyhood;
Characteristics of various ages need careful attention.

      (*Drama. Prescriptions for its composition.*
      a. *the play itself.*)

    Actions are either performed on the stage or reported from elsewhere.

180   What is conveyed to the ear makes a less vivid mark on the mind than
What is performed for the spectator's trustworthy eyes, who "reports it
Then to himself." But such actions as properly happen indoors you
Do not conduct on the stage; you remove many things out of sight and
Presently have them described by a speaker of eloquent language;

185   Just as Medea must not slay her children in sight of the viewers,
Impious Átreus must not cook the entrails of humans in public;
Never show Prócnē becoming a bird, nor old Cadmus a serpent.
Any such thing would leave *me* disbelieving as well as revolted.

    Nor shall a play that is meant for demand and for future revival

190   Ever have less than five Acts, or include any more than that either.

    Nor should a god intervene save in cases of crisis befitting
Such a deliverer. Nor should a fourth actor do any speaking.

      (b. *the chorus.*)

    See that the chorus is given an integral role in the story
Equal with actors, and see that it sings between Acts only things that

195   Further the unfolding plot and that properly suit with its nature.
See that it favors good men, standing ready to counsel them kindly,
Checking the wrathful and cherishing those who are fearful of evil.
Let it be always for food that is simple and frugal, for wholesome
Justice, for laws that are equal, for Peace with her wide-open portals.

200   Let it keep secrets its ears have received, let it pray to the gods for
Fortune's return to the wretched and present retreat from the haughty.

      (c. *Deterioration of the musical component of drama.*)

    There was a time when the flute, still unbanded with brass and not vying
Yet with the trumpet in sound, lent support to the chorus, its few stops
Gently producing their delicate tones which could perfectly carry

205   All through a theater not yet too crowded and teeming with viewers;
That was, of course, in the days when the listeners still could be counted
(They were so few), and they all were respectable, thrifty, and honest.

    After the victor began to expand his domains, and his cities
Broadened the scope of their walls, and his sponsoring god was revered in

210   Festivals marked by unchecked and permissive carousing by daylight,

Greater indulgence was shown to elaborate music and rhythms.
How would that matter to ignorant farmers on days free of work and
Thrown helter-skelter with city folk, ruffians mixed in with the gentry?
Thus to the flutist's original art there were added new movements,
Wanton parading on stage, and a trailing of robes out behind him.   215
Likewise the number of strings was increased on the simple old lyre and
Torrents of outpouring speech set a style never heard of, replete with
Precepts and saws about everyday life and predictions of future
Happenings such as would not be unfit for the priestess at Delphi.

    (d. *The Satyr play.*)

    He who competed at tragedy scripts for no more than a paltry   220
Goat had his countrified Satyrs soon strip to the skin, and severely
Keeping his dignity, set them to joking by way of a novel
Lure for his hearers to stay in their seats, now the festival rites were
Over, the sacrifice made, and the hearers both drunk and unruly.
Having the Satyrs thus laughing and joking, thus turning the solemn   225
Into the comic, is really commendable, but in so doing
See that a god or a hero appearing along with the Satyrs —
Recently clad in his purple and gold and effectively regal —
Does not descend to the gross kind of talk heard in lower-class taverns
Or, while avoiding the ground, climb sublimity-clouds and talk nonsense.   230
Tragedy's Muse is above any prattle of frivolous verses,
But, like a matron who dances from duty on sacred occasions,
May with propriety mingle a little with impudent Satyrs.

    I would not choose merely forthright and literal words and expressions,
Pisos, if I were to set about writing a play about Satyrs;   235
Nor would I strive for a style so distinct from the tragic that no one
Really could tell whether Davus the slave was the speaker, or daring
Pýthias when she was making a fortune by swindling old Simo,
Or old Silénus who tutored and tended the boy Dionýsus.
I would compose any poem of mine out of matter so widely   240
Known that whoever attempted to match it would labor and sweat in
Vain in attempting to match it: success lies with order and sequence,
And out of everyday usage arises the highest achievement.

    Fauns, I believe, when transferred to the stage from their woodlands, should never
Speak in the language of street boys, or even of Forum frequenters,   245
Nor should they dally like love-stricken youths over languishing verses,
Nor should they cackle obscenities, dwelling on off-color stories;
That would offend any man with a horse, an estate, and a father;
What gets approval from buyers of hot roasted chickpeas and chestnuts
Meets with disfavor and wins no awards from the persons of substance.   250

    (e. *The dramatic "trimeter."*)

    Any long syllable after a short one produces an iamb,
Lively of movement, and "trímeter" came to be used as the term for

Verses in which six iambics proceeded in unbroken sequence,
Each foot alike from the first to the last. All the same, in more recent
255 Times, to provide retardation and statelier cadence, iambics
Have been admitting the ponderous spondee to membership status,
Treating it kindly but not to the point of relinquishing to it
Either the second or fourth-foot positions. In Áccius's well known
Trimeters iambs are scarce, and the rarity of them in lines that
260 Énnius wrote for the stage — and excessively weighted and burdened —
Has been adjudged the result of his hasty and careless composing —
Or of unconscionable ignorance as to the art of poetics.

(f. *Only the Greek masters provide metrical standards.*)

Not every critic can tell when a poem is rhythmically faulty,
And there is undeserved leniency granted to Roman composers.
265 Counting on that, shall I *also* be slipshod at writing? and fancy
My faults will never be noticed? and warily tread within limits
Set by the hope of forgiveness? By that course I *may* escape censure
But I have *not* deserved praise. My advice to you, friends, is to keep on
Poring, by day and by night, over models the Greeks have established.
270 Yes, it is true that your forebears had praise for the meters and wit of
Plautus, on both counts too lenient, not to say foolish, in granting
So much esteem. Now if only we both, you and I, can distinguish
Nowadays what is mere crudeness and what is true wit, and can also
Count out an accurate cadence by ear and on well-calloused fingers!

(g. *Beginnings of tragedy and comedy; transition to a new topic.*)

275 Thespis is said to have been the inventor of tragedy, something
Not known before, and they say he transported his dramas in wagons,
Singers and actors performing with faces daubed over with wine lees.
After him, Aeschylus founded the usage of masks and of stately
Costumes, and laid out a stage of no very great size over trestles,
280 Setting a grandiose style and a pattern for strutting in buskins.
Next came Old Comedy, winning a great deal of praise, but its freedom
Overstepped limits and turned into license and virulence, such that
Curbing by law was in order; the law was enacted; the chorus,
Losing its power to harm, then disgracefully lapsed into silence.

(VI   *Roman literature and some of its problems.*)

285 Poets of ours have left *no* compositional form unattempted,
And not the least of their merits has been to abandon the pathways
Traced by the Greeks and to celebrate Roman achievements and exploits
Both in the purple-stripe tragedy and in the comedy toga.
Latium would not be more mighty in valor and weaponry than in
290 Language and letters, if only the painstaking use of the file were
Not so repugnant to all of its poets. You scions of royal
Numa Pompílius, censure, I bid you, the poem that has not

Many a day been worked over, with many erasures and changes,
And, with a closely pared fingernail, ten times retested for smoothness.

Just because genius was prized by Demócritus over mere lowly   295
Craftsmanship, just because *he* said no sane-minded poet could enter
Hélicon, many of ours will not bother to shave or to trim their
Fingernails; baths they avoid; they live all to themselves in some corner.
Name and renown as a poet can only be won if the head that
Three Anticýras could never make sane is in no case committed   300
Into the hands of the barber Licínus. — Oh, I am a fool to
Vent my bad temper and bile in this fashion when spring is approaching!
No other course would produce better poems. But that is no matter;
I shall be rather a whetstone which, though it is useless for cutting,
Can impart sharpness to iron: although I write nothing myself, I   305
Can define function and purpose of writing, explain whence resources
Are to be drawn, and show what provides poets with substance and form, and
What is in good taste or bad, where right or wrong judgment will lead them.

Clear understanding is foremost and first of the rules for good writing.
Concepts abound in the works of Socratic philosophers; once that   310
Matter is properly grasped, you will find all your words without effort.
One who has learned what he owes to his friends and his country, what sort of
Love is the due of a parent, how brother and guest should be cherished,
What is the trust and the duty of judges and statesmen advisors,
And how commanders in war must comport themselves: such a man cannot   315
Help but give all of his characters language appropriate to them.
Manners and life as they are, are the models to follow, O you who
Learnedly imitate: see that you speak with their actual voices.
Sometimes a play that is vivid at moments, with characters speaking
Lines that befit them, no matter if greatness and polish are lacking,   320
Interests an audience more, and turns out to be more entertaining,
Than the pretentious variety ever so prettily jingling.

Genius was granted the Greeks by the Muse, and the gift of a rounded
Utterance; nor did the Greeks ever suffer from greed, save the greed for
Praise, whereas schoolboys of Rome do examples with figures, converting   325
Twelfths of an *as* into terms of the decimal system: "Now, tell me,
Son of Albínus: if you had five twelfths of an *as* and subtracted
One twelfth, how much would be left? Can you give me the answer?" — "One
                                                                third." — "Ah,

You will make out! Say you added a twelfth, how much *then* would it come to?"
—"Half of an *as*." With a canker like that, and with grubbing for money   330
Steeping their minds, can we ever expect they will write any poems
Worth using cedar-oil paper and keeping in cypress-wood cases?

(VII   *Miscellaneous principles.*
a. *Poetry should entertain and instruct.*)

Poets seek either to profit the reader or else entertain him,
Or to combine both components, the charming and useful, together.

335   If you intend to convey certain teachings, be brief, so that minds may
       Readily seize on your statements and afterwards surely retain them:
       Any superfluous words only cause a full mind to brim over.
       Fictions composed to amuse should abide within plausible limits,
       Nor should a story demand a belief in capricious inventions:
340   Little boys eaten by Lamias are not extracted alive from
       Bellies of Lamias. Oldsters deride what does not teach a lesson;
       Young bucks ignore any work that is over-austere; but one who
       Mingles the sweet and the useful together will carry the vote with
       All of the parties by charming the reader while giving him counsel.
345   That kind of book brings in money for book dealers, such as the Sosii,
       That kind of book crosses seas and expands the renown of the author.

          (b. Some *flaws are inevitable; good works are those*
          containing a minimum of flaws.)

          There are defects, I admit, of a kind that deserve overlooking;
       Strings may not sound quite the note that the mind and the hand had intended,
       And, all too often, the flat that we try for comes out as a sharp, nor
350   Will the good marksman unfailingly hit every target he threatens.
       But, when a poem shows beauties preponderant, I am not one to
       Cavil and fret at occasional blemishes splotched by a careless
       Hand or unguarded against by the proneness of humans to error.
       What is my point, then? Why, this: that the copyist who, despite warnings,
355   Miswrites the same thing repeatedly cannot be pardoned, and any
       Harpist forever misplaying the very same note will be laughed at.
       I rank the frequently blundering poet with Chóerilus: when he
       Does produce two or three excellent lines I am startled to laughter,
       As I am taken aback by good Homer's occasional drowsing.
360   True, with a long piece of writing a drowsiness does steal upon you.
          Poems are often like pictures; with some you are much more delighted
       If you inspect them close up and with others if viewed from a distance;
       One needs a half-light, another is seen to advantage in full light,
       Having no fear of the sharpest inspection a critic may practice;
365   One pleases once, while another, ten times reexamined, still pleases.

          (c. *Mediocrity is failure.*)

          You, elder youth of the two, though you do have a father to guide you
       Rightly, and though you have wisdom yourself, bear in mind what I tell you:
       Only in limited areas can what is middling and passable ever
       Find its acceptance. A lawyer, in court or as counsel, with only
370   Middling abilities may lack the talents of brilliant Messála
       And he may not have the knowledge and skill of Cascéllius Aulus,
       Yet he can still serve a purpose, while *no* place is open to middling
       Poets, and neither mankind nor the gods nor the book-dealers want them.
       Just as an excellent banquet is marred by a discord of music,
375   Or by a perfume too coarse, or by poppyseed mixed with Sardinian

Honey, when things of that sort never ought to have been there at all: so
Too with a work that was born and created for charming all spirits:
Missing the heights by the least little trifle, it drops to the bottom.

(d. *Who should write? And when should he publish?*)

Someone not knowing the games on Mars' Field will stay out of the contests;
Lacking all skill with a ball or a quoit or a hoop, one abstains from   380
Playing those sports to avoid the derision of congregate viewers;
Yet, knowing nothing of poetry, people still write. And why not? — as
Long as a man is respectably born, of good family, rated
Wealthy enough to be titled a knight, and with nothing against him?

You, with your excellent judgment and mind, are not likely to say or   385
Do what your natural bent would forbid; but if some day you do try
Writing, I urge you: submit compositions to Máecius the critic,
Or to your father, or me, and take care that the work is for nine years
Privately kept in its manuscript. What is not published can then be
Simply destroyed; but beyond your recall is the word you have uttered.   390

(e. *The practical uses of poetry.*)

Men of the forests of old were deterred from their carnage and bestial
Fodder at words from the gods as delivered by consecrate Orpheus,
Whence he was fabled a tamer of tigers and ravening lions;
And of Amphíon, the founder of Thebes, it is told that he moved great
Stones by the sounds of his tortoise-shell lyre and emplaced them at will by   395
Sweetest entreaties of singing. For these were the uses of wisdom
Once: demarcation of public from private, profane things from sacred,
Ban on all mating at random, establishing rules about marriage,
Setting up organized towns, and inscribing of laws upon wood. Thus
Honor and fame came to dwell with prophetic and half-divine poets   400
And with their songs. After those came preeminent Homer, and also
Songs by Tyrtáeus, who roused up all masculine spirits to martial
Exploits. By poetry too there were oracles given, and ways and
Patterns of life were set forth; in Piérian song the good will of
Monarchs was courted, and festival games were invented, and games for   405
Closing the seasonal labors of men. I recall all these things lest
You feel ashamed of the lyrical Muse or of singer Apollo.

(f. *Talent and training are equally necessary.*)

Whether a poem of worth is the product of nature or art is
Quite undetermined. Without an abundance of talent I see no
Profit in study, nor any advantage in genius left raw, since   410
Each needs the help of the other and friendly conjunction of effort.
One who is anxious to get to the coveted goal in the foot race
Will have since boyhood endured and performed many things, with his sweats and
Chills and abstaining from women and wine. Any flutist in Pýthian
Contest has first known the rigors of training in dread of his teacher.   415

Nowadays one merely says, "I compose the most marvelous poems;
'Last after me gets the mange!', I'm disgraced if I'm left to the rear and
Have to confess that I simply don't know what I never have studied."

(VII   *Critics and criticism.*)

Just as a crowd will collect at an auctioneer's call to "Buy wares!", so
420   Toadies come flocking in hopes of their personal gain to a poet
Land-dowered, loaded with cash, every cent of it interest-bearing.
If there is someone, in fact, who can offer an excellent dinner,
Help some obscure little starveling with bail and extract him from tangled
Nets of a lawsuit, it *would* be a wonder to me if that happy
425   Man could distinguish a true friend amid the deceivers around him.
If there is someone indebted to you or about to become so,
Never invite him to listen to poems of yours at a thankful
Moment, because he will cry: "Oh, that's beautiful! Excellent! Perfect!"
One passage makes him turn pale, while another brings tears to his grateful
430   Eyes, he will leap for delight, he will stamp with his foot in his fury.
Just as hired mourners in funeral processions will wail and make gestures
Far more distracted with grief than the actual mourners, a scoffer
Puts on a show of intenser emotion than honest admirers.
Kings, it is said, have the habit of urging huge goblets of drink on
435   Someone, and testing his nature by wine, when they wish to make sure of
Character worthy of friendship; but if you write poems you never
Need such a ruse to discover the thoughts of your fox-like cajolers.
Had you but read to Quintílius, he would have advised you: "Improve on
This — and on this," and if *you* said you *could* not improve them, not even
440   After a second attempt and a third, he would bid you delete them
And to reforge the bad verses all over again on the anvil;
But, if you chose to defend a line rather than change or amend it,
Not a word more would he waste or admit any further discussion;
Then you were free to delight in yourself and your work without challenge.
445   Any good, competent man will go over your poems and censure
Lines that are flat, finding fault with the roughnesses, drawing a line with
Heavy black pen through an ill-expressed passage, excising pretentious
Ornament, forcing the clarification of any unclearness,
Pointing out all ambiguities, marking what needs to be changed, — in
450   Short, be your new Aristárchus; nor will he say, "Why take a friend to
Task over trifles?" Those trifles can ruin a poet, if after
Having quite wrongly been humored, he suffers derision in public.

(IX   *Poetic ecstasy is a fraud.*)

Wise people shun any man with the mange or the royal disease of
Jaundice, or one who is moonstruck, or given to frenzies of priestly
455   Dancing, as prudence shuns contact and touch of the lunatic poet:
Street urchins heckle him, only the recklessly curious trail him.
Belching up verses, he maunders around with his gaze to the skies, and

If, like the bird-catcher watching for blackbirds, he falls in a well or
Ditch and starts shouting for help at the top of his lungs, "Come and get me
Out of here, citizens! Help!", no one bothers to help him. If someone   460
Does come and throw him a rope, I will ask: "Are you sure that this fellow
Did not deliberately throw himself down there without any slightest
Wish to be rescued?", and I will proceed to relate how the famous
Poet in Sicily perished: Empédocles, having a mind to
Be like a god and immortal, quite coolly jumped down into Etna's   465
Raging volcano. Let suicide stand as an option for poets.
Saving their lives when they *don't* want them saved may amount to a murder.
This is by no means his only attempt, and if rescued, he will not
Be the more human or give up his love for a death with theatrics.
Nor has it ever been clear why he keeps on producing his poems;   470
Whether he pissed on his late father's ashes or came under curse from
Doing away with some sacred enclosure, he is, of course, mad, and
Much like a bear that has managed to smash through the bars of the bear-cage,
Out springs this ruthless reciter to pounce on the schooled and the unschooled;
And, when he gets them, he holds them and kills them by reading his poems,   475
Gorging on blood like a leech on the skin and not dropping till sated.

One omission strikes us in this long poem about literary composition: Horace offers no guidance for writing the kind of poetry he himself wrote. Lines 83–85 say that meters have been assigned by the Muses for various types of lyric poems, but he does not mention what those meters are. Yet lines 89–284—with some digressions—dwell on dramatic composition, a genre never attempted by Horace, as he himself admits. If the Pisos had playwriting in mind and requested information on that topic in particular, it is hard to understand why Horace supplied them with guidelines four centuries out of date. Morris, in his note to lines 220–250, about the Satyr play, says:

> This section also is in part traditional, but it is in part a real criticism of forms of drama which were on the stage in Horace's time, like mimes and *fabulae Atellanae* (clown farces) and which bore enough resemblance to the Satyr plays to justify Horace in treating them all as one kind of drama.

The present translator has tried very hard, but without success, to put himself in agreement with this opinion of Morris's. On the other hand, lines 89–284 raise more problems than they solve relative to the *history* of drama.

The poem as a whole is hardly a *letter* at all. As an "Art of Poetry," a Law of literature, it holds small appeal for the modern reader, who is baffled to know how the generations between the Renaissance and the Romanic era could view it with such awe. But if it is taken simply as "E.2.3," as a *sermo*, a *causerie* about literature by a literary man of high achievements, the poem has great charm. It flows easily from topic to topic, its wit sparkles, and its common sense reassures. And it reveals more about the speaker than it reveals about the mystery of creative writing.

Notes in abundance, perhaps in overabundance, are supplied to Horace's "E.2.3;" adequate notes to Horace's *Ars Poetica* would require a volume.

1–4   Horace intends a "super-grotesque." "Bird-women" were, in varying combinations, sirens, harpies, sphinxes, gorgons, and so on, but ancient art had no fish-tailed mermaids.

9–10   We are free to imagine that the objection is voiced by the Pisos themselves.

15 "Purple patch" (*purpureus pannus*) has become a set phrase in English critical vocabulary.

16–18 Actual (lost) poems are probably being cited; for example, "a view of the Rhine" may refer to "Alpínus's" poem about Gaul, which "turned the Rhine-mouth to mud" (S.1.10.37 and note).

20–22 That is, the artist was commissioned to paint a votive tablet, with one or more scenes depicting the swimmer's escape from drowning, to be hung in a shrine, as in S.2.1.32–33 and note.

32 "Gymnasium" means a gladiators' training school; the street side contained shops, the "last one of which as you are coming down from the Forum" being this particular bronzesmith's shop. So Morris interprets the single word *imus*, "lowest."

47–48 E.2.2.115–119 recommends revival of picturesque "Words the Cethéguses sounded of old and the speech of the Catos"; here the statement is qualified by "in adroit combination" (*callida . . . iunctura*).

51 "Wrap-loined" = *cinctutis*, a word almost certainly coined by Horace. "It means (says Morris) 'clad in the *cinctus*,' a kind of loincloth or kilt which was used before the tunic as an undergarment." Cethégus was consul in 204 B.C.

51–58 Latin had often borrowed Greek words, especially since 240 B.C., for example, Cicero's *philosophia*, but Horace usually "translates" the borrowed word: "hundred-handed Gyas" (*Odes* 2.17.14) is *centimanus*, from Greek *hekatógkheiros;* the Áufidus River (in *Odes* 4.14.27) is "bull-shaped," *tauriformis*, from Greek *taurómorphos*, (which we paraphrase as "raging like a bull").

Vergil was criticized in his lifetime and afterwards for being "too Greek" in his language. His Third Eclogue begins:

> Menalcas: Tell me, Damoetas, whose sheep are these? Meliboeus's?
> Damoetas: No, Aegon's; Aegon turned them over to me just the other day.

Donatus's *Vita* of Vergil around 350 A.D. quotes a parody of these two lines:

> Menalcas: Tell me, Damoetas, whose sheep are these? and is he Latin?
> Damoetas: No, Aegon's; our country people don't talk this way.

63–68 The interrupting thought is expanded to mention three admirable, but less than stupendous, engineering projects undertaken by Julius Caesar or by Augustus:

1. cutting a channel from the sea into the Lucrine Lake (S.2.4.31–34 and note) to create an inner harbor for the Roman fleet (a similar harbor was created at Ostia, the port of Rome at the mouth of the Tiber).
2. building the 19-mile canal through the Pontine marshes; see the note to S.1.5. 11–25, under "Itinerary." A small portion of the marshes was reclaimed for agriculture.
3. straightening the Tiber channel for flood-control; but note the small-scale project of the same kind on Horace's farm, in E.1.14.29–30.

73 Here Horace begins paraphrasing passages from a Greek handbook of rhetoric, which ancient commentator Porphyrio says was the treatise by Neoptólemus of the third century B.C.; from it, he adds, Horace chose only the most important sections.

Horace's procedure from line 73 to at least line 284 seems to have been to select a passage from Neoptólemus for paraphrase, then to digress into comments of his own at will until another passage from Neoptólemus caught his attention, and so on.

73–88 Certain meters are obligatory with certain genres of poetry:

• Epic, or, narrative, poems require Homer's dactylic hexameter; definition on p. 14.

• For a sad "elegy" "lines of dissimilar length" are required—meter unspecified. Mimnérmus, around 600 B.C., was usually said to be the originator of this couplet-form (E.1.6.65–66 and E.2.2.101 and notes); but, as explained in the note to E.2.2.91, the true elegy had turned into the "elegiac verses" of such contemporary poets as Tibullus and Propertius, who alternated dactylic hexameters with so-called "pentameters" in poems about love. Horace seems to refer to *epigrams* expressing "joy when one's wish had been granted."

· In the 650s and 640s B.C. Archílochus wrote poems of invective, for which he used "iambics," a term very clearly defined in lines 251–4 below; see the Introduction to Horace's *Epodes*, p. 96.

· Comedy and tragedy both adopted 6-foot iambics for passages of rapid dialogue.

Comedy actors wore a soft, low slipper ("sock," *soccus*); see Milton's *L'Allegro*, 132: "If Jonsons learned Sock be on," that is, if a *comedy* of Ben Jonson's is being performed.

Tragedy actors wore a thick-soled boot laced half way up the leg: Latin *cothúrnus,* English "buskin" (from "buckskin").

83–85   As if weary of paraphrasing Neoptólemus, Horace merely says that proper meters have been established "by the Muse" for:

· hymns to the gods and to heroes (*pueros deorum,* "lads of the gods");
· victory odes for athletes and horses, such as Pindar's; note to *Odes* 4.2.5–27;
· love poems;
· drinking songs.

For poets in the last two categories see the note to *Odes* 4.9.5–12, where the list includes: Simónides, Alcáeus, Stesíchorus, Anácreon, and Sappho.

92   The translator has ventured to place line 92 where it seemed to make better sense.

Compare the fixed categories of meters for medieval French narrative poems: 8-syllable couplets for "Arthurian" matter, and for "Charlemagne" matter 10-syllable lines in *laisses* ("bundles") with all lines in a *laisse* having the same rhyme-sounds.

90   Átreus (father of Agamémnon) took revenge on his own brother Thyéstes by killing the latter's sons and serving their flesh to Thyéstes at a banquet; *Odes* 1.16.17 and note.

93–94   Chrémes is likely to be identical with the unnamed father berating his profligate son in S.1.4.48–52. In Epode 1,33 a miser named Chrémes hid his money in the ground. In S.1.10.40–42 a Chrémes is outwitted by "Davus the slave and the artful young girl" in a (lost) play by Fundánius. We suspect that all three allusions are to the same comedy by Fundánius, for whom see the note to S.1.10.40.

95   Péleus (father of Achilles) lived in exile as a young man because he had killed his brother Phocus; see also the note to *Odes* 3.7.17.

Télephus, an illegitimate son of Hercules, was abandoned by his persecuted mother on a mountainside (or, in an ark committed to the waves), suckled by a doe, found and reared by cattlemen, and lived to see many adventures. Horace doubtless alludes to a lost play of Euripides in which Télephus, after being wounded by Achilles, came as a beggar to the Greek camp to obtain the cure which an oracle had told him was obtainable only from Achilles.

Both stories have to be pieced together from multiple sources.

97   "Booming," like the "booming with tragedy-thunder" of E.1.3.14, depends on the figure of blowing across the mouth of a jar (*ampulla*). Horace's *sesquipedalia verba* is regular Latin for "words a foot-and-a-half long," but we keep the outlandish term which English has adopted, from this line, to describe foolish pomposity.

105–107   It is difficult to reconcile these lines with the use of dramatic masks.

108–111   Speech in general, and dramatic speech in particular, relieve our emotions. Horace may be advancing his own version of Aristotle's doctrine of tragic "catharsis."

113   Horace puns on "cavalrymen (knights) and footsoldiers" and "knights (as a high social rank) and commoners."

114–118   A list of character "types," probably from the handbook of Neoptólemus. Line 118 contrasts two "barbarians," primitive versus effete Oriental, with two kinds of Greeks (for stylistic balance); Thebans and Argives fought each other in the Seven-against-Thebes story.

120–127   Probably a paraphrase from Neoptólemus again. For Ixíon (124) see *Odes* 3.11.21 and note. For the complex stories of the others, see Robert Graves: *The Greek Myths.*

128–135   A statement of the "classical" doctrine of "imitation." Most Roman plays on

Greek subjects were "translations," or rather, "free adaptations." Lines 133–4 say, literally: ". . . nor will you be at pains as a faithful interpreter (*fidus interpres*) to render word for word, nor, as an *imitator*, . . ."—*imitator* being Horace's Latin word.

136   "Cyclical poets," so called by scholars in Alexandria after 300 B.C., rounded out "the Trojan cycle" of story with six "epics" supplementing the *Iliad* and the *Odyssey: The Cyprian Lays,* the *Aethiopis,* the *Little Iliad,* the *Sack of Troy,* the *Returns,* and the *Telegony.* Surviving fragments of these inferior works are printed, in Greek and in English, in pp. 489–532 of the "Hesiod" volume of the Loeb Classical Library.

139   In Latin, this famous line reads: *Parturient montes, nascetur ridiculus mus.* Latin prosody enabled Horace to place *mus* in the final and *un*accented syllable for comic effect.

140–152   For Horace, Homer is the supreme poet and the *Odyssey* the supreme poem. Lines 141–2 repesent Horace's second free paraphrase of the opening lines of the *Odyssey,* the earlier version being in E.1.2.19–22.

Antíphates (*Odyssey* 10.100 ff.) is a cannibal giant, king over other cannibals.

Odyssey 12.87 ff. describes Scylla, a twelve-footed monster whose six snake-necks swoop down from her cliff-lair to seize sailors from passing ships and devour them. A bow-shot away Charýbdis the whirlpool sucks whole ships to the bottom of the sea.

Odyssey 9.160 ff. tells of the cannibal-ogre called the Cýclops ("One-eye"), whose particular name is Polyphémus. See S.1.5.63; E.2.2.125; *Odes* 1.4.8; and notes.

"Right to the heart of his story he plunges" (line 148) paraphrases the famous phrase *in medias res.*

155   In the 26 preserved Roman comedies (20 by Plautus, 6 by Terence), the final words *vos plaudite!* were usually assigned—so far as can be judged by the manuscripts—either to the last-speaking actor or to all three actors, that is, to "the company," but in eight of these cases the words are unassigned. What Horace means by "the singer" (*cantor*) is unclear. So far as is known, Greek comedies had no closing formula corresponding to *vos plaudite!*

158–179   That this passage is a digression is immediately clear, since in classical drama children appeared very rarely and only as nonspeaking characters, e.g., the two small daughters of Oedipus in the final scene of *Oedipus the King.* The four "ages" are: boy, youth, adult man, and old man.

From either direct knowledge or from report, Shakespeare was probably aware of these lines when he had Jaques report the *seven* "Ages of Man" in *As You Like It,* II,7.

"With praises for nothing but bygones" (173) = the admired phrase: *laudator temporis acti* ("a praiser of time past").

180 ff.   Resuming his paraphrase of the Neoptólemus handbook, Horace now proceeds to explain to the Pisos, his contemporaries, how to compose a classical tragedy in the manner of the Athenian stage of 400 years ago!

180–188   Not only were all Greek and Roman dramas performed in open-air theaters, but all action was represented as taking place out of doors, most commonly in front of a king's residence. All action "inside the palace" or elsewhere was reported, especially in the long and elaborate "messenger's speech" that usually led into the final scene.

On-stage violence was taboo—some scholars think because drama was a religious performance at a religious ceremony—but there was no limit to the violence that was permitted in oral report.

(French classical tragedy, which was performed indoors and which represented only indoors action, observed the same taboo and granted the same freedom to oral report. Its aristocratic propriety—*bienséance*—was, however, unknown to the Greeks and Romans.)

186   For Átreus see the note to line 90 above.

189–190   There is no wholly satisfactory explanation for this statement: literally, "Let a play not be less or more ample than a fifth Act . . ." (*Neve minor neu sit quinto productior actu/ fabula*). If by "Acts" Horace and/or Neoptólemus meant "acting sections" (as opposed to choral sections, as in line 194 below), then there are infractions of the rule even among the 33 preserved Greek tragedies of the 5th century B.C.

The 5-Act divisions in the 26 preserved Roman comedies of Plautus and Terence seem to be the work of "classical editors" superimposed upon the original texts.

Because of Horace's puzzling statement most serious dramas ("tragedy") in Europe—except in Iberia—between ca. 1575 and the 1860s were organized into five Acts.

191–192   A commonsense precept: do not get your characters into such straits that they have to be rescued by supernatural means (*deus ex machina*). Assuming, however, that the statement paraphrases Neoptólemus, we suspect that Neoptólemus objected to the way Euripides introduced divinities in certain final scenes, particularly in *Iphigenia in Tauris,* or even the means of the heroine's escape at the close of *Medea.*

192   Modern readers need to remind themselves that all classical dramas were performed by three actors—all adult male citizens, who, by rapid backstage changes of mask and costume, shared the up-to-ten roles of a play (not counting occasional "mute" figures).

Aeschylus used only two actors, until Sophocles began using three. But a fourth actor may have been used by Euripides (e.g., in *Hippolytus*), though this claim is disputed. As in the previous note, we are led to think that Neoptólemus was an anti-Euripidean purist who felt that Euripides had corrupted a great art-form.

Horace ignores the "mimes" of his own time (and since 300 B.C. in Greek) to which he himself alludes in S.1.2.2 and S.1.10.6 and in which actresses appeared, for example, the Arbuscula of S.1.10.77.

193   Fifteen adult male citizens, who in a given play might be costumed as men or as women, comprised the chorus of Athenian tragedy of the 5th century B.C. (and thereafter).(Comedy used a chorus of 24 men, who might be fantastically costumed as animals in some cases.) They sang the choral odes which alternated with the "acting sections" of the tragedy, remaining throughout the play in the "dancing-circle" ("orchestra," from Greek *orkheîsthai,* "to dance"), though their leader (a sixteenth person) might engage in dialogue with on-stage actors. About their music and choreography almost nothing is known, but collectively they were witness and party to all on-stage action.

In classical Greek times this "dancing-circle" was a full circle, up to 20 meters/65 feet in diameter, with a paved surface, in front of the stage and at perhaps a slightly lower level, though this point is moot. Roman theaters had a semicircular "orchestra," from which a few stones steps led up to the stage level.

193–201   Neoptólemus the purist must have objected to the perfunctory odes, borrowed or random-assigned by dramatists soon after the beginning of the 4th century B.C. (The 26 preserved Roman comedies have no chorus at all.)

To the audience, as to the on-stage actors, the chorus should express only morally right opinions (196–9).

In Euripides's *Hippolytus* Phaidra confides the guilty secret of her passion for her stepson to her nurse in the presence of the chorus of Trozénian women; the women keep this secret from other characters in the play. So should all choruses keep all secrets.

The chorus members, with their leader, constituted a single collective character *in* the play; at the same time they constituted what has been described as an "ideal spectator" speaking both *to* and *for* the audience. Thus the chorus was an intermediate entity between the dramatic illusion and the audience reality.

(The first operas, ca. 1600 A.D., intended a revival of ancient Athenian tragedy *with* chorus, but most operas have sought to "rationalize" the presence of the chorus and to restrict its appearances to certain scenes only. Very few have, like *The Beggars Opera,* kept the chorus in the spectators' view throughout the performance.)

202–205   The "flute" more nearly resembled a recorder rather than the transverse flute. Horace calls it a *tibia,* "shinbone,"—early flutes were made of bone; the Greek *aulós* ("something breathed into") was made of other materials, usually wood, and had a varying number of stops closed with the fingers.

Pictorial representations later than 400 B.C. show a "double flute" with a longer and a shorter pipe for bass and treble respectively, (Greek "male" and "female," Latin "left" and "right"), controlled by a single mouthpiece which was usually supported by a cheek-strap. (The "syrinx" or "Pan's pipe," made of graduated lengths of reed and blown across the open ends, was not used in the theater.)

The "flutist" must have "given the tone," kept the chorus on pitch, and maintained the rhythm. He also moved about the stage—at least in Roman times—to play accompaniment for actors performing a solo; see lines 214–5 below.

205–207 In the translator's opinion, the "degradation of the early flute" is likely to have been a complaint of Neoptólemus, and perhaps the "degradation of audiences" also. Horace then imagines both "degradations" as parallel to the deterioration described in E.2.1.139–155—and parallel to the general deterioration of human life since the "Golden Age."

208–210 The "victor" can only be Rome after the conquest of Greece (as in E.2.1.156) or after the Punic Wars (as in E.2.1.162 and note).

The "sponsoring god" (209) = *Genius,* as in E.2.2.187–9 and note.

Carousing by daylight (210) is reprehensible; compare S.1.4.51–52; *Odes* 2.7.6–7; E.1.14.34; and the notes to those passages.

211 The same complaint was made against Euripides. Possibly the change was something like that between Mozartean and Wagnerian opera.

216 Even with the very first lyre, invented by the infant Hermes (*Odes* 1.10.6 and note), ancient authorities disagreed as to the number of strings: 3, 4, or 7; *Odes* 3.11.4 (and note) specifies 7. In S.1.3.8 Hermógenes uses a four-string lyre. Musicologists say classical lyres had from 4 to 18 strings.

220–221 Horace takes Greek *tragōdía* ("tragedy") to be "goat-song," from *trágos,* "goat," + *ōdē,* "song," and he believes the term refers to the prize of "a paltry goat" for the winner of the annual tragedy-writing competition. The etymology of "tragedy" has been extensively debated, but with a reluctant, if general, return to the traditional "goat-song" interpretation. The goat is thought to have been more probably the sacrificial victim in the religious rites of which tragedy-performances were a part.

For the annual spring festival in honor of Dionysus poets prepared a set of three tragic plays, originally as a trilogy dealing with one theme, and a "Satyr play" also connected with the same theme, hence a total of four plays. A committee selected the three best sets of plays, and festival audiences then saw four plays a day for each of three days—a total of twelve. After the performances, first, second, and third prizes were awarded. Horace passes over this information as if the Pisos knew it without his explanation.

Satyrs (*Odes* 1.1.31; *Odes* 2.19.4 and note) were certainly devotees of Dionysus; in Jane Harrison's opinion (*Prolegomena,* . . , pp. 379–388) they were "mythologized" human backwoodsmen, lusty, sly, mischievous liars, but not vicious. Pictorial representations show them with black, bristly hair, snub noses, pointed ears, and sometimes horses' tails. Yet line 244 below equates them with fauns (*fauni*), *Italian* woodland godlings whose patron is the woodland *god* Faunus (*Odes* 1.4.11; 1.17.1; 2.17.28; 3.18.1).

220–250 About a "Satyr play" we may confidently say that it was: (a) a play whose chorus consisted of Satyrs; (b) comic yet distinct from the genre of comedy; (c) closely associated, at least originally, with tragedy and performed only after a sequence of tragedies; and (d) that it had nothing whatsoever to do with "satire." All else is conjecture. One complete Satyr play survives, Euripides's *Cyclops,* based on Book 9 of the *Odyssey.* In 1912 an ancient refuse heap in Egypt yielded up about half of a Satyr play by Sophocles, *The Trackers* (or *The Searching Satyrs*), based on the search for Apollo's stolen cows in the "Homeric Hymn to Hermes." Both plays date probably to the 440s B.C.

Soon after that decade the Satyr play is thought to have undergone a change, or to have been replaced by a non-tragic serious type of play, represented among preserved dramas by the *Alkestis* and the *Helena* of Euripides. After 400 B.C. it is thought that no further Satyr plays were composed. Thus Horace seems to debate, for the sake of the Pisos, the composition of a type of drama 350 years extinct.

Presumably, Horace is reporting what Neoptólemus said about Satyr plays, and presumably Neoptólemus was writing about Satyr plays before 450 B.C., possibly before 500 B.C., and about those lost works almost everything is uncertain. Some scholars think Satyr plays were a derivative from tragedy; others think they were the original tragedy-form oddly surviving side by side with their "descendant."

236–239 Horace emphasizes that the poetic style of a Satyr play must not duplicate the style of comedy, which is a wholly separate genre. The translator takes this to mean that the Satyr play is poetic and mythological, whereas comedy is "realistic."

Davus, Pýthias, and Simo are character types of the sort to be found in comedies of Terence, but no preserved comedy of Terence contains these particular names. See the note to lines 93–94 above, about Chrémes.

In both the *Cyclops* of Euripides and the *Trackers* of Sophocles Silenus appears as the father of the Satyrs and as chorus leader. In Vergil's Sixth Eclogue he is shown as obese, old, drunken, immensely learned, and a poet-singer of the highest skill.

240–243 In the prose version of E.2.3 by E. H. Blakeney these lines are transposed to come between lines 130 and 131, as if they were irrelevant to the Satyr-play discussion.

248 A "man with a horse, an estate, and a father" = "a citizen of standing." Ownership of a horse fit for military use was the original qualification of a "knight" (*Eques*). Having a *named* father indicated free-born status. Horace, for all his reverence for his father, never *names* his father, who, while still a slave, would have had only a "given name," perhaps only a nickname.

252–254 Horace does not explain why the 6-foot iambic line came to be called a "trímeter," which means a "3-foot line." Perhaps it was because the term "hexameter had been preempted to describe the *dactylic* hexameter (of Homer and of the present poem).

254–256 "In more recent times" = *non ita pridem*. This, as Morris remarks, is "not quite intelligible," since the iambic trimeter line had "from the earliest times" admitted spondees, that is, poetic feet consisting of two long syllables. See also the note to line 467 of the present poem.

268–269 This often-quoted statement reads: *Vos exemplaria Graeca/ nocturna versate manu, versate diurna.*

270–274 Here Plautus is termed a bad metrist, whereas actually he was a skilled metrist according to a "pre-classical" system which Horace did not understand. Cicero had also complained—for the same reason—that Plautus's meters were no meters at all. In an analogous case English taste of the early 18th century found that Chaucer did not scan and that Shakespeare often had too many syllables in a line.

The second objection is to Plautus's wit, and it means only that Horace found slapstick comedy distasteful. Essentially, it restates E.2.1.170–176, where Plautus was said to have composed bravura clown-roles without bothering to fit them into a rational overall plot.

In pairing Plautus with Epicharmus of Sicily (E.2.1.58 and note) Horace implies that both were clumsy beginners of a new genre.

Line 54 of the present poem credited Plautus with the coining of new words from the Greek.

Of line 274 Morris remarks that Horace "did not count the feet of his Alcaics on his fingers." The present translator stoutly disagrees.

275–277 It was a commonplace that Thespis (E.2.1.163 and note) was the inventor of tragedy—ca. 539 B.C. under circumstances that are less than clear. Since tradition agreed that tragedy originated in the "dithyramb," a singing and dancing ceremony in the springtime rites honoring Dionysus, it is thought that Thespis was the leader of such a "chorus" and that his innovation consisted of his impersonation of the god during the rite, so that the choral song *to* and *about* Dionysus became a hymn interrupted by speeches *by* the god Dionysus. No text by Thespis survives; the very drama-titles attributed to him are in doubt. Aristotle's *Poetics* does not mention his name.

His transportation of his dramas in wagons is mentioned only by Horace.

No Satyr plays are attributed to him. Indeed, the invention of the Satyr play is attributed to one Pratinas of Phlius, apparently in the 490s B.C. Yet the Satyrs and their joyous conclusion to tragedies may have been "there" all along and Pratinas may have been the first to compose *texts* for them. So thinks Sir Gilbert Murray in an excursus, pp. 341–363 of Jane Harrison's *Themis;* see pp. 344–5.

278–280 These innovations of Aeschylus (525–456 B.C.) tally with information from other sources. His first entry in tragedy-competition is reported as of 499 B.C. At some point in his career performances were given on the south slope of the Athenian acropolis, but the Theater of Dionysus now viewed there by tourists is essentially a structure from after 338 B.C.

"Masks" (278) = *personae,* Latin for "sound through," or possibly an Etruscan word. Later certainly, but perhaps in Aeschylus's time, the mask was a covering for the entire head, including hair, made of linen stiffened with wax, and containing a built-in mouthpiece for amplifying the voice.

"Costumes" = *pallae,* "(Greek-type) mantles" worn over other garments.

"Buskin" = *cothurnus,* as in line 80 above and note.

281–284 The origins of comedy are even more obscure than those of tragedy. For Greek "Old Comedy" see S.1.4.1–5 and note. Its first practitioner was said to be Epicharmus of Sicily, ca. 530–440 B.C., as in E.2.1.58 and note. Tiny fragments survive from his 36 plays.

After the political collapse of Athens in 404 B.C. the biting political satire of Old Comedy was necessarily abandoned and the much tamer Middle Comedy came into use; but there was no legal censorship, as Gilbert Norwood explains in detail—citing this passage from Horace—in *Greek Comedy,* 1931, pp. 26–29. Horace doubtless believed in a parallel with the censorship of Roman comedy, as in E.2.1.145–155 and note.

There is reason to think that the choral portions of drama diminished steadily almost from the beginning, in favor of longer "acting sections," and that the chorus was eliminated altogether in the course of the 4th century. In any case, the chorus was not legislated out of existence.

288 In patriotic Roman tragedies, such as Áccius's *Brutus,* statesmen wore the toga with the purple border (*toga praetexta*) and such works were distinguished from Greek plays by the term *fabula praetexta.*

Comedies with Roman settings and with characters wearing togas went by the name of *fabula togata,* as opposed to a *fabula palliata,* which had a Greek subject and Greek characters wearing the Greek mantle called *palla* or *pallium.*

290 "Painstaking use of the file" = *limae labor et mora.* English critical vocabulary has adopted the set phrase *labor limae* or "the labor of the file."

295 Demócritus (ca. 460 to ca. 362 B.C.) is "the absent-minded philosopher" of E.1.12.12–14 and note, and "the laughing philosopher" of E.2.1.194 and note.

297 Mount Hélicon is the Greek mountain home of the Muses (*Odes* 1.12.5), but here it is "poets' heaven," as in E.2.1.218; compare also the note on Mount Alba in E.2.1.27.

300 Anticyra, as in S.2.3.82–83 and note, was the region in Greece that produced the madness-curing plant hellebore.

301 The barber Licínus is unknown to us; some joke must have attached to the name.

301–302 The allusion is not to fine spring weather but to the mid-February purification ceremonies, which included house cleaning and the taking of cathartics.

304–305 The whetstone metaphor paraphrases a famous rejoinder by the Greek orator Isócrates (436–338 B.C.).

309 "Clear understanding" = simply *sapere,* as in E.2.2.141 and note.

310 "Socratic philosophers"—Plato, Xenophon, et al.—will furnish, not scenarios or literary themes, but "basic ideas." Morris believes the phrase stands for all philosophy.

316 "Characters" = *personae* (translated as "masks" in line 278 above).

324 The odd word "greed" here stands for a narrowly utilitarian education—of which it is the motivation.

326 Twelve *unciae* ("ounces") made one *as* (whence English "ace"), originally a pound of copper but long since depreciated to a small coin. Eight copper *assēs* comprised the monthly tuition fee to schoolmaster Flavius in S.1.6.75.

332 Cedar oil preserved the papyrus from bookworms; compare E.1.20.12. The text says "in polished cypress wood"; the translator supplies "cases" or *capsis,* as in S.1.10.63 and note.

333–334 This notion was elevated into literary Law in 18th-century Germany.

340 Greek *lámia* meant primarily a cannibal-ogre, Latin *lamia,* "witch, vampire," that is, a child-eating hag; see the note to lines 1–5 of *Odes* 3.17, to Lucius Aelius Lamia.

Keats's Lamia as a snake-woman derives from 17th-century Robert Burton's *Anatomy of Melancholy,* which in turn derived the notion from the 4th Book of the *Life of Apollonius (of Tÿana),* early 3rd century. The Lamiae of *Faust* 7696–7790 represent Goethe's independent variation of the ancient folklore figure.

341–342 "Oldsters" — *centuriae seniorum,* "centuries of senior (citizens)," a "century" being a block of 100 voters. King Servius Tullius (578–534 B.C.) was said to have organized the population into 193 such voting blocks, according to their wealth.

"Young bucks" = *celsi* ("haughty") *Ramnes,* the Ramnes/Rhamnes being a "century" of young knights (cavalrymen), said to have been organized by Romulus at the founding of Rome. In a different paraphrase: "our young aristocrats."

345 The Sosii were book dealers in the Vicus Tuscus, as in E.1.20.2 and note.

351 Here "poem" = *carmen,* "lyric poem; ode," not *poema,* the common word for a verse drama. (In line 276 Thespis "transported his *poemata* in wagons.")

354 "Copyist" = *scriptor librarius,* "book writer," that is, a slave assigned for the excellence of his handwriting to the task of copying texts. For the process see the "Note on Book Manufacture" at the end of the notes on E.1.20.

357 Chóerilus was liberally rewarded by Alexander the Great for a sincere but badly composed poem of praise (E.2.1.232–3).

359 For this phrase often misquoted as "(Even) Homer sometimes nods," the text has: . . . *quandoque bonus dormitat Homerus,* "whenever the good Homer drowses."

361 "Poems are often like pictures" = *Ut pictura, poesis:* "As (is) a picture, (so is) *poesis*"; Greek *poíēsis,* from *poiéō,* "to make," meant "a making; a forming, creating; the art of poetry; a poem."

Simónides of Ceos (556–ca. 466 B.C., "the Cean" of *Odes* 2.1.38 and 4.9.7) first remarked that painting was soundless poetry and that poetry was oral painting, and other Greek writers had expressed similar notions. Here in line 361 *Ut pictura, poesis* serves as a convenient transitional phrase and lines 361–5 restate a commonplace observation.

For two centuries the phrase served as the motto and Law of European literary criticism. Already cited with favor by Renaissance writers, it was the basic concept of Du Fresnoy's *De arte graphica,* 1668, and thereafter French, Swiss, English, and German critics claimed—on the revered authority of Horace—that "poetry" should be "painting in words." Various writers challenged the idea, but the systematic separation of "time art" (literature) from "space art" (painting) was the achievement of Lessing in his long essay *Laokoon* 1766. For the long debate Horace cannot be held responsible.

369–371 "In court or as counsel" = the two branches of the legal profession, courtroom lawyer and expert on law.

Marcus Valerius Messál(l)a "Corvínus" was a courtroom orator of almost legendary eloquence in the generation before Horace's; see S.1.10.28 and 85 and notes.

Aulus Cascéllius—Horace inverts the name, as frequently—was a distinguished legal expert contemporary with Messálla "Corvínus."

374 A "discord of music" = *symphonia discors,* of which *symphonia* is directly borrowed from the Greek; compare E.1.12.19: *concordia discors* (translated as "harmonious discord"). Lines 52–53 above recommended judicious borrowings from the Greek.

375 Seeds of the white *papaver* ("poppy") were delicate; Sardinian honey was coarse. Note that banquet food and banquet music are mentioned together: the Romans commonly had music at banquets.

380 Three *Greek*-type sports played on the Campus Martius before spectators. In S.2.2.9–13 three-handed catch and throwing the discus were disdainfully contrasted with Roman rabbit-hunting and horse-taming, and in S.1.6.126 Horace pointedly avoided going

there to play three-handed catch. He also avoided that sport in S.1.5.49. Greek *boys* trundled hoops—see the latter-5th-century gravestone of one Panaitios, now in the National Museum at Athens—but whether adults did so or not is uncertain. See *Odes* 3.24.54–58.

386   "What your natural bent would forbid" = *invita Minervā,* "Minerva unwilling." We follow Cicero's paraphrase in *On Duties* 1.31.110: *Adversante et repugnante naturā.* Compare *crassā Minervā* as "gifted with nature's own wisdom" in S.2.2.3 and note. The old Italian goddess Minerva, whose name is cognate with Latin *mens* and English "mind," is identified with Greek ideas about Athena.

384   Knights, as in E.1.1.57–59 and note, were required to have a minimum fortune of 400,000 sesterces.

387   Máecius the critic = Spurius Máecius Tarpa, head of the Board of Poets, called "arbiter Tarpa" in S.1.10.38 and note.

388   "Nine years," like the "nine months" of S.1.6.61, means "for quite some time" and should not be taken literally. Catullus 95, 1–2 says his friend Cinna's *Smyrna* was published at least "nine harvest-tides and nine winters after it was begun."

390   Compare E.1.18.71: ". . . a word once released is in flight beyond ever recalling." Also Longfellow's poem "I shot an arrow into the air . . ."

391–407   Recalling that E.2.3 was composed *before* E.2.1, this "defense of poesy" is the "forestudy" to E.2.1.5–17 and 118–138.

In stressing the social uses of literature Horace inevitably harks back to the theme of social evolution, as in S.1.3.99–112, *Odes* 1.10.1–6, and certain early stanzas of *Odes* 3.11.

The Orpheus of *Odes* 1.12.7–12 and 1.24.13–14 seemed more lyric-ecstatic than didactic. Here he resembles the Mercury of *Odes* 1.10.1–6. The rationalizing explanation of line 393 is surprising.

Amphíon's moving of the stones is mentioned in *Odes* 3.11.2, but E.1.18.41–44 presented him in quite a different aspect. The point of 391–6 is that Orpheus brought mankind out of nomadic savagery, whereas Amphíon built a civilized city, continuing the "social evolution."

The traditional list of pre-Homeric poets named, in this order: Orpheus, Linus, Musáeus, Thamyris of Thrace, and Amphíon of Thebes.

399   Tradition claimed that laws were first inscribed on wooden tablets.

401   Homer, in the *Iliad,* (now dated to 850–800 B.C.) celebrated war.

402–3   Tyrtáeus of Sparta, ca. 650 B.C., composed "war songs," of which a few fragments survive.

403–4   "Ways and patterns of life" were set forth by Hesiod in *Works and Days,* at some date "after Homer."

404–5   "Pindar, Bacchýlides, Simónides were all in some sense court poets," says Morris. They belong approximately to the century 550 to 450 B.C.

404   "Piérian," meaning "of the Muses," is explained in the note to *Odes* 3.4.40. In *Odes* 3.10.15 this translation substituted "Macedon" for *Pieria.*

408–411   Debate on this subject was age-old and Horace's conclusion was a commonplace.

412–415   Both athletic and musical contests were featured in Greek "Games," different sequences of which were held at Olympia, at Pytho/Delphi, at Neméa, and at Corinth.

Pytho was renamed Delphi after Apollo slew the snake-oracle Pytho; he himself then became "Pythian Apollo" and in his honor the "Pythian Games" were held there.

416–418   That is, nowadays people write with neither talent nor training—"Last after me gets the mange!" (*occupet extremum scabies*) paraphrases a challenge used in children's games—the reader may supply his own modern equivalent. An ancient commentator gives the expression in full: *hábeat scabiem quísquis ad me vénerit novíssimus!* ("May whoever gets to me last have the mange!"). Note the old Italian scansion by accents (as in Plautus's comedies), not by Horace's classical metrics imitated from the Greeks. Compare the children's jingle in E.1.1.60 and note.

421   See S.1.2.13 and note.

431–432 Women called *praeficae* were hired as mourners to accompany funeral processions with cries and gestures of grief, but Horace uses the masculine *conducti* to make his comparison consistent.

434–436 Like that other "habit of kings" in S.1.2.86–90, this practice of kings is mentioned only by Horace.

437 "Fox-like" = *sub volpe,* perhaps in allusion to Aesop's fable of "The Fox and the Crow"; Morris prefers the corresponding fable in Horace's contemporary Phaedrus (1.13). See S.2.5.56 and note.

438 This judicious critic Quintílius is the Quintílius Varus whose death in 24 B.C. evoked from Horace the lament of *Odes* 1.24. See the note to line 5 of that poem.

450 Aristárchus, the Homeric critic of the 2nd century B.C. in Alexandria, was proverbially severe.

453–455 Jaundice (not mentioned in the text) was "the royal disease" (*morbus regius*) for reasons unknown—possibly because the patient turns "yellow as gold."

"Moonstruck" (Shakespeare's "lunátic") stands for *iracunda Diana,* "(whom) angry Diana (afflicts)." The moon—"Diana"—was long believed to induce mental disorders.

"Frenzies of priestly/ Dancing" = *fanaticus error,* "madly ecstatic straying." The allusion is to the frenzied dancing in honor of the goddess Bellona (S.2.2.223 and note) or in honor of Cýbelē/Dindýmenē (*Odes* 1.16.7–9 and notes). The modern Western reader thinks of "whirling dervishes."

458 The "bird-catcher watching for blackbirds" alludes to some lost story of proverb.

464–466 Empédocles, the physicist-philosopher of the 5th century B.C. from Akragas /Agrigentum (now Agrigénto) in Sicily was said to have jumped into the crater of Mount Etna; of the varying reasons alleged for that action Horace selects one to suit his present purpose. In E.1.12.20 Empédocles was briefly mentioned as a representative of the Epicurean philosophy.

467 Among all the dactylic hexameters in Horace's works this is the only spondaic hexameter, that is, the only one to have a spondee (two long syllables) in the fifth foot.

472 A "sacred enclosure" was a spot struck by lightning and therefore taboo and enclosed with a wall, for example, the spot near the N end of the Forum called the *Puteal* ("the Puteal Curbing," S.2.6.35 and note; "Libo's/ Wall," E.1.19.8–9 and note).

473–476 A similar idea was expressed humorously in S.1.3.86–89, where a debtor had to listen to readings by his creditor, and disgust at competitive "readings" by poets marks E.2.2.91–101, but the near-fury of the present passage is unique in Horace's works. Whether any particular person was intended, is unknown, but compare the note to E.2.2.91–101.

Since the present poem was first published well before 16 B.C., the approximate year of Propertius's "disappearance from history," it is possible to spin a theory to make out that Propertius was suffering from mental disorders in the years 19–18–17 B.C., but such a notion is entirely speculative.

Since E.2 and *Odes* 4 were both published (apparently) in 13 B.C., it is not possible to identify Horace's "last composition." Tradition placed E.2 after *Odes* 4 in collections of Horace's complete works, but it is somewhat reassuring to know that, in any case, E.2.1 was composed later than this (republished) "Letter to the Pisos." Thus the career of a genial and eminently sane poet does not, truly, close with these lines of intense anger.

Appendices

The *"Life of Horace"* (*Vita Horatii*), by Suetonius

A hundred and twenty-five years after Horace's death the Emperor Hadrian began his reign, 117–138 A.D., and presently appointed a distinguished man of letters, Gaius Suetonius Tranquillus, to have charge of Roman libraries and archives and to act as his advisor in cultural matters. In 121 he made Suetonius imperial secretary, but in 122 Suetonius, then aged about fifty-three—or possibly in some later year—disappears from history. A Greek reference book compiled around 1000 A.D. lists nearly twenty works by him: "The Twelve Caesars," *Royal Biographies, Lives of Famous Whores, The Roman Year, Methods of Reckoning Time*, and so forth. The whole list is repeated by Robert Graves in the Foreword to his translation (in "Penguin Classics") of *De Vita Caesarum*, commonly known in English as "The Twelve Caesars" and the only book by Suetonius to survive intact. (The portion about Augustus is several times cited in our notes to Horace's poems.)

Digests of his *Illustrious Men (De Viris illustribus)* also survive, because ancient editors prefaced them to the works of Vergil, Horace, and Lucan. The *Vita Horatii* reads as follows:

1   Q(uintus) Horatius Flaccus of Venusia (was born), as he himself relates, of a
2 father who was a freedman and a collector of taxes, and even, it has been thought,
3 a dealer in salt fish, since in the course of a dispute someone once taunted him by
4 saying, "How many times I have seen your father wipe his nose on his arm!"
5 Called up for the Philippi campaign, he obtained a tribuneship of soldiers from
6 General M(arcus) Brutus, and when amnesty was granted by the winning side he
7 procured an appointment as scribe in a quaestor's office. But finding favor first
8 with Maecenas, then with Augustus, he held no ordinary place in the affections of
9 both. How greatly Maecenas esteemed him is sufficiently attested by this epigram:

10   *ni te visceribus meis, Horati,*
11   *plus iam diligo, tu tuum sodalem*
12   *Ninnio videas strigosiorem,*

> (If more than my own vitals, Horace,
> I do not cherish you now, may you see
> your boon companion more wasted than Ninnius)

but much more by this line in his final commendation to Augustus: "Look after   13
Horatius Flaccus as you would me" (*Horati Flacci ut mei esto memor*).   14
    Augustus also offered him the post of secretary, as witness this letter to   15
Maecenas:

> Formerly I could depend on myself for writing my personal letters, but ex-   16
> tremely busy as I am, and not well, I want to take our Horace away from you.   17
> From that parasites' table of yours he will come to this regal one and assist   18
> me in writing letters.   19

But not even when he refused did he get the least bit angry or cease to bear him   20
friendship. There are letters extant from which I have culled some items by way of   21
evidence:

> Make yourself at home with me as if you were a member of my household; you   22
> will be helping yourself, and not for nothing, whereas I have wanted the benefit 23
> of your company, if your health permits.   24

And again: 25

> My opinion of you you will be able to hear from our Septimius also, for I   26
> happen to have mentioned you in his presence. But if you have haughtily spurned 27
> our friendship, we do not for that reason *anthuperēphanoûmen* (Greek for "return 28
> haughtiness for haughtiness").   29

What is more, he often calls him, among other joking terms, the "neatest prick"   30
(*purissimum penem*) and the "nicest little man" (*homuncionem lepidissimum*), and he 31
enriched him with one precious gift after another.   32
    His writings he esteemed to the point where he felt they would endure for-   33
ever, so that he not only assigned him the composition of the *Centennial Hymn* but 34
also the celebration of the victory of his stepsons Tiberius and Drusus over the   35
Vindelici, obliging him to add a fourth Book, after a long interval, to his three   36
Books of Odes. After reading certain of his *sermones* and finding no mention of him- 37
self he complained: 38

> I want you to know I am angry with you for not addressing me in particular   39
> in most of your writings of this kind. Are you afraid posterity might hold it   40
> against you that you seem to be a friend of ours?   41

and he elicited from him the piece (*eclogam*) which begins: 42

> *Cum tot sustineas et tanta negotia solus,*   43
> *res Italas armis tuteris, moribus ornes,*   44
> *legibus emendes, in publica commoda peccem,*   45
> *si longo sermone morer tua tempora, Caesar.*   46

(E.2.1.1–4:
> Knowing how great and how many affairs you sustain, single-handed,
> Giving the state its defenses, . . . etc.)

    In his figure he was short and stout, as described by himself in his *Satires*   47
(*satiris*) and by Augustus in this letter: 48

49   Oniscus brought me your little book (*libellum*), which I find acceptable as an
50   apology, tiny as it is. You do seem afraid your little books (*libelli*) will be
51   bigger than you are, but though you lack height, you don't lack for bulk. Thus
52   you may write in pint-size, whereas the girth of your volumes is *ogkōdéstatos*
53   (Greek for "very well rounded"; pronounce: *ongk-*), as is your tummy (*ventriculi*).
54
55   (See note below.)
56   He lived mostly in his rural Sabine or Tiburtine retreats, and his house is
57   pointed out near Tiburnus's little grove.
58   I have also come across elegies (*elegi*) bearing his name and a prose letter of
59   self-recommendation to Maecenas, but I consider both to be spurious. The elegies
60   are banal and the letter unclear—faults all but non-existent with him.
61   He was born the sixth day before the Ides of December in the consulship of
62   L(ucius) Cotta and L(ucius) Torquatus (December 8, 65 B.C.) and died the fifth
63   day before the Kalends of December in the consulship of G(aius) Marcius Censo-
64   rinus and G(aius) Asinius Gallus (November 27, 8 B.C.), in his fifty-seventh year,
65   naming Augustus as his heir before witnesses (*palam*) when, because of extreme
66   weakness, he was unable to sign the tablets of his will. He was buried and interred
67   at the furthest edge of the Equiline Hill, next to the grave of Maecenas.

2   "Freedman" = *libertinus,* as in S.1.6.45 and 46: *libertino patre natum.* "Collector of
    taxes" = *exactionum coactor,* a minor official, but, in some manuscripts of the *Vita, actionum
    coactor,* a collector of money at auctions; see S.1.6.85–87 and note.

2–4   The connection between the occupation and the gesture is unclear.

5   "A tribuneship of soldiers" = *tribunus militum;* see S.1.6.48 and *Odes* 2.7.1–14 and notes.

7   "Procured" = *comparavit,* which may also mean "purchased"; Italian *compare,* "to
    buy." *Scriptum quaestorium* means "a job as clerk in the treasury department." Of 20
    annually elected *quaestors,* two served in Rome as public treasurers and custodians of
    public documents, four served elsewhere in Italy, the rest in the provinces abroad. The
    time would be, at most, 41 to 38 B.C., when Horace was aged 24 to 27.

9–12   "Epigram" (Greek *epígramma*) originally meant 'inscription" or "caption," later a
    short poem in the manner of an "inscription" or "caption." Hence the three lines quoted
    may represent the total poem. The meter is "hendecasyllabics," eleven-syllable lines in
    the pattern: | _ _ | _ ∪ ∪ | _ ∪ | _ ∪ | _ ∪ |, a form never used by Horace, but used by
    Sappho and Anacreon (among other Greek poets) and by Catullus in more than 40
    poems.

12   Ninnius is unidentified; ? = the legendary Ninus, Assyrian king of Nineveh after 700
    B.C., as in Ovid's *Metamorphoses* 4.88.

26   This Septimius is doubtless identical with the travel-eager Septimius addressed in *Odes*
    2.6 and with the one recommended in E.1.9 for a position on Tiberius's staff.

35   For the campaign against the Vindelici in 15 B.C. see the headnote to *Odes. Book 4.*

36   The ten-year interval, 23 to 13 B.C.; see the Introduction to *Odes. Book 4.*

37   *Sermones* must be a loose term for Horace's non-lyric works. The allusion is almost
    certainly to E.2.2 and E.2.3; see the Introduction to *Epistles. Book II.*

47   "Satires" must also be a loose term, like *Sermones* in the foregoing note, since Horace's
    self-description occurs, not in the "Satires," but in E.1.20.24, where he says "little of
    stature" (*corporis exigui*); Suetonius writes *brevis atque obesus.* See also S.2.3.309 and note.

49   Oniscus is unidentified. Some *Vita* manuscripts have *Onysius,* which looks like a hand-
    writing garble for "Dionysius," a plausible name for a (Greek) freedman.
       The "little book" is unidentified. *Libellus* meant: "pamphlet," "petition," "letter,"
    etc. Conceivably E.2.1 is meant, but more likely is some small selection of poems copied
    out especially for the emperor. "Tiny as it is" = a humorous *quantuluscumque.*

54–55   Here occur two sentences of Suetonius' text which editors have sometimes considered unauthentic; Morris's text of the *Vita* omits them outright. Reifferscheid's *C. Suetoni Tranquilli Reliquiae* (in the Teubner series, Leipzig, 1860, p. 47), prints:

> *ad res Venerias intemperantior traditur. nam specula in cubiculo scortans ita dicitur habuisse disposita, ut quocumque respexisset sibi imago coitus referretur.*

In matters sexual he is reported as somewhat intemperate. They say that when having sex he so arranged mirrors in his bedroom that the intercourse was reflected whichever way he looked.

56–57   Horace often speaks of Tibur (Tívoli), and in *Odes* 1.7.11–14 even mentions the "consecrate grove of Tibúrnus," but nowhere does he say that he *owned* a house there. The "Sabine farm" was situated 10–12 miles NNE of Tibur, too far to commute. But note Catullus's poem 44, addressed to *his* estate, which some people designate as "Sabine," others as "Tiburtine."

65   "He was buried and interred" = *Humatus et conditus est*, which may represent the common rhetorical embellishment called *hendiadys*, "one thing by means of two," but the Teubner text considers *humatus* a scribal intrusion. For what it may be worth: *conditus*, with a short i, means "buried" (among other meanings), whereas *condītus*, with a long i means "embalmed (with spices)."

A Note on Maecenas

In the thirty years of their friendship Horace addressed twenty-three individual poems to his patron; the name "Maecenas," in *Odes* 1.1.1 and 3.29.1, "encloses" the entire corpus of Horace's masterwork, save for the personal epilogue poem; and if Maecenas is mentioned only once in *Odes* 4 and not at all in E.2, those two final collections were put together at the emperor's behest and in a sense dedicated to him. Between the subsidizer and the subsidized this record is noteworthy. There must have been times when their friendship was strained—*Odes* 2.17 and E.1.7 poignantly reflect such strains—but the difficulties were always overcome. And after their deaths, a few months apart, they were buried side by side.

Moreover, Maecenas has his own place in history, not only as a patron of poets, but as astute diplomat, as statesman-advisor, and in three extended intervals as deputy chief of state. Yet the details of his life are in many respects unclear.

He was born, in all probability at Arretium (Arezzo), about 140 km/90 m almost due north of Rome in the heart of Etruria—the old territory of the Etruscans—on April 13th of some year between 74 and 70. Thus he was five to nine years older than Horace. In three poems Horace hails him as a descendant of Etruscan kings (S.1.6.1–4, *Odes* 1.1.1, and 3.29.1), and Propertius, another poet-pensioner, says the same in his own poem 3.9.1. *What* Etruscan kings is not said. For centuries Etruscan city-kings had ruled in Arretium and elsewhere, but all Etruscan power yielded to Roman power after 282 B.C. In S.1.6.3–4 Horace adds that Maecenas's ancestors, both paternal and maternal, "in the days of/ Yore held command over powerful legions"; despite the Roman term "legions" we get the impression that Etruscan armies are meant. Yet, apart from unspectacular careers for his father and grandfather, history records none of those illustrious forebears. He was already enormously wealthy as a young man, but the ultimate source of his inheritance is unknown. No other relatives of his are mentioned anywhere.

There is uncertainty about his very name. His Roman *praenomen*, "Gaius," may have been adopted in adulthood "for conformity's sake." It is usually said that his family name was Cilnius, which is Latinized Etruscan of unknown meaning and probably inherited, by Etruscan custom, from his mother. "Maecenas," sounded by him as "my-KANE-ahs" but in English as "my-SEEN-us," was likewise Etruscan and of unknown meaning, and it served as a *cognomen*, parallel to Horace's "Flaccus." Some scholars, however, see Cilnius as the given name and Maecenas as the family name, but there is no certainty either way.

It is surmised that his early years were spent in Rome, perhaps partly at Naples, and that he was living either in Athens or in Apollonia in 46–44 B.C. when he met Caius Octavius, the future Emperor Augustus, who was seven to eleven years his junior. The two of them may have returned to Italy together; if not, they met there again soon after their return. Their acquaintance had begun when the younger man was the relatively obscure Caius Octavius, and now that he was suddenly metamorphosed into Octavius Caesar his friend remained staunchly at his side through the grimly uncertain years 44 to 42, when young Caesar's failure would have meant death for Maecenas. Skillfully he represented young Caesar's interests on diplomatic missions to Mark Antony and other opponents, in 40, in 38—on the occasion when Horace accompanied the diplomatic party as far as Brundisium, as S.1.5 tells—and in 37 and in 36. During the war against Sextus Pompey in 36 he was Caesar's deputy head of state. Evidence conflicts as to whether he was or was not at the battle of Actium on September 2, 31, but it is certain that he again acted as deputy head of state through the two years from latter 31 until Caesar returned from Egypt and the East in 29. His duties included management of the secret police, and through them he thwarted an assassination plot and *coup d'état*. When, after a serious illness in 30, he reappeared at the theater the audience gave him an ovation, from which we infer that equitable rule as deputy had won approval of the citizenry. In 28–27 he steered Caesar toward policies of moderation in the new imperial regime then taking shape. Once Caesar, in January of 27, became "the August One," *Augustus*, Maecenas was virtually lieutenant emperor, and again, from late 27 to 24, he acted as deputy head of state while Augustus was in Spain directing the last phases of conquest of the Iberian peninsula. Then, in 23–22, came a painful crisis. The man history remembers as Varro Murena conspired to assassinate Augustus and restore the Roman Republic; Murena was foster brother to Maecenas's recently acquired wife, Terentia; Maecenas learned of the conspiracy, told his wife of it in time for her to warn Murena—who was apprehended anyway and executed. Augustus resented the "betrayal" and was cooler to his old friend after that, but amity and trust were not wholly destroyed. There were occasions when the emperor still consulted Maecenas on the most delicate matters of policy, but the intimately trusted advisorship passed gradually into the hands of capable Sallustius Crispus, grandnephew and adopted son of the historian Sallust. Attested facts are sparse for Maecenas's later years, but close to his death at a disputed date (perhaps September) in 8 B.C. he declared Augustus sole heir to all his estates and wealth. An anonymous elegy terms him "Caesar's right hand."

His patronage of Horace, of Propertius, of Caius Valgius Rufus and other poets, as well as of Vergil in the period when the *Georgics* were written, brought immense benefits to Latin literature. But he himself was also a writer of prose and verse which survived until at least the time of Isidore of Seville, who died in 636 A.D. The prose works included a *Prometheus*, an essay entitled *De cultu suo*, about his manner of living, and a *Symposium*, in which Vergil, Horace, and jurist Messala Corvinus appeared as speakers. Nine snippets of prose and about eighteen lines of verse are all that survive, in quotation by later authors, from his total production. A single printed page can contain the lot of them. Augustus is known to have laughed good-naturedly at these literary efforts of his old friend, while in the next century they were received with less good-natured laughter from the philosopher Seneca and the critic Quintilian.

The verse fragments show use of the less common meters and a preciosity of style. The sincere, if unbeautiful epigram to Horace is preserved by Suetonius in the *Vita Horatii*. Addressed to "Flaccus" are five lines quoted by Isidore, listing certain jewels that Maecenas is *not* seeking—the incomplete sentence fails to clarify *why* not. Both of these pieces are in hendecasyllabics reminiscent of Catullus. Striking, however, are the three and a half lines cited by Seneca as "thoroughly disgusting" (*turpissimum*). These turn up unexpectedly, paraphrased by LaFontaine in *Fables* 1.15 (*La Mort et le malheureux*), as

> Mécénas fut un galant homme:
> Il a dit quelque part: "Qu'on me rend impotent,
> Cul-de-jatte, goutteux, manchot, pourvu qu'en somme

> Je vive, c'est assez, je suis plus que content."
> Ne viens jamais, ô mort, on t'en dit autant.

The Latin is harsher:

> Make me feeble of hand, feeble of foot, of hip;
> Pile a hump on my back, knock my teeth loose;
> But so long as life remains, it is good. Sustain it for me
> Even if I am sitting on the sharp cross.

The last phrase refers to the torture of anal impalement. (Compare Catullus 97,5.)

Between 36 and 31 he built his lavish palace on the Esquiline Hill at the eastern extremity of the ancient city. From its unique tower, a century later, Nero was to watch Rome burn. Its gardens sought to bring the beauty of the countryside within the city limits, with special attention to birds and the decorative uses of water. Whether the palace was grand or garish, the gardens beautiful or fussily pretty, is a point not to be decided on the evidence. By ca. 100 A.D. the whole area was completly built over. Egyptian papyri attest that Maecenas also had an estate in Egypt. He traveled widely and doubtless had other residences besides, as wealthy Romans regularly did, either for seasonal residence or for their private "hotels" when on journeys.

In the "high house" on the Esquiline Caesar was often a guest, both before and after becoming "the August One"; Suetonius (72) says: "if he fell ill, he always took refuge in Maecenas's mansion." Vergil must have come up occasionally from Naples; Horace and Propertius were "regulars." Celebrities surely frequented his banquets, his literary gatherings, and his musicales, and there must have been times when *monde* rubbed elbows with *demi-monde*. Sometimes he may well have joined the latter in their own habitats. His parties were doubtless lively on occasion, but there is no cause to imagine them as orgiastic.

Surely too he collected pretty girls, as he collected art objects and gems, but love evaded him. A single clause in the *Annals* of Tacitus (after 100 A.D.) mentions a passionate attachment to the male ballet dancer and mime artist Bathyllus. Around 23, when he was approaching fifty, he married the lady Terentia, as mentioned. It was a stormy marriage, with repudiations and reconcilements, with Terentia's ultimate fate unknown. In the year 12 B.C. Maecenas was obliged to face a hostile court of law on charges of adultery.

He shunned public office, declined senatorial rank, and remained all his life, by choice, a knight (*eques*), that is, a member of the aristocracy of money. Thus he retained the rich man's dearest privilege, the freedom to choose his friends. Seneca, who was not born until four years after Maecenas's death, speaks with contempt of those friends, mentioning also that Maecenas wore his tunics absurdly long and that he was generally graceless about his personal appearance.

As he grew older a grave nervous disorder afflicted him. Pliny the Elder, writing some eighty years later, states that Maecenas never really slept in the last three years of his life and that he suffered "continual fever." His fear of death became obsessive. The lines scornfully quoted by Seneca express that terror, though we do not know at what period of his life they were written. For those undocumented years 13 to 8 B.C. one tends to imagine an unhappy picture: Horace, himself aging, unwell, and unsolaced by his lyre as he had hoped, comforting Maecenas as the latter advanced ever further into morbid depression, and being comforted by Maecenas in turn. The blind leading the blind, as it were. Yet the terms of Maecenas's will conveyed all his vast wealth, the mansion and gardens on the Esquiline, and the other estates, to the emperor. His last recorded words, however, were the request to Augustus: "Look after Horatius Flaccus as you would me."

The prim and the stern of mind have, in various ages, dismissed Maecenas as a shallow hedonist and made light of his loyalties to friends and given little weight to his powerful influence upon a tumultuous era. Others have admired his many-sidedness and the wisdom of his counsels, pointing out the acumen and the practical courage he displayed as deputy head of state in crucially dangerous times. To still others he is an interestingly problematical personality about whose career there is a regrettable lack of information. A fair evaluation of the total personality is presented by Jean-Marie André, in *Mécène* (Paris, 1967, pp. 26 ff.), under four heads: religion of joy, dread of death, cult of friendship, and concern for "rustic" nature."

A Note on the Emperor Augustus

To the man who became the Emperor Augustus Horace alludes some twenty-five times, before 27 B.C. as "Caesar," thereafter as "Caesar," as "Augustus," or as "Caesar Augustus." Only once does he speak to him directly as one human being to another, and then by invitation, in E.2.1, which is possibly his very last composition. The second-person address in the late *Odes* 4.14 and 4.15 is more nearly prayer than ordinary parlance.

The earlier allusions regard a great and remote personage who is a friend to Maecenas as Maecenas is a friend to Horace. The note of awe is first sounded in *Odes* 1.2, probably of 28 B.C. Disasters and omens of disaster have beset the Roman state, says that poem, which then asks (lines 25–26): "To what god shall people appeal for aid when/ Total ruin threatens?" Various divinities are suggested—Apollo, Venus, the deified Romulus—until the poet guesses it may be Mercury, the god of prosperity, who even now, in the guise of a mortal, is in charge of the state; deftly the lines shift to second-person invocation ending in the triumphal cry to "Caesar, our leader!"

To some degree this is playful riddling, but in *Odes* 1.12 the concluding three-stanza prayer to Jupiter states unequivocally that Caesar is the supreme god's earthly representative. *Odes* 3.3.9–12 accord him a place in heaven *now*, among other deified heroes:

> By upward striving Pollux and Hercules
> Attained the fiery stars and the heights of sky,
> With whom Augustus now reclines at
> Banquets and, crimson of lip, drinks nectar.

Odes 4.14.5–6 could go no further with: "O greatest Prince wherever the sun proceeds/ Across the world's inhabited lands and realms," nor *Odes* 4.15 which, in its entirety, exalts Augustus as a god of peace—on earth. In short, Horace addresses himself to the "living myth" of Augustus. But what was the stupendous accomplisher like in his everyday mortality?

He was born plain Caius Octavius, in Rome, on September 23, 63 B.C., the year when Cicero as consul prosecuted Catiline for attempted overthrow of the Roman Republic. Thus he was two years younger than Horace. The Octavii were lesser gentry from Velítrae (now Vellétri) in the Alban Hills southeast of Rome. His grandfather was a banker there, but his father had moved to the capital, gained senatorial rank, and served as praetor in 61 and subsequently as governor of Macedonia before his premature death. The widow immediately remarried, so that the boy was brought up in the household of his politically prominent stepfather, Lucius Marcius Philippus. The crucial link of kinship, however, was his mother's mother, Julia, the sister of Julius Caesar. We hear of the twelve-year-old boy's delivering the funeral oration for this grandmother in 51 B.C.

His great-uncle took note of him early, awarding him military honors at age sixteen, having him along on the Spanish campaign at age seventeen, and enrolling him as a Patrician. On December 13, 45 Julius Caesar made his will, the concluding lines of which named this grandnephew as his heir and stipulating that, as his "son," the lad should take the name of Caesar. By that date the young man was "in college" at Apollonia, a now-uninhabited site on the coast of Albania. By no coincidence Apollonia was also a staging area for the troops assembling for a campaign against the Parthians. The young Caesar-to-be was to get acquainted with the military leaders, clearly in anticipation of joining the Eastern venture.

Extremely important alliances were formed at Apollonia. One was with tall, lanky, dour Marcus Vipsanius Agrippa, an almost exact contemporary, whose family was—and remained—undiscoverable. A second near-contemporary was Quintus Salvidiénus Rufus. And either at Apollonia or on side trips to Athens acquaintance was made with the somewhat older Maecenas. Not one of these allies had a genuinely Roman name, yet within a year or so they were to be the prime supporters of Julius Caesar's heir.

News of the assassination reached Apollonia at the end of March, 44 B.C., in a letter from the youth's mother. He sailed at once for Italy, cautiously landing at the small town of Lupiae south of the garrisoned port of Brundisium. There he learned of his inheritance and also, in letters from his mother and stepfather, of the great perils inherent in accepting it. Without hesitation he met Fate's challenge, determined to avenge his "father's" murder and to continue his "father's" mighty work.

After a cordial reception by the Brundisium garrison the eighteen-year-old proceeded with all caution to Rome, where, on the day after his arrival around May 1st, he proclaimed himself Caesar's heir before the crowds in the Forum. Mark Antony was alarmed. As closest friend to the decreased he was obliged to pay this young man a certain deference—until he could find a way to destroy him. The anti-Caesarians were no less alarmed, but Cicero reassured them that "the boy" would be praised, honored, and discarded. All parties underestimated this "boy."

The struggle for power was engaged at once. Thirteen years later young Caesar was to stand unchallenged master of the Roman world. Antony, finding it politically impossible to do without him, became his partner in the war against the anti-Caesarians, and it was Antony, the seasoned soldier, who won the battle of Philippi in 42, while young Caesar fled in panic and hid in a swamp. Antony's taunts on that score were brutal. Once the Roman world was divided between these two Philippi victors and Anton took himself off to rule the eastern half of the empire, it was Agrippa and Salvidiénus who won young Caesar's wars in Italy— until Salvidiénus tried to desert to Antony and perished for his treachery. In 36 it was Agrippa who defeated Sextus Pompey, and in 31 it was Agrippa who won the sea battle in the final showdown against Antony and Cleopatra, but officially Octavius Caesar was the victor both times. Agrippa had no alternative: without the magic of the Caesarian name he was a nonentity. Maecenas, meanwhile, managed the strategy and the diplomacy.

In 40, at age twenty-three, Octavius Caesar married the lady Scribonia, who bore him his only child, the ill-starred Julia. He divorced her—for nagging, he alleged—to marry anew, on January 17, 38, with the lady whom history remembers as the Empress Livia; she was to live as his devoted spouse for fifty-two years and to survive him by fifteen years. This second marriage was of immense political advantage, and if it was also inspired by passion, the conjunction of circumstances was remarkable. Livia Drusilla was made available by divorcing her husband, Tiberius Claudius Nero, so that she brought to Caesar's house a son not yet four years old—the future Emperor Tiberius—while being in advanced pregnancy with a second son who, at his birth in Caesar's house, was named Drusus Claudius Nero. The new marriage throve, but without children. Cynics would later claim that, while Caesar ruled the world, Livia ruled Caesar, but that may have been mere wags' talk. Caesar honored and esteemed Livia, but he freely and frequently indulged in adulteries.

No Oriental king was more concerned about his dynasty than was this Caius Octavius of the lesser, rural gentry, now that his name had become Octavius Caesar. In 25, to minimize "alien blood" in his line, he married his only child, Julia, to his sister's son, Marcellus: their offspring would be his heir and successor. The plan failed. Two years later the nineteen-year-old son-in-law died without issue. The girl-widow was then married to Agrippa, whose power now rivaled Caesar's. (Maecenas advised that it was either this or assassinate Agrippa.) Two sons and a daughter of that union took the imperial name: Gaius Caesar (20 B.C. to 4 A.D.), Lucius Caesar (17 B.C. to 2 A.D.), and the younger Julia; a third son, known as Agrippa Posthumus, may have been retarded. Meanwhile young Tiberius married Agrippa's daughter (by a previous marriage), Vipsania, whom he dearly loved. There had been times when Augustus had given Tiberius hope of the succession, but now he was brother-in-law to the boy heirs, an honorable second place, as it were.

But in 12 B.C. Agrippa, worn out at age fifty, died, leaving sons Gaius and Lucius aged eight and five, respectively. At this point Augustus should have designated Tiberius as his heir. He knew that Tiberius was completely trustworthy, he had used him—and would continue to use him—for all sorts of tasks, but he did not much like him. Drusus, the younger stepson, was far more to his liking, but the elder brother could not, without trouble, be bypassed. Augustus doted on his grandsons and trusted they might succeed him. Time might resolve the problem. Time did nothing of the sort. In 9 B.C. Drusus died, and with brilliant success Tiberius assumed his dead brother's military command, proving himself more valuable than ever.

In 6 B.C. Augustus took a drastic step which would honor Tiberius "sufficiently" while simultaneously disposing of the widowed Julia and smoothing his grandsons' path to the imperial succession. Abruptly he ordered Tiberius to divorce his beloved Vipsania in order to marry the widow Julia, Tiberius's mother-in-law. Therewith Gaius and Lucius, hitherto Tiberius's brothers-in-law, became his stepsons—and wards. By 4 A.D., after ten unhappy years had passed for all parties concerned, the two young hopefuls were prematurely dead, the incompetent Agrippa Posthumus was next in line of succession, and new arrangements had to be made. The bitterly disappointed emperor now formally adopted Tiberius as his son and heir, with the new name of Tiberius Julius Caesar. Tiberius was then forty-six. He was to serve—and wait—for another ten years, until the death of Augustus on August 19, 14 A.D. Even then he delayed a full month before beginning his reign on September 19, by which time he had been securely informed that Agrippa Posthumus had been assassinated. That precaution may have been taken in advance by Augustus himself, though some people credited the Empress Livia with issuing the order in Augustus's name, with or without Tiberius's being aware of it. Still others felt sure Tiberius himself had arranged the murder.

Meanwhile the thrice-wedded Julia had come to grief. Tiberius, as her husband, honored her publicly, detested her privately, and after their only child died in infancy abandoned her altogether. In 2 B.C. she was brought to public trial on the charge of promiscuous adulteries. One of her lovers, Iullus Antonius, Mark Antony's son who had been reared in Augustus's own household, was executed, four others were exiled, and Julia herself was banished to a remote island to live under very harsh restraints. Later she was held at Rhegium (now Reggio di Calabria) at the toe of Italy, with some relaxation of restraints, but her father refused ever to see her again. Ten years later, in 8 A.D., the same fate overtook her daughter, the younger Julia. By strictest orders of Augustus neither daughter nor granddaughter was, under any circumstances, to be buried in the family mausoleum.

Public immorality was the official charge in both trials, but the fates of the "lovers" suggest that the real, never-admitted, charge was conspiracy to murder the father and grandfather. In that same year, 8 A.D., Augustus also banished the poet Ovid, nominally on the charge of composing immoral poems. In subsequent works Ovid more than once lamented his unintentional offense—without ever specifying what that offense was. He was never officially implicated with the younger Julia, and the nature of his crime has never been ascertained. Repeated pleas from exile failed to make Augustus relent and recall Ovid; nor did Tiberius yield to entreaties after 14 A.D., for Tiberius rigidly adhered to the policies of Augustus in all things.

In his public life, where our Caius Octavius Caesar Augustus bore himself imperially, his "lucky star" never failed him; in private life no such star shone. According to the extended portrayal by Suetonius we see him as a handsome man, of medium height (five feet, seven inches), with bad teeth and in latter years the hint of a rheumatic limp. He ate frugally, drank abstemiously, dressed in homespuns woven by his womenfolk, sparsely furnished his palace, and got along on less sleep than most people. He worked long hours at state business. He entertained at dinner only occasionally and served modest-scale menus. Collecting rare bronzes was one of his few extravagances, though he had a passion for gambling, and by his own account often allowed his winnings to go uncollected. No hardship was entailed thereby, since his private fortune came to exceed, perhaps by as much as four times, the total revenue of the Roman state. He owned Egypt outright after 30 B.C., for instance, and that was only one string to his financial bow.

In the political arena he was brave, resourceful, and tenacious, whereas amid physical danger he was a coward. He even hid in cellars when it thundered. In cold weather he shivered within several layers of clothing. His recurrent illnesses cannot be diagnosed now on the evidence. Rheumatism and kidney stones are understandable, but could he, in 23 B.C., really have been cured of abscesses on the liver by nothing more than cold-water baths? Moderns may suspect some psychosomatic problems. Moreover, he was superstitious, fretted over the meaning of his dreams, and shrank in horror from deformed persons.

He was a stickler for social protocol as he was a stickler for good grammar; he once retired a proconsular governor for a gross misspelling in a dispatch. With his slaves and freedmen he was kindly, affable, and generous with rewards for good service, but his punishments for misbehavior were cruel; for a secretary who accepted a bribe for revealing the contents of a message he ordered the man's legs broken. He deemed Roman citizenship too precious to extend to non-Italians except in the rarest of cases, even though this policy, especially in Gaul, worked to his political disadvantage.

By the standards of his time he was well educated. He had a good command of Greek, but he shrank from using the language publicly for fear of making mistakes; when he wrote it for official purposes he would have it checked by a native stylist. He enjoyed Greek and Roman literature of the past, particularly Greek Old Comedy, though not for a minute would he have tolerated the equivalent political satire in his own Rome. Horace idealizes but does not exaggerate in *Odes* 3.4.37–40 when he says:

> Exalted Caesar, once he has quartered all
> His weary cohorts safely in villages
> And seeks repose himself from labors,
>   Finds your (i.e., the Muses') Piérian recreations.

He sincerely cherished the works of "his" poets, Vergil and Varius, Horace and Propertius, but he took pleasure in other writers too, even to attending those public readings that Horace found so distasteful. He liked to distill maxims for practical behavior from books. And he was himself a writer, though his writings are all lost. They included a few poems, a never-finished tragedy called *Ajax*, and an autobiography in thirteen Books.

The personality of Augustus has been very differently assessed in different eras, and there is endless debate about his governmental, economic, and military policies. Aspects admired and imitated by Louis XIV, for instance, were neither admired nor recommended by Thomas Jefferson.

Here, we attempt no evaluations, since Horace attempted none. Horace exalted the "living myth" of the man who brought peace and national prosperity out of civil chaos and who spectacularly aggrandized Roman dominion. Before the man Augustus, in whose company he must have been many times, he remained humbly deferential, and any criticism of state policies he would have deemed unspeakable impudence. As for his poems of praise, they have poetic validity—a remarkable fact in itself, they have the ring of sincerity, and they seem to have expressed the majority opinion, if not universal opinion. The purity of his Roman patriotism was never questioned in centuries of study in schools, and he saw Augustus as the very soul of Rome.

Foreign Nations

Collected here are explanations about certain foreign nations mentioned by Horace, beginning with the Asiatic group eastward from the Euphrates. By far the most important of these were the Parthians, whom Horace, at will, terms "Medes," "Persians," or "Parthians."

I.1.   Medes

Medes: sing. *Medus*,   pl.   *Medi*;   *Odes*   1.2.51/1.27.5/1.29.5/2.1.31/2.9.21 /3.3.43/3.5.9/3.8.19/4.14.42/*Centennial Hymn* 54. A "book word" used by Horace and his contemporaries on the basis of Herodotus 1.95–130, et al, when they meant "Parthians."

The Medes were a blend of immigrant Iranians (Indo-Europeans) with indigenous, non-Indo-European peoples of NW Iran, first mentioned in Assyrian records as of 836–5 B.C. By 700 B.C. they had established a capital at Ecbátana (modern Hamadán) in control of "the Hamadán-Teherán-Isfahán triangle." They extended their power E into modern Afghanistan and W almost to the Aegean coast of modern Turkey, especially after 612, when they conquered Nineveh, capital of Assyria (modern Iraq). Herodotus (1.101) says one of their six tribes was the Magoi, or, the Magi. They dominated their close kinsmen, the Persians, to their south, until 550, when the Persian prince Cyrus II led a revolt to overthrow Median power and establish the great Persian empire of antiquity. Thereafter they were assimilated into the Persian population.

I.2.   Persians

Persians: *Persae; Odes* 1.2.22/1.21.15/1.38.1 (adj.)/3.1.44("Achemenids" in the text)/3.5.4/3.9.4/4.15.23 ("faithless")/also 2.12.21 "Achaemenes." Again, a "book word" from Herodotus.

Mentioned in Assyrian records even earlier than the Medes, the Iranian tribes collectively known as the Persians established themselves in SW Iran, to the E of the Persian Gulf, in "Persis" (modern Fars Province). In the early 600s they were dominated by the Medes and remained so until the revolt of Cyrus in 550. On October 29, 539 B.C. Cyrus, leading Medes and Persians, captured Babylon on the death of Babylonian King Belshazzar. Assuming the title of "Great King," Cyrus not only consolidated Median and Persian power but extended his dominion both to E and W. Under his successors the Persian Empire came to include all of

SW Asia as well as Egypt and portions of SE Europe. Called "Achémenids" from an alleged ancestor named Acháemenes, a succession of these "Great Kings" ruled uninterruptedly from 550 to 331 B.C.

For centuries of pre-history the various Iranian tribes had shared the polytheistic worship of such gods as Mithra and Varuna with their cousin-people, the Hindus, but by 550 many of them had accepted a quasimonotheistic reformation of that religion by Zoroaster (Zarathustra), whose preaching is usually dated to around 660 B.C. and localized in eastern Iran, beyond the deserts. Their language is recorded in two forms, west-Iranian "Old Persian" and east-Iranian "Avestan" (the dialect of the Zoroastrian books), both of which used cuneiform script.

Two successive "Great Kings," Darius I in 490 B.C. and Xerxes I in 480–479, attempted to conquer Greece, and Herodotus's *History of the Persian Wars*, written between 450 and 400, relates the story of those wars and the complex circumstances that led up to them. After 479 the power of the Achémenids, from the Mediterranean to the Himalayas, declined until Alexander the Great conquered the whole area in three brief years, 334–331 B.C. At Persepolis, near modern Shiraz, tourists visit the impressive remains of the last imperial palace of the "Great Kings," which Alexander laid in ruins.

I.3.   Parthians

Parthians: sing. *Parthus*, pl. *Parthi*, noun and adj. S.2.1.15/S.2.5.62/Epode 7,9/ *Odes*1.12.53/1.19.11/2.13.17–18/3.2.4/4.5.25/4.15.8/E.1.18.56 /E.2.1.112 and 256.

The Parthians were Iranians from around the SE corner of the Caspian Sea, first mentioned in Darius I's rock inscription of ca. 520 B.C. as constituting the sixteenth satrapy (province) of the Achémenid empire. After the death of Alexander the Great in 323 they came under nominal rule of Alexander's Greek successors in Asia, the Seleúcids (so named for King Seleúcus, the first of the line), but in the years 312–262 they allied themselves with Iranian Scyths called Dahae to their immediate N (i.e., E of the Caspian Sea) and began the establishment of an independent kingdom. By 247 (or so) they were in control of the large area of Khurasan (now divided among Iran, Afghanistan, and Soviet Turkestan) as far E as Qandahar. Their advances westward, into Iran proper and into Iraq, were slower. When the Romans defeated the last Seleucid ruler, Antiochus III, in 190–189, the Parthian king, Mithradates II (ca. 123–87) began alliances and conquests into what is now Turkey, where, after protracted struggles, he was defeated by Roman armies under Lucullus (see the note to E.1.6.40–44) and Pompey the Great.

In the battle of Carrhae, 54 B.C., the Parthians slew Roman General Lucius Licinius Crassus, took a large Roman army captive, and kept the Roman standards as trophies. By 20 B.C. internal dissention within the Parthian empire was such as to prompt an *entente* with Rome and the return of the standards to young Tiberius, Augustus's stepson and representative. (See E.1.3, 8, and 9.) To Parthian King Phraátes IV Augustus sent an Italian slavegirl named Musa, and although the eldest son of this union succeeded to his native throne, the subsequent children were brought to Rome as hostages. There Prince Vonones became so Romanized as to be unfit for ruling in Parthia when it came time for him to do so (7 A.D.). Thus Horace, in *Odes* 4.14, composed ca. 14 B.C., might stretch a point and claim the Parthian empire as "conquered" by Augustus.

A succession of Parthian capitals included the famous Hekatómpylos (Greek for "Hundred Gates"), the very site of which has not yet been ascertained SE of the Caspian Sea, while the last Parthian capital, attesting the westward shift of Parthian power, was at Ctesiphon on the middle Tigris, not far E of the ruins of ancient Babylon on the Euphrates.

Around 227 A.D. the Parthians succumbed before a new Iranian dynasty called Sasanian/Sassanian, who so effectively obscurred the memory of their predecessors that even the near-474 years of Parthian history were reckoned at less than half that period—until Arab historians discovered the deception. The reasons for such animosity are unclear.

Parthian documents and artifacts, sparse as they are, have at last come to the attention of scholars, who are now cautiously appraising the evidence. Parthian government seems to have been feudal in nature, so that Pliny the elder (before 79 A.D.) could speak of an affiliation of eighteen kingdoms. At least three languages were in use, as documents show, some being in Greek, some in Aramaic, and some official ones in a bizarre mixture of Aramaic and native Iranian; alphabets of these languages completely displaced cuneiform writing. A variety of religions was also tolerated, though the principal one was Zoroastrianism. Important blocks of story matter in the later Persian epic poems may have been the creation of Parthian entertainer-poets, though the Sasanians claimed all the credit. Parthian too may be the origins of the picturesque coats of arms and even the rudiments of the chivalric code later adopted by European knighthood, though it may have been once again the Sasanians who elaborated these ideas.

The latter centuries of Parthian rule involved almost constant warfare with Rome, so that Latin historians provide half, as it were, of the story of Parthian decline. Around 227 A.D. the Parthian vassal-king of Fars Province, the "Persian heartland," led a successful revolt that undid Parthian power and substituted for it a vigorous, intensely nationalistic dynasty called Sasanian that came close to reestablishing the boundaries of the old empire of the Achémenids. The arts flourished; books were composed in the Middle Persian (Pahlevi) language; the Zoroastrian religion became the state cult tended by a priestly caste (the Magi), fire temples dotted the landscape, and we hear of persecutions of Jews, Christians, and Buddhists; it was an era of glory, national pride, military prowess, palace intrigues, and the usual juxtaposition of splendor and poverty. Meanwhile the Roman empire, as of 227 A.D., had already entered into its age of slow, dismal deterioration. To Roman eyes the "new" Persians were simply the old Parthians under a new name. The wars went on, the frontiers in the Tigris-Euphrates region, and even west of there, shifted back and forth, but the overall course of Roman power was downward, while Persian power, for all its losses and gains, remained constant. After the fall of the western Roman empire in 476, the Byzantine empire continued the struggle. In the early 600s the Byzantines and the Persians fought each other to exhaustion, so that from 633 to 642 Moslem armies professing the new religion of Mohammed took almost the entire Sasanian empire and exterminated a dynasty.

I.4.   Hindu/ Ind/ India

Odes 1.12.56 expects that Augustus will yet conquer "men from the lands of sunrise, . . . Hindus" (*Indos*), or, in *Odes* 4.14.42, "the Hindu" (*Indus*). A land of wealth is indicated by "ivory of Ind" (*ebur Indicum*) in *Odes* 1.31.6 and by "treasure of Ind" (*divitis Indiae*) in *Odes* 3.24.2. In S.2.8.14 the slave Hydáspes bears the name of the "Indian" river now called the Jhelum.

Since Alexander's time, if not before, "India" was either the area of the Indus River (the core of modern Pakistan) or a country extending E from the Indus. (The ancient Hindus called the river Sindhu and their country Āryāvarta.) In 327–325 B.C. Alexander conquered to a short distance E of the Indus in the northern region called Punjab ("Five Rivers"), but the territory was partly lost at his death in 323. Seleúcus, his Greek successor in Asia (312–280) reinvaded the Punjab but ended by ceding some part of it to Hindu King Chandragupta in 304. His ambassador to Chandragupta, Megásthenes, spent considerable time, ca. 300, at Pataliputra (now Patna) on the Ganges and wrote a report on the actual India. A generation later the Emperor Asoka (273–233) sent Buddhist missionaries to all Greek rulers, including Seleúcus's successor, "Antiyaka, king of the Yavanas," that is, Antiochus, king of the Ionians, but shortly after Asoka's time the newly powerful Parthians severed communications between the Ganges valley and the coast of Syria.

The written account of "India" by ambassador Megásthenes, as well as accounts by Alexander's companions, Ptolemy (later King of Egypt) and Aristobulus, were accessible in Horace's time, though he shows no signs of having read them. They are lost to us, but much of their information was repeated by Horace's contemporary, the Greek historian Strabo, and by a series of later Roman geographers, particularly by Claudius Ptolemy around 150 A.D. and somewhat earlier by Arrian, who followed up his seven-Book *Anabasis of Alexander* with a one-Book *Indica*. In this latter we read of 118 Indian nations, seven social castes, a marked difference in physical types between northern and southern Hindus, elephant hunts, exotic animals, linen clothing, turbans, and much more.

Maritime commerce between the Mediterranean and India was just beginning in Horace's time. It was to continue until ca. 200 A.D., bringing Roman subjects, if not actual Romans, to India's west coast, to Ceylon, and even to Burma, Malaya, and the SE coast of China.

I.5.   Seres; "Chinese"

Seres (sing. and pl.)/ *Serae* (pl.); adj. *Sericus*, "of the Seres; silken." *Odes* 1.12.56 "men from the lands of sunrise,/ *Seras et Indos*"/ *Odes* 3.29.27/ *Odes* 4.15.22/ Epode 8,15 "silken cushions" (*sericos . . . pulvillos*)/ *Odes* 1.29.9 "Chinese (*Sericas*) arrows."

Also in Propertius's poem 4.8.23 *Serica carpenta*, "two-wheeled, roofed carriages with silken hangings."

The word *Seres* first appears in Latin in Vergil's *Georgics* 2.121: "and how the Seres comb delicate fleeces from leaves." The *Georgics* were composed between 37 and 30 B.C. while Vergil was living principally at Naples. Horace's *Epodes* were published in 30 B.C. We note that all allusions are by poets of the Maecenas circle; the word does not occur in the works of Tibullus, or even those of Ovid.

Pliny (before 79 A.D.) understood that the Seres lived at the terminus of the overland trade route to the East. Ptolemy's *Geography* located them in central Siberia, around the Yenisei River, but he also located the *Sinae* at the far end of the sea route to the East. In the 16th century it came to be realized that the Seres and the Sinae were, respectively, the north and south Chinese. The capital city of the Seres, called Seres or Sera, is uncertainly identified with various cities of NE China.

See Gibbon's discussion of the silk trade in Section 3 of Chapter 40 of *The Decline and Fall of the Roman Empire*; André Berthelot: *L'Asie ancienne . . . d'après Ptolémée*, Paris, 1930; pp. 238–247; J. K. Wright: *Geographical Lore . . .* , 1925; Dover reprint 1965; p. 271.

I.6.   Arabs; "Araby;" Saba

Odes 1.29.1 Araby the Blest/ibid., line 3 Saba/ *Odes* 1.35.32 "the Eastern and Red Sea regions"/ ibid., line 40 Arabs and Massagetae/wealth of the Arabs (or of Araby) *Odes* 2.12.24/3.24.2/ E.1.7.36/ "farthermost Arabs and Hindus" E.1.6.6.

The respective notes include the pertinent information, but it should be understood that in Horace's time all Arabs were in Arabia, principally along the Red Sea coast of the peninsula and around its SW corner, the region of Saba ("Sheba"), now the Yemen.

II. *The Southeast-European Group*

II.1. Scythians; Geloni; the River Tanaïs

Scyth(s)/Scythians: *Scythae/Scythes*; adj. *Scythicus*. *Odes* 1.19.10/ 1.35.10 "nomadic"/3.8.23–24 "entertaining thoughts of surrender"/ 3.24.9 "with their wagons that haul movable houses across/ Open steppes"/ 4.5.25 "icy"/4.14.42/ *Centennial Hymn* 55 "seek (Augustus's) pronouncements."

Geloni a tribe of Scyths. *Odes* 2.9.23 (their territory reduced)/ 2.20.19 "remote"/3.4.36 *pharetratos* (omitted in tr.), "armed with quivers." See also Vergil: *Georgics* 2.115 *pictos*, "tattooed"(T. E. Page)/*Aeneid* 8.725 "arrow-bearing."

The Tanaïs River (name used by Herodotus): the S-Russian Don. *Odes* 3.4.35–36 ". . . at the/Scythian river among Geloni"/3.29.28 and note; *Tanaïs discors*, tr as "the contentious Scythians"/ 4.15.24 "the folk who/ Issue from Tanaïs River regions."

The Romans, beginning with Vergil and Horace, regularly used the "book word" Scyth/Scythian when they meant Sarmatians. Much of Herodotus's Book IV is devoted to the Scyths.

The Scyths were a people of Iranian stock and language, occupying very large tracts of what has been termed *l'Iran extérieur*. First heard of around 750 B.C., they made extensive conquests. Under the name of Sakas they came to hold SE Iran; the Bible calls them the race descended from Ashkuz, miswritten in Genesis 10:3 as Ashkenaz (Richard N. Frye: *The Heritage of Persia*, World Publishing, 1963, p. 65); and passing to the E of the Caspian Sea, they rounded the northern coast of that Sea and displaced the Cimmerians of S Russia; Herodotus fixes their western limit at the Tanaïs River.

After 300 B.C. they were driven out of the S-Russian area by still another Iranian people, the Sarmatians, and apparently retreated into Asia. To the Romans, the Sarmatians seemed little different from the Scyths, allusions to them being often made in terms of their troublesome tribes, the Alani, the Roxolani, et al. The Sarmatians advanced farther up the Russian rivers than their predecessors, and though their territory included the subtropical fringe of the Black Sea coast, the Romans thought of them as inhabiting wintry lands.

II.2. Thrace; Thracian

Thracē (Greek *Thrakē*)/ *Thraca* (later Latin *-ia*); adjective *Thracus*/ *-ius*/*Threicius*/ *Thressus*. (Greek has similar variations.) Tribes called *Sithonius*, *Edoni*, *Bistonides* stand for Thracians in general. *Thraex* (later Latin *Thrax*): a gladiator using very heavy equipment, actual Thracian equipment.

Odes 1.18.9 and note (*Sithonius*)/ 1.24.14 "Thracian Orpheus"/ 1.25.11 "gales"/ 1.27.1 (drinking brawls)/ 2.7.27 (*Edoni*) "More madly than a Thracian"/ 2.16.5 "war-crazy Thracians"/ 2.19.16 "Thracian Lycurgus' downfall"/2.19.19 (*Bistonides*) "Thracian maenads"/3.9.9 "Thracian Chloe"/ 3.25.10 the lost maenad sees "snow-covered Thrace below,/ Hebrus River, and Rhódopē's (mountain chain)"/ 4.12.1 "breezes of Thrace"; (the Thracian story of Procnē follows)/ E.1.3.3 ". . . Thrace where the Hebrus lies shackled in ice"/ E.1.16.13 (the Hebrus) "Never flows colder . . . across Thrace."

S.2.6.44 "Thracian equipment"/ E.1.18.36 *Thraex*, tr as "Dueling arena performers."

The Thracians were an Indo-European people occupying the extreme SE corner of Europe between the lower Danube and the Aegean Sea (N-S) and from the River Strymon to the Black Sea (W-E). Originally they held the entire region from the Adriatic to the Black Sea, but before 1100 B.C. Illyrians forced them eastward, and after 480 B.C. they were forced further eastward, with the Greek Macedonians taking the lands between the Illyrians and the River Strymon. Despite Greek colonies on their Aegean coast, they remained "barbaric." The Romans, after taking Macedonia, found them troublesome. In Horace's lifetime they sponsored a native client kingdom, which disintegrated after the death of King Cotys in 14 A.D., and in 46 A.D. the Emperor Claudius annexed their territory to the Roman empire. The area is now divided among Bulgaria, Greece, and Turkey-in-Europe.

II.3.   Dacians

Dacus, pl. *Daci*. In *Odes* 1.35.9 ("the Dacian savage") and 2.20.18 the Dacians are said to fear Rome. The remaining allusions speak of Rome's fear of the Dacians and their king, Cotiso: S.2.6.53/ *Odes* 1.26.4 and note, "Kings that by terror may rule cold northlands"/3.6.14/ 3.8.18.

The Indo-European Dacians were Thracians who remained outside of Thrace. Their center was Transylvania, now a portion of W Rumania, not only N of the Danube but beyond a protective arc of the Carpathian Mountains; they also extended their power W into the plain of Hungary and N into Slovakia. A coalition of their tribes established a centralized kingdom from ca. 60 B.C. to ca. 44 B.C., but even after its early dissolution the Romans could not get direct control over the area. Against a second kingdom the Emperor Domitian (81–96 A.D.) fought inconclusive wars, but the Emperor Trajan defeated the Dacians completely in two wars, 101–102 and 105–106 A. D., driving many of them into what is now S Russia and introducing Roman settlers who ultimately became the modern Rumanians. Scenes of the Dacian wars are depicted sequentially in a spiral of reliefs 260 meters long on the 40-meter column erected by Trajan in 113 and still standing *in situ*.

II.4.   *Getae*

Odes 3.24.11 "Getae," followed by thirteen lines idealizing their nomadic existence/ in 4.15.22, where a singular was desirable in translation, we render "Getae" by an invented "Gett."

The Getae were another Thracian people, closely akin to the Dacians, but inhabiting on both sides of the Danube mouth, with Scyths to their immediate north. Conquered by Persian "Great King" Darius I in 513, they regained autonomy after 479, but in 335 they were conquered anew, in a single battle, by Alexander the Great. After 300 the Scyths to their north were replaced by Sarmatians, to whom the Getae became assimilated after 1 A.D. Yet the poet Ovid, in exile from ca. 7 to ca. 17 A.D. at Tomi (now Constanza, Rumania), reports whiling away the time by learning both the Getic and Sarmatian languages.

Into the area once Getic came the Germanic Visigoths after 150 A.D., with ensuing confusion of the two words "Getic" and "Gothic." In the 6th century the Goth Jordanes wrote a history of his Germanic nation, in Latin, under the title of *De origine actibusque Getarum*, "On the Origin and Feats of the 'Getts.' "